DESIGN
OF
DATABASE
STRUCTURES

DESIGN
OF
DATABASE
STRUCTURES

TOBY J. TEOREY
JAMES P. FRY

The University of Michigan

PRENTICE-HALL, INC., Englewood Cliffs, N.J. 07632

Library of Congress Cataloging in Publication Data

Teorey, Toby J.
  Design of database structures.

  (Prentice-Hall software series)
  Bibliography: p. 470
  Includes index.
  1. Database management.   2. System design.   I. Fry.
James P.   II. Title.   III. Series
QA76.9.D3T43   001.64   81-23375
ISBN 0-13-200097-0   AACR2

Editorial/production supervision
  and interior design by *Linda Mihatov Paskiet*
Cover designer: *Frederick Charles, Ltd.*
Manufacturing buyer: *Gordon Osbourne*

Prentice-Hall Software Series
Brian W. Kernighan, advisor

© 1982 by PRENTICE-HALL, INC.,
Englewood Cliffs, New Jersey 07632

Printed in the United States of America

10 9 8 7 6 5 4 3 2

ISBN 0-13-200097-0

Prentice-Hall International, Inc., *London*
Prentice-Hall of Australia Pty. Limited, *Sydney*
Prentice-Hall of Canada, Ltd., *Toronto*
Prentice-Hall of India Private Limited, *New Delhi*
Prentice-Hall of Japan, Inc., *Tokyo*
Prentice-Hall of Southeast Asia Pte. Ltd., *Singapore*
Whitehall Books Limited, *Wellington, New Zealand*

**TO
JULIETTE
AND
ROSEMARY**

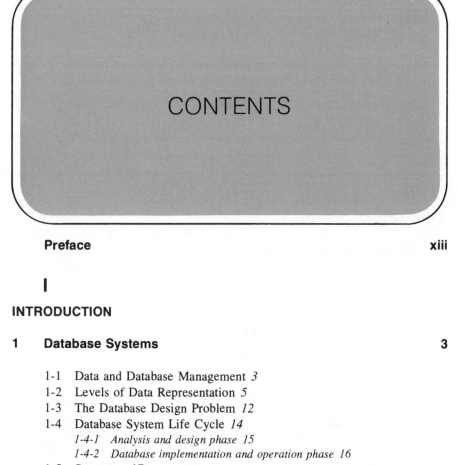

CONTENTS

II

CONCEPTUAL DESIGN

4   Conceptual Data Modeling   57

5   Entity Formulation and Analysis   76

6   Attribute Synthesis: An Example of Conceptual Design   97

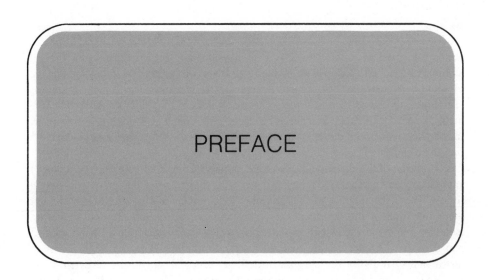

PREFACE

The purpose of this book is to establish a consistent framework for multilevel database design; to define a workable methodology; and to describe a set of general principles, tools, and techniques for database design at each level. The methodology uses the top-down (and iterative) design path, providing for evaluation at many points, allowing for redesign when necessary, and using the same basic terminology throughout. The goal of the design process itself is to formulate a database structure that accurately represents the real-world environment it serves, and one that can be efficiently implemented on an existing hardware/software system. System independence, however, is maintained as long as possible in the design process (i.e., the conceptual design step).

The methodology is illustrated throughout the text using detailed examples from statements of database system requirements through specification of logical and physical database structures that satisfy those requirements. The approach is applicable to network, relational, and hierarchical database systems.

Many steps in the database design process can be assisted with proper use of computer modeling techniques and other tools such as requirements analysis software. These tools range from documentation mechanisms to sophisticated design methodologies. Techniques such as simulation, graph theory, or mathematical optimization are commonly used, although simple expected-value estimates of performance have been found practical at various stages of database design. Categorized references are provided for the most appropriate tools at each design step.

Although emphasis is placed on the design of the database structure, its relationship to efficient program execution is also explored. Constraints for issues such as integrity, recovery, and security are discussed in terms of trade-offs with efficiency goals.

This book is for the professional database analyst, designer, database administrator, and application programmer. It could also be used for a one-semester senior or first-year graduate course in database design. The material is presented tutorially, and is supplemented with exercises and a bibliography, glossary of terms, index, and summary of variables. The level of mathematics is college algebra with a knowledge of some basic calculus. The reader is assumed to be familiar with data structures, searching and sorting techniques, and characteristics of the major database management systems (DBMSs). A course based on this text would naturally follow an introductory course on database management systems. Both theory and practice are presented, and their interaction is strongly emphasized.

The order of the chapters follows the database system life cycle steps (Chapter 1) very closely and presents the material in the order that a normal design process would follow. Part I (Chapters 1 to 3) is common to an understanding of all chapters, but thereafter each of the design phases is a complete entity and may be studied in isolation. For instance, a short course in physical design would follow Chapters 1 to 3 and 9 to 16. Chapter 18 presents an overview of the database design issues in distributed systems for the purpose of defining problems for future research.

Requirements analysis and conceptual design are illustrated with a common example (Chapters 3 and 6). Implementation design has a separate complete example (Chapter 8), and the physical design discussion contains smaller individual examples to demonstrate specific points. The examples serve to show that database design can be performed manually, but they also point out where computer-based tools can be effectively implemented.

Ann Arbor   *Toby J. Teorey*

James P. Fry

ACKNOWLEDGMENTS

We would like to express our gratitude for the various examples and manuscript critiques made by Larry Brown, Janis Bubenko, Bob Curtice, Jeffrey Hoffer, Alan Merten, Shamkant Navathe, Donna Rund, Mario Schkolnick, Dennis Severance, Diane Smith, John Smith, Dick Volz, and the several reviewers. Much of the design framework evolved from a course taught at the University of Michigan Engineering Summer Conference; it was also heavily influenced by the work at the 1978 NYU Symposium on Database Design and the 1978 Database Design Workshop in New Orleans. We acknowledge the contribution to our approach from our colleagues Sakti Ghosh, David Jefferson, Paul Jones, Bob Taylor, Vincent Lum, and Bing Yao.

At the University of Michigan we were assisted with software development, design tool evaluation, and manuscript revisions by the many able staff members of the Information Systems Research Group, including Ed Birss, David Chen, Rick Cobb, K. Sundar Das, Mark Deppe, Don DeSmith, Alberto Garcia, Eric Kintzer, Chris Merrill, Don Novak, Lew Oberlander, Don Swartwout, and Mike Wilens.

We thank Connie Allen, Pam Downie, Carol Dunn, and Izena Goulding for their help in manuscript preparation.

We appreciate the use of the library and technical facilities provided by the Department of Management Information Systems at the University of Arizona under Jay Nunamaker.

Exercises B5, B6, and B7 were contributed by Dennis Severance of the University of Michigan. Exercise B8 was suggested by William Weiler of Blue Cross/Blue Shield of Massachusetts, and Design Problem 3 in Appendix A was designed by Paul Helman and Marilyn Mantei of the University of Michigan. Design Problem 2 was revised from Chen [1978].

Finally, we wish to acknowledge the support and encouragement of our families, including Eunice L. and Thomas F. Teorey, Bessie May and Robert W. Teorey, and Anne J. and Palmer E. Fry.

DESIGN
OF
DATABASE
STRUCTURES

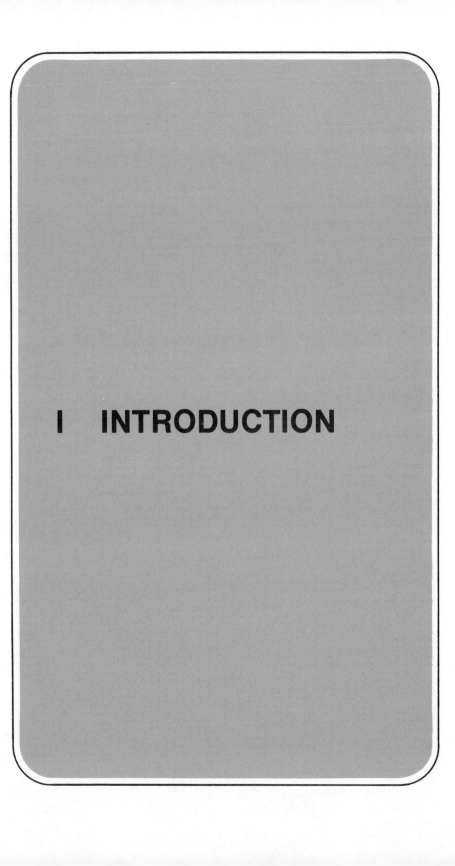

I INTRODUCTION

1 DATABASE SYSTEMS

Designing an integrated database is a difficult, time-consuming, and often un-structured process. It is a complex problem that pervades not only the data-process-ing function but eventually the entire organization. The quality of the resulting database structure is dependent upon the design methodology, the design techniques used in the steps of the methodology, the validity of the information requirements, and the commitment of the organization's developmental and operational resources to the endeavor.

In this chapter we begin to build the foundations for a practical database design methodology by establishing a standard set of terminology to be used throughout the text. We also review some of the basic concepts of data as used in the organization, as specified in application programs and database management systems, and as stored in computer systems.

1-1 DATA AND DATABASE MANAGEMENT

Data, as defined by Webster's is "a fact; something upon which an inference or an intellectual system of any sort is based" [Webster's, 1974]. The primitive compo-nents of data are the characters and numbers upon which a natural language is based, or their coded representations in strings of binary bits. A *data item* is the smallest unit of data that has meaning in the real world; it is the smallest named unit of data. A group of related data items treated as a unit by an application program is known as a *record,* and the collection of records of a single type is referred to as a *file.* Files can be manually stored or mechanized (electronically stored) on a computer. The distinc-tion between logical records, as viewed by the applications programmer, and stored records, as viewed by the storage devices and systems programmer/analyst, is emphasized throughout the text.

The remarkable continued growth in the use of computers for a wide variety of industrial, administrative, and scientific applications has led to the mechanization of extremely large quantities of data. During the late 1950s and early 1960s, businesses, government, and other organizations began to collect and store data on computer-accessible files. As each new need for data or data processing arose, a new file was created to meet that need. Individual groups within organizations developed their own computer applications and collected and maintained any required data in private files. The data files and applications programs were designed for one another, with much of the information being stored implicitly in the relationship of the program to the file.

Organizations eventually developed an awareness of the need for centralized management of data and applications. This awareness developed in several ways. Primarily, higher-level managers discovered that the information required to support their decision making was not easily obtainable. To fulfill a request for information, an application program had to be written to access several private files, with each file using its own format. The manager often canceled the request, either because the information would no longer be useful by the time it could be obtained, or because the information was not worth the cost involved. Second, decision making was hampered by the lack of data integrity. Computer reports conflicted because logically identical data items had different values. This was caused by data duplication among the private files, combined with inconsistent updating policies. There was also duplication of effort in the collection of data and the production of reports. Computer resources, both storage and processing, were being wasted. Finally, technology improved to the point where it became feasible to design, build, and operate large-scale collections of data in a computer environment. In summary, organizations realized that data were a valuable resource and needed to be centrally managed.

The concept of a database has thus emerged fully only in recent years. A *database* can be defined as a computerized collection of stored operational data that serves the needs of multiple users within one or more organizations. A key point is that the database is an integrated resource to be used by all members of the organizations who need information contained in it. Information is no longer implicit in the file-program combination but is stored explicitly in the database, which may include many different record types. The database is not single-program oriented as were private data files, but has an integrated requirements orientation.

Databases support managerial decision making in the following ways:

1. *Speed.* The computer system allows on-line querying for information.
2. *Total availability.* All the information contained within a database is available for use.
3. *Flexibility.* Previously unanswerable questions become answerable, and changes become relatively easy to implement.
4. *Integrity.* Data duplication is reduced and updating policies can be stand-ardized, resulting in consistent data.

Simply having a database does not entirely solve the organization's data-processing and decision-making needs, however. Since the database is an integrated resource for multiple users within an organization, it should be managed for the organization's benefit and from its viewpoint, not by individual users. Users naturally tend to develop applications for their own purposes, unconcerned about the impact that the new applications will have on other users. Without centralized management, the usefulness of a database declines over time.

Two additional concepts have been developed to solve the problem of controlling and managing the organization's database resource. Initially, software was developed to provide a common interface between all users and the integrated database. A common interface promotes privacy and data integrity. Also, users cannot store information implicitly and must use and modify data in a manner consistent with the organization's viewpoint. The software known as a database management system allows computer control of the data resource. A *database management system* (DBMS) is a generalized tool for manipulating a database; it is made available through special software for the interrogation, maintenance, and analysis of data. Its interfaces generally provide a broad range of languages to aid a wide variety of users. It also provides a convenient framework in which databases can be designed and used. A DBMS can be obtained by an organization through either a software vendor or in-house development.

The second concept is that of the *database administrator* (DBA). The DBA can be thought of as one or more individuals, possibly aided by a staff, who manage the organization's database resource. The DBA should be a dynamic and capable individual, primarily management oriented but also with a technical background. This person must be able to communicate with both upper-level management and data-processing users as well as manage the staff of technical specialists. The staff should include individuals experienced in a variety of areas, such as DBMS software, operating systems, computer hardware, applications programming, and system design. It is important that the staff also include individuals with a knowledge of the organization and its information requirements. The DBA's staff must be able to relate well to groups outside the data-processing department.

The DBA position was created when organizations recognized the need for centralized control of the data resource, data processing, and all other aspects that concern a database. The user community and individual users must be served as fairly as possible while keeping in mind the objectives of the organization as a whole. Thus, the DBA is responsible for determining all users' needs, designing a database, implementing the database, modifying or converting the database as needed, and assisting users with documentation and through education [Canning, 1972; DeBlasis and Johnson, 1977; Kent, 1978; Lyon, 1976a].

1-2   LEVELS OF DATA REPRESENTATION

At least three levels of abstraction are now recognized to exist in the specification of a database structure: the conceptual or enterprise administrator view, the implementation view of the applications programmer or end user, and the physical view of the systems programmer/analyst. Differences of opinion abound as to whether more levels of abstraction should be defined [Kerschberg et al., 1976; Senko et al., 1973] and whether a purely vertical definition of data representation is adequate [ANSI, 1978], but these three basic levels appear to be common to most discussions of data representation. A *data model* is a representation of data and its interrelationships which describes ideas about the real world. Data models have been used to present a conceptual view as well as an implementation view of data, but not a physical view, although the distinctions among these levels are often quite subtle.

Conceptual view. Figure 1-1 depicts the three basic levels of abstraction and some of their primary components. The conceptual schema or information structure is the name given to the data structure at the conceptual level. It is real-world-problem oriented and is completely system independent, that is, independent of the DBMS, the operating system (O.S.), and the computer hardware. In terms of the ANSI/SPARC three-level model of data, which is an operational model (versus our design model), the conceptual schema concepts are practically equivalent [ANSI, 1978] (see Fig. 1-2). Actually, many divergent viewpoints persist as to what the conceptual schema should be like and what it should represent, and the concept is still undergoing evolution. Our view will be, therefore, most pragmatic in nature, and more detailed distinctions are presented in Chapters 4 to 6.

The conceptual structure, or schema, consists of basic data elements of the real world (persons, things) called *entities;* other data elements which describe entities, called *attributes;* and associations between occurrences of data elements, called *relationships*. Figure 1-3 depicts this particular definition of a conceptual schema and illustrates alternative views of a problem within this framework. Typically, there are three types of (binary) relationships between occurrences of entities:

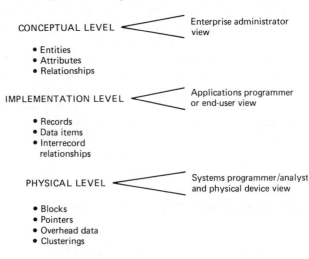

FIGURE 1-1   Levels of abstraction of data.

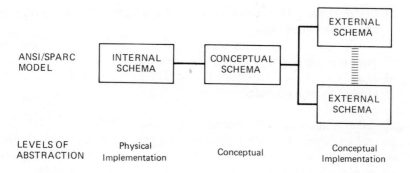

FIGURE 1-2 Correspondence between the ANSI/SPARC model and the levels of abstraction.

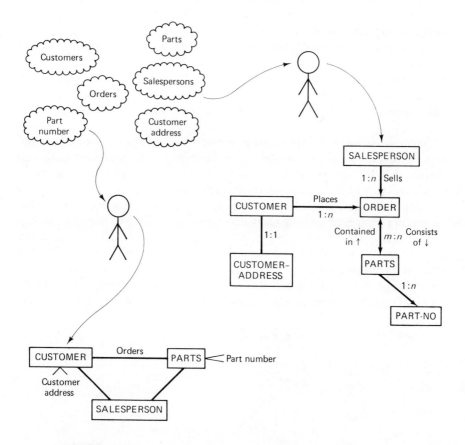

FIGURE 1-3 Two conceptual schemata to represent the same problem; different styles and data representations.

- *One-to-one (1 : 1)*. A customer has a unique family. (The uniqueness property exists in both directions.)
- *One-to-many (1 : n)*. A salesperson serves more than one customer, but a customer is assigned to exactly one salesperson.
- *Many-to-many (m : n)*. An order consists of many parts and each part may be ordered by many people.

Higher-order relationships are discussed by Codd [1970]. They can often be represented by several binary relationships, but only under restricted conditions. Most relationships in the everyday world, however, can be represented by simple or combined binary relationships.

A conceptual schema should maintain consistency of the relationships in terms of level of detail and time frame. With regard to level of detail, in the $m : n$ relationship example given above, an occurrence of the generic term ''part'' is a specific part type, whereas an occurrence of ''part type'' is an individual physical part (with a distinct serial number). An order consisting of physical parts is related to parts by $1 : m,$ not $m : n$. Time-frame consistency requires one to ask whether this relationship holds for the current time only or whether it holds for all time. The example assumes the relationship between customer and salesperson to be current. If it holds over a long period it will often become an $m : n$ relationship. This problem occurs, for example, with ''spouse'' or ''job title'' relationships, which could change over time.

Implementation view. The implementation view consists of (logical) records, their component data items, and their interrelationships. The three most commonly implemented data models are the hierarchical, the network, and the relational. A hierarchical view of the conceptual schema of Fig. 1-3 is given in Fig. 1-4. It consists of multiple record types in which one is designated as the root or entry record type. Each record consists of possibly many item types, some of which may become keys that uniquely identify each record. One-to-many (and sometimes one-to-one) relationships are defined between records in the hierarchy, with the ''one'' record designated as the parent and the ''many'' record designated as the child. A record may be a child in only one relationship, thus designating a unique parent for each record, but it may be a parent in many relationships. The root, however, may appear only as a

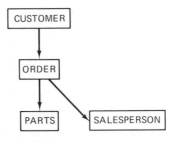

FIGURE 1-4   Hierarchical database structure.

parent record. In general, only one relationship may occur between two record types. The hierarchical data model is used in IMS and System 2000, although the underlying physical structures of these systems are quite different.

The network model is depicted in Fig. 1-5. It is similar to the hierarchical model, but it is more general in that any record may participate in any number of named relationships as a parent, child, or both. Consequently, there is no root node because any record may be defined as an entry point. Figure 1-6 shows the variety of relationships allowed, including mutliple relationships between two record types. The network model is implemented in CODASYL-like systems (IDMS, DMS 1100, DBMS-10, IDS-II, etc.) and others not conforming to the CODASYL data model (TOTAL, DMSII). Still other systems, usually categorized by their inverted file (physical) structure, can indirectly represent the network concept (Model 204, DATACOM/DB, ADABAS, etc.).

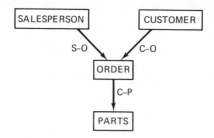

FIGURE 1-5   Network database structure.

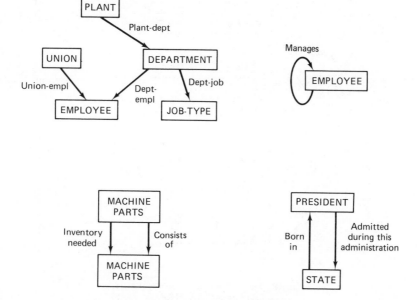

FIGURE 1-6   Network database configurations.

The relational data model (Fig. 1-7) is rapidly emerging as an implementable concept which is easy to understand and has many potential applications. Relational databases consist of "flat file" tables, called *relations,* which in turn are made up of *tuples* (record occurrences) and *attributes* (item types) whose values are drawn from a common *domain.* Relationships between relations are implicit in the overlapping domains used to define them, and thus we are allowed to design transformations among the major data models by using common information such as the unique key of a parent record to find its child records. In a relational database the parent–child relationship is implemented by defining a domain in a child record containing the key item type of the parent record. The relational model offers much more than simple transformations, however. It has mathematical properties that are useful for defining data manipulation languages and various levels of normal forms to increase the capability of maintaining data integrity and efficiency in a complex database. The three basic normal forms are illustrated in Fig. 1-8; however, fourth and even higher

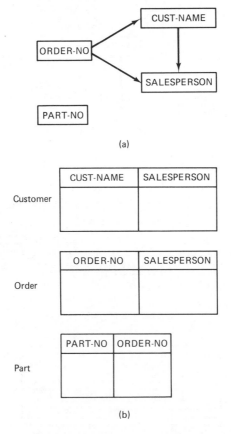

FIGURE 1-7 Relational database structure: (*a*) functional dependency diagram (1NF); (*b*) relations (3NF).

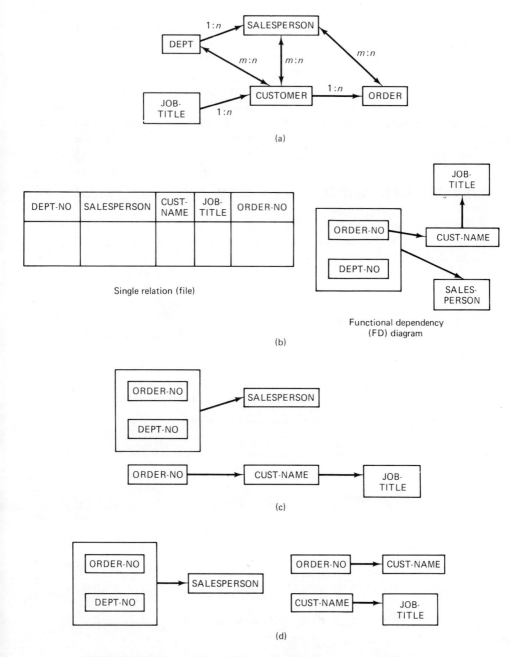

FIGURE 1-8 First, second, and third normal forms for relational databases: (*a*) unnormalized database—network database with all possible relationships shown, including redundancies; (*b*) first normal form (1NF); (*c*) second normal form (2NF)—nonfull dependency eliminated from the 1NF; (*d*) third normal form (3NF)—transitive dependency eliminated from the 2NF.

normal forms are also well known [Fagin, 1977, 1979]. Many relational systems have already been developed and some may soon supplant other types of systems in the commercial market.

Physical view. Physical structure is partially illustrated in Fig. 1-9. The basic components of physical databases are physical blocks, stored records, pointers, overhead data, and interblock gaps. Interrelationships among stored records through the use of clustering and index structures can also be considered part of physical structure.

1-3   THE DATABASE DESIGN PROBLEM

The combination of DBMS software, applications software, database implementation, and operating system/hardware environment brought together to provide information services for users is known as a *database system*. Although the technology for DBMS, operating system, and applications programming is well developed, little attention has been given to the effective use of these tools with alternative database structures. Thus, the major problem facing the database administrator is not whether to use this technology, but how to use it effectively [ACM/NBS, 1976]. This problem can be summarized by a number of issues that arise through the life cycle of an application:

1. What are the user requirements, and how can they be expressed?
2. How can these requirements be translated into an effective database structure?

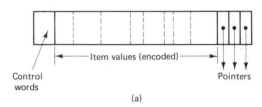

(a)

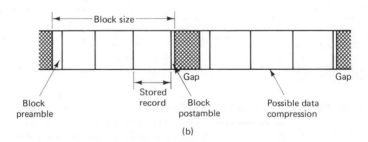

(b)

FIGURE 1-9   Physical database structure: (*a*) stored record; (*b*) physical blocks.

3. When should, and how can, the database structure be adapted to new and/or changing requirements?

The process of developing a database structure from user requirements is called *database design*. Many practitioners have argued that there are at least two separate steps in the database design process: the design of a logical database structure which is processible by the DBMS and describes the user's view of the data, and the selection of a physical structure that includes data representation or encoding, access methods, and physical clustering of data. Other than the logical/physical delineation, however, the overall structure of the design process has not been well defined, and even the logical/physical boundary has been open to considerable dispute. We wish to avoid this confusion by defining more concisely each step in the design process.

Database design, as currently practiced, shows many residual effects of its outgrowth from single-record-type file design methods. File design is primarily application-program dependent since the data have been defined and structured in terms of individual applications that use it. The advent of database management systems revised the emphasis in both the data and program design approaches. The concept of the integrated database serving multiple users was a direct result of the complex data structuring capabilities that the DBMS afforded. Data could now be viewed as a corporate resource instead of as an adjunct to a program, and consequently should have an integrated (multiuser) requirement orientation instead of a single-program orientation.

Achieving an acceptable level of database performance for all users has become a complex task. The database designer must be ever-conscious of the cost/performance trade-offs associated with multiple users of one or more integrated databases. Potential savings of storage space and expanded applicability of databases into organizational decision making should be accompanied by a critical analysis of potential degradation of service to some users. Such degradation is to be avoided if possible. Acceptable performance for all users should be the goal.

Another aspect of database performance is flexibility. Databases that are too tightly bound to current applications may have too limited a scope for many corporate enterprises. Rapidly changing requirements and new data elements may result in costly program maintenance, a proliferation of temporary files and sorts, and increasingly poor performance. A meaningful overall database design process should account for both integration and flexibility.

The major classes of inputs to and results from the database design process are designated in Fig. 1-10. General information requirements include a statement of the objectives of the database system, definition of the data elements to be included in the database, and a description of data element usage in the users' organizations. These requirements are not tied to any specific application; therefore, database structure design based on such requirements is considered to be advantageous for long-term databases that must be adaptable to changing applications.

Processing requirements consist of three distinguishable components: specific data items required for each application, the data volume (number of data item

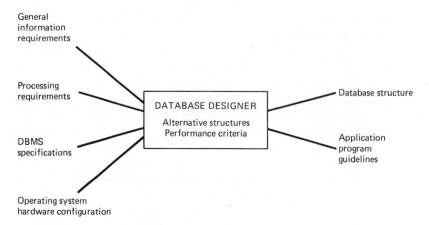

General
information
requirements

Processing
requirements

Database structure

DATABASE DESIGNER

Alternative structures
Performance criteria

DBMS
specifications

Application
program
guidelines

Operating system
hardware configuration

FIGURE 1-10   Database design process.

occurrences), and processing frequencies in terms of the number of times each application must be run per unit time. Each of these components is very important to a particular stage or step of the database design process. Other inputs, such as DBMS specifications or constraints and the operating system/hardware configuration, are also used by the designer.

Performance measures and performance constraints are also imposed on the database designer. Normally, the performance constraints are considered to be part of the system requirements and the actual performance measures used by the designer may be derived from these various constraints. Typical constraints include upper bounds on response times to queries, recovery times from system crashes, or specific data needed to support certain security or integrity requirements. Specific performance measures used to evaluate the final structure might include update, storage, and reorganization costs in addition to response-time requirements.

The two major results of the database design process are the complete database structure (including the so-called logical and physical components) and guidelines for application programmers based on database structure and processing requirements. As a whole, these results may be considered the specification for the final database implementation.

1-4   DATABASE SYSTEM LIFE CYCLE

The database system life cycle is a convenient and useful framework from which to view the database system as it evolves over time. This framework provides an ordered background to the functions of a database administrator and is divided into two separate phases: analysis and design and database operation. Collecting user requirements and designing the database takes place during the first phase; actual computer implementation and use occurs in the second phase. It is possible to make a further distinction as to the activities that take place during the life cycle by taking the viewpoint of a designer/user. The two phases are composed of the following steps:

- Analysis and design phase
  1. Requirements formulation and analysis
  2. Conceptual design
  3. Implementation design
  4. Physical design
- Database implementation and operation phase
  1. Database implementation
  2. Operation and monitoring
  3. Modification and adaptation

Each step in the analysis and design phase and the database implementation and operation phase is described below. At this point the reader should note that this viewpoint disregards two important design decisions—selection of system hardware and selection of system software—which are beyond the scope of this discussion.

1-4-1   Analysis and Design Phase

Requirements formulation and analysis is probably the most poorly defined, difficult, and time-consuming step of the entire process. It is, however, the most important because the majority of subsequent design decisions are based on this step; consequently, it has a cascading effect on the other steps of the analysis and design phase. The major task is collecting information content and processing requirements from all the identified and potential users of the database. Analysis of the requirements ensures the consistency of users' objectives as well as the consistency of their views of the organization's information flow.

Conceptual design addresses the design of a DBMS-independent information structure through the consolidation of the user information requirements specifications. The result of conceptual design is also called conceptual schema because it is a representation of the user's "world" view and independent of any DBMS software or hardware considerations.

Implementation design has two components, database and programs. The database structure resulting from implementation design is a DBMS-processible data definition or schema, usually expressed in a data definition language. It is also called the logical database strcture. If the data definition includes physical parameters (e.g., areas, page sizes, etc.), selection of appropriate characteristic values are deferred until the physical design step. The program design component addresses the development of structured programs using the host language and data manipulation language of the DBMS. The output is a functional specification of the program modules and a set of representative ad hoc queries to the database.

In the past the second and third steps were commonly referred to as logical design, but since this has led to much confusion in the literature we will drop the term "logical design" from our discussion and replace it with the more precise terms "conceptual design" and "implementation design."

Physical design consists of two components, as does implementation design: selection of the physical database structure and the fine tuning of the program modules specified in Step 3. The result is a complete, implementable database structure. For example, in a CODASYL system, the physical database structure could include a pointer array implementation of SETs, contiguous AREAs for multiple-record types, and entry-point access methods. The program component addresses the development of the structured data manipulation language programs for the given logical database structure. It produces a set of implementable algorithms.

We have briefly described the four steps of the analysis and design phase. It is important to realize that an inadequate analysis or decision in this phase will lead to improper implementation and ultimately to a nonresponsive application system.

1-4-2   Database Implementation and Operation Phase

Database implementation is concerned with the creation of the database and application programs based on the results of the three major database design steps, and the loading of the database with data. The actual database loading task is an often overlooked but costly effort. The existing data must be translated from their current form (logical and physical structure) to the new form resulting from the successful database design. Application program development is highly dependent on the host language selected, the existing logical structure, and to a lesser extent, on the physical structure. The objective of this component is to develop reliable and efficient database access programs to satisfy user processing requirements.

Operation and monitoring can be set up to collect (log) and summarize data about the actual system operation. The logging task will provide information about the validity of the user requirements; it will also help identify critical system performance areas which can be further evaluated. The resulting information can then be used for future revisions to the system. The integrity of the database must also be maintained, and any failure recovery must be handled efficiently.

Modification and adaptation addresses the changes in the design and tuning of the implementation (to the various degrees of freedom provided) as a result of new requirements, inputs from the monitoring phase, or analysis of user satisfaction with the current system. The objective is to optimize performance within the current system by reorganizing the database and/or changing the programs. Database reorganization is a broad term used to describe any change in the logical or physical structure of the database. Changes range from inversion of a relationship (restructuring) to the tuning of the physical structure (reformatting).

Finally, program adaptation refers to the process of modifying application programs, when necessary, to provide correct results from restructured databases.

Typically, this problem results from lack of logical data independence [Fry and Deppe, 1976; Fry and Kahn, 1976; Fry and Sibley, 1976], and the modifications include new sequences of data manipulation operations and changing variables to count logical records if blocking factors are changed.

1-5   SUMMARY

The concept of an integrated database has evolved because of the limitations of files and decentralized control of organizational data. Together with more complex data structure came the need for database management systems. However, this software is designed to define, load, and access data whose structure has been previously established, and is therefore separate from the database design process.

The central authority to design, implement, and control databases resides with the database administrator. The database design function is a complex and creative process that has many aspects: methodologies or general approaches, multiple levels of abstraction of data from the end-user view to the systems programmer and analyst view, analytical tools to assist in the design and analysis of database structures, and documentation techniques for tools or to be used directly by the database administrator.

The underlying framework for design and analysis is the database system life cycle and the breakdown of steps for design, implementation, and reorganization. Although the major phases of database design are well defined, the individual steps, their sequence, iterative refinement, and choice of performance measures are dependent upon design preferences, and in general allow for flexibility in this creative process.

2 THE DATABASE DESIGN PROCESS

2-1 THE CONCEPT OF A DESIGN METHODOLOGY

A method is an orderly and logical procedure for performing a particular task. A methodology is a system of methods, applying the basic principles of reasoning to scientific inquiry. In terms of databases, a *design methodology* can be thought of as a collection of tools and techniques employed within an organizational framework that can be applied consistently to successive database structure development projects [Wasserman, 1980]. Since a database system consists of programs as well as data, a database design methodology is considered to be an integral part of an overall software system methodology.

What are the goals of a "good" database design methodology? First, it should produce a useful database structure within a reasonable amount of time and with a reasonable amount of effort. A useful database is one that meets user objectives (i.e., high performance and adaptability to future processing needs, security, integrity, etc.), adheres to system constraints, such as storage space limitations, and is represented by a simple data model to enhance user comprehensibility and acceptance.

Second, a methodology should have enough generality and flexibility to not only be used by persons with different levels of design experience, but also for persons constrained by different data models or database management system software. Finally, a methodology should be reproducible so that two persons (or programs) applying the methodology to the same problem will produce the same or approximately the same result.

The statement of these goals is much simpler than the evaluation required to determine when they are met. The easiest to prove, but the most difficult to attain, is reproducibility. The gradual refinement of individual design techniques so that they can be integrated and automated as design tools would be the ultimate test of reproducibility. Flexibility could be demonstrated through experimentation (testing) with a wide range of data models used and design experience allowed. The evaluation of the final database structure implies use of the scientific method of problem statement, hypothesis formation, experimental design, data collection, interpretation of results, and the drawing of conclusions for each of the individual design techniques as well as for the methodology as a whole. Analytical models of database structures can be validated with live test data on operational systems. Validation of a methodology is much more subjective, however, in that a sufficient number of test cases under different conditions must be carried out to demonstrate a particular confidence level of performance.

To satisfy these goals, a database design methodology should have the following set of basic components [Novak and Fry, 1976]:

1. A design process that consists of a series of steps, each of which requires a choice among several design alternatives
2. Design techniques to perform the enumeration required in the design process, and evaluation criteria to select an alternative at each step
3. Information requirements for input to the design process as a whole and to each step
4. A descriptive mechanism to represent the information input and the results of each design step

Using the framework of the database system life cycle, let us look at each of these components in more depth. We first note that the remainder of this text is devoted to a detailed presentation of the major proposed steps and performance analysis of the techniques used.

Design Process

The design of a database can benefit greatly from the variety of well-known methodologies for software system design [Boehm, 1976; Wasserman, 1980]. In particular, top-down design with successive refinement is quite applicable to database structures. In the initial stage, a conceptual model of data set forth to represent data elements and relationships in the real world is successively refined to produce a DBMS-processible database structure. The design process itself is well structured in that each step produces a clearly defined result, but also in that it allows for iteration to repeat previous steps if the current design is unable to meet user objectives or system constraints, or if additional requirements are imposed. Iterative successive refinement, in the most general sense, allows the designer to return to any prior step for redesign. In practice, the cost of redesign increases significantly if one must repeat previous design steps after some implementation has already taken place; therefore, iteration within the preimplementation design steps is useful. Although iteration can significantly reduce the total development cost of the database, it makes the reproducibility goal of the design methodology more difficult to attain. For the current state of the art, however, iteration is a most necessary and useful technique (see Fig. 2-1) and will be assumed to be available for each step in the database design process.

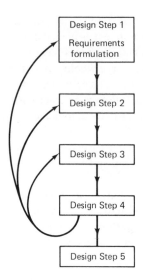

FIGURE 2-1 Forward and iterative design options (for Step 4) in a top-down successive refinement methodology.

Associated with this design process is a multistep *design review methodology,* involving techniques such as structured walkthroughs for the database structure as well as the applications software. Design reviews are being widely implemented specifically for database systems [Brown, 1977], using the strategies proposed for more general information systems [IBM, 1973; Yourdon, 1979]. The objective of a review is to find system design errors and correct them early in the life cycle so as to reduce the cost of system development. A review team is composed of experienced personnel from the database administration group, the software development group, and each applications area represented in the proposed system. Each review team selects a leader who is empowered to hand out assignments and run meetings. Meetings generally are recommended to last an hour or an hour and a half, but a meeting that is unproductive can be suspended and rescheduled by the team leader.

Typically, design reviews are called for at least four times in the life cycle:

1. After requirements analysis and information structure design (i.e., conceptual design)
2. After detailed system design
3. After implementation but before production use of the system
4. After production has begun and meaningful performance data have been collected

Each successive review requires more detailed documentation or test data, but the meeting formats are similar. Documentation is distributed to the review team a few days in advance of each meeting so that members may come prepared with questions and suggestions for alternative approaches for the database structures thus far designed. A formal presentation is made in the meeting summarizing the approach taken in the design process thus far, and responses by the review team are made verbally and in writing. The second review often requires more than one session to complete, and if the system is very large, major components of the system can be reviewed, one at a time. The third and fourth reviews have the benefit of statistical data to accompany the usual written documentation. Deviations from proposed performance guidelines (or required performance) are subjected to explanation and possibly to further analysis.

Design Techniques and Evaluation Criteria

Each step in the design process is characterized by a set of design techniques and alternative evaluation criteria. Although design techniques may be analytical, heuristic, or procedural in nature, any technique that can be implemented in software is designated as a *design tool* and as such is subject to very little fluctuation in designer "style."

Evaluation criteria used in design techniques are necessary to select a database structure from among several alternatives in a consistent and useful way. It can be said that most of the problems and confusion in database design stem from an imprecise view of what constitutes an optimal database design. Currently, and for the foreseeable future, variability in selection criteria comprises a weak link in the database design chain.

Difficulties in specification of criteria for the selection of alternatives are caused primarily by two factors. First, an almost infinite number of different database structures can be constructed from the same set of system requirements. An alternative selection criterion should be able to differentiate all of the alternatives available at that point. Description and identification of alternatives are important to ensure that potentially superior alternatives are not omitted from consideration. The second problem is that the alternatives are extremely difficult to evaluate. There are many dimensions to optimality, some of which are the unmeasurable and unquantifiable properties which are difficult to incorporate in an objective function. Evaluation criteria can thus be classified into quantitative and qualitative categories. Some of the criteria that may be grouped under each heading are shown in Fig. 2-2.

One of the difficulties in evaluating trade-offs lies in the different time frames and sensitivities of the criteria. The efficiency-type criteria are generally short term since they are extremely sensitive to usage changes, whereas things such as convertibility and adaptability require a longer perspective and are much less sensitive to short-term fluctuations of the environment.

Information Requirements

Information requirements pervade the entire design process of stepwise refinement of the database structure. It has often been found helpful to classify the information available to the design process into the information structure perspective and the usage perspective [Kahn, 1976].

Quantitative	Qualitative
Query response time	Flexibility
Update cost	Adaptability
Storage cost	Understandability of the
Creation time	design to new users
Reorganization cost	Compatibility with other
	systems
	Convertibility to new
	environments
	Recovery/restart
	capability
	Partitionability or
	capacity for modular
	growth

FIGURE 2-2 Database evaluation criteria.

Information classed in the *information structure perspective* (ISP) describes the natural and conceptual relationships of all data in the database and is not bound to any processes or applications. ISP information depicts the mapping of the real-world referents into entities and attributes and the mapping of the interrelationships between the real-world referents into relationships between data elements. ISP-type information always exists in an organization even though it may be difficult to quantify and collect. An example of the type of information that might be collected is shown in Fig. 2-3.

Information classed in the *usage perspective* (UP) defines the organization's processing requirements. It describes the data and relationships that are used in applications, as opposed to the data and relationships that exist naturally. This information reflects the processing requirements of the current applications and the estimated requirements of known future applications. It may be that the applications' data usage is not quantifiable if the applications are unstructured queries or unanticipated applications. Sample UP information is shown in Fig. 2-4.

Information	Example
Entity Description	
Name	Employee
Cardinality	100
Attribute Description	
Name	Social security number
Length	9
Value set	0-999,999,999
Probability of existence	1.0
Repetition factor	1
Relationship Description	
Name	Employed-by
Entities defined over	Employee, department
Cardinality	100
Mapping	1:1
Probability of existence	0.95

FIGURE 2-3 ISP information.

Information	Example
Process Description	
Name	Payroll
Frequency of occurrence	Weekly
Probability of occurrence	1.0
Priority	High
Data required	Employee, time card pay rate
Volume of data	100 employees
Operators	
Operator	FIND
Search criteria	Employee
Number of instances retrieved	All
Associations used	Status active
Probability of occurrence	1.0
Probability of retrieved instance being used	0.95

FIGURE 2-4 UP information.

There is a high degree of overlap between the two perspectives. The data items used by applications, which are collected in the UP, will be a proper subset of the data elements that exist in the ISP if the ISP information is complete and consistent.

A database designed from information provided by the ISP perspective will differ markedly from one designed from the UP perspective. The use of ISP-type, application-independent data elements has several implications for database design. The use of ISP information ensures that the database structure will be able to support the full range of current and future applications since the data items specified by the UP are a subset of the ISP data elements. Because of this, the ISP information provides a basis for handling unstructured, varying, and unknown queries and applications (applications whose data requirements cannot be accurately predicted). Since a database is expected to serve different uses over time, this adaptability is highly desirable.

Information from the UP has a different effect on the design. Basing the design on current and anticipated usage, it is possible to achieve a highly efficient design since the database structure can be tailored to reflect highly used access paths. In the past this has received more emphasis due to program-oriented design.

Each perspective affects the resulting design along a different dimension; ISP provides flexibility and adaptability and UP provides efficiency. The reason that UP-oriented design has been so popular is that the benefits from an efficient design are immediate and easily measured. The benefits of flexibility and adaptability, however, may be much greater than that of current efficiency because efficiency-oriented designs are very sensitive to changes in both usage mix and data requirements and would probably have to be reorganized more frequently to maintain efficiency and completeness. Flexibility benefits are more long term in nature and are more difficult to quantify. An ISP-oriented design is sensitive to changes in the real-world referents that define the data requirements and which typically have much longer life spans than do application programs.

The desirability of having both flexibility and efficiency has led to the formulation of design methodologies that use both ISP and UP information [Kahn, 1978; Novak and Fry, 1976]. The common framework specifies that the ISP information should be used to form the initial information structure and the UP information used to refine the information structure for processing efficiency as desired. Thus, the utility of including ISP information should be clear: at small cost in terms of the current performance of known, structured applications, the flexibility of the system can be increased to handle more unstructured and unknown applications. These unstructured and new applications will probably be inefficient if they deviate widely from the current applications' access patterns; but being able to do them inefficiently is much better than not being able to do them at all. Recognition of this point has done much to improve the potential of database systems. Without the inclusion of ISP information, a database merely allows a larger number of users to share the limitations of being bound and restricted by their file designs.

Descriptive Mechanisms

Both requirements specifications and target database structures at all steps need to be represented by a simple model or series of related models, understandable at one level by the end user of the data, at another level or levels by application programmers, and at one or more levels by systems programmers and analysts. Stepwise refinement of the basic structure demands consistency in how the data are viewed and manipulated at all levels.

There are three basic classes of descriptive mechanisms necessary for a design methodology. First, the final product of the implementation design process is expressed using the DBMS's Data Description Language (DDL). DDLs are fully developed for existing DBMSs, and some prototype specifications for terminology and definitions of general DBMSs exist in the ANSI/SPARC Interim Report [ANSI, 1978].

The second class is the description of the information inputs to be discussed in Chapter 3. Collection and information analysis aids currently in prototype use are all similar in that they provide formats for specification of both ISP- and UP-type information and perform basic consistency checking. The identification of synonyms, homonyms, and overlapping definitions for data elements and their relationships is not an easy task to automate and probably will remain a human activity with basic assistance from the software aids.

The third class of descriptive mechanisms describes the results of intermediate steps between the information inputs and the DDL. The major intermediate result is the entity diagram (Fig. 1-3), which acts as a bridge between conceptual design and implementation design. Many design techniques use a normalized relational-type representation, which has also been found to be quite useful.

2-2 OVERVIEW OF DATABASE DESIGN: THE BASIC STEPS

The basic objectives of database design are to enable users to obtain the exact data they need to perform their duties within the organization and to make the data available in a reasonable amount of time. The first objective requires that the elements in the database represent the complete data needs of the user organizations based upon their overall goals, internal organizational structure, and projected data access requirements. The second objective, performance, requires that the database structure resulting from the design process allow fast-enough access to data such that those who need the data can perform their duties effectively. Performance has present and future aspects, however. The early design-phase goal could be to produce a flexible database structure that should be adaptable to a changing user environment, whereas the later design phase may emphasize tuning to optimize performance for known processing requirements.

A stepwise database design methodology can now be formulated that derives a database structure from a set of user information and processing requirements. The evolution of database design methodologies is currently a dynamic process, and there is no general agreement on a "best" approach. A practical methodology must therefore rely on generally accepted principles and should not be dependent upon narrow viewpoints and assumptions. In this spirit we offer the following design steps, which represent the major principles developed in the currently known general design methodologies. Particular emphasis is given to the methodologies of Sheppard [1974; Rund, 1977], Kahn [1976; Fry and Deppe, 1976], Tozer [1976], Chen [Chen and Yao, 1977], Bubenko [Bubenko et al., 1976], and Gerritsen [1975a, b]. These steps should be considered as flexible guidelines or checkpoints for the database administrator or database designer, not formal rules that encompass all possible design situations. The general interconnections between steps are illustrated in Fig. 2-5. Note that the step numbering system is consistent with the database system life cycle discussed in Chapter 1.

STEP 1: REQUIREMENTS FORMULATION AND ANALYSIS

This activity involves the establishment of organizational objectives, derivation of specific database requirements from those objectives or directly from management and nonmanagement personnel, and documentation of those requirements in a form that is agreeable to both end users and database designers. The technique normally used is personal interviews with various levels of management and key employees involved in the processing of goods, services, and data in the organization. The result of an interview should be a flow of the data elements associated with that process, interfaces between processes, and a verification that both the interviewer and employee agree on the flow model semantics. Specific objectives and database requirements should be obtained at the highest possible level in the organization.

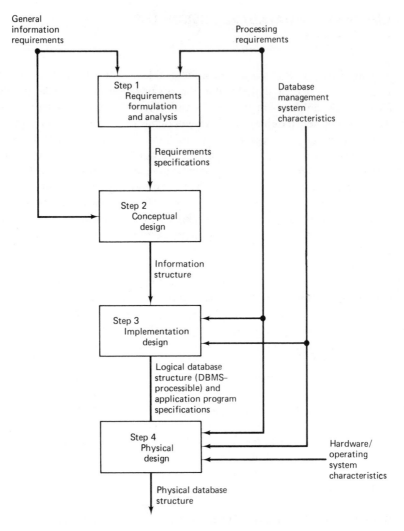

FIGURE 2-5 Basic database design steps.

Among the requirements collected and documented should be information regarding constraints due to security, reliability, technology available, as well as political and bureaucratic constraints. Organizational policies regarding personnel, operational activities, and future growth should also be assessed. Documentation can be done manually, through requirement statement languages, or with automated data dictionary facilities. It may be helpful to separate the process-dependent requirements (i.e., those associated with specific database applications) from the process-independent requirements at the documentation stage for future reference [Kahn, 1976].

STEP 2: CONCEPTUAL DESIGN

The conceptual design phase concerns itself with the description and synthesis of diverse users' information requirements into a preliminary database design. This phase results in a high-level representation of these requirements such as an entity–relationship diagram. The focal point of the diagram would be a set of entities that represent or model a particular information aggregate specified in the requirements. Entities can be described by attributes that provide detailed information about the entity and one or more of which might serve as an identifier to distinguish different entity instances. Relationships between entities depict the functional aspects of the information represented by the entities [Chen, 1977a; Chen and Yao, 1977].

There are a number of approaches to the formulation of entity–relationship diagrams; the commonality among these approaches is the set of four basic design decisions or steps:

1. Selection of entities
2. Selection of entity attributes
3. Identification of key attributes for entities
4. Selection of relationships between entities

Although some commonality exists in these steps to create an information structure, no agreement exists as to the order in which these steps are to be performed. The main point to remember is that the initial information structure should be at least partially process independent to provide a basis for long-term flexibility in the design structure.

The approach to conceptual design normally taken assumes a single-user view, or perhaps assumes that the database administrator/designer understands the requirements of all users of the proposed database system and that he or she has combined their requirements into a single complete set of consistent specifications. An alternative approach is to perform this "view integration" as part of the conceptual design process [Navathe and Schkolnick, 1978; Yao, 1978; Yao and De Jong, 1978; Yao et al., 1978].

View modeling. Each user's requirements are analyzed and represented in some common form. Associated with each view is a set of entities, attributes, and inter-relationships among entities that describe objects and events in the system being modeled.

View integration. The individual user's requirements, specified in a standard form such as entity–relationship diagrams [Chen, 1977a, b; Chen and Yao 1977; Sowa, 1976], are then consolidated into a single global view. Inconsistencies and redundancies must be recognized and resolved. If the eventual target system provides a subschema mechanism, the individual results of view modeling might be used to design the subschemas, while the result of view integration would, after further processing, become the schema.

STEP 3: IMPLEMENTATION DESIGN

Given a representation of the information structure, the refinement of this structure is addressed next. The primary objective of the implementation design step is to use the results of the conceptual design phase and the processing requirements (usage perspective) as input to create a DBMS-processible schema as output. Although the placement of the dividing line between conceptual design and implementation design is open to some debate, as is the relationship of logical and physical design, the distinction we make here is important to developing a practical stepwise methodology.

First, the processing requirements are analyzed for data content. The format of the local information structures for processes is the same as the initial structure produced in Step 2. After each process has been represented, the initial structure from conceptual design can be consolidated with all local structures based on processing into a revised information structure. Then, using the combined insight gained from the consolidated and revised information structures, processing data relationships, and allowable DBMS record type characteristics, initial record types can be formulated.

The logical database structure (schema) thus formed can now be evaluated based on quantitative information and performance measures such as logical record access counts, total bytes transferred to satisfy an application, and total bytes in the database. These measures attempt to predict physical database performance in terms of elapsed time and physical storage space as closely as possible.

Finally, the schema is refined for better efficiency. In some cases it may be useful to "look ahead" at those DBMS features such as indexes, hashing, or system entry points. However, if the schema cannot be refined without modifying the information content, the schema design is terminated. All refinements are subjected to the same evaluation as the initial schema.

STEP 4: PHYSICAL DESIGN

The practice of physical database design has advanced through several stages of development from file design to the design of physical database structures for integrated database schemas in the popular DBMSs today. This progression encompasses the various known techniques for storage structure, search mechanisms, and record segmentation. Fortunately, today's DBMSs have underlying physical structures and access methods that rely heavily on the file design technology, and many of the old techniques still apply.

We can classify the major decision classes of physical design into at least three categories.

Stored record format design. This includes all forms of data representation and compression in stored records. It also includes partitioning of data items in a record to different physical locations, depending on size and usage characteristics.

Clustering analysis and design. Clustering involves the placement of record occurrences into contiguous physical extents, allocation across secondary storage devices, and block-size selection for efficient retrieval.

Access path design. This encompasses any parameter that has a significant effect on the number or cost of accesses required to retrieve or update data (e.g., the logical ordering of records, pointer options, access methods, and overflow techniques). Note that these issues are also important in Step 3; hence the overlap between implementation and physical design.

Application program guidelines and the incorporation of security and integrity constraints are also an integral part of physical design as well as implementation design. However, the order in which all the physical design decisions should be considered is not fixed. In general, the most available performance data at this level are for I/O service time, the most designer-controlled component of elapsed time for database applications. Minimization of I/O service time and storage space are meaningful objectives for this step. Minimization of CPU time is also good, but that is better controlled by good application program design than by the database structure design.

Software system design, consisting of program and database design components, has been undergoing rapid evolution through the "structured" analysis, design, and programming techniques advocated by Dijkstra and others [Dijkstra, 1976; Mills, 1972; Parnas, 1972; Wirth, 1971, 1974] and developed commercially [Caine and Gordon, 1975; Gane and Sarson, 1979; Jackson, 1975; Orr, 1976; Ross and Schoman, 1977; Yourdon and Constantine, 1979]. Experience has shown that program and database design components undergo various stages of specification and stepwise refinement in parallel (overlapping) paths, where each step in either component relies on the current working alternative designs of the other components. Although our emphasis in this text is on the database structure component, it is important to be continually aware of the implication of a database structure refinement or new integrity constraint, for example, on program structure and its efficiency.

The basic program–database interrelationships during system design are shown in Fig. 2-6, which specifies many of the popular documentation "tools" used today to describe program and data structure. The outermost box represents the most abstract (highest level) view early in system design, and the innermost box represents the least abstract (lowest level or system dependent) view when the system is implemented. Connecting arrows indicate where influence is exerted across and within the design components.

2-3   DESIGN ISSUES

The major issues to be considered in the database design process are integrity, consistency, recovery, security, efficiency, and the effects of projected future growth. These issues are defined in the following sections, where their interactions with other issues are addressed. These issues are aggregated into the following groups [Lum et al., 1979a]:

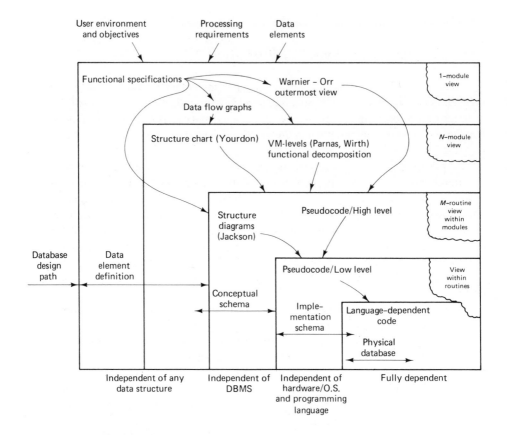

FIGURE 2-6 Correspondence between software and database development.

GROUP 1. Integrity, consistency, recovery

GROUP 2. Security

GROUP 3. Efficiency, growth, size, and performance constraints

This partitioning into groups reflects the degrees of freedom allowed the database designer. Group 1 usually reflects users' demands and consists of narrow constraints within which the designer must work. In groups 2 and 3 there are usually more alternatives available to the designer to satisfy these requirements. The trade-offs among the group 3 issues are mostly (but not entirely) within the designer's prerogative when a feasible solution for the requirements has been found.

The nonefficiency issues, in particular, need to be resolved early for smooth evolvability. If these issues are not considered in the development of the implementation schema, for example, they must be specified elsewhere (operating system, database procedures at the application level, etc.) Decentralized treatment of these issues leads to coordination, enforcement, and flexibility problems.

2-3-1   Integrity, Consistency, and Recovery

A database is defined to have the *integrity* property when it satisfies certain specified data value constraints and preserves this property under all modifications (update, add, or delete) of the database [Lum et al., 1979a; Verhofstad, 1978]. As an example, suppose that an integrity constraint "salary of an employee cannot be greater than that of his manager" is defined for an employee database. To initialize the constraint the salary of every employee in the database is checked against that of his or her manager. If an employee does not satisfy this constraint, that employee's record is deleted from the database. After initialization, the constraint is checked whenever an employee record is added to the database or the salary field is modified for any employee. The nature of this constraint implies that it does not have to be enforced during a deletion operation on the database. There are constraints that need to be enforced during either update or deletion operations or both.

A database is defined to have the *consistency* property with respect to multiple users when at any instant of time the database will respond in the same manner (i.e., the answer to a particular query is the same) to all users. As an example, consider an employee file shared by a number of users in a time-shared environment. Suppose that the salary administrator is adjusting salaries and that at the same time the controller is preparing the budget from the database. If the salary administrator does not have the capability of locking the database (i.e., excluding all other users) for the complete duration of a transaction, the controller will wind up receiving an incorrect budget. On the other hand, if locking capabilities are available to both the salary administrator and the controller, and are used properly, both will receive consistent results from the database. There are many techniques for preserving consistency in a database.

Integrity and consistency are important properties of databases and thus are important factors for database designers. The major parameters are as follows:

1. *Integrity*
   a. Constraints
   b. Rules for enforcing constraints
   c. Rules for dealing with data when an integrity constraint test fails
   d. Efficient enforcement of constraints
2. *Consistency*
   a. Methods for modifying data:
      (1) Waiting time before modification enforced
      (2) Waiting time for other active users when modification enforced
      (3) The domain of influence of the modification
      (4) The algorithm for modification of data
   b. Number of users of the database at the instant the modification takes place

Recovery is the designed capability of the DBMS to restore the integrity of the database following any type of system failure. The recovery design process involves the establishment of adequate check systems to avoid losing transactions and data. If a system failure occurs, the major objective is to restore the state of transactions and data to their former position within a reasonable amount of time. The time for recovery may be specified as a quantitative objective in the user requirements. However, such an objective must include a clear definition of who initiates the recovery: a transaction, DBMS, operating system, or console operator. This will, of course, depend on the source of failure: transaction failures, operating system failures, or hardware failures.

Interactions with Other Design Issues

Implementation of integrity and consistency has a major impact on the efficiency of a DBMS. Intelligent implementation of integrity and consistency can reduce the overhead for enforcing these two components in any DBMS and thus increase efficiency. For example, if implementation of consistency is so designed that locking is confined to a minimum domain of influence of the data modification, it will affect the response time of the smallest set of users, thus increasing the efficiency of the overall system.

In general, however, enforcing integrity and consistency will increase response time. Intelligent methods and algorithms can only minimize the increase. If the enforcement of integrity and consistency can be scheduled during system idle time, the increase in response time can be reduced to zero. Thus, their effect on the efficiency of the system is dependent extensively on the design methods of implementation. To evaluate the effect of integrity on efficiency, for instance, one may determine the frequency and unit cost of integrity processing in terms of computer resources (e.g., CPU and I/O time) and treat integrity software as a new type of application in addition to end-user applications. Consistency, recovery, and security can also be evaluated in this manner.

A primary trade-off exists between recovery and another design issue, performance. The more sophisticated and the faster the recovery, the greater the on-line costs. Search operations may recover faster and more reliably, but update transactions will run more slowly. A secondary but very important trade-off is with efficiency/ size/growth. One can define independently recoverable subschemas such that transactions can update only one subschema. Depending on the problem, this may lead to a more (or less) flexible system for growth: the requirement to maintain user independence may or may not give a more flexible system. Depending on the partition, the resulting system may be larger in size, but it may be easier to maintain because of better defined interfaces.

2-3-2   Security

Security refers to the protection of data against intentional or unintentional disclosure, modification, or loss. The major objective of database security is to prohibit unauthorized access to data at minimum cost. Therefore, access control is the most important implementation problem. Access control can be implemented through subschemas that allow individual users to see only that portion of the logical database structure they need to see. Within that structure, refinements of access control (read only, write, append, etc.) may be specified within locking mechanisms. Most DBMSs allow locks to be placed on databases, records, or data items. Choosing where to put security locks on the data will have a profound influence on efficiency. Locks at the database level are easy to implement but may deny users access to many nonsensitive (and quickly needed) data. Security locks at the item level offer the most flexibility but involve a large overhead in processing data items.

The basic trade-off, then, appears to be in the extra processing overhead to enforce greater security at a detailed level. Consequently, it is crucial to have security constraints clearly specified in the requirements, together with performance constraints (for response time, etc.) so that a reasonable compromise can be achieved in the database schema design.

Designing and implementing security will also have to take into account the implementation techniques and algorithms used in integrity and consistency. The system has to be designed in such a manner that integrity is enforced for all users who are authorized to modify the database, whereas such enforcement may be unnecessary for those users who do not have the authorization for modification.

2-3-3   Efficiency

The efficiency aspects of the design of a DBMS-processible logical database structure (schema) are the use of computer resources to execute the database applications and the elapsed execution (or response) time. Three classes of efficiency objectives can be distinguished:

1. The schema designed must support the execution of each application in a minimum elapsed time. The focus is on on-line applications whose response time is set by the user. The response time for terminal users depends to a large extent on the number of secondary storage accesses. Projected future applications and database growth should also be accounted for in terms of continued acceptable response time.
2. The schema designed should require a minimum of secondary storage to store the database. The restrictions on the size of the database are called *size constraints*. Moreover, the execution of the applications must require a minimum data transfer volume between secondary and main storage.
3. The applications should be executable with a minimum of processing time and main storage requirements.

Before we look more deeply at the issue of efficiency, let us consider why efficiency of the database operation is used to evaluate the database structure. First, almost any real database has size constraints and its applications have maximum allowable response times. Second, although the other aspects of the design (integrity, consistency, recovery, security) can be more easily satisfied if efficiency is ignored, this could lead to an unacceptably inefficient design.

From the efficiency point of view the design of a schema can be viewed as an optimization problem. The problem is to construct a DBMS-processible schema such that:

1. The schema is in the solution space determined by the integrity, consistency, recovery, and security constraints as well as some DBMS restrictions.
2. The schema is optimum with respect to the efficiency objectives within these constraints.

This point of view implicitly subordinates the efficiency to the satisfaction of the integrity, consistency, recovery, and security constraints. Two arguments can be advanced in favor of this. One is that the main objective of a schema is to provide a global view of the database. The other argument is that the schema does not determine the physical database structure with enough detail to support a thorough performance analysis.

The trade-off between efficiency and other design issues is exemplified by the design for efficient retrieval, efficient update, and maintenance of consistency constraints. For example, whereas the use of redundancy in the schema may reduce response time for retrieval, it increases updating costs and introduces consistency problems. In addition, redundancy in the schema may imply a need for more secondary storage for the database. In general, it is worthwhile to pay a small update penalty for faster retrieval. Nevertheless, the predominance of retrieval or update for a particular database is the decisive factor in balancing the trade-offs discussed above.

Possibly the most serious obstacle to performance analysis is the lack of an adequate measure of the physical structure performance in terms of the schema. The currently used measures are the number of logical records accessed, the volume of data in the logical records transferred between main storage and secondary storage, and the secondary storage space needed if the stored records are equal to the logical records. Although all three measures can be very useful, they can also lose adequacy when the physical structure differs from the schema.

3 REQUIREMENTS FORMULATION AND ANALYSIS

Donna L. S. Rund

When database applications were first introduced, they tended to be simple and the databases small. As a result, designers were concerned primarily with optimizing the appropriate physical parameters in the databases (e.g., block size and access method). In this environment the information required to design a database usually consisted of some simple statistics (such as frequency of usage, volume of data, etc.). Today, database applications are very broad and very sophisticated. Many diverse applications may run on the same integrated database.

In this new environment, the design of a database to support all the applications becomes very complex. A design will not be valid, of course, without sufficient information to support the analysis that led to it. As a result, requirements analysis has been thrust to the forefront of the database design process.

In this chapter we investigate the objectives and techniques for information requirements formulation and analysis through an example, based upon a successful methodology applied to a number of large businesses. The information structure perspective (ISP), described in Chapter 2, is used here because in the most general case all the organizational data needs are defined, independent of a particular application. One might justifiably argue that data usage in an application is implied by the organizational "data needs," and therefore the usage perspective (UP) data are implicit here as well. Therefore, we make the distinction that the ISP represents the organizational model, data to be loaded into the database, and long-term usage implied by the "data needs"; whereas the UP represents explicit data required in reports, ad hoc queries, and update transactions to be done either manually or by computer. Ideally, the UP data are a proper subset of ISP data, but in practice not all the applications can be anticipated in advance and adjustments to the database structure must be made, preferably in the early design stages.

3-1 INTRODUCTION TO REQUIREMENTS ANALYSIS

Requirements analysis encompasses, among other things, an analysis of the organization's needs without any concern for constraints other than the manner in which the organization does its business. For example, the fact that a company has to report income tax in accordance with certain rules and regulations must be accomplished regardless of the procedure and system used to fulfill this need. Also, the fact that the company has decided to use a more automated process to support this application is independent of the computer or the database system to be used. The global decisions are usually made by top management, which determines the organization's goals and the strategies to achieve them.

After top management has stated policy, middle management will execute the strategies. Middle management probably will determine what computers and systems are appropriate for user applications. For example, should the system be a network of distributed computers, or should it be a single computer at company headquarters? It is expected that this kind of decision will be made by middle management in consultation with and subject to the approval of top management. (Of course, in many cases, this kind of decision as well as those from the top management may have already been made through, or constrained by, prior commitments.) The systems analyst, using additional information provided by operations-level users, will define the complete processing and information needed and derive an appropriate database structure.

The basic needs for systems analysts are first, the provision of a methodology to help capture the pertinent information needed for database design purposes, and second, the provision of tools to help them define their applications easily and precisely. These two topics are addressed in this chapter.

Requirements analysis involves the user, where the user may range from a clerk performing a business operation such as processing invoices, to a top-level manager responsible for formulating corporate goals and strategies. Thus, we focus our attention on the primary issue: communication between people with very different roles, objectives, and perceptions of the information system. However, it should be understood that requirements analysis is very closely related to other design steps; that is, preliminary metadata (data description and definition) are provided to develop or refine a conceptual model, which is then used as a guide to gathering and analyzing more metadata. Without such a guide it is unlikely that the collected metadata will be reliable; the volume of metadata will be higher and there will be insufficient structure for errors to be detectable.

As indicated in Chapter 2, information on organizational constraints, data elements, and processes are among the basic inputs to the database design process. In this chapter it is assumed that each application will be independently defined by either the analysts or the professionals in that particular area. Thus, the payroll department employees, who may be accountants by profession, will define the payroll applications; the personnel specialists will define the applications in the personnel department. Each department will perform its tasks without external constraints; it is assumed that each individual process will be defined in terms of a local view of the data without concern to the views of users of other applications.

3-1-1   Need for Corporate Requirements Analysis

The data elements and their relationships that are manipulated by database analysts cannot be easily deduced from basic business principles; there is too much diversity among organizations. Basic business principles provide a framework, but details should be provided by users from all levels of the organization. Data items and their relationships, which will be refined during the later phases of database design, must be defined and conflicts are at least recognized, if not resolved, during corporate requirements analysis. The problem is largely one of communication and understanding: different departments use different names for the same things, and the same names for different things, so that a preliminary common view of data and processes must be available before later steps can provide reliable results. Such a common view can be derived only in cooperation with users, and thus must be derived during corporate requirements analysis. However, this common view will not necessarily bear resemblance to the final database structure, but provides a framework for the collection of metadata. View integration occurs later [Lum, 1979a].

The importance and difficulty of communicating with the users should not be underestimated. Data models and data manipulation languages must be chosen very carefully for each user (e.g., a system flow diagram for an operations person, and a hierarchical diagram for a manager). An interviewer must provide feedback to the user in understandable terms, for example, by providing simple English-language statements of the major implications of the user's statements. This emphasizes the importance of iteration among the different design steps, as well as the distinction between corporate requirement analysis and other database design steps which are isolated from direct contact with the end users.

It might be argued that data elements, data relationships, and processes can be derived from analysis of an existing system. However, such a derivation requires two preliminary steps: first, functions must be abstracted from implementations, and second, business operations (which may be unchanged by a new information system) must be separated from control and planning (which will be changed greatly by a new information system). Performance of these two steps also requires considerable interaction with users.

3-1-2   Requirements Formulation and Analysis Steps

The methodology presented in this chapter consists of three basic substeps within the database system life cycle:

- *Step 1-1.* Defining the scope of the database (both current and future).
- *Step 1-2.* Collecting information about data usage ("data needs").
- *Step 1-3.* Translating the information collected into a form usable by the methodology analysis.

Each of these is described in detail in the following three sections.

3-2   DEFINING SCOPE

Ideally, the scope of a database system should cover all functional areas of an organization and be developed separately from any single application design effort. Rarely, however, has management approved the rather large budget required to develop logical or physical databases that encompass the entire organization. Instead, databases have been designed and implemented on an application by application basis. The data-processing environment that has resulted from this fragmented approach closely resembles that of the file environment, with the added cost and complexity of DBMS software. Consequently, we will concentrate on a method to define the potential scope of a database required to support a current application design effort while minimizing the possibility of creating a restrictive file environment.

Assuming that one or more databases are to be developed for a current application system, it is necessary to determine which functional areas of the company, outside of the application's scope, should be added to the design effort. If available, the best source of this information is the organizational *information plan*. Although plans vary widely in content, they should contain a definition of the organization's current and future management information strategy, a discussion of each system's scope, and definition of the dependencies between major systems (both automated and manual) and groups of data. Utilizing such a definition as a guideline, it is possible to determine which functional areas should be included in the design's scope. The example in Fig. 3-1 shows a portion of the systems and data groups required to support a distribution company, using data flow diagram format [Gane and Sarson,

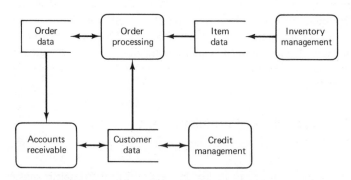

FIGURE 3-1   Sample information plan-data and system dependencies.

1979]. Assuming that the database was being developed for the accounts receivable application, the diagram would be used first to identify the major groups of data required to support accounts receivable: order data and customer data; and then to identify other applications which require at least some of the same data: order processing and credit management. The scope of the accounts receivable conceptual design effort would be defined to include the functional areas of accounts receivable, order processing, and credit management, as well as other areas in real systems.

If an organization does not have an information plan or if the plan does not contain diagrams of systems and data dependencies, it is the responsibility of the designer to determine the scope of the design effort. To accomplish this, persons within the functional areas for which the application is being designed should be interviewed to determine how they are related to the rest of the organization. Additional interviews could then be conducted in the newly identified areas to determine the extent to which they share data with the application under design.

Another factor that should be considered when defining scope is future changes to the business. Such changes include major changes in the business (e.g., new products, markets, etc.), major changes in operating policy (e.g., centralized versus decentralized purchasing and warehousing), and major changes in the governmental/regulatory environment. Each of these possible changes should be identified and defined further to determine if they could potentially change the definition, usage, or relationships between data. If it is determined that a future change could affect the database, the scope of the design effort should be expanded to consider the effects of the possible change.

3-3   COLLECTING INFORMATION ABOUT DATA USAGE

Once the scope of the database has been defined, the task of collecting information about data usage may begin. Before discussing methods to collect and document such information, it will be helpful to specify the relationship between data and the organization in which it is created and utilized. Then it will be easier to understand why some information is collected and documented in a highly structured manner and other information is either casually documented or not collected at all. To accomplish this, let us review a hypothetical organization and the changes it could undergo over time.

Assume that an organization was established by two brothers in the early 1920s to manufacture and sell nuts and bolts:

- One brother purchased the raw materials, manufactured the products, and shipped or delivered them to the customers.
- The other brother obtained customer orders, collected the money owed, and maintained the books.
- Business was conducted in a barn on their property.
- Except for occasional delivery boys, no other person worked for the company.

Further assume that the company is still in business but has expanded greatly:

- The company is publicly held and now employs over 4000 persons.
- There are two manufacturing locations and sales offices across the country.
- Most of the manufacturing is done using highly automated machinery.
- Computers are used to enter an order, plan the operations, and in general, track productivity.

To say that change has taken place in this business is obvious: volume has increased enormously, the manufacturing process has been automated, and sales personnel enter orders on-line. In trying to gain an understanding of the relationship of data to this organization, it is easy to concentrate on the number and effect of each change. Taking this viewpoint could be highly misleading, however, as many things have remained constant (Table 3-1). Specifically, these include:

- The operating functions that must be performed to conduct business (i.e., selling, manufacturing, maintaining accounts, etc.) are the same as those performed in the early 1920s.
- The relationship between operating functions has also remained fairly constant (i.e., an order must be placed before an item will be shipped, before an invoice is created, before a balance is posted to accounts receivable, etc.).
- Each of the operating functions still generates or uses a relatively constant set of data (i.e., customer name, account number, invoice number, invoice date, and amount billed are still required to post payments).

Two major conclusions may be drawn from these observations:

- Given that an organization remains in the same type of business, it will perform the same operational functions and generate or use the same basic operational data to conduct that business. Consequently, a stable database environment can be created if the logical database structure is based upon data relationships as created through the operational functions of a business.

TABLE 3-1   Changing and Constant Factors in a Business

Changed	*Remained Fairly Constant*
How functions are done (i.e., technology)	Functions performed to do business (take orders, maintain accounts, etc.)
Number of products and markets	
Number of employees—more management functions	Type of business being conducted
	Relationship between various operating functions
Information required to manage	Data generated and required to perform basic
Government regulations: taxes, social security, safety	operating functions ·

- The needs of management in controlling and planning the business will change according to "how" the business is being conducted and not "what" is being accomplished (e.g., "how" is automated versus manual; "what" is taking an order). In addition, the control and planning functions of management are almost always concerned with the operational functions of the business. Consequently, if a database structure is based on the data relationships created by the operational functions, almost all the data required to serve the changing needs of management will be provided.

The type of information to be collected about an organization's usage of data will be divided into the two categories of operational functions and control and planning functions and collected in two entirely different ways.

3-3-1 Operational Functions of the Business

The information collected about the operational functions of an organization and their usage of data provides the basic input to the database design process. Consequently, it is essential that the information be collected in a precise and thorough manner. To accomplish this, a highly structured interview and documentation technique should be used.

Before discussing how the interviews should be conducted, it is necessary to determine who should be interviewed. Since the purpose of the interview is to identify operational functions, it is best to start by identifying the organizational areas within the scope of the database design effort which perform functions essential to conducting business. For example, shipping, selling, and manufacturing all represent functions that must be performed to conduct business. On the other hand, the inventory control, market analysis, and auditing functions are essential to controlling or planning a business but are not necessary to conducting business. Once the organizations that perform operational functions have been identified, the persons that should be interviewed can be specified. The best way is to send each supervisor a questionnaire requesting the following information:

- The job titles of persons within his or her area of responsibility
- The operational functions performed in each job
- A brief idea of the objective of doing the job

Once the results of the questionnaires are received, a list of all job titles, functions performed, and their objectives should be developed (Table 3-2). Each job should then be reviewed and classified as either operational, control, or planning. The supervisor of each operational job should then be contacted and asked to select two persons with that job to be interviewed.

TABLE 3-2   Sample Job Titles, Functions, and Objectives

Job Title	Function	Objective
Order Picker*	Gather items for an order from warehouse	Fill customer's orders
Inventory Planner*	Buy items to stock inventory	Maintain inventory
Inventory Manager†	Determine optimum amount and time to buy items	Minimize investment in inventory
Order Clerk*	Create order	Take customer's order

*Represents a basic function of the organization.
†Represents a control function and should not be included at this time.

3-3-2   Conducting Interviews

The objectives of conducting operational interviews are threefold:

- Identify each operational function.
- Identify its data.
- Identify the explicit and implicit rules as to when and how each function occurs.

The following procedures will ensure that the required information is collected (as well as properly documented) in each interview.

Begin each interview by asking the interviewee to describe, in detail, the functions, or tasks, that are performed on a daily or potentially daily basis. As the interviewee describes the major actions, decisions, and interfaces, document them in a flowchart format (Fig. 3-2). Subsequently, utilize the flowchart as a feedback mechanism to the interviewee to verify that all the operational functions and their sequence are correct. Repeat the same procedure for weekly, monthly, quarterly, and yearly functions.

Second, as the flowchart is being developed, probe to determine what documents, files, or informal references are used to perform each function and note them in a separate list. The following list of information could have resulted from the flowchart shown in Fig. 3-2.

1. Order
2. Item book
3. Warehouse call (item number, quantity ordered, quantity available, and expected date of next shipment)
4. Salesperson's call (item number not available, alternate item number)

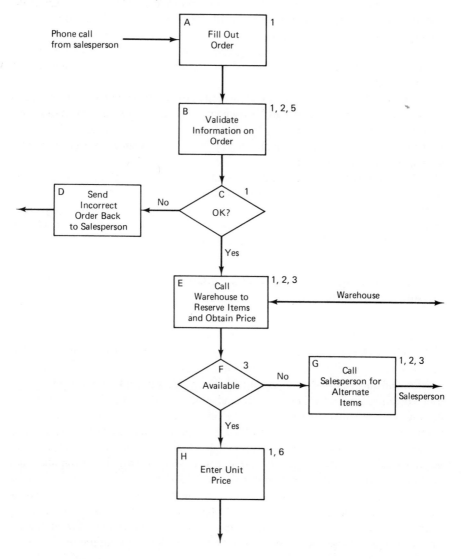

Jim Brown, Order Entry Clerk—Division Ordering Dept.
Daily activity—volume 450

Phone call
from salesperson

| A | Fill Out Order | 1 |

| B | Validate Information on Order | 1, 2, 5 |

| D | Send Incorrect Order Back to Salesperson |

C OK?   1   No

Yes

| E | Call Warehouse to Reserve Items and Obtain Price | 1, 2, 3 |

Warehouse

F Available   3   No

| G | Call Salesperson for Alternate Items | 1, 2, 3 |

Salesperson

Yes

| H | Enter Unit Price | 1, 6 |

FIGURE 3-2 Document flowchart of operational functions, document XREF, and function identifiers.

5. Customer log
6. Pricing form

Third, once the interviewee understands and agrees to the contents of the flowchart, discuss each specific action (e.g., Fill Out Order), decision (e.g., Available?), and interface point (e.g., Call Warehouse) to determine what specific documents or references are required. Using the information list created during the interview, place the number of the specific information (e.g., 2 for Item Book) next to each symbol on the flowchart (Fig. 3-2). After this has been accomplished, request a copy of each document that has been discussed. If none exists, such as in the case of a phone call, record the data content next to the reference itself (see Warehouse Call in the example).

Finally, associate the data elements actually utilized or created on each document to each function on the flowchart. To accomplish this, assign each symbol on the flowchart a unique identifier (e.g., A, B, C, etc., on Fig. 3-2). Place the identifier next to each specific data element actually utilized or created on each document associated with that function.

There is no specific format to document the explicit and implicit rules associated with when and how each of the flowcharted steps is performed (e.g., a salesperson can submit orders only to the warehouse in his or her region). It is essential, however, that such rules be recorded. If convenient, a second piece of paper may be attached to each flowchart or the notes may be put on the flowchart itself.

3-3-3   Management Interviews for Control and Planning Functions

The second type of information required to develop the conceptual database includes an in-depth understanding of the organization's explicit and implicit operating policies, a definition of the control and planning functions and the data they require, and an idea of business changes that may occur in the future. Such information is obtained from interviews with top and middle management. Since the nature of the information collected will vary according to the organization and the person involved, there is no rigid format in which the interview should be documented. It is recommended, however, that each interview be taped, if possible, and then transcribed to minimize the possibility of losing or missing information. If taping is not possible, thorough and readable notes should be taken.

Top-management interviews should be conducted with persons whose responsibilities include defining the goals and objectives of the business, formulating strategies to achieve these goals, and managing plans to implement these strategies. The objective of these interviews is to gain an overall understanding of:

- The basic components of the business and how they interact with one another
- The internal environment (i.e., organizations, locations, etc.)
- The external environment that affects the business directly or indirectly (regulatory agencies, type of markets, etc.)
- Explicit or implicit operating policies that determine how business is conducted (*Note:* Some of these may be identified when discussing the internal and the external environment)

- Information currently used or required to plan the business (obtain examples if available)
- Forecasted changes that may affect either the type of the business, the scope of the business, or how it is being conducted

Middle-management interviews should be conducted with persons directly responsible for the performance of one or more operating areas. The objective of these interviews is to gain a more thorough understanding of:

- The interfaces between various operating areas
- The rules and policies governing day-to-day operations
- The types of information currently used or required to measure and control performance
- The potential effect of forecasted changes on the operational areas

3-4   REQUIREMENTS INFORMATION TRANSFORMATION

The process of translating the information collected during the interviewing process into a form usable in the methodology analysis involves five major steps:

1. Compiling a list of all the data elements created and utilized
2. Defining the operational tasks of the organization, their characteristics, and their usage of data
3. Defining the control and planning tasks of the organization, their characteristics, and usage of data
4. Developing a list of all implicit and explicit operating rules and policies
5. Developing a list of potential future changes and the way in which they may affect operations

These steps are described in more detail below.

3-4-1   Identifying Data Elements

The problem most often encountered in developing a list of all data elements created and utilized by the operational functions flowcharted in the interviews is identifying which data elements are, or are not, redundant. One way to reduce the magnitude of this problem is to extract individual data elements from the documents obtained and categorize them in generic lists (such as dates, amounts, inventories, names, etc.). Two major goals are accomplished by following this procedure. First, the process of categorizing reduces the possibility of listing duplicate data elements.

Second, questions regarding the definition of each data element can be resolved by referencing the context, (i.e., the document and function) in which each is used.

Once generic lists have been developed and questions of redundancy and definition resolved, each data element should be put into a data dictionary and assigned both a unique identifier and description (see Table 3-3).

3-4-2   Identifying Operational Tasks

Once a dictionary of unique data elements has been created, it is possible to analyze the flowcharts developed during the interviews and define operational task/ data relationships. As previously mentioned, the operational functions of an organization provide the basis upon which a relatively stable set of data relationships can be defined. To accomplish this it is necessary to identify the lowest level of work that requires, on a repetitive basis, a unique set of data. Such a level of work is called a *task* and is defined as:

- A unique unit of work
- Consisting of a set of serially performed steps
- All steps directed toward a common goal
- All steps utilizing or creating a common set of data

A task/data relationship is then defined as the unique relationship created between data items when they are used to perform a specific task. These relationships provide the primary input to conceptual design analysis. Consequently, it is critical that they be defined carefully and thoughtfully.

The process of defining task/data relationships begins with analyzing the flowcharts developed during the interviews. The following rules should be applied to analyze each flowchart and divide it into a series of unique tasks:

- A task must be performed within one functional area of the business (i.e., tasks are always defined within each flowchart and will never span two or more).
- Each task must consist of a set of serially performed steps (or serially positioned symbols on the flowchart). If a decision point occurs and one path

TABLE 3-3   Sample List of Data Elements

ID Number	Name	Definition
1	Order Number	Uniquely defines each order throughout the company
2	Quantity Ordered	Defines the order quantity of a specific item on an order for one customer

of the decision involves a new action, the first task ends and a new one begins (see Fig. 3-3, tasks 2 and 3).

- Each step within a task must be performed within the same time frame (e.g., if a significant amount of time could elapse between two steps, such as in symbols E, F, and G on Fig. 3-3, more than one task should be defined).

- Each step within the task must utilize the same set of data. (*Note:* The specific data elements used must be the same and not just the information reference number that appears on the flowchart.) If new data are created in one step of

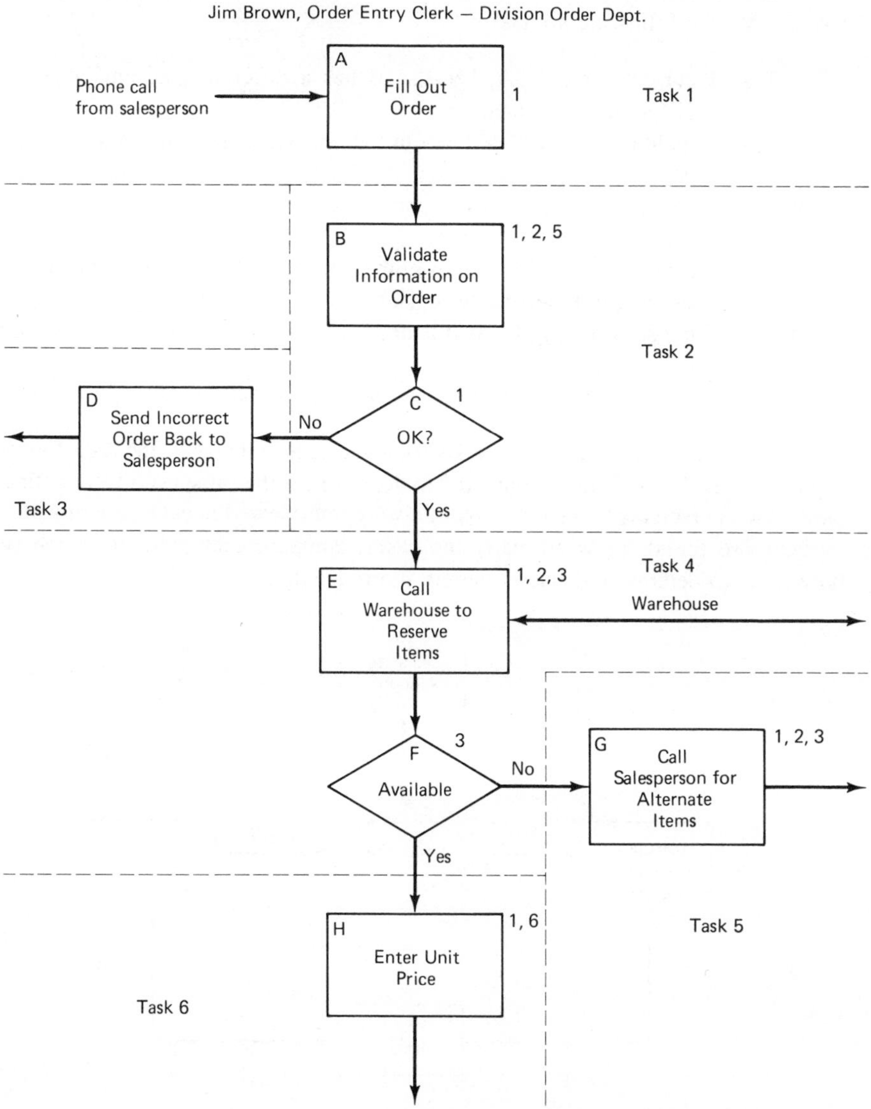

FIGURE 3-3 Dividing the flowchart into tasks.

the task, and utilized in the next step, they may be considered as the same set
of data.

- Each step within a task must always be performed. There is one exception to
  this rule, which is due to the level of detail that may be shown on the
  flowchart. If the flowchart contains a decision such as that shown in Fig. 3-4,
  all paths in the decision should be included in the same task because no path
  causes a change in goals or new data, or includes different steps.

Using the rules above as guidelines, the flowchart shown in Fig. 3-3 has been
divided into the following six tasks:

- *Task 1* consists of only A, because B has a different goal and requires a
  different set of data.
- *Task 2* includes B and C, as they utilize the same data and share the same
  goal.
- *Task 3* consists of only D, as it represents one path of a decision that is not
  always executed.
- *Task 4* consists of E and F, as they both try to attain the goal of reserving items
  and utilize the same set of data.
- *Task 5* consists of only G, as it is not performed all the time and has a goal
  other than those of E, F, and H.
- *Task 6* consists of H, as it utilizes a new set of data.

After all flowcharts have been analyzed and divided into tasks, the tasks for each
duplicate interview should be compared to determine if the same tasks were defined.
(*Note:* Two persons with the same job title were interviewed in each department.) If
conflicts are found (as is normally the case), compare each symbol on the two
flowcharts to determine if one is merely more detailed:

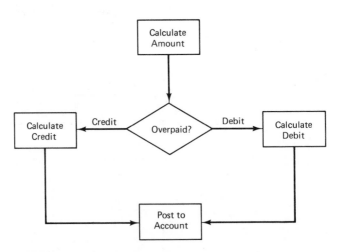

FIGURE 3-4   Example of both decision paths that should be included in
the same task.

1. If the flowcharts appear to be the same, but on different levels of detail, choose the one that best defines a complete unit of work.
2. If real functional differences are found, review the documents associated with each (and the accompanying notes); sometimes people with like titles do perform different functions due to seniority or competency. When such a situation is found, separate the unique tasks and add them to the list.
3. If it is difficult to determine why differences exist, call the supervisors and ask if they would review the task definitions (*Note:* Do not bring the interviews, as that could possibly destroy the confidentiality that should have been developed between the interviewer and the interviewee.)

Once all conflicts between definitions have been resolved, task/data relationships may be documented. Because it is highly likely that other redundant tasks have been defined, it is best to arrange the flowcharts by department or organization. This arrangement increases the likelihood that redundant tasks will be identified by the person doing the documentation for each organizational group. The documentation process should include the following (see Table 3-4):

- Each task should be assigned a numeric identifier.
- Each task should be briefly defined through a "verb-object" command such as "Take Order," "Reserve an Ordered Item," and so on.
- All tasks should be classified as either operational, control, or planning. (*Note:* Except in an unusual circumstance, all tasks extracted from the flow-charts are operational.)
- The frequency and volume of each task (documented on the upper part of the flowchart) should be identified.
- Each task should be related to a specific functional area of the organization such as order processing, manufacturing, and so on. (*Note:* Do not use organization or department names, as they usually do not represent the functions being performed across two or more departments.)

TABLE 3-4   Example of Task/Data Relationship Documentation Format

Task Number	Task Definition	Type	Frequency	Volume	Department	Data Elements
1	Create Order	Operational	Daily	2,000	Order Entry	1, 45, 50, 67
2	Validate Order	Operational	Daily	2,000	Order Entry	4–17, 22, 27, 50, 117, 120–124, 202
3	Fill Out Error Report	Operational	Daily	25	Order Entry	4–10, 200–204
4	Reserve Item from Warehouse	Operational	Daily	8,000	Order Entry	7–9, 62, 65
5	Request Alternate Items	Operational	Daily	50	Order Entry	2, 7–9, 15
6	Look Up Unit Price	Operational	Daily	7,950	Order Entry	15, 62, 65, 75

Because of the high volume of information created by defining data elements and task/data relationships, an automated system such as a data dictionary should be used to store, report, and update all such information.

3-4-3   Identifying Control and Planning Tasks

Control and planning tasks are identified by reviewing management interviews and highlighting the areas that pertain to a control or planning function. Take the following excerpt from an interview of a logging supervisor as an example:

> My boss judges me on the productivity of my loggers. Each and every day I get them to fill out a card that tells me how many trees they cut, how big they are, and how many broke. My secretary takes these cards and runs a tab on each *crew* so I can see how well they have done. This way I can get on their back if *logging productivity* falls.

An analysis of this excerpt shows that the logging supervisor performs the control task "Tracking Crew Logging Productivity." To accomplish this task, the supervisor is using the following data elements: days of work, number of trees cut, size of trees, number of trees broken, and crew identification.

> My boss judges me on the productivity of my loggers. Each and every *day* I get them to fill out a card that tells me *how many trees they cut, how big they are,* and *how many broke*. My secretary takes these cards and runs a *tab on each crew* so I can see how well they have done. This way I can get on their back if logging productivity falls.

The control task that resulted from this analysis should be added to the list of operational tasks with the "type" designated as control. The process described above should be repeated for all management interviews with appropriate type of control or plan included in the task. If new data elements are defined through this process, add them to the data dictionary so that they may be properly cross-referenced through a numerical identifier.

3-4-4   Identifying Current and Future Operating Policies

The process of identifying operating policies and future changes is very similar to that of identifying control and planning tasks as they are simply extracted from interviews. The product of this process will be two lists, with one containing statements of policies and the other statements of possible future changes.

Operating policies define the way in which business must be conducted or how different parts of the organization must relate. When reviewing the interviews for policies, look for statements that put parameters around how something is to be done. For example, the following interview contains two policies:

> We are a very decentralized organization. All *salespeople* report to a *specific region* and can sell only out of that region's *warehouse*. In addition, each *customer* is *treated* on a *region*-by-region basis. Consequently, customer *X* may have one *sales agreement* in region 1 and another in region 2. We choose this organization because competition changes so drastically from one area to another.

Reviewing the underlined areas, the following policies should be extracted and added to the list:

- Salespeople are assigned to specific regions and cannot sell items not stocked in that region's warehouse.
- Customers are treated on a regional basis, implying that they have a different sales agreement in each region in which they purchase goods.

Future changes include anything that may affect the scope of the business, present operating policies, or the relationship of the business to the external environment (regulatory agencies, etc.). To identify changes, scan each interview and highlight any treatment that implies change, and, if possible, the effect of the change. For example:

> We currently have a purchasing department at each warehouse. We did this so that each regional manager could have total control over his or her profit and loss picture. As prices are rising, however, it looks as if we may be able to get better price breaks through *central purchasing* of *higher-volume items.* Who knows. That's a radical change and you know how slow management moves sometimes.

The possible future change ''Purchase certain high volume items on a centralized versus a decentralized basis'' should be added to a list of changes.

This completes the requirements formulation step of database design. A description of conceptual design terminology and techniques is presented in the next three chapters.

3-5   TOOLS FOR FORMULATING AND DOCUMENTING REQUIREMENTS

Two primary problems are involved in training and tools. Training the information system specialists (who act as liaison between users and the technical persons designing the database) is necessary so that they can communicate effectively with people of different levels and extract the pertinent information. Communication problems arise not only because of the imprecision and qualitative rather than quantitative nature of natural language, but also because unstated rules and policies, things that everyone but the interviewer knows, are necessary parts of the corporate requirements. Such vague rules and policies must be made explicit and their consequences verified by the users. Tools are needed to enable different nondatabase professionals to specify clearly what their applications do. Both of these problems require good data models and methodologies.

A data model must be simple and "natural" to be acceptable to the end users, who are professionals of various disciplines. Because of this, models acceptable for an implementation schema design may not be suitable here. Note that a model that may lack mathematical foundation in some aspects may well be suitable. The reason is that although it is desirable to have all the processes, views of the data, and other information directly specified by the end users, the analysts and designers still play an active role. It is expected that they will help cleanse the information before it is ready for further processing by a design system.

Because of the high degree of interaction between people, and the limitations of current methodologies and tools, corporate requirement analysis is unquestionably a labor-intensive and error-prone process, requiring many iterations to achieve reliable results. Software engineering methodologies and tools are often either too general to be applicable, or are oriented toward processes rather than data. Clearly, there is a need for methodologies and tools that would assist both the database and program designers. Such methodologies and tools would have to deal with the realities of information systems—incomplete and changing requirements are the rule, rather than the exception. "Ballpark" and precise requirements must somehow be combined to obtain a reasonable basis for design.

The Problem Statement Language/Problem Statement Analyzer (PSL/PSA) [Hershey et al., 1975; Teichroew and Sayani, 1971; Teichroew et al., 1974; Teichroew and Hershey, 1977] is a complex but valuable computerized tool. A user of PSL/PSA describes the problem (in the Problem Statement Language, or PSL) as a collection of objects within the proposed database system, attributes of these objects, and relationships between these objects. Commentlike descriptions of objects are accepted and stored as part of their definitions. Objects are of several types. ENTITY and RELATION objects connected by the RELATED relationship may be used to represent the information structure of the proposed database system. In a manufacturing company database, for example, the PLANT and EMPLOYEE entity classes may be represented by corresponding PSL ENTITY objects. There would also be a RELATION object called "WORKS-IN" (or some variation) between these EN-TITY objects. WORKS-IN would be declared to have connectivity 1 to 100,000 since a particular employee works for exactly one plant and at most 100,000 employees (all of them) work for a particular plant. More detailed information concerning data to be stored for each ENTITY and RELATION may also be specified. Usage specifications may be made in terms of PROCESS, INPUT, OUTPUT, and other types of objects. A PROCESS object is a transaction or report type to be run on the proposed system.

The PSL/PSA system stores user-supplied system description information in a database. Facilities are provided for performing consistency checks and for printing various kinds of documentation in reports from the stored system description.

The CASCADE system [Aanstad et al., 1972] is another requirements analysis system that may be used to perform a bookkeeping function for database system requirements. It may be used in a manner essentially similar to the way in which PSL/PSA is used. Information to be stored in the database is represented as a collection of related permanent information, permanent information set, and permanent message objects. Application programs are represented as process objects, and are related to the information description objects that they manipulate.

Like PSA, CASCADE keeps system description information in a database, and will produce documentation reports based on the database contents on demand.

Data Dictionaries

The requirements analysis, logical and physical design, and implementation steps of the database system life cycle make heavy use of the catalog function. Resulting from the requirements formulation and analysis step is a set of validated data and processing requirements which serve as input to the remaining steps of this phase. Although there are no "off-the-shelf" packages specifically for documenting processing requirements, there are several software packages for documenting data requirements, called data dictionaries/directories. The data dictionary/directory (DD/D) function provides the centralized management of the data about the database. Its processing function is to store and retrieve these metadata (e.g., narrative data definitions) and to provide reports for the database administrator.

Over the past few years a number of DD/D packages have become available in the marketplace. Although no one DD/D package provides all functions, and packages are being extended to include program (process) inventory, the following are considered basic functions [Canning, 1974].

1. *Storage of data definitions.* The storing of symbolic and encoded data definitions for multiple databases, both machine-processible and not.
2. *Interrogation of data definition.* The preparation of reports of data item definitions and relationships for both the database administrator and the user.
3. *Generation of database quality procedures.* The creation of input validation programs, program test data, and sample output programs from the data definitions.
4. *Performance of security and integrity functions.* The control of the access to the DD/D and the preservation of the definitions as to the standards and conventions of the corporation.
5. *Maintenance of statistics on utilization.* The recording and storage for each element in the database of a profile of its usage and the programs that use it.
6. *Processing of definition.* The generation of encoded data definition for database management systems (e.g., DBD and PSB for IMS), the redefinition of existing elements, and the addition of new elements.

Tools for End Users

Realizing that tool users might be experts in each application area but are not necessarily very knowledgeable in computer systems and their functional capabilities, tools should be built in such a way that usage of tools will not require sophisticated computer system knowledge. Software engineering [Boehm, 1973; Hebalker and Zilles, 1979; Ross, 1977; Ross and Schoman, 1977; Wasserman, 1980] in some cases helps in addressing this area. Generally, it tends to stop at too high a level to provide adequate information for database design purposes. Existing work in database design seldom addresses the collection and analysis of corporate requirements in a manner that will provide us with a foundation to build tools.

Although there is a need to represent the processes, the associated views of the data, and the related information for later analysis, the information provided should be accurate but not overly restrictive. For example, although specifications written in current programming languages such as COBOL or PL/I may be very accurate, they tend to distort the view of the applications; the intent will be hidden and will be practically impossible to detect, particularly by automated means. What is needed is a tool with a very high level language based on a model that is simple and familiar to its users but completely independent of any systems.

Given such tools, end users can be induced to state all applications in a precise and accurate way so that database analysts and designers can easily incorporate this information with other information obtained through interviews. More important, information specified with the use of such tools is easily processible by the computer and can be used as direct inputs to the other areas. One may question if such tools can be devised. Observing the progress made in high-level database languages such as QBE, SEQUEL, QUEL, CONVERT, and so on [Chamberlin and Boyce, 1974; Shu et al., 1977; Stonebraker et al., 1976; Zloof, 1975], it is possible that very high level application specification languages may be created with the desired characteristics.

In the future, many developments may greatly reduce present problems: (1) the emerging role of the database administrator as an interface between users and computer specialists; (2) the development of general information-oriented models of organization; (3) an increased exposure of managers to computers, particularly in schools of business administration; (4) the increased attention that computer specialists are devoting to human factors, as opposed to computer efficiency; and (5) the development of other software technology that will have applications in our area. These developments, together with the development of tools for designing databases, will provide much help in relieving the problems faced by today's database analysts and designers.

II CONCEPTUAL DESIGN

4 CONCEPTUAL DATA MODELING

As detailed in Chapter 2, database design can be divided into four reasonably distinct phases: requirements analysis, conceptual design, implementation design, and physical design. Whereas Chapter 3 addressed the topic of requirements analysis, the next three chapters focus on conceptual design.

4-1 FRAMEWORK FOR CONCEPTUAL DESIGN

Conceptual design deals with information independent of any actual implementation (i.e., any particular hardware or software system). It is the objective of conceptual design to represent information in a form that is comprehensible to the user independent of system specifics, but implementable on several systems.

Representation of Information

A number of database design techniques and requirements description mechanisms have been developed in recent years. However, most of these techniques have addressed only a part of the problem and are awkward to use. One of the major stumbling blocks, therefore, lies at the interface between the representation mechanism used to specify the users' information requirements and the first steps of the design methodology.

To be useful, the representation mechanism should reflect the perspective and sophistication of the users. The problem is that representation mechanisms that are user oriented tend not to be very database oriented, while representation mechanisms that are design oriented force the users to make many representation decisions in order to get the information into a processible form. In many cases these representation decisions mask important design decisions which are not recognized as such by the design methodology, thus restricting the scope and power of the design process.

Motivation for a High-Level Representation
Mechanism

In most representation mechanisms, the users describe their information needs in terms of entities, attributes, and relationships (entity–relationship, or E–R diagrams, discussed in Section 4-3), or in the terms of records, items, and sets using a DBMS's data description language. It is obvious that a great deal of generality and potential design optimality are lost when the user is restricted to a particular low-level data description language instead of a higher-level entity diagram to specify their information requirements. Although these diagrams are a high-level representation, many design decisions are still implicitly made when users specify their needs in this form. For example, the modeling of information in Fig. 4-1 indicates at least three different entity structures can be used to represent the fact that an employee is assigned to a given project.

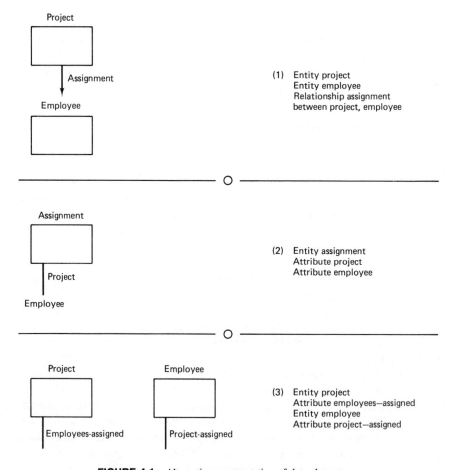

FIGURE 4-1   Alternative representation of data elements.

Depending on the perspective of the user, a work assignment could be viewed as a relationship (1), an entity (2), or an attribute (3). In a given design environment it is quite likely that multiple users are involved and have specified the same basic information in a variety of ways.

One of the most difficult aspects of multiple user environments is the consolidation of user views. This is quite difficult to do, even within a particular class of structures such as entities alone, or relationships alone. When different structures can be used to represent the same concept as well, the resolution is twice as difficult. As a result, there are two major reasons for a designer to use a high level of abstraction in the design process. Entities, attributes, and relationships are not always explicitly distinguished and the design decisions are often fuzzy. Second, the problem of consistency checking would be simplified if a common, high-level information representation structure for conceptual information structures could be developed.

One additional issue remains to be addressed. Would a representation mechanism that does not distinguish among entities, attributes, or relationships be accepted by the user community? We hope that it would be acceptable and eventually be preferable to users. This may seem counterintuitive to those of us on the designer's side of the fence. We often forget, though, that users are not interested in how the information is stored. They are only interested in receiving answers to interrogation. It has been accepted that users are not interested in nor care to understand physical database design since it does not help them solve their immediate problems. The same is true of the information at the DDL and entity structure levels. Only the information *content* is helpful to the users; information *structure* has no significance for users. This is not to say that in writing application programs to use the database the user's programmers do not need to know the structure of the database. In database design, though, the application programmers are not the ones who specify the required content of the database. Hopefully, the end user who has no interest in "how" of database design, but has the best understanding of what is needed, will specify the necessary content.

Design Perspective

Conceptual design will be approached here from two perspectives. Based on level of information representation, Fig. 4-2 indicates these perspectives to be object representation and entity modeling.

The first perspective is the formulation, definition, and integration of high-level data objects pertinent to model information. This perspective focuses on the integration of concepts by representing them as objects. Simply stated, the technology for this activity blends elements together without reference to their parts. These elements will be represented as objects that are blended together in the form of hierarchies. The design decisions for the object representation level are:

1. What are the objects?
2. What are the contexts for these objects?

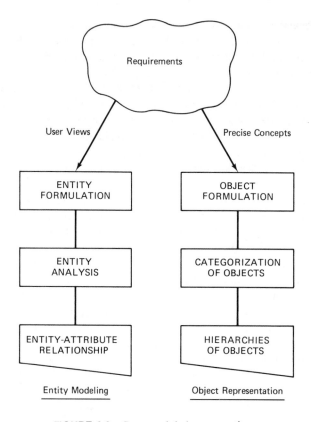

FIGURE 4-2 Conceptual design perspectives.

3. What are descriptive properties of each object?
4. What are identifying properties for each object?

The second perspective from which conceptual design can be approached, entity modeling, is the representation and integration of user views in terms of entity diagrams. Techniques for formulating entity diagrams, while mostly informal, result in the specification of entities, attributes, and relationships.

Four basic design decisions (steps) of entity information structure design are concerned with the representation of the users' information requirements. The four decisions are:

1. Selection of entities
2. Selection of entity attributes
3. Selection of key attributes for entities
4. Selection of relationships between entities

4-2 OBJECT REPRESENTATION

The conceptual approach to information systems design had its beginning in the ANSI/SPARC database study group work of the 1970s [ANSI, 1978]. Although it has received much attention in the literature [Falkenberg, 1976; Nijssen, 1977; Senko et al., 1973], as yet there is no common consensus as to the appropriate concepts and axioms. Rather than debate the issue, we focus on the information representation techniques, which have a good deal of commonality in their approach to the work of Smith and Smith [1978] and the research of Novak [Novak and Fry, 1976].

This perspective is directed to the idealization of the conceptual design level. It assumes the availability of a "clean" set of concepts that are to be integrated. They are "clean" in the sense that they have distinct meanings which are understood by the designer.

This perspective focuses directly on the central activity of conceptual design—concept integration. To appreciate this approach, it is necessary to understand the notion of an abstraction which people often use to "think about" or model the complex structures of the real world.

Abstraction

The dictionary definition of the term "abstract" is "disassociated from any specific instance; difficult to understand, ideal" [Webster's, 1974]. Using the principal definition, it is a fundamental premise of this approach that abstractions are the basis by which human beings understand and manipulate complex systems. An abstraction is a collection of details about a particular thing which can conveniently be viewed and named as a whole.

For example, a book names a collection of typed pages which are bound together; a postal address is a reference to a physical building which is a collection of rooms. Abstractions come in two forms: abstraction of the state of a system (i.e., abstract objects) and abstractions of the transformation of a system (i.e., abstract operations).

For the purposes of database design we are concerned with abstract objects or concepts. The goal of conceptual design is to define the relative structure of abstract objects. A database does not usually consist of independent objects; normally, objects are related to other objects in two ways, as a class and a collection. Correspondingly, there are two methods for object formalization: aggregation and generalization. *Aggregation* forms an object as a relationship between other objects. *Generalization* forms an object from a class of other objects.

Aggregation

In a mathematical sense aggregation corresponds to the Cartesian product. Objects in this case are formed as a relationship between other objects.

Figure 4-3 provides some examples that illustrate the idea of aggregation. In the

Relationship between objects	Aggregate object
A person reserves a room in a hotel for a certain date	Reservation
Instructor offers a course during a semester	Class (offering)
A vehicle has a load from a destination to a source	Haulage (trip)

FIGURE 4-3 Aggregation.

first case the relationship among the four objects, PERSON, ROOM, HOTEL, and DATE, is expressed by the object RESERVATION. That is to express the fact that a person reserves a room in a hotel for a particular date. In this particular aggregation the names of the individual objects are suppressed and the relationship is named as a whole.

Another way to view this is to think of an aggregation as the noun form of the verb in the relationship. For example, RESERVATION is the noun form of the verb "to reserve." This, however, is not always the case, as in the university example of a CLASS, which is a better name for the aggregation of "an instructor offers a course during a semester" than OFFERING. Consequently, the names of the aggregated relationships must be chosen carefully since they carry the semantics of the aggregation. It is important to note that each component of an object is a *simple* object, not a *set* of objects. For example, an INSTRUCTOR and a COURSE are both valid components of CLASS, but the set of STUDENTS in the CLASS is not a valid component.

Generalization

Figure 4-4 illustrates the idea of generalization. For example, the class of objects {DOG, CAT, ELEPHANT} can be generalized to the object ANIMAL. In this generalization, individual differences among the objects DOG, CAT, and ELEPHANT are being ignored (e.g., dogs bark, elephants have trunks), and their common "animal" nature is being emphasized. In general, if the class $\{O_1, \ldots, O_n\}$ can be generalized to O, then O_i is said to be a *category* of O. For example, DOG is a category of ANIMAL. Notice that it is impossible to determine whether O is a generalization of $\{O_1, \ldots, O_n\}$ unless each object is named. It is these names that carry the semantics of generalization.

Class of Objects	Generic object
{dog, cat, elephant}	animal
{car, truck, bicycle, ...}	road vehicle
{apple, pear, banana}	fruit

FIGURE 4-4 Generalization.

The objects resulting from aggregation and generalization are not special in any way. An aggregate object may be the generalization of some class of objects, in which case it will also be a generic object. A generic object may be the aggregation of some relationship between objects, in which case it will also be an aggregate object. In general, each object is both an aggregate object and a generic object. However, some components or categories of the object may not be of interest and thus do not appear in the conceptual model. An object is called *primitive* when no components or categories are of interest.

Abstraction Hierarchies

When generalization and aggregation are repeatedly applied to objects, hierarchies of objects are formed. Figure 4-5 illustrates a generalization hierarchy over various categories of vehicles. The class {VW-TRUCK, FORD-TRUCK, GM-TRUCK} is generalized to TRUCK. The class {TRUCK, LINER, PLANE} is generalized to MOTOR VEHICLE. The class {ROAD VEHICLE, MOTOR VEHICLE, AIR VEHICLE} is generalized to VEHICLE. The object MOTOR VEHICLE is crosshatched because it will be used as a common object throughout several examples.

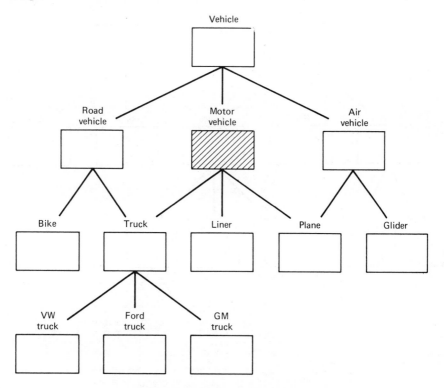

FIGURE 4-5 Generalization hierarchy.

There are two important things to observe about the structure of generalization hierarchies. First, notice that some categories are shared between several objects. For example, TRUCK is shared between ROAD VEHICLE and MOTOR VEHICLE, and PLANE is shared between MOTOR VEHICLE and AIR VEHICLE. Second, a generalization hierarchy may have several roots, not just a single root. Whereas the hierarchy in Fig. 4-5 has only one root, if this root is removed, the resulting hierarchy has three roots: ROAD VEHICLE, MOTOR VEHICLE, and AIR VEHICLE.

As required by aggregation, there is a functional (1 : *n*) correspondence between each object and its components in Fig. 4-6. For example, a HAULAGE determines a unique MOTOR VEHICLE, a unique SITE, and a unique LOAD. This is a characteristic property of aggregation hierarchies which distinguishes them from other kinds of hierarchies. In particular, given two objects, the functional correspondence can be used to decide whether one object can be a component of the other. For example, MOTOR VEHICLE cannot be a component of MAKER since a maker produces many motor vehicles.

It is worthwhile comparing Figs. 4-5 and 4-6, to note the different structural contexts in which the object MOTOR VEHICLE appears. Figure 4-5 is concerned with categories only—a MOTOR VEHICLE is a category of VEHICLE, not a

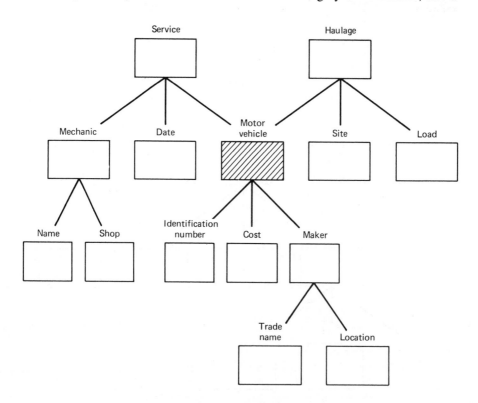

FIGURE 4-6   Aggregation hierarchy.

component of VEHICLE. Figure 4-6 is concerned with components only—a COST is a component of MOTOR VEHICLE, not a category of MOTOR VEHICLE. If it is desired to give an interpretation to edges in these hierarchies, then an edge in a generalization hierarchy may be read as "is-a," and in an aggregation hierarchy as "is-part-of." For example, a MOTOR VEHICLE is a VEHICLE, and a COST is-part-of a MOTOR VEHICLE.

A conceptual model must include the aggregation and generalization hierarchies for all concepts needed to support the application views. In principle, the aggregation hierarchy and the generalization hierarchy for a conceptual model could be defined separately. However, more modularity is achieved if the structure of each object is defined as a single unit. To distinguish the components from the categories in this structure, it is helpful to place the components in the plane of the paper, and the categories in a plane perpendicular to the paper. For example, Fig. 4-7 presents the structure of MOTOR VEHICLE in this way.

Such three-dimensional diagrams can be extended recursively to include the structure of components and categories. This is often a very clear way to present conceptual structure and is used in later sections. However, since any two objects can (in principle) be generalized or aggregated, conceptual models do not always fit neatly onto a three-dimensional grid system. Some examples of this situation are presented later.

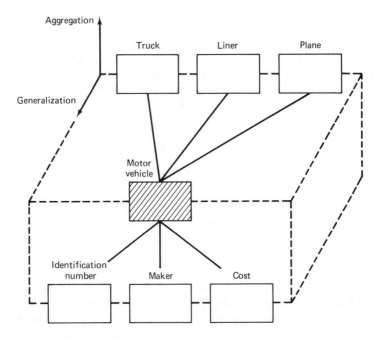

FIGURE 4-7   Consolidation of aggregation and generalization hierarchies.

User Views

Figure 4-6 shows an aggregation hierarchy that involves MOTOR VEHICLE. This hierarchy will be described by working from top to bottom. A SERVICE has three components: the MECHANIC who performed the service, the DATE of the service, and the MOTOR VEHICLE receiving the service. Notice that MOTOR VEHICLE is a component that is shared between SERVICE and HAULAGE. A MOTOR VEHICLE has its own components; its IDENTIFICATION NUMBER, the COST of its purchase, and the MAKER who produced it. The components of MECHANIC and MAKER are self-explanatory.

The previous description of Fig. 4-6 is unbiased with respect to a user's viewpoint. Suppose, instead, that the viewpoint of a user interested in motor vehicles is taken. This user will regard MOTOR VEHICLE as an entity, SERVICE as a relationship (i.e., a mechanic services a motor vehicle on a date), HAULAGE as a relationship (i.e., a motor vehicle hauls a load to a site), and IDENTIFICATION, NUMBER, COST, and MAKER as components, as in Fig. 4-8(a). On the other hand, a user interested in makers would regard MAKER as an entity, MOTOR VEHICLE as a relationship (i.e., a maker assigns a cost and identification number to a chassis), and TRADE NAME and LOCATION as components, as in Fig. 4-8(b). Finally, a user who is interested in services as entities (e.g., the service manager) would regard MECHANIC, DATE, and MOTOR VEHICLE as components [Fig. 4-8(c)].

There is a very important conclusion that can be drawn from the previous paragraph. It is inappropriate to assign a fixed interpretation of relationship, entity, or component to an object. Such an interpretation should only be made relative to the viewpoint of a particular user. If a user views an object as an entity, then its "parent" objects appear as relationships and its "child" objects appear as components. Different users may view different objects as entities. A representation for conceptual models that requires a fixed interpretation will artificially constrain concept integration. Artificial constraints usually manifest themselves in increased complexity and anomalous update properties.

4-3   ENTITY MODELING

The other perspective from which conceptual design can be viewed is entity modeling. It is probably the most widely known and practiced of all the views. It began with the early use of database management systems in the mid-1960s and was first reported by Bachman in 1969 in relation to the use of data structure diagrams. A graphical notation, consisting of boxes and arrows, was developed to describe the information structure for the I-D-S database management system. The formalization and extension of this notation was undertaken by Senko and colleagues in 1973, which resulted in the development of the entity set model. Hall et al. [1976] performed further work in this area, as did Chen [1976], who introduced the entity–relationship model as a simple extension to data structure diagrams and developed a design methodology.

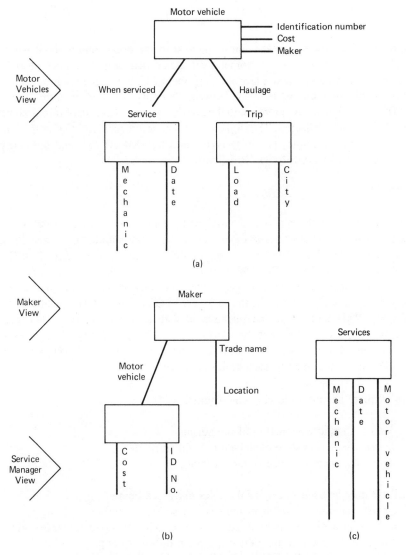

FIGURE 4-8 Different conceptual views of a vehicle system.

More recently, the notion of categories of entities has been introduced by Bachman and Daya [1977] in the role model and by Palmer [1978] in record set types.

Using the entity–relationship model, the representation of information at this level is accomplished through the modeling constructs: entities, attributes, and relationships. The fundamental construct is the entity. The user delineates real-world things of interest by using entities, then defines the properties of entities by using attributes, and finally describes the correspondence between entities by using relationships.

Entities

The entity is a fundamental point of interest to the organization about which information is to be collected. It becomes a vehicle or focal point to collect information. An entity may be a person, place, or thing about which information is desired to be stored. A distinction must be made between an entity type and an entity occurrence. The *entity type* is the reference to the homogeneous collection of things about which information is collected. The *entity occurrence* references a particular thing in the collection. For example, an entity type could be EMPLOYEE and the entity occurrences would be John Jones, Bill Smith, Jane Jones, ...

Attributes

The means by which properties are assigned to entities is through attributes. An *attribute* is a named characteristic of an entity. Its name should be unique for a particular entity type, but could be the same for different entity types (e.g., COLOR can apply to many entities—PERSON, VEHICLES, etc.). Although entities exist in their own right, attributes are used to specify what information is to be collected about an entity. Examples of attributes for the entity EMPLOYEE are NAME, ADDRESS, DATE-OF-BIRTH, and so on. The fundamental distinction between type and occurrence is also germane. The attribute type DATE-OF-BIRTH has many occurrences or values, such as May 1, 1940; September 29, 1971; and so on. Only one attribute value, however, is assigned to each entity occurrence.

An attribute has the following characteristics:

1. *Name.* Unique designation of the attribute.
2. *Description.* Narrative explanation of the attribute.
3. *Role.* The particular use of the attribute.

An attribute may be used in any of the roles discussed below.

The most common role of an attribute is to describe a property of an entity (i.e., delineate the information of interest). Another important role is one of identification; an attribute may be used to uniquely distinguish different entity occurrences. For example, the attribute EMPLOYEE NUMBER, which has a unique set of values, distinguishes different occurrences of the entity EMPLOYEE, even if they had the same name. Other attribute roles include (1) the representation of interentity relationships, (2) use in derived values, and (3) to supply information regarding operation in a specific environment [Bachman and Daya, 1977]:

- Value domain/type
- Existence
- Number of occurrences
- Lengths
- Units of measure

Relationships

A relationship is an association between one or more entity types. Entities are related in the real world and the relationship mechanism is used to model this fact. A number of characteristics are important to understanding and using relationships: name, association, degree, optionality exclusivity, sequence, time, and identifier.

A relationship has a *name*. The choice of a name does embody some meaning. For example, the relationship OCCUPIED-BY does provide information to the user. It also can imply some directionality, as in the house OCCUPIED-BY people, pets, and rodents. In the case of the relationship between the entities EMPLOYEES and SKILLS, the direction indicates a collection of all skills with a particular employee to skills possessed. On the other hand, EMPLOYEES-WITH-SKILL would employ the reverse direction of the relationship, associating each skill with the employees who had particular skills.

Graphical Notation

Besides its name there are a number of additional characteristics of a relationship which can be easily understood through the use of a graphical notation. The entity type is represented by a box labeled with the entity name. Each relationship is represented by an arc or line between two entities (boxes). The arc is assigned a name that indicates the name of the relationship. Figure 4-9 depicts a relationship R between two entities EMPLOYEES and PROJECTS.

Associativity/Exclusivity Characteristics

The exclusivity characteristic of a relationship indicates the degree of the association of the entity types [Everest, 1977]. If an entity Z instance is related to *at most one* instance of another entity (Y), the relationship is exclusive on this entity type. In mathematical terms such a relationship is termed a function; that is, given any instance of Z, a unique instance of Y is determined.

The associativity of a relationship is defined upon the exclusivity in the other direction on Z. In general, there are four possibilities for the association of an entity Z to another entity Y: one-to-one, one-to-many, many-to-one, and many-to-many.

If the relationship is exclusive in both directions (i.e., both entity types), it is a *one-to-one* relationship, as indicated in Fig. 4-10(a). If the relationship is exclusive

FIGURE 4-9   Relationship
R between two entities.

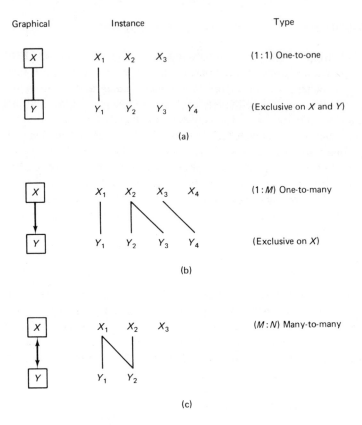

Graphical	Instance	Type

X X_1 X_2 X_3 (1 : 1) One-to-one

Y Y_1 Y_2 Y_3 Y_4 (Exclusive on X and Y)

(a)

X X_1 X_2 X_3 X_4 (1 : M) One-to-many

Y Y_1 Y_2 Y_3 Y_4 (Exclusive on X)

(b)

X X_1 X_2 X_3 (M : N) Many-to-many

Y Y_1 Y_2

(c)

FIGURE 4-10 Exclusivity of relationships.

on X, a one-to-many association exists between X and Y, which is also indicated in Fig. 4-10(b). When no exclusivity exists, a many-to-many association exists between X and Y [Fig. 4-10(c)].

For design purposes it is useful to know the cardinality or size of the relationship. For example, is the one-to-many relationship 1:3 or 1:1000? If the cardinality cannot be exactly specified, a frequency distribution is a reasonable approximation. It is also useful to know the rate of shift of the distribution's mean. Is the number of Y's increasing or decreasing over time?

Optionality (Exhaustibility, Dependency)
Characteristic

The optionality characteristic of a relationship existence criterion addresses the membership rules for the participating entity instances [Palmer, 1978].

1. *Optional.* The existence of either entity in the relationship is not dependent on the relationship.

2. *Contingent*. The existence of one of the entities in the relationship is dependent on the relationship.
3. *Conditional*. The existence of one of the entities is specified by a boolean criterion. This is a special case of the contingent relationship. When this occurs the arrow is labeled with the condition of existence.
4. *Mandatory*. The existence of both entities is dependent upon the relationship.

Figure 4-11 provides examples of these characteristics. The optionality characteristic is very important in maintaining the integrity and consistency in the database.

Exclusivity Characteristic

Additional environmental constraints may be described by the exclusivity of the relationships, as indicated in Fig. 4-12. To model the fact that warehouses store either finished goods or raw materials, but not both, the exclusivity characteristics would be used.

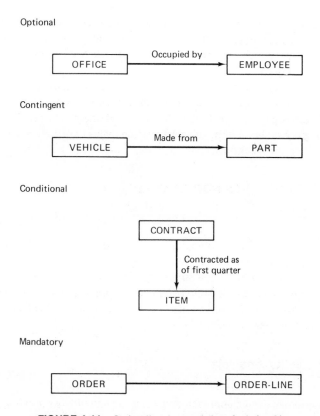

FIGURE 4-11 Optionality characteristics of relationships.

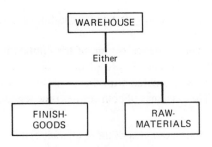

FIGURE 4-12 Either/or relationship.

Entity Identification Characteristic

Another characteristic is the case of the relationship in entity identification. As mentioned in the discussion of entities, the most common method of identification is the use of one or more entity attributes, whose values serve to uniquely distinguish one entity occurrence from another. Relationships are used to identify entities in two ways:

1. *In combination with attributes.* In this case the attributes values are not unique across the database and the "owner" of the relationship serves to distinguish uniquely the member occurrence. The attributes are unique within all occurrences designated by the "owner" entity.
2. *Two or more relationships.* In a confluence relationship the subordinate entity exists only when there are two corresponding occurrences of the parent relationships. In effect, the "owners" of the relationship determine the existence of the subordinate entity. Often in this case there are data associated with the intersection.

4-4 METHODOLOGIES FOR CONCEPTUAL DESIGN

Having delved into the basic principles and concepts for selected design approaches, we are now in a position to look at methodologies for utilizing these principles in the design of conceptual information structures. The various approaches to conceptual database design can be distilled into two major design methodologies: entity analysis and attribute synthesis. These can also be informally categorized as top-down and bottom-up approaches, respectively.

4-4-1 Entity Analysis

This top-down design approach divides the design process into four stages: view modeling, consolidation of views, schema mapping and analysis, and physical design. Only the first two are of interest in conceptual design.

View Modeling

The view modeling stage is directed to the modeling of the information required for the database as seen through the various perspectives of the organization. The categories or types of views to be represented are the corporate enterprise view, the application view, the information view, and the event view. Corresponding to each of the categories, the various types of information are represented as follows:

- *Organizational objectives/constraints.* The business goals of the organization as expressed in terms of the information required. Various constraints on the information, such as reporting requirements, auditing needs, regulation requirements, and privacy considerations.
- *Processing information.* Extant or future applications that need to be performed. This is the actual predictable processing that has to be performed on the database.
- *Information structures and relationships.* The modeling of the corporate information relationships: the actual data item, the aggregation of data items, and relationships that are necessary to support the operational business. This provides the basis for ad hoc or unanticipated requests.
- *Events and scheduling.* When actual information has to be presented: the due date for various reports, when applications have to be run. These are the undefined (ad hoc) as well as the predefined information activities of the organization.

View modeling is then the actual gathering of information at the various levels in the organization according to the four perspectives encountered. It includes the inputs from executives, managers, and end users.

Consolidation of Views

The consolidation of views is the process of integrating the various perspectives modeled in the preceding stage into a single conceptual view of the organization information and processing requirements. This conceptual view is represented in a high-level information structure diagram. The integrated view and the high-level information structure diagram comprise the bedrock of the database management approach. The construction of the conceptual view is therefore an essential, in fact perhaps the most important part of the design process. In previous approaches this step has often been omitted, or if attempted, improper shortcuts have been taken or ad hoc design decisions have been made.

The primary objective of the consolidation of user views is to identify and emphasize the commonality among the various views and to detect and resolve their major differences. This involves analysis and decisions at several levels:

- *Name inconsistency.* The identification of synonyms and homonyms among the data elements.

- *Identification differences*. The resolution of multiple identification mechanisms (e.g., employees may be uniquely distinguished by social security number in one application or employee number in another application).
- *Aggregation inconsistencies*. The delineation of different groupings of elements at the structural level or the operation on the element values at the instance level (e.g., "Total Sales" is the total for the region, country, world).
- *Mutual subsets*. The distinguishing of the complementary subsets of data, such as part-time employees, full-time employees, and retired employees.
- *Conflicting update requirements*. The detection of inconsistent insertion/deletion rules among different user perspectives.
- *Conflicting integrity constraints*. The identification of differing integrity rules for the data. For example, each new project creates a new occurrence of the EMPLOYEE entity, causing duplicate instances.

Details and specific steps are formulated in Chapter 5.

4-4-2   Attribute Synthesis

This methodology is described as bottom-up because it begins with the low-level data attributes from which higher-level entities and relationships are formed. There are four stages to this methodology: classification of attributes, composition of entities, formulation of relationships, and graphical representation.

Classification of Data Elements

Resulting from the requirements analysis described in Chapter 3 is a complete list of data elements used by the various tasks of the organization. Based on a series of heuristic rules, these data elements are classified with respect to type of attribute and membership in entities. A data element is categorized as being one of two types of attributes. An identifier attribute is a data element that is unique across all tasks and other data elements, and may also be used to access other attributes. A nonidentifier attribute is dependent upon an identifier attribute for access and cannot exist (meaningfully) on its own. In essence, it is "owned" by a single entity (identifier).

Composition of Entities

Attributes belong to two types of entities: unique entities and nonunique (dependent) entities. Unique entities stand alone, have at least one identifying attribute, and are not dependent on any attribute or other entity for existence. In nonunique entities there is a natural dependency on other entities for existence and other attributes for meaning.

Formulation of Relationships

After creating the two types of entities, other information, such as company policy and interviews, is used to develop relationships among the entity types and also to assign additional attributes to entities.

Graphical Representation

As a final step, the aforementioned attributes, entities, and relationships are expressed graphically in terms of an entity–relationship model. The following steps are used: express all unique and nonunique entities, display all relationships between entities, and represent all interentity relationships.

The details and specific steps of the attribute synthesis methodology are formulated in Chapter 6.

5 ENTITY FORMULATION AND ANALYSIS

5-1 INTRODUCTION

Chapter 4 addressed the representation of information for the conceptual design phase and introduced two modeling schemes: a high-level object representation and the traditional entity-based representation. Using the traditional modeling approach, this chapter develops a "methodology" for formulating conceptual schemas. Chapter 4 developed the basic modeling constructs and this chapter provides the steps for using these constructs, which are necessary to develop a conceptual schema.

We divide conceptual design into two subphases: design perspective modeling and perspective consolidation.* Although there have been a number of research contributions to conceptual design, few concrete results have been obtained. In addition to the modeling work surveyed in Chapter 4, the following research investigations have influenced the development here: the view modeling work of Navathe and Schkolnick [1978], view integration of Navathe and Gadgel [1980], and the data analysis approach developed by Davenport [1978] and Palmer [1978].

5-1-1 Design Objectives and Scope

The starting point, regardless of the design methodology, is the delineation of the scope of the design. Ordinarily, a compromise is dictated because too broad a scope leads to fuzzy and complex designs, and too narrow a scope leads to fragmentation of data and limits the integration of the database. Ideally, the scope should cover all the related functional areas of the organization. Management, however, does not usually

*This follows the 1978 New Orleans Data Base Design Workshop formulation [Lum et al., 1979a], which in turn had its roots in the 1978 NYU Symposium on Database Design [Yao et al., 1978], an informal workshop at IBM Research in San Jose, and the work of the Database Systems Research Group at the University of Michigan [Novak and Fry, 1976].

approve expenditures large enough or schedule enough time to embark on such a massive task. As a result, in very large organizations there will probably be more than a single integrated database. Unfortunately, extreme generalization of this fact leads to the microscopic view of one database per application. This approach results in nonintegration and fragmentation of database structure.

In order to form a compromise, consideration should be given to the technical sophistication of the organization, its commitment to the database approach in terms of dollars and people, the complexity of the data being modeled, and the degree of integration. Ideally, the scope decided upon should be comprehendible by the designer and have explicit relationships to the other databases.

A useful approach to this problem is to develop an overall information plan for the organization. Once the functional areas of the organization are depicted, it is relatively easy, by information flow analysis, to decompose these areas into databases of manageable size and scope.

5-1-2   Definition of Design Perspectives

Another technique used to simplify the conceptual design process is to partition the vast amount of information that goes into the process. To accomplish this, and to capture some specific and unique information, we approach the modeling of information requirements from several perspectives. This is an extension of the work of Kahn [1976] and Chen [1977a]. Our approach is to use four perspectives: corporate, information, application, and event. Each perspective represents a different viewpoint of the information requirements.

Corporate Perspective

The corporate perspective reflects senior and middle management's view of the organization's information requirements. It is based on how the organization operates and is structured to do business. This is an important perspective since many of the final entities in the design will result from it.

Application Perspective

The application perspective represents the processing that must be performed by the enterprise to meet their business goals. It comprises the reports that have to be produced, the transactions that have to be processed, and the general processing that is performed.

Information Perspective

The information perspective depicts the generic information relationships necessary to support decision making and long-term information requirements. It is represented by user ad hoc queries, long-range information plans, and general management requirements.

Event Perspective

The event perspective deals with the time and scheduling requirements of the enterprise. It represents when things happen, such as transaction arrival time, or when processing has to be accomplished, such as report XYZ due every Friday or the fact that application ABC is performed biweekly.

5-2 MODELING OF DESIGN PERSPECTIVES

This phase of our conceptual design methodology is the modeling and subsequent representation of the information necessary to support the four basic design perspectives. It is the representation of information on a local or individual basis which is necessary to support the enterprise, its users, applications, and management.

5-2-1 Model Constructs

From Chapter 4 we choose the modeling constructs of entities, attributes, and relationships to represent each of these perspectives. To review, an *entity* is a real object of interest—person, place, thing, event—about which information is collected. A *relationship* is an association between the occurrences of two or more entities. An *attribute* is a property of interest that the designer wishes to record. The core or heart of the entity–attribute–relationship model is a graphical representation system consisting of boxes and arrows. The boxes are used to represent entities and the arrows are used to represent relationships, with the ''head'' indicating direction. Attributes are indicated as lines (no arrows) emitting from the boxes, as depicted in Fig. 5-1. To represent a relationship between SALESPERSON and CUSTOMER,

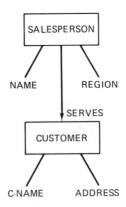

FIGURE 5-1 Information diagram for entity, attribute, and relationship.

an arrow would be drawn from the entity SALESPERSON to the entity CUSTOMER, indicating that a salesperson serves or calls on many customers. The attributes NAME and REGION describe salespeople, and the attributes C-NAME and ADDRESS serve to describe the entity CUSTOMER.

Basic Premises/Rules

The following is a general set of rules which are provided as a foundation for modeling these perspectives.

- The design perspectives are modeled by three types of constructs: entity, attribute, and relationship.
- Each component of information in the design perspective is represented by one and only one construct.

5-2-2   Formulation of Design Perspectives

The modeling of the design perspectives consists of a sequence of steps that results in a model of a local perspective. The following steps relate to all the design perspectives.

STEP 1: IDENTIFY THE LOCAL VIEWS

For each design perspective established, there is a set of "subperspective" or local views. These would correspond to self-contained areas of data that are related to functional areas. For example, in an order entry system some of the local views would be order entry, customer billing, order history, and new products. The selection of a local view will depend on the particular perspective and the size of the functional area. Factors to be considered in formulating local views include minimum dependence on or interaction with other views, and manageable scope. Based on these factors, a local view may cross applications, functional areas, or even perspectives.

STEP 2: FORMULATE ENTITIES

For each local view, one can formulate the entities that are required to capture the necessary information about the local view. At this step the designer is confronted with two important problems. The first deals with the population of entity instances and is addressed by using the concept of type or role. For example, the population of the entity EMPLOYEE could be categorized into employees of type: truck driver, secretary, and engineer. At this stage in the conceptual design process it is important to capture the relevant types and model each as a specific entity. The generalization of these types into the generic entity EMPLOYEE is considered in the next phase of conceptual design: consolidation of perspectives (see Section 5-3).

The second problem is the use of the construct, entity. Often a piece of information can be modeled as an attribute, entity, or relationship. For example, the fact that two employees are married can be modeled using the entity MARRIAGE, the relationship IS-MARRIED-TO, or the attribute CURRENT-SPOUSE. At this point in the design process the designer should be guided by two rules. The first rule is to use the construct that seems most natural; if this is the wrong construct, it will be factored out in subsequent design steps. The second rule involves our assumption that one and only one construct is used to model a piece of information in the local view: redundancy in the use of modeling constructs is to be avoided.

With regard to the number of entities used to represent the local view, there is a result from information theory coined "the magic number seven plus or minus two" [Miller, 1956]. This result states that the number of facts (information clusters) that a person can manage at any one time is about seven, give or take two. Applying this to the database design process, the number of entities a local view should have is at most nine, but probably closer to six or seven. If this is violated, perhaps the scope of the local view is too large.

Another consideration is the selection of the name for an entity. Since an entity represents a fact of information, a precise name should be given to this fact. This is also important to the consolidation stage, where homonyms and synonyms are dealt with. If we have fuzzy naming of concepts, the integration and consolidation processes will be equally fuzzy.

STEP 3: SELECT IDENTIFYING ATTRIBUTES FOR EACH ENTITY

Although a particular collection of attributes may be used as the basis for formulating entities, the significant attribute at this point in the design process is the identifier, which serves to distinguish uniquely the individual entity instances. The entity identifier is composed of one or more attributes whose value set is unique. This is also important to the consolidation phase because the identifying attribute values are in one-to-one correspondence with the entity instances. Therefore, two entities with the same identifiers may to some degree be redundant. This depends, however, on their descriptive attributes and the degree of generalization.

STEP 4: SPECIFICATION OF RELATIONSHIPS

In this step additional information is added to our local view by the formulation of associations among the entity instances. As developed in Chapter 4, there are several types of relationships: optional, contingent, mandatory, exclusive, and conditional. An informal procedure for approaching this step is to take each entity in the local view and pair it with all other entities contained in that view [Davenport 1978]. For each pair, ask if a meaningful question can be proposed involving both entities or if both entities may be used in the same transaction. If the answer is yes, determine the type of relationship that is needed to form the association. Next determine which relationships are most significant and which are redundant. Unfortunately, this can be done only with detailed understanding of the design perspective under consideration. For example, in Fig. 5-2(a) there appears to be a redundancy in the relationships x, y, and z between entities A, B, and C. As indicated by Fig. 5-2(b), the RECEIVES

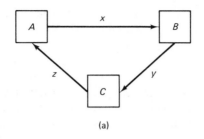

(a)

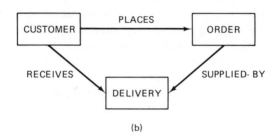

(b)

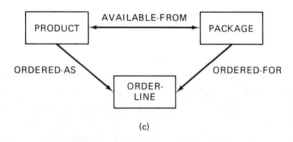

(c)

FIGURE 5-2 Analyzing redundant relationships.

relationship is normally redundant because a DELIVERY is not made unless an ORDER is placed. In Fig. 5-2(c), however, the AVAILABLE-FROM relationship associates all possible combinations of PRODUCTS and PACKAGES; consequently, it is needed to define the correct ORDER-LINE in the relationships ORDERED-AS and ORDERED-FOR [Kent, 1977, 1978].

STEP 5: ADD DESCRIPTIVE ATTRIBUTES TO ENTITIES

Attributes can be divided into two classes: those that serve to identify entity instances and those that provide the descriptive properties of the entity. In the final step of local view modeling, we add the descriptive attributes to the previously defined entities. The implication of the criterion that the identifier attributes serve to identify instances completely is that the descriptive attributes must be dependent (i.e., functionally dependent) upon the entity identifier. Another criterion is that only single-valued attributes are allowed for the description of an entity. In relational terms this means that the entity is in first normal form and all repeating attributes have been removed. Consider, for example, the entity CUSTOMER, which is identified by the attributes NUMBER and NAME and described by the attributes BALANCE and ADDRESS, where ADDRESS is composed of STREET, CITY, STATE, and POSTAL-CODE. The case where the CUSTOMER has multiple locations violates the normalization principle that repeating groups are not allowed. In this case, another entity can be formed, say LOCATION, to contain the attributes STREET, CITY, STATE, and POSTAL-CODE. An association is formed between CUSTOMER and LOCATION and named by the relationship CUSTOMER-ADDRESS.

Another issue that needs to be addressed is the case where one attribute is used in multiple entities. In this case the attribute is redundant and a rule needs to be established, such as applying the frequency of use with the identifier. Examination of the processing transactions indicates which identifier the particular attribute used most frequently and the attribute is assigned to that entity.

We have now completely defined the five steps of local view modeling which are to be repeated for each basic design perspective. Although not scientific by any means, this procedure provides a design sequence that is utilized by some practical (expert) designers. The analysis for consistency, integrity, and integratability is performed next.

5-3   CONSOLIDATION OF USER VIEWS

Now that each perspective has been formulated and represented by an entity–relationship diagram, the next step in the conceptual design process is the consolidation of these perspectives into a single global information structure. This structure not only mutually satisfies each perspective but also represents a reasonably succinct and integrated database.

We wish to develop a global information structure that supports all the input perspectives of the users, management, and business processes as well as the policy constraints of the enterprise.

As indicated in Fig. 5-3, the global information structure is developed from the various input perspectives—corporate, application, information, and event—and policy guidance. The input perspectives capture the information required to perform the business, and the policy guidance (rule) describes the legal and government constraints on doing business. All of these inputs are represented by the information diagrams of the entity–relationship model according to the stepwise procedure developed in Section 5-2.

There are only two outputs from perspective consolidation, one major and the other ancillary. The major output is the global information structure, which is the result of the consolidation process. It is the integration of the corporate, application, information, and event perspectives in so far as possible. The ancillary results indicate the degree to which integration has been achieved. They are comprised of the unresolved conflicts and nonintegrated components. Naturally, the objective of the

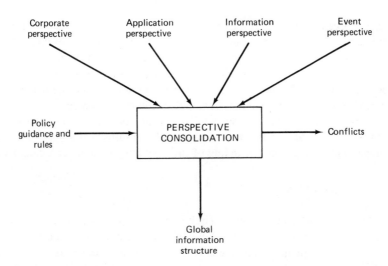

FIGURE 5-3 Model for perspective consolidation.

consolidation process is to minimize this output. Although the model does not directly reflect iteration, the consolidation process is a highly iterative one, often bound by constraint and conflict.

5-3-1 Concepts and Principles
for Consolidation

There are three underlying concepts that form the basis for the consolidation of design perspectives: identity, aggregation, and generalization. The various ways in which the required components of these concepts may be apportioned among local user views form the interrelationship types, which are presented in Section 5-3-2.

Identity

Identity is the simplest and most straightforward of the three concepts. Two or more elements are said to be identical if they have the same semantic meaning. It is not necessary, however, for identical elements to have the same syntactic representation. Another way of describing an identity relationship is to say that two or more elements are synonyms.

Although the identity concept is quite simple, the determination of synonymous instances is not. Owing to our inadequate data representation methods, knowledge of data semantics is quite limited. Typically, an in-depth understanding of the user environments is required to determine if any identical synonyms exist. The mapping of element descriptions onto occurrences of the element in the real-world system is difficult because the instances of a descriptive element in the population may constitute a subset of potential instances. In this case it is difficult to determine if the element description is too vague or if the instances really do represent a subset of the element description. Moreover, the instances of two element descriptions that are candidates for identity relationships may form an intersection instead of a union. It is difficult to decide if either or both of the element descriptions are able to cover the union of the instances. Similar, rather than identical elements exist under these conditions. Determining whether similar definitions may be resolved to identical definitions, or if one of the other element relationships really applies, requires an in-depth and detailed understanding of the user organizations and data needs.

Aggregation

The aggregation concept is also quite straightforward and it occurs frequently in practice, as does the identity consolidation. As developed in Chapter 4, aggregation refers to a concept in which a relationship between elements is considered to be another, higher-level element. For example, the element EMPLOYEE may be thought of as an aggregation of NAME, SOCIAL-SECURITY-NO, and ADDRESS (Fig. 5-4).

Many aggregations are easy to identify since the major data models incorporate syntax that can represent aggregation.

Generalization

This is the most difficult concept to grasp and is easily confused with aggregation. Whereas aggregation may be thought of as constituent parts making up a ''whole,'' generalization is concerned only with ''wholes.'' It refers to an abstraction process in which a group of similar elements is thought of as a generic element by suppressing the differences between them (see Chapter 4). For example, EMPLOYEE may be thought of as a generalization of FACTORY-WORKER, OFFICE-WORKER, and EXECUTIVE. An instance of any of these three types is also an instance of the generalized EMPLOYEE. The reference to similar elements (identities) in the preceding section applies here. In many cases it appears that similar elements should not be forced into an identity relationship, but instead should be represented as a generalization.

Aggregation and generalization are quite similar in structure and application and

FIGURE 5-4   Aggregation.

may be easily confused since one element may participate in both aggregation and generalization relationships (Fig. 5-5).

Also, inferences may be drawn about the aggregation dimension from the generalization dimension, and vice versa. In Fig. 5-5 it can be inferred that each instance of EXECUTIVE is also an aggregation of NAME, SOCIAL-SECURITY-NO, and ADDRESS, since all the characteristics of the generalized EMPLOYEE also apply to the more specific elements that EMPLOYEE represents.

5-3-2   Consolidation Types

There are three consolidation types, each based on one of the underlying concepts. These may be combined in various ways to construct any type of relationship between objects (elements) in different user views. Each consolidation type will now be discussed, followed by a discussion and example of how they may be used together to represent complex consolidations (consolidations that involve more than one consolidation primitive type).

Two important assumptions are required in order to deal with the consolidation of user views. First, it must be assumed that each user view, or set of requirements, is complete and consistent. This requires that all of the necessary objects be specified (completeness) and that no consolidation of intrauser objects is required. In other words, it is assumed that the user can ensure the following:

1. The set of objects specified is complete for the user's needs.
2. All objects are uniquely named (no homonyms allowed).
3. No synonyms exist (no identity consolidation required).

Implicit consolidations of aggregated and generalized objects are allowed and are desirable. The consistency/completeness assumption serves to simplify the inter-user-consolidation process by eliminating intrauser consistency checks.

The other assumption is one of simplification and convenience. It will be

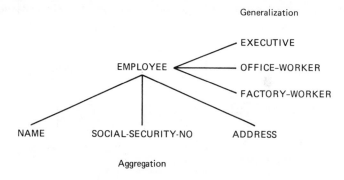

FIGURE 5-5   Aggregation and generalization.

assumed that only binary consolidation will be attempted; that is, only two user views will be consolidated at a time. This makes the search for combinations of consolidation alternatives easier, and eliminates any potential problems with the order of consolidation in a *n*-ary consolidation. Also, it appears that in most cases it is more efficient to consolidate views in a binary method. This is discussed in Section 5-3-3.

Identity Consolidation

Identity consolidation is based on the identity concept introduced previously. Two objects may be semantically identical synonyms, with the additional option of having identical names. Homonyms must be guarded against, as well as similar, but not identical objects. Similarity is probably best expressed using aggregation and generalization.

As a check on the consistency of the consolidation and on user views, it can be asserted that if an object from user 1's view is found to be identical to an object from user 2's view, neither of these objects can participate further in any other identity consolidations between these two views. This is true because each object is assumed to be unique in the context of its local user view.

The notation introduced here to represent the consolidation types will be used throughout the remainder of the text. User view 1 will consist of objects $A_{(1\text{-}N)}$ and user view 2 will consist of objects $B_{(1\text{-}N)}$. A global, or consolidated result will depict the global object(s) that are used to represent the consolidation process. Figure 5-6 shows the identity consolidation process. A global object G_{AB} is created to indicate that it is an identity consolidation of $A_{(X)}$ and $B_{(X)}$. The relationship that results in the global object can be represented by a set relationship. In this case, $A_{(X)}$ is equated to $B_{(X)}$ and $G_{(AB)}$.

Aggregation Consolidation

Aggregation may occur in two forms. The difference between them is whether or not one of the users has specified the aggregated "whole" object. To take the simpler case first, assume that the situation in Fig. 5-7 exists. Here user 1 has specified a

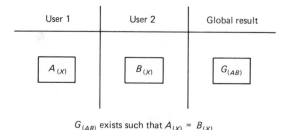

$G_{(AB)}$ exists such that $A_{(X)} = B_{(X)}$

FIGURE 5-6   Identity consolidation.

```
        User 1                          User 2
   (inventory view)                  (sales view)

HANDLEBARS

WHEELS

SEATS                                 BICYCLES

FRAMES
```

FIGURE 5-7   Aggregation of inventory and sales view.

number of objects without making any distinct consolidation-type relationships between them. This is not an error or omission on his part. This user's information needs do not include any need for the designation of an explicit consolidation between the objects. It is likely that there are associations or groupings that involve one or more of these objects. These relationships, however, do not represent a higher-level (aggregate) object.

User 2 has specified an object (among others) that is an aggregation of user 1's objects. To create a scenario for this example, it could be that user 1 represents an inventory function for parts in a bicycle factory and user 2 represents a sales function for the assembled bicycles.

In a consolidation, the two views could be merged without explicitly stating that BICYCLE is an aggregation of the listed parts. However, this does not enhance the sharability of data very much and is equivalent to a physical data merge in which distinct data are stored in the same file structure but are not logically related. The more powerful and preferred alternative is to perform a logical data merge in which semantics and definitions are merged conceptually as well as physically. This enhances data sharability by enabling the system designer to create access paths and references between the users' views, thus improving the database content and long-term flexibility in information needs.

The conceptually more difficult version of aggregation occurs when neither user has specified some or all of the constituent parts of the unmentioned "whole." A scenario for Fig. 5-8 could be that separate inventory functions are maintained for basic, nonvariable parts (FRAMES, WHEELS) and for parts that may be substituted by customer request (SEATS, HANDLEBARS). This type of aggregation is more difficult to recognize since neither has visualized a BICYCLE object.

It may be argued that since neither user has specified an aggregated BICYCLES, it is not proper for the consolidation process to create a global object to represent it.

```
          User 1                          User 2
  (interchangeable parts)            (replacement parts)

          WHEELS                           SEATS

          FRAMES                         HANDLEBARS
```

FIGURE 5-8   Aggregation of component parts.

This argument ignores the possibility of synergistic effects among data definitions. The objects in the individual views are necessary but not sufficient conditions for BICYCLES to be created. Together, though, the sufficient conditions are met and BICYCLES is necessary to relate the two sets of parts for logical data merging. If the aggregated object is not created, only a physical data merge will occur.

The resolution of the two types of aggregation is shown in Fig. 5-9. Type 1 aggregation refers to Fig. 5-7 and type 2 aggregation refers to Fig. 5-8 and uses a "virtual" consolidated object that is created by the aggregation process. The global result consists of a global object and a list of global-specific objects that represent the objects in the source views. The arrows can be taken to mean "is an aggregation of." In set notation, the individual view objects are a subset, possibly an improper one, of the global object. While necessary and sufficient conditions may be met by the union of the two views, other objects may still be added to the aggregation list by other users, such as SPOKES and CHAINS.

Generalization Consolidation

There are two forms of generalization, as there are with aggregation. The difference, again, lies in whether either of the users has specified the generalized or generic object. The same arguments regarding logical data sharing and the synergistic

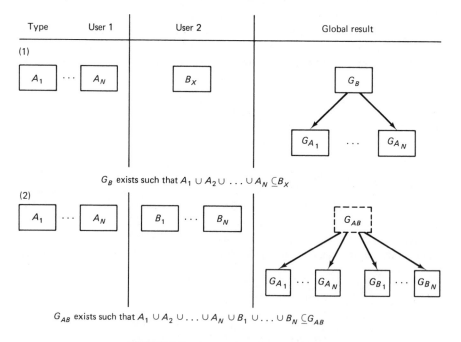

FIGURE 5-9   Aggregation of types 1 and 2.

effects of consolidation mentioned for aggregation also apply to generalization. The two examples in Figs. 5-10 and 5-11 illustrate the generalization types.

In the first case, user 2 has specified the generic object CYCLES, whereas user 1 has specified subsets, or instances, of the cycles concept. In the second example neither user has recognized the generic CYCLES. Although it is conceptually possible to conceive of the generic object from one or two instances, it is not likely to occur in practice. Only when brought together are the instances sufficient to trigger recognition of the generic relationship between the specific object types.

A number of global implementations are possible for representation of the results of a generalization. The introduction of a "TYPE" object is a potential implementation since the objects from which a generic object is drawn are similar in many respects and identical in other respects. In the bicycle example, the generic object CYCLES could be described by a CYCLE-TYPE object that would have codes or some other values that could distinguish among bicycles, tricycles, and tandems.

Other implementations include linking a list of the specific objects to the generic with or without the TYPE object. The choice of an implementation has not been resolved and it is debatable which best serves users and designers. Figure 5-12 documents the generalization process using the TYPE object and a list of specific objects linked to the TYPE object. The generic object can be viewed as the intersection of the definitions of the specific objects. This is contrasted with aggregation, where the aggregated object is viewed as the union of the specific objects' definitions.

Complex Semantic Relationships

Up to this point, each type of consolidation has been discussed in isolation. Each individual view object and global object may, however, participate in multiple consolidation types. Also, no mention has been made of the implicit and explicit aggregations and generalizations that may occur within an individual view. By combining consolidation types, powerful and complex relationships can be rep-

User 1	User 2
BICYCLES	
TRICYCLES	CYCLES
TANDEMS	

FIGURE 5-10   Generalization Example 1.

User 1	User 2
BICYCLES	TRICYCLES
TANDEMS	

FIGURE 5-11   Generalization Example 2.

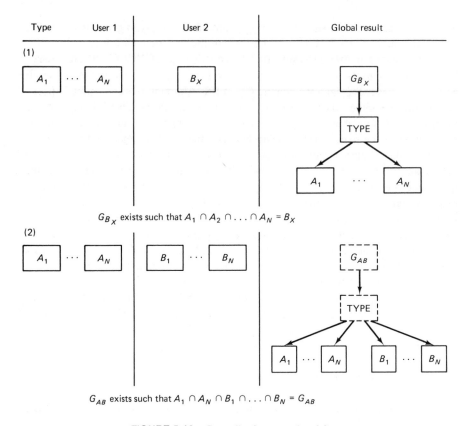

Type	User 1	User 2	Global result

(1)

GB_X exists such that $A_1 \cap A_2 \cap \ldots \cap A_N = B_X$

(2)

G_{AB} exists such that $A_1 \cap A_N \cap B_1 \cap \ldots \cap B_N = G_{AB}$

FIGURE 5-12   Generalization types 1 and 2.

resented. Indeed, it is hoped that most, if not all, semantic relationships can be represented by some combination of the consolidation primitives.

This is best exemplified by an illustration. Figure 5-13 presents two user views for the bicycle example. In this case there is no clear distinction between what the users perceive; varying and overlapping object definitions and levels of abstraction are evident. For instance, user 1 has a lower-level view of TRICYCLES and BICYCLES than does user 2, who perceives a generic object CYCLES. Both users see their (BI) (TRI)CYCLES as consisting of parts of varying levels of abstraction. User 1, who has the more detailed view with respect to CYCLES, has the more general view toward WHEELS (user 2's RIMS and TIRES). Also, user 2 has defined an additional part, SEAT-POST, that does not correspond to any objects in user 1's view. In this example both users' views can be regarded as primarily aggregation-type relationships. In a broader context, many user relationships will not represent either aggregation or generalization. There are many relationships that represent processes, procedures, and conditional associations. For the sake of clarity these types of user relationships are omitted from the diagram in this section.

Figure 5-13 probably represents a fairly typical situation in that there is a high

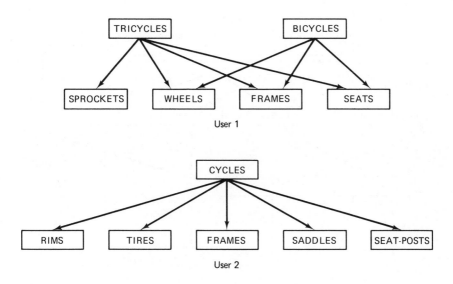

FIGURE 5-13   Sample user views.

degree of overlap between the local views in terms of objects and relationships specified, and dissimilar levels of abstraction for aggregation and generalization are visualized. Figure 5-14 shows how the consolidated end product should look to combine the two views accurately. All the information specific to user 1 and user 2 is contained in the consolidated form, as well as the additional synergistically created information resulting from the logical data merger that has been performed.

This consolidated user 1–2 view can easily be generated and documented with the four consolidation primitives, as illustrated in Fig. 5-15. Given the global links provided by the consolidation expressions (dashed lines in Fig. 5-15), it would be a

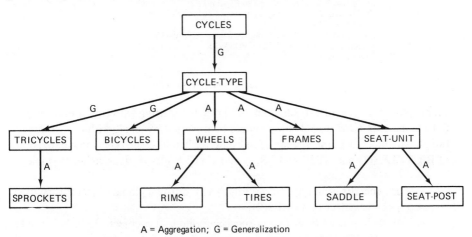

A = Aggregation; G = Generalization

FIGURE 5-14   Proposed consolidation specification.

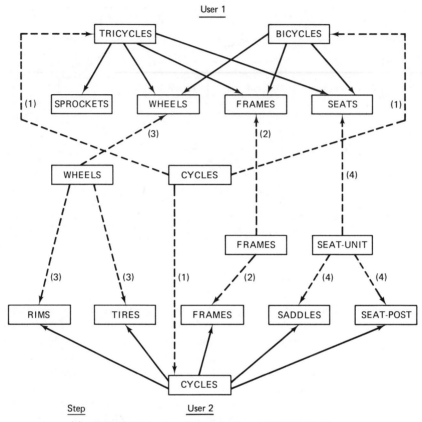

Step   **User 2**

(1) CYCLES (2*) is a type 1 generalization of TRICYCLES (1)
     and BICYCLES (1).
(2) FRAMES (1) is identical to FRAMES (2).
(3) WHEELS (1) is a type 1 aggregation of RIMS (2) and
     TIRES (2).
(4) SEAT-UNIT (2) is a type 2 aggregation of SEATS (1)-
     SADDLES (2) with SEAT-POST (2).
* User number

FIGURE 5-15   Complex consolidation examples.

simple process to generate the diagram of Fig. 5-14. Starting with the global objects,
links to the user 1 and user 2 objects could be traversed by an algorithm to build the
full global object diagram. A rough procedure for handling the type 1 generalization
of BICYCLES(1) and TRICYCLES(1) into CYCLES(2) is given as an example.

1. For generalization type 1 [(1), Fig. 5-15], create a global object for the user
   x generic object [CYCLES(2)].
2. For each user y object that is specific to the user x object [TRICYCLES(1)
   and BICYCLES(1)], create a corresponding global object.

3. Link the global object created in step 2 to the global object that is the "type" object for the generic object (CYCLE-TYPE).

4. For each object in user *y* that is used by *all* the objects in user *y* related to the generic object in an aggregation context, create corresponding global objects and link them to the global "type" object. [Link WHEELS(1), FRAMES(1), and SEATS(1) to CYCLE-TYPE.]

5. For each object in user *y* that is *not* used by all of the objects in user *y* related to the generic object in an aggregation context, create corresponding global objects and link them to the global equivalent of the parent, aggregated object. (Create the global SPROCKETS and link it to global TRICYCLES.)

It should be possible to develop algorithms along this line that permit us to take any set of consolidation statements and create a consistent, complete global specification from them. It must be emphasized that this proposal merely sets forth a model for consolidation and a means of representing various types of similarity among user views. No attempt is made at this point to automate the identification of instances of these consolidation types in a user view. Our lack of semantic representations precludes any attempt to replace the human element with an algorithm in the near future.

5-3-3 Consolidation Process

Up to this point we have been concerned only with binary consolidation for reasons of simplicity. In most real-world situations, though, numerous users will be involved with the design of a database. How, then, should the consolidation process proceed?

One alternative is to perform a single *n*-ary consolidation step. This may be feasible, but it is not desirable. It would be both algorithmically and conceptually complex and there would be a large chance for errors and omissions to occur. It would also be quite time consuming, since to perform a single identity search for one object in user 1's view, all of objects in users 2 through *N* would have to be checked. With a large number of users and a large number of objects, this is highly inefficient. The human heuristic thought processes can help to eliminate some of the brute-force nature of the search, but for very large systems, it is still probably beyond the capabilities of a single person.

The obvious alternative is to perform an *n*-ary consolidation, where *n* is less than the number of users involved. It will be shown that binary consolidation is the logical conclusion of the scaling down of the magnitude of *n*. As a result, the consolidation process would resemble a binary tree in which the leaf nodes would represent the users' views, the root node would be the final, global view, and the interior nodes would represent subconsolidations.

Conceptually, it is simpler because only two views are involved, and it is more likely that the database administrator, or whoever is coordinating the consolidation process, will have a good understanding of the semantics of the user views involved. This approach fits well with the hierarchical organization structures commonly found in business because lower-level personnel can direct lower-level consolidations for which their detailed expertise is needed, and higher-level personnel can direct the consolidation of higher-level subconsolidations for which generalization and aggregation abstractions would probably be more evident. The outline of this process is diagrammed in Fig. 5-16.

In terms of efficiency, the shape of the binary consolidation tree is important, as is the ordering of the leaf node individual views. The advantage that binary consolidation has over n-ary consolidation is that the results of any binary consolidation of N objects with M objects will probably be $N + M - X$, instead of $N + M$ objects, where X corresponds to the degree of overlap in object definitions between the views. An n-ary consolidation would result in a bigger value of X but would have the disadvantage of sharply higher comparison rates in the early stages of consolidation.

An advantage is gained by shaping the tree as symmetrically as possible so as to minimize the number of objects in the domains of the two views being consolidated at intermediate steps. Figure 5-17 illustrates this concept. The "poor" example brings in new, unconsolidated users at each step and lessens the X advantage since the number of comparisons at any node is the product of the number of objects at the prior nodes.

The ordering of the nodes of the tree is important because proper grouping of the initial and subconsolidations will maximize the degree of overlap between views and result in a larger X factor, thus minimizing the number of objects to be considered in later steps of the consolidation process. In other words, it makes sense to consolidate closely related functional units within an organization whenever possible. In most organizations this will correspond with the hierarchical structure, which is equivalent to a tree structure. Careful thought in the planning phase can help to minimize the efforts expended for the admittedly difficult and time-consuming consolidation process.

To simplify the design process, conceptual design has been viewed from a series of perspectives: information, application, event, and corporate. To simplify the

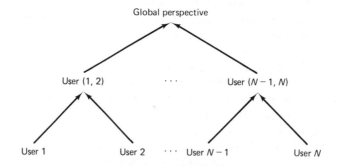

FIGURE 5-16   Binary consolidation.

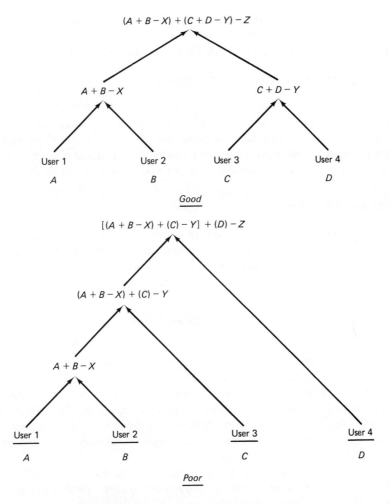

FIGURE 5-17 Alternative consolidation structures.

modeling process, these perspectives have been further partitioned into a series of local views. Now it is time to integrate all the information into a single global information structure.

Normally, the consolidation process can proceed through the design perspectives in the following order. Begin the design with the information perspective, add the application perspective, consider the event perspective, and finally, merge the corporate perspective. The rationale for this is the following. We begin with the information perspective because it is the richest perspective in terms of constructs and it will probably yield the majority of the final information constructs. Therefore, it is a logical place to begin. The application perspective relates the reality of the processing to the design and thus provides a realistic balance to the information perspective.

Next, the times of events, processes, and applications are considered to provide a feasible design. Finally, the corporate constraints are added to complete the design.

The consolidation process is divided into the following steps:

STEP 1: SELECTION OF PERSPECTIVE

It is important first to confirm the design perspective ordering as the sequence for consolidation. Since a general ordering was given, this should be checked with the goals and utilization of the database being designed. If, for example, you are designing a database for a process-oriented industry, you might consider the key perspectives to be the application and event perspective and thus begin the process with these.

STEP 2: ORDERING OF LOCAL VIEWS

Once the design perspectives have been ordered and selected, the consolidation process focuses on local views within the perspective. Several views comprise the perspective chosen, and this step orders the views for the consolidation process. These views are ordered as to importance with respect to the specific design objectives for this database.

STEP 3: CONSOLIDATION OF LOCAL VIEWS

This step constitutes the heart of the consolidation process. For simplicity and convenience we use binary consolidation. That is, we integrate only two user views at a time and avoid the potential problems of n-ary consolidation. The order of consolidation is determined by Step 2 and the process proceeds as follows. First, take the top two views in the particular perspective and consolidate these using the basic consolidation principles. Next, following the prescribed order of two, take the next local view and merge it with the previously consolidated local views. The process is continued until the last view is merged.

When the consolidation process is completed for the first design perspective, the next design perspective is introduced and the process continues until all perspectives are integrated.

STEP 4: CONFLICT RESOLUTION

Conflicts arise in the consolidation process for a number of reasons, principally because of the number of people involved and the lack of semantic power in our modeling constructs. Conflicts may also be caused by incomplete or erroneous specification or interruption of requirements. The majority of these conflicts are dealt with in the consolidation step using the rules developed. If there are remaining conflicts that have to be dealt with by designer decisions, they are taken care of in this step. When a design decision is made, it is important to "backtrack" to the point in the consolidation process where the constructs were entered into the design. At this point the implications of the design decision are considered, as are their propagation effects on the consolidation process.

6 ATTRIBUTE SYNTHESIS: AN EXAMPLE OF CONCEPTUAL DESIGN

Donna L. S. Rund

Chapters 4 and 5 introduced the basic terminology and techniques of conceptual design. This chapter continues the requirements analysis methodology described in Chapter 3 as an example of conceptual design in practice.

The major design steps in this particular methodology (within the life-cycle framework) are:

- *Step 2-1.* Selection of entities and attributes.
- *Step 2-2.* Identification of data relationships.
- *Step 2-3.* Representing the information structure in graphical form.
- *Step 2-4.* Interpreting the information structure for verification.

Let us now investigate each step in more depth in the following sections.

6-1 THE BASIC MODEL

The objective of this phase of the analysis is to identify the components of the conceptual data model selected. The entity–relationship model will be used, implying that the analysis should identify the following components:

1. Entities are represented by data elements that are used in the organization to identify objects, create other data elements, or reference other data elements. The analysis should identify two types of entities: *unique entities,* represented by a data element that identifies a particular or distinct thing or object (such as social security number and order); and *nonunique entities,* created when two or more unique entities are used to identify a set of data elements.

The existence of a relationship may create a new entity, which derives its identity through two or more entity keys. Such entities are represented by a rectangle with a double bottom line: they derive their identity from two or more other entities and cannot exist if any of the owning entities do not exist. For example, in Fig. 6-1 each occurrence of INVENTORY must be related to an existing ITEM and an existing WAREHOUSE. If either ITEM or WAREHOUSE is removed, the INVENTORY associated with that ITEM and WAREHOUSE may no longer exist.

   2. Attributes are represented by data elements that must be related to either a unique or a nonunique entity to have meaning (e.g., ADDRESS has no useful meaning unless it is qualified by the entity CUSTOMER).

   3. Relationships represent dependencies between two or more data elements. Three types of relationships will be identified through the analysis:

   a. *Entity relationship* describes the qualified or unqualified ownership between entities. For example, the entity VENDOR owns (in an unqualified sense) VENDOR-ITEM. This relationship implies that a vendor's ITEM can never appear in a database unless it is related to a VENDOR. In a qualified relationship, ownership is dependent upon a specific condition or status. For example, a LINE-ITEM is owned by the ORDER entity as long as the LINE-ITEM is "not shipped." As soon as the LINE-ITEM "is shipped," the INVOICE entity and not the ORDER owns the LINE-ITEM. Consequently, the relationship between LINE-ITEM and either the ORDER entity or the INVOICE entity is qualified by the status of the LINE-ITEM (see Fig. 6-2).

   b. *Entity–attribute relationship* describes the data elements directly owned by one or more entities. Like entity relationships, the ownership may be qualified or unqualified. If an attribute is related to only one entity, the ownership is unqualified. In a qualified relationship, the attribute will always be owned by one main entity and further qualified by one or more secondary entities. For example, QUANTITY-ON-HAND is owned by the entity ITEM, but is further qualified by WAREHOUSE, as it defines the specific location of an instance of the attribute QUANTITY-ON-HAND.

   c. *Attribute relationship* represents the unqualified ownership between attributes that belong to the same entity or entity relationship. For example, the entity

FIGURE 6-1   Graphical notation of entity created through the relationship of two or more other entities.

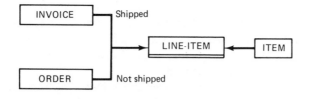

FIGURE 6-2   Graphical notation of either/or relationship.

ACCOUNTS-RECEIVABLE owns two attributes, TOTAL-BALANCE-OWED and 30-DAY-OVER-DUE-BALANCE. In order to exist, TOTAL-BALANCE-OWED is dependent upon the existence of an ACCOUNTS-RECEIVABLE entity. 30-DAY-OVER-DUE-BALANCE, however, is dependent on the existence of the attribute TOTAL-BALANCE-OWED. Implied is that the attribute 30-DAY-OVER-DUE-BALANCE will never exist unless TOTAL-BALANCE-DUE exists.

6-2   ANALYZING INFORMATION TO IDENTIFY THE COMPONENTS OF THE INFORMATION (CONCEPTUAL) STRUCTURE

The analysis methodology to be presented in this section focuses on translating the task/data relationships into the components described above. One may assume at this stage in the design that, having completed both the interviews and the analysis of the interviews, the designer could easily identify the model's components without further analysis. Although this may be possible for a database of very narrow scope, it should not be attempted for the following reasons:

- It is nearly impossible to analyze all possible data relationships if the number of tasks and data elements exceeds about 30.
- The results of the analysis rely very heavily on the prejudices of the designer (i.e., the designer's specific view of the world).
- It is likely that nonunique entities and qualified relationships will not be properly identified because they are generally exceptions to the rule and difficult to single out, even with a rigid analysis technique.

The analysis is divided into two main phases. The objective of the first phase (Step 2-1) is to identify unique and nonunique entities and attributes. During this same phase, attributes will be divided into those that may relate to an unique entity and those that may relate to a nonunique entity. The second phase of the analysis (Step 2-2) will use the results of the first phase to identify the relationships between entities, between entities and attributes, and between attributes.

6-2-1   Identifying Entities and Attributes (Step 2-1)

The first phase of the analysis is based upon a series of hypotheses that were developed as a result of analyzing the characteristic data elements as they are used within the tasks of an organization. These hypotheses are as follows:

1. A data element will probably be an *unique entity* if it displays the following properties:

    a. It is used by a large number of tasks.

    b. It is used with a large number of other data elements.

    c. Its joint usage with other individual data elements is low in comparison with the total number of times it is used across all tasks (later referred to as the *usage ratio*).

2. A set of two or more data elements will be candidates for a *nonunique entity* if:

    a. Each data element in the set has first been classified (or came close to being classified) as a unique entity.

    b. Each data element in the set appears together in a high percentage of the total tasks in which each appears.

    c. Across the tasks in which the set of data elements appears, there is a high degree of joint usage with the other data elements.

3. A data element will probably be an *attribute related to a unique entity* if it displays the following properties:

    a. It is used in a relatively small number of tasks.

    b. It is used with a relatively small number of other data elements.

    c. Its joint usage with other data elements is generally high in comparison with the total number of times it is used across all tasks (usage ratio).

4. A data element will most likely be an *attribute related to a nonunique entity* if it displays the following properties:

    a. It is used in an average (i.e., neither high nor low) number of tasks.

    b. It is used with an average number of other data elements.

    c. Its joint usage with other data elements is average in comparison with the total number of times it is used across all tasks (usage ratio).

Important note: It is possible that the collection of data elements may not contain a particular entity name, i.e., the aggregate name for a collection of attributes (c.f. Section 4-2), but only its attributes' names. In such a case the attribute that uniquely identifies that entity (i.e., its key) will be identified as the entity by the above classification. When this occurs, the identifying attribute is said to represent the entity; however, an actual entity name must be created to represent the aggregation of the identifying attribute and all associated nonidentifying attributes.

The first part of the analysis (Step 2-1-1) will identify unique and nonunique entities and classify attributes as belonging to either a unique or a nonunique entity. To accomplish this it is necessary to define the value to complete the matrix in Fig. 6-3. When completed, these values will be used as the criteria to classify all data elements.

To define these values, individual data relationships defined by each operational task must be combined and analyzed in a five-step process. The first step of the process is to reflect each task/data relationship in a matrix that displays all data relationships. This process is best shown through an example.

Assume that the following three task/data relationships were identified through the interview analysis:

	Usage across task	Joint usage with other data elements	Usage ratio
High			
Average			
Low			

FIGURE 6-3 Classification criteria for data elements.

- *Take Order,* using data elements 1, 3, 4, 7, 9.
- *Check Credit,* using data elements 1, 3, 5, 6, 9.
- *Reject Order,* using data elements 1, 2, 4.

The process begins by reflecting the data relationships of each task in a matrix. At the same time, a tally is kept of the number of tasks in which each data element is used. Thus:

1. Define a matrix (called the *relationship matrix*) whose rows and columns are equal to the total number of data elements used across all tasks (i.e., nine for the three tasks).
2. Define a vector in which the tally of task usage will be kept for each data element.
3. Perform the following for each task/data relationship:
   a. For each task, fill in the task usage vector by adding to the appropriate cell a "1" for each data element used by the task. For example, the task "Take Order" uses data elements 1, 3, 4, 7, and 9. Consequently, a "1" should be added to cells 1, 3, 4, 7, and 9 [Fig. 6-4(a)]. Figure 6-4(b) shows the content of the vector after the second task has been added, and Fig. 6-4(c) shows its contents after the third task has been added.
   b. For each task, enter all of its data relationships into the relationship matrix. This is accomplished by entering the relationships of each data element to all other data elements used by the task. For example, task 1, "Take Order," uses data elements 1, 3, 4, 7, and 9. Take the first data element, 1, and set the current position to row 1 in the matrix. Add a "1" to the columns of row 1 that represent data elements 3, 4, 7, and 9 [Fig. 6-5(a)]. Once the relationships of data element 1 have been entered, position yourself at row 3, for data element 3, and add a "1" to columns 1, 4, 7, and 9. Repeat this process for all the data used in task 1. Figure 6-5(b) shows the relationship matrix after task 1 has been entered, Fig. 6-5(c) shows its contents after task 2 has been entered, and Fig. 6-5(d) shows its contents after all three tasks have been entered.

Note: Cell number relates
to the data element
reference number

Task usage		Task usage		Task usage	
1	1	1	2	1	3
2	0	2	0	2	1
3	1	3	2	3	2
4	1	4	1	4	2
5	0	5	1	5	1
6	0	6	1	6	1
7	1	7	1	7	1
8	0	8	0	8	0
9	1	9	2	9	2
(a)		(b)		(c)	

FIGURE 6-4 Task usage vector: (*a*) contents of task usage vector after first task, "Task Order," has been entered; (*b*) contents of task usage vector after second task, "Check Credit," has been entered; (*c*) contents of task usage vector after all three tasks have been entered.

In summary, the relationship matrix, R, can be formulated as follows, given the individual task usage vectors, u, v, and w for each of the three tasks:

$$R_{ij} = (u_i u_j^T + v_i v_j^T + w_i w_j^T)\, \delta_{ij} \qquad (6\text{-}1)$$

where vector element u_i represents the usage of data element i in task u, T is the transpose, and

$$\delta_{ij} = \begin{cases} 0 & \text{if } i = j \\ 1 & \text{if } i \neq j \end{cases}$$

Having reflected all data relationships in the matrix, the second step of the analysis (Step 2-1-2) develops a vector that shows the total number of data elements to which each data element is related. To accomplish this, a tally of the number of nonzero cells is made for each row (or data element) of the matrix. The result is placed in the *total data relationship vector* (Fig. 6-6).

The third step of the analysis (Step 2-1-3) uses the relationship matrix and the two vectors to form a third vector, which will contain each data element's *usage ratio*. The following must be accomplished to compute this ratio:

1. The first step involves translating each cell in the relationship matrix from a count of data relationships [e.g., data element 1, row 1, is related to data element 3, column 3, twice; see Fig. 6-5(d)] to a percentage of total usage (e.g., data element 1 is

Note: Row and column numbers relate to the data element reference numbers

Column

	1	2	3	4	5	6	7	8	9
1	0	0	1	1	0	0	1	0	1
2	0	0	0	0	0	0	0	0	0
3	0	0	0	0	0	0	0	0	0
4	0	0	0	0	0	0	0	0	0
5	0	0	0	0	0	0	0	0	0
6	0	0	0	0	0	0	0	0	0
7	0	0	0	0	0	0	0	0	0
8	0	0	0	0	0	0	0	0	0
9	0	0	0	0	0	0	0	0	0

(Row)

(a)

Column

	1	2	3	4	5	6	7	8	9
1	0	0	1	1	0	0	1	0	1
2	0	0	0	0	0	0	0	0	0
3	1	0	0	1	0	0	1	0	1
4	1	0	1	0	0	0	1	0	1
5	0	0	0	0	0	0	0	0	0
6	0	0	0	0	0	0	0	0	0
7	1	0	1	1	0	0	0	0	1
8	0	0	0	0	0	0	0	0	0
9	1	0	1	1	0	0	1	0	0

(Row)

(b)

Column

	1	2	3	4	5	6	7	8	9
1	0	0	2	1	1	1	1	0	2
2	0	0	0	0	0	0	0	0	0
3	2	0	0	1	1	1	1	0	2
4	1	0	1	0	0	0	1	0	1
5	1	0	1	0	0	1	0	0	1
6	1	0	1	0	1	0	0	0	1
7	1	0	1	1	0	0	0	0	1
8	0	0	0	0	0	0	0	0	0
9	2	0	2	1	1	1	1	0	0

(Row)

(c)

Column

	1	2	3	4	5	6	7	8	9
1	0	1	2	2	1	1	1	0	2
2	1	0	0	1	0	0	0	0	0
3	2	0	0	1	1	1	1	0	2
4	2	1	1	0	0	0	1	0	1
5	1	0	1	0	0	1	0	0	1
6	1	0	1	0	1	0	0	0	1
7	1	0	1	1	0	0	0	0	1
8	0	0	0	0	0	0	0	0	0
9	2	0	2	1	1	1	1	0	0

(Row)

(d)

FIGURE 6-5 Relationship matrix: (*a*) contents of the relationship matrix after the first data element and its relationships have been entered; (*b*) contents of the relationship matrix after all data relationships from task "Take order" have been entered; (*c*) relationship matrix after all data relationships of tasks 1 and 2 have been entered; (*d*) contents of the relationship after the three task/data relationships have been entered.

used in three tasks in the first cell of the task usage vector; consequently, it is used with data element 3, column 3, 66% of the time; see Fig. 6-7).

2. The second step in computing the usage ratio involves tallying for each row of the matrix the total number of cells that exceed a parameter u which defines high usage. *(Note:* An appropriate starting value for u might be 70% for this example. If the

Total data
relationships

	Total data relationships
1	7
2	2
3	6
4	5
5	4
6	4
7	4
8	0
9	6

Note: Each cell number corresponds to a data element reference number

FIGURE 6-6 Total data relationship vector.

Column

Row	1	2	3	4	5	6	7	8	9
1	0	33%	66%	66%	33%	33%	33%	0	66%
2	100%	0	0	100%	0	0	0	0	0
3	100%	0	0	50%	50%	50%	50%	0	100%
4	100%	50%	50%	0	0	0	50%	0	50%
5	100%	0	100%	0	0	100%	0	0	100%
6	100%	0	100%	0	100%	0	0	0	100%
7	100%	0	100%	100%	0	0	0	0	100%
8	0	0	0	0	0	0	0	0	0
9	100%	0	100%	50%	50%	50%	50%	0	0

FIGURE 6-7 Content of relationship matrix after each cell has been changed to reflect percent of time used together rather than a count of times used.

number of task/data relationships are small, the parameter should be increased. Conversely, it should be decreased for an extremely large sample.) The results of the tally of each row should be placed in the appropriate cell of the *usage tally vector* (Fig. 6-8).

3. The final step in computing the usage ratio is to divide each cell of the usage tally vector (i.e., the tally of high usage data relationships) by the corresponding cell in the total data relationship vector. The results should be converted to a percentage and placed in the corresponding cell in the *usage ratio vector* (Fig. 6-9).

The fourth step of the analysis (Step 2-1-4) uses three vectors to develop histograms. These histograms will be used to select the values that define high, average, and low within the categories of:

	Usage
1	0
2	2
3	2
4	1
5	4
6	4
7	4
8	0
9	2

Cell number

	Usage ratio
1	0%
2	100%
3	33%
4	20%
5	100%
6	100%
7	100%
8	0
9	33%

Cell number

FIGURE 6-8 Contents of usage tally vector after the total number of cells exceeding the high-usage parameter has been tallied for each data element.

FIGURE 6-9 Contents of the usage ratio vector after the usage ratio has been computed.

- Usage across tasks
- Usage with other data elements
- Usage ratio

Figures 6-10 to 6-12 show the histograms for each of the vectors. It should be noted that, except for the usage ratio, intervals of 1 have been selected due to the small number of task/data relationships used in this example. In a normal-size database design effort, the interval for usage across tasks should be set at 5 and the interval for

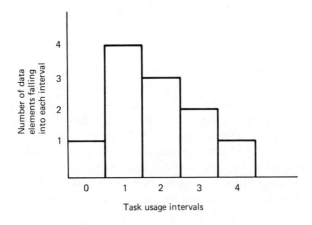

FIGURE 6-10   Histogram of data usage across tasks [from Fig. 6-4(c)].

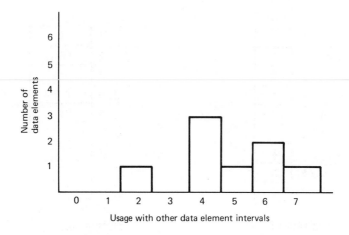

FIGURE 6-11   Histogram of usage with other data elements (from Fig. 6-6).

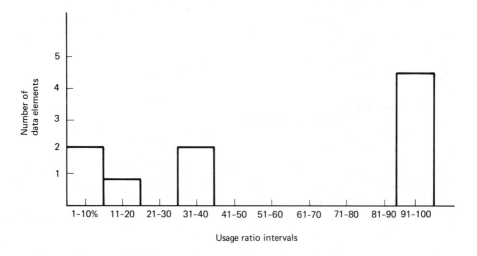

FIGURE 6-12   Histogram of usage ratio (from Fig. 6-9).

usage with other data elements at either 5 or 10. Once developed, the histograms are used visually to select the values that will define each category discussed previously. Because the histograms shown in Figs. 6-10 to 6-12 are based on three tasks only, they are not representative of a real database design effort. The distribution shown in Fig. 6-13 displays the type of curve that will almost always be found in a "usage across tasks" analysis and a "usage with other data elements" analysis. Note that the division of this curve into high, average, and low is at the cutoff points, where real differences in usage occur. Using the types of cutoffs shown in Fig. 6-13, the following categories would be defined for Figs. 6-10 and 6-11:

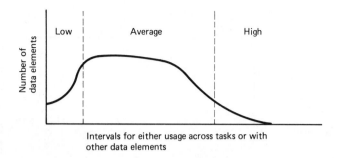

FIGURE 6-13 Typical curve when analyzing usage across tasks or usage with other data elements.

- Usage across tasks would be defined as:
  High, ≥3
  Average, >1 and <3
  Low, ≤1

- Usage with other data elements would be defined as:
  High, ≥7
  Average, >2 and <7
  Low, ≤2

The curve normally found in a usage ratio analysis is shown in Fig. 6-14. Because this ratio attempts to isolate high usage, the curve is normally divided into two distinct parts. Using the types of cutoff points shown in Fig. 6-14, the usage ratio categories are defined in Fig. 6-15 (using this example).

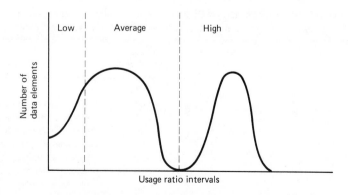

FIGURE 6-14 Typical curve for a usage ratio analysis.

	Usage across	Usage with other data	Usage ratio
Entity	$\geqslant 3$	$\geqslant 7$	$\leqslant 11\%$
Attribute referenced by nonunique entity	$>1, <3$	$>2, <7$	$>11\%, <41\%$
Attribute referenced by unique entity	$\leqslant 1$	$\leqslant 2$	$\geqslant 41\%$

FIGURE 6-15   Summary of classification criteria.

Depending upon the number of task/data relationships and the scope of the database, it is advisable that two or three different cutoff points be identified to see if they have an effect on the classification of data elements into the categories of entities, or attributes referenced by one or more than one entity. If numerous differences are identified, Step 2-1 should be performed for each department classification, defined across all tasks. These separate analyses will allow the designer to determine the entities of each department and consequently to identify the cutoff points for the design as a whole. (*Note:* In a large design it is very possible that some entities will be identified in a department classification analysis but not in the overall analysis. Consequently, both types of analysis should be performed.)

To complete the fourth step of the analysis, the three vectors should be combined by data element so that all their values can be viewed together, and each data element can be classified according to the criteria of high, average, and low (Fig. 6-15 and Table 6-1).

TABLE 6-1   Classification of Data Elements by Entity, Attribute Referenced by Unique Entity, and Attribute Referenced by Nonunique Entity

Data Element	Usage Across Tasks	Usage with Other Data	Usage Ratio (%)	Classification
1	3	7	1	Entity
2	1	2	100	Attribute by unique entity
3	2	6	33	Attribute by nonunique entity
4	2	5	20	Attribute by nonunique entity
5	1	4	100	Borderline—but probably attribute by unique entity
6	1	4	100	Borderline—but probably attribute by unique entity
7	1	4	100	Borderline—but probably attribute by unique entity
8	0	0	0	Never used
9	2	6	33	Attribute by nonunique entity

The fifth and final step in the first phase of the analysis (Step 2-1-5) is to utilize the list of entities and task/data relationships to identify possible nonunique entity combinations. Continuing our example, let us assume that the five entities shown in Table 6-2 had been identified during the fourth step of the analysis and that these entities are used in the tasks shown in Table 6-3. Utilizing the list of tasks (Table 6-3) and entities (Table 6-2), the following steps should be performed to identify candidates for nonunique entities.

1. Identify the entities associated with each task and create a list of the combinations formed, such as:

Task 1	10, 61, 86
Task 2	10, 22, 61
Task 3	10, 86
Task 4	10, 61
Task 5	10, 68, 86

2. Further analyze the combinations to determine all possible pairings (Table 6-4, column 2).
3. Determine the number of times each combination of entities appears (Table 6-4, column 2).

TABLE 6-2   Five Entities Identified through the Analysis

Data Element Reference Number	Description
10	ITEM
86	WAREHOUSE
61	CUSTOMER
22	SALESPERSON
68	VENDOR

TABLE 6-3   Correspondence between Tasks and Data Elements*

Task Reference Number	Description	Data Element Reference Number
1	Check Available Inventory	<u>10</u>, 57, 69, <u>86</u>, 107, 89, <u>61</u>
2	Write Order	<u>61</u>, 8, 9, <u>10</u>, 57, 6, 18, <u>22</u>
3	Receive Items	<u>86</u>, 69, <u>10</u>, 89
4	Quote Price	<u>10</u>, 67, 106, <u>61</u>, 16
5	Order Items	<u>10</u>, 69, <u>86</u>, 89, 57, <u>68</u>

*Unique entities are underlined.

4. Using the total number of tasks (i.e., five in the example) as the basis, compute the percentage of the time that each combination appears (Table 6-4, column 3).

5. Select as candidates for nonunique entities those combinations that appear frequently (begin by selecting those that occur over 50% of the time). *Note:* There is no fixed rule for choosing a threshold percentage of the time to use because of the variability of each corporate environment. For example:

- ITEM (10) and WAREHOUSE (86) appear together 60% of the time and are used in tasks 1, 3, and 5.
- CUSTOMER (61) and ITEM (10) appear together 60% of the time and are used in tasks 1, 2, and 4.

6. For each of the candidates (e.g., ITEM/WAREHOUSE and CUSTOMER/ ITEM, review the specific data elements with which they appear (Table 6-5). As can be seen, there is a high degree of common usage among data elements used with ITEM (10) and WAREHOUSE (86), whereas there is little if any overlap between the data elements used with ITEM (10) and CUSTOMER (61). This analysis shows that

TABLE 6-4   Analysis of Candidates for Nonunique Entities

Nonunique Entity Candidates	*Number of Joint Appearances*	*Frequency (%) (Column 2/Total Number of Tasks)*
10, 86	3	60
10, 61	3	60
86, 61	1	20
10, 86, 61	1	20
61, 22	1	20
10, 22	1	20
61, 10, 22	1	20
10, 68	1	20
86, 68	1	20
10, 86, 68	1	20

TABLE 6-5   Data Elements Used by Candidates for Nonunique Entities

Candidates for Nonunique Entity	*Tasks in Which Appear*	*Other Data Elements*
10, 86	1	57, 69, 89, 107
	3	69, 89
	5	57, 69, 89
10, 61	1	57, 69, 89, 107
	2	6, 8, 9, 18, 57
	4	16, 67, 106

. ITEM/WAREHOUSE should be classified as a nonunique entity, whereas ITEM/
CUSTOMER should not.

The identification of nonunique entities completes the first phase of the analysis
for the information structure. The flowchart in Fig. 6-16 summarizes the major five
steps of this phase.

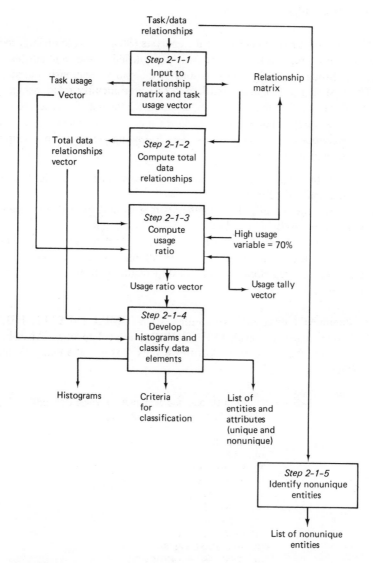

FIGURE 6-16   Summary of the first phase of conceptual design (Step 2-1),
selection of entities and attributes.

6-2-2 Identifying Relationships (Step 2-2)

Three types of relationships were defined in Section 6-1:

- Relationships between entities
- Relationships between entities and attributes
- Relationships between attributes

The objective of the second phase of the analysis (Step 2-2) is to identify these three types of relationships so that the previously identified entities and attributes can be expressed through the graphical notations of the entity–relationship model.

The first step in this analysis (Step 2-2-1) is to identify relationships between entities. To accomplish this, it is necessary to match the list of unique and nonunique entities to the policy statements defined during management interviews and develop a list that describes entity relationships. The following step-by-step example shows how this should be accomplished:

1. Begin by creating a list of all unique and nonunique entities defined in the first phase of the analysis (Table 6-6).
2. Review the list of policy statements that were extracted from management interviews (Table 6-7).
3. Analyze each policy statement in Table 6-7 to determine if it defines ownership between entities or defines the attributes referenced through a nonunique entity. The following list describes the relationship resulting from analyzing the policy statements in Table 6-7.

- Statement 1 discusses two entities, CUSTOMER and SALESPERSON. It further states that each CUSTOMER is related to one SALESPERSON, implying that the entity SALESPERSON "owns" the entity CUSTOMER (line 1, Fig. 6-17).

TABLE 6-6 List of Unique and Nonunique Entities Defined
in the First Phase of the Analysis

15.	ORDER
10.	ITEM
22.	SALESPERSON
86.	WAREHOUSE
61.	CUSTOMER
106.	INVOICE
68.	VENDOR
54.	VENDOR-ITEM
110.	PURCHASE ORDER
10.	ITEM; 86. WAREHOUSE
15.	ORDER; 10. ITEM; 106. INVOICE
22.	SALESPERSON; 61. CUSTOMER

TABLE 6-7   Sample of Operating Policies Extracted from
Management Interviews

1. A customer is always assigned to one salesperson.
2. Each item could appear in any inventory, so we have to track quantity by specific warehouse.
3. We accept a customer's order only after we have formally reviewed his or her credit, established an account, and assigned a salesperson.
4. We purchase from many vendors, so we maintain complete lists, by vendor number, of all the items each sells.
5. Often, the same item can be purchased from different vendors, so we reference all vendors' items through our item numbers.
6. Sometimes the individual line items of an order are filled through more than one warehouse. We do this to increase service.
7. Each line item of an order is invoiced as soon as it is shipped.

- Statement 2 discusses two entities, ITEM and WAREHOUSE. It also identifies as INVENTORY the attributes owned between this pair of nonunique entities. This implies that the combination of ITEM and WAREHOUSE owns the attributes making up INVENTORY (line 2).
- Statement 3 includes three entities, CUSTOMER, ORDER, and SALESPERSON, and defines two relationships, that between the SALESPERSON and the CUSTOMER and that between the CUSTOMER and the ORDER (line 3).
- Statement 4 directly discusses the entity VENDOR and indirectly discusses the entity VENDOR-ITEM. It implies but does not explicitly state a relationship between VENDOR and VENDOR-ITEM (line 4).
- Statement 5 discusses a relationship between ITEM and VENDOR-ITEM (line 5).
- Statement 6 refers to two entities, ORDER and WAREHOUSE. The statement itself implies that the relationship between these two entities is through LINE-ITEM. Since ORDER and WAREHOUSE are not a nonunique entity, it is not clear through this statement alone exactly how the relationship should be defined. Two things can be recorded, however, and hopefully clarified later. This includes the fact that LINE-ITEMs are "filled" from WAREHOUSEs (possible conditional relationship) and that ORDERs have, or own, LINE-ITEMs (line 6).
- Statement 7 helps to clarify the cloudy relationships implied in statement 6. Included in this statement are two entities, ORDER and INVOICE, and the unidentified group of attributes, LINE-ITEMs. Reviewing the list of nonunique entities (Table 6-6) the combination ORDER, ITEM, and INVOICE will be found. It seems safe to assume that LINE-ITEM is probably identified through these entities. In addition, the relationship of LINE-ITEM to ORDER is conditional upon being "not shipped" and the relationship of LINE-ITEM to INVOICE is conditional upon "being shipped" (line 7).

Once the policy statements have been analyzed, the list of nonunique entities should be reviewed to determine if all attribute groupings have been defined (e.g., the

Owning entity	Owned entity	Identification of nonunique entities owned	Conditions of ownership and other comments
(1) 22. SALESPERSON — — —61. CUSTOMER			
(2) 10. ITEM — — — — — 86. WAREHOUSE — —	— — — — — — — — — —> INVENTORY — — — — — — — — — —>		
(3) 22. SALESPERSON — — — —> 61. CUSTOMER 61. CUSTOMER — — — — —> 15. ORDER			
(4) 68. VENDOR — — — — — —> 54. VENDOR- ITEM			
(5) 10. ITEM — — — — — — —> 54. VENDOR- ITEM			
(6) 86. WAREHOUSE — — — — — — — — — — — — —> LINE-ITEM (not clear what nonunique entity identifies LINE-ITEM)			Filled from
15. ORDER — — — — — — — — — — — — — — — — —> LINE-ITEM			
(7) 15. ORDER — — — — — — — — — — — — — —| 106. INVOICE — — — — — — — — — — — — — —> LINE-ITEM 10. ITEM — — — — — — — — — — — — — — —|			ORDER relationship only when "not shipped." INVOICE relationship only "after shipped."
(8) 22. SALESPERSON 61. CUSTOMER			Relationship defined (lines 1 and 3) but no group of attributes formed.

FIGURE 6-17 Definition of entity relationships.

attribute grouping INVENTORY was defined through the nonunique entity ITEM and WAREHOUSE. If an attribute grouping has not been defined, add the nonunique entities to the bottom of the list of entity relationships, noting that the specific relationship has not yet been defined (line 8, Fig. 6-17). Even though entity relationships have been identified through the preceding analysis of policy statements, it is very likely that one definition may contradict another. Such contradictions will be identified as graphical notations of the information structure.

Having identified entity relationships, the second step in this phase (Step 2-2-2) involves identifying relationships between entities and attributes. In preparation for doing this, three lists should be developed. The first list should contain all data elements classified as attributes referenced by an unique entity, and the second should contain all data elements classified as attributes referenced by a nonunique entity

(Table 6-8). The third list should show, for each data element, all the data elements it is related to, and the percentage of the time they are used together. [*Note:* This list is just a more readable version of the matrix shown in Fig. 6-7. If the analysis performed earlier was automated, this list should be generated automatically (see Table 6-9 for an example).]

With these three lists in hand, the following steps should be performed:

1. All attributes referenced by a unique entity should be worked with first. The purpose of the following steps is to determine which unique entity owns each attribute.

   a. Take the first attribute, ITEM-DESCRIPTION (i.e., 14 in Table 6-8), and look at the data relationship list (Table 6-9) to determine what entities it is used with. In this example, the only entity it is used with is ITEM. Because ITEM-DESCRIPTION is not related to another entity, it should be assigned to the entity ITEM [Table 6-10(a)].

   b. If the attribute was shown in the data relationship list as being related to more than one entity, the following must occur:

     (1) Compare the percentage of the time the attribute is used with each of the entities, and eliminate from consideration any entity with a low percentage, as an attribute is usually referenced through its owning an entity a very high percentage of the time. For example, CUSTOMER-ADDRESS is used with CUSTOMER 100% of the time and with INVOICE 8% of the time. Because of the low percent of usage, the entity INVOICE would be eliminated and CUSTOMER-ADDRESS would be assigned to CUSTOMER.

     (2) If, after the elimination of low percentage entities, it is still not clear which owns the attribute, review all tasks in which the attribute is created (in the CUSTOMER-ADDRESS example—it would be a task such as "Establish Customer Account"). Review all data elements associated with the creating task to determine which are entities.

TABLE 6-8   List of Attributes by Classification

Attributes Referenced by a Unique Entity	*Attributes Referenced by a Nonunique Entity*
12. ITEM-NUMBER	
14. ITEM-DESCRIPTION	42. QUANTITY-ON-HAND
16. CUSTOMER-NUMBER	
18. CUSTOMER-ADDRESS	56. REORDER-POINT
21. TERRITORY-CODE	67. AMOUNT-ORDERED
25. ORDER-NUMBER	
34. TOTAL-BALANCE-OWED	69. AMOUNT-SHIPPED
35. 30-DAY-OVERDUE-BALANCE	70. SALES-AGREEMENT-DATA
19. CUSTOMER-ZIP-CODE	71. SALES-AGREEMENT-DURATION
78. VENDOR-NUMBER	
87. WAREHOUSE-ID	

TABLE 6-9   Example Data Relationship List

Used With	Percent of Time Used
14. ITEM-DESCRIPTION	
20. ITEM-WEIGHT	90
10. ITEM	100
94. ITEM-SIZE	80
152. UNIT-COST	65
18. CUSTOMER-ADDRESS	
19. CUSTOMER-ZIP-CODE	100
72. CUSTOMER-SHIPPING-DAYS	42
61. CUSTOMER	100
44. CUSTOMER-STATE	98
106. INVOICE	8
42. QUANTITY-ON-HAND	
67. AMOUNT-ORDERED	30
43. QUANTITY-ON-ORDER	61
10. ITEM	100
56. REORDER-POINT	46
86. WAREHOUSE	98
15. ORDER	21
70. SALES-AGREEMENT-DATE	
71. SALES-AGREEMENT-DURATION	96
22. SALESPERSON	98
117. SALES-AGREEMENT-TERMS	92
61. CUSTOMER	100

TABLE 6-10   Assignment of Attributes

Attributes related to: 10. ITEM

  14. ITEM-DESCRIPTION

(a) Beginning of a list of attributes owned by item

Attributes related to:

10. ITEM	61. CUSTOMER
14. ITEM-DESCRIPTION	18. CUSTOMER-ADDRESS
	34. TOTAL-BALANCE-OWED
	35. 30-DAY-OVERDUE-BALANCE
	19. CUSTOMER-ZIP-CODE
22. SALESPERSON	
21. TERRITORY-CODE	

(b) After all attributes referenced by a unique entity have been assigned

In most cases, only one entity will appear in a task, which creates an attribute referenced by a unique entity. If only one exists, assign the attribute to that entity. If more than one exists, and if the attribute is related to each entity a high percentage of the time, ask the following question: If each of the entities is deleted, which one would cause the attribute to be meaningless? In the previous example, deleting INVOICE would not make CUSTOMER-ADDRESS meaningless, but deleting

CUSTOMER would. Consequently, assign the entity to CUSTOMER, but note that it is a questionable assignment and should be reviewed after all attributes have been assigned.

2. Once all attributes referenced by an unique entity have been assigned [Table 6-10(b)], those referenced by a nonunique entity may be assigned. Before trying to determine what nonunique entity they should be related to, review the list of entity relationships (Fig. 6-17) and create a new list which shows all nonunique entities, and where defined, the name of the attribute grouping they reference (Table 6-11). Then perform the following steps: Take the first attribute from Table 6-8, 42. QUANTITY-ON-HAND, and look at the data relationship list to determine which entities it is used with (Table 6-9). Look up these entities (10. ITEM, 86. WARE-HOUSE, and 15. ORDER) on the list of nonunique entities (Table 6-11) to determine if they have been classified as a nonunique entity. If none exists, as in this example, review the percentage of the time the attribute is related to each entity and eliminate those with a low percentage (ORDER in this example). Repeat the process of looking at the list of nonunique attributes. This time a match is found and QUANTITY-ON-HAND is assigned to the attribute group INVENTORY, which is identified through the nonunique entity ITEM and WAREHOUSE.

3. Most of the remaining attributes can be assigned using the same process to assign QUANTITY-ON-HAND. If, while assigning an attribute to a nonunique entity combination, however, a name has not been associated to the attribute grouping (as in the case of SALESPERSON and CUSTOMER, Table 6-11), attempt to determine the nature of the grouping from the attributes themselves. For example, the attribute SALES-AGREEMENT-DATE should clearly be assigned to the non-unique entity SALESPERSON and CUSTOMER. Since this attribute, and the others with which it is associated, all reference a "Sales Agreement," that name should be used to identify the attribute groupings.

Table 6-12 shows all attributes after they have been assigned to either a unique entity or a nonunique entity.

The last step in the second phase of the analysis (Step 2-2-3) involves identifying relationships between attributes. Although identification of attribute relationships is a

TABLE 6-11   List of Nonunique Entities and the Name of the
Attributes They Reference

Entities Making Up a Nonunique Entity	Name of Attributes They Reference
{ 10. ITEM 86. WAREHOUSE	INVENTORY
{ 15. ORDER 106. INVOICE 10. ITEM	LINE-ITEM
{ 110. PURCHASE-ORDER 54. VENDOR-ITEM	?
{ 22. SALESPERSON 61. CUSTOMER	?

TABLE 6-12 All Entity–Attribute Relationships

Attributes Related to: 10. ITEM

   14. ITEM-DESCRIPTION

Attributes Related to: 22. SALESPERSON

   21. TERRITORY-CODE

Attributes Related to: LINE-ITEM

   (15. ORDER, 106. INVOICE, 10. ITEM)

   67. AMOUNT-ORDERED
   69. AMOUNT-SHIPPED

Attributes Related to: 61. CUSTOMER

   18. CUSTOMER-ADDRESS
   34. TOTAL-BALANCE-OWED
   35. 30-DAY-OVERDUE-BALANCE
   19. CUSTOMER-ZIP-CODE

Attributes Related to: INVENTORY

   (10. ITEM, 86. WAREHOUSE)

   42. QUANTITY-ON-HAND
   56. REORDER-POINT

Attributes related to: SALES-AGREEMENT

   (22. SALESPERSON, 61. CUSTOMER)

   70. SALES-AGREEMENT-DATE
   71. SALES-AGREEMENT-DURATION

---

part of the logical design process, it has a minor role because they do not influence the basic database (information) structure. Their major importance is realized when physical (stored) records are developed. Therefore, the process to identify attribute relationships is less structured and relies, to a great extent, on common sense.

The following procedure should be used to identify and document relationships between attributes. (*Note:* Attribute relationships exist between attributes owned by either a unique or a nonunique entity. Consequently, this procedure should be repeated once for each entity attribute relationships shown in Table 6-12.) The attributes related to CUSTOMER will be used as an example.

1. Identify all tasks associated with the four attributes of the unique entity CUSTOMER (Table 6-13).
2. Review each task to identify attribute relationships (refer to Table 6-14 to see how each relationship is documented).

- The first task, Create New Customer, shows that there is a high relationship between 18. CUSTOMER-ADDRESS and 19. CUSTOMER-ZIP-CODE.
- The second task, Post to Customer Account, shows no new relationship.

TABLE 6-13 Tasks Associated with
Attributes of CUSTOMER

Tasks Associated with
CUSTOMER-ADDRESS and CUSTOMER-ZIP-CODE

Create New Customer
   18. CUSTOMER-ADDRESS
   61. CUSTOMER
   19. CUSTOMER-ZIP-CODE

Tasks Associated with
TOTAL-BALANCE-OWED

Post to Customer Account
   61. CUSTOMER
   34. TOTAL-BALANCE-OWED

Tasks Associated with
30-DAY-OVERDUE-BALANCE

Age Customer Account
   61. CUSTOMER
   34. TOTAL-BALANCE-OWED
   35. 30-DAY-OVERDUE-BALANCE

TABLE 6-14 Format for Documenting Attribute Relationships

CUSTOMER-NUMBER	
Highly Related Attributes	Attributes with Dependencies
18. CUSTOMER-ADDRESS	34. TOTAL-BALANCE-OWED
19. CUSTOMER-ZIP-CODE	35. 30-DAY-OVERDUE-BALANCE

- The third task, Age Customer Account, shows a definite relationship and dependency (identified through common sense) between 30-DAY-OVER-DUE-BALANCE and TOTAL-BALANCE-OWED.

The identification and documentation of attribute relationships complete the second phase of the analysis. A flowchart of the steps performed during this phase is shown in Fig. 6-18.

6-3 EXPRESSING ENTITIES, ATTRIBUTES, AND RELATIONSHIPS THROUGH THE GRAPHICAL NOTATIONS OF THE ENTITY-RELATIONSHIP INFORMATION STRUCTURE (STEP 2-3)

The objective of this phase of information structure design is to express the entities, attributes, and relationships identified in the analysis phase through the graphical notations of the entity–relationship model. The process involved in developing the graphical data structure is divided into three main steps and includes expressing

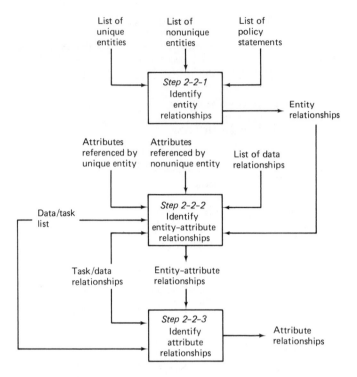

FIGURE 6-18 Summary of the second phase of conceptual design (Step 2-2), identification of data relationships.

- All unique and nonunique entities (Step 2-3-1)
- All relationships between entities (Step 2-3-2)
- All relationships between attributes and between entities and attributes (Step 2-3-3)

As described in Section 6-1, entities are displayed through the use of rectangles, with unique entities having a single bottom line and nonunique entities having a double bottom line. Figure 6-19 shows some of the entities defined in Table 6-6.

Once all entities have been graphically displayed, their relationship to each other may be added to the diagram. To accomplish this, the definition of entity relationships (Fig. 6-19) developed during the analysis will be referenced and the following performed:

- Line 1 of Fig. 6-17 shows that the SALESPERSON entity *owns* the CUSTOMER entity. This relationship should be displayed by drawing an arrow from SALESPERSON to CUSTOMER [Fig. 6-20(a)].
- Line 2 identifies the nonunique entity INVENTORY and its identifying entities ITEM and WAREHOUSE. This relationship should be displayed by drawing one arrow from ITEM to INVENTORY and another arrow from WAREHOUSE to INVENTORY [Fig. 6-20(b)].

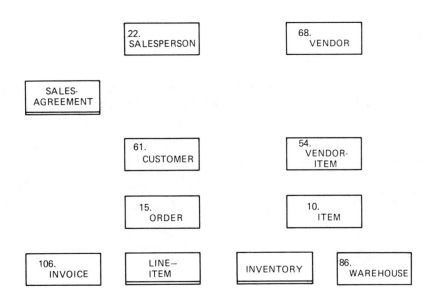

FIGURE 6-19 Graphical display of unique and nonunique entities.

• Line 3 identifies two relationships: one being between SALESPERSON and CUSTOMER, and the other being between CUSTOMER and ORDER. Both of these relationships are displayed in Fig. 6-20(c).

• Line 4 defines a relationship between VENDOR and VENDOR-ITEMs and is displayed in Fig. 6-20(d).

• Line 5 defines a relationship between ITEM and VENDOR-ITEM and is displayed in Fig. 6-20(e).

• Line 6 defines a relationship between WAREHOUSE and the nonunique entity LINE-ITEM. In addition, it places the parameter "filled from" on the relationship and makes it a conditional relationship. Also defined is a relationship between ORDER and LINE-ITEM. These relationships are displayed in Fig. 6-20(f).

• Line 7 further defines the nonunique entity LINE-ITEM through two conditional relationships and one normal relationship. The normal relationship is between ITEM and LINE-ITEM; the remaining two depend on the status of the LINE-ITEM as "not shipped" or "shipped." Because a LINE-ITEM cannot "be shipped" and "not shipped" at the same time, the relationship of LINE-ITEM must be shown as belonging to either ORDER or INVOICE but not to both. This relationship is shown in Fig. 6-20(g).

At the time entity relationships were defined, it was unclear if the nonunique entity SALESPERSON and CUSTOMER (line 8, Fig. 6-17) existed, as the group of attributes it defined had not been identified. To determine if this relationship should be included in the data structure model, it is necessary to review the list of entity–attribute relationships (Table 6-12). It can be seen from this list that the attribute grouping SALES-AGREEMENT has been defined and implies a relationship be-

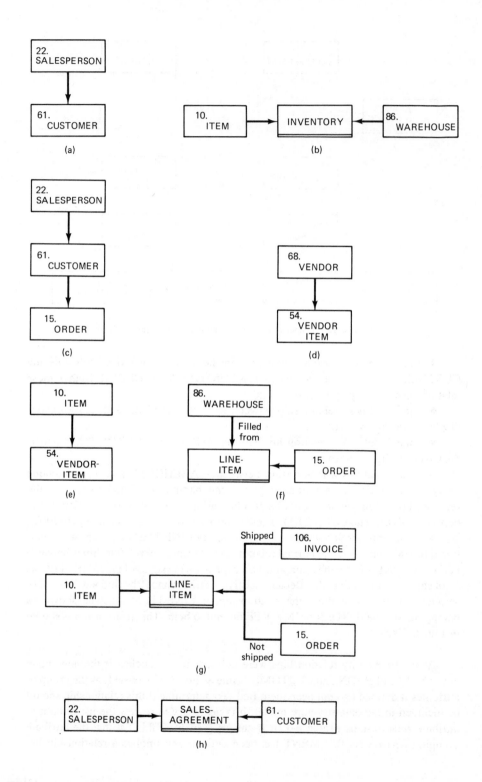

(a)

(b)

(c)

(d)

(e)

(f)

(g)

(h)

FIGURE 6-20 (*Opposite*) Sample data relationships for the target database: (*a*) relationship between SALESPERSON and CUSTOMER; (*b*) relationships among components of a nonunique entity, INVENTORY; (*c*) relationships among SALESPERSON, CUSTOMER, and ORDER; (*d*) relationship between VENDOR and VENDOR-ITEMS; (*e*) relationship between ITEM and VENDOR-ITEM; (*f*) conditional relationships between WAREHOUSE and the nonunique entity, LINE-ITEM; (*g*) conditional and either/or relationship between INVOICE, ORDER and LINE-ITEM and a normal relationship between ITEM and LINE-ITEM; (*h*) relationship between SALESPERSON and SALES-AGREEMENT and between CUSTOMER and SALES-AGREEMENT.

tween SALESPERSON and SALES-AGREEMENT. This relationship is displayed in Fig. 6-20(h).

Having displayed the individual entity relationships with the correct notations, the next step involves developing an overall information structure by combining individual relationships. The resulting structure is shown in Fig. 6-21.

After the basic information structure has been developed, entity–attribute and attribute relationships are expressed in a graphical format. Unlike entity relationships, entity–attribute and attribute relationships are displayed through the use of hierarchical diagrams. To develop each hierarchy, the attribute relationship lists (Table 6-14) developed during the analysis should be referred to determine how attributes group together [e.g., the highly related attributes CUSTOMER-ADDRESS and CUSTOMER-ZIP-CODE in Fig. 6-20(h) should be grouped under the heading ADDRESS] or how they depend upon one another (e.g., 30-DAY-OVERDUE-BALANCE in Table 6-14 is shown as being dependent upon TOTAL-BALANCE-OWED). The hierarchical diagram shown in Fig. 6-22 displays the relationships between the entity CUSTOMER and all its attributes. Such diagrams should be developed for the attributes of all unique and nonunique entities.

The combination of the basic information structure—consisting of unique entities, nonunique entities, and entity relationships—and the hierarchical diagram of attribute and entity–attribute relationships constitutes the full information structure.

6-4 INTERPRETING THE INFORMATION STRUCTURE SO THAT IT MAY BE VERIFIED BY ALL USERS (Step 2-4)

The process of developing the information structure necessarily involves summarizing and interpreting large amounts of data concerning how different parts of an organization create and/or use data. The reason the design methodology is so structured is that it is extremely difficult to identify and understand all data relationships and the condition under which they may or may not exist. Even with this degree of

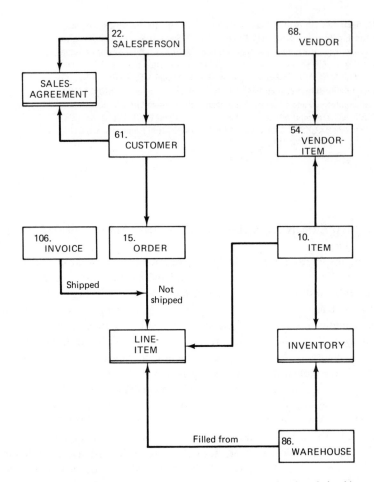

FIGURE 6-21 Completed information structure showing all entity relationships.

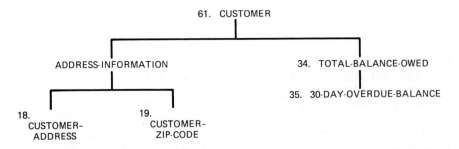

FIGURE 6-22 Hierarchical diagram of attribute relationships and entity–attribute relationships.

structure it is highly probable that some relationships were missed and that some were expressed incorrectly. In addition, the development of the information structure is the only mechanism that defines explicitly how different parts of an organization use and manage their data. Consequently, it is reasonable to expect that management, with this newfound knowledge, will want to be made aware of their current environment and possibly consider some changes. Because of this, it is necessary to provide them with an understanding of the data relationships shown in the information structure and how these relationships affect the way in which business is, or can be, conducted. To accomplish this, each relationship in the design and each relationship excluded from the design must be identified and expressed in very clear statements that can be reviewed and approved by management. Following management's review, the design, if necessary, will be adjusted to reflect their decisions.

The following steps should be performed to interpret the information structure (all examples are based on Fig. 6-21).

Step 2-4-1 involves stating what each entity is dependent upon (i.e., if any arrow points to it). For example:

- Each CUSTOMER must be assigned to a SALESPERSON before an account may be established.
- All ORDERs must be from CUSTOMERs with established accounts.
- All INVENTORies must reside at a predefined WAREHOUSE and may contain only ITEMs currently on the company's books.

Step 2-4-2 defines the implications of each arrow (note that each arrow implies a one-to-many relationship). For example:

- Each SALESPERSON may serve an unlimited number of CUSTOMERs.
- Each CUSTOMER may be served by only one SALESPERSON.
- Each CUSTOMER may have an unlimited number of ORDERs.
- Each ORDER must be from only one CUSTOMER.
- Each WAREHOUSE may have an INVENTORY that contains all or part of the ITEMs sold by the company.
- Each ITEM may be in all or some of the WAREHOUSE INVENTORies.

Step 2-4-3 defines what information cannot exist if an occurrence of each entity is removed from the database. For example:

- If a SALESPERSON is replaced, all CUSTOMERs must be immediately reassigned to a new SALESPERSON and all SALES-AGREEMENTs renegotiated.
- If a CUSTOMER-ACCOUNT is deleted or inactivated, all current ORDERs from that customer will be removed and the SALES-AGREEMENT nullified.

- If an ITEM is discontinued or otherwise deleted, all of its INVENTORY, across all WAREHOUSEs, is also deleted.
- If a WAREHOUSE is sold, or removed, no INVENTORY can reside at that location.

Step 2-4-4 involves defining what each entity is not dependent upon (note that there is no directly connecting arrow). For example:

- A SALESPERSON has no direct relationship to VENDORs, INVOICEs, ITEMs, or WAREHOUSEs.
- CUSTOMERs have no direct relationships to INVOICEs, VENDORs, ITEMs, or WAREHOUSEs.
- INVENTORies have no direct relationships to VENDORs, INVOICEs, ORDERs, CUSTOMERs, or SALESPERSONs.

The four steps defined above should also be performed to interpret the hierarchical diagram of each entity. All statements created through this process should be added to the previous lists.

Prior to presenting the translation of the information structure to management, the implication of possible future changes (previously extracted from management interviews), should be checked against the design and areas of potential problems noted. Assume that some of the possible changes extracted from management interviews include:

- Allowing CUSTOMERs to share an ORDER to realize freight savings (e.g., many CUSTOMERs to one ORDER)
- Assigning SALESPERSONs to a specific WAREHOUSE, implying that they cannot sell ITEMs from another WAREHOUSE
- Allowing a CUSTOMER to have blanket orders that cover a period of 6 to 12 months

Each of the preceding statements of potential future change must be analyzed:

1. To determine if the current information structure can absorb the change.
2. To define and diagram the changes that would have to take place to accommodate new requirements.
3. To define, through clear statements, the implications of such changes.

The following paragraphs describe how these steps would be performed for each of the three possible future changes.

Change 1: More Than One Customer to an Order

The first potential change implies that more than one CUSTOMER may own an ORDER. Since the current information structure explicitly shows that each ORDER must belong to only one CUSTOMER (e.g., the arrow originates from CUSTOMER in Fig. 6-21 and points to ORDER), the current design could not accommodate this change.

To accommodate more than one CUSTOMER to an ORDER, each ORDER must be divorced from a CUSTOMER, and ORDERs and CUSTOMERs must be related to specific LINE-ITEMs (e.g., ORDER one owns LINE-ITEMs 1 to 20, while CUS-TOMER A may own LINE-ITEMs 1 to 10 and CUSTOMER B may own LINE-ITEMs 11 to 20). The structure to support this change is shown in Fig. 6-23.

The implications of this change may be stated as follows:

- The attributes related to the ORDER entity describe such things as date of shipment and delivery address. Since ORDER nò longer relates to a specific CUSTOMER, such attributes would have to appear with each LINE-ITEM.
- Since no direct relationship is shown between an ORDER and a CUSTOMER, it is possible that an invalid ORDER may enter the system (e.g., an ORDER for which no CUSTOMER exists).
- INVOICEs, which were implicitly related to a CUSTOMER through their relationship to LINE-ITEM (which was owned by ORDER and CUS-TOMER), must now be explicitly related to both CUSTOMER and LINE-ITEM (e.g., an arrow from CUSTOMER would have to point to INVOICE).

Change 2: Assigning Salespeople to a Warehouse

The second change disallows a SALESPERSON from taking an order that cannot be supplied by the warehouse he or she is served by. Since the current information structure shows no explicit relationship between SALESPERSON and WARE-HOUSE and allows each LINE-ITEM to be "filled from" any WAREHOUSE, it cannot easily accommodate this change.

To assure that a SALESPERSON sells only from the WAREHOUSE assigned, several major changes must occur in the data structure. First is the addition of a relationship between WAREHOUSE and SALESPERSON. Adding this relationship implies that because a SALESPERSON belongs to a WAREHOUSE, so do his or her CUSTOMERs and their ORDERs. Since this future change did not state that CUS-TOMERs could order only from one WAREHOUSE (meaning they could deal with one SALESPERSON from each WAREHOUSE), the relationship between SALES-PERSON and CUSTOMER would have to be discontinued and SALESPERSON must be directly related to the ORDER. In addition, the relationship between SALESPERSON and SALES-AGREEMENT would have to be changed to WARE-HOUSE and SALES-AGREEMENT. This allows a CUSTOMER to have a different SALES AGREEMENT with each WAREHOUSE. The last change must be the

FIGURE 6-23   The information structure required to support the first possible change.

removal of the "filled from" relationship between WAREHOUSE and LINE-ITEM. The data structure supporting these changes is shown in Fig. 6-24.

The implications of the second change are as follows:

- A CUSTOMER is no longer confined to a specific SALESPERSON or WAREHOUSE. A CUSTOMER can purchase from any WAREHOUSE but must deal through a different SALESPERSON for each.
- CUSTOMERs may enter into separate SALES-AGREEMENTs with each WAREHOUSE, implying that ORDERs may be priced in several different ways.
- Each WAREHOUSE can have one or more SALESPERSONS but each SALESPERSON can sell for only one WAREHOUSE.
- A SALESPERSON does not have direct responsibility for any customer but does have responsibility for the ORDERs he or she takes.
- All ORDERs taken by a SALESPERSON must be filled from the WARE-HOUSE to which he or she is assigned.

Change 3: Inclusion of Blanket Orders

The third change describes the duration over which a customer may have an open ORDER. Since this change does not define new relationships, and the existing structure allows LINE-ITEMs to be INVOICEd "as shipped," the existing design can easily accommodate the inclusion of a BLANKET-ORDER.

Once the information structure has been translated into statements and the impact of all future changes has been identified, a report should be prepared for management. Because a great deal of material is contained in such a report, it is recommended that it

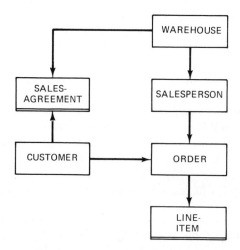

FIGURE 6-24   Information structure to support
the second possible change.

be arranged by entity topic and explicitly ask questions concerning hazy areas or the value of accommodating future changes (Table 6-15). Once individual managers have had the time to review and comment (give them space to write on the report), their collective comments should be examined and the following analysis performed.

1. If a majority of managers disagreed with a statement and gave the same corrected "restatement," simply reflect their statement in the design. For example, if all managers disagreed with statement 7 in Table 6-15, and said that "an invoice must be explicitly related to one customer," add an arrow from CUSTOMER to INVOICE.
2. If a few managers disagreed, or many different viewpoints were expressed,

TABLE 6-15 Example of Report to be Given to Management for Approval

CUSTOMER INFORMATION

Statements About How Customer Information Is and Is Not Used in the Current Operating Environment

1. Each customer must be assigned to a salesperson before an account may be established.
   COMMENTS: _____

2. All orders must be from customers with established accounts.
   COMMENTS: _____

3. Each customer can be served by only one salesperson.
   COMMENTS: _____

4. Each customer may have an unlimited number of orders.
   COMMENTS: _____

5. If a salesperson is replaced, all customers must be immediately reassigned to a new salesperson and all sales agreements renegotiated.
   COMMENTS: _____

6. If a customer is deleted or inactivated, all of the customer's current orders will be removed and sales agreements nullified.
   COMMENTS: _____

7. Customers have no direct relationship to invoices, vendors, item numbers, or warehouses.
   COMMENTS: _____

8. More than one customer may be on a given order.
   AGREE _____
   DISAGREE _____

9. A customer buys from a warehouse and not a salesperson. Consequently, each customer may have a sales agreement with each warehouse.
   AGREE _____
   DISAGREE _____

present the viewpoints and their implications to a number of top management to obtain a decision. (*Note:* Do not expect an immediate decision, as managers are not used to thinking about the impact of data on their business.) Reflect the decision in the information structure.

3. The decision to accommodate future changes that require an adjustment to the information structure must be made by top management. Follow the same procedure as described previously.

Once all decisions have been made and both the diagram and the statements adjusted, the information structure, the result of conceptual design, is complete. Before turning the result over to the persons responsible for developing the logical database structure, it is appropriate to present the final design (just the statements) to the group of managers who performed the review. By following this procedure, all managers can be apprised of the rules under which their areas will be required to operate.

III IMPLEMENTATION DESIGN

7 IMPLEMENTATION DESIGN CONCEPTS

The boundary between conceptual and physical database design is difficult to assess because of the lack of a standard terminology. There seems to be general agreement, however, that conceptual design encompasses a DBMS-independent view of data and that physical design results in a specification for the database structure as it is physically stored. The in-between design phase that produces a DBMS-processible schema will be called implementation design. Refinements to the database structure that occur during this design phase are developed from the viewpoint of satisfying DBMS-dependent constraints as well as the more general constraints specified in the user requirements.

The major objective of implementation design is to produce a DBMS-processible schema that satisfies the full range of user requirements from integrity and consistency constraints to efficiency for projected database growth and complexity. However, there must be considerable interaction with the application program design activities that are going on simultaneously with database design. High-level program specifications are analyzed, and program design guidance should be supplied to correspond to the proposed database structure.

In this chapter we investigate the major implementation design issues, describe a design process for schemas and subschemas, and look at detailed efficiency analysis required for schema design. An example in Chapter 8 illustrates the schema design decisions required.

7-1 IMPLEMENTATION DESIGN COMPONENTS

A diagram of the spectrum of inputs to and outputs from the implementation design is shown in Fig. 7-1 [Lum et al., 1979a]:

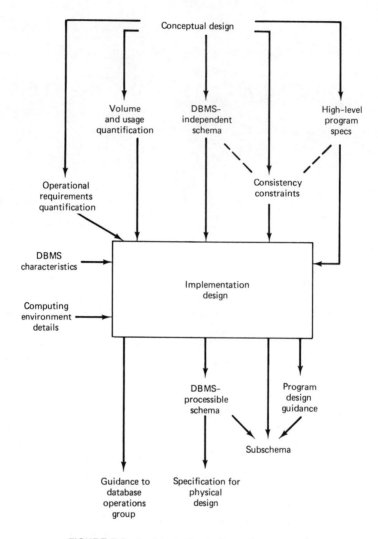

FIGURE 7-1 Implementation design environment.

Inputs

1. *DBMS-independent schema.* The major result of the conceptual design phase, to be constrained and refined by the implementation design phase.
2. *Operational requirements quantification.* Specifications for integrity, recovery, security, response time limits, and growth projection for volume and new structures.
3. *Volume and usage quantification.* Database size in terms of data occurrences and application frequencies.

4. *Consistency constraints.* Rules for keeping data elements mutually consistent, rules for dealing with inconsistent data while resolution takes place, and constraints on duplicates and ordering of update operations.
5. *High-level program specifications.* Result of program requirements analysis.
6. *DBMS characteristics.* Rules for formulating DBMS-processible schemas and subschemas and program syntax.
7. *Computing environment details.* Hardware/software capacity and configuration limitations.

Outputs

1. *DBMS-processible schema.* Specifications for a database structure that can be implemented with a specific DBMS; does not include (or use defaults for) the more physical parameters that specify clustering of records or block-size considerations; however, it does include some access path parameters such as ordering, pointers, and search mechanism.
2. *Subschemas.* DBMS-processible database structure consistent with individual user views and security constraints.
3. *Specifications for physical design.* Fully documented schema and subschemas with volume, usage, and hardware/software environment information for use in the physical design phase.
4. *Program design guidance.* Suggestions on access path selection for application programmers based on the proposed database structure.
5. *Guidance to the database operations group.* A summary of requirements, constraints, and available data on the hardware/software environment to the database administrator and staff.

The role of the implementation design is to document thoroughly all available volume data, requirements, and constraints in the schema so that there is no question or confusion about what is allowed in future design iterations.

7-2   IMPLEMENTATION DESIGN STEPS

A number of implementation schema design processes have been proposed in the literature, ranging from completely manual processes to partially automated schemes [Chen, 1977b; Fry et al., 1978a; Jones, 1976; Yeh et al., 1978a]. For the purpose of exposition a general set of schema design steps is indicated in Fig. 7-2. Although presented in an algorithmic context to indicate an overall sequence, these steps are by no means complete nor are there sufficient criteria for evaluation or convergence of the schema design process in general or its individual steps. It should be noted that schema design, perhaps more than any other area, requires interaction with the other database design steps and the outside area of program design.

The step numbering scheme used here has been kept consistent with the global

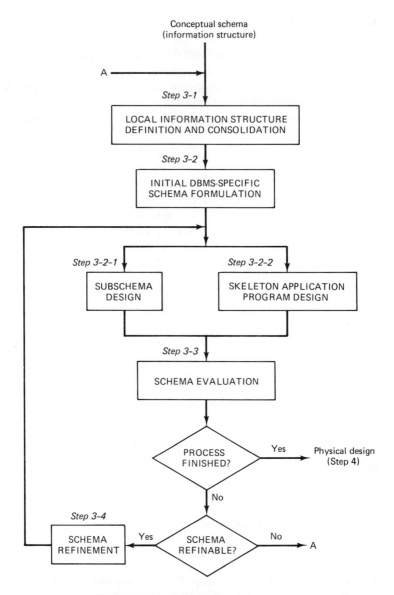

FIGURE 7-2 Implementation design steps.

numbering scheme defined in Chapter 2. The first steps are perhaps the most straightforward and easiest to perform. The major input to these steps is the conceptual schema (information structure) which has already been formulated. The objective is to formulate a DBMS-processible schema that is isomorphic to the conceptual schema. To perform this mapping we need an additional input: the data model characteristics of the particular DBMS. In the case of the network or relational data model, the mapping of a conceptual schema to a DBMS-processible schema is straightforward with a set of simple rules. For example, rules are needed for handling *M : N* relationships by link records (in network data model) or new relations (in the relational data model) or the creation of entry points. The hierarchical data model and variations thereof require additional rules: for example, for removing multiple-parent relationships and for treating *M : N* relationships.

Local Information Structure Definition and Consolidation (Step 3-1)

The processing requirements can be analyzed for data content, both for the source (basis) of retrieval or update and for the target data retrieved or updated. An appropriate subset of the initial information structure is selected, if possible, to satisfy the data requirements of each application, such as a report, ad hoc query, or update transaction. The format of the local information structures is the same as the initial structure produced in Step 2. After each application has been represented, the initial structure from Step 2 can be consolidated with all local structures based on processing, into a revised information structure. In some cases the local structures will extend the initial structure because new entities and relationships may have to be defined. Thus, the revised structure may look quite different from the original one.

After the formulation of the initial DBMS schema the design process branches into two parallel steps, as shown in Fig. 7-2.

Using the combined insight gained from the consolidated information structure in this step, processing/data relationships, and allowable DBMS-record-type characteristics, initial record types can be formulated. In the simplest case, entities become record types directly, and attributes become item types. In more complex cases, entities can be split or consolidated to form new record types. This step begins the consideration of DBMS-specific rules and constraints on database definition, although the more physical components of schemas, such as might be in the proposed CODASYL Data Storage Description Language [CODASYL, 1978], are not considered until physical design.

Subschema Design (Step 3-2-1)

This branch of the design process is in actuality an analog of view integration performed in Step 2, information structure design. The objective of this step is to design the schema interface (a subschema) for the application programs. The subschema is a working subset of the schema that allows for efficient access to data by a particular user without compromising security. Rules for schema design and evaluation apply to subschemas.

Application Program Design (Step 3-2-2)

The other branch of the design process is the interface to application program design. It is not our objective to perform a complete application program design, for this is a formidable task. Rather, we can develop a program outline or skeleton. For each transaction, enough details are sketched to perform the data access function and provide the interface with the procedural logic. This step can provide valuable input to the next step, schema evaluation.

Schema Evaluation (Step 3-3)

The logical database structure (schema) can now be evaluated based on quantitative information and performance measures. *Processing volume* is defined as the combination of two parameters: processing frequency and data volume. *Processing frequency* is the frequency at which an individual application is required to be run. *Data volume* is the number of occurrences of each record type currently stored in the database. Database growth is reflected in increases to both processing frequency, sometimes referred to as "usage," and data volume.

Performance measures at this point are limited to logical record access counts, total bytes transferred to satisfy an application, and total bytes in the database. These measures attempt to predict, as closely as possible, physical database performance in terms of elapsed time and physical storage space. This task tends to be more successful for navigational-type database structures (i.e., networks and hierarchies) and less successful for entry point structures (inverted) unless indexes are represented as additional record types. Relational structures may be analyzed in this step under the same assumption for indexes. Consequently, this step can be described in terms of either implementation or physical design, depending on the designer's orientation.

At this point in the design process it is appropriate to ask if the design is complete. Again it is difficult to establish precisely what a complete schema design is, but simplistic criteria such as conformance to the conceptual schema and satisfaction of the application program interface (subschema) with minimal transport volume may be sufficient. If the criteria are not satisfied, the schema refinement step is executed; otherwise, the process is completed and physical design commences.

Schema Refinement (Step 3-4)

The purpose of this step is to adapt the schema to a different representation of the information. In this case we are utilizing those DBMS features such as indexes or hashing functions. Under no circumstances is the information content of the database to be modified. If the schema cannot be refined without modifying the information content, the schema design is terminated and requirement analysis is entered. All refinements are subjected to the evaluation described in Step 3-3 (Fig. 7-2).

7-3 LOGICAL DATABASE STRUCTURE
   PERFORMANCE

Logical record access (LRA) counts are made to estimate the expected number of occurrences of each record type retrieved explicitly in the course of executing an application. When weighted by processing frequencies, these figures show which application will probably require the most I/O accesses to and from the database. Furthermore, by noting which applications are dominant in terms of frequency of execution or LRAs per unit time, one can determine where design improvements will be most effective.

If LRAs can be specified for each application by record type, it is easy to use their results to calculate transport volume or the total amount of data flow between the application programs and the database management system. The transport volume due to one record type in one application is just the product of the size of that record and its number of LRAs in that application. This may be summed over all record types to calculate the transport volume in bytes for the application. Finally, the various transport volumes for the applications may be weighted by the application frequencies and summed to obtain the global transport volume.

Transport volume should be used to supplement LRAs in making information structure refinement decisions because simple minimization of LRAs alone will lead to extremely large record types. Other limitations of LRAs as objective functions are their inability to assess time/space trade-offs at the physical level (e.g., more indexes can reduce access time), and their orientation toward navigational systems such as CODASYL or IMS and not toward inverted index systems such as ADABAS or System 2000. The latter handicap can be overcome, however, by extending the concept of navigational access path to include indexes as well as user data, with index "record types."

7-3-1 Logical Record Access Approach

Performance measures for logical database structures or schemas can be defined in terms of standard units as follows [Teorey, 1980]:

• *Logical record access (LRA)*
Accesses for application i are given by

$$\text{LRA}_i = \sum_{j=1}^{N} \text{LRA}_{ij} \qquad (7\text{-}1)$$

where N equals the number of record types in the database and LRA_{ij} is the accessed number of logical records of record type j for application i.

Accesses per unit time equal

$$\text{LRA} = \sum_{i=1}^{M} \sum_{j=1}^{N} \text{LRA}_{ij} \times F_i \qquad (7\text{-}2)$$

where M equals the total number of applications for this database and F_i is the frequency (number) of executions of application i per unit time.

• *Transport volume*
Transport volume (in bytes) per application i is given by

$$TRVOL_i = \sum_{j=1}^{N} LRA_{ij} \times RECSIZE_j \qquad (7\text{-}3)$$

where $RECSIZE_j$ equals the average size of logical record type j in bytes.
   Transport volume (in bytes) per unit time equals

$$TRVOL = \sum_{i=1}^{M} \sum_{j=1}^{N} LRA_{ij} \times RECSIZE_j \times F_i \qquad (7\text{-}4)$$

• *Storage space*
Data storage space (bytes) equals

$$DSTOR = \sum_{j=1}^{N} RECSIZE_j \times NREC_j \qquad (7\text{-}5)$$

where $NREC_j$ equals the number of occurrences of record type j in the database.
   Pointer storage space (in bytes) equals

$$PTRSTOR = \sum_{j=1}^{N} NREC_j \times PS \times NPTR_j \qquad (7\text{-}6)$$

where PS is pointer size in bytes and $NPTR_j$ is the average number of pointers stored with record type j.
   Once a candidate schema has been defined and processing volume information collected, all the parameters defined above are known except LRA_{ij}, which must be estimated for each application i on the database. Applications can be very complex, often involving a series of database accesses that are closely related to each other. In such cases it is helpful to classify individual components of an application in terms of a starting point (depending on DBMS "currency" rules) and whether the next record retrieval is of one of the following types:

• Find a unique record occurrence of type j.
• Find all record occurrences of type j (associated with a parent record of type k).
• Find some subset of record type j occurrences based on specified boolean criteria.

Based on these general types or classes of retrievals, the LRA count is typically either 1, $NRECR_j$, or $NRECR_j/2$, where $NRECR_j$ represents the average number of record type j occurrences in a particular relationship (usually, as a child record under a specific parent record, or cardinality of a relation).
   Designers with more experience may wish to analyze record occurrence distributions instead of expected values in terms of child record occurrences per parent record

occurrence, although best case/worst case comparisons may be considerably simpler and often just as meaningful. For example, if, in a hierarchy, two parent records of type *B* (Fig. 7-3) have respectively, 10 and 50 occurrences of child record occurrences *C*, then the average of 30 child records may not be meaningful for this particular case, but it may be a reasonable estimate for a large sample of *B* records. If the variance of record occurrences of *C* per occurrence of parent *B* is quite large, the expected value approach should consider worst-case performance. The technique of expected value LRA computations will be illustrated here.

Consider the three candidate hierarchical schemas shown in Fig. 7-4 to satisfy some given database requirements and constraints. We wish to evaluate all schemas

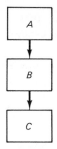

FIGURE 7-3   Simple hierarchy of three record types.

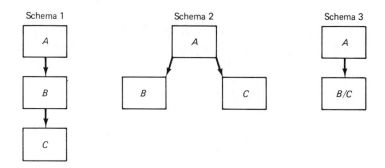

Schema 1: $NREC_A$ = 100, $NREC_B$ = 200 per *A*, $NREC_C$ = 5 per *B*

Schema 2: $NREC_A$ = 100, $NREC_B$ = 200 per *A*, $NREC_C$ = 1000 per *A*

Schema 3: $NREC_A$ = 100, $NREC_{B/C}$ = 1000 per *A* (5 *C*'s per *B*; *B*'s are redundant)

$RECSIZE_A$ = 100 bytes, $RECSIZE_B$ = 200 bytes, $RECSIZE_C$ = 50 bytes, $RECSIZE_{B/C}$ = 250 bytes

Pointers assumed: Forward, parent, first child

FIGURE 7-4   Candidate schemata and data volume.

using our basic performance measures for the following applications, each executed
once per unit time period.

1. Find random occurrence of record *A*
2. Find random occurrence of record *B*
3. Find random occurrence of record *C*
4. Find all *A*'s
5. Find all *B*'s associated with a *given A*.
6. Find all *C*'s associated with a *given B*.
7. Find all *A*'s associated with a *given C*.

For simplicity we assume that applications 1 through 4 use record type *A* as the entry
point and that only sequential access is allowed between record occurrences. We are
not concerned at this time with how the candidate schemas were derived or with their
physical significance.

Total LRAs for each application per time period are shown in Table 7-1. Finding
random records involves an expected search distance of one-half the number of record
occurrences in the list to be searched. For a sequential list, finding all records takes
only twice as long as finding one. Faster random access searches can be obtained with
indexed or hashing access methods, and these may be modeled with the LRA
approach. One possible method is to represent an index as a new record type in the
schema and assign an LRA to each index entry accessed. Transport volume can then
be computed according to the size of each index entry. Hashing can be modeled by
assigning one LRA for each random access. At this point in the design we cannot
model synonym collisions or overflow because physical parameters such as block size
and percent fill have not yet been considered. Thus, the LRA approach is limited in its
predictive capability for random-access-method performance.

According to Table 7-1, Schema 1 minimizes the LRA count. However, we still
have other performance measures to consider. Tables 7-2 and 7-3 summarize transport volume and storage space for our candidate schemas. They show that Schema 1
also minimizes transport volume but is only a close second in storage space minimization; thus, access speed is traded off with storage, and selection of the "best" schema

TABLE 7-1   LRA Counts for Candidate Schemas in Fig. 7-4

Application	Schema 1	Schema 2	Schema 3
1	50 *A*	50 *A*	50 *A*
2	50 *A* + 100 *B*	50 *A* + 100 *B*	50 *A* + 500 *B/C*
3	50 *A* + 100 *B* + 3 *C*	50 *A* + 500 *C*	50 *A* + 500 *B/C*
4	100 *A*	100 *A*	100 *A*
5	200 *B*	200 *B*	1000 *B/C*
6	5 *C*	1 *A* + 1000 *C*	4 *B/C*
7	1 *B* + 1 *A*	1 *A*	1 *A*
Total	251 *A* + 401 *B* + 8 *C* = 660	252 *A* + 300 *B* + 1500 *C* = 2052	251 *A* + 2004 *B/C* = 2255

TABLE 7-2   Transport Volume for Candidate Schemas in Fig. 7-4*

Application	Schema 1 (kB)	Schema 2 (kB)	Schema 3 (kB)
1	5	5	5
2	25	25	130
3	25.15	30	130
4	10	10	10
5	40	40	250
6	0.25	50.1	1.25
7	0.3	0.1	0.1
Total	105.7	160.2	526.35

*kB = kilobytes.

TABLE 7-3   Data Storage Space for Candidate Schemas in Fig. 7-4*

	Schema 1	Schema 2	Schema 3
Total records	$100\,A + 20{,}000\,B$ $+ 100{,}000\,C$	$100\,A + 20{,}000\,B$ $+ 100{,}000\,C$	$100\,A +$ $100{,}000\,B/C$
Data storage	9.01 MB	9.01 MB	25.01 MB
Pointer storage	1.04 MB	0.96 MB	0.80 MB
Total storage	10.05 MB	9.97 MB	25.81 MB

*MB = megabytes; pointer = 4 bytes (parent has one pointer, child has two pointers).

depends on the cost function the designer places on access count and storage space. In this case, however, Schema 1 is clearly the most efficient and should be preferred unless there is a strict storage space limitation of 10.0 megabytes.

The tabular data point out how some applications are inherently much more expensive than others to run, and that processing volume or frequency is also important to consider. Other factors, such as priority of applications or response time constraints, may dictate that dominating applications may not be based solely on LRA counts. This is where proper establishment of system objectives plays an important role in implementation design.

7-3-2   Relationship Between Logical and Physical Performance

The relationship between logical record accesses and physical I/O depends on many factors, including block size and physical clustering. However, some general rules of thumb can be stated here. If we define physical I/O to consist of a series of random physical block accesses (PBA_r) with expected time to access and transfer each random block TRBA, and sequential physical block accesses (PBA_s) with expected time to access and transfer each sequential block (TSBA), our task is to translate LRA count into functions of PBA_s and PBA_r, and again to translate physical accesses into total I/O service time, TIO_s and TIO_r. For example:

To search a physical sequential file:

$$PBA_s = \left\lceil \frac{LRA}{BF} \right\rceil \quad \text{sequential block accesses} \qquad (7\text{-}7)$$

where BF is the blocking factor and $\lceil \ \ \rceil$ is the ceiling function,

$$TIO_s = PBA_s \times TSBA \qquad \text{seconds} \qquad (7\text{-}8)$$

For direct access to a record:

$$PBA_r = LRA = 1 \text{ random block access} \qquad (7\text{-}9)$$

and thus

$$TIO_r = PBA_r \times TRBA = TRBA \qquad \text{seconds} \qquad (7\text{-}10)$$

Note that in these cases TIO does not account for buffering or for the possibility that a block to be accessed is already in main storage. Therefore, TIO as used here represents the worst case. Note also that values for TSBA and TRBA depend on whether the block accesses occur in a stand-alone or a shared environment. Typically, the shared environment implies that each block access, random or sequential, is randomized by the interference due to other users. The stand-alone environment implies that random accesses are confined to the extent of the data stored, whether stored in one cylinder or in several devices, and sequential accesses may possibly be synchronized through record interlacing or other techniques to improve performance. For example, typical expected disk service times for the stand-alone environment are

$$TSBA = ROT/2 + BKS/TR \qquad (7\text{-}11)$$

$$TRBA = SEEK(NCYL) + ROT/2 + BKS/TR \qquad (7\text{-}12)$$

where ROT is the full rotation time, BKS the block size in bytes, TR the transfer rate in bytes per second, and SEEK(NCYL) the expected seek time over a database extent of NCYL contiguous cylinders. The expected disk service time for a multiuser shared environment is typically

$$TSBA = TRBA = SEEK(CPD) + \frac{ROT}{2} + \frac{BKS}{TR} \qquad (7\text{-}13)$$

where SEEK(CPD) is the expected seek time over the extent of the entire disk of CPD cylinders.

These expressions do not necessarily hold under all circumstances but are the most typical cases. One obvious variation is to use a device control unit hardware scan to find a particular identifier value in a record. For this case, TSBA = BKS/TR, because each block is scanned as fast as it is passed by the read–write heads; occasionally, however, a cylinder boundary is crossed and an additional delay occurs.

The important point to observe between logical and physical database performance is that the measures can be related analytically. Extreme caution must be used, however, because those relationships can be quite complex and must be carefully formulated for a given hardware/software environment.

Another note of caution should be made concerning the use of the LRA count as the only performance measure. In Fig. 7-5 two simple cases are presented for the "find all A" application. In case 1 the application requires 100 LRA, 100 PBA$_r$, and 100 TRBA time. Since transport volume is the same (disregarding unused block space), the differences between the two cases lie in the number of block accesses and the type of block accesses. Random block accesses are typically more time consuming than are sequential block accesses.

Because the LRA count cannot predict block accesses, it is limited in its ability to predict accurately absolute physical performance. However, it is very useful for predicting relative performance for schemas when the available access methods for each schema are similar.

Variations of the LRA approach have been reported to be useful in hierarchical as well as network database structure design [Bubenko et al., 1976; Chen et al., 1979; Oren and Aschim, 1979]. One approach estimates the total operational cost associated with retrieval, update, and report generation, including restructuring of data and sort/merge activity required to produce reports, but is currently limited to hierarchical databases [Chen et al., 1979]. A serious drawback of all these techniques is their lack of formal validation against live test data from real implementations. This applies generally across almost all analytical models of database structures, evaluators, or designers.

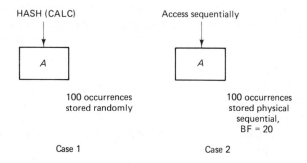

FIGURE 7-5   Two schemata with the same LRA count for "find all A" records application.

7-4 ALTERNATIVE IMPLEMENTATION DESIGN TOOLS

Given a candidate DBMS-independent database structure, there are currently two major categories of design tools available for producing a DBMS-processible schema: schema evaluators and schema designers. A schema evaluator is usually simpler because it is given a DBMS-processible structure, already manually designed, and evaluates its efficiency (usually in terms of access path length and storage space) for a given workload of application program functions and frequencies. The LRA approach of Section 7-3 is typical of this class of tools.

A schema designer usually must also do some kind of evaluation, but has the additional task of designing a feasible or possible "optimal" structure according to established performance criteria. Schema designers vary widely in their approaches and objectives, and as yet have not been effectively analyzed for relative applicability and validity. In this section some of the better known tools are presented to exemplify the range of approaches currently being developed.

Schema design techniques fall roughly into four categories: the pragmatic (manual) approach, algorithms for clustering of data attributes together to form records, optimization of relationship implementations, and theorem proving techniques [Fry et al., 1978a]. The pragmatic approach is exemplified by the entity–relationship synthesis of database schemas [Chen, 1977a,b; Chen and Yao, 1977]. In this approach, entity types become record types, and 1 : N relations become set types within their corresponding record types, one owned by each record type, and both having as a member type a special link record type unique to this relation representation. Thus, data items are grouped into record types according to the DBMS-independent entity diagram derived earlier.

It may sometimes be more efficient to partition an entity's attributes among several record types, or to combine the attributes of several entities into a single record type. Several researchers have proposed matrix techniques for clustering attributes into record types. Typically, an N by N matrix is developed, where N is the number of attributes in the information structure and element (i, j) of the matrix is the frequency at which attributes i and j will be processed together. Large frequencies indicate attribute pairs that should perhaps be placed in the same record type. Belford's method [Belford, 1975] uses a "nearest centroid algorithm" to associate an attribute with others with which it is often required simultaneously. An attribute may be assigned to several such clusters (and so will be stored redundantly). Hoffer's method [1975; Hoffer and Severance, 1975] uses the *bond energy algorithm* (BEA) to cluster attributes. The BEA produces a matrix of pairwise similarity measures for the attributes. Attributes are clustered by identifying submatrices of the similarity matrix whose element values are high.

Hubbard and Raver [1975] discuss a technique for automating logical database design. This technique consolidates the information structure views of the several applications (called "local views"). These local views are expressed in the form of lists of data elements, binary associations between data elements, and descriptions of the associations. Some of the data elements are distinguished as keys, and other data elements are termed attributes. The technique clusters the data elements in accordance with the associations in such a way that each cluster contains exactly one key. Associations between keys become associations between their clusters. If the technique is used to design for the CODASYL data model, the clusters are implemented as record types, and the intercluster associations are implemented in accordance with their cardinalities. A $1 : n$ association becomes a set type and an $m : n$ association becomes a link record type and a pair of set types, one owned by each of the two record types corresponding to the two clusters, and both containing the link record type as its member type. This technique has been implemented in software for IMS as IBM's Database Design Aid (DBDA).

An early contribution to the techniques of relationship implementation optimization was the automated approach of Mitoma [1975; Mitoma and Irani, 1975]. This technique accepts a list of data items and descriptions of their interrelationships as input, and implements the described information structure as a CODASYL schema. Each relationship may be implemented in one of 12 ways. An integer programming approach is used to find an allowable combination of relationship implementations that minimizes an expected access cost measure subject to a constraint on the amount of storage used. Extensions of this model for real systems, including IMS as well as CODASYL systems, have been developed by Purkayastha [Irani et al., 1979]. Berelian and Irani [1977] also extended it for a paging environment.

A model called DESIGNER uses artificial intelligence methods in an approach to CODASYL logical database structure design [Gerritsen, 1975b, 1978]. DESIGNER uses a theorem-proving technique to synthesize a CODASYL logical structure from the queries to be processed by the proposed dastabase system. Queries are translated by the system into a set of assertions about the structural interrelationships among the data elements referenced. New assertions are derived as theorems from older ones. These assertions specify feasibility constraints on the logical structure and are used to generate a logical structure capable of representing all information required by queries.

8   AN EXAMPLE SCHEMA DESIGN PROBLEM

The following problem is a revision of the case study originally proposed by Bubenko [Bubenko, 1977a,b]. It illustrates many of the major problems the implementation schema designer faces when trying to maximize performance for a multiuser integrated database [Teorey, 1980].

8-1   REQUIREMENTS SPECIFICATIONS (STEP 1)

A manufacturing firm wishes to develop a computer-based information system for labor and employee management of the firm's several plants. The firm has 50 plants located in 40 states. The company has approximately 100,000 employees. Each plant is divided into departments and further subdivided into work stations. There are 100 departments and 500 work stations in the company. In each department there is an on-line time clock at which employees report their arrival and departure. A work task is associated with one of 20 different job types. Each job type can be performed at each plant. During a given day, an employee may perform more than one work task, each associated with a different job type, and each work task can be performed (and reported) at a different work station. Each work station has an on-line data entry device at which an employee reports activity carried out on a work task. There are five worker unions represented in the company, and every employee belongs to exactly one union. Although the size of the company remains stable, about 20% of the employees leave each year and are replaced by new personnel.

Processing Requirements

To support these information needs, the following input transactions are necessary:

    T1. The day an employee is hired, input employee number, name, address, birthdate, plant name, union name, and date of hire.

T2. The day an employee is terminated, input employee name, employee number, and date of departure. Employee records are deleted and a separate file is maintained on former employees.

T3. When a work task is completed, input employee number, work station number, job type, current date, and hours worked.

An initial analysis of the labor and employee management information needs of the firm was performed. As a result, the following reports were described as being necessary to support the firm's activity:

R1. Each quarter, the company has to report to the worker unions, for each union: the company name, the number of its members having worked in that quarter, total working hours, and total earnings; in addition, for each union, a list of its members' names, addresses, social security number (SSN), days worked, and average monthly salary for that quarter.

R2. Each year a report to the states listing for each employee living in those states: name, SSN, and total earnings.

R3. Every month a report to those states where a plant is located: the company name, plant names in state, the number of employees hired, the number of employees who left the company, and the number of employees the last day of the month.

R4. To company management each month for each plant: plant name, total employee hours worked, and total salary amount; within each plant for each job: hours worked and job description.

R5. To plant management daily: employee name, SSN, a breakdown of hours worked for every job, and total hours reported at work stations (for all employees by job type).

R6. To plant payroll each month for employee: employee name, address, SSN, and earnings.

R7. To personnel management, on-line request for a particular employee: name, days worked this year, earnings this year, and hours reported (up to date of this request).

From the various requirements specified above, the objectives of the database design are summarized as follows: to provide fast access to data in support of on-line data entry devices that report employee completion of a particular task; to provide timely reports to various levels of management on a daily, monthly, or sometimes longer basis; and to allow on-line queries about individual employees. Both random and sequential applications must be supported, and although some must be completed within seconds, others have less restrictive turnaround requirements. Performance constraints are not explicitly stated; therefore, typical values will be assumed when appropriate.

Fortunately, for our example this phase of the analysis is greatly simplified by the existence of a single concise statement of the problem. All assumptions made must be based on information contained in the problem statement, and because there are no real-life users with whom to review the specifications, revisions will not be needed.

8-2 CONCEPTUAL DESIGN (STEP 2)

The first activity is to analyze the general information requirements and formulate an initial information structure (i.e., conceptual schema). This will provide a starting point for stepwise refinement toward a logical database structure and a basis for long-term flexibility in the design. In general, consolidation may be required if more than one user view is expressed at this level.

The basic information structure presented in Fig. 8-1 is the result of our analysis of the natural relationships in the manufacturing firm described in the requirements specification. The concept of a $1 : M$ relationship is illustrated by the potential association of several departments within a plant. Although a particular plant may have only one department, the relationship is defined for the general case. A $1 : 1$ relationship exists between CLOCK and DEPARTMENT to indicate uniqueness of an on-line clock to each department. The $M : N$ relationship between EMPLOYEE and WORK-STATION represents the fact that a work station may contain many employees, and that an employee may work at many work stations over a given day or longer period.

The initial information structure is based on many assumptions about the data and should be verified as soon as possible. For example, although not explicitly stated in

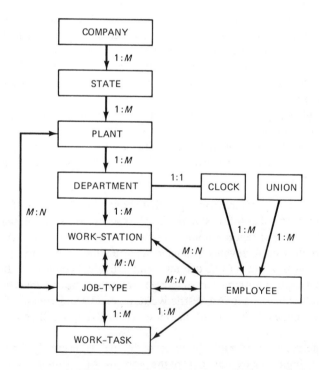

FIGURE 8-1 Initial information structure.

the problem, we assume that each WORK-STATION may be associated with many JOB-TYPEs because many plants in our experience are known to have such a configuration. This assumption, and others of similar character, are implicit in the information structure and can be derived from it for future reference. Note also that this step is greatly simplified in this example because only a single conceptual view is presented in the requirements specifications; thus, conceptual view integration is not necessary. In Step 3, however, we will see that the many processing views require integration.

Although data volume is not relevant to our design until Step 3, it is easily derived at the entity level from the general information requirements and is recorded for future reference. Actually, it does have an immediate use as a verification that the proposed relationships are meaningful.

8-3   IMPLEMENTATION DESIGN (STEP 3)

STEP 3-1: DEFINE AND CONSOLIDATE LOCAL INFORMATION STRUCTURES

The next activity starts with analysis of each processing requirement for data content. Then an appropriate local information structure (entities, relationships, and their attributes) that satisfies the data requirements of each application (i.e., a report or update transaction result) can be drawn. The initial information structure can be used as a basis for formulating the local structures, but usually the processing requirements require extensions to the initial structure. If the objective is strictly short-term efficiency, the initial structure can be discarded after this step. Local information structures are then consolidated into a single global structure that eliminates most redundant entities and their attributes, but satisfies the access path requirements for the processing.

The manufacturing firm processing requirements define seven reports and three update transactions that must be satisfied by the database. To that list we discover (sooner or later) that at least one "implied" transaction must also be defined: modify the effective date and amount of any salary increase (possibly quarterly) that occurs for any employee. Other updates, such as employee address changes, occur infrequently and are not considered here, although in practice they should be noted. The local information structures for all applications are presented in Fig. 8-2. Attributes of entities are defined and are designated on the right side of each entity box. No distinction is made between attributes of entities and data items that make up logical records in this simplified methodology. However, we do not yet assume that entities represent individual logical record types. Sometimes new entities must be defined or split off from other entities, while other entities may be consolidated from existing ones.

The analysis of processing data content is enhanced by a processing matrix such as the one shown in Fig. 8-3. Each transaction and report is represented in terms of the data elements (attributes) required. This matrix is used to centralize for quick refer-

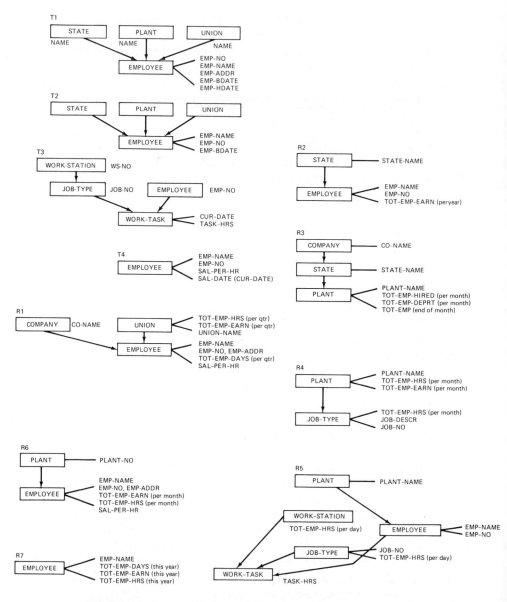

FIGURE 8-2 Local information structures based on processing data content.

ence what is known about processing requirements. It is not our intention to indicate whether data are derived from or stored explicitly in the database, merely to display in one place all data needed by the applications.

The consolidation of local information structures into a single global information structure is accomplished by a step-to-step integration of each local structure with every other local structure or with the initial information structure. As an example,

Data elements	Transactions				Reports/Queries						
	T1	T2	T3	T4	R1	R2	R3	R4	R5	R6	R7
1. CO-NAME					X	X	X				
2. CUR-DATE			X	X							
3. CUR-TIME			FUTURE?								
4. DEPT-NAME	FUTURE?										
5. EMP-ADDR	X				X					X	
6. EMP-BDATE	X										
7. EMP-DDATE		X									
8. EMP-HDATE	X										
9. EMP-NAME	X	X		X	X	X			X	X	X
10. EMP-NO	X	X	X	X	X	X			X	X	
11. JOB-DESCR								X			
12. JOB-TYPE			X					X	X		
13. PLANT-NAME	X						X	X	X	X	
14. SAL-PER-HR				X	X					X	
15. SAL-DATE				X							
16. STATE-NAME						X	X				
17. TASK-HRS			X						X		
18. TOT-EMP							STATE/MO				
19. TOT-EMP-DAYS					EMP/QTR					EMP/YR	
20. TOT-EMP-DEPRT							STATE/MO				
21. TOT-EMP-EARN					UNION/QTR	EMP/YR		PLANT/MO		EMP/MO	EMP/YR
22. TOT-EMP-HIRED							STATE/MO				
23. TOT-EMP-HRS					UNION/QTR			PLANT; JOB/MO	EMP; JOB/DAY	EMP/MO	EMP/YR
24. UNION-NAME	X				X						
25. WS-NO			X						X		

Aggregate data per unit entity per unit time (brace spanning rows 18–23)

FIGURE 8-3 Processing matrix.

consider transactions T2 and T3 in Fig. 8-2, which contain the common entity EMPLOYEE. Consolidation of these two applications merely involves taking the union of entities and relationships, as shown in Fig. 8-4. In other cases it can be more complex, as when the entities or entity relationships do not coincide. Observing Report R5, which is to be consolidated with the structure in Fig. 8-4, WORK-STATION has a direct relationship with WORK-TASK. The next consolidation adds this new relationship to the structure, but further analysis is required to determine if both the direct and indirect relationships between WORK-STATION and WORK-TASK are needed. This is resolved by noting that the indirect relationship through JOB-TYPE results in a needless redundancy of JOB-TYPE records (i.e., 20 per WORK-STATION, or 20 × 500 in all). Since transaction T3 can easily use the direct relationship, the relationship between WORK-STATION and JOB-TYPE is eventually eliminated. Such a decision, however, should be delayed until all applications have been analyzed.

The final result of this step-by-step procedure is shown in Fig. 8-5, a revised (global) information structure. Note that the entities COMPANY, DEPARTMENT, and CLOCK are left out because they have no immediate use in terms of the current processing requirements. COMPANY is justifiably eliminated because there is only one occurrence of it (i.e., one company) and its name can easily be supplied as part of

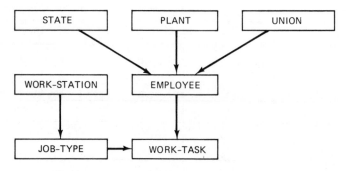

FIGURE 8-4 Consolidation of transactions T2 and T3.

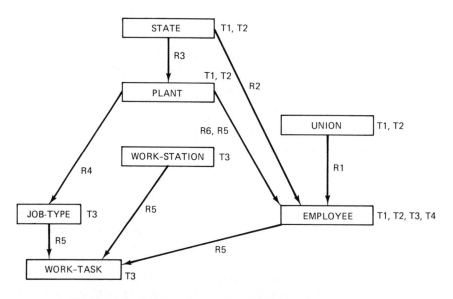

FIGURE 8-5 Consolidated and revised (global) information structure.

the application programs. Its name is not likely to change often. CLOCK is eliminated because the changing time is not meaningful in the database. Attributes such as "current time" (CUR-TIME) denote the time of an event and are adequate substitutes for CLOCK in this database. Also, the recording of daily clock-in and clock-out times for employees is not used for any of the current reports and can be delegated to a separate file or database at this early stage of decision making. The entity DEPART-MENT is also not used by any current reports, but its elimination could prove dangerous in the future if management decides that department-level reports are needed. Therefore, the solution shown in Fig. 8-5 is considered to be of short-term utilization only.

Additional assumptions needed to support the derivation of this structure are:

1. EMP-NO = SSN (social security number).
2. The task history is not needed once it is summarized at the end of each day.
3. Report R4: "total salary amount" represents the total employee earnings that month.
4. An employee lives in the same state where he or she works (could be too simplifying).
5. Old salary rates for individual employees need not be stored in the database.

These assumptions, and all others regarding designer objective, information requirement, and processing data content, should be completely verified at this stage.

In the local information structures some attributes were easily defined as the natural attributes of existing entities. Other attributes, however, had to be derived from existing data in order to store aggregate data over various time periods. Aggregate data, such as TOT-EMP-HRS, are necessary in this database because the same data must be reused for daily, monthly, interim, and annual reports. Since it would not be efficient to allow data to accumulate indefinitely (i.e., storage space and access-time degradation would be significant), they are often aggregated as soon as they are used in the earliest report for which they were designed. Thus, employee hours on a task are reported daily and then added to monthly cumulative employee-hour totals for the monthly reports, and so on. In Fig. 8-2 the potential aggregate values are shown in the local information structures to represent what is needed for the reports. The decision to store these values directly or to derive them from more detailed data is deferred until processing volume is considered in Step 3-4.

STEP 3-2: FORMULATE THE DBMS-SPECIFIC LOGICAL DATABASE STRUCTURE

DBMS specifications are now considered, and the information structure is further refined into a DBMS-specific logical database structure (or schema). Particular attention should be given to record content constraints and how entry points can be specified.

The revised information structure shown in Fig. 8-5 is a network structure, the most generalized form of relating entities. The conversion of this diagram to a CODASYL network schema, for example, is quite simple, particularly in the absence of any explicit $M : N$ relationships. At this point we will assume each entity results in a separate record type. A feasible DBMS-specific schema is now produced and the schema is refined according to performance objectives set forth in the system requirements. Entities are very often split and/or consolidated into record types at various points in the design process in order to maximize efficiency or meet constraints on security, integrity, and so on. No modifications are required in Fig. 8-5 to represent a feasible CODASYL schema except the designation of entry points. The processing requirements designate potential entry points on all seven record types. Other records are accessed relative to at least one of the foregoing entry records. Note that in the conversion to a CODASYL schema, the relationships represent possible access paths. In general, relationships may or may not be implemented as access paths, although in practice there is usually a significant correspondence.

Record types and their contents for this schema are summarized in Fig. 8-6. Key data items are also denoted. Their selection depends on the uniqueness of identifying data elements (primary keys) which describe entities and their usage in accessing data for individual applications [Rund, 1977].

The conversion of the network information structure to nonnetwork DBMS-specific structures requires further analysis. For example, Fig. 8-5 suggests a hierarchical design with the exception that EMPLOYEE and WORK-TASK are subordinate to several record types: legal in network databases, but illegal in hierarchies. However, in IBM's IMS, for instance, one of the relationships between parent and child record types can be specified as a "logical" relationship (with "logical" pointers) within one or across two "physical" databases. Relations in a relational database are also suggested by the record types denoted in Fig. 8-5. The interrecord relationships explicitly shown must be transformed to duplicate data in the existing relations (record types) or used to create new relations that contain composite keys of the two record types related [Fagin, 1977; Martin, 1977]. A reasonable alternative approach for relational databases would be to begin design at this step by determining a feasible database in normal form [Bernstein, 1976; Codd, 1970] and optimizing LRAs or transport volume within the constraints of the level of normalization desired.

RECORD	STATE		2 CHAR	
	ITEM	STATE-NAME	2 CHAR	KEY
RECORD	PLANT		58 CHAR	
	ITEM	PLANT-NAME	20 CHAR	KEY
	ITEM	TOT-EMP-HIRED/MO	5 CHAR	
	ITEM	TOT-EMP-DEPRT/MO	5 CHAR	
	ITEM	TOT-EMP	6 CHAR	
	ITEM	TOT-EMP-HRS/MO	10 CHAR	
	ITEM	TOT-EMP-EARN/MO	12 CHAR	
RECORD	UNION		20 CHAR	
	ITEM	UNION-NAME	20 CHAR	KEY
RECORD	EMPLOYEE		96 CHAR	
	ITEM	EMP-NAME	20 CHAR	KEY
	ITEM	EMP-NO	10 CHAR	KEY
	ITEM	EMP-ADDR	24 CHAR	
	ITEM	EMP-BDATE	6 CHAR	
	ITEM	EMP-HDATE	6 CHAR	
	ITEM	TOT-EMP-HRS/DAY	4 CHAR	
	ITEM	TOT-EMP-HRS/MO	4 CHAR	
	ITEM	TOT-EMP-HRS/YR	4 CHAR	
	ITEM	TOT-EMP-DAYS/QTR	4 CHAR	
	ITEM	TOT-EMP-DAYS/YR	4 CHAR	
	ITEM	TOT-EMP-EARN/YR	10 CHAR	
RECORD	WORK–STATION		3 CHAR	
	ITEM	WS-NO	3 CHAR	KEY
RECORD	JOB-TYPE		26 CHAR	
	ITEM	JOB-NO	2 CHAR	
	ITEM	JOB-DESCR	20 CHAR	KEY
	ITEM	TOT-EMP-HRS/MO	4 CHAR	
RECORD	WORK-TASK		10 CHAR	
	ITEM	TASK-HRS	4 CHAR	
	ITEM	CUR-DATE	6 CHAR	

FIGURE 8-6   Simple logical record definitions.

STEP 3-3: EVALUATE THE LOGICAL DATABASE
STRUCTURE SCHEMA FOR PROCESSING VOLUME

Processing requirements are now analyzed in great detail for data volume and processing frequency. For each application, performance measures such as logical record accesses, transport volume in number of bytes transferred, and storage space required should be computed. Then one can identify critical applications that have strict priority or turnaround requirements, and dominant applications that access the largest number of records or total bytes over a given time period. Total records accessed is dependent on the number of records accessed per application execution multiplied by the frequency of execution per specified time period. A trace of access paths through the consolidated information structure (Fig. 8-5) for each application results in the summary data shown in Table 8-1. Each application is characterized by its frequency and logical record accesses (LRAs). LRAs are categorized by record type to illustrate where the heaviest concentration of activity is taking place. It also allows easy computation of the transport volume as the weighted sum of LRAs and record sizes, excluding pointers.

A basic assumption made for these LRA computations is that applications of the

TABLE 8-1   Summary of Logical Record Accesses (LRAs) for Database Applications Using the Revised Information Structure (Fig. 8-5)*

Application	Frequency	LRAs	LRAs per Application	LRAs per Day	Transport Volume per Day
T1	100/day	1 EMPLOYEE + 1 PLANT + 1 UNION + 1 STATE	4	400	17.6k
T2	100/day	1 EMPLOYEE + 1 PLANT + 1 UNION + 1 STATE	4	400	17.6k
T3	200k/day	1 EMPLOYEE + 1 WORK-TASK + 1 WORK-STATION + 1 JOB-TYPE	4	800k	27,000k
T4	120k/year	1 EMPLOYEE	1	500†	48k
R1	Quarterly	5 UNION + 100k EMPLOYEE	100k	1.7k	160k
R2	Annually	40 STATE + 100k EMPLOYEE	100k	0.4k	40k
R3	Monthly	40 STATE + 50 PLANT	90	4.5	0.1k
R4	Monthly	50 PLANT + 50 × 20 JOB-TYPE	1050	53	1.4k
R5	Daily	50 PLANT + 100k EMPLOYEE + 200k WORK-TASK + 200k JOB-TYPE + 200k WORK-STATION	700k	700k	17,600k
R6	Monthly	50 PLANT + 100k EMPLOYEE	100k	5k	480k
R7	1000/day	1 EMPLOYEE	1k	1k	96k

*LRAs = 1.51×10^6 per day; transport volume = 45.5×10^6 bytes per day; data storage space = 11.63×10^6 bytes; pointer storage space (minimum) = 4.01×10^6 bytes; total storage space = 15.64×10^6 bytes.

†Assumes 240 workdays per year.

"get single record" category will be implemented with an access method that does all its searching in indexes or via a hashing (CALC) algorithm, the details of which must be analyzed at the physical design step. Also, applications implementable by batch processing (i.e., T1 and T2) are not analyzed as such until later. The first assumption provides a fixed-lower-bound estimate on LRAs and simplifies the analysis somewhat. Records stored or accessed via hashing, for example, ideally require only one LRA; the possibility of collisions and overflow are not considered until physical design. If, on the other hand, we disallow the assumption of some direct access, the search to a random target record could be much longer. We must use the expected search-length approach from Section 7-3-1. It should also be noted in Table 8-1 that transactions T1, T2, and T3 involve insertions and deletions. These operations are typically implemented by first accessing the parent record occurrences associated with child record occurrences to be inserted or deleted, possibly modifying the parents' pointers (as is done here), and then finding predecessor and/or successor sibling records and modifying their pointers. Of course, there are many implementations of parent–child relationships, and their true evaluation will have to await physical design (Step 4). We shall assume for this level of analysis that the parent record directly references the child record.

STEP 3-4: REFINE THE SCHEMA FOR GREATER EFFICIENCY

It is readily seen from Table 8-1 that the overwhelmingly dominant applications, in terms of LRAs per day, are T3 and R5. The other reports are not as seriously considered in terms of designing for minimum LRAs or transport volume. However, other factors, such as priority or elapsed-time constraints, could cause the dominance list to be reordered. Query R7 could easily fall into this category because of its on-line nature.

Transaction T3 and report R5, the dominant applications, can be made more efficient by moving WORK-STATION data to WORK-TASK records. This change is largely possible because the WORK-STATION record is so small that an obvious reduction in pointer space can be made by consolidating it with the WORK-TASK records. LRAs and transport volume are also reduced because the WORK-STATION records are no longer separately accessed. Slightly more data space is required, however, because the WORK-STATION number (WS-NO) is now redundant in the WORK-TASK records.

The reduction in LRAs for this change (as well as the other changes discussed here) is shown in Table 8-2, which summarizes LRA performance for the final schema in Fig. 8-7. The fifth column indicates where LRAs have increased or decreased from the revised information structure in Fig. 8-5. Transport volume can easily be derived from the table using the LRA components and record-size statistics from Fig. 8-6.

Another change that will reduce transport volume in application T3 and R5 is the splitting of EMPLOYEE records into two record types, one with active data

TABLE 8-2   Summary of Logical Record Accesses for Database
Applications Using the Final Logical Database Structure (Fig. 8-7)*

Application	Frequency	LRAs	LRAs per Application	LRAs per Day (Change)	Transport Volume per Day
T1	100/day	1 PLANT + 1 EMPLOYEE + 1 EMP-DATA	3	300(↓)	16.6k
T2	100/day	1 PLANT + 1 EMPLOYEE + 1 EMP-DATA	3	300(↓)	16.6k
T3	200k/day	1 EMPLOYEE + 1 WORK-TASK + 1 JOB-TYPE	3	600k (↓)	22,600k
T4	120k/year	1 EMPLOYEE	1	500	37k
R1	Quarterly	100k EMPLOYEE + 100k EMP-DATA	200k	3.4k (↑)	176.7k
R2	Annually	50 PLANT + 100k EMPLOYEE	100k	0.4k	30.8k
R3	Monthly	50 PLANT	50	2.5(↓)	0.1k
R4	Monthly	50 PLANT + 50 × 20 JOB-TYPE	1050	53	1.4k
R5	Daily	50 PLANT + 100k EMPLOYEE + 200k WORK-TASK + 200k JOB-TYPE	500k	500k (↓)	15,400k
R6	Monthly	50 PLANT + 100k EMPLOYEE + 100k EMP-DATA	200k	10k (↑)	530k
R7	1000/day	1 EMPLOYEE	1k	1k	74k

*LRAs = 1.11×10^6 per day; transport volume = 38.9×10^6 bytes per day; data storage space = 12.43×10^6 bytes; pointer storage space (minimum) = 3.21×10^6 bytes; total storage space = 15.64×10^6 bytes.

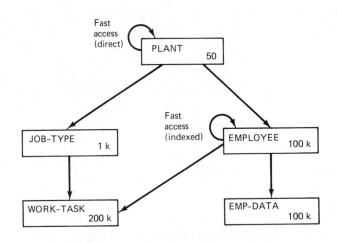

FIGURE 8-7   Final logical database structure.

(EMPLOYEE) and one with fairly inactive data (EMP-DATA). The inactive data would include employee address, birthdate, and date hired. A trade-off is necessary here in that LRAs are increased for reports R1 and R6, and the pointer storage space is increased—but not seriously relative to the cost reductions in the dominant applications (see Table 8-2).

Other less dramatic improvements can also be made. Moving STATE data into PLANT records will reduce space due to pointers as well as reduce LRAs for report R3 by 40. Slightly more data space is required because 10 of the 40 states are redundant in PLANT records; however, this is more than offset by the decrease in pointer space needed for separate record types implemented as CODASYL sets.

Pointer space, LRAs, and transport volume in transactions T1 and T2 can also be reduced by moving UNION data into EMPLOYEE records, but at a significant cost in increased storage space due to redundant union name data. At 20 characters per union name, repeating it in 100 k EMPLOYEE records results in 2 megabytes of redundant storage. This can be significantly reduced (down to 200 kilobytes) if the union name can be reduced to two characters using a data compression scheme. The same compression can be used for the plant name which is also allotted 20 characters, although its effect is not as dramatic as for the dominantly active EMPLOYEE record.

The final (CODASYL-type) schema resulting from these design decisions of entity splitting, consolidation, and data compression is shown in Fig. 8-7. We have now reduced the complexity of the structure to five record types and five set types plus two singular set types for database entry points. The new values for the various performance measures are shown at the bottom of Table 8-2 for comparison with Table 8-1. A 20 to 30% reduction in LRAs and transport volume was obtained with only a 7% increase in data storage space. If minimum pointer storage space (one "next" pointer for each record occurrence and one child pointer for each parent record occurrence) is added to data storage space for the two schemas in Fig. 8-5 (Table 8-1) and Fig. 8-7 (Table 8-2), the total storage is the same for both schemas.

It should be noted that the original definition of aggregate item types in the schema of Fig. 8-6 are unchanged in the final schema. As an example of the reasoning behind these types of decisions, consider the item TOT-EMP-HRS/MO in the PLANT record, which is required by report R4. In the current implementation it is convenient for application R5 to update PLANT records anyway. The alternative is to omit TOT-EMP-HRS/MO from PLANT records and derive it each time R4 is required (i.e., monthly), taking the sum of TOT-EMP-HRS/MO for each EMPLOYEE. This involves 100 k additional EMPLOYEE record accesses each time R4 is run. It is not too serious a problem since R4 is only a monthly report, but our first implementation is much more efficient.

8-4 SUMMARY OF THE MAJOR DESIGN ISSUES

The manufacturing firm example addressed many important implementation design issues facing the database designer, including the following:

STEP 3-1

- Construction of an information structure for individual processing applications.
- Determination of implied transactions.
- Verification of assumptions about what data can be aggregated and what need to be saved in the database after aggregation.
- Resolution of multiple views of processing; consolidate data and resolve redundant relationships.
- Determination of whether to eliminate some or all entities not used by current applications.
- Identification of potential primary keys.

STEP 3-2

- Conversion of consolidated and refined information structure into a DBMS-specific schema.
- Use of controlled redundancy to satisfy DBMS constraints.
- Specification of initial record contents.
- Determination of initial entry points from processing requirements.

STEP 3-3

- Determination of which performance measures should be used for the logical database structure or schema.

STEP 3-4

- Coordination of processing applications for more efficient overall processing time; when updates are best done; maximizing processing for records already accessed to avoid reaccessing.
- Determination of which entities should be consolidated to improve performance.
- Determination of which entities should be split when the activity level varies widely among items within records.
- Determination of where permanent data compression could be most useful in reducing storage space.
- Determination of where access path length could be reduced by a better choice of entry points, pointer options, and record ordering (based on minimizing LRAs for this step).

Other design issues occur in the requirements step and physical design step and are discussed in [Lum et al., 1979a; Schkolnick, 1978]. There are also several other problems that must be addressed by the logical designer, usually in Step 3-4, some of which can be classified as purely logical and others that overlap the decisions made by the physical designer. We do not make such a distinction here, but wish to point out that some physical design decisions can be tentatively made at the logical level (Step 3 at least, which to many designers is considered physical design anyway) and then verified or refined at the physical level. These other issues include the following:

Normalization within records. The consolidation of multiple entities into single record types results in the possibility of unnormalization of these records, thus creating the potential for the same types of update anomalies that occur in first, second, and even third normal-form relations [Codd, 1970; Date, 1975]. The designer must evaluate the trade-off between efficient performance now and potential inefficiencies later due to extra processing updates.

Nonintegrated database options. After consolidation of multiple user views (conceptual and processing) into an integrated database structure, certain characteristics of the design problem may result in the formation of multiple databases (i.e., determine the most efficient configuration of databases and files). This is frequently caused by widely varying levels of data volatility and retrieval frequencies, or by the presence of a great deal of historical data. First, a partition of the database for the most efficient use of computer resources (time and space) is necessary, and then the incorporation of constraints (usually security) on individual user views is to be performed. In the manufacturing firm example, multiple database options should be considered if daily employer clock-in and clock-out times are to be maintained, if daily TASK-HRS are to be retained after aggregation summation at the end of each day for report R5, and if the salary history of each employee is to be maintained.

Program design. Application program specifications should be produced as a result of the implementation design step. This should be very straightforward because detailed analysis of each application and its potential interrelationships with other applications has already been accomplished for the logical record access evaluation in Step 3-3 (Fig. 8-7). For example, while report R5 is being produced, daily updates to TOT-EMP-HRS/MO in PLANT records can be made for eventual use in producing report R4. Otherwise, a separate application must be developed. Advice to programmers in the form of efficient access path selection is the important contribution here.

Batch processing. Transactions T1 and T2 in our example are typical of updating operations that should be batched. Approximately 200 updates are required daily, but the new data are not needed immediately unless the new employee starts working the same day hired. In that case the update transaction T1 must be performed before any work tasks are completed (i.e., T3) by that employee. The actual efficiency resulting from batch processing cannot be determined until the physical design step, when I/O time and CPU time can be effectively estimated.

Selection of hardware/software environment. Normally, database designers work within the constraints of a given hardware/software (DBMS/OS) environment. Occasionally, this selection process is part of the database system design problem.

Using the life-cycle framework, database design is done independently of DBMS through Steps 1, 2, and 3-1. After Step 3-1, candidate DBMSs should be evaluated for this design in Steps 3-2, 3-3, 3-4, and 4. Some elimination of grossly inefficient choices (based on this design problem) of DBMSs can usually be made at the end of Step 3. At that point other issues involving nonefficiency considerations should be addressed and a decision can be based on an assessment of both efficiency and nonefficiency requirements of the organization [CODASYL, 1976]. Selection of hardware and system software should be made such that compatibility with the DBMS is maintained, but also with consideration of other non-DBMS applications to be run on the system.

IV   PHYSICAL DESIGN

9 PHYSICAL DATABASE DESIGN PRINCIPLES: BASIC CONCEPTS

9-1 INTRODUCTION TO PHYSICAL DESIGN

The third and lowest level of abstraction of a database is at the physical level. The physical organization of data has a major impact on database system performance because it is the level at which actual implementation takes place in physical storage. Performance is measured primarily in terms of operational costs to perform daily work loads and occasional reorganizations. It is less concerned with long-term information requirements, which guide the earlier design phases. Performance improvements are easier to measure at this level (e.g., 2:1 and 3:1 decreases in operational cost are possible because of improved physical organizations).

Current emphasis is on the design of physical structures for large-scale (integrated) multiple-record-type database systems. However, we find that single-record-type design techniques provide us with the fundamental tools that we need to analyze complex structures. In many cases, particularly with access methods, the multiple-record-type physical structure is a collection of single-record-type structures and search mechanisms.

The basic unit of data in physical structures is the stored record. A *stored record* is a collection of related data items (attributes) that correspond to one or more logical records, and includes all necessary pointers, record length and other overhead data, and coding schemes for character representation. In other words, the stored record extends the concept of logical record to include actual storage format. A *file* is a set of similarly constructed stored records of a single type. Stored records in a file may or may not be of the same length. A *physical database* is a collection of interrelated data stored together as one or more types of stored record. Files can be considered as degenerate forms of physical databases in which the number of stored record types is one. In this and succeeding chapters we use the term "file" to represent single-record-type physical databases. A *file organization* or *file structure* is a representation of stored records that make up a file which shows the intrarecord relationships (record format), logical and physical ordering, potential access paths such as indexes, and physical device allocation. Similarly, we can use the term *physical database organization* or *physical database structure* to represent stored record format, logical and physical ordering, potential access paths, and device allocations for a multiple-record-type database. The term *storage structure* can be interchanged with file structure or physical database structure.

Armed with these fundamental definitions, we can now approach the question: What is file design? In general, *physical database design* (or physical design) is the process of developing an efficient, implementable physical database structure from a given logical database structure that has been shown to satisfy user information requirements. Physical design frequently includes the satisfaction of certain operational constraints such as storage space limitations and response-time-distribution requirements. *File design* is the process of developing an implementable file structure that satisfies the various operational requirements specified by the user community. Physical database structure is composed of stored record format, access path structure, and record placement on physical devices. Substeps in the physical design process address these major components as well as several others.

9-1-1 Physical Design Steps

As we have seen in the earlier phases of the database design process, the physical design phase can also be categorized into distinct steps based on groups of related design decisions. However, once again, the proper ordering of these steps is open to conjecture, owing to the fairly strong dependencies between these groups of design decisions. Practical experience has shown that neither the starting point nor the order of steps can be definitely stated for a given design problem. On the other hand, the physical design phase can be regarded as an iterative process of initial design and refinement. Each of the proposed steps needs to be performed several times, but each succeeding analysis should be done more quickly because the procedure is known and the number of unchanging performance variables should be increasing between iterations. Typically, two or three passes through the substeps will result in convergence to a solution. The relative importance of each step toward system performance becomes obvious through experience and careful documentation of the entire analysis.

The following five steps include three that represent the major categories of physical database structure design and two that involve constraints and program design. Succeeding chapters focus on the first three steps in considerable detail.

STEP 4-1: STORED RECORD FORMAT DESIGN

Assuming that the logical record structure has been defined, this process addresses the problem of formatting stored data by analysis of the characteristics of data item types, distribution of their values, and their usage by various applications.

Decisions on redundancy of data, derived versus explicitly stored values of data, and data compression are made here.

Certain data items are often accessed far more frequently than others, but each time a particular piece of data is needed, the entire stored record, and all stored records in a physical block as well, must be accessed. *Record partitioning* defines an allocation of individual data items to separate physical devices of the same or different type, or separate extents on the same device, so that total cost of accessing data for a given set of user applications is minimized. Logically, data items related to a single entity are still considered to be connected, and physically they can still be retrieved together when necessary. An *extent* is a contiguous area of physical storage on a particular device.

STEP 4-2: STORED RECORD CLUSTERING

One of the most important physical design considerations is the physical allocation of stored records, as a whole, to physical extents. *Record clustering* refers to the allocation of records of different types into physical clusters to take advantage of physical sequentiality whenever possible. Analysis of record clustering must take access path configuration into account to avoid access-time degradation due to new placement of records.

Associated with both record clustering and record partitioning is the selection of physical block size. Blocks in a given clustered extent are influenced somewhat by stored record size, but also by storage characteristics of the physical devices. Furthermore, larger blocks are typically associated with sequential processing and smaller blocks with random processing. Thus, we see that although block size is closely related to clustering, it is also dependent on access path, type of applications, and hardware characteristics. Consequently, choice of block size may be subject to considerable revision during an iterative design process.

STEP 4-3: ACCESS METHOD DESIGN

An access method provides storage and retrieval capabilities for data stored on physical devices, usually secondary storage. The two critical components of an access method are storage structure and search mechanisms. Storage structure defines the limits of possible access paths through indexes and stored records, and the search mechanisms define which paths are to be taken for given applications. Intrarecord design and device allocation aspects of storage structure are not used here, whereas index design and interrecord connections are quite relevant.

Earlier, we defined a stored record as consisting of a collection of attributes. An *attribute* is an item type; it may be used as a primary key, secondary key, or nonkey. A *primary key* uniquely defines a record (i.e., it has no duplicate values in the database). A *secondary key* is an attribute used as an index to records, but it does not uniquely identify those records (i.e., the same key value can appear in more than one record occurrence). A *nonkey* is an attribute that is not used as a primary or secondary key for indexing or other search mechanism for records.

Access method design is often defined in terms of primary and secondary access path structure. The primary access paths are associated with initial record loading, or placement, and usually involve retrieval via the primary key. Individual files are first designed in this manner to process the dominant application most efficiently. For the same reason, physical databases may require several primary access paths. Secondary access paths include interfile linkages and alternate entry-point access to stored records via indexes on secondary keys. Access time can be greatly reduced through secondary indexes, but at the expense of increased storage space overhead and index maintenance. These trade-offs are considered in more detail in Chapters 12 through 16.

STEP 4-4: INTEGRITY AND SECURITY CONSIDERATIONS

As in implementation design, trade-offs among integrity, security, and efficiency requirements must be analyzed.

STEP 4-5: PROGRAM DESIGN

The goal of physical data independence, if met, precludes application program modifications due to physical structure design decisions. Standard DBMS routines should be used for all accessing, and query or update transaction optimization should be performed at the systems software level. Consequently, application program design should be completed when the logical database structure is known. When physical data independence is not guaranteed, program modification is likely. For example, a program based on a navigational access method (such as in the IMS or CODASYL system) would have to be radically changed if entry-point access methods were introduced for the first time during the physical database design phase.

Design decisions are also required in other areas, many of which are quite system dependent. Some examples are selection of buffer pool size, redundancy of stored records, and differential files. These issues appear to be equally important and difficult to analyze for both physical database structure and file design.

9-1-2   Physical Design Environment

The design environment is basically the same for both file design and physical database design. However, many design decisions for files are much simpler than for multiple-record-type databases. First, the major categories of inputs and outputs for the physical design phase are illustrated in Fig. 9-1. The logical database structure resulting from the implementation design phase defines the framework from which the physical designer works. It will remain unchanged during physical design unless some catastrophic inefficiency is detected during this phase or processing requirements change in some way. Again, one might regard physical design as a further refinement of this structure. In general, physical design considers new parameters, but previous tentative decisions on access paths and record allocation are finalized in this phase. Parameters regarding data volume, application processing frequency, and

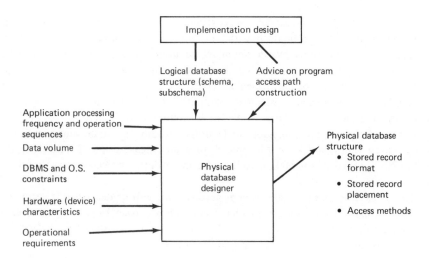

FIGURE 9-1 Physical design environment.

sequences of operations in application programs are the same as those required for implementation design. New parameters introduced at this stage are those specific to DBMS and operating system (O.S.) access methods, those specific to describe physical device capacity limitations and timing characteristics, and all operational requirements. Operational requirements are constraints typically imposed on integrity, security, and response time under static conditions and possibly for dynamic growth projections. Detailed parameters in these categories are presented as needed in the following sections.

The visible components of the resulting physical database structure are the stored record format, stored record placement specification, and access method specification. Underlying these specifications is the satisfaction of all operational requirements and hardware/software system constraints. During the design process, consideration of efficiency issues can take place only after the various constraints are satisfied and a feasible solution has been obtained. Normally, the feasible region is still large enough for significant differences in daily operational performance due to variations in physical design parameters. The remainder of this chapter is devoted to basic concepts regarding performance, and succeeding chapters continue this discussion in addition to describing techniques for finding feasible physical structures in constrained environments.

9-1-3 Performance Measures

The determination of performance measures for physical design is most critical to the design process. It affects not only the design choices, but also the techniques we employ to determine those choices. Our approach is to present a top-down description of database system cost, and define what cost components the database designer has at least some control over, particularly within the constrained feasible region of physical database structure solutions. We do not advocate any single measure of performance as completely dominant or desirable, but recommend a group of measures that provide different views of performance. Trade-off analysis will be required when different individual measures result in conflicting design decisions, and only the person making the final design can take into account the qualitative factors such as corporate policies on obtaining additional storage capacity or penalties for occasional slow response times, and so on. Multiple performance measures provide the designer with flexibility for decision making for both the initial design procedure and for future modifications.

Let us assume that database system performance will be described in terms of *cost*. At various times cost may be given in terms of time, space, or possibly monetary value. Returning to our discussion of the database system life cycle, we can describe the total cost of the life cycle in terms of the following:

- Planning cost
- Design cost: programs, databases
- Implementation and testing cost: programs, databases
- Operational costs: users, computer resources
- Maintenance costs: program errors, data integrity loss

Planning, design, implementation and testing, and maintenance costs are well defined for general software systems and are not considered further here. The major problem that the physical database designer must address is how to minimize present and future operational costs in terms of user needs (such as timely, accurate data) and computer resources.

Next, we investigate operational costs in more detail. Assuming that database schema redesign and application program redesign are considered as part of (re)design and maintenance in the life cycle, and are therefore analyzed in the conceptual or implementation database design phases, operational costs are unique to physical design and can be categorized as follows:

- Query response time
- Update transaction cost
- Report generation cost
- Reorganization frequency and cost
- Main storage cost
- Secondary storage cost

Each of these cost components is important to the designer, but priorities shift with individual working environments. Let us take each component and analyze it in terms of the most basic units of cost: bytes, seconds, and so on.

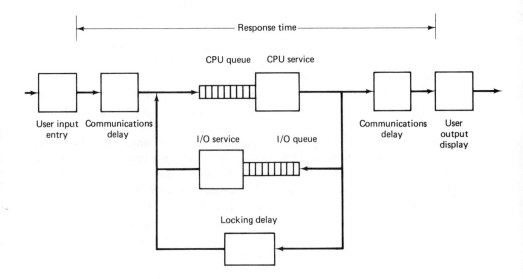

FIGURE 9-2 Query response time components.

Query Response Time

Response time is defined as the elapsed time between query initiation and the initial display of the query result. Contributors to response time are CPU service time, CPU queue waiting time, I/O service time, I/O queue waiting time, lockout delay, and communications delays (Fig. 9-2). Read and write time at the user interface level are not included in the strict definition given here. This simplifies the analysis and eliminates from consideration the wide variation of data entry and data display techniques that are not relevant to the database design problem.

The CPU queue and I/O queue waiting times are heavily influenced by the total mix of jobs in the computer system. In a system dominated by nondatabase applications, these delays are completely out of the control of the database designer. In a system dominated by database applications, there may be some control over these delays if the system can take advantage of parallelism in the hardware to manage concurrent user processes effectively, or the database designer can find ways to reduce effective CPU and I/O service times for user processes. Queue waiting times are normally functions of service times at those resources as well as other factors. Communication delays are independent of the database structure in a centralized database system and cannot be reduced through better design. This is not true, however, in a distributed database system, where one has a choice between sending intermediate data as well as final results across a network.

Delays due to lockout mechanisms for database integrity purposes are dependent upon the DBMS software decisions made prior to the database design problem. Lockout at a high level, such as at the database level, tends to cause longer internal queues for data retrieval, but it has lower CPU overhead and shorter physical resource queues. Lockout at the item level causes the opposite situation: shorter internal queues, but more CPU overhead and potentially longer physical resource queues. The trend is toward lower-level lockout because of improved overall response time (i.e., the internal queue wait time tends to dominate total response time). The database designer has little control here if lockout is at the item level. At higher levels of lockout, the designer may distribute records or databases in such a way as to allow for greater concurrency.

CPU service time has several components: system overhead to initiate and terminate I/O calls, DBMS and O.S. routines to retrieve and update data, and user application program processing of records. The database designer has no control over the amount of time any routine requires, once called. However, there is some control over the number of system software calls made if data are clustered efficiently into records, blocks, and extents. A good application program design to correspond with the database structure design is also beneficial toward reducing CPU service time.

I/O service time can be reduced through effective use of data compression techniques, access path selection, and record placement. Once I/O time is reduced, secondary benefits can often be felt in the reduction of CPU service time and consequently in a potential reduction of both I/O and CPU queue delays. As a result, the dominant performance measure component of query response time, in terms of database designer control, appears to be I/O service time. It is less DBMS or O.S. dependent than CPU service time and is feasible to predict with analytical methods.

A word of caution is needed here. Reliance on I/O service time alone as a predictive measure of total system performance can be dangerous. It is true that reduction of I/O service time will undoubtedly reduce response time, but the magnitude of response-time reduction may be insignificant and not justify the cost of reorganizing the database. There is always the very real possibility that system bottlenecks are not at the I/O devices, in which case the database structure performance is dominated by inefficiencies elsewhere. Under such circumstances detailed performance measurement and system tuning should be provided by systems programming personnel. For practical purposes it is desirable to collect data on as many individual components of response time as possible so that proper adjustments can be made in the database system design. In the absence of such data, I/O service time is the measure most controllable by the database designer and must always be accounted for during the design process.

Update Transaction Cost

Update cost is measured in elapsed time from initiation of the transaction until completion. It may be part of a larger application program and therefore not easily measured without special software. The elapsed-time components are the same as for a query response, but with more emphasis on resource usage. Updates may require additional processing for index modifications and such things as block or file rewrite, including write verification. However, these additional processing activities can be completely described by the basic measures given above for determining response time.

Report Generation Cost

Report generation is a special form of query retrieval in which large amounts of structured data are presented as output. Elapsed-time components of report generation are the same as for query and update (from the end of data entry to the beginning of data display), but the intermediate CPU and I/O service is more complex. Report generation can be depicted as having four major steps: retrieval, restructuring, sorting, and display of results. A detailed example is given in Section 12-4.

Reorganization Frequency and Cost

Some access methods (e.g., ISAM), although efficient for static databases, degrade severely under dynamic growth conditions. Growth projections in both data volume and processing frequency should be seriously considered in the design process so that frequent reorganizations are not required. Growth not only affects the choice of loading factor (the proportion of each block initially filled with stored records), but also the choice of access method. The cost of reorganization is again similar to the cost of queries and updates; reorganization is really a long series of database updates, involving retrieval and rewriting. The designer's role is to consider the cost of reorganization and its probable frequency against the alternative choices of access methods and their potential reorganization costs. Dynamically reorganized access methods, such as VSAM [IBM 1976, 1977], minimize such discrete reorganization costs at the expense of some system overhead to split blocks and update pointers during normal operating periods. The overhead appears to be worthwhile if long overflow chains can be avoided and reorganization is less frequent. Evaluation techniques presented below can be used to verify this assertion.

Main Storage Space

Main storage occupancy in database systems consists of programs and data. Program space must be allocated for user applications, DBMS routines, and O.S. support routines. Procedures for allocating program space are in the domain of the O.S. software and vary widely among systems, particularly between virtual and nonvirtual storage systems and between paged and nonpaged systems. Data space must be allocated for application program work areas, DBMS and O.S. work areas, and buffers for indexes and data. The database designer may possibly have some control over buffer allocation, but little else. Database performance is usually improved with increases in buffer space unless all data are processed sequentially. In the sequential case two buffers per process in execution are usually adequate. Even with random processing, however, an overallocation of buffers to a database application may seriously degrade the performance of the rest of the computer system. Main storage is frequently the most critical resource in a multiprogramming system, and its use must be fairly allocated to all active applications.

Secondary Storage Space

Secondary storage occupancy consists of blocked data and indexes. Some overhead in blocks exists for flags, counters, pointers, and free space for database expansion. The designer has a great deal of control here. Index size, loading factors, pointer options, data representation, and data redundancy are choices that the designer can make that affect secondary storage space. In most large-scale systems, secondary storage space is becoming less expensive relative to CPU and I/O time costs, and thus it will continue to be less important as a cost factor. In small systems, and in some large ones, secondary storage space is very limited and can be a critical problem in database design. This variation in importance of storage space from system to system will continue into the foreseeable future, and therefore is a major design consideration. In some cases it can be disregarded, but we do not believe that this should be done without evaluating its consequences.

In summary, database systems have many performance measures that should be considered on an individual basis. Composite or utility functions have not proven effective as yet. Among the variety of performance measures, we find that the database designer has a significant amount of control over only two:

- I/O service time
- Secondary storage space

Limited control is possible over

- Lockout delays
- CPU time
- Main storage space

Measures that are completely or almost completely independent of database designer control include

- CPU and I/O queue waiting time
- Communications delays for centralized databases

From these three groups of components the designer can derive values for query response time, update elapsed time, report generation elapsed time, and reorganization time. Monetary costs can be obtained in terms of resource usage, weighted by unit costs of usage which are installation dependent. Additional monetary costs are possible in terms of response-time delays or deadlines missed. In the remainder of this chapter we take a detailed look at the two controllable performance measures: I/O service time and secondary storage space.

9-2 PERFORMANCE COMPUTATION

We now turn our attention to the computation of the important performance measure I/O service time. At this point we have not developed any models for access methods, record placement, and so on, and we will consider our development here as basic in the sense that it is independent of database structure more complex than purely sequential or purely random. Models for more complex structures are discussed, in turn, after the basic concepts are presented. We start with an ideal model that derives I/O service time which is independent of physical device characteristics. This gives us a clear point of departure for considering more advanced hardware developments. The model is then extended for movable-head disks to illustrate computation in terms of actual milliseconds. The disk model is generalized to include variations in the computing environment that have an effect on the magnitude of I/O service time.

Once these detailed relationships have been established, we can focus on a higher level of abstraction in the remainder of our analysis. We will see that physical database performance can henceforth be described in terms of physical block accesses, sequential or random, and block size in bytes. Transformation of physical block accesses into I/O service time is always done in a consistent way using the approach given in the following section.

Note that performance will be estimated in terms of *expected values*. Although it is preferable to obtain distribution properties on performance, including mean and variance, theoretical results helpful to deriving distributions of performance have been lacking, owing to the complexity of the database problem. Distributions exist in the database (occurrences of child records per occurrence of a parent record, etc.), in the processing requirements (number of conjunctions in a query), and in the computing system (current mix of database and nondatabase tasks). However, because of the complex interrelationships between user applications, databases, DBMS, O.S., and hardware, the overall analysis has been done successfully only through simulation techniques [Hulten and Soderlund, 1977], which tend to be expensive. They are also, of necessity, system dependent. Queuing techniques have been applied to O.S. models [Kleinrock, 1975; Kobayashi, 1978], but specific applications to database systems have not yet been made. Thus, for simplicity and flexibility, we adhere to the expected value approach. Also, at this point, we are interested only in I/O service time, because of designer control limitations.

The analytical approach is reasonable when we can specify certain bounds on performance due to some practical definitions of worst-case and best-case conditions. The following sections illustrate the conditions of single-user versus multiuser environments, dedicated versus shared secondary storage devices, and how they affect CPU time and I/O time relationships in physical block processing. These bounds provide better perspectives for real performance than the development of a single performance equation under strict assumptions.

9-2-1 I/O Service Time: The Basic Model

The implementation design phase was characterized by performance measures such as logical record accesses (LRAs). Appropriately, the physical design phase is characterized by physical block accesses (PBAs), which can be subdivided into sequential block accesses (sbas), fast (or "flying") sequential block accesses (fbas), and random block accesses (rbas). Blocks are sequentially accessed if they are accessed in the same contiguous order in which they are stored (i.e., physical sequential). Fast sequential access occurs when a search command is issued to the storage control unit, and identifier searching is done by hardware as data pass by the read/write heads. There is no transfer of data from secondary storage to main storage. Ordinary sequential access, by contrast, implies that each sequential block is transferred from secondary storage to main storage, where its contents are analyzed. Blocks are randomly accessed if the order of retrieval is totally independent of the order of storage. This implies that blocks stored in a physical sequential manner can be randomly accessed to service simple ad hoc queries, and blocks retrieved in logical sequential order may be accessed randomly because they were originally loaded in random order. A transformation is required to obtain physical block accesses from logical record accesses, and another transformation is required to determine expected I/O service time from physical block accesses.

Consider a sequential database (or file) containing NR stored records of equal size and format. To search the entire database in a sequential manner we have the following relationships:

$$LRA = NR \qquad \text{logical record accesses} \qquad (9\text{-}1)$$

$$PBA_s = PBA_f = \left\lceil \frac{LRA}{BF} \right\rceil \qquad \text{sequential block accesses (sbas)} \qquad (9\text{-}2)$$

where BF is the blocking factor. If we now consider a random file of NR records and each record is accessed exactly once, we have

$$LRA = NR \qquad (9\text{-}3)$$

$$PBA_r = LRA \qquad \text{random block accesses (rbas)} \qquad (9\text{-}4)$$

To compute I/O service time for these two cases, let us first define TSBA as the expected time to access and transfer a sequentially accessed block between secondary storage and main storage (i.e., the I/O service time per block). TFBA is the expected time for a device read/write head to pass over a sequentially accessed block as if it were transferring that block to main storage. Then let TRBA be the expected time to access and transfer a randomly accessed block between secondary storage and main storage. The expected I/O service time to search the entire database is

$$TIO_s = PBA_s \times TSBA \qquad \text{for sequential block accesses} \qquad (9\text{-}5)$$

$$TIO_f = PBA_f \times TFBA \quad \text{for fast sequential block accesses} \quad (9\text{-}6)$$

$$TIO_r = PBA_r \times TRBA \quad \text{for random block accesses} \quad (9\text{-}7)$$

Up to this point we have assumed nothing about the existence of buffers. For sequential accesses the ideal model assumes only single buffering. The advantage of multiple buffering for sequential databases is that one can obtain overlap between input (I), compute (C), and output (O) processes [Hellerman and Smith, 1970; Teorey, 1978]. So far we have only defined the input process (retrieval) and have assumed that no CPU time and no database writes are required. Under general conditions of read–compute–write, multiple buffering can dramatically improve performance, with the optimum number of buffers dependent on the number of CPU and I/O devices available and the relative magnitudes of CPU service time and I/O service time required [Sherman and Brice, 1976a; Teorey, 1978; Towsley et al., 1978].

Buffers are quite useful for random accesses as well. There is a close analogy with paging systems, in that increasing the number of buffers for randomly organized databases, like increasing the page allocation for a process, improves the probability that the next block (or page) requested is already in main storage. Assuming independence between successive requests in a randomly organized database, Eq. (9-7) for expected I/O service time is modified to

$$TIO_r = (1 - PMS) \times PBA_r \times TRBA$$
$$= (1 - NBUF/NBLK) \times PBA_r \times TRBA \quad (9\text{-}8)$$

for random access to all records, where PMS is the probability that the next random block requested is already in main storage, NBUF is the number of buffers allocated to this application, and NBLK is the number of blocks required to contain the database.

In general, when total access involves a combination of random and sequential steps, we see that

$$TIO = \sum_S PBA_s \times TSBA + \sum_F PBA_f \times TFBA$$
$$+ \sum_R (1 - NBUF/NBLK) \times PBA_r \times TRBA \quad (9\text{-}9)$$

where S is the set of all sequential portions of data access, F is the set of all fast sequential portions of data access, and R the set of all random portions of data access.

When direct access is made to a randomly organized database, $PBA_s = PBA_f = 0$ and $PBA_r = 1$. When using a hardware search of a sequential database for a random record, $PBA_s = PBA_r = 0$ and $PBA_f \simeq (1 + [LRA/BF])/2$. The equation is not exact because the final block may not be completely full. The exact value, although mathematically interesting [Yao, 1977b], is much more complicated and improves the accuracy by only a negligible amount.

9-2-2   I/O Service Time for Disk Storage

The equations for I/O service time given in the previous section are device independent and access method independent. Different access methods will require individual expressions for block accesses. Different hardware devices will require individual expressions for TSBA, TFBA, and TRBA. Well-known expressions for a movable-head disk with a single disk arm mechanism are as follows:

$$\text{TSBA} = \text{ROT}/2 + \text{BKS}/\text{TR} \qquad (9\text{-}10)$$

$$\text{TFBA} = \text{BKS}/\text{TR} + \text{MINSK}/\text{BLKPC} \qquad (9\text{-}11)$$

$$\text{TRBA} = \text{SEEK(NCYL)} + \text{ROT}/2 + \text{BKS}/\text{TR} \qquad (9\text{-}12)$$

where

ROT = full rotation time (milliseconds)
BKS = block size (bytes)
TR = transfer rate (kilobytes per second)
MINSK = minimum seek time to traverse one cylinder
BLKPC = number of blocks to be stored sequentially in a cylinder
SEEK(NCYL) = the expected seek time, randomly selected over the extent of the database, NCYL contiguous cylinders

Seek time is assumed local to the database extent. This restriction is investigated in the next section. Equation (9-10) also assumes that additional delays due to occasional sequential block accesses that require crossing a cylinder boundary are negligible and commonly overlappable with CPU processing, and can be ignored. For the interested reader, a derivation of an exact expression is given in [Yao, 1977b]. Equation (9-11) does account for the crossing of a cylinder boundary every BLKPCth block sequentially accessed because this overhead typically accounts for a significant proportion of total time, TFBA. In addition to Eq. (9-11), if fast sequential scanning covers many disk tracks and cylinders, it is more accurate to compute fast sequential access time as

$$\text{TFBA} = \text{ROT}/\text{BLKPT} + \text{MINSK}/\text{TPC} \qquad (9\text{-}13)$$

where
BLKPT = number of blocks to be stored sequentially on a single disk track
TPC = number of usable tracks per cylinder on this device

Equation (9-12) does not consider the cylinder boundary problem because all random block accesses are assumed to be on different cylinders. Once again, this assumption is based on the idealistic randomness of the stored data and the negligible error that occurs occasionally when two consecutive accesses are made to the same cylinder. The probability of this occurring is 1/CPD, where CPD is the number of usable cylinders per disk spindle.

Data channel time (CHT) associated with disk access time is either ROT/2 + BKS/TR or BKS/TR, depending on whether the rotational latency is included in or excluded from channel utilization, respectively.

Example 9-1: What is the disk and channel time needed to access a 4096-byte page sequentially and randomly on an IBM_{3350} disk given the following?

SEEK(CPD) = 25 milliseconds

ROT = 16.7 milliseconds

TR = 1198 kilobytes per second

BKS = 4096 bytes

Channel time does not include rotational latency

TSBA = 16.7 / 2 + 4096 / 1198 = 11.8 milliseconds

TRBA = 25 + 16.7 / 2 + 4096 / 1198 = 36.8 milliseconds

TFBA = CHT = 4096 / 1198 = 3.4 milliseconds

9-2-3 Dedicated and Shared Computing Environments

Performance of database systems is contingent on the type of computing environment. Most analysis of database structures is done with a stand-alone (single user) configuration, because it is easier to validate and the designer has greater control over the variables. The multiuser configurations contain many complex interactions that are stochastic in nature and difficult to analyze [Wiederhold, 1977]. Some attempts of analysis have been made with simulation models [Hulten and Soderlund, 1977; Lum et al., 1970; Nakamura et al., 1975]. In this section we take an expected-value approach and limit our analysis to I/O service time as a function of the computing environment.

The computing environment can be expressed in terms of three user configurations, assuming that a movable-head disk is the standard for secondary storage:

1. Single user with dedicated device (SUDD)
2. Multiuser with dedicated device (MUDD)
3. Multiuser with shared device (MUSD)

The single-user configuration implies that each application is run stand-alone on the entire computing system. Multiuser systems involve multiprogramming and time sharing, with potentially a mixture of database and nondatabase applications. A dedicated device implies that each database resides on a set of contiguous blocks, called an extent. On a multiuser shared device the database may or may not be on contiguous blocks, but the device contains many databases belonging to different users, so that the position of the read/write head on the device can be regarded as a random variable. In the worst case, this has the effect of making each physical block access a random access regardless of where a user's previous block access occurred. On a single- or multiuser dedicated device the read-write head position would be unchanged since the previous block access. The single-user shared device configuration need not be considered separately because a single user will have exclusive access to owned databases regardless whether the device is shared or dedicated.

Sequential Database Access

The equation for expected sequential block access time, Eq. (9-10), can now be modified to account for the computing environment. Under the basic assumption that CPU time to process records, plus other delays, cause the rotational position of a disk track to be randomized for successive I/O requests, we have

$$\text{TSBA(SUDD)} = \text{ROT}/2 + \text{BKS}/\text{TR} \tag{9-14}$$

$$\text{TSBA(MUDD)} = \text{ROT}/2 + \text{BKS}/\text{TR} \tag{9-15}$$

$$\text{TSBA(MUSD)} = \text{SEEK(CPD)} + \text{ROT}/2 + \text{BKS}/\text{TR} \tag{9-16}$$

The only variation from the original equation, which occurs in the MUSD case, is due to randomization of the read/write head position between block accesses; thus, a seek is required for each block. This does not occur on dedicated devices.

If we now relax the restriction that CPU time and other delays are assumed to be much larger than disk rotation time, we may have a situation in which there is a constant synchronization between read requests. Values for TSBA(SUDD) could then fall in the range

$$\text{BKS}/\text{TR} + \text{MINSK}/\text{BLKPC} \leq \text{TSBA(SUDD)} < \text{ROT} + \text{BKS}/\text{TR} \tag{9-17}$$

The lower bound represents the case when CPU time plus all resource delays fall within the time to span interblock gaps. The upper bound represents the fact that in the worst case the CPU time and resource delays take a fraction of a second beyond the interblock gap leading the next block to be retrieved. Thus, an entire extra rotation is required to access the next block. Block size, BKS, can be any size and the inequality (9-17) will hold.

The computation of expected I/O service time follows simply for each of the three cases by applying Eq. (9-5). Response time to access and process the entire sequential database is also the same form for all three cases:

$$TRESP = TIO_s + PBA_s \times TCPUB + WAIT + COMMDELAY \qquad (9\text{-}18)$$

$$= PBA_s \times (TSBA + TCPUB) + WAIT + COMMDELAY$$

where TCPUB is the expected CPU time associated with the processing of a single block, WAIT is the expected total wait time in the resource queues, and COMM-DELAY is the expected total communication delay. When there is a single user, WAIT = 0. Lockout delays are assumed to be included in WAIT.

Fast Sequential Database Access

Contrary to ordinary sequential access, fast sequential access time is not subject to variations in the computing environment:

$$TFBA(SUDD) = BKS/TR + MINSK/BLKPC \qquad (9\text{-}19)$$

$$TFBA(MUDD) = BKS/TR + MINSK/BLKPC \qquad (9\text{-}20)$$

$$TFBA(MUSD) = BKS/TR + MINSK/BLKPC \qquad (9\text{-}21)$$

In this mode the storage control hardware services the requests, so in the dedicated device environment it has the same characteristics as sequential database access, in which all internal processing takes place within the time to traverse interblock gaps [i.e., as shown by the lower bound of Eq. (9-17)]. The shared disk case is no different from the dedicated disk case, because the storage control search commands may be chained to avoid interruption by another process (i.e., another channel program) until the search terminates after possibly many block accesses.

The analysis throughout assumes that sequential access is to be used, and the analyst can substitute fast sequential access where it is known to be appropriate for a particular computer system configuration.

Random Database Access

When random accesses are needed to process a database, the synchronization of rotational position is not a factor because seek time dominates the total I/O service time. The expected time to process random blocks (for the three basic computing environments) is

$$TRBA(SUDD) = SEEK(NCYL) + ROT/2 + BKS/TR \qquad (9\text{-}22)$$

$$TRBA(MUDD) = SEEK(NCYL) + ROT/2 + BKS/TR \qquad (9\text{-}23)$$

$$TRBA(MUSD) = SEEK(CPD) + ROT/2 + BKS/TR \qquad (9\text{-}24)$$

The only variation in random organizations occurs for dedicated devices in which the accesses are confined to the extent of the data base; thus, a local seek, SEEK(NCYL), is designated. Depending on the size of the database, the following bounds on SEEK are specified:

$$0 \leq \text{SEEK(NCYL)} \leq \text{SEEK(CPD)} \tag{9-25}$$

The lower bound represents the database residing on a single cylinder, and the upper bound represents a database that encompasses all cylinders. To determine the expected seek time over an extent of NCYL cylinders, we apply the same argument used to determine SEEK(CPD) over the entire disk. We assume that a randomly organized database allocated over NCYL cylinders is evenly (uniformly) distributed over those cylinders. Because the last cylinder may only be partially full, this assumption is not exact. However, for NCYL $\geq$ 5, the error is negligible. For NCYL $<$ 5 the specific probability of traversing certain distances between accesses can be easily computed. We first compute the seek distance:

$$\text{SDIST} = \sum_{x=0}^{\text{NCYL}-1} x \times P(\text{Dist} = x) \tag{9-26}$$

The probability distribution of seek distance is represented by

$$P(\text{Dist} = x) = \frac{2(\text{NCYL} - x)}{\text{NCYL}^2} \tag{9-27}$$

Equation (9-27) can be derived by observing each of the NCYL possible current read/write head positions and possible distances in both directions that can be traversed from that position, given that the next request will be on any cylinder with probability 1/NCYL. Substituting (9-27) into (9-26), we have [Martin, 1967]

$$\begin{aligned}
\text{SDIST} &= \sum_{x=0}^{\text{NCYL}-1} \frac{2x \times (\text{NCYL} - x)}{\text{NCYL}^2} \\
&= \frac{\text{NCYL}^2 - 1}{3(\text{NCYL})}
\end{aligned} \tag{9-28}$$

To convert expected seek distance to seek time, we assume a linear seek time function as shown in Fig. 9-3. Then

$$\text{SEEK(NCYL)} = \begin{cases} 0 & \text{for NCYL} = 1 \\[2ex] \text{MINSK} + \Delta\text{SK}\left[\dfrac{\text{NCYL}^2 - 1}{3(\text{NCYL})} - 1 \right] & \text{otherwise} \end{cases} \tag{9-29}$$

where MINSK is the minimum (one cylinder) seek time, and ΔSK is the slope of the linear seek time function, or

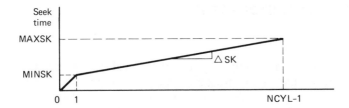

FIGURE 9-3 Movable-head disk linear-seek-time approximation.

$$\Delta SK = \frac{MAXSK - MINSK}{NCYL - 2}$$

where MAXSK is the maximum seek time over $NCYL - 1$ cylinders and $NCYL > 2$. For $1 < NCYL < 5$, an exact computation can be made using

$$SEEK(NCYL) = \sum_{x=0}^{NCYL-1} P(\text{Dist} = x) \times SEEK(x) \qquad (9\text{-}30)$$

Expected I/O service time and response time to process an entire database are computed in the same manner as in the sequential database organization:

$$TIO_r = (1 - NBUF/NBLK) \times PBA_r \times TRBA \qquad (9\text{-}8)$$

$$TRESP = TIO_r + PBA_r \times TCPUB + WAIT + COMMDELAY \qquad (9\text{-}31)$$

The expected block access and transfer times are summarized in Table 9-1.

TABLE 9-1   Expected I/O Service Time per Physical Block

	Sequential Access	*Fast Sequential Access*	*Random Access*
Single-user dedicated device (SUDD)	ROT/2 + BKS/TR (no synchronization) Lower bound (with synchronization): BKS/TR + MINSK/BLKPC Upper bound: ROT + BKS/TR	BKS/TR + MINSK/BLKPC	SEEK(NCYL) + ROT/2 + BKS/TR
Multiple-user dedicated device (MUDD)	ROT/2 + BKS/TR	BKS/TR + MINSK/BLKPC	SEEK(NCYL) + ROT/2 + BKS/TR
Multiple-user shared device (MUSD)	SEEK(CPD) + ROT/2 + BKS/TR	BKS/TR + MINSK/BLKPC	SEEK(CPD) + ROT/2 + BKS/TR

9-3 SECONDARY STORAGE SPACE

We recall that in addition to I/O service time, secondary storage space is the only other cost measure that is significantly controlled by the database designer. The importance of storage space varies widely from system to system; it is a very critical resource when it is saturated on a system, and it has a very low cost when it is not saturated. This nonlinear relationship between storage required and storage cost is difficult to quantify, and perhaps is better expressed as a constraint. The decision as to whether this is a cost or a constraint is a policy matter requiring consultation with the installation manager. We confine our analysis to the computation of storage space only; then the application of a constraint condition or cost factor can be done separately.

9-3-1 File Storage

At the conceptual level we defined entities and their relationships without regard to physical size. The implementation-level design process, however, considered item size and data volume for each relationship to determine total bytes of data required. Pointer space was also estimated, albeit separately from data space, by considering implementation relationships as potential access paths. Pointer options of "next," "prior," "parent," "first child," and others are considered at the implementation level, particularly for systems that allow navigational access through the database. Indexing is not considered yet, so many sources of pointers are unaccounted for at this level. Just as logical record accesses are used to predict real performance, without verification, so the computation of total bytes for data and pointers provides a rough estimate of the lower bound of physical storage space required. If total bytes at this design phase are already greater than available space, redesign should be done on the logical database structure before considering physical parameters.

There are several units of measure of storage at the physical level. If the measurement must be device independent, the basic unit, bytes, is still appropriate. However, bytes should be computed as the product of bytes per block and the number of blocks. For multiple block sizes we can express total block storage as

$$\text{BLKSTOR} = \sum_{k=1}^{\text{NBKS}} \text{BKS}_k \times \text{NBLK}_k \qquad \text{bytes} \qquad (9\text{-}32)$$

where NBKS = number of distinct block sizes (or types)
  BKS_k = block size of the kth block type (bytes)
  NBLK_k = number of blocks of type k in the database

Integrated databases naturally allow varying block sizes. File systems normally specify a single block size for data records, but indexes and overflow areas are potential sources of different block sizes. At least the internal formats of these types of blocks are different from data blocks, so computation of the usable space must proceed differently.

Device-dependent storage space is better computed in terms of natural (discrete) units of storage such as tracks or cylinders. Calculations of bytes alone can be misleading, just as it would be misleading to count records instead of blocks and ignore the overhead needed for physical storage. Therefore, total secondary storage space is computed as the sum of primary data space, overflow data space, and index space.

We first derive an expression for primary data storage space in terms of each of the possible units of measure described above. Let us consider a simple file with NR fixed-size stored records. Each stored record is assumed to contain data items, pointers, and other record overhead as needed. Stored record size is SRS bytes. (Variable-size records are considered in the next section.) The total storage due to stored records is

$$\text{SRSTOR} = \text{NR} \times \text{SRS} \qquad \text{bytes} \qquad (9\text{-}33)$$

Here

$$\text{SRS} = \sum_{i \in I} \text{IS}_i + \text{NPTR} \times \text{PS} + \text{ROVHD} \qquad (9\text{-}34)$$

where IS_i = size of the ith element of the set I of item types for this record type (bytes)

     NPTR = number of pointers in this record type

        PS = pointer size (bytes)

  ROVHD = record overhead (bytes)

Data compression, if used, is implied in IS_i, PS, and ROVHD.

The total number of blocks is estimated by

$$\text{NBLK} = \left\lceil \frac{\text{NR}}{\left\lfloor \dfrac{\text{BKS}}{\text{SRS}} \right\rfloor} \right\rceil \qquad (9\text{-}35)$$

where BKS is the block size in bytes and $\left\lfloor \dfrac{\text{BKS}}{\text{SRS}} \right\rfloor$ is the number of stored records in each block (i.e., the blocking factor). This rather idealized case does not consider block overhead and loading factor. Let us define the block overhead, BOVHD, as the storage space required to specify all information needed for block management by the operating system. It often includes a control word and record counts when records are of variable size. The loading factor, LF, specifies the maximum proportion of usable block space, after overhead is allocated, to be filled with stored records at the initial load time. Figure 9-4 illustrates the case of a block containing 100 bytes, a loading factor of 0.8, an overhead of 10 bytes, and stored

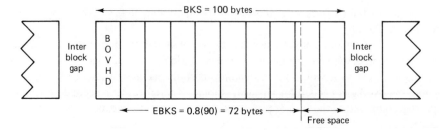

FIGURE 9-4 Example block allocation at initial file load.

record size of 10 bytes. For this configuration we are allowed a blocking factor of 9 and an initial load of 7 records per block. Actual block utilization is 70%.

Applying block overhead and loading factor to the computation of the number of blocks required to hold the database, we obtain the effective number of stored records per block (effective blocking factor) as

$$EBF = \left\lfloor \frac{(BKS - BOVHD) \times LF}{SRS} \right\rfloor \qquad (9\text{-}36)$$

where

$$EBKS = (BKS - BOVHD) \times LF \qquad (9\text{-}37)$$

is the effective block size and the number of blocks is

$$NBLK = \left\lceil \frac{NR}{EBF} \right\rceil = \left\lceil \frac{NR}{\left\lfloor \dfrac{(BKS - BOVHD) \times LF}{SRS} \right\rfloor} \right\rceil \qquad (9\text{-}38)$$

The total number of bytes is therefore

$$BLKSTOR = NBLK \times BKS \qquad \text{bytes} \qquad (9\text{-}39)$$

Ideally, the total number of tracks can be estimated by

$$NTRK = \left\lceil \frac{NBLK}{\left\lfloor \dfrac{BPT}{BKS} \right\rfloor} \right\rceil \qquad (9\text{-}40)$$

where BPT is the maximum track size in bytes and $\lfloor BPT/BKS \rfloor$ is the allowable number of blocks per track.

$$TRKSTOR = NTRK \times BPT \qquad (9\text{-}41)$$

TABLE 9-2   IBM 3350 Disk Storage Track Capacity (KS = 0)

Physical Blocks per Track	Maximum Bytes per Block	Physical Blocks per Track	Maximum Bytes per Block
1	19,069	9	1,954
2	9,442	10	1,740
3	6,233	11	1,565
4	4,628	12	1,419
5	3,665	13	1,296
6	3,024	14	1,190
7	2,565	15	1,098
8	2,221	16	1,018

Practically speaking, most disk systems allow blocks per track to be specified in a different way to take into account track overhead and block overhead. Table 9-2 shows the relationship between block size and allowable blocks for the IBM 3350 [IBM, 1979]. The equation is

$$\text{TRACK CAPACITY (in equal-length blocks)} = \frac{19,254}{C + KS + BKS}$$

where $C = \begin{cases} 185 & \text{if KS} = 0 \\ 267 & \text{if KS} = 0 \end{cases}$ is the count of record length

KS = key length or size (bytes)
BKS = block size (bytes)

The constant C accounts for home address and other block overhead; the constant 19,254 is the total number of bytes on a track.

The total number of cylinders is given by

$$NCYL = \left\lceil \frac{NTRK}{TPC} \right\rceil \tag{9-42}$$

where TPC is the number of usable tracks per cylinder for this device.

Example 9-2:   Given a 1,000,000-record file where stored records are 50 bytes each, maximum blocking factor is 30, and the device is an IBM 3350, what is the error in total bytes in computing storage in terms of stored records only and actual track space? Assume that LF = 0.9 and BOVHD = 12 bytes.

Stored record: $SRS = 50 \times 10^6 / 0.9 = 55.5 \times 10^6$ bytes

Block size: $BKS = 30 \times 50 + 12 = 1512$ bytes

Effective blocking factor: $EBF = [(1512 - 12) \times 0.9 / 50] = 27$

Total blocks: $NBLK = \lceil 10^6 / 27 \rceil = 37,038$

From Table 9-2, and for a block of 1512 bytes, the number of blocks per track is 11.

Total tracks: NTRK = $\lceil 37,038 / 11 \rceil$ = 3368

Track storage: TRKSTOR = 3368 × 19,069 = 64.2 × 10^6 bytes

$$\% \text{ Error} = \frac{64.2 - 55.5}{64.2} \times 100 = 13.5\%$$

Overflow data blocks and index blocks can be described with the same set of parameters as primary data blocks. Typical index entries consist of key item values and pointers, but overhead data and free space can also occur in indexes.

9-3-2   Database Storage: Multiple-Record Types

Secondary storage space in database systems consists of primary data storage, overflow data storage, and index storage. These are the same basic components as those found in file systems; however, the file design problem is usually simplified by a constant record size and block size. On the other hand, integrated databases must often deal with multiple record types, variable record sizes, nonhomogeneous block contents, and multiple block sizes.

If physical blocks are homogeneous in record type and records are fixed size, the problem reduces to one of computing the number of blocks (or tracks) for each record type and summing the results. If blocks are homogeneous in record type, but record sizes are variable, or if blocks are nonhomogeneous with variable-size records, the problem is much more complex than the fixed-size record case. When both blocks and records are of variable size, the total storage required for each block size is computed separately, then summed. The basic problem, then, is to determine how much storage is required for an extent of fixed-size blocks containing variable-size records. The record sizes either exhibit certain recognizable patterns or are considered random within some bounds. If patterns exist, such as a record of a certain size (parent) followed by a fixed number of records of another size (children), they can be manually analyzed in the straightforward manner presented in Section 9-3-1. The random case is more difficult—even impossible to analyze when the exact record size distribution is not known.

An example will help illustrate the possible extreme values. Suppose that there are 500 stored records of length 200 bytes and 500 stored records of length 900 bytes. The block size is 1000 bytes. If we let LF = 1 and BOVHD = 0, and if the ordering specifies that all the large records come first and all the small records come second, this pattern would result in a database size of

$$\text{NBLK} = \left\lceil \frac{500}{\left\lfloor \frac{1000}{900} \right\rfloor} \right\rceil + \left\lceil \frac{500}{\left\lfloor \frac{1000}{200} \right\rfloor} \right\rceil = \left\lceil \frac{500}{1} \right\rceil + \left\lceil \frac{500}{5} \right\rceil = 600 \text{ blocks}$$

for the best case. On the other hand, an ordering that alternated large and small records would result in a database of 1000 blocks, the worst case. Any other ordering (including a random ordering) would produce a database size somewhere between these two extremes. For very large databases this nearly 2:1 ratio in physical size will greatly affect performance as well as storage cost. The range of possible record distribution conditions is discussed in the following cases.

Case 1: The example above illustrates the simple case where the record size distribution is known and an easily recognizable pattern exists. The solution to finding the total number of blocks required to store the database is to define all the possible block compositions (orderings); compute the number of blocks, NBLK, for each composition; and take the weighted sum. The fixed-size-record problem is a degenerate subcase of this case.

Case 2: The record size distribution is known, as in Case 1, but no recognizable pattern exists [i.e., the physical ordering is (or appears to be) random]. Let us assume in this case that the maximum stored record size is much smaller than block size: SRS(max) $\ll$ BKS. Under these conditions it is known that the maximum amount of unused space in each block, after initial load, is less than the size of the largest stored record, assuming that overhead and loading factor have already been accounted for. Let the effective block size be defined as

$$\text{EBKS} = (\text{BKS} - \text{BOVHD}) \times \text{LF} \tag{9-37}$$

so that if EBKS is used to estimate the expected used space in each block, the maximum error will be SRS(max). For a truly large distribution of record sizes, a better estimate of expected used space is EBKS − ESRS, where ESRS is the expected stored record size over all record types. This estimate would be most accurate for a normal distribution of record sizes, but it is still reasonable for many other distributions that occur in practice.

Case 3: This case is similar to Case 2 except that SRS(max) is allowed to be comparable in size to BKS, so the approximation approach of Case 2 is no longer valid. Even under these conditions an exact solution approach is not known. However, a multiple-record-size analysis technique by Oberlander [Oberlander, 1979] provides a good approximation. The technique (and algorithm) assumes that the size of any record in the database is independent of its neighbors. This is assumed to hold for all blocks regardless of the fact that the first record of block j may be the first record that did not fit into block $j - 1$ at database load time. Thus, independence does not always occur, but the error due to the independence assumption is usually small. Let us illustrate the technique with an example.

Let a database be defined to consist of 300 records with an expected record size of 200 bytes. Assume that BOVHD = 0 and LF = 1 for simplicity. Block size is given as 300 bytes. The actual distribution of record size is

Record Type	SRS (BYTES)	Record Occurrences
A	100	100
B	200	100
C	300	100

For this simple configuration a random distribution of records and record types across the database results in the seven possible arrangements of records in a block shown in Fig. 9-5, occurring with probability $P_i, i = 1, 2, \ldots, 7$. From the data in Fig. 9-5 we can compute the expected value of used space in each block and then compute the database size.

$$E[\text{used space}] = \sum_{i=1}^{T} P_i \times \text{USED}_i = 248 \text{ bytes/block}$$

$$\text{SRSTOR} = \sum_{j=1}^{3} \text{SRS}_j \times \text{NR}_j = 100 \times 100 + 200 \times 100 + 300 \times 100$$
$$= 60{,}000 \text{ bytes}$$

$$\text{NBLK} = \left\lceil \frac{60{,}000 \text{ bytes}}{248 \text{ bytes/block}} \right\rceil = 242 \text{ blocks}$$

Alternative (nonrandom) orderings:

1. *ABCABCA* . . . sequence: NBLK = 200 (global minimum)
2. *AA* . . . *ABB* . . . *BCC* . . . *C* sequence: NBLK = 233
3. *ACACAC* . . . *ACBBB* . . . *B* sequence: NBLK = 300 (global maximum)

A hand simulation of 300 random record orderings produced an allocation of 230 blocks. The value of 242 blocks, the estimate for NBLK for the Case 3 method, represents a 5% error from the simulation results.

The computational complexity of this method increases rapidly with larger block sizes and more record types. Above 10 record types the manual computation becomes unwieldy and a computer implementation of the algorithm is needed. Complexity is polynomial and computationally feasible for most database specifications, although it could be quite expensive for large databases with over 200 record types. As the block

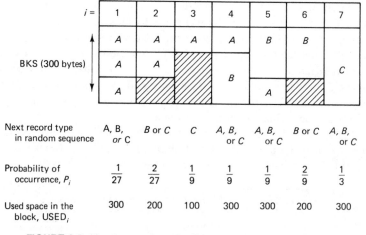

FIGURE 9-5   Random sequence distribution of record types in blocks.

size becomes significantly larger than stored record size, the approximation approach in Case 2 becomes more realistic to use.

Case 4:   The distribution of record sizes is unknown, although the expected record size is known. Assuming a fixed record size (the expected size) is a dangerous practice and could lead to a grossly underestimated storage requirement. A better approach might be to assume a uniform distribution of record sizes from 1 byte to 2 $\times$ SRS $-$ 1 bytes, with a mean value at SRS. Depending on block size, the methods of Case 2 or 3 can be applied.

9-4   SUMMARY

The major components of physical database structure design are stored record format design, stored record clustering, and access method selection. Constraints are also imposed for integrity and security, as we have already noted in the implementation design phase. The accompanying program design process should be independent of the database design process at this point, to maximize physical data independence.

Performance measures abound, but the database designer has most control over I/O service time and secondary storage space. Storage space encompasses stored record data, block overhead data, pointers, overflow records, and indexes for access methods. Multiple-record-type database size estimates are much more difficult to obtain than file size because of the nonhomogeneous block contents.

The computation of I/O service time is dependent upon the type of user environment from single user and dedicated device to multiuser and shared device. Both extremes need to be investigated when using the expected-value approach to performance estimation. The transformation from access-path-length estimation to I/O service time is done in two steps: development of expressions for physical block accesses for sequential and random components of access methods, and estimation of I/O service time from physical block accesses. The second transformation was discussed in this chapter, and the first transformation is to be addressed in Chapters 12 to 16. A discussion of CPU time estimation is given in Chapter 16.

10 RECORD STRUCTURE DESIGN

An important step in the database design process is the design of physical (stored) record content and structure. Basic record content, and item types and lengths, are defined in the implementation design step; and the option exists to keep the record content unchanged in the mapping from logical record to stored record. However, additional modifications may be made during physical design as performance measures become more realistic and can be validated with an operating database system. Two major types of record modification are available: data encoding and record partitioning.

Data encoding is a term that represents a broad class of techniques for encoding item values in normal or reduced formats in the same way that abbreviations are alternative bit representations. The objective of data compression is to save space in addition to reducing data retrieval cost. Record partitioning (often called record segmentation) is a form of allocation in which the logical database structure, or schema, is unchanged, but items within the record can be clustered and reallocated to separate physical extents. Analytical techniques used to determine how to cluster items into logical records are often just as applicable to the clustering of items into stored records. The difference lies in the performance measures and some additional independent variables in the physical design process. The objective of record partitioning is to reduce data retrieval and update costs.

In this chapter we analyze and compare various approaches to data encoding, compression, and record partitioning in terms of physical database performance. We shall begin to see that the design process involves gradual refinement of the database structure beyond the logical schema and reuse or extension of some of the refinement techniques discussed earlier.

10-1 DATA ITEM ENCODING AND COMPRESSION

Despite the many advances in storage technology, the reduction of storage space and data transfer time will continue to be a major consideration in the design of a physical database. These components of total system cost are significantly affected by the way in which data are represented in storage. In Fig. 10-1 the basic stored record components are shown: data items, pointers, and record overhead. Overhead data such as control bits and record-length indicators are encoded in a manner consistent with the implementation hardware and software. Similarly, pointers are encoded to facilitate fast retrieval as well as to reduce space. For example, pointers that designate absolute addresses may be specified as displacements with a common base if the use of displacements reduces the pointer size significantly. The database designer may have some degree of control over data item representation, so we now concentrate our investigation on this aspect of record design.

10-1-1   Data Item Representation

It has been shown that there exist at least four basic primitive techniques for the storing of data items in stored records [Maxwell and Severance, 1973; Olle, 1968]: positional, relational, indexed, and labeled. These techniques are shown in Fig. 10-2. The first three techniques require the data item representations to be used in the same order in each record, and the fourth technique allows representation in any order. In the first three cases the item type is implicit and only the value needs to be physically represented. In the labeled technique both the label (an encoding for the item type) and the data value are explicitly represented.

The positional technique uses fixed-length fields for item values, which makes

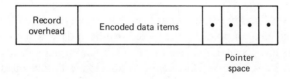

FIGURE 10-1   Stored record components.

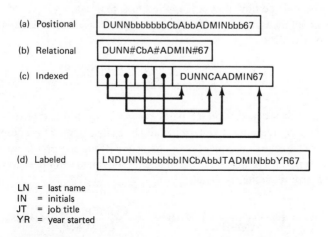

FIGURE 10-2   Data item representation techniques for stored records.

the retrieval software more efficient but can be wasteful in storage space. When values are smaller in length than their field widths, the fields are blank filled after right or left justification takes place. Wasted space may be reduced by the relational or indexed techniques. The relational technique replaces blanks with a single special character, not used elsewhere in the database, that delimits items. The indexed approach uses a pointer array to specify the beginning (and implicitly the end) of item values. Pointers can be absolute addresses, relative displacements, or possibly an array of data item lengths. The labeled technique is efficient when a record has many defaulted item values and only the nondefaulted values need to be explicitly stored. Additional representations are described in [Maxwell and Severance, 1973].

Within the framework of these primitive data item storage techniques there is also the option of character representation as a sequence of binary bits. The most commonly used character codes are ASCII (7 bits/character; American National Standards Institute, ANSI), EBCDIC (8 bits/character; IBM), fieldata (6 bits/character; U.S. Army), BCD (6 bits/character; CDC), and Baudot code (5 bits plus shift characters) [Martin, 1970, 1977; Wiederhold, 1977]. Standardized encoding helps simplify both the initial design and system conversion efforts. The ASCII codes are summarized in Table 10-1. Compression techniques may be designed within the framework of standard codes or may convert from standard codes to special condensed codes, as we will see in the next section.

10-1-2   Compression Techniques

There are many ways to reduce storage space in stored records. We have already mentioned the encoding of pointers and record overhead data, while redundancy of item types should have been eliminated in the conceptual structure and implementation design steps (Steps 2 and 3). Data item encoding is a well-developed science that has been described quite adequately in earlier texts and surveys [Aronson, 1977; Martin, 1977; Wiederhold, 1977]. Let us examine the major categories of compression techniques and see how they are applied to actual data.

The dominant measure of performance of a compression technique is the compression ratio, COMPR:

$$\text{COMPR} = \frac{\text{data size without compression}}{\text{data size with compression}} \qquad (10\text{-}1)$$

where the unit of data depends on the particular problem. It could be an individual character, if the compression is fixed, or it could be an entire file if the compression is variable across characters or sequences of characters. If the compression is variable, COMPR represents an average value per character. Given the compression ratio, the expected data size reduction is given by

$$\text{REDUC} = \left(1 - \frac{1}{\text{COMPR}}\right) \times 100\% = \frac{\text{COMPR} - 1}{\text{COMPR}} \times 100\% \qquad (10\text{-}2)$$

TABLE 10-1 ASCII Character Coding*†

Bit positions 4321	000	001	010	011	100	101	110	111
0000	NUL	DLE	blank	0	@	P	`	p
0001	SOH	DC1	!	1	A	Q	a	q
0010	STX	DC2	''	2	B	R	b	r
0011	ETX	DC3	#	3	C	S	c	s
0100	EOT	DC4	$	4	D	T	d	t
0101	ENQ	NAK	%	5	E	U	e	u
0110	ACK	SYN	&	6	F	V	f	v
0111	BEL	ETB	´	7	G	W	g	w
1000	BS	CAN	(	8	H	X	h	x
1001	HT	EM	)	9	I	Y	i	y
1010	LF	SUB	*	:	J	Z	j	z
1011	VT	ESC	+	;	K	[	k	{
1100	FF	FS	,	<	L	\	l	|
1101	CR	GS	−	=	M	]	m	}
1110	SO	RS	.	>	N	^	n	~
1111	SI	US	/	?	O	—	o	DEL

(header positions: *765* above columns, *4321* for rows)

*Bit numbering is right to left within a character.

† ACK Acknowledge
BEL Audible signal
BS Backspace
CAN Cancel
CR Carriage return
DCx Device control
DEL Delete
DLE Data-link escape
EM End of medium
ENQ Enquire
EOT End of transmission

ESC Escape
ETB End of trans-
     mission block
ETX End of text
FF Form feed
FS File separator
GS Group separator
HT Horizontal tabulate
LF Line feed
NAK Negative acknowledge

NUL Null
RS Record separator
SI Shift in
SO Shift out
SOH Start of heading
STX Start of text
SUB Substitute
SYN Synchronous idle
US Unit separator
VS Vertical tabulate

Abbreviations

Abbreviations fit more into the broader category of data encoding than of compression because the encoding either takes place before the database is loaded or during reorganization. Several examples of abbreviations are given in Fig. 10-3. The data reduction obtainable is quite dramatic, but the decoding process often requires a prohibitively large storage table if the number of item values is quite large. Quite often the decoding is done manually with the tables in hard copy. Also, great care must be taken when different classes of abbreviation codes are placed into a single item type [e.g., CANADA (CA) and CALIFORNIA (CA) have the same two-character abbreviations]. Finally, we note that abbreviations can be used only when the data can be predetermined, or are static, so that the abbreviations can be made unique.

States (2 bytes)		Cities (2 bytes)		Three-letter agencies (3 bytes)
Arizona	AZ	Anaheim	C1	CIA
California	CA	Burbank	C2	DIA
Michigan	MI	Hollywood	C3	DOD
New Jersey	NJ	Los Angeles	C4	FBI
New York	NY	San Diego	C5	NSA

Dates			
June 15, 1968	6.15.68	3256	(days since 1.1.60)
(13 bytes)	(6 bytes)	(12 bits)	

FIGURE 10-3 Abbreviation codes ($2 \leqq COMPR \leqq 10$).

Null Suppression

Null suppression is the term used for techniques that suppress zeros and blanks. Although compression ratios attainable are not as good as some of the other methods, they can take advantage of certain types of data in which zeros or blanks are dominant.

One way of obtaining null suppression is by extending the relational technique for storing data items. This is illustrated in Fig. 10-4. Sequences of zeros and blanks are represented by a special character followed by a number that indicates the length of the sequence. Obviously, sequences of two or one are not efficiently represented in this manner and are normally left unchanged during encoding.

Another approach to null suppression is to use a bit map. This is a variation of the indexed technique for data item representation. When a unit of data is fixed, such as a word or byte, null or zero data values can be denoted by a 0 bit, and nonnull and nonzero values can be given by a 1 bit. The bits are stored at the beginning of a data file and their positions correspond exactly to the positions of characters, words, or some other unit in the data file. An example of the use of the bit map is illustrated in Fig. 10-5.

Original data: DUNNbbbbbbCbAbb450000b55
Compressed data: DUNN#6CbAbb45@4b55
          COMPR = 24/18 = 1.33
          REDUC = 25%

FIGURE 10-4 Null suppression with length indicators.

Original data:

Item 1	0	0	Item 2	0	Item 3	0

Compressed data:

1001010	Item 1	Item 2	Item 3

FIGURE 10-5 Zero suppression using a bit map (COMPR = 1.75, REDUC = 43%).

Pattern Substitution

Pattern substitution is a class of techniques in which sequences of characters which are often repeated become defined as patterns, which are then represented by shorter codes. Figure 10-6 illustrates the use of a pattern table that must be referenced when the data characters are scanned. When a match occurs between the latest sequence of characters and a pattern table entry, a substitution is made. In general, the pattern table may be stored with the data or with the encoding software. Many sophisticated techniques exist for substitution of one character for two or more characters in a pattern and are discussed in detail elsewhere [Aronson, 1977; Martin, 1977].

Statistical (Variable-Length) Encoding

Statistical encoding is another class of data compression methods which can be used by itself or combined with a pattern substitution technique [Aronson, 1977]. Statistical encoding takes advantage of the frequency distribution of characters, so that short representations are used for characters that occur frequently, and longer representations are used for characters that occur less frequently. When combined with pattern substitution, short representation may be used for some frequently occurring pairs or other groups of characters. Morse code, for example, uses short code groups for the common letters, and longer code groups for the others.

When binary ones and zeros are used to represent a message in variable-length codes, there must be a way to tell where one character of pattern ends and the other begins. This can be done if the code has the *prefix property,* which means that no short code group is duplicated as the beginning of a longer group. Huffman codes [Huffman, 1953] have the prefix property, and in addition are minimum redundancy codes; that is, they are optimal in the sense that data encoded in these codes could not be expressed in fewer bits.

Figure 10-7 shows the combinatorial techniques used to form Huffman codes. The characters, listed in descending order of frequency of occurrence, are assigned a sequence of bits to form codes as follows. The two groups with the smallest frequencies are selected and a 0 bit is assigned to one and a 1 bit is assigned to the other. These values will ultimately be the value of the rightmost bit of the Huffman code. In this case the rightmost bit of A is 1, while that of B is 0, but the values of the

Original data	Compressed data	Pattern table	
CED3690000BB52X0	#369?/52X0	CED	#
CED3700000BB86X0	#370?/86X0		
CED3710000BB12X3	#371?/12@	0000	?
		BB	/
		X3	@

FIGURE 10-6   Pattern substitution $(1.6 \leqslant \text{COMPR} \leqslant 1.8)$.

Character	Frequency (%)	Step 1	Step 2	Step 3	Huffman code Step 4
E	60				0
T	20			0	10
4	10		0	10	110
B	6	0	10	110	1110
A	4	1	11	111	1111

FIGURE 10-7 Formation of a Huffman code (COMPR = 4.71, REDUC = 79%). An 8-bit character is assumed [Aronson, 1977].

bit assignments could have been interchanged. Next, the two groups, A and B, are then treated as if they were but one group, represented by BA, and will be assigned a specific value in the second bit position. In this way both A and B receive the same assignment in the second bit position. The above process is then repeated on the list E, T, 4, BA, where BA represents groups A and B and has a frequency of 10%. The two least frequently occurring groups, represented by 4 and BA, are selected, and a 0 bit is assigned to character 4 and a 1 bit is assigned to BA. These values will be the values of the second bit from the right of the Huffman code.

The partial code assembled up to this point is represented in the step 2 column of Fig. 10-7. In each of steps 3 and 4 the process is repeated, each time forming a new list by identifying the two elements of the previous list that had just been assigned values, and then assigning 0 and 1 to the two least frequently occurring elements of the new list. In this example, data written in the Huffman codes require only 1.7 bits per character on the average, whereas 3 bits would be required in fixed-length representations.

The general case for the construction of a Huffman code for characters $c_1, \ldots,$ c_n with probabilities $p_1, \ldots, p_n$, respectively, involves generating a binary tree in which each of the n characters is represented as a terminal node and the other (internal) nodes are formed in the following manner. First, from the two nodes with the smallest probabilities, say c_1 and c_2, a new node $c_{1,2}$ with probability $p_1 + p_2$ is formed to be the parent of c_1 and c_2. With the reduced set of $n - 1$ nodes, which consists of $c_{1,2}, c_3, \ldots, c_n$ with probabilities $p_1 + p_2, p_3, \ldots, p_n$, respectively, repeat the procedure above until the reduced set consists of only two nodes.

Now consider the binary tree that consists of the terminal nodes and all the new nodes formed by the foregoing process. For each successive pair of branches, starting at the root, assign the values 0 and 1 to each link of the branch. The resultant code for each of the characters is the sequence of assigned values obtained by tracing the tree from the root to each of the terminal nodes. Each aggregate causes the items so chosen to have a code length of one more binary digit; the average length of the code is minimized by giving this extra digit to the least probable aggregate (subtree).

The method is illustrated in Fig. 10-8. Let the characters be $c_1, c_2, c_3, c_4,$ and c_5, and have probabilities 0.3, 0.3, 0.2, 0.15, and 0.05, respectively. In the tree that results from this method the terminal nodes are represented by squares, the internal nodes by circles, and in each node is its probability of occurrence. The Huffman code for each of the characters is:

$$c_1 = 00 \quad c_4 = 110 \qquad \text{COMPR} = 3.6 \ (2.2 \ \text{bits/character})$$

$$c_2 = 01 \quad c_5 = 111 \qquad \text{REDUC} = 72\%$$

$$c_3 = 10$$

10-2   RECORD PARTITIONING

Stored record partitioning has been extensively studied in a variety of computing environments [Babad, 1977; Clark and Hoffer, 1979; Eisner and Severance, 1976; Hammer and Niamir, 1979; March and Severance, 1977]. Let us examine some of the more successful techniques and their underlying assumptions. From this examination we should be able to apply the appropriate tools to typical existing design problems. The most restrictive case is the optimal segmentation algorithm of March and Severance [March and Severance, 1977], in which items in a stored record are partitioned into a primary and a secondary segment. Although theoretically interesting, it should be noted that this technique is restricted to systems that can support physical partitioning. Clark and Hoffer [1979] and Hammer and Niamir [1979] have examined the more general problem of data item clustering of multiple-record types in an integrated database.

10-2-1   Record Segmentation Algorithms

The record segmentation algorithm of March and Severance [1977] is based somewhat on the generally accepted phenomenon that 80% of data retrieved from a database consists of only 20% of the stored data items (the "80/20 rule"). Therefore,

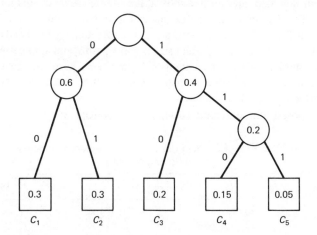

FIGURE 10-8   Binary Tree for Huffman code construction [Aronson, 1977].

the theory goes, it is possible to significantly increase the efficiency of a file or database by partitioning data items into primary and secondary "segments" (hence the name segmentation) or extents according to the amount of activity they generate by virtue of their use as selection criteria or display in reports. The *primary segment* is to hold the most active data items and is normally allocated to the fastest storage device. Roughly (but not necessarily) 20% of the data items would reside there. The *secondary segment* is to hold the least active data items; it may be located on the same type of device as the primary segment, but could also be assigned to a slower type of device. Each segment can then be referred to as a subfile. All data requests generate access to the primary segment. If the data are not found, a second access is made to the secondary segment. Available buffer space in main storage is then allocated to the primary and secondary subfiles in a way that minimizes the total cost of the database applications to be run on the system. Performance is measured in terms of physical I/O accesses for retrieval and update, and for storage space, with all measures weighted by monetary costs (per unit access or byte of storage).

This design problem was first analyzed by Eisner and Severance [1976] in terms of individual record retrieval from a secondary segment. Primary segment records are blocked to fill main storage buffer space. March and Severance model the more general case when the primary and secondary subfiles are arbitrarily blocked, subject to the constraint of main storage buffer space. System cost reductions of 65% to 80% are claimed, with the March–Severance algorithm performing 20 to 30% better than the Eisner–Severance algorithm. March and Severance formulate the record segmentation as a network flow problem and produce an efficient branch-and-bound procedure for its solution. Solution time grows proportionately to $(m + n)^2$, where m is the number of data items in the original record definition and n is the number of user applications that reference those data items. Details of the algorithm can be found in March and Severance [1977].

We shall now take an intuitive look at the March–Severance algorithm design philosophy. The data item information needed for record segmentation is shown in tabular form in Table 10-2. Each row represents a data item type (d_i) and each column represents a user application (u_j). Item size is shown as IS_i and application frequency is given as F_j. Individual matrix elements indicate when a particular data item is used in an application. No indication is made as to whether a data item is used in the selection criteria or for data display.

The proposed stored record structure will consist of two record segments:

TABLE 10-2   Data Item Usage in a Single-Record-Type File
to Be Segmented

Data item	Item size, IS_i	Frequency, F_j =	15	2	55	10
d_1	10		×		×	
d_2	12		×	×		
d_3	38					×
d_4	4				×	

primary and secondary. If we designate the set of record items as $D = \{d_1, \ldots, d_i,$ $\ldots, d_m\}$ and user applications as $U = \{u_1, \ldots, u_j, \ldots, u_n\}$, a record segmentation A is defined by the subset $D_A \subseteq D$ of data items allocated to the primary segment. The length of the primary segment is given by

$$SRS_1 = \sum_{d_i \in D_A} IS_i \qquad (10\text{-}3)$$

and the length of the secondary segment is given by

$$SRS_2 = \sum_{d_i \in D - D_A} IS_i \qquad (10\text{-}4)$$

where $SRS_1 + SRS_2 = SRS$, a constant.

Associated with segmentation A is a set of users $U_A \subseteq U$ whose data content requirements are satisfied by the data items assigned to the primary segment. The cumulative frequency of applications involving *satisfied users* over some predesignated time period is

$$F_s = \sum_{u_j \in U_A} F_j \qquad (10\text{-}5)$$

and the cumulative frequency of applications involving *dissatisfied users* (users whose data items are in the secondary segment) is given by

$$F_d = \sum_{u_j \in U - U_A} F_j \qquad (10\text{-}6)$$

where $F_s + F_d = F$, a constant.

Applications are stated in terms of retrieval only; and retrieval of a primary segment involves access plus data transfer. If an application requires one or more data items in the secondary segment, an additional retrieval is required. Even if all data items are in the secondary segment, retrieval of both primary and secondary segments is required. This restriction, although not realistic, is necessary to make the mathematical formulation tractable. We claim that the effect on potential solutions is negligible due to the dominance of the data items in the primary segment.

The record segmentation problem can be stated as

$$
\begin{aligned}
\text{minimize TCOST} = NR\Bigg[&\left(\frac{CA_1}{BKS_1} + CT_1\right) \times SRS_1 \times F \\
&+ \left(\frac{CA_2}{M - BKS_1} + CT_2\right) \times SRS_2 \times F_d \\
&+ CS_1 \times SRS_1 + CS_2 \times SRS_2 \Bigg]
\end{aligned}
\qquad (10\text{-}7)
$$

where TCOST is the total retrieval and storage cost per unit time period T. Also, we have

NR = number of records in the file

M = main storage buffer size; it is shared between the primary and secondary subfiles

BKS_1 = block size of the primary subfile ($BKS_2 = M - BKS_1$)

CA_1 = cost of a single access to a primary subfile

CT_1 = cost of data transfer from a primary subfile (per byte)

CS_1 = cost of primary subfile storage over time (per byte)

Similarly CA_2, CT_2, and CS_2 are defined for a secondary subfile. The dependent variables in Eq. (10-7) are SRS_1, SRS_2, and BKS_1.

We illustrate the application of the record segmentation algorithm to the following problem. Suppose that a personnel file is designed with the item type and user application characteristics summarized in Table 10-3. Other system parameters are given in Table 10-4. The test results for the March–Severance and Eisner–Severance algorithms are shown in Table 10-5. Applying the 80/20 rule as a heuristic, we can examine the sensitivity of the total cost to variations in solution parameters. Of the 30 data items listed, the highest 6 (highest 20%) in terms of frequency of access represent 74% of the application executions and the highest 7 data items represent 84% of the application executions. These values were found by taking the sum of the user application frequencies for each data item and ordering data items by total frequency.

The total cost for the partition (1, 2, 5, 9, 11, 12, 14), (3, 4, 6–8, 10, 13, 15–30) is $7282, which is near the worst case; thus the 80/20 rule alone is not a good heuristic in this case. Choosing only the highest six data items comes nowhere near minimizing total cost. However, we find that the top eight data items (27%) represent 94% of the application executions. Above eight data items there is a dramatic decrease in effect: the top nine represent 95% of executions. Therefore, we are led to choose the highest eight data items for an efficient partition. According to Table 10-5, it is in fact the optimal partition.

This procedure suggests the following heuristic (if one is unable to implement the full algorithm): apply the 80/20 rule to obtain an initial partition. Evaluate that partition. Then test the sensitivity of the total cost to variations of data item allocation near the original partition, stopping where the marginal increase in application execution frequency is no longer significant. Pick the best partitioning of the data items from the candidates evaluated. Each evaluation is based on an assumed value of SRS_1 and SRS_2 and solving the resulting single-variable expression in BKS_1 by simply taking the derivative and solving the quadratic equation in BKS_1, verifying that it is truly a minimum. In cases where the 80/20 rule is not applicable, a more exhaustive search will be required. Problems with up to 40 data items and 40 user applications were solved quickly with the March–Severance algorithm on a CDC Cyber-74 computer.

TABLE 10-3   Retrieval Data Content from a Personnel Database
[March and Severance, 1977]

Data item, d_i			User requests, u_j									
			1	2	3	4	5	6	7	8	9	10
			User frequencies, F_j									
Number	Name	IS_i	1	1	10	5	10	10	50	500	300	300
1	Employee name	30	×	×	×	×		×	×	×		
2	Pass number	6	×		×				×		×	×
3	Social security	9	×		×			×				
4	Pay rate	6	×			×		×				
5	Employee status	1	×	×	×	×	×	×	×	×		
6	Security code	1	×		×				×			
7	Skill codes	6	×				×					
8	Division code	2	×	×	×			×	×	×		
9	Department codes	4	×	×	×			×	×	×	×	
10	Assigned projects	8	×					×		×	×	
11	Project hours	12	×					×		×		×
12	Overtime hours	12	×					×	×	×		×
13	Shift	1	×					×	×			
14	Absentee data	10	×							×	×	
15	Deduction data	15	×					×				
16	Dependents	2	×					×				
17	Office address	5	×	×								
18	Office telephone	4	×	×								
19	Date hired	6	×									
20	Date made permanent	6	×									
21	Date terminated	6	×									
22	Position history	30	×			×			×			
23	Salary history	30	×			×						
24	Confidential data	20	×			×						
25	Marital status	1	×			×						
26	Sex	1	×			×						
27	Birth date	6	×			×						
28	Education	60	×									
29	Home telephone	10	×	×								
30	Home address	50	×	×								

10-2-2   The Bond Energy Algorithm

A more general problem than record segmentation is the clustering of data items in stored records in an integrated database. This problem can be reformulated for clustering of data items into logical records by merely changing the measures of performance from physical characteristics to logical record accesses (LRAs). It can also be used to find efficient clusterings of record types into physical areas as an

TABLE 10-4 System and Database Parameters for the Personnel
Database [March and Severance, 1977]

	Primary device	Secondary device
System cost parameters		
Access cost ($/access), CA	1.54×10^{-3}	1.54×10^{-3}
Transfer cost ($/char), CT	5.2×10^{-8}	5.2×10^{-8}
Storage cost ($/char/month), CS	6.0×10^{-7}	6.0×10^{-7}
Data set parameters		
Length of a record (char)	360	
Number of records	100,000	
Main memory constraint: buffer space available (char)	13,000	

TABLE 10-5 Test Results for the Personnel Database
[March and Severance, 1977]

Record segmentation solution specifications

Relative cost savings	
Unblocked secondary over fully blocked unsegmented	41.5%
Optimal blocking over fully blocked unsegmented	55.3%
Optimal blocking over unblocked secondary	23.7%

Segmentation type	Data item assignment		Segment size		Buffer allocation		Cost per month
	Primary	Secondary	Primary	Secondary	Primary	Secondary	
Fully blocked unsegmented	1, . . . , 30		360	0	13,000	0	$7,305.76
Unblocked secondary (Eisner–Severance)	1, . . . , 16, 22	17, . . . , 21, 23, . . . , 30	155	205	12,795	205	$4,278.22
Optimal blocking (March–Severance)	1, 2, 5, 9, . . . , 12, 14	3, 4, 6, . . . , 8, 12 15, . . . , 30	83	277	8,698	4,302	$3,266.24

alternative to the techniques discussed in Chapter 11. The *bond energy algorithm* (BEA) is a cluster analysis method that has been developed to identify natural groupings (clusters) that occur in complex data arrays; it permutes the rows and columns of the arrays in a way that groups the larger array elements together for easier identification [McCormick et al., 1972]. The BEA has now been applied to the record partitioning problem by Hoffer and others [Hoffer, 1975; Hoffer and Severance, 1975; Clark and Hoffer, 1979].

The philosophical basis for the BEA is that data attributes which are used together should be stored in the same physical subfile. If one views the joint usage in user applications as a form of "bond" that holds attributes together, a measure of the cohesiveness could be derived in terms of attribute (data item) similarity. The BEA makes use of a formal notion of a pairwise attribute similarity measure based on joint usage in applications. The similarity values form the data elements of an $m \times m$ array where m is the number of data items identified for the database.

The sequence of steps shown in Fig. 10-9 illustrates the role of the BEA and human creativeness in the stored record design process. The derivation of the similarity matrix S, which is the major input to the BEA, requires careful study of the user environment and methodical data collection to obtain the probabilities of coaccess of all attributes i and j. The BEA produces a permutation of array S, called S', which maximizes or nearly maximizes the chosen measure of effectiveness (i.e., similarity) for the whole database. (BEA is a heuristic algorithm and capable of near-optimal solutions.) The human designer must then determine the actual clusters from the permuted similarity matrix S', taking into account possible constraints on stored record size, security level of the data, and relationships between key items and nonkey items. It must be emphasized that the BEA is considered a suboptimization method and the overall design process for record content is subject to designer variability. The accuracy of the estimates of relatedness of attributes is another source of variability.

Data Collection and Parameter Determination

The basic parameter required for cluster analysis of attributes is the probability of access of attribute i in user application u, P_{iu}. It is computed from

$$P_{iu} = \frac{\text{NVAL}_{iu}}{\text{NIV}_i} \tag{10-8}$$

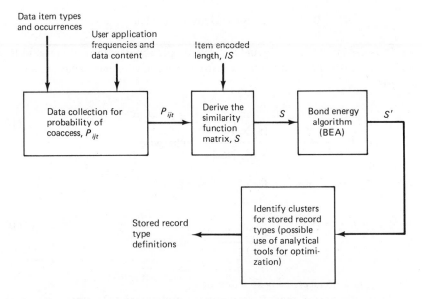

FIGURE 10-9   Stored record design through cluster analysis.

where NVAL_{iu} is the number of values of item type i required by application u and NIV_i is the number of occurrences of item type i in the database. Independence across records and executions of application u is assumed. Values for NVAL_{iu} and NIV_i are obtainable through user estimates, hardware or software execution time monitors, or program input/output analysis. Program input/output analysis is recommended because it identifies the source and volume of data usage within programs without incurring the overhead of monitors or subjectiveness of user estimates [Clark, 1977; Clark and Hoffer, 1979].

Derivation of the Similarity Function

Given access probabilities P_{iu} and P_{ju} for attributes i and j in application u, the probability of the coaccess of the two attributes in the same application is

$$P_{iju} = \begin{cases} 1 & \text{if } P_{iu} = P_{ju} \neq 0 \\ 0 & \text{if } P_{iu} = 0 \text{ or } P_{ju} = 0 \\ \overline{P}_u & \text{otherwise} \end{cases} \tag{10-9}$$

where P_{iu} is given by

$$P_{iu} = \begin{cases} 1 & \text{for attributes in the selection criteria} \\ \dfrac{\text{NVAL}_{iu}}{\text{NIV}_i} & \text{for attributes identified for display} \\ 0 & \text{for attributes not used} \end{cases} \tag{10-10}$$

and $\overline{P}_u$ is the minimum of P_{iu} and P_{ju}. The proportion of information useful to user application u which would be retrieved from a subfile with only values for attributes i and j is

$$C_{iju} = \begin{cases} 0 & \text{if } P_{iu} = P_{ju} = 0 \\ \dfrac{\text{IS}_i \times P_{iu} + \text{IS}_j \times P_{ju}}{(\text{IS}_i + \text{IS}_j) \, \max(P_{iu}, P_{ju})} & \text{otherwise} \end{cases} \tag{10-11}$$

If $P_{iu} = P_{ju}$, the expression for C_{iju} is simplified as

$$C_{iju} = \begin{cases} 0 & \text{if } P_{iu} = 0 \\ \dfrac{\text{IS}_i + P_{iju} \times \text{IS}_j}{\text{IS}_i + \text{IS}_j} & \text{otherwise} \end{cases} \tag{10-12}$$

where C_{iju} is a nondecreasing function of P_{ijt}.

As similarity measures, P_{iju} represents simplicity and C_{iju} represents a measure that encompasses the combined effect of attribute size and probability of access. Many other measures are definable with the characteristic that they are nondecreasing functions of the probability of coaccess. Let us apply P_{iju} as our measure of similarity and derive the S matrix by taking the weighted sum of coaccess probabilities for each application u according to its frequency of execution, F_u:

$$
S_{ij} = \begin{cases}
\displaystyle\sum_{u=1}^{U} F_u P_{iju} & \text{for } i \neq j \\[2em]
\displaystyle\sum_{u=1}^{U} F_u & \text{for } i = j
\end{cases}
\tag{10-13}
$$

Cluster Identification

The BEA of McCormick [McCormick et al., 1972] has the following useful characteristics: it identifies and groups together values of S_{ij} that are similar, it identifies secondary interrelationships between clustered groups for potential further grouping, and it has a computation time of $O(\text{NIT}^3)$ where NIT is the number of item types, or attributes, in the database. The algorithm uses as a measure of nearest-neighbor bond strength, BOND:

$$
\text{BOND} = \frac{1}{4} \sum_{i=1}^{\text{NIT}} \sum_{j=1}^{\text{NIT}} S_{ij} \, (S_{i,j-1} + S_{i,j+1} + S_{i+1,j} + S_{i-1,j})
\tag{10-14}
$$

where $S_{i,0} = S_{0,j} = S_{i,\text{NIT}+1} = S_{\text{NIT}+1,j} = 0$ for all i and j. The algorithm groups similar attributes by permuting (exchanging) rows and columns of S to maximize BOND. Thus, if S_{ij} is large, it will be surrounded by other large values, and if S_{ij} is small, it will be surrounded by other small values.

Equation (10-14) can be simplified by taking advantage of the fact that the pairwise similarity measure is symmetric (i.e., $S_{ij} = S_{ji}$), so that only the column bonds need to be computed:

$$
\text{BOND} = \frac{1}{2} \sum_{i=1}^{\text{NIT}} \sum_{j=1}^{\text{NIT}} S_{ij} \, (S_{i,j-1} + S_{i,j+1})
\tag{10-15}
$$

Figure 10-10 illustrates the algorithm steps. In Fig. 10-10(a) the S matrix is given for attributes A, B, C, and D. First, one of the (attribute) columns is chosen arbitrarily; in this case attribute A. The remaining NIT $-$ 1 attributes are tested being adjacent to column A and the pairwise bond strengths $\sum_{i=1}^{\text{NIT}} S_{iA} S_{ix}$ for $x = B, C, D$ are computed. The column with the largest bond strength is chosen [see column D, Fig. 10-10(b)]. Then the remaining NIT $-$ 2 attributes are tested on either side of the existing columns and again the arrangement with maximum pairwise bond strength is chosen [Fig. 10-10(c)]. Ties can be broken arbitrarily or by considering the succeed-

(a) S matrix

	A	B	C	D
A	3	1	1	3
B	1	3	2	0
C	1	2	3	1
D	3	0	1	3

(b) initial column

	A	
A	3	$AB = 8$
B	1	$AC = 11$
C	1	$AD = 19$
D	3	

(c) two columns

	A	D	
A	3	3	$DB = 5$
B	1	0	$DC = 9$
C	1	1	$BA = 8$
D	3	3	$CA = 11$

(d) three columns

	C	A	D	
A	1	3	3	$DB = 5$
B	2	1	0	$BC = 13$
C	3	1	1	
D	1	3	3	

(e) four columns, fully permuted

	B	C	A	D
A	1	1	3	3
B	3	2	1	0
C	2	3	1	1
D	0	1	3	3

(f) rows and columns fully permuted

	B	C	A	D
B	3	2	1	0
C	2	3	1	1
A	1	1	3	3
D	0	1	3	3

FIGURE 10-10 Bond energy algorithm in a four-attribute database: (*a*) *S* matrix; (*b*) initial column; (*c*) two columns; (*d*) three columns; (*e*) four columns, fully permuted; (*f*) rows and columns fully permuted.

ing possible arrangements and maximizing over the combination of arrangements. The completed permuted columns are shown in Fig. 10-10(e). Finally, the row permutations are carried out to provide complete symmetry [Fig. 10-10(f)]. An exhaustive enumeration of BOND for NIT columns would require NIT(NIT − 1) evaluations. These are shown in Table 10-6(b) for NIT = 4 and with the BOND value given in Eq. (10-15). The BEA greatly reduces the work required to find an efficient permutation of rows and columns in the similarity matrix.

The database designer is now given the subjective task of drawing boxes [as shown in Fig. 10-10(f)] along the main diagonal so that attributes with common usage are grouped together. Numbers within a box should be large compared with those numbers immediately outside the box. In this example, attributes *B* and *C* are put together and *A* and *D* are put together in two subfiles, assuming that no further constraints disallow this partitioning. The selection of boxes is simplified in this example; in general, however, it is subject to a large degree of variation by different designers. On the other hand, experiments by Clark and Hoffer [1979] have shown

TABLE 10-6   BOND Values for All Nonredundant
Four-Attribute Arrangements

Pairwise bonds	Four-attribute BOND values, Eq. (10-15)	
$AB = BA = 8$	$ABCD = 30$	$BACD = 28$
$AC = CA = 11$	$ABDC = 22$	$BADC = 36$
$AD = DA = 19$	$ACBD = 29$	$BCAD = 43$ (optimal)
$BC = CB = 13$	$ACDB = 25$	$BDAC = 35$
$BD = DB = 5$	$ADBC = 37$	$CABD = 24$
$CD = DC = 9$	$ADCB = 41$	$CBAD = 40$

that small variations in cluster definitions for complex databases can be tolerated in the overall analysis. Also, boxes may be drawn both on and off the diagonal. Those off the diagonal represent further possible relationships that may exist with other groupings on the main diagonal and may be combined to form composite boxes. Those data items boxed on the diagonal are immediate candidates for subfiles. There may also be a great deal of overlap among boxes, and it may be advantageous to combine overlapping boxes, where possible, to achieve larger and more efficient attribute clusters. Additional analysis may be conducted by enumerating more partitions manually, using a simulation program, or an optimum-finding technique [Clark and Hoffer, 1979; Hoffer, 1975].

10-2-3   A Heuristic Partitioning Model

An alternative heuristic approach to record partitioning has been proposed by Hammer and Niamir [1979]. Although the design goals are the same as for the BEA approach (i.e., nearly optimal record partitioning based on joint usage of data items in user applications), the design process is largely automated by a software package that evaluates candidate partitions in terms of physical page accesses required to execute user applications. The computing environment modeled is a multiuser relational database system with virtual storage (paging) software and hardware. Considerable effort is made to model efficient transaction-processing techniques in relational systems.

The partitioning heuristic begins with a candidate partitioning and attempts to move toward an optimum point based on stepwise page-access minimization. As with the BEA technique, the partitioning heuristic examines pairwise groupings in its first phase, but in this case it is done at the level of blocks of attributes. Each block contains a set of attributes such that blocks are pairwise disjoint and all attributes exist in the blocks. The second phase looks for performance improvements by moving attributes across blocks in the partitioning, and continues until no variation can further improve performance. The two phases alternate until no improvement occurs over a complete cycle. A fast version of this technique is claimed to be much faster than the BEA [i.e., $O(m^2)$] and still give efficient nearly optimal solutions.

11   RECORD CLUSTERING

Each time a stored record is loaded into a database it is placed according to one of many options under the control of the designer and the DBMS. Logical ordering has already been mentioned as a primary consideration; however, physical ordering, or degree of contiguity, is also very important. Physical ordering may be subject to the clustering of stored records in a collection of physical extents, which we call *record clustering*. This is quite different from record segmentation, where data items are allocated to different extents (see Chapter 10), although in both cases the extents themselves may be allocated to different physical devices to decrease I/O processing time, and also allocated different block sizes. In this chapter we investigate record clustering in both hierarchical and network logical database structures.

The record clustering problem is one of determining how to store database records, for a given data model, in order to minimize the access time for typical operational work loads. Access time is typically measured in terms of I/O service time and CPU service time; however, we shall assume that CPU time is negligible for the normal search procedures implemented in current systems. (See Chapter 16 for CPU time estimation.) Also, we need only represent access time in terms of physical block accesses and refer to Chapter 9 for the transformation from block accesses to I/O service time.

Proper clustering can make significant differences in the efficiency of a database system because it takes groups of data that are to be frequently accessed together and allows them to be stored physically in a way that maximizes sequential access and minimizes random access. For example, I/O service time improvements of 5:1 have been known to occur due to a shift from a random access path to a sequential access path configuration for a student registration system at a leading university. In general, the optimal clustering is difficult to find in a complex integrated database where data accessed by different application programs overlap, and trade-offs between sequential and random access must be evaluated. However, recent research results have made the hierarchical database clustering problem computationally feasible and hold promise for at least a heuristic approach for network structures.

11-1 CLUSTERING IN HIERARCHICAL DATABASES

The record clustering problem for hierarchical databases (such as IMS) is important to understand because it has immediate application to many existing databases, and it forms the basis for the more general network database placement specifications. A straightforward, yet very fast technique for solving this problem has been developed by Schkolnick [1977, 1978]. Because of its wide applicability, we will take a close look at how it works and what insights can be gained by using it.

Consider the hierarchical structure shown in Fig. 11-1. Each box represents a record type and the arrows represent the 1 : m relationships between record types that form the hierarchy. Within each box are numerical values for the stored record size (SRS) and the total number of occurrences of this record type (NR). For simplicity we assume that child record occurrences are equally distributed over parent records, so that, for example, there are an average of five occurrences of record B per occurrence of the parent record A. More realistic distributions can be considered after the simple model is fully understood [Schkolnick, 1978]. The arrows under the boxes and along the relationship paths designate the directions of record occurrence transition for database applications, and the number associated with each arrow is the number of times a record occurrence transition is made per unit time.

Horizontal arrows denote successor (sibling) record transition for a single record type, and vertical arrows denote parent-to-child record transition across record types. These transition values can easily be determined from known database operation sequences or by collecting access statistics from the daily (hourly, etc.) work load on a database. For example, let $F(A, A)$ be the frequency of transition of a record A occurrence from another record A occurrence. The command GET ALL B would result in $F(A, A) = 10$, $F(A, B) = 10$, and $F(B, B) = (5 - 1)10 = 40$. All other frequencies would be zero. The value for $F(A, A)$ represents the initial access to the root record type and all succeeding accesses to records of that type. For each record A, the path AB is taken once. Finally, for each record B accessed from A, four additional

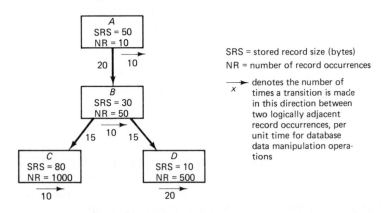

FIGURE 11-1 Hierarchical database structure.

B records are accessed sequentially. The basic assumptions we make for this computation are that the data records are stored in hierarchical preorder fashion: $A_1, B_{1,1},$ $C_{1,1,1}, \ldots, C_{1,1,20}, D_{1,1,1}, \ldots, D_{1,1,10}, B_{1,2}, C_{1,2,1}, \ldots, C_{1,2,20}, D_{1,2,1}, \ldots, D_{1,2,10},$ $B_{1,3}, \ldots, B_{1,10}, A_2, \ldots$; and pointers are implemented for direct parent-to-first-child transition, child-to-child transition, and last-child-to-successor-parent transition.

The record clustering problem in a hierarchical database is the determination of an allocation of record types to contiguous extents (e.g., data set groups in IMS or areas in CODASYL systems) to minimize the number of I/O accesses for a given set of user applications. One or more record types are in an extent, and all occurrences of a record type are allocated to that extent. Within each extent the records are assumed to be stored in hierarchical order, so that each possible clustering of records in extents could result in a new physical sequence of records. As an example, if A and B are grouped together, and C and D are separately allocated, the three resulting *groups* in this *clustering* are:

1. $A_1, B_{1,1}, \ldots, B_{1,10}, A_2, \ldots$
2. $C_{1,1,1}, C_{1,1,2}, \ldots, C_{10,5,20}$
3. $D_{1,1,1}, D_{1,1,2}, \ldots, D_{10,5,10}$

This clustering of three groups will be much more efficient than the original clustering of one group into a single extent when $F(B,B)$ is very large, as in a GET ALL B command. In the original clustering B occurrences are scattered among C and D records, but in the second clustering B occurrences are kept close together in physical sequential order. The original clustering tends to be more efficient when all the data are to be accessed in their natural hierarchical order for report generation purposes.

The determination of an optimal clustering of records to physical extents first involves defining and estimating the value of the expected distance $D(I,J)$ between a record of type I and its first child record of type J and the expected *distance* $D(I,I)$ between a record of type I and its sibling successor record of type I, in a group:

$$D(I,I) = \text{SRS}(I) + \sum_{J \in S_1} D(J,J) \times \text{ANC}(I,J) \tag{11-1}$$

where

$$\text{ANC}(I,J) = \text{NR}(J) / \text{NR}(I) \tag{11-2}$$

$$D(I,J) = \text{SRS}(I) + \sum_{K \in S_2} D(K,K) \times \text{ANC}(I,K) \tag{11-3}$$

In Eq. (11-1) $D(I,I)$ is the length of record type I plus the sum of the distances (lengths) of the intervening descendent records of I. S_1 is the set of direct (descendent record types of I, and the sum is taken over all record types J which are in S_1; ANC(I, J) is the average number of child records of type J per occurrence of parent record type *I*. In Eq. (11-3) $D(I, J)$ is the sum of the length of record type *I* and the total distance (record lengths) across descendent records *K* in S_2. S_2 is the set of direct descendent record types *K* of record type *I* that are to the left of *J* and in the same group as *I* and *J*. Distance functions are illustrated in Fig. 11-2 for a purely hierarchical ordering of a hierarchical database.

The expected number of physical block accesses associated with a transition from *I* to *J* is given by

$$\text{PBA}(I, J) = \begin{cases} \min [D(I, J)/\text{EBKS}, 1] & \text{within the same group} \\ 1 & \text{across different groups} \end{cases} \quad (11\text{-}4)$$

whree EBKS is the effective block size. EBKS represents the usable portion of a block associated with the effective blocking factor EBF and is given by

$$\text{EBKS} = \text{EBF} \times \text{SRS} \quad (11\text{-}5)$$

The expected number of block accesses in the transition from one record occurrence to another is less than 1 when the distance between the records is less than the effective block size. When the distance is greater than the block size, at most one block access is required. Schkolnick defines this problem within a paging environment, where all block accesses are random (rba) and the hierarchical pointers allow one to go directly to the next block without scanning intervening blocks. In a nonpaging environment the interblock distances may be characterized by some pattern that is potentially more efficient than random. We will assume a paging environment for this analysis and refer the reader to Chapter 9 for the time-distance relationships.

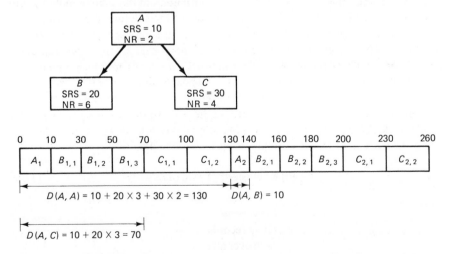

FIGURE 11-2   Basic distance functions in a hierarchical database.

The total number of block accesses for a particular clustering of records in extents is given by

$$\text{PBA (clustering)} = \sum_{I \in S} [F(I,I) \times \text{PBA}(I,I) + \sum_{J \in S_1} F(I,J) \times \text{PBA}(I,J)] \quad (11\text{-}6)$$

where S is the set of all record types I in the clustering and S_1 is the set of direct descendents J of record type I. The sums of block accesses for individual types of record transitions are weighted by the frequencies of those transitions. Applying Eq. (11-6) to the hierarchy in Fig. 11-1 we obtain for a single clustering of the database:

$$\begin{aligned}\text{PBA (clustering)} \quad &= F(A,A) \times \text{PBA}(A,A) + F(A,B) \\ &\times \text{PBA}(A,B) + F(B,B) \times \text{PBA}(B,B) + F(B,C) \\ &\times \text{PBA}(B,C) + F(B,D) \times \text{PBA}(B,D) + F(C,C) \\ &\times \text{PBA}(C,C) + F(D,D) \times \text{PBA}(D,D) \end{aligned} \quad (11\text{-}7)$$

For other databases we could write the cost in a similar manner, but to illustrate the efficiency of the solution technique it is helpful to rewrite Eq. (11-6) in a different but equivalent way:

$$\text{PBA (clustering)} \quad = C(R) \quad\quad\quad\quad\quad\quad\quad\quad\quad\quad\quad\quad\quad\quad (11\text{-}8)$$

$$= F(R,R) \times \text{PBA}(R,R) + \sum_{J \in S_1} [F(R,J) \times \text{PBA}(R,J) + C(J)]$$

where $C(R)$ is the cost for the root R of the tree comprising clustering, in physical block accesses. S_1 is the set of record types directly descended from type R; that is, the child record types of R, and $C(J)$ is the cost contribution of the subtree rooted at J to the expression $C(R)$. Note that the cost for the root of a tree defines the cost of the tree itself. Note also that Eq. (11-8) is recursive in that the cost of a tree (hierarchical) structure is a linear function of the costs of the component subtrees. Such a rule is possible only with hierarchical (and not network) structures in which members of each group in a clustering must be direct descendents and ancestors of each other. While other groupings are still legal in IMS secondary data set groups, for example, they are not normally implemented because their transitions are usually inefficient [Schkolnick, 1977]. The normal grouping alternatives are shown in Fig. 11-3. Applying Eq. (11-8) to our example in Fig. 11-1, we obtain

$$\text{PBA (clustering)} = C(A) \quad\quad\quad\quad\quad\quad\quad\quad\quad\quad\quad (11\text{-}9)$$

where

$$C(A) = F(A,A) \times \text{PBA}(A,A) + F(A,B) \times \text{PBA}(A,B) + C(B) \quad (11\text{-}9a)$$

$$\begin{aligned}C(B) &= F(B,B) \times \text{PBA}(B,B) + F(B,C) \times \text{PBA}(B,C) + C(C) \\ &\quad + F(B,D) \times \text{PBA}(B,D) + C(D) \end{aligned} \quad (11\text{-}9b)$$

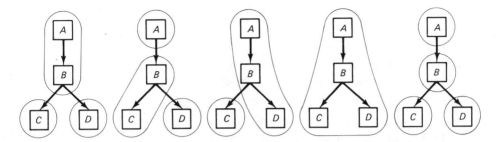

FIGURE 11-3 Examples of alternative groupings of records to form clusterings.

$$C(C) = F(C, C) \times \text{PBA}(C, C) \qquad \text{(11-9c)}$$

$$C(D) = F(D, D) \times \text{PBA}(D, D) \qquad \text{(11-9d)}$$

Using Eq. (11-9), and in the general case for Eq. (11-8), we find that we can compute PBA (clustering) by starting at the leaves of the tree in this clustering and by working bottom up, build reusable temporary results as we go along.

Let us denote a clustering as a binary function of pairs of record types in the database. For example, let us define A and B as the first potential pairing. If A and B are grouped together, the pairing AB is given a value of 1; otherwise, pairing AB is given a value of 0.

Now we can compute total cost in physical block accesses for all candidate clusterings in our example structure (Fig. 11-1). Pair grouping notation can be simplified by listing all the legal pairings of record types in the order to be used for the binary representation: AB, BC, BD. The three pairings and all combinations of them can be represented by a three-digit binary number. For example, 100 represents $AB = 1$ (grouped), $BC = 0$ (not grouped) and $BD = 0$ (not grouped). Taken as a whole, the clustering 100 is represented by AB, C, D. The purpose of the binary notation is to facilitate reference to groupings in a large complex database where it would be tedious to list all possible groupings with lettering or record names; also, it is easier to implement in a computerized design aid with the binary notation.

Let us now compute cost for two of the legal clusterings of Fig. 11-1, assuming that EBKS = 1000 bytes:

Clustering ABCD (111):

$$C(C) = F(C, C) \min [D(C, C)/\text{EBKS}, 1] = 10 \min [80/1000, 1]$$
$$= 10 \times 0.08 = 0.8$$

$$C(D) = F(D, D) \min [D(D, D)/\text{EBKS}, 1] = 20 \min [10/1000, 1]$$
$$= 20 \times 0.01 = 0.2$$

$$C(B) = F(B, B) \times \text{PBA}(B, B) + F(B, C) \times \text{PBA}(B, C) + C(C) + F(B, D)$$
$$\times \text{PBA}(B, D) + C(D)$$
$$= 10 \times \min [30 + 20 \times 80 + 10 \times 10/1000, 1] + 15 \min [30/1000, 1]$$
$$+ 0.8 + 15 \min [30 + 20 \times 80/1000, 1] + 0.2$$

$$= 10 \times 1 + 15 \times 0.03 + 0.8 + 15 \times 1 + 0.2$$
$$= 26.45$$

$$C(A) = F(A,A) \times PBA(A,A) + F(A,B) \times PBA(A,B) + C(B)$$
$$= 10 \min [50 + 5 \times 30 + 5 \times 20 \times 80 + 5 \times 10 \times 10/1000, 1]$$
$$+ 20 \min [50/1000, 1] + 26.45$$
$$= 10 + 20 \times 0.05 + 26.45$$
$$= 37.45$$

PBA (clustering $ABCD$) $= C(A) = 37.45$ rba

Clustering AB, C, D (100):

$$C(C) = 0.8, \qquad C(D) = 0.2$$

$$C(B) = 10 \min [30/1000, 1] + 15 \times 1 + 0.8 + 15 \times 1 + 0.2$$
$$= 0.3 + 15 + 0.8 + 15 + 0.2 = 31.3$$

$$C(A) = 10 \min [50 + 5 \times 30/1000, 1] + 20 \times 0.05 + 31.3$$
$$= 2 + 1 + 31.3 = 34.3$$

PBA (clustering AB,C, D) $= C(A) = 34.3$ rba

Table 11-1 displays the cost figures for all the legal clusterings for Fig. 11-1. The optimal cost solution is seen to be the clustering ABD, C (101), which is a 24% decrease in block accesses from the next best clustering (100) and a 50% decrease from the worst case (000). Thus, we see that with a simple enumeration method we can readily determine the optimal clustering for the given work-load frequencies and logical database structure. Unfortunately, the number of possible legal clusterings in a hierarchy with n record types is 2^{n-1} (i.e., exponential in n), so, for example, when $n = 21$ there are over 10^6 possible clusterings to enumerate. Manual analysis would be limited to about six record types and computer analysis might extend the enumeration capability to about 20 to 35 record types, depending on the computing power available.

Schkolnick demonstrated a faster procedure that takes time proportional to n [1977]. If we take the view that a tree with root x can be regarded as a subtree of

TABLE 11-1   Expected Distance $D(A,A)$ and Total Cost $C(A)$
in rba for Candidate Record Clusterings in Fig. 11-1

Clustering	Binary code	$D(A,A)$	$C(A)$
A, B, C, D	000	50	51.80
A, BD, C	001	50	38.25
A, BC, D	010	50	46.95
A, BCD	011	50	46.95
AB, C, D	100	200	34.30
ABD, C	101	700	25.75
ABC, D	110	8200	37.45
ABCD	111	8700	37.45

some larger tree with root y, it is possible to develop a heuristic procedure that eliminates nonoptimal clusterings in the subtree at x from further consideration in the whole tree at y. It can be shown that a clustering having both $D(x, x)$ and $C(x)$ equal to or greater than another clustering in x can be eliminated from further consideration beyond the current subtree. Thus, in our example, we can avoid full enumeration of all eight clusterings by first evaluating the subtree with root at B. The result of this evaluation is shown in Table 11-2. Clusterings 10 and 11 are both eliminated due to the disqualification criterion

$$D(B, B)_i \geq D(B, B)_j \quad \text{and} \quad C(B)_i \geq C(B)_j \quad \quad (11\text{-}10)$$

for some other clustering j.

TABLE 11-2   Expected Distance and Total Cost for Subtree
at B in Fig. 11-1

Clustering	Binary code	$D(B, B)$	$C(B)$	Action
B, C, D	00	30	31.30	Keep
BD, C	01	130	17.75	Keep
BC, D	10	1630	26.45	Eliminate
BCD	11	1730	26.45	Eliminate

Returning to Table 11-1, we see that all clusterings ending in 10 or 11 need not be considered further. This means that for the tree rooted at A, evaluations are needed only for clusterings 000, 001, 100, and 101. When this process of elimination is continued through the larger subtrees, the savings in computation time increases dramatically. The fast clustering algorithm is claimed to be flexible enough to incorporate more general distributions of child records per parent (with mean of ANC) and more general cost functions that include storage space and I/O time functions dependent on device allocation.

Blocking factor BF (and EBF) determines effective block size, EBKS, which is used to directly compute the cost of a group transition [see Eq. (11-4)]. Thus, the blocking factor has a significant effect on the choice of record clustering. For example, an extremely small block size rules out any advantage of physical sequential records in area clusters, so that in a paging environment no clustering could improve on the simplest single grouping of the entire database. If each area cluster could have a different block size, the computational complexity of the record clustering algorithm would be very high.

11-2   CLUSTERING IN NETWORK DATABASE STRUCTURES

The record clustering technique we have analyzed for hierarchical databases in Section 11-1 can be applied to a limited degree to network databases. We focus our analysis on the CODASYL data model [CODASYL, 1971a], which represents a widely used class of network DBMSs. A CODASYL physical database structure is specified in the Data Storage Description Language (DSDL) presented in the CODASYL *Journal of Development* [CODASYL, 1978]. Existing CODASYL implementations do not necessarily provide all the features and options described in the DSDL. However, CODASYL's division of database structure specification into a schema (in the DDL) and storage schema (in the DSDL) provides a convenient and practical way to avoid the ambiguities concerning the meanings of logical and physical database structure. In the context of the CODASYL data model, implementation design results in a DDL schema and physical design results in a DSDL schema.

Record placement in CODASYL is controlled primarily by the PLACEMENT clause in the DSDL. One of three kinds of placement specification may be chosen for each record type:

1. *CALC*. One or more data item values are hashed to produce a storage address.
2. *CLUSTERED VIA SET s*. A new member occurrence r_1 of SET type s is stored near existing member occurrence r_2 of the same occurrence of SET type s. r_1 is close to r_2 in the SET occurrence's logical ordering.
3. *SEQUENTIAL*. Occurrences are stored in physical sequential order, based on specific data item values.

These options are mutually exclusive.

Each possible placement option for a given record type r specifies that the physical placement of record occurrences of type r is to be guided by some logical access path to type r record occurrences, either a direct logical access path (CALC), a SEQUENTIAL logical access path, or a SET-implemented logical access path (CLUSTERED). In choosing record placement options, the database designer is choosing one logical access path per record type to be favored in the placement of record occurrences.

Within the CLUSTERED VIA SET option, the OWNER and DISPLACEMENT phrases allow the designer to specify the relationship between the storage placement of record occurrences CLUSTERED VIA SET s and the location of the corresponding owner occurrences of the SET s occurrences. The designer may specify that the clustered members be placed NEAR OWNER, at a specified displacement from the owner, or at a location independent of the owner's. If record type r is CLUSTERED VIA SET s, but not NEAR OWNER, each newly stored r occurrence will be stored near other r occurrences which belong to the same SET s occurrence; this cluster of related r occurrences will not be placed near the owner occurrence. Figure 11-4 illustrates the effects of including or omitting NEAR OWNER in record type y's CLUSTERED VIA SET s phrase, where x is the owner type for SET s [Oberlander, 1979].

Clustered records may be allocated to CODASYL areas, each of which typically corresponds to a file and is stored in a contiguous extent on secondary storage. The unit of physical access is typically a page. All pages in an area are constrained to be the same size, although different areas can have different page sizes. It is assumed that

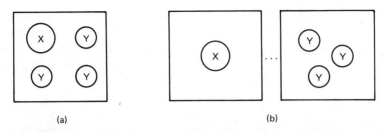

(a)   (b)

FIGURE 11-4 Effect of NEAR OWNER phrase on physical placement: *(a)*
NEAR OWNER; *(b)* not NEAR OWNER.

record occurrences cannot span pages. Area design consists of choosing a page size
and number of pages for each area. If an area is to be accessed sequentially, it may be
desirable to reserve storage for insertions in each page during initial loading. The
storage eligibility relationship between areas and record types is in general $m : n$.
Occurrences of record type A may be scattered among several areas, although any one
record occurrence is stored in just one area, and occurrences of several record types
may be stored in a given area.

The task of choosing the number and content of areas is clearly related to the
record placement problem discussed above. In order to allow the DBMS to follow
placement rules specified for the various record types, it is necessary that clusters of
record types connected by SET types named in CLUSTERED VIA SET NEAR
OWNER placement specifications be stored within the same area or areas. Record
types that are not so connected may be stored in different areas.

Figure 11-5 illustrates how CODASYL record placement and area definition
relate to the hierarchical clustering model in Section 11-1. When clustering is
specified NEAR OWNER [Fig. 11-5(a)], record types A and B are stored in hierarchi-

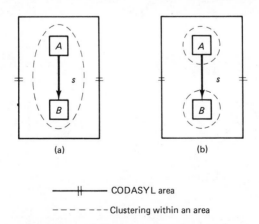

(a)   (b)

————╫———— CODASYL area

— — — — — — Clustering within an area

FIGURE 11-5 Clustering using CODASYL placement options and areas: *(a)* Clustered via set *s* NEAR
OWNER; *(b)* clustered via set *s* not NEAR OWNER.

cal sequence in a single clustering AB. When clustering is not NEAR OWNER [Fig. 11-5(b)], record types A and B are clustered separately as A, B, although both clusterings are maintained in a single area. Although clusterings and areas appear to be separate design decisions, this separability suggests a stepwise heuristic algorithm for CODASYL record placement:

STEP 1 Find the optimal ''minor'' clustering using Schkolnick's technique: first break the network structure down into its (possibly overlapping) hierarchical components. Then find the optimal hierarchical clustering for each component and resolve the overlapping components by trial-and-error enumeration.

STEP 2 Design areas by enumeration. Given the optimal ''minor'' clusterings and their overlap resolution, evaluate candidate ''major'' clusterings within areas. Reduce the solution space by considering only the dominant user applications and by setting an upper limit on physical area size. A simpler design philosophy is to assign one area to each cluster on a 1 : 1 basis.

An example network database structure with potential clusterings for its component hierarchies is shown in Fig. 11-6. The network clustering problem is more complex than the hierarchical problem because areas are not confined to record types directly descended from one another, but may be selected in any combination over the entire database; that is, if there are n record types in the database, the number of possible clusterings is given by the rapidly increasing Bell function [Aigner, 1979]:

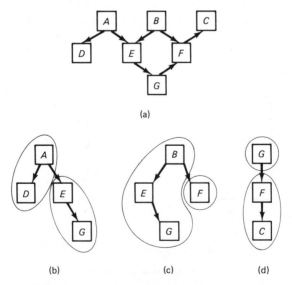

(a)

(b)   (c)   (d)

FIGURE 11-6   Network schemata and component hierarchical schemata with potential clusterings: (a) original network; (b) hierarchy 1; (c) hierarchy 2; (d) hierarchy 3.

$$B_0 = 1, B_{n+1} = \sum_{k=0}^{n} \binom{n}{k} B_k \qquad (11\text{-}11)$$

Sample values for B_n are given in Table 11-3.

TABLE 11-3   Number of Potential Clusterings in Hierarchical and
Network Databases with n Record Types

n	Hierarchical database	Network database
1	1	1
2	2	2
3	4	5
4	8	15
5	16	52
6	32	203
7	64	877
8	128	4140
15	16,384	1.38×10^9
$\vdots$	$\vdots$	$\vdots$
n	2^{n-1}	$B_n = \sum_{k=0}^{n-1} \binom{n-1}{k} B_k \quad (B_0 = 1)$

Let us now apply our simple heuristic to determine "minor" clusterings and areas for Fig. 11-6. Assume that the three hierarchies have optimal clusterings given by Fig. 11-6(b)–(d):

$$\left.\begin{array}{l} \text{Hierarchy 1: } AD, EG \\ \text{Hierarchy 2: } BEG, F \\ \text{Hierarchy 3: } G, FC \end{array}\right\} \text{optimal "minor" clusterings}$$

Overlap occurs between EG, BEG, and G; between F and FC. AD has no overlap and is automatically made a valid grouping within the network. The potential clusterings to be evaluated over the entire network are:

$$\left.\begin{array}{ll} 1.\ AD,\ BEG,\ F,\ C & 5.\ AD,\ BE,\ G,\ F,\ C \\ 2.\ AD,\ BEG,\ FC & 6.\ AD,\ BE,\ G,\ FC \\ 3.\ AD,\ B,\ EG,\ F,\ C & 7.\ AD,\ B,\ E,\ G,\ F,\ C \\ 4.\ AD,\ B,\ EG,\ FC & 8.\ AD,\ B,\ E,\ G,\ FC \end{array}\right\} \begin{array}{l} \text{candidate} \\ \text{"major" clusterings} \end{array}$$

The total number of enumerations is $O(n)$ for each of the hierarchies plus the eight candidate network clusterings (i.e., 19 enumerations). A brute-force evaluation of all possible network clusterings requires 877 enumerations. Clearly, we have a need for a computer program to accomplish the evaluations. Assuming that a program has been run and determines that clustering 2 (AD, BEG, FC) is optimal, the potential areas we can define are:

	Area 1	*Area 2*	*Area 3*
1.	AD	BEG	FC
2.	AD, BEG	FC	—
3.	AD, FC	BEG	—
4.	BEG, FC	AD	—
5.	AD, BEG, FC	—	—

These can be easily enumerated in the same manner as hierarchical clusterings except that blocks inside the areas are only random within the areas, not across the whole storage device.

Clearly, this algorithm is purely heuristic and could be subject to a cycling effect (i.e., nonconvergence) if it attempted to solve for a global optimum set of clusterings. A more general (and much more complex) methodology for CODASYL record placement and area design using heuristic algorithms, a graph theoretical model, and an optimization technique has been investigated but not validated in an operating environment [Oberlander, 1979]. Other applicable methodologies include the bond energy algorithm discussed in Chapter 10 [Clark and Hoffer, 1979] and the heuristic approach of Hammer and Niamir [1979]. There is a great deal of similarity between the optimal network clustering problem and the optimal record partitioning problem, but their exact relationship has not yet been shown.

12 PRIMARY
ACCESS METHODS:
SEQUENTIAL PROCESSING

12-1 INTRODUCTION

The salient design decisions that relate implementation design to physical design are those associated with access paths. At the conceptual level, entities and relationships are described in terms of data associations without regard to how the data are accessed. Then, when the DBMS implementation is considered, the information structure is refined to accommodate various system constraints and minimize access path lengths over the entire set of user applications. The simplest transformation from information structure to DBMS-processible logical database structure converts entities to records directly so that associations between entities form the basis for navigational access paths. Of course, restricting ourselves to such an arrangement puts severe limitations on our ability to be flexible about conceptual design. Nevertheless, entity relationships do suggest possible starting points for thinking about access paths, although many other considerations should be made that may in fact create new database structures totally different from the original conceptual model.

The logical database structure or schema design is based primarily on constrained minimization of access path length, so is closely related to the final physical structure. The physical structure considers the schema to form the basis of navigational accessing, if needed, and imposes other entry-point access methods if justifiable in terms of generally agreed upon performance measures. In this manner logical record accesses (LRAs) and transport volume, which were used to predict relative system performance, evolve to physical block accesses and eventually to I/O service time as further measures of relative performance. Response time, composed of I/O service time and many other resource service and delay times, is a predictor of absolute performance, which is subject to validation under controlled experimentation with live test data.

In this chapter we take a close look at evaluation techniques for database access methods to predict relative performance. A simple model of sequential and random data access is used as a descriptive mechanism for the myriad of approaches discussed in the literature and sometimes implemented in real systems. Using this approach, we describe how access paths can be evaluated for both retrieval and updating operations and investigate trade-offs between access methods, necessary to make intelligent selection decisions. The major classes of access methods are addressed, as well as hybrid cases, based on their values of basic descriptive parameters. Another objective of the analysis is to provide enough concepts for future evaluation of access methods not yet known.

12-1-1   Access Method Terminology

The term "access method" will be defined in its generic sense; that is, we will provide a general definition that is not construed to be associated with a particular access method implemented by a DBMS or O.S. vendor. An *access method* is a technique that provides storage and retrieval capabilities for data stored on physical devices, normally secondary storage. Access methods have two major components: storage structure and a search mechanism. The storage structure (as defined in Section 9-1) provides the framework for establishing access paths to data. The *search mechanism* is an algorithm that defines a specific access path to be taken within the storage structure framework and indicates how many steps must be taken along that access path.

To illustrate these definitions, consider a sequential file. The storage structure defines the potential access path as being along the physical sequential ordering of the file, whereas a retrieval search mechanism could be described as either a sequential search, a binary search, or a hashing function, for example. For each of these search mechanisms the number of steps (block accesses) varies considerably along the same basic access path. One might reasonably argue that in fact there are at least three access paths here, not one, but the definition presented here suits our purpose better for consistency and readability of the evaluation technique. It is easier to describe nonsequential access along a sequential structure in terms of steps required. Access in a random structure, such as a tree or network, is often naturally nonsequential in terms of physical ordering, but is sequential in terms of following the "next" pointer from block to block or record to record.

A binary search or hash address scheme to locate a record stored physically sequentially is to be considered as a random block access, but the randomness is constrained to the extent of the database. Performance of access methods will be evaluated in this chapter in terms of physical block accesses for user application workloads. Chapter 9 showed how I/O service time could be deduced from these values, given that block sizes and user computing environment are known.

12-1-2   Classification of Access Methods

A database access path can be viewed as a sequence of sequential and random accesses to stored records. Differences among access methods, due to variations in storage structure and search mechanisms, have the effect of changing the order sequence of sequential and random accesses and the length of each sequence. Accesses are made first to blocks and then to stored records within blocks. Because accesses to blocks require tens of milliseconds of I/O time and search time within blocks is typically in the range of microseconds of CPU time (with current technology), our analysis concentrates on the dominant measure of processing time, block access, and transfer time. On the other hand, while intrablock search methods are becoming more important as main storage capacities increase, they are based on the same set of access methods already applied to data manipulated within main storage, such as symbol tables and page tables in systems software. We will discuss the full range of access methods in the context of secondary storage, although the concepts are applicable to any storage level.

A taxonomy of access method classes was proposed by Severance and Carlis [1977] on the basis of the type of user application to be processed. Those methods that fall into each class represent the most efficient approaches to service that type of application. The three major classifications are:

1. *GET ALL or MANY*

    This class of applications requires access of a significant proportion of the database, usually between 10 and 100% of the records. Sequential processing, large report generation, and batch processing usually fall into this class. The lower bound of 10% represents a frequent crossover point for ad hoc queries, above which a sequential database search is usually more efficient than an index search of *target records* (i.e., those records that satisfy the qualification conditions of the query).

2. *GET UNIQUE*

    This class represents the opposite extreme. Access is made to a single target record if it exists. The spectrum of random access techniques and indexing based on a primary key fall into this class.

3. *GET SOME*

    The third class of applications covers the intermediate ground of access to target records that make up somewhere between 0 and 10% of the entire database. Ad hoc queries are the most common application type, and secondary indexing becomes an important implementation technique.

This classification has the distinct advantage of allowing the designer to focus quickly on those techniques that will best satisfy response time requirements and constraints on storage space for a given set of user applications. Other types of classification are possible, and we introduce some further distinguishing characteristics to further subclassify currently known access methods. It will be seen that a large number of hybrid techniques exist that cross the boundaries of our three major categories. We readily acknowledge that many access methods implemented in real systems represent an attempt to compromise several types of user applications that predominate in a particular system. Such methods are clearly identified in this classification scheme. Table 12-1 summarizes the major classifications discussed in this chapter. Note the absence of system-dependent access methods. Some of these will be treated explicitly in the examples, but most others should be constructable from the basic components illustrated below.

TABLE 12-1   Major Access Method Classifications

User Application Class	*Access Methods*
GET ALL, GET MANY (10–100%)	Sequential Physical sequential (contiguous storage) Linked sequential (noncontiguous storage)
GET UNIQUE (one or none)	Direct access Random (identifier hashing) Full index (indexed random) Indexed sequential Binary tree B-tree Radix search tree (TRIE)
GET SOME (0–10%)	Multilist Inverted Cellular inverted Doubly chained tree

12-2   PHYSICAL SEQUENTIAL PROCESSING: GET MANY, GET ALL

The most efficient physical structure for high-volume sequential processing is physical sequential. The contiguous records allow for physical blocking and thus minimize the access time to the data. Low-volume processing is often most efficient with linked allocation, especially when data volatility is high. We investigate each of these organizations in terms of their performance for many types of retrieval and update, and obtain some expressions for the basic trade-offs frequently encountered.

It should be emphasized that physical sequential and linked sequential organizations are the foundation for a very large class of access methods, including indexed sequential, multilist, inverted, and various tree search mechanisms. More complex structures, which are synthesized from these two basic organizations, will be subsequently analyzed more easily when we more fully comprehend the salient characteristics and limitations of sequential organizations.

12-2-1   Physical Sequential Retrieval

The physical sequential structure is perhaps the simplest organization to analyze. However, there are a significant number of parameters involved in processing data stored sequentially, each of which has continued importance for more advanced physical organizations:

- *Type of work load.* Sequential processing, random retrieval and update, batch retrieval and update, report generation.
- *Order of data records.* Allows batch processing; avoids sorting if report order is the same as file order.
- *Blocking factor.* Affects sequential processing efficiency.
- *File size (number of records).*
- *Loading factor.* Allows growth without excessive overflow and consequent reloading.
- *Search mechanism.*

An example of physical sequential organization is shown in Fig. 12-1.

The basic physical sequential structure has a single level of NR contiguous records. It may be ordered or unordered. Ordering can be ascending or descending according to a single primary key and its set of nonredundant values. Records are assumed to be of constant size and to contain nonkey elements. No pointers are required.

An unblocked sequential organization (file or subfile) has NR blocks; that is, each record is contained in a separate block. In general, there are NBLK = ⌈NR/EBF⌉ blocks, where EBF is the effective blocking factor. Files with variable-size records have no established blocking factor, but contain NBLK blocks computed from the distribution of record size, as shown in Section 9-3-2. Assuming that the error due to an unfilled final block is negligible, the expected number of physical blocks accessed in the retrieval of a random record is

$$\text{PBA (GET UNIQUE, seq search)} = \frac{1 + \text{NBLK}}{2} \qquad \text{sba} \qquad (12\text{-}1)$$

where sba specifies that the unit of measure is in sequential block accesses. Similarly, rba denotes random block accesses.

Equation (12-1) applies to an unordered file as well as an ordered file if the target record exists. If it does not exist, the search length is still the same for an ordered file, but would be NBLK blocks for an unordered file because every record would have to be checked. Thus, an unordered file is only inefficient for random retrieval when the search fails.

A binary search of NBLK blocks for a unique record requires that the file be ordered and reasonably long, so that a sequential search is not justifiable. In a binary search, once a candidate block is accessed it is searched internally for the target record. The expected binary search length for a file of NBLK blocks is [Knuth, 1973]

$$\text{PBA (GET UNIQUE, bin search)} = \log_2 \text{NBLK} - 1$$

$$= \log_2 (\text{NBLK}/2) \qquad \text{rba} \qquad (12\text{-}2)$$

| BESSIE | BETSY | BONNIE | CAROL | EUNICE | JANE | JULIETTE | KELLY | KRISTIN | MARILYN | MERILEE |

FIGURE 12-1 Physical sequential organization.

for NBLK $\geq$ 50. For NBLK $<$ 50, a more exact formula is given in Martin [1977]. In general, the upper bound has been shown to be $\lfloor \log_2 NBLK \rfloor + 1$ under any circumstances. Note that random block accesses are required for a binary search, but the number of accesses is constrained by the extent of the file. Note also that all blocks are assumed to be equally filled.

Retrieval of all records (GET ALL) is the same amount of work for ordered and unordered files:

$$PBA \ (GET \ ALL) = NBLK \qquad sba \qquad (12\text{-}3)$$

where NBLK = $\lceil NR/EBF \rceil$ for fixed-size records and constant effective blocking factor. Equation (12-3) holds for all sequential applications, including boolean queries based on secondary keys.

A variation of sequential processing is popular for batch retrieval of RPBR records. To process the RPBR records most efficiently, they are placed in a transaction file in the same order as the master file, and merged. Records in the master file that match keys with transaction records are saved and processed during the merge operation. The component block accesses required for the transaction file (tf) and master file (mf) are

$$PBA \ (GET \ BATCH)_{tf} = \left\lceil \frac{RPBR}{EBF_{tf}} \right\rceil \qquad sba \qquad (12\text{-}4)$$

$$PBA \ (GET \ BATCH)_{mf} < NBLK_{mf} + RPBR \qquad sba \qquad (12\text{-}5)$$

where the first term represents a sequential file scan and the second term represents a restart delay after each target record is found. Inequality (12-5) is not very useful. To obtain an exact expression for PBA (GET BATCH)$_{mf}$, we assume that the RPBR records are randomly distributed across the master file. The following theorem is proved for logical record accesses in a continuous environment, and is then applied to block accesses for batch processing.

THEOREM 12-1 Given a set of k randomly distributed records to be retrieved from a file of n records, the expected search length is $kn/(k + 1)$ records.

PROOF. We shall assume that n is large enough to approximate this discrete environment with a continuous model. Let $X_1, X_2, \ldots, X_k$ be independent random variables over the interval $[0, n]$. Then we must find the expected value of a, $E(a)$, where $a = \max (X_1, X_2, \ldots, X_k)$. Let

$$F(a) = \text{Prob}(X_1 \leq a \wedge X_2 \leq a \wedge \ldots \wedge X_k \leq a)$$

$$= \text{Prob}(X_1 \leq a) \cdot \text{Prob}(X_2 \leq a) \cdot \ldots \cdot \text{Prob}(X_k \leq a)$$

$$= \left(\frac{a}{n}\right)_1 \left(\frac{a}{n}\right)_2 \cdots \left(\frac{a}{n}\right)_k$$

$$= \left(\frac{a}{n}\right)^k \qquad \text{for the cumulative distribution function}$$

Then the density function is

$$f(a) = \frac{dF(a)}{da} = \frac{d\left(\frac{a}{n}\right)^k}{da} = \frac{ka^{k-1}}{n^k}$$

Finally, the expected value of a is

$$E(a) = \int_0^n af(a)\ da$$

$$= \int_0^n \frac{aka^{k-1}}{n^k}\ da$$

$$= \frac{k}{n^k} \int_0^n a^k da$$

$$= \frac{k}{n^k} \frac{a^{k+1}}{k+1}\ \Big|_0^n = \frac{k}{n^k} \cdot \frac{n^{k+1}}{k+1} = \frac{kn}{k+1}$$

Applying this result to our problem, assuming a large value of NR, we obtain

$$\text{LRA (GET BATCH)}_{mf} = \frac{\text{NR} \times \text{RPBR}}{\text{RPBR} + 1} \tag{12-6}$$

When $\text{RPBR} = k = 1$, there is only one record in the batch, and the batch problem is equivalent to a single random retrieval. Accordingly, Eq. (12-6) reduces to $\text{LRA}_{mf} = \text{NR}/2$ for random record retrieval. Assuming fixed-length records, we convert expected record accesses to expected block accesses using

$$\text{PBA (GET BATCH)}_{mf} = \frac{\text{LRA}_{mf}}{\text{EBF}_{mf}} + \text{RPBR sba} = \frac{\text{NR} \times \text{RPBR}}{\text{EBF}_{mf}(\text{RPBR} + 1)} + \text{RPBR sba}$$

$$\tag{12-7}$$

Total block accesses for the entire batch retrieval is

$$\text{PBA (GET BATCH)} = \text{PBA (GET BATCH)}_{tf} + \text{PBA (GET BATCH)}_{mf} \tag{12-8}$$

$$= \frac{\text{RPBR}}{\text{EBF}_{tf}} + \frac{\text{NR} \times \text{RPBR}}{\text{EBF}_{mf}(\text{RPBR} + 1)} + \text{RPBR} \qquad \text{sba}$$

12-2-2   Physical Sequential Update

Sequential file updating requires creation of a new master file. Consequently, the old master file must be read, any transaction file that exists must be read, and the new master file must be written. To perform this expensive set of operations for random updates would be prohibitive, and is severely restricted, for example, in IMS HSAM. Batch updates are the normal mode of operation for physical sequential files, and their access cost is simply computed as

$$\text{PBA (UPDATE BATCH)} = NBLK_{mf(old)} + NBLK_{tf} + NBLK_{mf(new)} \qquad \text{sba}$$

(12-9)

where

$$NBLK_{mf(new)} = \left\lceil \frac{NR + RPBI - RPBD}{EBF_{mf(old)}} \right\rceil,$$

RPBI is the total number of records to be inserted, and RPBD is the total number of records to be deleted in the batch. The physical sequential retrieval and update operations are summarized in Table 12-2.

If the writing of a new master file requires write verification, each of the

TABLE 12-2   Database Operation Cost [in Physical Block Accesses (PBAs)] for Physical Sequential Organizations*

Operation	*Ordered File†*		*Unordered File†*	
GET ALL	$\lceil NR/EBF \rceil$	sba	$\lceil NR/EBF \rceil$	sba
GET UNIQUE SEQUENTIAL (found)	$\dfrac{1 + NBLK}{2}$	sba	$\dfrac{1 + NBLK}{2}$	sba
SEQ′ (not found)	$\dfrac{1 + NBLK}{2}$	sba	$NBLK$	sba
BINARY (found)	$\log_2 \dfrac{NBLK}{2}$	rba	N/A	
BINARY′ (not found)	$\lfloor \log_2 NBLK \rfloor + 1$	rba	N/A	
DIRECT (found)	1	rba	N/A	
DIRECT′ (not found)	1	rba	N/A	
GET NEXT	$1/EBF$	sba	$1/EBF$	sba
GET PRIOR	$1/EBF$	sba	$1/EBF$	sba
GET SOME (boolean query)	Same as GET ALL		Same as GET ALL	
GET BATCH	$\left\lceil \dfrac{RPBR}{EBF_{tf}} \right\rceil + \dfrac{NR \times RPBR}{EBF_{mf}(RPBR + 1)}$ $+ RPBR$	sba	N/A	
UPDATE BATCH	$NBLK_{mf(old)} + NBLK_{tf}$ $+ \left\lceil \dfrac{NR + RPBI - RPBD}{EBF_{mf(old)}} \right\rceil$	sba	N/A	

* NR   Number of records in the file
  EBF   Effective blocking factor
  RPBR   Number of target records per batch retrieval
  RPBI   Number of target records per batch update (insertion)
  RPBD   Number of target records per batch update (deletion)
  NBLK   Number of blocks containing the file
    tf   Transaction file
   mf   Master file
  N/A   not applicable
† Expected number of block accesses.

$NBLK_{mf(new)}$ blocks must be reread immediately after being written. These extra reads are considered to be sequential block accesses because only rotational delays are incurred (i.e., a write is followed by a read on the same track). If CPU and other delays are significant between block write and reread, the sequential access model of Section 9-2 is used and PBA_s (write verify) $= NBLK_{mf(new)}$. Otherwise, if the other delays are negligible, the reread operation requires an integral number of disk rotations $k \times ROT$, where $k = \lceil BKS / BPT \rceil$, the number of tracks required to contain a block. Most systems do not allow block size to exceed track size, so $k = 1$ under normal conditions.

12-2-3   Trade-offs in Physical Sequential Organizations

The most common trade-offs to be considered in the design of physical database structures involve the proper choice of block size and selection of primary key for the ordering of the data. Each of these design problems is illustrated with examples.

Block Size

Sequential processing of sequentially stored data becomes more efficient when block size is larger because the number of physical accesses is fewer. As block size increases, however, there is more data to transfer per block. Fortunately, although each block requires more transfer time as block size increases, the number of blocks decreases and the savings in block access time can be quite dramatic.

Direct or random access to individual records can be most effectively accomplished with unblocked records because it minimizes the amount of unused data accessed. A trade-off exists when a physical sequential file or subfile is to be processed sequentially with probability P and accessed directly with probability $1 - P$. Given a file of NR records with LF = 1 and BOVHD = 0, we see that EBF = BF, and the number of block accesses to sequentially process the file is precisely the number of blocks in the file:

$$PBA = NBLK = \left\lceil \frac{NR}{EBF} \right\rceil \quad sba \qquad (12\text{-}10)$$

The number of block accesses to directly access the file is exactly 1. Combining the two cases, weighted by their respective probability of occurrence, we obtain the expected number of block accesses:

$$PBA = P\left\lceil \frac{NR}{EBF} \right\rceil \quad sba + (1 - P) \quad rba \qquad (12\text{-}11)$$

The expected I/O service time is therefore

$$\text{TIO} = P \left\lceil \frac{\text{NR}}{\text{EBF}} \right\rceil \text{TSBA} + (1 - P)\text{TRBA} \tag{12-12}$$

Substituting Eqs. (9-16) and (9-24) into Eq. (12-12) for a shared disk (worst case) environment, we obtain

$$\text{TIO} = P \left\lceil \frac{\text{NR}}{\text{EBF}} \right\rceil \left[\text{SEEK(CPD)} + \frac{\text{ROT}}{2} + \frac{\text{BKS}}{\text{TR}} \right]$$
$$+ (1 - P) \left[\text{SEEK(CPD)} + \frac{\text{ROT}}{2} + \frac{\text{BKS}}{\text{TR}} \right] \tag{12-13}$$

Noting that BKS = EBF × SRS, we rewrite (12-13) as

$$\text{TIO} = P \left\lceil \frac{\text{NR}}{\text{EBF}} \right\rceil \times \left[\text{SEEK(CPD)} + \frac{\text{ROT}}{2} + \frac{\text{EBF} \times \text{SRS}}{\text{TR}} \right]$$
$$+ (1 - P) \left[\text{SEEK(CPD)} + \frac{\text{ROT}}{2} + \frac{\text{EBF} \times \text{SRS}}{\text{TR}} \right] \tag{12-14}$$

To find the value of EBF that minimizes I/O service time, we assume continuous approximation and drop the ceiling function of the block count. Then taking the derivative of TIO with respect to EBF and setting it to zero, we obtain

$$\text{TIO} = \frac{P \times \text{NR}[\text{ROT}/2 + \text{SEEK(CPD)}]}{\text{EBF}^2} + \frac{P \times \text{NR} \times \text{EBF} \times \text{SRS}}{\text{EBF} \times \text{TR}}$$
$$+ \text{SEEK(CPD)} + \text{ROT}/2 + \frac{\text{EBF} \times \text{SRS}}{\text{TR}} - P \times \text{SEEK(CPD)}$$
$$- P \times \text{ROT}/2 - P \times \text{EBF} \times \text{SRS}/\text{TR}$$

$$\tag{12-15}$$

$$\frac{d\ \text{TIO}}{d\ \text{EBF}} = \frac{-P \times \text{NR}[\text{ROT}/2 + \text{SEEK(CPD)}]}{\text{EBF}^2} + \frac{\text{SRS}}{\text{TR}} - \frac{P \times \text{SRS}}{\text{TR}} = 0$$

$$\frac{\text{SRS}(1 - P)}{\text{TR}} = \frac{P \times \text{NR}[\text{ROT}/2 + \text{SEEK(CPD)}]}{\text{EBF}^2}$$

$$\text{EBF} = \left[\frac{P \times \text{NR}[\text{ROT}/2 + \text{SEEK(CPD)}]\text{TR}}{\text{SRS}(1 - P)} \right]^{1/2}$$

The second derivative is positive, so we have a minimum if the feasible positive root EBF stays positive and finite. This does hold true for $0 < P < 1$. A fractional value for EBF can be resolved either up or down to the nearest integer by substituting the two candidate values back into Eq. (12-13) for TIO as a manual check on whether or not the function is minimized. For example, if we let $P = 10^{-4}$, NR $= 10^5$ records, SEEK(CPD) $= 25$ milliseconds, ROT $= 16.7$ milliseconds, TR $= 1198$ KBS, and SRS $= 100$ bytes, the resulting optimum blocking factor is

$$\text{EBF} = \left[\frac{10^{-4} \times 10^5 (8.35 + 25 \text{ ms}) \times 1198 \text{ bytes/ms}}{100 \text{ bytes} \times (1 - 10^{-4})} \right]^{\frac{1}{2}}$$

$$= 19.99$$

$$\simeq 20$$

The effective blocking factor is fairly high despite the extremely low proportion of sequential processing applications in this example. Because of the extremely large I/O service time to execute the sequential applications, it still is a dominating factor in overall performance. In general, a practical upper bound must be placed on blocking factors, such as track size or buffer size limitations. A graph of I/O service time is plotted for this problem in Fig. 12-2. From the graph we see that the total I/O service time flattens out for EBF > 10 and begins to rise slowly at EBF $= 20$; thus, a wide range of blocking factors will produce a near minimum total cost. The graph clearly points out the benefit of having at least some blocking factor implemented for sequential processing. Blocking also increases the utilization of disk tracks or magnetic tape by decreasing the block overhead, a positive function of the number of blocks.

Key Order Selection

Let us assume that our file has n candidate keys for initial ordering. Some keys may have unique values for every record and some may not. We wish to select that key for ordering that minimizes total I/O processing cost for all applications. Extra

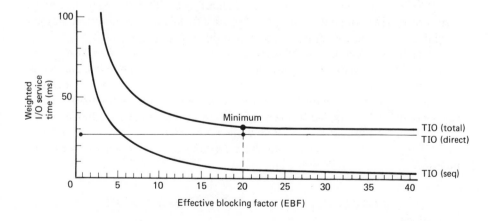

FIGURE 12-2   Weighted I/O service time for a sequential file.

costs will be incurred for resorting the file before certain applications can be completed or final reports printed. If there are n ways to order the file, the total I/O processing cost of ordering by key k is

$$\text{COST}(k) = f_k \times \text{CIO}_k + \sum_{\substack{j=1 \\ j \neq k}}^{n} f_j\, (\text{CIO}_j + \text{CSORT}_j) \qquad (12\text{-}16)$$

where f_k = fraction of time applications are run, using key k, thus requiring no sorting of records

CIO_k = I/O processing cost of applications using key k

f_j = fraction of time applications are run, using key $j \neq k$, thus requiring additional sorting time

CIO_j = I/O processing cost of applications using key $j \neq k$

CSORT_j = I/O processing cost of a sort on key j

We wish to find k that minimizes total I/O processing cost. Rewriting Eq. (12-16) to include $f_k \times \text{CIO}_k$ in the summation, we find that each cost has a constant term $\sum_{j=1}^{n} f_j \times \text{CIO}_j$:

$$\text{COST}(k) = \sum_{j=1}^{n} f_j \times \text{CIO}_j + \sum_{\substack{j=1 \\ j \neq k}}^{n} f_j \times \text{CSORT}_j \qquad (12\text{-}17)$$

Therefore, the total cost is minimized by the key k that minimizes the sum $\sum_{j=1,\ j\neq k}^{n}$ $f_j \times \text{CSORT}_j$, or more simply, the key k that maximizes $f_k \times \text{CSORT}_k$. If sorting time is constant, total cost is minimized by ordering by key k whose fraction of applications f_k is the largest. The analysis is greatly simplified in this last case, and it is interesting to note that only frequency of execution of applications is important, not the cost of executing them.

The trade-off, if any, comes from the product $f_k \times \text{SORT}_k$ to be maximized when sorting time varies with initial file order. The most frequently used key order may not minimize cost if the cost of sorting to obtain that order is low.

Note that we assumed that I/O processing cost for each type of application had equal weight with every other application, which simplified our problem considerably. In practice, the true "cost" may be more complicated. For example, a certain application may have to be run in a certain amount of time (i.e., a deadline) or else a heavy penalty will be imposed. A penalty factor could be introduced into the model, Eq. (12-17), by a weight WT_j to be multiplied times SORT_j. If the sum of $\text{CIO}_j +$ CSORT_j is greater than the time at which the deadline occurs, the penalty cost will be imposed.

$$\text{COST}(k) = \sum_{j=1}^{n} f_j \times \text{CIO}_j + \sum_{\substack{j=1 \\ j \neq k}}^{n} f_j \times \text{CSORT}_j \times \text{WT}_j \qquad (12\text{-}18)$$

where
$$WT_j = \begin{cases} 1 & \text{if } CIO_j + CSORT_j < \text{deadline time} \\ \text{penalty cost} & \text{otherwise} \end{cases}$$

The cost of an m-way merge sort on randomly ordered records has been investigated in depth by Knuth [1973]. The total sort consists of an initial sort phase and X_{min} merge phases, where X_{min} is the minimum value of X that satisfies the inequality $m^X \geq$ NBLK, where NBLK blocks hold all the data in the file. If each phase or pass requires a read and write of each block in the file, the total physical block accesses for all phases is

$$PBA(SORT) = 2 \times NBLK(1 + X_{min}) \qquad (12\text{-}19)$$

12-3   LINKED SEQUENTIAL PROCESSING

12-3-1   Linked Sequential Retrieval

Sequential processing is often performed on nonphysical sequential (noncontiguous) data. Linked data allow dynamic storage allocation to be performed when many processes are contending for storage space or when the data are highly volatile. A logical representation of the linked sequential organization is given in Fig. 12-3.

The main difference between linked sequential and physical sequential organizations is the use of pointers instead of contiguous storage. This has the effect of disallowing the binary search option because the data are no longer densely packed and midpoint addresses cannot be computed.

Each record in the linked list is potentially located in a different block from its predecessor record. The probability that they are in the same block, given random placement, is $(EBF - 1)/(NR - 1)$, where $EBF - 1$ represents the number of other records in the current block and $NR - 1$ represents the total number of other records in the file. In a multiple-record-type database this probability is much more complex. We assume, for now, that the probability of being in the same block is negligible and specify each record access in a linked list to be a random block access. For sequential access to all the records in the file,

$$PBA(GET\ ALL) = NR \qquad rba \qquad (12\text{-}20)$$

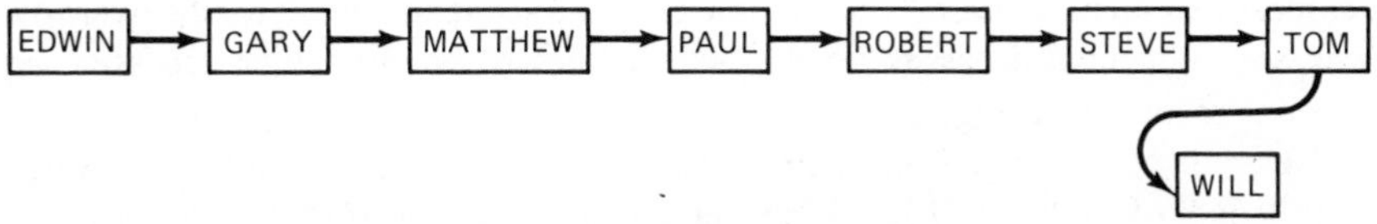

FIGURE 12-3   Linked sequential organization.

Batch processing of RPBR records requires

$$\text{PBA(GET BATCH)} = \frac{\text{RPBR} \times \text{NR}}{\text{RPBR} + 1} \quad \text{rba} + \left\lceil \frac{\text{RPBR}}{\text{EBF}_{tf}} \right\rceil \quad \text{sba} \qquad (12\text{-}21)$$

assuming that the transaction file is physical sequential. Retrieval of a random record is given by the expected block accesses:

$$\text{PBA(GET UNIQUE)} = \frac{1 + \text{NR}}{2} \quad \text{rba} \qquad (12\text{-}22)$$

when the file is ordered, and whether the target record exists or not. When the file is unordered and the target record exists, the expected block accesses is given by Eq. (8-22). If the record does not exist, we have

$$\text{PBA(GET UNIQUE}') = \text{NR} \quad \text{rba} \qquad (12\text{-}23)$$

12-3-2   Linked Sequential Update

Update operations for linked lists have been studied in great detail for random-access storage and secondary storage. The simple model we have looked at is quite useful for summarizing these concepts. Here we assume the list to be ordered; unordered lists are discussed in Section 12-3-3.

Record insertion for a linked list is done after a successful search has found the record that succeeds the record to be inserted. Expected search cost for that record is $(1 + \text{NR})/2$ random block accesses. If there is no room for an insertion in the same block as the successor record, several options are available. First, a new (empty) block can be allocated for the new record; this necessitates a single random write for the new block and a sequential block rewrite for the predecessor record. Second, an overflow block may already be designated; this produces a random block read and sequential rewrite for the overflow block plus a sequential rewrite for the predecessor record. Third, the first block can be split into two blocks; this requires two block writes: one random write for the new block and one sequential rewrite for the old block. For these three options a maximum of three block accesses is required for insertion into this ordered list after the search operation has been completed.

A two-way linked list requires the blocks containing the newly inserted record, its successor (NEXT), and predecessor (PRIOR) records to be rewritten. This results in at most four block accesses: one random read and sequential write for the overflow block and sequential accesses for the two rewrites of blocks for predecessor and successor records (see Fig. 12-4).

Deletion of a record from a linked sequential organization takes an average search length of $(\text{NR} + 1)/2$ blocks to find the target record. If the delete operation consists of flagging the record, only a single rewrite is necessary for the block

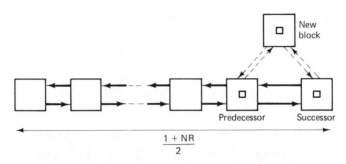

FIGURE 12-4 Insertion into a two-way linked block list.

containing the deleted record. If the delete operation consists of resetting the next pointer of the previous record, only that block must be rewritten after the pointer change is made.

A two-way linked list delete operation requires an additional random block read and sequential rewrite for the successor block to modify its prior pointer. Any block immediately written after reading (and some CPU processing) is considered to be sequentially accessed. All other accesses are considered to be random.

A record modification (change) causes a single rewrite of the block containing that record after it is accessed. Write verification, if required, causes a reread of any block just written, and it is considered to be a sequential block access.

In summary, the conditions that must be evaluated for linked sequential update are:

- One-way or two-way linkage.
- Type of operation: insertion, deletion, change.
- Ordered or unordered list.
- Is free space allocated in blocks to allow easy insertion?
- How is overflow handled for insertions?
- Is write verification required?
- Is deletion handled by setting a flag or resetting pointers?

Example 12-1: A linked sequential file with 100 records is ordered by a primary key (ascending). It is two-way linked, and any insertion requires block splitting and write verification. What is the expected number of random and sequential block accesses for an insertion operation, a deletion operation, and a change to a record? Compare these costs to the initial cost to locate the target record.

PBA_1 = expected block accesses to find the next higher (successor) record, based on key value

$$= \frac{100 + 1}{2} = 50.5 \text{ rba}$$

Assuming that enough buffer space is allocated to keep the predecessor block in main storage, no further block reads are needed to reset pointers in the predecessor and successor records. After block splitting, the two blocks are written back to secondary storage.

$PBA_2 =$ block accesses for rewrite after insertion

$= 1$ rba $+ 1$ sba

$PBA_3 =$ block accesses for write verification after insertion

$= 2$ sba

Therefore, the expected total number of block accesses for insertion is

$$PBA(INSERT) = PBA_2 + PBA_3 = 1 \text{ rba} + 3 \text{ sba}$$

Assuming that deletion is accomplished by pointer modification, we have

$PBA_4 =$ block accesses for deletion after record is located

$= 1$ rba $+ 2$ sba

to rewrite the block containing the predecessor record plus a random read and sequential rewrite for the block containing the successor record whose pointer must be reset. If $PBA_5 = 2$ sba for write verification after deletion, we have the total delete cost

$$PBA(DELETE) = PBA_4 + PBA_5 = 1 \text{ rba} + 4 \text{ sba}$$

The record change results in a single rewrite of the block changed plus a sequential reread for write verification:

$$PBA(CHANGE) = 2 \text{ sba}$$

Obviously, the search cost is dominant, but of course is dependent on the size of the file. The cost for updates, after search is completed, is independent of file size.

12-3-3   Trade-offs in Linked Sequential Organizations

Two types of trade-off problems are discussed in this section: pointer options for linked organizations and the effect of loading factor on avoidance of overflow. Each problem involves a time–space trade-off and a retrieval–update trade-off.

Pointer options

One-way and two-way linked lists were discussed in Section 12-3-2 with regard to updates. We can identify the differences between these two options if we can specify the individual cost, in block accesses, for each type of retrieval and update operation. Furthermore, storage space can be compared. These costs are summarized in Table 12-3. The table shows that the one-way linkage has better performance for insertions and requires less storage space, but the two-way linkage is significantly better for the GET PRIOR record operation, which is useful in deletions and backward searching. The delete operation that requires a pointer change is done efficiently with a one-way linkage if the predecessor record is available in the buffer, where it was placed during the search phase. If it is not in the buffer, the search must be completely restarted.

Most file operations for unordered lists have the relationships shown in Table 12-3, except for GET UNIQUE (record not found) and INSERT (new block needed). These costs are shown in Table 12-4. The first case when a record is not found, the unordered list search, takes longer (i.e., it must proceed through the entire list). In the second case insertion is easier for an unordered list because it may be done at the head of the list. Thus, search time for an insertion is minimal and predecessor pointer resetting is not necessary. On the other hand, an ordered list is needed if batch processing is desired.

Another important pointer option in many systems is the parent pointer, which allows direct access of a parent record of the current record just accessed. In CODASYL, for example, this is known as the OWNER pointer and it is accessed via the GET OWNER command. IMS has options for either symbolic or direct parent

TABLE 12-3   File Operation Cost in PBAs and Storage Cost in Bytes for
Ordered Linked Organizations (without Write Verification) *

Operation	One-Way Linked		Two-Way Linked	
GET ALL	NR	rba	NR	rba
GET UNIQUE (found or not)	$(1 + NR)/2$	rba	$(1 + NR)/2$	rba
GET NEXT	1	rba	1	rba
GET PRIOR	Max. $= NR/2$	rba	Max. $= 1$	rba
GET SOME	NR	rba	NR	rba
GET BATCH	$\dfrac{RPBR \times NR}{RPBR + 1}$ rba $+ \left\lceil \dfrac{RPBR}{EBF_{tf}} \right\rceil$ sba		Same as one-way	
UPDATE BATCH	Batch retrieval cost $+$ RPBI(indiv. insert cost) $+$ RPBD(indiv. delete cost) $+$ RPBC(indiv. change cost)		Same format as one-way	
Updates after search is completed				
CHANGE nonkey item	1	sba	1	sba
INSERT (same block)	1	sba	1	sba
INSERT (new block needed)	Max. $= 1$ rba $+ 2$ sba		1 rba $+ 1$ sba	
DELETE (set flag)	1	sba	1	sba
DELETE (change pointers)	Min. $= 1$ sba, max. $= NR/2$ rba $+ 1$ sba		1 rba $+ 2$ sba	
Storage space per stored record	RS $+$ ROVHD $+$ PS bytes		RS $+$ ROVHD $+ 2$ $\times$ PS bytes	

* NR   Number of records in the list (file)
  RS   Logical record size (bytes)
ROVHD   Stored record overhead (bytes)
  PS   Pointer size (bytes)

TABLE 12-4   Database Operation Cost (PBA) for Unordered Linked
Organizations That Differ from Ordered Linked Organizations

Operation	One-Way Linked	Two-Way Linked
GET UNIQUE' (not found)	NR rba	NR rba
INSERT (new block needed)	Search is 1 rba Max.: 1 rba + 1 sba	Search is 1 rba Max.: 1 rba + 1 sba

pointers (see Section 9-1). Parent pointers take advantage of the many database applications that search "upward" from a child record occurrence to its unique parent record occurrence of a specified record type. These operations are common to hierarchical and network databases in particular. Relational databases do not model the parent–child relationships in the same manner. It could be implemented within a single relation or across separate relations. Traversal across relations could be done with a combination of JOIN, SELECTION, and PROJECTION commands in a relational algebralike language; traversal within a relation can be done with a combination of SELECTION and PROJECTION commands.

As is true with other pointer options, the faster access to certain (in this case, parent) records is obtained at the price of additional pointer storage space in each child record occurrence of that record type. Fortunately, neither the other retrieval operations nor the update operations are seriously affected by the use of the parent pointer. The added pointer space contributes to a slightly larger transport volume, but neither CHANGE nor DELETE operations cause additional block accesses to maintain parent pointers. For the INSERT of a new child record occurrence, the parent record must be located to set the child's parent pointer to the proper address. If the child's position was located via the parent, the parent record is usually still "current," so its location is saved. If, on the other hand, the child's position was located via a direct entry point to its predecessor records, the parent may have to be found via an additional GET UNIQUE retrieval operation. Update software should be written to avoid this double retrieval if possible.

Loading Factor

Variations of sequential file organizations, such as indexed sequential, can avoid costly overflow operations if sufficient free space is initially allocated to blocks to allow for projected database growth. Physical sequential files can avoid the overflow problem by batching updates periodically and rewriting the entire file once per batch. Linked sequential organizations do not experience a heavy degradation of performance due to overflow. This can be seen by observing the difference in block accesses between INSERT (same block) and INSERT (new block needed) in Tables 12-3 and 12-4. The worst degradation for unordered lists is one extra random block access per insertion. For ordered lists the worst case is one random and two sequential block accesses extra. Search cost is the same for all combinations of order and linkage, assuming that the target record exists.

Extra block accesses can be reduced by allowing free space in the blocks at initial load, and thus we have a time–space trade-off. For a given loading factor LF the storage space required is computed by

$$\text{BLKSTOR} = \text{BKS} \times \text{NBLK} \qquad (9\text{-}39)$$

$$\text{NBLK} = \left\lceil \frac{\text{NR}}{\text{EBF}} \right\rceil \qquad (9\text{-}38)$$

where EBF is the effective blocking factor as computed in Eq. (9-36). As LF decreases, EBF decreases and NBLK increases; that is, more physical blocks are required to hold the database when free space increases. This increase in storage space must be evaluated against the decrease in block accesses for insertions we have gained. The exact relationship between loading factor and expected overflow cost is very complex; it depends on the distribution of insertion key values and the number of insertions made. See Section 13-2-2 for a detailed analysis.

12-3-4   Storage Space for Sequential Organizations

Storage space is estimated for physical sequential and linked sequential using the same expression. In both cases it is a function of stored record size, SRS. Stored record size could vary considerably among sequential organization options such as physical sequential, linked one-way, linked two-way, and so on. Derivation of the storage space requirement was shown in Chapter 9. We apply that basic approach to each access method in terms of physical block storage. Other storage unit computations, such as number of tracks and cylinders, are illustrated in Section 9-3.

$$\text{BLKSTOR} = \text{NBLK} \times \text{BKS} \qquad (9\text{-}38,\ 9\text{-}39)$$

$$= \lceil \text{NR}/\text{EBF} \rceil \times \text{BKS}$$

$$= \left\lceil \frac{\text{NR}}{\left\lfloor \dfrac{(\text{BKS} - \text{BOVHD}) \times \text{LF}}{\text{SRS}} \right\rfloor} \right\rceil \times \text{BKS} \qquad \text{bytes}$$

where

$$\text{SRS} = \begin{cases} \text{RS} + \text{ROVHD bytes} & \text{for physical sequential} \\ \text{RS} + \text{ROVHD} + \text{PS bytes} & \text{for one-way linked sequential} \\ \text{RS} + \text{ROVHD} + 2 \times \text{PS bytes} & \text{for two-way linked sequential} \end{cases}$$

12-4   REPORT GENERATION: TOTAL COST

Report generation is a special case of retrieval (GET ALL) where the output is to be structured in a manner often unlike the original schema. The basic operations of retrieval, restructuring, sorting, and display of results are sequenced as shown in Fig.

12-5. The retrieval and report writing operations are obligatory and the restructuring and sorting operations are optional, depending on the source schema structure and target report schema structure.

Example 12-2: Consider the CODASYL-like schema in Fig. 12-6(a) for a database consisting of instructors, classes, and students. Suppose that the following report is required:

1. LIST ALL STUDENTS IN ALPHABETICAL ORDER.
2. FOR EACH STUDENT, LIST ALL CLASSES AND INSTRUCTOR FOR EACH CLASS.

The report schema desired is shown in Fig. 12-6(b). In order to produce the report schema from the database schema, all three record types must be retrieved. The original schema must be restructured to correspond to the report format, student records must be sorted by full name, and the final report must be displayed. Each step requires detailed analysis to obtain CPU and I/O service times.

Let us now develop some expressions for I/O service times (as usual) for this problem. CPU time is discussed in Section 16-4.

Retrieval. This is a simple case of sequential access, similar to what we have studied throughout this chapter. Let us assume that there are 2500 instructors, 5000 classes, and 35,000 students. Let us further assume that each class has an average of 35 students and that each student enrolls in an average of 5 classes. Therefore, we have a total of $5 \times 35,000 = 35 \times 5000 = 175,000$ student contact units for all of the classes. At the schema level we have

$$LRA(GET\ ALL) = 2500I + 5000C + 175,000S = 182,500 \qquad (12\text{-}24)$$

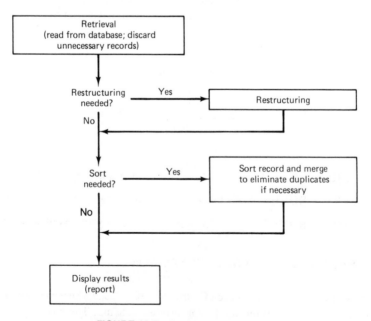

FIGURE 12-5   Report generation process.

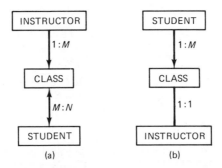

FIGURE 12-6 Database schemata for report generation application: (*a*) database schema; (*b*) report schema.

where I = instructor, C = class, and S = student. At the physical level the I/O service time is also a function of effective blocking factor:

$$\text{PBA(GET ALL)} = \left\lceil \frac{2500}{\text{EBF}(I)} \right\rceil + \left\lceil \frac{5000}{\text{EBF}(C)} \right\rceil + \left\lceil \frac{175{,}000}{\text{EBF}(S)} \right\rceil \quad \text{sba} \qquad (12\text{-}25)$$

We have also assumed here, for simplicity, that the data have been stored in hierarchical physical sequential order. This is an ideal case, whereas random block accesses are often required in real problems. If we let $\text{EBF}(I) = 20$, $\text{EBF}(C) = 50$, and $\text{EBF}(S) = 10$, Eq. (12-25) becomes

$$\begin{aligned}
\text{PBA(GET)ALL} &= \left\lceil \frac{2500}{20} \right\rceil + \left\lceil \frac{5000}{50} \right\rceil + \left\lceil \frac{175{,}000}{10} \right\rceil \\
&= 125 + 100 + 17{,}500 \\
&= 17{,}725 \text{ sba}
\end{aligned}$$

Restructuring and sorting. These operations are closely related in the sense that a report generation algorithm considers both restructuring and sorting simultaneously. In our example, for instance, there are many alternative approaches to the transformation from source schema to target report schema, three of which are described here.

1. Each STUDENT record retrieved is to be inserted physically sequential into a new area, removing duplicate records, and maintaining the new order required for the final report. Assume that the new records contain combined information on students, classes, and instructors; this new record type we designate as S'. Because $S' > S$, let us assume an $\text{EBF}(S') = 7$. Note that this approach combines restructuring and sorting as a single operation from the viewpoint of I/O service.

The local operations required for the restructuring and sorting are 175,000 passes through a sorted file whose average length is 35,000/2 records. We see that 20% of the passes result in a new insertion and shifting of the remaining records, and 80% of the passes (duplicate STUDENT records) require only an insertion of new class and instructor data. Thus, we have

$$\begin{aligned}
\text{LRA(RESTR/SORT)} &= 0.2 \times 175{,}000(35{,}000/2) + 0.8 \\
&\quad \times 175{,}000(35{,}000/4) \\
&= 1837.5 \times 10^6
\end{aligned}$$

$$\text{PBA(RESTR/SORT)} = \left\lceil \frac{\text{LRA}}{\text{EBF}(S')} \right\rceil = \left\lceil \frac{1837.5 \times 10^6}{7} \right\rceil = 262.5 \times 10^6 \text{ sba}$$

2. Each STUDENT record retrieval is to be inserted physically sequential into a new area, removing duplicate records but maintaining no particular order. A sort is then required for the 35,000 STUDENT records placed in the area.

$$\begin{aligned} \text{LRA(RESTR ONLY)} &= 0.2 \times 175{,}000(35{,}000/4) + 0.8 \\ &\quad \times 175{,}000(35{,}000/4) \, S' \\ &= 1531.4 \times 10^6 \, S' \end{aligned}$$

$$\text{PBA(RESTR ONLY)} = 1531.4 \times 10^6/7 = 218.75 \times 10^6 \text{ sba}$$

From Eq. (12-19) we obtain an estimate of physical block accesses for the sorting of 35,000 records (5000 blocks). Let us assume a 6-way ($m = 6$) merge sort is possible.

$$m^x \geqslant \text{NBLK} = 5000$$

$$X_{min} = \lceil \log_6 5000 \rceil = 5$$

$$\begin{aligned} \text{PBA(SORT)} &= 2 \times \text{NBLK}(1 + X_{min}) \\ &= 2 \times 5000 \times 6 \\ &= 60{,}000 \text{ sba} \end{aligned}$$

$$\begin{aligned} \text{PBA(RESTR/SORT)} &= \text{PBA(RESTR ONLY)} + \text{PBA(SORT)} \\ &= 218.81 \times 10^6 \text{ sba} \end{aligned}$$

Thus, for this case, the sorting cost is dominated by the restructuring cost. The total cost is less than the cost for case 1.

3. Each STUDENT record retrieved is to be inserted physically sequential into a new area in the same order retrieved, including duplicates. A sort on the 175,000 records is then performed.

$$\text{LRA(RESTR ONLY)} = 175{,}000S'$$

$$\text{PBA(RESTR ONLY)} = \left\lceil \frac{175{,}000}{7} \right\rceil = 25{,}000 \text{ sba}$$

For the sort phase, we have

$$m^x \geqslant \text{NBLK} = 25{,}000$$

$$X_{min} = \lceil \log_6 25000 \rceil = 6$$

$$\begin{aligned} \text{PBA(SORT)} &= 2 \times \text{NBLK} \times (1 + X_{min}) \\ &= 2 \times 25{,}000 \times 7 \\ &= 350{,}000 \text{ sba} \end{aligned}$$

$$\begin{aligned} \text{PBA(RESTR/SORT)} &= \text{PBA(RESTR ONLY)} + \text{PBA(SORT)} \\ &= 25{,}000 \text{ sba} + 350{,}000 \text{ sba} \\ &= 375{,}000 \text{ sba} \end{aligned}$$

This is by far the most efficient method and is the one that we assume will be used.

Display of results. Assuming that S' records are ready for retrieval, it is a simple matter to produce the report format:

$$\text{LRA(DISPLAY)} = 35{,}000S'$$

$$\text{PBA(DISPLAY)} = \left\lceil \frac{35{,}000}{7} \right\rceil = 5000 \text{ sba}$$

The total cost in physical block accesses is summarized in Table 12-5. It shows that in this example, and potentially in other cases, the initial retrieval cost is

TABLE 12-5   Report Generation Cost (Example 12-2)

	LRA	PBA
Retrieval	$25000I + 5000C + 175,000S$	17,725 sba
Restructuring	$175,000S'$	25,000 sba
Sort	$7 \times 350,000S'$	350,000 sba
Display of results	$35,000S'$	5,000 sba
Total	2.8425×10^6	397,725 sba

a small portion of total cost for a formal report. Expressions for variations in retrieval, sorting, and display of results are well known and are explained earlier in this chapter. General expressions for restructuring operations are not well known, although active development is under way [Chen et al., 1979; Navathe and Fry, 1976; Swartwout et al., 1977a]. However, most restructuring operations can easily be expressed as a sequence of database retrievals and updates, and thus the restructuring cost can be taken as the sum of the cost of the individual lower-level operations.

13 PRIMARY ACCESS METHODS: RANDOM PROCESSING

The term *random processing* refers to combinations of database organization and target record selection by user applications that result in a random target record physical location with respect to the immediately preceding target record location. In one instance the data may be organized (initially loaded) in an arbitrary fashion so that they have no recognizable order. Thus, a sequence of GET NEXT commands, based on key order, results in a series of random accesses to data. In another instance the data may be ordered, even physical sequential, but the sequence of retrieval commands specify randomly located target records, as in simple ad hoc queries. The term "GET UNIQUE" implies that the retrieval command refers to (at most) a single target record. If a small set of physically contiguous records is specified, the search can be partitioned into a GET UNIQUE command for the first record and a GET ALL command for the remaining records in the set.

The random access to records stored in physical sequential order may be accomplished with a sequential search or binary search, as shown in Chapter 12. In this chapter we consider a number of alternative approaches. We shall see that no single approach is optimum for all types of database applications, even when restricted to random access operations, because of different emphasis on retrieval, update, and storage space efficiency.

13-1 DIRECT ACCESS

The sequential search of a database for a single record represents one extreme among search mechanisms. Direct access represents the other extreme. If the database designer can allocate a separate record storage location for every possible unique primary key value, then a simple key-to-address transformation function can be devised to store and retrieve each record in exactly one random block access. This can be accomplished by assigning a relative block number (a relative physical address) for each set of key values of records residing in a physical block. The data are actually stored in key order and the relative block numbers are implicitly assigned to the stored data in sequential order.

Figure 13-1 illustrates a simple case where a company has 30 departments, numbered in consecutive order from 1 to 30. Department records are stored five to a block, so that six blocks are required. The key-to-address (KTA) transformation function is

$$\text{relative block address } = \left\lceil \frac{\text{DEPT\#}}{5} \right\rceil \qquad (13\text{-}1)$$

For example, the record for Department 12 is located in relative block 3. This absolute correspondence between key and relative block address is the main characteristic of the direct access method. Thus, it is most appropriate when the keys can be controlled in a way that wasted space is kept to a minimum. In this example, storage utilization is 100%.

Consecutive key values are not always possible for real data, and often a more complex transformation function is required. For example, suppose that products being manufactured by a company are numbered PB2000 to PB2999 and QN500 to QN1499 for their 2000 products. Direct addresses can be efficiently generated according to the following rules:

1. If the first two characters are PB, subtract 1999 from the numeric value.
2. If the first two characters are QN, add 501 to the numeric value.

We now have addresses ranging from 1 to 2000 in a one-to-one correspondence with product numbers. This is illustrated in Fig. 13-2.

So far, we have seen that direct access can be extremely efficient in retrieval time and storage space under the right conditions. All retrieval requires 1 rba (random block access), while storage space is dependent on all possible transformed values of keys. Minimal CPU processing time is used to make each KTA transformation, and update operations are simple because there are no access path restrictions (see Table 13-1).

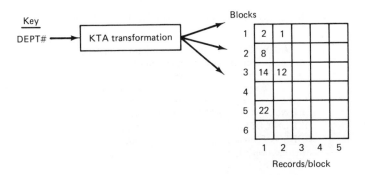

FIGURE 13-1   Direct access storage and retrieval for DEPT records.

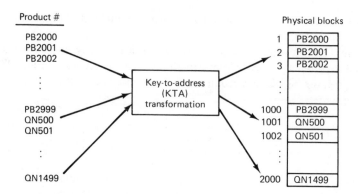

FIGURE 13-2 Direct access transformation of noncontiguous key values.

If all applications had easily controllable key values, this access method would be much more prevalent than it is today. However, lack of key controllability is a common problem in most corporate databases. As an example, suppose that a company with 100,000 employees uses social security number (SSN) as the primary key for employee records. There are no obvious subsets of the 10^9 possible key values that can be eliminated; storage space cannot be reduced. Consequently, only one record location out of 10^4 will be used, a gross inefficiency in storage space.

Using employee full name as the key has similar drawbacks. If 20 characters are allocated to names, 26^{20} key values are possible. Of course, we know that most combinations of characters are unusable, but no one wants to assume the responsibility for choosing and discarding unusable names. Furthermore, duplicate names are inevitable, making it impossible to maintain the uniqueness of the block addresses generated by the transformation.

Storage space

$$\text{BLKSTOR} = \left\lceil \frac{\text{number of key values}}{\text{EBF}} \right\rceil \times \text{BKS} \qquad \text{bytes} \qquad (13\text{-}2)$$

where each key value denotes one record position or slot to be allocated.

TABLE 13-1 Database Operation Cost (PBA)
for the Direct Access Method

Operation	Direct Access
GET ALL, NEXT, PRIOR	N/A
GET UNIQUE(found or not)	1 rba
GET SOME(Boolean query)	N/A
After the search is completed:	
CHANGE	1 sba
INSERT	1 sba
DELETE	1 sba

Addressing

Before leaving our discussion of direct access, let us clarify the meaning of addresses implied here. The primary key value used as input to the KTA transformation function can be considered to be a symbolic address. The output of the KTA transformation is a relative physical address which must be again transformed into an absolute physical address (DEVICE#, CYLINDER#, TRACK#, etc.) by the operating system (see Fig. 13-3). Separation of these transformations enhances physical data independence so that physical movement of data does not affect the DBMS addressing software. Stored addresses, such as direct pointers, often consist of relative block (or page) numbers instead of absolute physical addresses. Symbolic pointers are considered to be even another level higher than direct pointers, although both types of pointers may appear explicitly in stored records.

In summary, the important considerations in the design of a direct access file are:

- *Type of work load.* Random retrieval (GET UNIQUE) and update; physical sequential retrieval.
- *Key-to-address transformation function.* Affects CPU processing time.
- *Number of possible key values.* Determines the size of the database.
- *Level of data addressing used.* Affects CPU processing overhead and data independence.

13-2   IDENTIFIER HASHING (RANDOM ACCESS)

Identifier hashing is a widely used access method for fast random retrieval and update of records. We have already seen that the direct access method is highly dependent upon the controllability of key values, and it often requires an unwieldy amount of overhead in storage-space cost. Identifier hashing provides efficient retrieval and

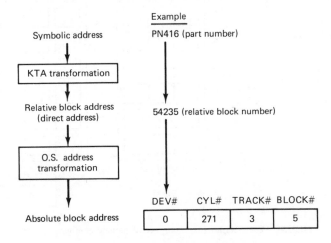

FIGURE 13-3   Levels of data addressing.

update for individual records accessed on the basis of primary key value. The cost of this advantage is the loss of file order and the potential for batch processing or report generation based on primary key ordering. Note that secondary key hashing is also a valid technique and is implied as relevant to the following discussion.

We begin the discussion on identifier hashing by establishing a basic terminology. An *identifier* is an attribute that uniquely defines each occurrence of some real-world entity. In the context of a database or file, an identifier is an item type that uniquely identifies occurrences of a particular record type (i.e., a primary key). *Identifier hashing*, or simply *hashing*, is an access method that directly addresses data by transforming a key value into a relative or absolute physical address. The key transformation is often called a *hashing function*. The alternative term for hashing, *random access*, properly indicates that a class of randomizing functions is used to transform a possibly nonuniform of key values into a uniform set of physical addresses. The direct access method takes a set of key values of size KS bytes on a vocabulary of size V and requires a separate physical address for each of the V^{KS} possible key values [Severance, 1974]. If only NR distinct key values are actually used in the database, the identifier density is NR/V^{KS}. Hashing is a method that attempts to map a large set of V^{KS} values fairly uniformly into a smaller, more manageable set of $O(NR)$ physical addresses. The mapping for direct access is 1:1, but for hashing it is m:1. Furthermore, because of the nature of randomization functions, two or more keys may transform to the same physical address, called the *home address*. If this occurs, those keys are referred to as *synonyms*, and the transformation to an already occupied home address results in a *collision*. The direct access method avoids synonyms and collisions at the cost of enormous storage overhead. Once a collision occurs during database load, or insertion after initial load, the hashing access method must resolve where to store the new record containing the synonym key.

Figure 13-4 illustrates a common way to implement a hashing organization. The

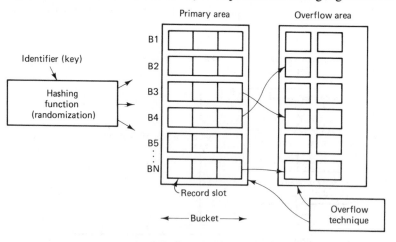

FIGURE 13-4   Hashing (random) access method configuration.

addressing space that can be directly accessed by a hashing function is partitioned into fixed-size areas called *buckets*. A bucket can be a cylinder, track, block, page—whatever unit can be conveniently addressed as a whole. A bucket, in turn, may consist of smaller physical units of data, such as a track, block (or page), or stored record. The smallest subunit of a bucket used in performance analysis is the (stored) *record slot* or *cell*.

Resolution of synonym collisions involves two steps. First, the bucket is scanned to see if room is available beyond the first record slot for the new record. If there is room, no further scanning is required. If the bucket is filled, the second step must be taken, the handling of overflow. Let us define the area containing the buckets as the *primary area* and the rest of available storage as the *overflow area*. An *overflow handling technique* is now invoked to store the new record efficiently. The evaluation of overflow handling techniques is one of the major concerns of this section.

Before we investigate the hashing access method in detail, let us note the major factors involved in its design:

- *Type of work load.* Random retrieval and update only.
- *Key value distribution.* Affects distribution of home addresses and number of synonyms.
- *Hashing (randomization) function.* Affects distribution of home addresses and number of synonyms.
- *Initial loading order.* Affects overall performance if open overflow method is used; does not affect chained overflow performance.
- *Address space (number of buckets).* Affects the number of synonyms; also may change the addresses for keys, requiring modification of the hashing function.
- *Bucket size (number of record slots).* Allows flexibility of handling collisions without necessarily using the overflow area; similar to the use of a loading factor.
- *Loading factor.* Controls probability of overflow.
- *Overflow handling technique.* Affects I/O service time for load, retrieval, and update operations.

Each of these factors is considered in the following analysis.

13-2-1   Hashing Functions

An identifier transformation or hashing function performs best when it maps NR key values exactly into NR home addresses without synonyms. There are NR! ways to accomplish this ideal assignment, but considering the NR^{NR} total possible ways of assigning NR keys to NR home addresses, the random probability of an ideal assignment is minuscule. Practical experience leads us to concentrate on the development of hashing functions that perform reasonably well, randomizing the key values over the entire address space.

A considerable amount of research has been conducted on the construction of efficient hashing functions [Knuth, 1973; Severance, 1974; Severance and Duhne, 1976]. Efficiency can be measured by the CPU time to compute the transformation and by the I/O service time to access the bucket. In general, the CPU time is insignificant compared to the I/O time required to access the data, and we emphasize the fact that the ability of a hashing function to randomize the key values over the entire address space is the more important aspect. If it fails to accomplish this, there will be many synonyms (collisions) and degradation in performance due to overflow area searching. Fortunately, one of the simpler transformation functions has proved to have excellent performance. Lum et al. [1971] studied the more common hashing functions and found that no one transformation method was always "best" in terms of randomization because the distribution of key values, or identifiers, greatly affected the home address distribution. However, the division hashing method and its variations performed consistently well, and because of their simplicity, were recommended as the best methods for general use. We illustrate the concept of division hashing with some simple examples.

Example 13-1:   Given key values 36, 26, 12, 5, 95 and an address space of 10 buckets, design a hashing function that does not produce collisions (see Fig. 13-5). If we number the buckets 1 through 10 and use the simple division hashing function, $f = $ Identifier(mod 10) + 1, we see that 36 and 26 are synonyms; both map to bucket 7. Also, 5 and 95 are synonyms, mapping to bucket 6. The loading of

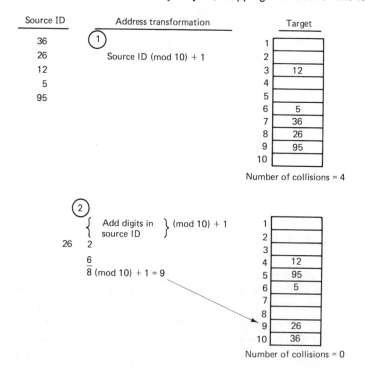

FIGURE 13-5   Simple division hashing function.

these five keys produces at least two collisions. However, if we change the identifier transformation function to sum-of-digits(mod 10) + 1, we obtain key value (home address) pairs as follows: 36(10), 26(9), 12(4), 5(6), and 95(5). This approach is a combination of folding (adding the digits) and division hashing. We see that each key in this case is mapped to a unique address and there are no collisions. Although this function may fail for certain key sequences such as 36, 72, 27, 54, 63, it does have a good randomizing effect for large key value sets.

Note that in this example the physical addresses are relative block addresses. It is sometimes preferred to compute absolute addresses directly, particularly when the hashing is performed by low-level O.S. routines.

Example 13-2:   Derive a hashing function that maps social security numbers (SSN) into specific disk track addresses. Assume that 32 IBM 3350 disks are available and distribute the SSNs uniformly across the devices.

First, we note that SSNs have the form xxx-xx-xxxx, so that 10^9 values are theoretically possible. Let us assume that currently only 0.2×10^9 numbers have been issued. The secondary storage available can be described in terms of 32 devices, $32 \times 555 = 17,760$ cylinders, or $32 \times 555 \times 30 = 532,800$ tracks. The maximum storage allowed is 10.14×10^9 bytes for 3350 disks, so approximately 50 bytes can be allocated for each of the 0.2×10^9 entries.

The algorithm we choose to use here is another form of folding and division hashing in which we take different sums of the digits and divide by each of the three moduli: one for device number, one for cylinder number, and one for track number. Application of the algorithm to the key 527-45-6783 is shown in Fig. 13-6. The first part of the address is $(527 + 45 + 6783) \bmod 32 = 27$, the second part is $(527 + 456 + 783) \bmod 555 = 101$, and the final part is $(6 + 7 + 8 + 3) \bmod 30 = 24$. For this type of problem, in which the address space cannot be described as a continuum by a single sequence of numbers, each part of the address must be derived separately.

13-2-2   Overflow Techniques

Overflow occurs when all record slots for a given bucket are filled with synonym records and a new synonym record is to be inserted. Selection of overflow handling technique is one of the most important decisions in the design of a random access method. Approaches for analysis of these techniques are applicable to the other access

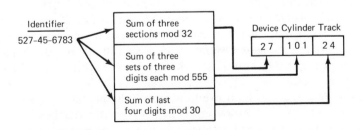

FIGURE 13-6   Hashing function with absolute addresses.

methods as well, including indexed sequential. The basic types of overflow techniques are given by [Knuth, 1973; Severance and Duhne, 1976]:

1. *Open overflow*

This method stores an overflow record in the first unused or open record slot in the next unfilled bucket. The search proceeds through succeeding block addresses in the buckets until either an open slot is found or the original bucket has been accessed again (i.e., the search cycles unsuccessfully). This type of search is called *linear search* or *linear probe*. The number of buckets accessed before the record is stored is called the *displacement* of the record. When clusters of records are transformed as synonyms, the displacement of some records tends to be quite large with respect to what one might expect to see on the average. Also, when the loading factor (LF) approaches 1.0, the expected linear search distance increases very rapidly. Note that all overflow records are placed into the existing primary area rather than a separate overflow area.

2. *Nonlinear search*

Although the term ''open overflow'' has the common connotation that the linear search is used, many types of search are actually possible to find an open slot in the existing primary area. To avoid some of the clustering and high-density problems associated with the linear search, other methods have been proposed to access buckets in a nonlinear (nonsequential) fashion. *Rehashing* uses a sequence of identifier transformation functions to find an open slot to either store a new record or retrieve that record later. Early development in such an approach is attributed to V. A. Vyssotsky [McIlroy, 1963]. Another approach, called *quadratic searching*, was introduced by Maurer [1968]. In this method, when a collision occurs, successive addresses are generated from a quadratic equation of the form $Ai^2 + Bi + C$ (modulo the address space size), where i is the probe number, C is the home address of the initial probe, and A and B are arbitrary constants.

3. *Coalesced chaining*

This method provides for a group of unused buckets at initial load to allow for overflow. When bucket A is filled with synonym records, an overflow record is placed in an unfilled bucket (B) and the overflow bucket B is linked to the home address bucket A. Additional overflows from A are stored in B until B is filled. At that time bucket B is removed from the free space list. Then the free space list (of unfilled buckets, all part of the primary area) is searched for a new overflow bucket C, the first available bucket. Although bucket B handles overflow from bucket A, it may also be a home address bucket for other records. Consequently, when B overflows, the synonym chains of A and B coalesce and both overflow to bucket C. This is a form of global overflow in which overflow buckets (and blocks) are nonhomogeneous in terms of types of record chains. Overflow buckets are still considered to be part of the primary area because they also serve as home address buckets if necessary.

4. *Separate chaining*

This method allocates local overflow record buckets for each home address bucket. The congestion of overflow chains in global overflow buckets is eliminated, but at the cost of potential wasted storage space in overflow buckets containing only a few records. Some overhead is required to remove an overflow record that is stored in a bucket subsequently needed as a home address. This form of overhead can be avoided if the overflow buckets are allocated to a separate overflow area and are not to be used as home addresses. If a separate area is used, a design decision must be made regarding the use of buckets, blocks, or just record slots in the overflow area.

Figure 13-7 illustrates the basic types of overflow techniques in terms of a simple database example. In each of the four approaches, the overflow record is placed

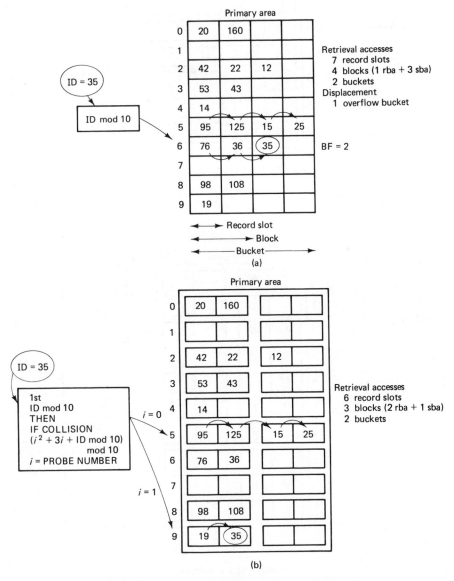

FIGURE 13-7   Hashing overflow techniques: (*a*) open overflow; (*b*) nonlinear search (quadratic); (*c*) coalesced chaining; (*d*) separate chaining.

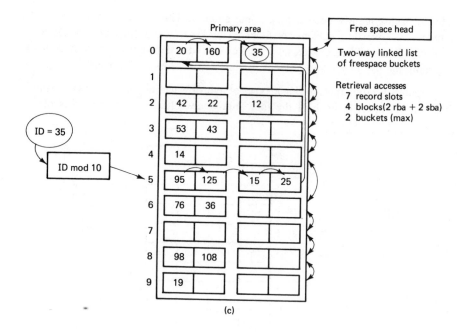

(c)

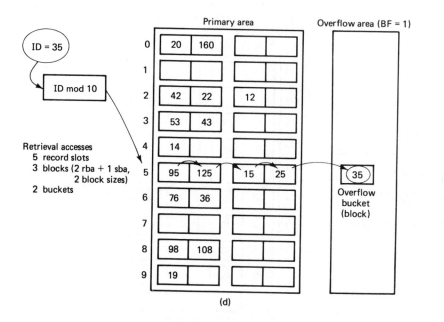

(d)

FIGURE 13.7 continued

differently. The three measures of "retrieval accesses" computed in the figure reveals an important point: the measurement of hashing access method performance by record accesses does not take into account the effect of blocking and bucket size. We know that block accesses, and their sequentiality or nonsequentiality, are more closely related to a standard cost measure, I/O service time, than are record accesses. For example, if the primary area had a blocking factor of four, all four overflow techniques would store the new record with the same number of record accesses as before, but they would now all use exactly two block accesses. On the other hand, the proximity of successive block accesses and block size still varies among overflow techniques. Consequently, the comparative I/O service time performance is not easily predicted by record, block, or bucket accesses alone. Comparative analysis can be truly only made in terms of I/O service time.

Example 13-3: Assume a random block access (rba) over the whole disk averages 40 milliseconds (ms) and a sequential block access (sba) averages 10 ms for the database indicated in Fig. 13-7. What overflow technique minimizes I/O service time when (a) the primary area and overflow area reside on a single cylinder, and (b) when each bucket is a track on a random cylinder and the overflow area is on a random cylinder? Note that rba (single cylinder) = sba. Applying the analysis of Section 9-2 and the access counts of Fig. 13-7, we have Table 13-2.

Theoretical results obtained by Knuth [Knuth, 1973] and others [Severance and Duhne, 1976] are summarized in Fig. 13-8 under very restrictive conditions. The measure is in terms of record accesses for our four basic overflow techniques, and the bucket size is limited to one record. Records are retrieved with equal probability. Although comparative values of record accesses should be evaluated carefully, the dramatic degradation of performance of open overflow and rehashing for loading factors between 0.9 and 1.0 are significant. From this figure we see that the separate chaining technique has potentially good performance for all loading factors exhibited, while open overflow and rehashing have poor performance for loading factors in excess of 0.9. The rehashing technique may have significantly worse performance than open overflow for LF > 0.5 because each probe is typically a random access over a significant proportion of secondary storage. Experimental results for more realistic bucket sizes are shown in Tables 13-4, 13-7, and 13-8.

TABLE 13-2   Performance of Overflow Techniques

Overflow Technique	Number of Record Accesses	Number of Block Accesses	Number of Bucket Accesses	I/O Service Time (1 cylinder) (ms)	I/O Service Time (random) (ms)
1. Open overflow	7	4	2	40	70
2. Nonlinear search	6	3	2	30	90
3. Coalesced chaining	7	4	2	40	100
4. Separate chaining	5	3	2	30	90

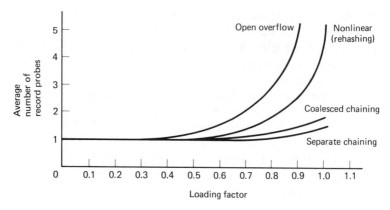

FIGURE 13-8 Comparison of overflow techniques for large NR and bucket size of one record [Severance and Duhne, 1976].

In addition to measures of I/O service time, Severance and Duhne [1976] observed that the open overflow method requires less complex software because it neither stores nor manipulates pointers. This tends to reduce CPU time overhead as well, and its effect on overall performance could be significant. They also observed, however, that despite the pointer space savings in open overflow, overall storage space will not necessarily be minimized. Chained overflow requires only one pointer per bucket, a small amount of overhead. Furthermore, the loading factor is a much more significant parameter, and the open overflow technique needs a relatively low loading factor to maintain good performance. Hence, the open overflow trade-off is between simplicity and CPU time savings as advantages, and increased I/O service time and storage space as disadvantages. The relative importance of these trade-off factors depends, of course, on the system requirements, work load, and computing environment.

Further analysis of these overflow techniques is needed to appreciate the details of these performance trade-offs. In recent years both analytical and simulation models of hashing overflow have been developed; however, they differ considerably in their assumptions and performance measures. Furthermore, most of the models are too complex to present here in detail. However, we can summarize the major results, and for consistency, apply these concepts to develop performance expressions for the more realistic configurations and performance measures we have studied for all the access methods.

A hashing function that truly randomizes the keys produces the effect that each key has an equal probability of mapping to any home address (bucket):

$$P(\text{assigned bucket} = k) = 1/\text{NB} \qquad \text{for } 1 \leq k \leq \text{NB buckets} \qquad (13\text{-}3)$$

The assumption of randomization has two advantages: first, it is straightforward to analyze; and second, its performance is quite good (i.e., the probability of accessing a target record in one block access is high). Application of randomization produces a binomial distribution for the number of records, X, mapped to a bucket:

$$P_{\text{NR,NB}}(X = r) = \binom{\text{NR}}{r}\left(\frac{1}{\text{NB}}\right)^r \left(1 - \frac{1}{\text{NB}}\right)^{\text{NR}-r} \tag{13-4}$$

For reasonably, and practically large values of NR and NB, we can use the Poisson approximation,

$$P_{\text{RPB}}(X = r) = P(r) \simeq \frac{e^{-\text{RPB}}\text{RPB}^r}{r!} \tag{13-5}$$

where RPB = NR/NB, the average number of records per bucket. This theoretical distribution can be used to estimate the probability of overflow and analyze alternative overflow handling techniques.

Given the separate chaining overflow technique, we can proceed to derive the expected number of logical record accesses, or probes, for a successful search of a record in either a primary or overflow bucket. First, the probability that a bucket will contain at least i records is

$$
\begin{aligned}
\text{PRI} &= \sum_{r=i}^{\infty} P(r) \\
&= \sum_{r=i}^{\text{NR}} P(r)
\end{aligned}
\tag{13-6}
$$

for sufficiently large NR so that the infinite series converges to within acceptable tolerance for some $r < \text{NR}$. In practice, the series converges quite rapidly as we see in the examples below. Next, the number of accesses to the i th record in a bucket is

$$\text{LRAB}_i = i \times \text{PRI} = i \sum_{r=i}^{\text{NR}} P(r) \tag{13-7}$$

and the total logical record accesses summed over all records in the bucket are

$$\text{LRAB} = \sum_{i=1}^{\text{NR}} \text{LRAB}_i = \sum_{i=1}^{\text{NR}}\left[i \sum_{r=i}^{\text{NR}} P(r) \right] \tag{13-8}$$

Since the NR records are assumed to be randomly distributed over all buckets, the expected number of LRAs to any given bucket for any record is

$$E[\text{LRAB}] = \frac{\text{total accesses to a bucket for all records}}{\text{expected number of records in a bucket}}$$

$$= \frac{LRAB}{NR/NB}$$

$$= \frac{NB \sum_{i=1}^{NR} \left[i \sum_{r=i}^{NR} P(r) \right]}{NR}$$

$$= \frac{\sum_{i=1}^{NR} \left[i \sum_{r=i}^{NR} P(r) \right]}{LF \times RSPB}$$

(13-9)

where $LF = NR/(NB \times RSPB)$ and RSPB is the number of record slots per bucket.

Example 13-4:   Given any large database where $NR = NB$, $LF = 1$, $RSPB = 1$, and $RPB = 1$, we have Table 13-3 to illustrate the computation of expected number of LRA probes to a random record.

TABLE 13-3   Overflow Computation in LRAs for the Separate Chaining Technique*

r	$P(r)e^{RPB}$	i	$PRI \times e^{RPB}$	PRI	$LRAB_i$
0	1.0	0	2.7183	1.0	0
1	1.0	1	1.7183	0.6321	0.6321
2	0.50	2	0.7183	0.2642	0.5284
3	0.1667	3	0.2183	0.0803	0.2409
4	0.0417	4	0.0516	0.0190	0.0760
5	0.0083	5	0.0099	0.0036	0.0180
6	0.0014	6	0.0016	0.0006	0.0036
7	0.0002	7	0.0002	0.00007	0.0005
8	0.000025	8	0.00003	0.00001	0.0001
9	0.0000027	9	0.000003	0.000001	0.00001
10	0.0000003	10	0.0000003	0.0000001	0.000001
					1.4996

* LRAB $= 1.50$
$E[LRAB] = 1.50/1.0 = 1.50$ bucket accesses

When $RSPB = 1$ all LRA probes are bucket accesses, assuming that each overflow access is a separate bucket access. When $RSPB > 1$, only one bucket access is required for the first RSPB synonym records mapped to the bucket. In general, a bucket having $RSPB + k$ records mapped to it is filled and has k overflow records or buckets. The total number of accesses to the $RSPB + k$th record is $1 + k$ bucket accesses. The expected number of bucket accesses to a random record is derived from Eqs. (13-7) to (13-9) by substituting the function, number of bucket accesses to the ith record, BA_i, for i:

$$E[BA] = \frac{\sum_{i=1}^{NR} \left[BA_i \sum_{r=i}^{NR} P(r) \right]}{LF \times RSPB}$$

(13-10)

where

$$BA_i = \begin{cases} 1 & \text{for } i = \text{RSPB} \\ 1 + i - \text{RSPB} & \text{for } i > \text{RSPB} \end{cases}$$

From Eq. (13-10) we can produce Table 13-4, which coincides with the work reported by others [Knuth, 1973; Severance and Duhne, 1976].

TABLE 13-4   Expected Bucket Accesses for a Successful Search Using the Separate Chaining Overflow Technique

	LF									
RSPB	*0.2*	*0.5*	*0.7*	*0.9*	*1.0*	*1.1*	*1.5*	*2.0*	*3.0*	*5.0*
1	1.10	1.25	1.35	1.45	1.50	1.55	1.75	2.00	2.50	3.50
2	1.02	1.13	1.24	1.36	1.43	1.50	1.82	2.25	3.17	5.10
3	1.01	1.08	1.18	1.32	1.40	1.49	1.90	2.50	3.83	6.70
4	1.00	1.05	1.14	1.29	1.38	1.48	1.98	2.75	4.50	8.30
5	1.00	1.04	1.12	1.27	1.37	1.48	2.07	3.00	5.17	9.90
10	1.00	1.01	1.06	1.21	1.33	1.50	2.49	4.25	8.50	17.90
20	1.00	1.00	1.02	1.15	1.31	1.55	3.33	6.75	15.17	33.90
50	1.00	1.00	1.00	1.08	1.29	1.71	5.83	14.25	35.17	81.90
100	1.00	1.00	1.00	1.04	1.28	1.97	10.00	26.75	68.50	161.90

Going one step further, we extend Eqs. (13-9) and (13-10) to the case where either or both the primary and secondary overflow areas are blocked:

$$E[\text{PBA}] = \frac{\sum_{i=1}^{NR}\left[\text{PBA}_i \sum_{r=i}^{NR} P(r) \right]}{\text{LF} \times \text{RSPB}} \tag{13-11}$$

where PBA_i is the discrete function given in Table 13-5.

TABLE 13-5   Physical Block Accesses in a Successful Search to the *i*th Record in a Bucket (Dedicated Environment)

i	PBA$_i$*
1	$1\ \text{rba}_1$
2	$1\ \text{rba}_1 + \left(\left\lceil \dfrac{i}{\text{EBF}_1} \right\rceil - 1 \right)\ \text{sba}$
⋮	
RSPB	$1\ \text{rba}_1 + \left(\left\lceil \dfrac{i}{\text{EBF}_1} \right\rceil - 1 \right)\ \text{sba}$
RSPB + 1	$1\ \text{rba}_1 + \left(\left\lceil \dfrac{\text{RSPB}}{\text{EBF}_1} \right\rceil - 1 \right)\ \text{sba} + 1\ \text{rba}_2$
RSPB + k	$1\ \text{rba}_1 + \left(\left\lceil \dfrac{\text{RSPB}}{\text{EBF}_1} \right\rceil - 1 \right)\ \text{sba} + \left\lceil \dfrac{i - \text{RSPB}}{\text{EBF}_2}\ \text{rba}_2 \right\rceil$

*rba$_1$ Random access to the home address bucket
 rba$_2$ Random access to the overflow bucket from the home address bucket or another overflow bucket

A search is unsuccessful when all records associated with a home address bucket have been accessed and the target record is not found. The primary area is organized as physical sequential, so an unsuccessful search terminates at the first empty record slot. The overflow area is organized as linked sequential; an unsuccessful search in the overflow area will terminate at the last record, which has a null pointer value. Letting $E[LRAB']$ denote the expected number of LRA probes for an unsuccessful search, we obtain

$$E[\text{LRAB}'] = \sum_{r=0}^{\text{RSPB}-1} P(r)(r + 1) + \sum_{r=\text{RSPB}+1}^{\text{NR}} P(r)r \qquad (13\text{-}12)$$

More useful expressions for bucket accesses, when overflow records are unblocked are

$$E[\text{BA}'] = \sum_{r=0}^{\text{RSPB}} P(r) + \sum_{r=\text{RSPB}+1}^{\text{NR}} P(r)(r - \text{RSPB} + 1) \qquad (13\text{-}13)$$

and block accesses, when both primary and overflow areas may be blocked, are

$$E[\text{PBA}'] = \sum_{r=0}^{\text{NR}} P(r)\text{PBA}_r \qquad (13\text{-}14)$$

where PBA_r is given in Table 13-6. Application of Eq. (13-13) produces Table 13-7, which was derived similarly in [Knuth, 1973].

Only the separate chaining method uses an overflow area that is completely separate from the primary area. The other overflow methods presented above use only the primary area to store new records after a collision has occurred. Consequently, neither the binomial distribution nor the Poisson approximation are applicable to these configurations. Let us take a quick look at each of the other overflow techniques and apply the physical block access approach wherever possible.

TABLE 13-6   Physical Block Accesses in an Unsuccessful Search to a Bucket with r Synonym Records, Using the Separate Chaining Overflow Technique

r	PBA_r
0	$1\ \text{rba}_1$
1 to RSPB $-$ 1	$1\ \text{rba}_1 + \left(\left\lceil \dfrac{r+1}{\text{EBF}_1} \right\rceil - 1 \right)\ \text{sba}$
RSPB $+ k$ for $k \geqslant 0$	$1\ \text{rba}_1 + \left(\left\lceil \dfrac{\text{RSPB}}{\text{EBF}_1} \right\rceil - 1 \right)\ \text{sba} + \left\lceil \dfrac{r - \text{RSPB}}{\text{EBF}_2} \right\rceil \text{rba}_2$

TABLE 13-7   Expected Bucket Accesses in an Unsuccessful Search
Using the Separate Chaining Overflow Method

	Loading Factor									
RSPB	0.10	0.20	0.30	0.40	0.50	0.60	0.70	0.80	0.90	0.95
1	1.0048	1.0187	1.0408	1.0703	1.1065	1.1488	1.197	1.249	1.307	1.3
2	1.0012	1.0088	1.0269	1.0581	1.1036	1.1638	1.238	1.327	1.428	1.5
3	1.0003	1.0038	1.0162	1.0433	1.0898	1.1588	1.252	1.369	1.509	1.6
4	1.0001	1.0016	1.0095	1.0314	1.0751	1.1476	1.253	1.394	1.571	1.7
5	1.0000	1.0007	1.0056	1.0225	1.0619	1.1346	1.249	1.410	1.620	1.7
10	1.0000	1.0000	1.0004	1.0041	1.0222	1.0773	1.201	1.426	1.773	2.0
20	1.0000	1.0000	1.0000	1.0001	1.0028	1.0234	1.113	1.367	1.898	2.3
50	1.0000	1.0000	1.0000	1.0000	1.0000	1.0007	1.018	1.182	1.920	2.7

Open Overflow

An analysis of open overflow is given in [Knuth, 1973] for "internal" (main storage) searching:

$$E[\text{LRA}] \simeq \tfrac{1}{2}\left(1 + \frac{1}{1 - \text{LF}}\right) \qquad \text{for a successful search} \qquad (13\text{-}15)$$

$$E[\text{LRA}'] \simeq \tfrac{1}{2}\left[1 + \left(\frac{1}{1 - \text{LF}}\right)^2\right] \qquad \text{for an unsuccessful search} \qquad (13\text{-}16)$$

When there is only a single record slot per bucket (RSPB = 1), Eqs. (13-15) and (13-16) are easily extendable for physical block accesses:

$$E[\text{PBA}] = \frac{E[\text{LRA}]}{\text{EBF}_1} \qquad \text{for a successful search} \qquad (13\text{-}17)$$

$$E[\text{PBA}'] = \frac{E[\text{LRA}']}{\text{EBF}_1} \qquad \text{for an unsuccessful search} \qquad (13\text{-}18)$$

However, when RSPB > 1, each bucket may contain several record slots, and expressions (13-17) and (13-18) no longer apply.

The expected number of bucket accesses for a successful "external" (secondary storage) search with linear probing is

$$E[\text{BA}] = 1 + t_{\text{NB}}(\text{LF}) + t_{2\text{NB}}(\text{LF}) + t_{3\text{NB}}(\text{LF}) + \ldots \qquad (13\text{-}19)$$

where

$$t_n(\text{LF}) = e^{-n\text{LF}} \sum_{n=0}^{\infty} \frac{(\text{LF} \times n)^n}{(n + 1)!}$$

The series normally converges in a few steps. If each bucket contains exactly the same number of blocks, NBPB, then physical block accesses are given by

$$E[PBA] = 1 \text{ rba} + (E[BA] - 1) \times \text{NBPB sba} < E[PBA] \leq 1 \text{ rba} + E[BA] \times \text{NBPB} \tag{13-20}$$

Application of Eq. (13-19) produces the values listed in Table 13-8.

TABLE 13-8   Expected Bucket Accesses in a Successful Search Using the Open Overflow Method (Linear Probing) [Knuth, 1973]*

	Loading Factor									
RSPB	0.10	0.20	0.30	0.40	0.50	0.60	0.70	0.80	0.90	0.95
1	1.0556	1.1250	1.2143	1.3333	1.5000	1.7500	2.167	3.000	5.500	10.5
2	1.0062	1.0242	1.0553	1.1033	1.1767	1.2930	1.494	1.903	3.147	5.6
3	1.0009	1.0066	1.0201	1.0450	1.0872	1.1584	1.286	1.554	2.378	4.0
4	1.0001	1.0021	1.0085	1.0227	1.0497	1.0984	1.190	1.386	2.000	3.2
5	1.0000	1.0007	1.0039	1.0124	1.0307	1.0661	1.136	1.289	1.777	2.7
10	1.0000	1.0000	1.0001	1.0011	1.0047	1.0154	1.042	1.110	1.345	1.8
20	1.0000	1.0000	1.0000	1.0000	1.0003	1.0020	1.010	1.036	1.144	1.4
50	1.0000	1.0000	1.0000	1.0000	1.0000	1.0000	1.001	1.005	1.040	1.1

*Reprinted with permission.

Nonlinear Search

This method has only been analyzed for RSPB = 1 [McIlroy, 1963; Severance, 1974].

$$E[LRA] \simeq -1/LF \times \log_e (1 - LF) \qquad \text{for a successful search} \tag{13-21}$$

Because each probe is considered to be a random access over the extent of the database, $E[PBA] = E[LRA]$ rba.

Coalesced Chaining

This method has also been analyzed for only the RSPB = 1 case [Knuth, 1973]:

$$E[LRA] \simeq 1 + \frac{1}{8 \times LF}(e^{2 \times LF} - 1 - 2 \times LF) + \tfrac{1}{4} \times LF \tag{13-22}$$
$$\text{for a successful search}$$

$$E[LRA'] \simeq 1 + \tfrac{1}{4}(e^{2 \times LF} - 1 - 2 \times LF) \quad \text{for an unsuccessful search} \tag{13-23}$$

As in the nonlinear search, each probe is considered to be a random access over the extent of the database, so $E[PBA] = E[LRA]$ and $E[PBA'] = E[LRA']$.

13-2-3 Performance Characteristics

Retrieval Performance

Random retrieval of records is best analyzed when both levels of primary data and overflow data are taken into account as a single access path, as shown in Section 13-2-2. Rewriting Eq. (13-11) after substituting Eq. (13-5) into it, we have

$$\text{PBA(GET UNIQUE, key found)} = \frac{\sum_{i=1}^{NR}\left(\text{PBA}_i \sum_{r=i}^{NR} \frac{e^{-\text{RPB}}\text{RPB}^r}{r!}\right)}{\text{LF} \times \text{RSPB}} \quad (13\text{-}24)$$

where PBA_i is given in Table 13-5. Furthermore, applying Eq. (13-14), we obtain

$$\text{PBA(GET UNIQUE', key not found)} = \sum_{r=0}^{NR} \frac{e^{-\text{RPB}}\text{RPB}^r}{r!} \times \text{PBA}_r \quad (13\text{-}25)$$

where PBA_r is given in Table 13-6.

Another retrieval operation relevant to hashing is sequential processing of primary and overflow areas. The data are unordered, so the most efficient method is to scan sequentially the primary area and the overflow area:

$$\text{PBA(GET ALL)} = \text{NB} \times \left\lceil \frac{\text{RSPB}}{\text{EBF}_1} \right\rceil \quad \text{sba} + \text{NBLKOV} \quad \text{sba} \quad (13\text{-}26)$$

where NBLKOV is the number of blocks in the overflow area. In this case we ignore the initial random block access to the first bucket because it is an insignificant part of the total search. Boolean queries can also be processed by sequentially scanning all blocks.

Commands such as GET NEXT might be allowed for synonyms associated with the same home address.

$$\text{PBA(GET NEXT)} \simeq \frac{p}{\text{EBF}_1} \quad \text{sba} + (1-p) \times 1 \quad \text{rba} \quad (13\text{-}27)$$

where p is the proportion of synonyms that are located in the primary area, and $1-p$ is the proportion of synonyms that are located in the overflow area.

$$p = \frac{\text{RPB} - \text{OVFLCH}}{\text{RPB}} = \frac{\text{RPB}_1}{\text{RPB}} \quad (13\text{-}28)$$

where OVFLCH is the expected overflow chain length and is given by

$$\text{OVFLCH} = \sum_{r=1}^{NR-RSPB} P(\text{RSPB} + r)r \quad (13\text{-}29)$$

and $P(RSPB + r)$ is the Poisson probability function for the overflow chain length r. $RPB_1 = RPB - OVFLCH$ is the expected number of primary data records currently allocated to the bucket.

Update Performance

The foundation for update analysis has been presented in earlier sections for physical sequential and linked sequential organizations. Record update in the hashing access method is therefore very straightforward. If the update involves a change of a nonkey value, only one extra sequential block access (after retrieval) is needed to rewrite the changed block:

$$PBA(\text{CHANGE nonkey}) = 1 \text{ sba} \tag{13-30}$$

An insertion of a new record in the primary area also requires only a block rewrite in addition to the initial retrieval. This occurs with probability p. An insertion into the overflow chain is equivalent to the insertion in a one-way linked list. Applying Table 12-4 for insertions, we obtain

$$PBA(\text{INSERT}) = p \times 1 \text{ sba} + (1 - p)(1 \text{ rba} + 1 \text{ sba}) \tag{13-31}$$

Deletion is computed similarly. If the record to be deleted is in the primary area, only a single block rewrite is necessary, assuming that it must be either flagged or erased to accomplish the deletion. If it is in the overflow area, only its predecessor record's pointer need be reset. If the predecessor record is still in a buffer, we would use the best-case expression, applying the analysis of Section 12-2.

$$PBA(\text{DELETE}) = p \times 1 \text{ sba} + (1 - p) \times 1 \text{ sba} = 1 \text{ sba} \tag{13-32}$$

Update involving a key change implies a deletion of the record from its current position and insertion into a new position, governed by the new value of the key:

$$PBA(\text{CHANGE key}) = PBA(\text{DELETE}) + PBA(\text{GET UNIQUE}) \\ + PBA(\text{INSERT}) \tag{13-33}$$

The total block accesses to retrieve and change a key is PBA(GET UNIQUE) + PBA(CHANGE key).

Storage Space

Secondary storage space for the random access method consists of a primary area and an overload area. Assuming blocking factors of EBF_1 and EBF_2, respectively, where

$$EBF_i = \left\lfloor \frac{(BKS_i - BOVHD_i) \times LF_i}{SRS_i} \right\rfloor \quad \text{for } i = \begin{cases} 1 & \text{for the primary area} \\ 2 & \text{for the overflow area} \end{cases}$$

we obtain

BLKSTOR(primary area) = (number of buckets) × (blocks per bucket)
× (bytes per block)

$$= NB \times \left\lceil \frac{RSPB}{EBF_1} \right\rceil \times BKS_1 \qquad \text{bytes} \qquad (13\text{-}34)$$

$$\text{BLKSTOR(overflow area)} = NBLKOVFL \times BKS_2 \qquad \text{bytes} \qquad (13\text{-}35)$$

13-2-4   Scatter Tables

The notion of physical database independence in virtual memory systems was analyzed by Morris [1968] with the concept of scatter tables. An extra level of mapping was proposed for hashing organizations in which keys would be transformed into addresses in a table that contained pointers to actual records in the primary data area. The extra level of indirection has the advantage that the data file could be loaded in some order to facilitate sequential batch processing (see Fig. 13-9). On the other hand, because the physical location of the data record would be independent of the key value, or identifier, and its hashed address, a data file could be physically

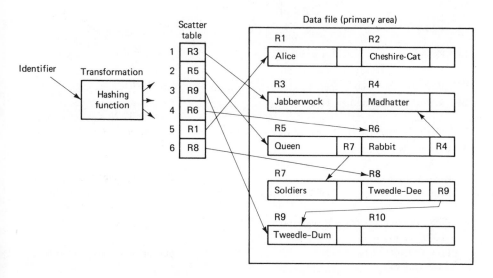

FIGURE 13-9   Scatter table organization.

reorganized without complete reloading. Also, variable-length records would be more easily accommodated, and records could easily be found on the basis of values from more than one identifier. The apparent disadvantages of the scatter table are the extra storage space required for the additional scatter table (record pointers), an additional block access for random retrievals, and update overhead in the scatter table to maintain proper order in a volatile data file.

We wish to illustrate more precisely some of the advantages and disadvantages of scatter tables. First, let us modify our hashing (random) access path model to encompass a scatter table (see Fig. 13-9). The chained overflow method is assumed to be used, consistent with Morris' model, although other alternatives such as open overflow could be used as well. The execution I/O performance characteristics are summarized in Table 13-9. We can refer to the table to compare scatter table performance with the hashing access method represented in Fig. 13-6. Random retrieval is always longer with a scatter table, but the ordered data file increases the potential for batch processing of simple queries and updates. Most updates are equivalent in both access methods, assuming that the scatter table entries are not affected by insertions and deletions after initial loading. However, changing a key value in a record accessed by a scatter table could result in a reorganization of the data file if a specific physical ordering is required. Reorganization may be deferred if overflow is allowed for the data file.

TABLE 13-9   Database Operation Cost (PBA) for Hashing Access Methods*

Operation	Hashing (Random Access)	Hashing with Scatter Table
GET ALL	$NB \left\lceil \dfrac{RSPB}{EBF_1} \right\rceil$ sba + NBLKOV sba	Same as hashing
GET NEXT	$p \times \dfrac{1}{EBF_1}$sba + $(1 + p)$ rba	Same as hashing
GET PRIOR	N/A	N/A
GET UNIQUE(key found)	Eq. (13-24)	GET UNIQUE(hashing) + 1 rba
GET UNIQUE'(not found)	Eq. (13-25)	GET UNIQUE(hashing) + 1 rba
GET RPBR(Batch retrieval)	N/A	Same as physical sequential (Table 12-2)
GET SOME(Boolean query)	Same as GET ALL	Same as hashing
After the search is completed		
CHANGE nonkey	1 sba	Same as hashing
CHANGE key	GET UNIQUE(key found) + INSERT + DELETE	Possible reorganization of the data file and the scatter table
INSERT record	p sba + $(1 - p)(1$ rba + 1 sba)	Same as hashing
DELETE record	1 sba	Same as hashing
UPDATE BATCH (after batch retrieval)	N/A	Sum of individual record updates

*$$p = \frac{RPB_1}{RPB_1 + OVFLCH} = \frac{RPB_1}{RPB}.$$

Storage space increases with a scatter table by an amount equal to the product of pointer size (PS) and the number of entries in the scatter table. If the scatter table is blocked, blocking overhead must be taken into account as well.

13-3   FULL INDEX (INDEXED RANDOM)

Indexing is a widely used concept in manual retrieval systems such as dictionaries or card catalog systems for libraries. It has important implications for computerized data that must be efficiently stored and retrieved because it suggests an alternative approach to direct access for random processing. For instance, when data are stored physically sequential but are accessed by GET UNIQUE commands, it is usually more efficient to search a file of only its primary keys to find the target key, particularly when the key size is small relative to the stored record size. After a match of search key and index key value is found, the record can then be accessed via the pointer to it, which is stored next to the target key value entry in the index. If no match is found, the search terminates at the index level. No assumption of order is made, although ordered key values provide the proper structure for a binary search of the index. Random access via hashing to the index is also possible, as is done in DMS-II [Burroughs, 1974].

A *full index* is a file organization in which an index entry is provided for each individual record occurrence in the file or subfile. An index entry consists of a primary key value and a pointer to the record containing that value. In general, there is usually some ordering to the index to facilitate a fast search, but no order or physical contiguity is necessarily associated with the stored records. Physical sequential stored records are a special case of this type of organization. An example of full index entries is given in Fig. 13-10. The term "indexed random" is equivalent to full index.

The important considerations for a full index file are:

- *Type of work load.* Random retrieval, random update, sequential processing.
- *Blocking factor (index, data).* Affects sequential processing efficiency and index search time.
- *Loading factor.* Allows index insertions without excessive overflow or index reordering.
- *File size (number of records).* Affects storage space and index size.
- *Order of records and index entries.*

Retrieval and Update Performance

Arbitrary ordering of data records has the advantages of physical data independence at the stored record level and low update cost. The major disadvantage of arbitrary ordering of data records occurs when the user application specifies GET ALL and requires the data in the report to be in a specified order. Efficient organizations for GET ALL commands were discussed in Section 12-2.

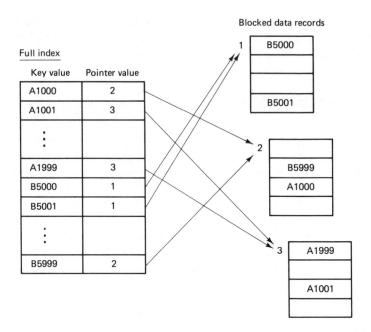

FIGURE 13-10 Full index access method.

Arbitrary ordering for index entries (each entry can be considered an "index record") has the same advantages and disadvantages as any physical sequential file. First, unsuccessful searches for key match require that the entire index be scanned. Second, only sequential searches are possible. On the other hand, ordered indexes greatly increase the potential for fast access for GET UNIQUE commands and batch retrieval operations. Unfortunately, full indexes are dense; update operations, especially insertions of new keys and key changes, require retrieval and rewrite of the entire index. Deletions can be flagged to avoid rewrites each time.

The cost of basic database operations for ordered and unordered indexes and data records is summarized in Table 13-10. Most table entries can be extracted from Table 12-2 because the full index is a direct application of a physical sequential file.

It should be noted that the total block accesses for a database operation is the sum of block accesses for the index and block accesses for data records (i.e., two columns in Table 13-10). The retrieval costs are derived from physical sequential database performance and are applicable for full indexes. The update operations require further explanation, however. Changing a nonkey value is accomplished by accessing the block containing the data record, making the change in the main storage work area, and rewriting the same block with the changed record. Changing the key is more complex when the index is ordered. Whether in the index or data blocks, the change is accomplished by a search and delete of the old (index or data) record and then a new search and insertion of the new record. This requires a full read and full rewrite of the ordered (index or data) file.

Similarly, an insertion of a new record implies that there now exists a new key

TABLE 13-10 Database Operation Cost (PBA) for Full Index Organizations*

Operation	Ordered Index	Unordered Data Rec.	Unordered Index	Ordered Data Rec.
GET ALL(no sort)	0	$\lceil NR/EBF_2 \rceil$ sba	0	$\lceil NR/EBF_2 \rceil$ sba
GET NEXT(in order)	$1/EBF_1$ sba	1 rba	$\left(\left\lceil \dfrac{NR}{EBF_1} \right\rceil + 1\right)/2$ sba	1 rba
GET PRIOR	$1/EBF_1$ sba	1 rba	Same as GET NEXT	1 rba
GET UNIQUE (key found) Sequential index search	$\dfrac{\left\lceil \dfrac{NR}{EBF_1} \right\rceil + 1}{2}$ sba	1 rba	Same as GET NEXT	1 rba
Binary index search	$\log_2 \dfrac{NR}{2EBF_1}$ rba	1 rba	N/A	1 rba
Direct index search	1 rba	1 rba	N/A	1 rba
GET UNIQUE'(key not found) Sequential index search	$\dfrac{\left\lceil \dfrac{NR}{EBF_1} \right\rceil + 1}{2}$ sba	0	$\lceil NR/EBF_1 \rceil$ sba	0
Binary index search	$\left\lfloor \log_2\left(\dfrac{NR}{EBF_2}\right) \right\rfloor + 1$	0	N/A	0
Direct index search	1 rba	0	N/A	0
GET SOME(Boolean query) After search is completed	0	$\lceil NR/EBF_2 \rceil$ sba	0	$\lceil NR/EBF_2 \rceil$ sba
CHANGE nonkey	0	1 sba	0	1 sba
CHANGE key	$2\left\lceil \dfrac{NR}{EBF_1} \right\rceil$ sba	1 sba	1 sba	$2\left\lceil \dfrac{NR}{EBF_2} \right\rceil$ sba
INSERT key and data	$2\left\lceil \dfrac{NR}{EBF_1} \right\rceil$ sba	1 rba + 1 sba	1 rba + 1 sba	$2\left\lceil \dfrac{NR}{EBF_2} \right\rceil$ sba
DELETE key and data	1 sba (if flag is set)	0	1 sba (if flag is set)	0

*EBF_1 Effective blocking factor for index records
  EBF_2 Effective blocking factor for data records
  NR Number of records in the file

value and thus we need a key insertion as well. The insertion into an ordered (and dense) file requires a full read and rewrite of that file. The rewritten file contains one more record than the original file, but the effect of one record on performance is assumed to be negligible. Therefore, we use the same expressions for insertion to an ordered file and a change to that file, whether index or data. Insertion to an unordered file requires a sequential block write for the old block (before block splitting), which now points to the new overflow block (assuming that overflow takes place), and a random block write for the new block. If overflow does not occur, only the sequential rewrite of the old block is needed. As seen in Section 12-2, many overflow options exist, and each must be analyzed separately.

Deletions are simple if we assume that index records are merely flagged when deleted; only a rewrite of the flagged entry is needed. A flagged index entry effectively deletes the data record because it erases the pointer to that record.

Storage Space

Storage space needed for the full index access method is the sum of index blocks and data blocks:

$$\text{BLKSTOR} = \text{NBLK(index)} \times \text{BKS(index)} + \text{NBLK(data)} \times \text{BKS(data)}$$

$$= \left\lceil \cfrac{\text{NR}}{\left\lceil \cfrac{(\text{BKS}_1 - \text{BOVHD}_1) \times \text{LF}_1}{\text{KS} + \text{PS}} \right\rceil} \right\rceil \times \text{BKS}_1$$

$$+ \left\lceil \cfrac{\text{NR}}{\left\lceil \cfrac{(\text{BKS}_2 - \text{BOVHD}_2) \times \text{LF}_2}{\text{SRS}} \right\rceil} \right\rceil \times \text{BKS}_2 \qquad \text{bytes}$$

(13-36)

where the subscript 1 represents index file parameters and the subscript 2 represents data file parameters.

13-4   INDEXED SEQUENTIAL

The direct, random, and full index access methods provide efficient retrieval capabilities for GET UNIQUE commands under certain restricted conditions. The direct access method is very efficient when keys are controllable and storage overhead can be kept low. The random access method is usually more practical for database configurations requiring high-volume random access and update. Also, the full index access method can retrieve single records efficiently with an ordered index, and updates are simple when data records are unordered. Suppose that we wish to build a file organization that efficiently allows both sequential and random processing to take place. To do this we need an ordered index and ordered data records. This can be accomplished with the full index method; however, update I/O processing is costly for both index and data records. Furthermore, the storage cost for a full index of a very large database may be excessive.

The indexed sequential access method provides a reasonable compromise among retrieval, update, and storage costs. It is efficient for combined sequential and random applications, and it reduces the index overhead in update and storage space from the full index approach. (As we shall see, it still retains the ordered data record update inefficiencies that plague the full index and physical sequential organizations, but new overflow handling techniques are helping to alleviate this problem.) First, let us consider the potential reduction of index storage space and sequential access time through the use of block indexes. A *block index* is an ordered index of primary key values, where each entry represents the highest key value of all records in a given block. Associated with each key value in the index is a pointer to the appropriate block. A block index is illustrated in Fig. 13-11.

Ordering must be preserved in a file using ordered block indexes. Ordering allows each index entry to specify the bounds on each block: the key value represents the upper bound (i.e., the highest key value of the block), and the pointer represents the lower bound by addressing the block and implicitly addressing the first record in the block, which contains the lowest key value.

An *indexed sequential* access method consists of an ordered physical sequential file and a hierarchy of block indexes, each ordered by primary key values in the same way in which the data file is ordered. Each key value in an index of any level j represents the highest key value in an index block or data block at level $j + 1$. A sequential search is conducted at each level of index and data until the requested record is located or found to be missing. We see that the indexed sequential file generalizes the block index concept to include many levels. This allows fast access to very large databases or files in which a single index may be too large for an efficient search or update. A binary search of each index and data block would increase the efficiency of the indexed sequential access method if the database is static in size, or if new records can always be contained in the proper blocks without overflow. Volatile files usually require overflow chains, and this loss of denseness and physical order inhibits the effectiveness of the binary search. Consequently, the standard search mechanism for indexed sequential files is the sequential search.

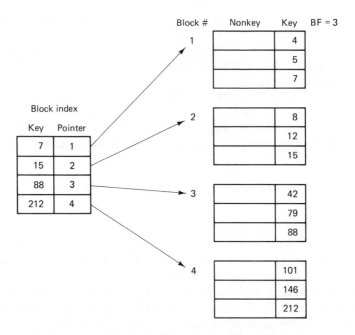

FIGURE 13-11   Block index (indexed sequential) organization.

An example of indexed sequential organization is given in Fig. 13-12. The example contains three levels of indexes, one level of data records, and one level of chained overflow records. Actual implementations of indexed sequential organizations may vary considerably from this example in terms of number of index levels, search length per level, type of search, and overflow method. However, the basic index architecture and internal structure is consistent with the example.

IBM's ISAM [IBM, 1966] can be represented as shown in Fig. 13-12. Level 1 represents a master index that may be located in main storage during file processing. Level 2 is the cylinder index, and level 3 is the track index, both of which may contain many blocks. Data records occur at level 4 and overflow records occur at the final two levels. At the track index level, each pointer to data records addresses a whole track on the same cylinder as the track index.

In general, overflow may be handled by designating free space to be allocated at the block, track, cylinder, or device level. In each case the records are usually chained and not reordered physically until the file is reorganized. Details of overflow handling are quite implementation dependent.

The design of an indexed sequential file requires careful consideration of the following:

- *Type of work load*. Retrieval, update, random vs. batch operations, sequential processing.
- *Ordering*. Allows faster searching, batch processing, avoids sorting if report order is the same as file order.
- *Blocking factor (index and data)*. Affects sequential processing efficiency and storage space for index entries.
- *File size (number of records)*. Affects storage space needed for indexes.
- *Loading factor*. Allows file growth without excessive overflow; affects storage space required.
- *Index levels*. More levels can reduce access time to data.
- *Index size*. Affects retrieval and update time for index entries.
- *Overflow technique*. Proper choice reduces degradation of performance for retrieval and update; lessens the need for reorganization.

13-4-1   Retrieval from an Indexed Sequential File

Access to data in an indexed sequential file is accomplished by traversing each index sequentially until the key value equals or exceeds the search key, and then by following the associated pointer to the next level. At the data level the search continues until the target record is located, determined to be missing, or an overflow search is required. The distance between the data blocks and overflow records, and the method of storing overflow records, is dependent on the overflow technique. Typically, loading factors can be established for blocks, tracks, and cylinders, or

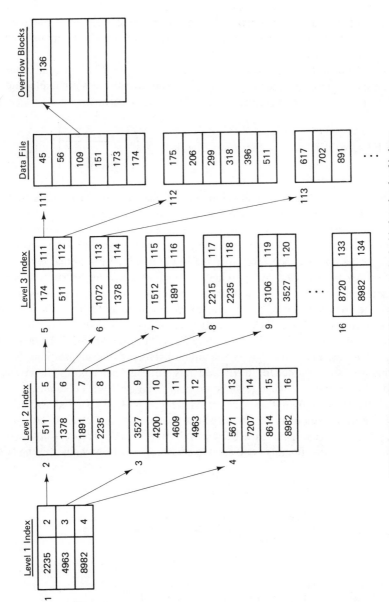

FIGURE 13-12 Indexed sequential access method with three levels of indexes.

some combination of them. Within blocks, new records are considered to be contiguous with regard to that block. Within track and cylinder overflow areas, however, records are usually chained and unblocked. Therefore, each record is linked to another record, but because it is usually within the same cylinder, each access (rba) is made without movement of the disk arm. Many alternative overflow techniques may be used, and it should be recognized that variations of our simple model may be required for each technique.

Using the example configuration represented in Fig. 13-12 and assuming that no overflow has occurred yet, the expected access path to retrieve a randomly selected record is the sum of the interlevel and intralevel block accesses:

$$\text{PBA(GET UNIQUE, no overflow)} = n \text{ rba} + \sum_{i=1}^{n} \left(\left\lceil \frac{\left\lceil \frac{(1 + NR_i)}{2} \right\rceil}{EBF_i} \right\rceil - 1 \right) \text{ sba} \tag{13-37}$$

where $n = NIL + 1$, NIL is the number of index levels, and NR_i is the number of (data or index entry) records at level i. The first term represents the interlevel accesses for indexes and data records, each of which may require a separate evaluation of ''rba'' to estimate I/O service time. The second term represents the remaining intralevel block scanning to be done at each level after the initial block access to that level.

Overflow is evaluated by applying the separate chaining overflow model of hashing to the indexed sequential method, where each block is taken to be a home address and overflow records from that block are assumed to be on a chain that belongs exclusively to that block. To apply the hashing model, we first define NR_0 as the number of records in the database (originally) at initial load. NR is the current database volume and includes $NR - NR_0$ additional records due to insertions. Record deletions are also accounted for in NR, which is reduced when records are physically deleted, but not reduced when records are only ''flagged'' for deletion.

The overflow configuration is illustrated in Fig. 13-13. After initial load, random record insertions eventually fill up the primary data block and cause overflow. The primary block is analogous to a bucket with $BF_n - EBF_n$ record slots, and the overflow chain is functionally equivalent to a hashing overflow chain. Letting NR −

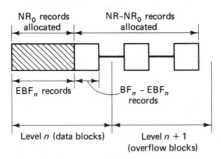

FIGURE 13-13   Indexed sequential basic overflow configuration.

NR_0 be the total number of new records in the database, we apply Eq. (13-11) to the indexed sequential configuration and obtain the expected number of overflow block accesses:

$$E[\text{OVPBA}] = \frac{\sum_{i=1}^{NR-NR_0}\left[\text{PBA}_i \sum_{r=i}^{NR-NR_0} P(r)\right]}{\text{RPB}} \tag{13-38}$$

where

$$\text{RPB} = \frac{NR - NR_0}{\left\lceil \dfrac{NR_0}{\text{EBF}_n} \right\rceil}$$

the expected number of new records per data block. $P(r)$ is given in Eq. (13-5), and

$$\text{PBA}_i = \begin{cases} 0 & \text{if } 1 \leq i \leq \text{BF}_n - \text{EBF}_n \\ k \text{ rba} & \text{if } i = \text{BF}_n - \text{EBF}_n + k \end{cases} \quad \text{for } k \geq 0$$

There are no additional block accesses as long as new records can fit into the unused area of the data block. Once overflow occurs, each new access is a random access within the extent of the overflow area.

We now combine the two components of random retrieval in an indexed sequential organization from Eqs. (13-37) and (13-38):

$$\text{PBA(GET UNIQUE, key found)} = n \text{ rba} + \sum_{i=1}^{n}\left(\left\lceil \frac{\left\lceil \dfrac{(1 + NR_i)}{2} \right\rceil}{\text{EBF}_i} \right\rceil - 1\right)\text{sba} \tag{13-39}$$

$$+ \frac{\sum_{i=1}^{NR-NR_0}\left[\text{PBA}_i \sum_{r=i}^{NR-NR_0} P(r)\right]}{\text{RPB}}$$

Equation (13-39) represents the case where the search was successful. An unsuccessful search involves a search of all records in the block plus a search of all overflow records:

$$\text{PBA(GET UNIQUE', key not found)} = n \text{ rba} + \sum_{i=1}^{n}\left(\left\lceil \frac{\left\lceil \dfrac{(1 + NR_i)}{2} \right\rceil}{\text{EBF}_i} \right\rceil - 1\right)\text{sba} \tag{13-40}$$

$$+ \sum_{i=0}^{NR-NR_0} P(i)\text{PBA}_i$$

where

$$PBA_i = \begin{cases} 0 & \text{if } i \leq BF_n - EBF_n \\ k & \text{if } i = BF_n - EBF_n + k \end{cases} \qquad \text{for } k \geq 0$$

A GET ALL command bypasses the indexes and results in accessing the data records directly. Ignoring the initial access and occasional new cylinder accesses, we obtain

$$PBA(\text{GET ALL}) = \left\lceil \frac{NR}{EBF_n} \right\rceil \text{sba} + \left\lceil \frac{NR}{EBF_n} \right\rceil E[\text{OVPBA}] \text{ rba} \qquad (13\text{-}41)$$

A GET SOME command, such as a boolean query, also requires a full file scan as given by Eq. (13-41).

Batch retrieval based on an ordered transaction file is very efficient, particularly when overflow is negligible. Each target record in the batch requires a minimum of n block accesses, as does a random retrieval, but some or all of those blocks could still be residing in buffers from previous recent accesses. Therefore, the actual I/O time for indexed sequential batch retrieval can be much lower than an equivalent set of random retrievals (which occur over a much longer time interval, typically, and have less chance of referencing data still in the buffers) and possibly lower than batch retrieval over a physical sequential file without indexes. For extremely large batch sizes it may be preferable to do a sequential scan and omit the index searching.

We wish to determine the expected index and data block accesses to service a batch of RPBR target records out of NR total records using the indexed sequential organization. Let us assume that there are two levels of indexes, cylinder indexes and track indexes. The total number of cylinder index entries (or records) is NRC and the total number of track index entries (or records) is NRT. We derive the number of data blocks from the relationship NBLK = [NR/EBF].

An interesting paper by Yao [1977b] provides the analytical relationship we need to specify the number of blocks that must be accessed at each level to process the entire batch. Assuming a random distribution of batched requests, we need to know the expected number of index and data blocks to be accessed. In the worst case, RPBR block accesses would be required at the data level. For simplicity in the notation of Theorem 13-1 we let $n = NR$, $m = NBLK$, and $k = RPBR$. The theorem addresses the problem of random drawing without replacement, a realistic assumption regarding the nature of batch processing. Simpler expressions can be derived when random drawing with replacement is assumed.

THEOREM 13-1 [Yao, 1977b]   Given r records grouped into b blocks ($1 < b \leq r$), each contains r/b records. If k records are randomly selected from the r records, the expected number of blocks "hit" (blocks with target records) is given by

$$\text{PBA(blocks hit)} = b \left(1 - \prod_{i=1}^{k} \frac{rd - i + 1}{r - i + 1} \right) \qquad \text{where } d = 1 - \frac{1}{b} \quad (13\text{-}42)$$

PROOF. Let X be a random variable representing the number of blocks hit and let I_j be a random variable where $I_j = 1$ when at least one record in the jth block is selected, and $I_j = 0$ otherwise. The jth block has $p = r/b$ records and there are $r - p$ records not in the jth block. The probability that no records are selected from the jth block is

$$C_k^{r-p} / C_k^r \quad \text{or} \quad C_k^{rd} / C_k^r \qquad \text{where } d = 1 - \frac{1}{b}$$

It follows that the expectation of I_j is

$$E[I_j] = 1 - \frac{C_k^{rd}}{C_k^r}$$

Hence the expected number of blocks hit is

$$E[X] = \sum_{j=1}^{b} E[I_j] = b \left(1 - C_k^{rd} / C_k^r \right)$$

Using the identity

$$C_y^x = \frac{x!}{y! \, (x - y)!}$$

we have

$$E[X] = b \left[1 - \frac{(rd)! \, (r - k)!}{r! \, (rd - k)!} \right]$$

$$= b \left(1 - \prod_{i=1}^{k} \frac{rd - i + 1}{r - i + 1} \right)$$

COROLLARY. If $k > r - r/b$ or $b = 1$, then all m blocks are hit.

Let us now apply Theorem 13-1 to analyze the expected improvement in performance from random retrievals to batch retrievals of RPBR target records.

$$\begin{aligned} \text{PBA(batch retrieval, indexed seq.)} &= \text{PBA(cylinder index)} \\ &+ \text{PBA(track index)} + \text{PBA(data record)} \\ &+ \text{PBA(overflow)} + \text{PBA(transaction file)} \end{aligned} \qquad (13\text{-}43)$$

The cylinder index is the first-level index. It contains

$$\text{NBLKC} = \lceil \text{NCYL} / \text{EBF}_1 \rceil \qquad \text{blocks} \qquad (13\text{-}44)$$

If the batch contains RPBR randomly selected records, the expected number of blocks used in the cylinder index to process the batch is

$$\left\lceil \frac{NCYL}{EBF_1} \cdot \frac{RPBR}{RPBR + 1} \right\rceil$$

Random retrieval of each record consists of a random access to the first block in the cylinder index plus the sequential search of the remaining blocks in approximately half the index. This is repeated RPBR times since each access to a data record is independent of the previous access. Batch retrieval is different. Because buffers are normally available to hold at least the latest cylinder index blocks accessed, and the batch is ordered by physical address, each block is accessed at most only once. If the cylinder index is on a different device than the data blocks (i.e., a dedicated device), each block access after the first block is an ordinary sequential access. If the cylinder index is on the same device as the data blocks (i.e., a shared device), each block access is a random access. These differences are defined in Chapter 9, so for now we assume a dedicated device and represent the total cylinder block accesses for the entire batch as

$$PBA(GET\ BATCH,\ cylinder\ index) = 1\ rba + \left(\left\lceil \frac{NCYL}{EBF_1} \cdot \frac{RPBR}{RPBR + 1} \right\rceil - 1 \right) sba$$

$$(13\text{-}45)$$

The track index is the second-level index. Each track index has entries for the data tracks for a given cylinder, and may also designate overflow tracks. There are NCYL track indexes, one for each entry in the cylinder index. Each track index contains $\lceil (NTRK/NCYL)/EBF_2 \rceil$ blocks. Therefore, the total number of blocks in all the NCYL track indexes is

$$NBLKT = \left\lceil \frac{NTRK/NCYL}{EBF_2} \right\rceil \times NCYL \qquad (13\text{-}46)$$

According to Theorem 13-1, the expected number of track index blocks that will be needed to refer to RPBR randomly selected records (without replacement) is

$$NBLKT \left(1 - \prod_{i=1}^{RPBR} \frac{NTRK \times d_1 - i + 1}{NTRK - i + 1} \right)$$

where $d_1 = (NBLKT - 1)/NBLKT$.

Each block is accessed only once since the batch is ordered by physical address and we assume that each track index is held in a buffer until all the records it refers to have been accessed. Each block access is considered to be random because it is definitely nonsequential unless the batch size is comparable to the file size. However, the random access distance between consecutive records in the batch is low because of batch ordering, and I/O service time is much lower than a random access over the whole device. The expected access distance between records in a batch is NCYL(track indexes)/(RPBR − 1) cylinders. Using this value and the methods of Section 9-2, we can compute expected I/O service time. For now, however, we are only concerned with physical block accesses:

PBA(GET BATCH, track indexes) = 1 rba

$$
+ \left\lceil \text{NBLKT} \times \left(1 - \prod_{i=1}^{\text{RPBR}} \frac{\text{NTRK} \times d_1 - i + 1}{\text{NTRK} - i + 1} \right) \right\rceil - 1 \quad \text{rba}_2
$$

(13-47)

where

$$
d_1 = \frac{\left\lceil \dfrac{\text{NTRK}}{\text{EBF}_2} \right\rceil - 1}{\left\lceil \dfrac{\text{NTRK}}{\text{EBF}_2} \right\rceil}
$$

and the subscript on rba_2 denotes a different expected random access distance (than CPD or NCYL) that must be accounted for.

Applying Theorem 13-1 again, we can derive the expected block accesses for the RPBR data records in the batch:

PBA(GET BATCH, data records) = 1 rba

$$
+ \left\lceil \text{NBLK} \times \left(1 - \prod_{i=1}^{\text{RPBR}} \frac{\text{NR} \times d_2 - i + 1}{\text{NR} - i + 1} \right) \right\rceil - 1 \quad \text{rba}_3
$$

(13-48)

where

$$
d_2 = \frac{(\text{NBLK} - 1)}{\text{NBLK}}
$$

and rba_3 denotes a limited random access whose expected distance is NCYL(data records)/(RPBR − 1).

Overflow chains are accessed next. If each data block has an expected number of overflow accesses equal to $E[\text{OVPBA}]$, and each record in the chain is typically nonsequential relative to its predecessor in the chain, we have

PBA(GET BATCH, overflow)

(13-49)

$$
= \left\lceil \text{NBLK} \times \left(1 - \prod_{i=1}^{\text{RPBR}} \frac{\text{NR} \times d_2 - i + 1}{\text{NR} - i + 1} \right) \times E[\text{OVPBA}] \right\rceil \quad \text{rba}_4
$$

Finally, the cost of accessing the transaction file is given in Sec. 12-2:

$$PBA_{tf} = \left\lceil \frac{RPBR}{EBF_{tf}} \right\rceil \qquad sba \qquad (12\text{-}4)$$

The total physical block accesses for batch retrieval for indexed sequential files with a cylinder and track index is the sum of Eqs. (13-45), (13-47) to (13-49), and (12-4).

By contrast with batch retrieval, random retrieval uses a random access to each level of index and data plus a sequential search at each level to find the target entry.

$$\begin{array}{l} PBA(GET\ UNIQUE, \\ \qquad cylinder\ index) \end{array} = \left[1\ rba + \left(\left\lceil \frac{(1 + NCYL)/EBF_1}{2} \right\rceil - 1 \right) \quad sba \right] \times RPBR$$
$$(13\text{-}50)$$

The search of the track index is similar to the search of the cylinder index, except that the track index is limited to a single track. Therefore, access to a random entry on that track requires a single random access.

$$\begin{aligned} PBA(GET\ UNIQUE,\ track\ index) &= [1\ rba] \times RPBR \\ &= RPBR \qquad rba \end{aligned} \qquad (13\text{-}51)$$

Furthermore, because track index entries point to data tracks individually, the data record access is also limited to a single random access.

$$\begin{aligned} PBA(GET\ UNIQUE,\ data\ record) &= [1\ rba] \times RPBR \\ &= RPBR \qquad rba \end{aligned} \qquad (13\text{-}52)$$

$$PBA(GET\ UNIQUE,\ overflow) = \lceil RPBR \times E[OVPBA] \rceil \qquad rba_4 \qquad (13\text{-}53)$$

The total physical block accesses for random retrieval of RPBR records for indexed sequential files with a cylinder and track index is the sum of Eqs. (13-50) to (13-53) and (12-4).

> *Example 13-5:*   Assume a file of 10^6 fixed size records of length 100 bytes, block size of 1000 bytes, and effective blocking factor of 10 (when LF = 1 and BOVHD = 0). Assume that the index block size is equivalent to the data block size, but that the index blocking factor is 100. Let NCYL = 100 cylinder index entries (records) and NTRK = 10,000 track index entries (records) so that there are NTRK/NCYL = 100 entries in each track index, NR/NTRK entries on each data track, and NCYL = 100 entries per cylinder index. Also assume that the file has just been loaded and no overflow has occurred. If RPBR is the number of records to be retrieved (in the batch), compare random and batch retrieval performance for RPBR = 10^i for i = 0, 1, ..., 6. Do not consider the transaction file for now, because it is a fixed cost for both cases. What if sequential batch processing were used instead of indexed sequential batch processing?

SOLUTION. $\text{NBLK} = \lceil \text{NR/EBF}_3 \rceil = 10^6/10 = 10^5.$

GET UNIQUE (indexed sequential):

$\text{PBA} = \text{PBA(cylinder index)} + \text{PBA(track index)} + \text{PBA(data record)}$
$\qquad + \text{PBA(overflow)}$

$$= \left[1 \text{ rba} + \left(\left\lceil \frac{(1 + 10^2)/10^2}{2} \right\rceil - 1 \right) \text{ sba} \right] \times \text{RPBR}$$
$$+ \text{RPBR rba} + \text{RPBR rba} + 0 \text{ rba}_4$$

$$= 3 \times \text{RPBR} \qquad \text{rba}$$

GET BATCH (indexed sequential):

$\text{PBA} = \text{PBA(cylinder index)} + \text{PBA(track index)} + \text{PBA(data record)}$
$\qquad + \text{PBA(overflow)}$

$$= \left[1 \text{ rba} + \left(\left\lceil \frac{10^2}{10^2} \cdot \frac{\text{RPBR}}{\text{RPBR} + 1} \right\rceil - 1 \right) \text{sba} \right]$$

$$+ \left[1 \text{ rba} + \left(\left\lceil 10^2 \left(1 - \prod_{i=1}^{\text{RPBR}} \frac{10^4(0.99) - i + 1}{10^4 - i + 1} \right) \right\rceil - 1 \right) \text{ rba}_2 \right]$$

$$+ \left[1 \text{ rba} + \left(\left\lceil 10^5 \left(1 - \prod_{i=1}^{\text{RPBR}} \frac{10^6(0.99999) - i + 1}{10^6 - i + 1} \right) \right\rceil - 1 \right) \text{ rba}_3 \right]$$

$$+ \left[\left\lceil 10^5 \left(1 - \prod_{i=1}^{\text{RPBR}} \frac{10^6(0.99999) - i + 1}{10^6 - i + 1} \right) \right\rceil \times \frac{0}{2} \right]$$

$$= 3 \text{ rba} + \left(\left\lceil 10^2 \left(1 - \prod_{i=1}^{\text{RPBR}} \frac{10^4(0.99) - i + 1}{10^4 - i + 1} \right) \right\rceil - 1 \right) \text{ rba}_2$$

$$+ \left(\left\lceil 10^5 \left(1 - \prod_{i=1}^{\text{RPBR}} \frac{10^6(0.99999) - i + 1}{10^6 - i + 1} \right) \right\rceil - 1 \right) \text{ rba}_3$$

When $\text{RPBR} = 1$, the two methods of retrieval have equal cost. Each method requires exactly three random block accesses of the same type (extent).

GET BATCH (physical sequential): We use Eq. (12-8), omitting the transaction file cost.

$$\text{PBA} = \left\lceil \frac{\text{RPBR}}{\text{RPBR} + 1} \cdot \frac{\text{NR}}{\text{EBF}_3} \right\rceil \text{ sba} + \text{RPBR sba}$$

$$= \left\lceil \frac{\text{RPBR}}{\text{RPBR} + 1} \times 10^5 \right\rceil \text{sba} + \text{RPBR sba}$$

We wish to plot the approximate relationship between access cost and RPBR. The weights we can use are $\text{rba} = 40 \text{ ms}$, $\text{rba}_2 = \text{rba}_3 = 20 \text{ ms}$, and $\text{sba} = 10 \text{ ms}$, with a block size of 1000 bytes.

Figure 13-14 shows that random processing is never better than batch processing for the indexed sequential organization. However, batch processing with indexed sequential is only better than simple sequential batch processing (without indexes) up to approximately 20,000 records per batch, or 2% of the file. After that point the use of indexes does not pay off. It is less efficient than sequential processing of only the data file.

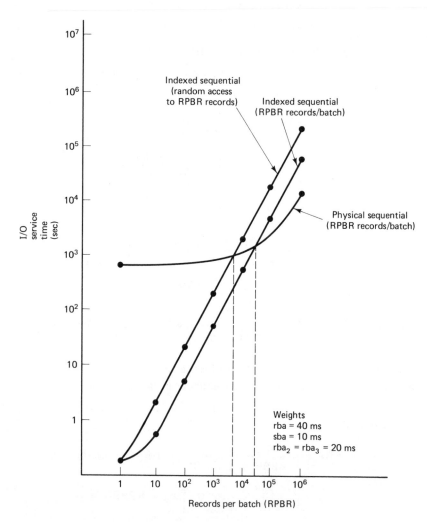

FIGURE 13-14   Indexed sequential performance for sequential and batch retrieval application.

13-4-2 Update to an Indexed Sequential File

Indexed sequential file update costs are computed in a straightforward way. The simplest change to a record is one in which only nonkey data are to be modified. This is accomplished by first retrieving the target record, making the change in the user work area, and rewriting the changed record and the rest of its block back to secondary storage. After retrieval, only a single sequential block write is required. This represents no change from the full index approach.

Modification of a key value is a much more complicated change to a record. If the change is so small that the data record need not be moved to another block, only a simple block rewrite is necessary. For a more significant key value change, the data record must be deleted from its current position and inserted to its new position in another block. Separate searching is required for the deletion and insertion suboperations. Then all levels of indexes must be checked to see if the deleted and reinserted key value affects the block key values stored there. If it does, index modifications must also be made. To evaluate this operation we need to define PRMV as the probability that the data record must be moved to a new block, $PRDEL_i$, as the probability that the old key value is listed in index level i, and $PRINS_i$ as the probability that the new key value must now be listed in index level i.

The costs of these suboperations in block accesses are:

1. *Search for the target record:*

$$PBA_1 = n\ \text{rba} + \sum_{i=1}^{n} \left(\left\lceil \frac{(1 + NR_i)/2}{EBF_i} \right\rceil - 1 \right) \text{sba} + E[OVPBA]\ \text{rba} \tag{13-54}$$

2. *Data record change:*

$$PBA_2 = PRMV \times (\text{delete and reinsert data record})\ \text{pba}$$
$$+ (1 - PRMV) \times 1\ \text{sba} \tag{13-55}$$
$$= PRMV \times (PBA_3 + PBA_4)\ \text{pba} + (1 - PRMV)\ \text{sba}$$

where pba represents physical block accesses when it is not yet known whether the accesses are random or sequential.

3. *Data record deletion* (after the search, flag as deleted, and rewrite):

$$PBA_3 = 1\ \text{sba} \tag{13-56}$$

4. *Data record insertion* (after the search is completed):

$$PBA_4 = OVFLPR \times (1\ \text{rba} + 2\ \text{sba}) + (1 - OVFLPR) \times 1\ \text{sba} \tag{13-57}$$

If overflow occurs, an overflow block must be read and rewritten, and the data block where overflow occurs must have its pointer set and the block rewritten. If overflow does not occur, only the data block with the new record needs to be rewritten.

If we wish to know the probability that overflow occurs for a given bucket (OVFLPR), the simplest method is first to find the probability that overflow does not occur, $1 - \text{OVFLPR}$. This is obtained by summing the probabilities for number of records in a bucket, x, for $x \leq \text{RSPB}$.

$$1 - \text{OVFLPR} = \sum_{x=1}^{\text{RSPB}} P(x) \tag{13-58}$$

Rearranging terms, we get

$$\text{OVFLPR} = 1 - \sum_{x=1}^{\text{RSPB}} P(x)$$

$$= 1 - \sum_{x=1}^{\text{RSPB}} \frac{e^{-\text{RPB}} \times \text{RPB}^x}{x!} \tag{13-59}$$

5. *Access to all levels of indexes* for possible deletion or insertion of key values:

$$\text{PBA}_5 = \text{NIL rba} + \sum_{i=1}^{\text{NIL}} \left\lceil \frac{(1 + \text{NR}_i)/2}{\text{EBF}_i} - 1 \right\rceil \text{sba} \tag{13-60}$$

6. *Index record insertion:*

$$\text{PBA}_6 = \sum_{i=1}^{\text{NIL}} \text{PRINS}_i \, \text{sba} \tag{13-61}$$

If a change is necessary, the currently accessed index block is changed and rewritten.

7. *Index record deletion:*

$$\text{PBA}_7 = \sum_{i=1}^{\text{NIL}} \text{PRDEL}_i \, \text{sba} \tag{13-62}$$

The total cost for a key change is

$$\text{PBA(CHANGE key)} = \text{PBA}_1 + \text{PBA}_2 + \text{PBA}_5 + \text{PBA}_6 + \text{PBA}_7 \tag{13-63}$$

An insertion operation requires insertion of both data record and possibly the key in one or more indexes if it is the highest value key in the block.

$$\text{PBA(INSERT)} = \text{PBA}_1 + \text{PBA}_4 + \text{PBA}_5 + \text{PBA}_6 \tag{13-64}$$

A deletion operation requires that the data record be flagged and its block rewritten. Also, if the deleted entry had its key value listed in one or more indexes, those values must be changed to the next highest key value in the respective blocks.

$$\text{PBA(DELETE)} = \text{PBA}_1 + \text{PBA}_3 + \text{PBA}_5 + \text{PBA}_7 \tag{13-65}$$

Batch updates are generally more efficient using an indexed sequential organization than a physical sequential organization because the indexes can be used to access target records without scanning the entire file. The search component is equivalent to batch retrieval, Eq. (13-48), and the update component is equivalent to the corresponding random processing update operations specified in Eqs. (13-55) to (13-65). The advantage of batch processing is that the search time is reduced because of the proximity of successive target records in the ordered batch.

13-4-3 Storage Space for Indexed Sequential Organizations

Storage space consists of index blocks (levels 1 to NIL) plus data blocks (level $n = $ NIL $+ 1$) and overflow blocks (level $n + 1$).

$$
\begin{aligned}
\text{BLKSTOR} = \sum_{i=1}^{\text{NIL}} &\left\lceil \frac{NR_i}{\left\lfloor \dfrac{(BKS_i - BOVHD_i) \times LF_i}{KS + PS} \right\rfloor} \right\rceil \times BKS_i \\
+ &\left\lceil \frac{NR_n}{\left\lfloor \dfrac{(BKS_n - BOVHD_n) \times LF_n}{SRS} \right\rfloor} \right\rceil \qquad (13\text{-}66) \\
\times &\left[BKS_n + \left\lceil \frac{E[OVPBA]}{\left\lfloor \dfrac{(BKS_{n+1} - BOVHD_{n+1})}{SRS} \right\rfloor} \right\rceil \times BKS_{n+1} \right] \text{bytes}
\end{aligned}
$$

where NR_i is the number of index entries at level i.

13-4-4 Trade-Off Analysis in Indexed Sequential Organizations

Indexed Sequential versus Full Index

Let us assume that the full index access method is implemented with an ordered index and unordered data file. We can now apply our analysis to compare their respective performance. The two access methods have equivalent performance for GET ALL operations, assuming that no overflow occurs. If ordered data are required, based on primary key value, the indexed sequential file need not be sorted. The unordered full index implementation always requires sorting according to the report specifications.

The full index organization does not allow for overflow, but reorders the index to accommodate any new insertion. GET UNIQUE is very efficiently handled with both methods, with some variation due to search mechanism implementation. Also, changes involving nonkey values are simply done with a single block rewrite with both access methods.

GET NEXT and GET PRIOR are much more efficiently handled by indexed sequential because of the physical contiguity of records. Also, indexed sequential is the only method that can efficiently execute batch processing because it keeps the data file ordered. Although deletion is easier using a full index if we allow deleted index entries to be flagged, insertion and key change operations are difficult with either method because of the massive index updating required. Storage space is lower with indexed sequential due to the block index concept.

Example 13-6:   Given a 10^6 record file with 100 bytes each, key size is 6 bytes, pointer size is 4 bytes, and block size (BKS) is 1000 bytes. Let LF = 1 and BOVHD = 0 for simplicity. Compare the storage space difference between a full index organization and indexed sequential organization with two levels of indexing having 10^2 and 10^4 index entries, respectively. Assume that there are no overflow records. If the work load is one random retrieval, one random insertion, and one random deletion per unit time, what is the difference in total I/O service time using the two access methods? Allow the full index method to use a binary search for its 10^6 entry index.

$$\text{BLKSTOR(full index)} = \text{BLKSTOR(Index)} \quad + \text{BLKSTOR(Data)}$$

$$= \left\lceil \frac{10^6}{\left\lfloor \frac{1000}{10} \right\rfloor} \right\rceil \times 1000 \; + \left\lceil \frac{10^6}{\left\lfloor \frac{1000}{100} \right\rfloor} \right\rceil \times 1000$$

$$= 10^7 + 10^8 = 110 \times 10^6 \text{ bytes}$$

Full index: $NR_1 = 10^6$, $NR_2 = 1$.
Indexed sequential: $NR_1 = 10^2$, $NR_2 = 10^2$, $NR_3 = 10^2$.

BLKSTOR(indexed seq.)

$$= \left\lceil \frac{100}{\left\lfloor \frac{1000}{10} \right\rfloor} \right\rceil \times 1000 + \left\lceil \frac{10,000}{\left\lfloor \frac{1000}{10} \right\rfloor} \right\rceil \times 1000 + \left\lceil \frac{10^6}{\left\lfloor \frac{1000}{100} \right\rfloor} \right\rceil \times (1 + 0) \times 1000$$

$$= 10^3 + 10^5 + 10^8$$

$$= 100.101 \times 10^6 \text{ bytes} \qquad \text{(a 9\% reduction from the full index storage cost)}$$

$$\text{PBA(full index)} = \text{PBA(retrieval)} \times 3$$
$$+ \text{PBA(insertion)} + \text{PBA(deletion)}$$

$$= [\log_2(5000)] \times 3 \text{ rba} + (2 \times 10^4) \text{ sba} + 1 \text{ rba}$$
$$+ 1 \text{ sba} + 1 \text{ sba}$$

$$= 12.29 \times 3 + 1 \text{ rba} + 2 \times 10^4 + 2 \text{ sba}$$

$$= 37.87 \text{ rba} + 20002 \text{ sba}$$

PBA(indexed seq.) = PBA(retrieval) $\times$ 3
                   + PBA(insertion) + PBA(deletion)

$$= \left(3 \text{ rba} + \left(\left\lceil \frac{(1 + 10^2)/2}{100} \right\rceil - 1\right) \text{ sba}\right.$$

$$+ \left(\left\lceil \frac{(1 + 10^2)/2}{100} \right\rceil - 1\right) \text{ sba} + 0 \left.\right) \times 3$$

$$+ 1 \text{ sba} + 2 \text{ rba} + \left(\left\lceil \frac{(1 + 10^2)/2}{100} \right\rceil - 1\right) \text{ sba}$$

$$+ \left(\left\lceil \frac{(1 + 10^2)/2}{100} \right\rceil - 1\right) \text{ sba}$$

$$+ 0.11 \text{ sba} + 1 \text{ sba} + 2 \text{ rba}$$

$$+ \left(\left\lceil \frac{(1 + 10^2)/2}{100} \right\rceil - 1\right) \text{ sba}$$

$$+ \left(\left\lceil \frac{(1 + 10^2)/2}{100} \right\rceil - 1\right) \text{ sba} + 0.11 \text{ sba}$$

where $PRINS_i = 1/EBF_{i+1}$ and
$PRDEL_i = 1/EBF_{i+1}$

$$= (3 \text{ rba}) \times 3 + 1 \text{ sba} + 2 \text{ rba} + 0.11 \text{ sba} + 1 \text{ sba}$$
$$+ 2 \text{ rba} + 0.11 \text{ sba})$$

$$= 13 \text{ rba} + 2.22 \text{ sba}$$

Using the disk characteristics of Chapter 9 (IBM 3350 disk), we obtain

$$\text{rba} = 25 + 8.35 + 16.7/16 = 34.4 \text{ ms}$$
$$\text{sba} = 8.35 + 16.7/16 = 9.4 \text{ ms}$$
$$\text{TIO(full index)} = 37.87 \times 36.4 + 20{,}002 \times 9.4 = 189.4 \times 10^3 \text{ ms}$$
$$\text{TIO(indexed seq.)} = 13 \times 36.4 + 2.22 \times 9.4 = 0.49 \times 10^3 \text{ ms}$$

This workload is much more efficiently serviced with an indexed sequential organization. I/O service time is dramatically reduced, owing to the very inefficient index insertion time for the full index method. Retrieval was also significantly faster using indexed sequential despite the binary block search of the full index. Finally, we note that storage space is also lower using indexed sequential. Although deletion is faster in a full index organization, the total time for search and deletion is larger than it is for indexed sequential. Therefore, there appear to be no real trade-offs between these two access methods for large files of 1 million records. Indexed sequential is clearly superior over the full index approach for this work load and database.

Optimum Index Configuration

The selection of an optimum number of indexes and optimum size of each index is a complex problem that is highly dependent on the proportion of file retrievals, insertions, deletions, and changes. Let us only consider retrieval block accesses and develop a simple model. Let NR be the total number of records in the file, EBF_2 the effective blocking factor of data blocks, and EBF_1 be the effective blocking factor of a one-level index. Therefore, $NBLK = \lceil NR/EBF_2 \rceil$ and $NBLKI = \lceil NRI/EBF_1 \rceil$, where NBLKI is the number of index blocks required and NRI is the number of entries in the block index. From the description of this file we know that $NRI = NBLK$ (i.e., there is one entry in the index for each block in the data file). The expected retrieval access path length (excluding overflow) in block accesses is given by

$$PBA(retrieval) = 1\ rba + \left(\frac{1 + NBLKI}{2} - 1 \right) sba + 1\ rba \qquad (13\text{-}67)$$

This function is minimized with $NBLKI = 1$. In general, any n-level index organization minimizes retrieval time when the block size at each level is maximized. Therefore, the recommended index block size is the largest practical size allowed in the system, possibly a quarter, half, or full disk track. A large data block size is also recommended because it makes sequential processing more efficient and reduces the number of entries required.

Given a maximum data block size, BKS, and a maximum index block size, IBKS, we now wish to find the optimum number of index levels. If n is the number of index levels, we know that a minimum of $n + 1$ random block accesses are required to obtain a data block, one for each of the n levels of indexes plus the data record level. Additional sequential block accesses are required at each level where the index or data file is too large for a single block. If at any given level j, more than 30 sequential block accesses are required, it is usually better to add a level of indexing. The cost of an additional level is 1 rba and the gain is the elimination of 30 sba at level j. (The relative cost of rba to sba is known to be about 4:1 for block sizes in the range 2^{10} to 2^{12} bytes for IBM 3350-like disks. Ultimately, a top-level (master) index that resides in main storage can be justified in terms of I/O time reduction any time the next lower level index requires more than one block to store it. The cost for a master index is in the permanent main storage space occupied. No additional update cost should occur for additional levels of indexes because the search component of update is reduced and the block index update operations are minimal in terms of block accesses. Verification of this assertion can be done with the relationships derived above for updates and retrieval for various index configurations.

14 PRIMARY ACCESS METHODS: SEARCH TREES AND RANDOM PROCESSING

Access methods whose foundations are explicit tree structures have been used for searching main storage tables and lists for many years. More recently, however, their application has been extended to random retrieval of secondary storage data, thus competing with the more classical methods such as indexed sequential and hashing. In this chapter we investigate three basic classes of tree structures and some of their variations: binary search, B-tree, and the TRIE structure. The search mechanism used for these structures is normally a linked sequential method; thus we find that the type of structure is the distinguishing characteristic of interest for study and evaluation.

14-1 BINARY SEARCH TREES

Binary search trees are an important class of physical database structures that provide a reasonable compromise among both random and sequential retrieval applications and high update volume. Data records can be organized as an ordered linked sequential file to enhance report processing and batch transaction processing. An additional pointer in each stored record facilitates fast tree searching for random retrieval, which is the more common use of this organization. Insertion and deletion operations are fast, after searching has been completed, because only pointer values are changed and no storage reallocation is required. A *binary tree* T_{NR} is an ordered triple (T_l, R, T_r) where R is the root node and T_l and T_r are the left and right binary subtrees of R. T_l and T_r contain l and r nodes, respectively. We note that $l \geq 0, r \geq 0$, and $l + r = NR - 1$ nodes. A *binary search tree* over NR names (identifiers) is a binary tree T_{NR} in which each node is labeled with a distinct name and is in lexicographic order; that is, for any node i, the names of nodes in its left subtree lexicographically precede node i and the names of nodes in its right subtree. The search mechanism for a binary search tree visits the root node (R) first and compares the search key, k, with the key value at the root, k_R. If $k = k_R$ the search terminates successfully. If $k < k_R$ lexicographically, the search continues recursively through the left subtree of R. If $k > k_R$ lexicographically, the search continues recursively at the right subtree of R. If the algorithm continues to a leaf node i, and $k \neq k_i$, the search ends unsuccessfully. A *leaf* node is any node in the binary search tree that has no subtrees (i.e., a terminal node).

In a binary search tree each node consists of a node value, left pointer, and right pointer. The node value consists of the full primary key and possibly several nonkey elements; each node is equivalent to a stored record. The insertion mechanism makes use of the binary tree search mechanism to attempt to find the node (record) that contains the search key value. When the search ends ''unsuccessfully'' at a leaf node j, the new node is inserted as the left or right subtree of leaf node j, depending on whether the key value (or name) is less than or greater than k_j, respectively. With this algorithm the path length to an identifier is dependent upon the order in which identifiers are stored, and consequently the shape of the resulting tree can be anywhere from a linear list [Fig. 14-1(a)] to a perfectly balanced tree [Fig. 14-1(b)]. Other shapes in between the two extremes are also common [Fig. 14-1(c)].

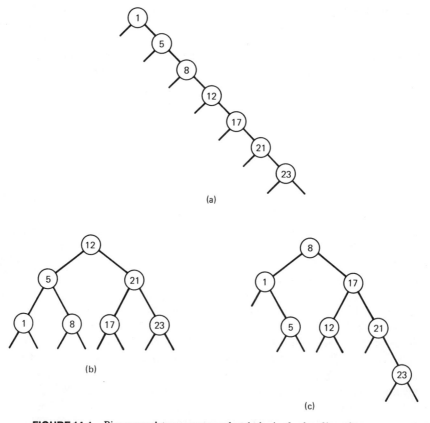

(a)

(b)

(c)

FIGURE 14-1   Binary search trees constructed on the basis of order of insertions.

Given a set of NR identifier values to be stored, the expected path length to an identifier varies from $(1 + NR)/2$ for the linear list to approximately $\log_2 NR - 1$ for a balanced tree [Severance, 1974]. Hibbard [1962] showed that a random ordering would result in an expected path length of $1.4 \log_2 NR$ for a successful search and $1.4 \log_2 (NR - 1)$ for an unsuccessful search. He also analyzed updates and storage space.

The notion of "balance" in a binary search tree is important to the design of efficient tree structures for database retrieval and update. Before we consider this concept, however, let us define some additional terms. The *level* of a node or leaf *i*, L_i, is the path length from the root of T_{NR} to node *i*. The root is considered to be level 0. The *height* of a tree is the maximum level of any of its nodes. A tree is considered *balanced* when the difference in height between the root and any two leaves (terminal nodes) is at most one. Balanced trees minimize the expected access path length when there is an equal probability for each node being referenced. Under such ideal conditions it would be important to be able to easily construct balanced trees.

When the database is volatile, an alternative binary search tree organization, called an AVL tree, was proposed and studied by Adelson-Velskiy and Landis [1962], Foster [1965], and others. This class of trees is also known as "height-balanced trees." T_{NR} is a *height-balanced (AVL) tree* if for every node *i*, the height of its left and right subtrees differ by at most one. Several examples are given in Fig. 14-2. This is a much less restrictive definition of balance than for perfectly (fully) balanced binary search trees. In fact, in an *m*-level AVL tree the maximum difference in length between any two paths is $m/2$. However, the expected successful search length is only approximately $\log_2 NR + 1$ probes. This is only slightly larger than the optimum expected search length for a fully balanced binary search tree. A summary of the performance differences, in terms of access path length (logical record accesses), is shown in Table 14-1.

Many other types of balanced trees have been proposed to deal efficiently with both retrieval and update; included are "weight-balanced trees" and generalized height-balanced trees with a difference $d > 1$ in path length between subtrees. Summaries of work on binary search trees are given in Knuth [1973] and Nievergelt [1974].

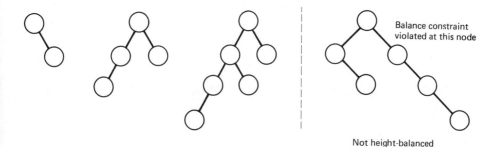

Balance constraint violated at this node

Not height-balanced

FIGURE 14-2   Height-balanced (AVL) trees [Nievergelt, 1974].

TABLE 14-1   Comparison of Search Lengths (LRA) for Binary Search
Trees with NR Nodes*

	LINEAR	UNBAL	BAL	AVL
Best search length	1	1	1	1
Expected search length	$(1 + NR)/2$	$1.4 \log_2 (NR - 1)$ (successful) $1.4 \log_2 NR$ (unsuccessful)	$\log_2 (NR + 1) - 2$	$\log_2 (NR + 1)$
Worst search length	NR	Not defined	$\log_2 (NR + 1)$	$1.44 \log_2 (NR + 1)$

*LINEAR   Linear (linked) list; the worst case of an unbalanced binary search tree
 UNBAL   Unbalanced; random ordering of insertions
   BAL   Fully balanced binary search tree; path length from root to any two leaves differs by no more than one
   AVL   Height-balanced (AVL) tree; sibling subtrees differ in height by no more than one

The major factors to be addressed in the design of binary search trees are:

- *Data volatility*. Relative importance of update and retrieval affects the type of balance required in a tree.
- *Record identifier access frequency distribution*. Affects the type of tree balance required.
- *Record insertion sequence*. Affects degree of balance; retrieval time.
- *Storage device level*. Secondary storage file could benefit from record clustering (e.g., top nodes in contiguous storage).

14-1-1   Retrieval Performance

The access path representation of binary search trees is illustrated in Fig. 14-1. At each level there is only one node to access, and a random access is assumed as the default value for secondary storage implementations. If an implementation clusters nodes in some nonrandom way, further investigation would be needed to determine the "weight" (in distance or time) associated with each random access. Using the expected LRA for random search times in Table 14-1, we obtain the expected search costs:

$$
\text{PBA(GET UNIQUE)} = \begin{cases} 1.4 \log_2 (NR - 1) \text{ rba} & \text{for UNBAL} \\ \log_2 (NR + 1) - 2 \text{ rba} & \text{for BAL} \\ \log_2 (NR + 1) \text{ rba} & \text{for AVL} \end{cases} \tag{14-1}
$$

When the search is unsuccessful:

$$
\begin{aligned}
&= 1.4 \log_2 \text{ NR rba} &&\text{for UNBAL} \\
\text{PBA(GET UNIQUE')} \quad &\leq \log_2 (\text{NR} + 1) \text{ rba} &&\text{for BAL} &&(14\text{-}2) \\
&\leq 1.44 \log_2 (\text{NR} + 1) \text{ rba} &&\text{for AVL}
\end{aligned}
$$

GET NEXT and GET PRIOR require one or more random block accesses via tree pointers to the right subtree and left subtree, respectively. In the worst case it may traverse the entire height of the tree. GET ALL requires a traversal of the entire tree, and it applies to both sequential processing and for boolean query processing:

$$
\text{PBA(GET ALL)} = \text{NR rba} \qquad (14\text{-}3)
$$

Efficient implementations of binary search trees will typically include a blocking factor and store records in blocks in their natural order of insertion. This is called *sequential allocation* [Muntz and Uzgalis, 1970; Nievergelt, 1974]. *Grouped allocation* tries to cluster a new node (record) near its parent node (record). If the block (or page) containing the parent node is full, a new block (page) is allocated to the new node. Simulation experiments give some support to the argument that the grouped allocation scheme tends to have fewer block accesses. The trade-off is that grouped allocation requires more data storage space because of the sparsely populated new blocks allocated when child records cannot be placed near parent records (i.e., placed in the same block). Some reduction of storage space can be realized if overflow records are allocated to sparsely populated overflow blocks that have already been allocated.

The best grouped allocation of EBF records to a block will reduce each set of $\log_2$ EBF record accesses to a single block access. Therefore, in the best case,

$$
\text{PBA(GET UNIQUE, grouped alloc.)} = \frac{\text{PBA(GET UNIQUE)}}{\log_2 \text{EBF}} \quad \text{rba} \qquad (14\text{-}4)
$$

Similarly, the best case for an unsuccessful search can be specified. In the case of unordered sequential processing, however, the sequential allocation scheme is very efficient. The best case possible is

$$
\text{PBA(GET ALL, unordered, seq. alloc.)} = \left\lceil \frac{\text{NR}}{\text{EBF}} \right\rceil \quad \text{sba} \qquad (14\text{-}5)
$$

Ordered sequential processing can be accomplished with random accesses to (1) nodes in the proper sequence, Eq. (14-5), or (2) sequential accesses to nodes in arrival sequence, Eq. (14-3), plus the accesses to sort the records, whichever of (1) or (2) costs less. Muntz and Uzgalis [1970] derived the expected number of block accesses for sequential allocation for the UNBAL configuration to be

$$\text{PBA(GET UNIQUE, UNBAL, seq. alloc.)} = 0.75 + \frac{1.5 \times EBF}{NR} \tag{14-6}$$

$$+ 1.4 \log_2 \left(\frac{NR}{2 \times EBF} \right)$$

14-1-2   Update Performance

The binary search tree configurations in Table 14-1 all exhibit the same characteristics for updating after the search has been completed. The simplest form of update is to change a nonkey value at a node. This is the same as a linked sequential organization change:

$$\text{PBA(CHANGE nonkey)} = 1 \text{ sba} \tag{14-7}$$

Changing a key value in a record in a binary search tree implies that a reallocation of the tree nodes is highly likely. If the change is so small that no reallocation is necessary, the cost is equivalent to a change of a nonkey value. If, however, the change is made to another random key value, it is equivalent to a random deletion, followed by a random insertion in the search tree. Let us now proceed to derive the cost of those operations.

We need to develop expressions for record insertion and deletion for the various configurations of binary search trees discussed above. The UNBAL configuration, inserting records in the natural (random) order of arrival, is interesting because it illustrates that the least cost of updates occurs when the tree is not required to be balanced. We will also see that fully balanced (BAL) trees are very difficult to update, and the AVL trees provide a reasonable compromise between retrieval and update.

The UNBAL configuration, by definition, easily combines search and insertion in an efficient way. The search is performed until a terminal node is located that ends the so-called "unsuccessful" search for a node containing the key to be inserted. The terminal node is the parent of the new node, and the child is inserted as the left or right subtree of the parent, depending on whether the new key is lexicographically smaller than or larger than the parent key, respectively. If the block containing the parent record has space for a new record, and if the blocking strategy allows such an insertion, the cost of insertion is a sequential block access to the parent block already traversed. For all other conditions, an additional random block access is required for the new child record:

$$1 \text{ sba} \leq \text{PBA(INSERT, UNBAL)} \leq 1 \text{ sba} + 1 \text{ rba} \tag{14-8}$$

Deletion of a record in an UNBAL configuration is simple if the deletion operation only involves setting a flag in the stored record. This requires only a single sequential access (sba) to rewrite the block accessed by the search mechanism in a so-called ''successful'' search. However, the more typical case is deletion by reset-ting pointers, and this requires some movement of a lower-level node up to the deleted node position to maintain the binary tree structure. An algorithm to accomplish this type of deletion has been proposed by Knuth [1973]. The activity of this algorithm is illustrated in Fig. 14-3, where node 12 is to be deleted. If both subtrees of node 12 are null, the deletion is simply accomplished by nullifying node 22's left pointer. If either the left or right subtree of node 12 (but not both) is null, the other subtree can be moved up to the deleted node position merely by setting node 22's left pointer to the root node of that subtree.

Figure 14-3(a) shows the most difficult case when the node to be deleted has both left and right subtrees. In this case a search is conducted to the right subtree and recursively following its left pointers until a terminal node is found. This node (node 13) has the smallest key value in this subtree; it is, of course, larger than any key value in the left subtree of the deleted node. Also, it has no subtrees, by definition, so reallocation is kept to a minimum. This node (node 13) is deleted from its current position and inserted in place of the original node to be deleted (node 12) in a sequence that properly saves the critical pointers until they are no longer needed. Node 13 now

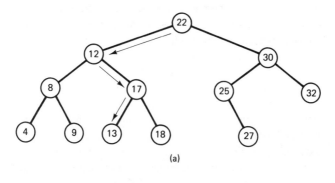

(a)

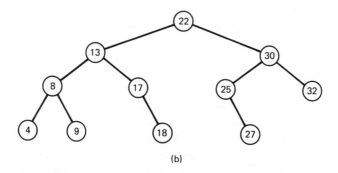

(b)

FIGURE 14-3 Deletion of a record from a randomly constructed binary search tree (UNBAL): (*a*) before deletion of node 12; (*b*) after deletion of node 12.

points to nodes 8 and 17, node 22 points to node 13, and node 17's left pointer is nullified. If node 17 did not have a left subtree, it would replace node 12 directly. The final positions of nodes after the operation is completed is shown in Fig. 14-3(b).

The cost of this deletion operation varies from the simplest case when only node 22's left pointer must be reset (1 sba), to the most complex case when additionally the root must be deleted and the entire height of the right subtree must be searched. Therefore, the limits on deletion cost are

$$1 \text{ sba} \leqslant \text{PBA(DELETE, UNBAL)} \leqslant 1.4 \log_2 (\text{NR} - 1) - 1 \text{ rba} + 1 \text{ sba}$$

$$(14\text{-}9)$$

The fully balanced configuration (BAL) is more complex than the unbalanced ones because the strict balance constraint must be maintained after each insertion or deletion. The AVL trees have a much less restrictive constraint of balance; therefore, they require fewer transformations (node reallocations), and each transformation usually requires less time to perform than for a fully balanced tree. For example, Fig. 14-4 shows a binary search tree that is height-balanced and fully balanced. The insertion of a node E creates a new tree that is still height-balanced but not fully balanced. The constraint violation occurs because the path from L to E is of length 4, and other paths of length 2 still exist. No transformation would have been required for a height-balanced tree. In contrast, the transformation to maintain full balance changed the position of every node in the tree. In general, a transformation requires $O(n)$ steps, each involving a node position change. It is then with good reason that AVL trees are more attractive to implement in real systems, where databases are likely to be reasonably volatile.

Let us look more closely at AVL tree update and the maintenance of height balance. Figure 14-5 illustrates an insertion operation that requires a common type of transformation, called a *rotation*. The initial subtree is height-balanced. The symbols with the nonterminal nodes are condition codes denoting the current state of balance before insertion. The symbols ''/,'' ''−,'' and ''\'' indicate a left subtree with greater height, equal left and right subtree heights, and right subtree with greater height, respectively, for this node. After node E is inserted, the balance constraint is violated at node M and a transformation is required to restore height balance. The rotation preserves the relationship between nodes C, E, and G; and also between M and Q. The rotation actually occurs between G and M, and because G may have only two subtrees, by definition, node J must be moved to be M's left subtree to preserve the proper ordering among G, J, and M.

An example of a double-rotation-type transformation is shown in Fig. 14-6. In the subtree N, the height-balance constraint is violated at node D when the insertion of node E is made. During the transformation many of the node relationships are unchanged. However, two rotations are required: node I is rotated with node D, and then it is rotated with node N. In the first rotation the left subtree E, H of node I is moved to be the right subtree of node D. In the second rotation between nodes I and N, node L is moved to be the left subtree of node N.

Insertion in height-balanced trees requires at most either a single or double

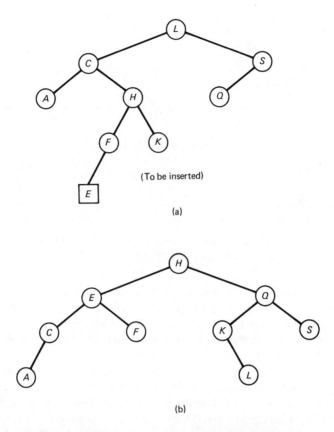

FIGURE 14-4 Fully balanced tree transformation for insertion: (a) fully balanced before insertion of node E; (b) after insertion and rebalancing transformation.

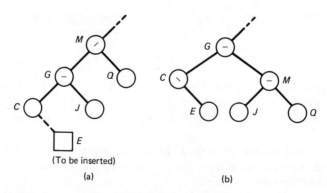

FIGURE 14-5 Height-balanced tree transformation for insertion: (a) initial subtree; (b) after "rotation" to restore balance.

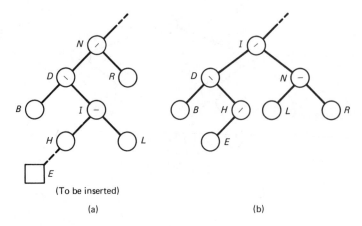

(To be inserted)

(a)   (b)

FIGURE 14-6 Height-balanced tree double rotation: (a) initial subtree; (b) after "double rotation" to restore balance [Nievergelt, 1974].

rotation. A detailed explanation of height-balanced tree updates, in terms of logical record accesses, is given by Knuth [1973]. Knuth also provides an algorithm for search and insertion, its mathematical (complexity) analysis, and probability tables for single and double rotations as a function of path length from where the balancing constraint was violated to the point of insertion.

In view of the recognized complexity of analyzing AVL tree insertions, let us consider only the bounds on physical block accesses. The lower bound is exemplified in Fig. 14-4, where no rotations are required for height balance and only one pointer needs to be set in the parent node. If both parent and new child nodes are in the same block, only one sequential block rewrite is required. If they are allocated to different blocks, the parent block needs a sequential rewrite and the new child block needs a random write.

Lower bounds:

$$\text{PBA(INSERT, AVL)} = \begin{cases} 1 \text{ sba} & \text{if parent and new child are in the same block} \\ 1 \text{ sba} + 1 \text{ rba} & \text{if in different blocks} \end{cases} \qquad (14\text{-}10)$$

The upper bound is somewhat more complex. In the worst case there will be a double rotation involving three nodes, plus the movement of two subtrees across parent nodes (as in Fig. 14-7). The following basic steps are required:

1. After the search is completed to where the insertion is to be made, a random write is necessary (at most) for the insertion, plus the sequential rewrite to update the parent pointers.
2. Assuming that a stack is used to preserve node addresses traversed to find the point of insertion, no further secondary storage searching is needed to relocate

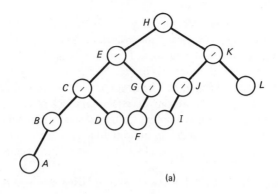

(a)

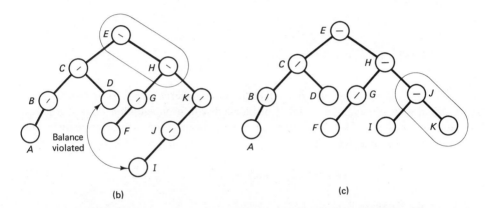

(b)

(c)

FIGURE 14-7 Deletion of a record from an AVL tree: (*a*) before deletion of node *L*; (*b*) first rotation, *E* and *H*; (*c*) second rotation, *J* and *K*.

the nodes where rotation is required. These nodes are located in the stack using the rebalancing algorithm.

3. Pointers must be reset in the three nodes involved in the rotation, plus the parent node of the subtree under transformation. If they all reside in separate randomly placed blocks (the worst case again), four random reads and sequential rewrites are required here.

Upper bounds:

$$\text{PBA(INSERT, AVL)} = \begin{cases} 1 \text{ sba} & \text{if all nodes to be updated are in the same block} \\ 5 \text{ sba} + 5 \text{ rba} & \text{if all nodes are in separate randomly placed blocks} \end{cases} \quad (14\text{-}11)$$

Deletion of records in an AVL tree may require up to $\log_2$ NR transformations. This is considerably more complex than insertion, and very little mathematical algorithmic analysis exists on the subject. To visualize the problem a little better, observe that deletion of node L in the tree of Fig. 14-7 requires two single rotations of separate pairs of nodes: E, H and J, K. The lower bound is simple; if the deletion is to a leaf node and balance is not upset, only a sequential block rewrite is necessary for the parent node. The upper bound computation must consider $\log_2$ NR rotations, three nodes per transformation (two nodes in the rotation, plus the parent of the subtree transformed), and possibly separate blocks to be read and rewritten.

$$1 \text{ sba} \leq \text{PBA(DELETE, AVL)} \leq \log_2 \text{NR}(3 \text{ sba} + 3 \text{ rba}) \qquad (14\text{-}12)$$

The performance characteristics of binary search trees are summarized in Table 14-2.

14-1-3 Storage Space

Storage space depends on whether the binary search tree is stored unblocked, blocked with sequential allocation, or blocked with grouped allocation. We define stored record size first, assuming that record format and size are homogeneous throughout the tree structure.

$$\text{SRS} = \text{KS} + \text{NKS} + 2 \times \text{PS} \qquad \text{bytes} \qquad (14\text{-}13)$$

When the database is unblocked,

$$\text{BLKSTOR} = \text{SRS} \times \text{NR} \qquad \text{bytes} \qquad (14\text{-}14)$$

When sequential allocation and blocking is used,

$$\text{BLKSTOR} = \left\lceil \frac{\text{NR}}{\text{EBF}} \right\rceil \times \text{BKS} \qquad \text{bytes} \qquad (14\text{-}15)$$

Grouped allocation blocking has a variety of implementations that result in a wide range of low- to high-density packing of records in blocks. Certainly, the lower bound is defined by Eq. (14-15). A gross upper bound is defined by NR blocks, but we can reduce this estimate by noting that in the worst case, each full block has only one "overflow" record in a separate block, so that the combined number of records in two blocks are EBF + 1, or the average per block is (EBF + 1)/2. Consequently, the bounds on storage space required for grouped allocation are

$$\left\lceil \frac{\text{NR}}{\text{EBF}} \right\rceil \times \text{BKS} \leq \text{BLKSTOR} \leq \left\lceil \frac{\text{NR}}{(\text{EBF} + 1)/2} \right\rceil \times \text{BKS} \qquad \text{bytes} \qquad (14\text{-}16)$$

TABLE 14-2 Database Operation Cost (PBA) for Binary Search Trees*

	Linear	*Unbalanced*	*Balanced*	*AVL*
GET ALL	←——————————————— $\left\{\begin{array}{l}\text{UB: NR rba} \\ \text{LB: NR/EBF sba}\end{array}\right.$ ——————————————→			
GET NEXT GET PRIOR	←——————————————— $\left\{\begin{array}{l}\text{UB: } \log_2 \text{NR rba} \\ \text{LB: } \quad 0\end{array}\right.$ ——————————————→			
GET UNIQUE (key found)	$(1 + \text{NR})/2$	UB: $1.4 \log_2 (\text{NR} - 1)$ rba	UB: $\log_2 (\text{NR} + 1) - 2$ rba	UB: $\log_2 (\text{NR} + 1)$ rba
	←——————— $\left\{\begin{array}{l}\text{LB: } \dfrac{\text{PBA(GET UNIQUE)}}{\log_2 \text{EBF}} \text{ rba}\end{array}\right.$ ———————→			
GET UNIQUE' (key not found)	$(1 + \text{NR})/2$	UB: $1.4 \log_2 \text{NR}$ rba	UB: $\log_2 (\text{NR} + 1)$ rba	UB: $1.44 \log_2 (\text{NR} + 1)$ rba
	←——————— $\left\{\begin{array}{l}\text{LB: } \dfrac{\text{PBA (GET UNIQUE')}}{\log_2 \text{EBF}} \text{ rba}\end{array}\right.$ ———————→			
GET RPBR (batch)	←——————— Same as linked sequential (Table 12-3) ———————→			
GET SOME (boolean query)	←——————————— Same as GET ALL ———————————→			

After the search is completed:

	Linear	*Unbalanced*	*Balanced*	*AVL*
CHANGE nonkey	←————————————— 1 sba —————————————→			
CHANGE key	←——————— GET UNIQUE + DELETE + GET UNIQUE + INSERT ———————→			

INSERT record
  LB:
  UB:
	
	1 sba
	1 rba + 2 sba
		
		1 sba
		1 rba + 1 sba
			
			1 sba
			0(NR) rba
				
				1 sba
				5 rba + 5 sba

DELETE record
  LB:
  UB:
	
	1 sba
	1 sba
	+ NR/2 rba
		
		1 sba
		$1.4 \log_2$
		$(\text{NR} - 1) - 1$
		rba + 1 sba
			
			1 sba
			0 (NR) rba
				
				1 sba
				$\log_2 \text{NR}(3 \text{ rba}$
				$+ 3 \text{ sba})$

UPDATE BATCH	←——————— Sum of individual updates of RPBR records ———————→			

*UB   Upper bound
 LB   Lower bound

14-2 B-TREES

The B-tree is a very popular structure for organizing and maintaining large indexes. Like the binary search tree, it offers very good random retrieval and update performance, while allowing occasional sequential processing without having to reorganize the data. B-trees fall into the category of multiway trees, those that allow more than two branches from any node. The indexed sequential access method is another form of multiway tree in which each index can be considered to be a node with a branch for each (block) key value stored in the index. The B-tree generalizes this notion, allowing many possible node sizes, branches, and node levels. Each node in a B-tree consists of a set of primary key values, index pointers, and associated data. The index pointers are used to branch to the next lower level of nodes in the B-tree index. The "associated data" in each node are typically a set of data pointers which are used to locate data records whose key values appear in the current index node. Although the data records could feasibly reside directly in the index nodes, it is not an efficient way to implement very large databases. B-trees are normally used for indexes only, and the data records reside in a separate area where random access can be made.

B-trees were studied in the early 1970s by Bayer and McCreight [1972; Bayer, 1972] and others [Comer, 1979b]. The B-tree structures showed early promise for efficient storage of very large indexes on secondary storage and allowed very fast random retrieval of records. Some of the B-tree concepts have been implemented in IBM's access method, VSAM [Comer, 1979b; IBM, 1976, 1977; Keehn and Lacy, 1974; Wagner, 1973]. A great deal of attention has focused on these structures in recent years, and their applications continue to evolve today.

The major advantages of B-trees are:

1. Secondary storage space utilization of better than 50% at all times. Storage space is dynamically allocated and reclaimed, and no service degradation occurs when storage utilization becomes very high.
2. Random access requires very few steps (physical block accesses) and is comparable to hashing and multiple index methods.
3. Record insertions and deletions are efficiently handled on the average, allowing maintenance of the lexicographic (natural) order of keys for sequential processing and proper tree balance to maintain fast random retrieval.
4. Allows efficient batch processing by maintaining key order.

The major disadvantage of B-trees is their undeveloped application to secondary key retrieval. However, we expect to see future secondary access methods incorporate B-tree structures as part of the overall scheme, such as the index search components.

Definition

A *B-tree* is a generalization of a binary tree in which two or more branches may be taken from each node. A B-tree of *order k* has the following properties:

1. Each path from the root node to a leaf node has the same length, h, also called the height of the B-tree (i.e., h is the number of nodes from the root to the leaf, inclusive).

2. Each node, except the root and leaves, has at least $k + 1$ child nodes and no more than $2k + 1$ child nodes.
3. The root node may have as few as two child nodes, but no more than $2k + 1$ child nodes.
4. Each node, except the root, has at least k keys and no more than $2k$ keys. The root may have as few as one key. In general, any nonleaf (branch) node with j keys must have $j + 1$ child nodes.

From these properties we can see that an order 1 B-tree, in which each branch node has exactly two branches, is a fully balanced binary search tree. B-trees tend to be more flexible than binary trees because of the variable number of keys allowed in nodes. Thus, many insertions and deletions may occur without any transformation of the tree. In some instances transformations are required (see Section 14-2-2).

A B-tree *branch node* is organized similarly to the physical sequential structure illustrated in Fig. 14-9. In a typical implementation, each block (or page) consists of a single node; blocking factor, to be meaningful at all, is measured in terms of the maximum number of key entries, NKEY = $2k$. In Fig. 14-8 the actual number of key entries is NK $\leqslant 2k$; thus, NKEY − NK key positions and their associated pointers are unused. Key values are denoted by k_i, index pointers are shown by p_i, and associated data (or pointers to data) are designated by α_i. In this section we assume that α_i represents a pointer to the data record in a random access file.

A collection of nodes comprising an order 1 B-tree is shown in Fig. 14-9(a). Here, actual key values are explicitly shown, and pointer branches are drawn to illustrate access path directions. Associated data are common to all nodes and omitted from the diagram. Order 2 and order 3 B-trees are presented in Fig. 14-9(b) and (c). Note that node utilization varies dramatically between k and $2k$ keys, and that the leaves all occur at the same level. Each B-tree is always kept fully balanced in terms of height. Note also that the root is allowed to have as little as one key, regardless of the order of the B-tree.

Comparing Fig. 14-9 with the binary search tree of Fig. 14-3, the height of the B-tree tends to be smaller, particularly as the order increases. Thus, the B-tree has potentially a much faster retrieval time than a binary search tree, given each node is placed in a separate block or page. The search mechanism for the B-tree proceeds similarly to the binary search tree except that multiple branches are possible. The algorithm scans the ordered keys in a node until the stored (index) key is equal to or larger than the search key. If they are equal, the search is successful and the data pointer is used to locate the data record. If a larger stored key is found in position i, the previous index (p_{i-1}) pointer is followed to the next level node, which is scanned in the same manner. If all stored keys are smaller than the search key, the rightmost index

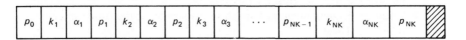

FIGURE 14-8   B-tree branch node with NK keys currently stored.

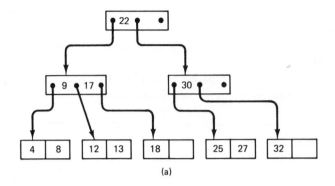

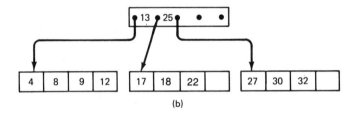

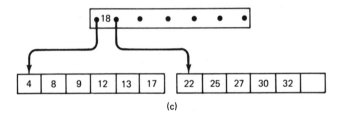

FIGURE 14-9 B-tree configurations for a 12-key file: (*a*) order 1 B-tree
(*h*=3); (*b*) order 2 B-tree (*h*=2); (*c*) order 3 B-tree (*h*=2).

pointer (p_{NK}) is taken to the next level. If no key match is found in a leaf node, the
search terminates unsuccessfully. Observing Fig. 14-9, the search for key 25 requires
three accesses in (a), one access in (b), and two accesses in (c).

The design of a B-tree index requires careful consideration of the following
factors:

- *Type of work load*. Random retrieval and update are most appropriate; sequential and batch processing are possible; boolean query processing is slow.
- *Volatility*. High frequency of updates is well suited to the B-tree structure and
  rules of balance.
- *B-tree order*. Affects search time significantly; controls block (node) utilization and flexibility for efficient insertions.

- *File size, NR.* B-tree is efficient for very large files.
- *Key length fixed or variable.*
- *Pointer size.*
- *Update (overflow) techniques.*

These factors are discussed in the analysis sections below.

14-2-1   Retrieval Performance

The wide variation in B-tree implementation configurations makes derivation of expected access path length quite difficult. Recall that each node in the order k B-tree may contain between k and $2k$ keys, inclusive, and this variation drastically affects the shape of the tree structure. Furthermore, the shape is constantly changing due to insertions and deletions, so the expected value can vary significantly over time. Under these circumstances the bounds on path length are a more stable measure of performance. Also, because of the multiway formation, the vast majority of keys are at the h level of the tree. Consequently, the expected path length is very near the maximum path length. Let us first determine bounds on the height of a B-tree. Then retrieval performance bounds can be easily found.

Height of a B-tree: Upper Bound

The worst-case configuration that maximizes the height of an order k B-tree for NR keys is illustrated in Fig. 14-10(a) for $k = 2$. In this case the root node has a minimum of one key and all other branch nodes have the minimum of k keys per node. A summary of the number of nodes and keys at each level is given in Table 14-3. If the height of the tree is h, then all of the nodes at level h are occupied by at least k keys and the *minimum sum* of keys through levels 1 to h is less than or equal to NR:

$$1 + 2k + (2k)(k + 1) + (2k)(k + 1)^2 + \ldots + (2k)(k + 1)^{h-2} \leq NR$$

$$1 + (2k)[1 + (k + 1) + (k + 1)^2 + \ldots + (k + 1)^{h-2}] \leq NR$$

$$1 + (2k) \left[\frac{(k + 1)^{h-1} - 1}{(k + 1) - 1} \right] \leq NR \qquad (14\text{-}17)$$

$$1 + 2[(k + 1)^{h-1} - 1] \leq NR$$

Rearranging terms, we have

$$(k + 1)^{h-1} \leq \frac{NR + 1}{2}$$

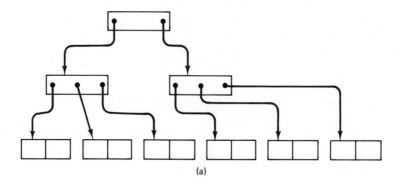

(a)

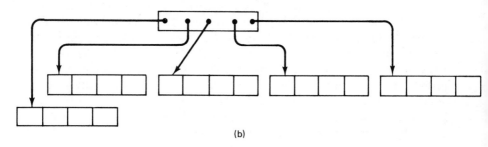

(b)

FIGURE 14-10 B-tree height extremes for $k=2$ (order 2 tree): (a) maximum height tree characteristics for $k=2$; (b) minimum height characteristics for $k=2$.

and taking the $\log_{k+1}$ of each side yields

$$h \leq \log_{k+1}\left(\frac{NR + 1}{2}\right) + 1 \qquad \text{and } h \text{ integer} \qquad (14\text{-}18)$$

Therefore,

$$h \leq \left\lfloor \log_{k+1}\left(\frac{NR + 1}{2}\right)\right\rfloor + 1 \qquad \qquad (14\text{-}19)$$

TABLE 14-3   Maximum Height B-Tree Characteristics

Level	Number of nodes	Number of keys
1	1	1
2	2	$2k$
3	$2(k + 1)$	$(2k)(k + 1)$
4	$2(k + 1)^2$	$(2k)(k + 1)^2$
$\vdots$	$\vdots$	$\vdots$
h	$2(k + 1)^{h-2}$	$(2k)(k + 1)^{h-2}$

Height of a B-tree: Lower Bound

The characteristics of a minimum height B-tree are shown in Fig. 14-10(b) and summarized in Table 14-4. In this case the maximum of $2k$ keys are used in each node, including the root node. If the height of the tree is h, then the maximum sum of keys through level h is greater than or equal to NR, the total number of keys stored:

$$2k + (2k)(2k + 1) + (2k)(2k + 1)^2 + \ldots + (2k)(2k + 1)^{h-1} \geq \text{NR}$$

$$2k[1 + (2k + 1) + (2k + 1)^2 + \ldots + (2k + 1)^{h-1}] \geq \text{NR} \qquad (14\text{-}20)$$

$$2k \left[\frac{(2k + 1)^h - 1}{(2k + 1) - 1} \right] \geq \text{NR}$$

$$(2k + 1)^h \geq \text{NR} + 1$$

$$h \geq \log_{2k+1}(\text{NR} + 1) \text{ and } h \text{ integer} \qquad (14\text{-}21)$$

Therefore,

$$h \geq \lceil \log_{2k+1}(\text{NR} + 1) \rceil \qquad (14\text{-}22)$$

For example, if NR = 17 keys, the bounds on h for an order 2 B-tree are

$$\left\lceil \log_5(17 + 1) \right\rceil \leq h \leq \left\lfloor \log_3 \left(\frac{17 + 1}{2} \right) \right\rfloor + 1$$

$$2 \leq h \leq 3$$

If NR = 24 keys, the bounds are

$$\left\lceil \log_5(24 + 1) \right\rceil \leq h \leq \left\lfloor \log_3 \left(\frac{24 + 1}{2} \right) \right\rfloor + 1$$

$$2 \leq h \leq 3$$

TABLE 14-4   Minimum Height B-Tree Characteristics

Level	Number of nodes	Number of keys
1	1	$2k$
2	$2k + 1$	$(2k)(2k + 1)$
3	$(2k + 1)^2$	$(2k)(2k + 1)^2$
4	$(2k + 1)^3$	$(2k)(2k + 1)^3$
$\vdots$	$\vdots$	$\vdots$
h	$(2k + 1)^{h-1}$	$(2k)(2k + 1)^{h-1}$

Each of these cases can be verified intuitively. If NR = 17, we see that h must be at least 2 from Fig. 14-10(b), and at most 3 (at 100% utilization) in Fig. 14-10(a). If NR = 24, we can still fit all keys into $h = 2$ levels [Fig. 14-10(b)] with 100% utilization, and no more than $h = 3$ at less than 100% utilization [Fig. 14-10(a)]. The minimum number of keys needed to require $h = 4$ levels as an upper bound is seen from Table 14-3: $(2k)(k + 1)^2 = 36$ for $k = 2$. Note that in an AVL tree the expected search length, h, is $\log_2 (24 + 1) = 4.65$. We see that even a well-balanced binary search tree has longer random retrieval time than a B-tree.

Retrieval performance consists of h accesses to the node containing the address of the data record plus one access to the data record. If the search is unsuccessful, however, the final block access is not performed. Assuming that each node in a B-tree is a physical block, we derive retrieval performance (upper bound) as

$$\text{PBA(GET UNIQUE)} = h + 1 \leqslant \left\lfloor \log_{k+1} \left(\frac{NR + 1}{2} \right) \right\rfloor + 2 \text{ rba} \qquad (14\text{-}23)$$

The lower bound occurs when a match is found with one of the keys in the root node. In this case two random block accesses are required, one to the root node (index search) and one to the data record block. For an unsuccessful search, the upper and lower bounds are equivalent:

$$\text{PBA(GET UNIQUE}') = h \leqslant \left\lfloor \log_{k+1} \left(\frac{NR + 1}{2} \right) \right\rfloor + 1 \text{ rba} \qquad (14\text{-}24)$$

Sequential processing, as in binary search tree sequential processing, uses a form of postorder search that visits the left subtree, the root, then the right subtree. When there are multiple paths from a subtree root node, the subtrees are visited from left to right with the root accessed in between subtrees so that the lexicographic order is maintained. In practice, the root would be maintained in a buffer so that it would only have to be accessed once. Using this scheme the buffer area would have to be large enough to hold $h + 1$ nodes or blocks. For the maximum node B-tree each node has only k keys (except the root, which has one key). In a minimum node tree, each node has $2k$ keys. Therefore, the bounds on sequential processing for NR randomly placed data records are the sum of index node accesses and data record (block) accesses:

$$\frac{NR}{2k} + NR \leqslant \text{PBA(GET ALL)} \leqslant \frac{NR}{k} + NR \qquad \text{rba} \qquad (14\text{-}25)$$

If data records are blocked, the bounds could be significantly reduced.

The operation GET NEXT (and equivalently GET PRIOR) is used for each of the NR components of GET ALL:

$$\text{PBA(GET NEXT)} = \text{PBA(GET ALL)}/NR \qquad (14\text{-}26)$$

Batch retrieval is possible with B-trees when the transaction file is also in lexicographic order. If the batch contains RPBR records, then in the worst case, RPBR data blocks plus all B-tree nodes must be accessed:

$$PBA(\text{Batch retrieval, RPBR}) = PBA(\text{GET ALL}) - (NR - RPBR)\text{ rba}$$
$$(14\text{-}27)$$

14-2-2   Update Performance

B-tree update has many of the same characteristics of binary search trees because some form of balance constraint must be maintained. In the worst case for insertions and deletions, transformations could be propagated through the entire height of the tree. The simplest update, as usual, is the change of a nonkey item in a record after the record has been accessed by the search mechanism. Only a simple block rewrite is required to store the updated record back into the database:

$$PBA(\text{CHANGE nonkey}) = 1\text{ sba} \qquad (14\text{-}28)$$

The change of a key item has a minimum cost of a single data block rewrite (sba) and index block rewrite (sba) if the change to the new key value is small enough to not cause rearrangement of key values in a B-tree node. The more typical case, at maximum cost, occurs when the key value changes to a randomly selected new value so that an index entry deletion must be executed, followed by a search and index entry insertion, and then a data block rewrite:

$$2\text{ sba} \leqslant PBA(\text{CHANGE key}) \leqslant PBA(\text{DELETE index value})$$
$$+ PBA(\text{GET UNIQUE}) + PBA(\text{INSERT index value}) \qquad (14\text{-}29)$$
$$+ PBA(\text{rewrite the data block})$$

The deletion and insertion components are defined below.

The INSERT operation consists of finding the appropriate index block, inserting the new key value into the index block and rewriting it, allocating space for the new data block, and writing the data record into its block location. First let us analyze the data block operation. Allocating space is accomplished by system software and requires only internal processing. The write operation for the new data record requires a single random block access (rba). If the data records are blocked, the block must be read first (rba), the insertion made in the main storage work area, then rewritten (sba). Thus, the extra work for blocked data records is 1 sba for insertion.

The B-tree index insertion operation is more complex because several alternative operations are possible once the search is completed. The search itself is exactly h steps in all cases because the initial insertion can be made only at a leaf node. Once the search is completed, there are four types of possible situations.

Case 1:   The simplest case occurs when there is room in the leaf node to accommodate the new key value. After the initial access of the node, only a sequential rewrite (sba) is necessary to return the updated node to its proper physical position.

Case 2:   If the leaf node is full of $2k$ keys, it must be split into two nodes, each containing k keys. After the insertion there are $2k + 1$ keys, but one of them is inserted into the parent node for the node being split. Assuming that the parent node is not full, we have the following suboperations:

a. Insert to parent node (already in a buffer) and rewrite: 1 sba.
b. Rewrite the node being split: 1 sba.
c. Create a new node and write it with k keys: 1 rba.

Case 3:   The third possibility occurs when the parent node is also full. It too must be split, and in the worst case the split can propagate up to the root, thus adding one to the height of the tree. In the worst case, suboperation 2a is executed for the new root, and suboperations 2b and 2c are executed h times. Each of the first three cases are illustrated in Fig. 14-11: Case 1 (key 7), Case 2 (key 37), and Case 3 (key 57).

Case 4:   As an alternative to splitting a node each time it becomes full and an insertion is requested, the right sibling of that node is accessed to see if it has some free space for possible rearrangement of keys with the full node. If it has at least two empty key positions, the full node can shift over the appropriate number of keys through the parent node and right sibling to maintain both lexicographic order and approximately equal utilization between the two sibling nodes. This concept is illustrated in Fig. 14-12. We see that the insertion of a single key requires three suboperations:

a. Shift the new value to the parent node (already in a buffer) and rewrite the block: 1 sba.
b. Rewrite the "overflow" node: 1 sba.
c. Access the right sibling and rewrite with the insertion(s): 1 rba + 1 sba.

The cost of "overflow" redistribution is actually higher than a split, provided that the split does not propagate upward. On the other hand, use of both splitting and "overflow" redistribution methods could be more efficient by avoiding extra splits whenever possible. Knuth describes a variant of the B-tree, sometimes called a B*-tree (but not to be confused with the B*-trees of Section 14-2-4), that allows each node to be a minimum of almost two-thirds full; it splits both an overflow node and its right sibling, if both are full, into three nodes. This has the effect of increasing storage utilization and decreasing the expected height of the tree. Update cost may or may not be improved.

From the discussion above we can summarize the four cases for insertion as follows:

PBA(INSERT) = PBA(INSERT index key) + PBA(INSERT data record)

$$(14\text{-}30)$$

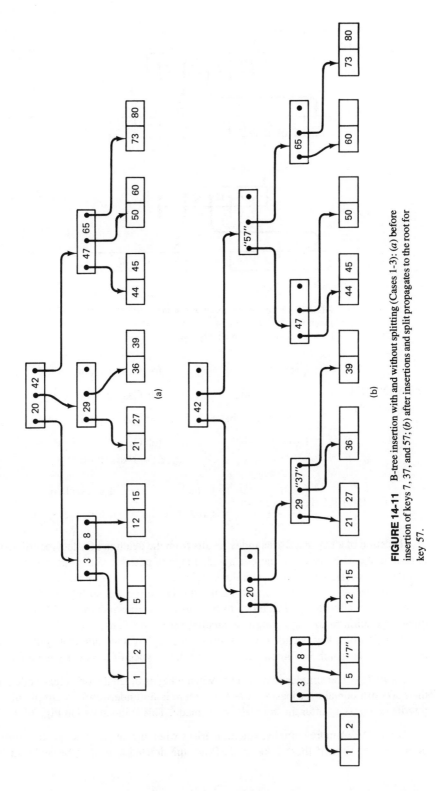

FIGURE 14-11 B-tree insertion with and without splitting (Cases 1-3): (*a*) before insertion of keys 7, 37, and 57; (*b*) after insertions and split propagates to the root for key 57.

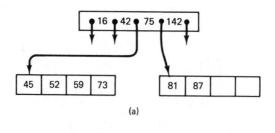

(a)

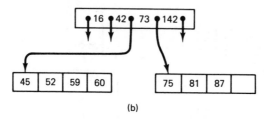

(b)

FIGURE 14-12 B-tree insertion causing overflow—redistribution technique (Case 4): (*a*) before insertion of key 60; (*b*) after insertion and redistribution.

$$\text{PBA(INSERT index key)} = \begin{cases} 1 \text{ sba} & \text{for Case 1: same block} \\ 1 \text{ rba} + 2 \text{ sba} & \text{for Case 2: split once} \\ 1 \text{ sba} + h(1 \text{ rba} + 1 \text{ sba}) & \text{for Case 3: split } h \text{ times} \\ 1 \text{ rba} + 3 \text{ sba} & \text{for Case 4: overflow} \\ & \quad\quad\quad\quad \text{redistribution} \end{cases} \quad (14\text{-}31)$$

$$\text{PBA(INSERT data record)} = \begin{cases} 1 \text{ sba} & \text{if unblocked} \\ 1 \text{ rba} + 1 \text{ sba} & \text{if blocked} \end{cases} \quad (14\text{-}32)$$

Deletion of a key in a B-tree index results from the deletion of a data record in the data area. As with insertion, there is a wide range of possible situations to consider. The deletion of the data record, if unblocked, is accomplished automatically when the key is deleted from the index; therefore, no I/O is required. Possibly some CPU time is needed to reallocate the data block to free storage. If data records are blocked, the delete operation results in a single sequential rewrite of that block.

Deletion of a key occurs after a successful search to the node that contains the key. After the search is completed, there are three types of possible situations:

Case 1:   The simplest case occurs when a key is deleted from a leaf node and the node still contains at least *k* keys (i.e., there is no underflow). A simple block rewrite is necessary after the key deletion is made. This is illustrated in Fig. 14-13.

Case 2:   A more complex situation arises when the key is to be deleted from a branch node. Even if there is no underflow, the deleted key must be replaced by

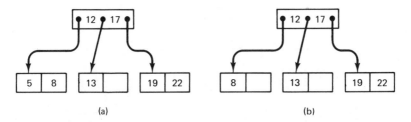

FIGURE 14-13 B-tree deletion of a key from a leaf node (Case 1): (*a*) before deletion of node 5; (*b*) after deletion.

another key to maintain the right subtree of the key deleted. The replacement key is obtained from the leftmost leaf node of the right subtree of the key to be deleted. (Note that this is the same procedure used to delete keys from a randomly constructed binary search tree, UNBAL.) This requires a maximum search of h nodes if the key is to be deleted from the root node. Once the leaf node is found, the leftmost key is deleted and then reinserted at the new node. If the leaf node deletion does not cause underflow, the operation is complete. We summarize the activity described above by:

a. Find the leftmost leaf node in the right subtree: 1 rba (min.); h rba (max.).
b. Delete key from leaf node (no underflow): 1 sba (see Case 3 if underflow).
c. Delete key from branch node and replace with the new key taken from the leaf node: 1 sba.

An example of Case 2 is shown in Fig. 14-14.

Case 3: When a leaf node key deletion causes underflow (fewer than k keys remain in the node), a key may be borrowed from a left or right neighboring (sibling) node. With no extra I/O, however, one may borrow more keys to obtain a balanced distribution of keys between the two neighboring nodes. This last step requires the existence of at least $2k$ keys, total, in the two nodes. If there are fewer than $2k$ keys available, the nodes are *concatenated*. This means that all keys are transferred to one of the nodes and the other node is completely deleted from the tree. Concatenation is the opposite of splitting. It implies that the associated key in the parent node that separates the two neighboring sibling nodes must also be moved to the remaining sibling node. This deletion of a key from the parent node may, unfortunately, cause underflow there as well, and in the worst case the underflow could propagate back to the root node. The possible operations for underflow are summarized as:

a. Redistribution of the keys from sibling nodes requires a read of the sibling node not yet accessed, sequential rewrites for both sibling nodes, and a rewrite of the parent node: 1 rba + 3 sba.
b. One level concatenation requires a read of the sibling node not yet accessed, a rewrite of the parent node, and a rewrite of the single remaining sibling node: 1 rba + 2 sba.
c. In the worst case a concatenation propagates to the root, an $h - 1$ level concatenation. At each level a new read of a sibling node is required, plus a

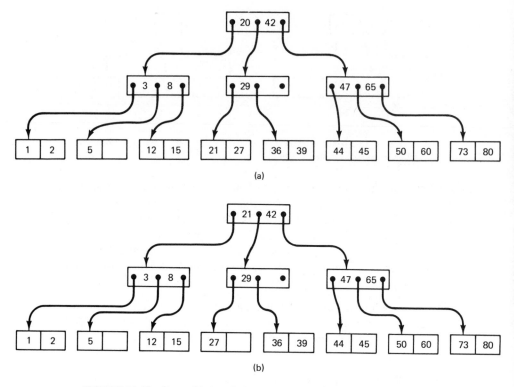

FIGURE 14-14 B-tree deletion of a key from a branch node (Case 2): (*a*) before deletion of branch node 20; (*b*) after deletion of node 20 and replacement by leaf node 21.

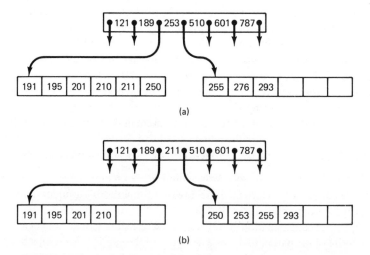

FIGURE 14-15 B-tree deletion of a key from a leaf node causing underflow: redistribution technique (Case 3a): (*a*) before deletion of key 276; (*b*) after deletion of key 276 and redistribution of keys in neighboring sibling nodes.

rewrite of the remaining node. The parent node is not rewritten yet because it becomes one of the siblings at the next level of concatenation: $(h - 1) \times$ (1 rba + 1 sba). Figures 14-15 to 14-17 show examples of each of the three underflow situations for Cases 3a, 3b, and 3c, respectively.

$$\text{PBA(DELETE)} = \text{PBA(DELETE index key)} + \text{PBA(DELETE data record)} \tag{14-33}$$

$$\text{PBA(DELETE index key)} = \begin{cases} \text{1 sba} & \text{for Case 1: leaf node,} \\ & \quad \text{no underflow} \\[6pt] \text{2 sba + search for re-} & \text{for Case 2: branch node,} \\ \text{placement key} & \quad \text{no underflow} \\ \text{(1 rba to } h \text{ rba)} & \\[6pt] \text{1 rba + 3 sba} & \text{for Case 3a: leaf node} \\ & \quad \text{redistributed} \\[6pt] \text{1 rba + 2 sba} & \text{for Case 3b: leaf node} \\ & \quad \text{concatenated} \\[6pt] (h - 1)(\text{1 rba + 1 sba}) & \text{for Case 3c: leaf node} \\ & \quad \text{concatenated up to the root} \\ & \quad \text{(worst case)} \end{cases} \tag{14-34}$$

$$\text{PBA(DELETE data record)} = \begin{cases} 0 & \text{if unblocked} \\ \text{1 sba} & \text{if blocked} \end{cases} \tag{14-35}$$

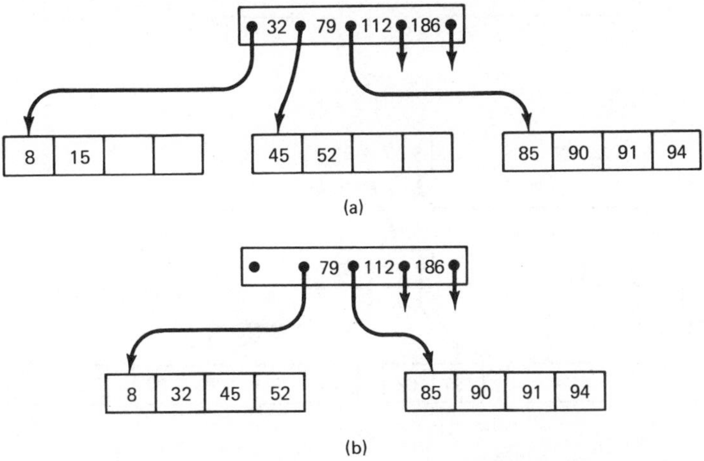

(a)

(b)

FIGURE 14-16   B-tree deletion of key from a leaf node: concatenation technique (Case 3b): (*a*) before deletion of key 15; (*b*) after deletion of key 15 and concatenation of two sibling nodes.

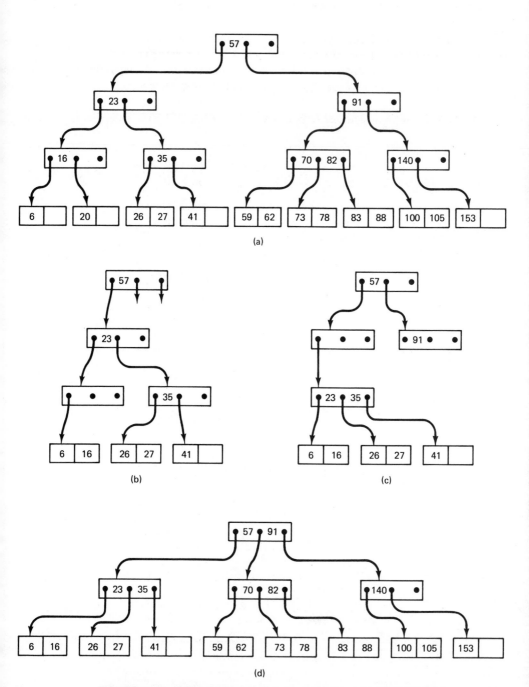

FIGURE 14-17 B-tree deletion of a key from a leaf node requiring multiple concatenations up to the root (Case 3c): (a) before deletion of key 20; (b) after first concatenation of keys 6 and 16; (c) after second concatenation of keys 23 and 35; (d) final B-tree after third concatenation of keys 57 and 91 and new root node.

14-2-3 Storage Space

Block storage for B-tree files consists of branch nodes (BNODES), leaf nodes (LNODES), and data blocks. Each of these three components has potentially different block sizes and internal formats:

$$BKS_1(BNODES) = (2k) \times KS + [(2k + 1) + (2k)] \times PS \qquad (14\text{-}36)$$
$$+ \ BOVHD_1$$

$$BKS_2(LNODES) = (2k) \times KS + (2k) \times PS + BOVHD_2 \qquad (14\text{-}37)$$

$$BKS_3(\text{data blocks}) = KS + NKS + BOVHD_3 \qquad (14\text{-}38)$$

where $BOVHD_i$ contains a flag to distinguish leaf nodes from branch nodes and data blocks.

Given NR total keys and an order k B-tree, the number of leaf nodes varies as:

$$2(k + 1)^{h_1-2} \leqslant LNODES \leqslant (2k + 1)^{h_2-1} \qquad (14\text{-}39)$$

where

$$h_1 = \left\lceil \log_{2k+1}(NR + 1) \right\rceil \qquad \text{and} \qquad h_2 = \left\lfloor \log_{k+1}\left(\frac{NR+1}{2}\right) \right\rfloor + 1$$

as given by Eqs. (14-19) and (14-22). These are the final terms for level h in Tables 14-3 and 14-4. Bounds on branch nodes can then be derived from the relationship

$$\frac{NR}{2k} \leqslant LNODES + BNODES \leqslant \frac{NR}{k} \qquad (14\text{-}40)$$

and the inequality LNODES $>$ BNODES for B-trees. Thus, total storage space is given by

$$BLKSTOR = BKS_1 \times BNODES + BKS_2 \times LNODES + BKS_3 \times NR \qquad \text{bytes}$$
$$(14\text{-}41)$$

14-2-4 B*-Trees

The most prominent variant of the B-tree is the B*-tree (or B$^+$-tree), which is characterized by all the keys and associated data residing in the leaf nodes and accessed via a B-tree index. In a B*-tree the initial separators in the index are a subset of the keys in the leaf nodes, and they are organized as a B-tree. Thus, some keys are actually redundantly stored in this organization; but placing all keys and records in

leaf nodes, connected in a linked sequential *sequence set,* allows for faster sequential processing.

The major similarities and differences between a B*-tree and a B-tree are listed below [Bayer and Unterauer, 1977; Comer, 1979b; Wedekind, 1974]:

1. Index loading is carried out in a bottom-up fashion for B-trees and B*-trees. The first keys are loaded at level h (initially $h = 1$), and after a split occurs a separator key is placed in a node at level $h - 1$, and so on, until all the initial keys have been loaded. The B-tree constraint that each node must have from k to $2k$ keys applies to B*-trees as well; the exception of the root holds in both cases.

2. Leaf nodes in a B-tree consist of $k \leq NK \leq 2k$ keys and associated data or pointers to data. Leaf nodes in a B*-tree consist of $k \leq NK \leq 2k$ keys and associated data, and a single pointer to the next sibling leaf node. A two-way pointer option is possible for this sequence set of leaf nodes. Thus, leaf nodes may have different formats and different sizes for the two physical organizations.

3. Branch nodes in B-trees and B*-trees have essentially the same format. However, in the initial loading (and any insertion) process, B*-trees differ in that all keys are stored in leaf nodes and keys stored in the index are duplicates. The index contains only enough separator values to ensure fast access to the leaf nodes. An example of the steps of B-tree and B*-tree loading is shown in Fig. 14-18. When a split occurs, the middle key value is moved to the parent node in both cases. A B*-tree additionally places a copy of the middle key at the left end of the right leaf of the parent node. Splitting of branch nodes is the same for both organizations.

4. Retrieval in a B*-tree always takes h steps to a leaf node. If the search key value matches a stored key value in an index node, the right subtree is accessed next and the search continues to a leaf node. Contrariwise, a B-tree search may terminate at midtree if a match is found.

5. In a B*-tree deletion operation, only the key value in a leaf node needs to be deleted. Any copy of that key in the index may remain there as long as it is useful to the retrieval process. Thus, B*-tree indexes can have nonkey values as separators. On the other hand, any deletion requiring redistribution or concatenation may result in deletion of any key in a parent index (branch) node. Examples of possible deletion scenarios are shown in Fig. 14-19.

Let us now analyze the performance of B*-trees relative to B-trees. The format is somewhat simpler than for the B-tree because of the absence of associated data (pointers to data) at the branch nodes. This means that B*-tree branch nodes, if the same physical size as B-tree nodes, can hold more keys. This trades off with the negative effect of redundant keys in the index (see Fig. 14-18).

Random retrieval is probably not significantly affected by these minor differences in the two organizations, especially since they counterbalance each other. On the other hand, an 80–20 nonuniform distribution in which 80% of the retrievals were to the 20% of the keys nearest the root of the tree, would be better implemented with a B-tree organization. The GET NEXT operation (and also GET PRIOR if a two-way pointer is implemented) for the B*-tree is a single random access across the sequence

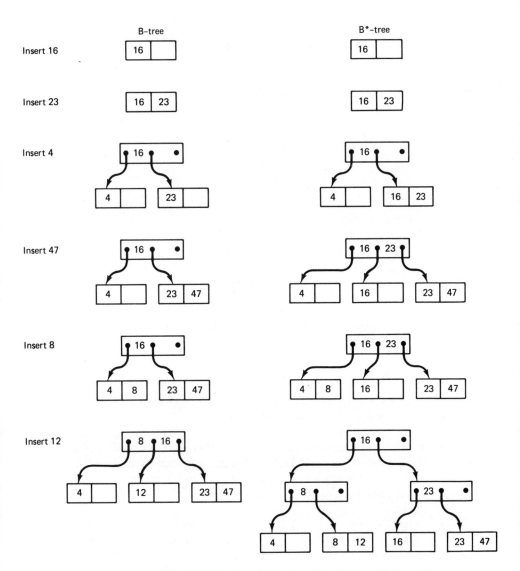

FIGURE 14-18 Example loading (insertion) sequence for a B-tree and B*-tree of order 1.

set. The GET ALL operation requires a single visit to each of the leaf nodes, bounded by the values in Eq. (14-32). This is more efficiently done with B*-trees through the sequence set.

Update operations for B*-trees are almost exactly the same as for B-trees, with a few exceptions for insertions and deletions. A summary of B*-tree and B-tree performance is shown in Table 14-5. Let us briefly discuss those differences.

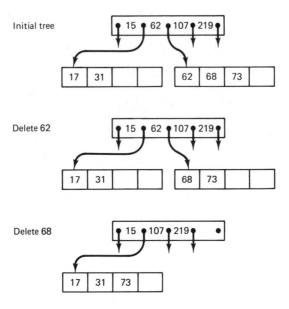

FIGURE 14-19 Successive keys (and record) deletions from a B*-tree of order 2.

Change. The same relationships, Eqs. (14-30) and (14-31), apply to both organizations. However, the search to the data record in the B*-tree is exactly h nodes, whereas in a B-tree it may be any length.

Insert. A B*-tree keeps all keys in leaf nodes after a leaf node split, but this does not affect the number of physical I/O (block access) operations to insert an index key. However, the B*-tree requires the insertion of a key and its associated data into the same block, so only a single block rewrite is needed.

Delete. In a B*-tree, keys can only be deleted from leaf nodes, so Case 2 for B-tree deletion does not apply. Otherwise, the key deletion operations are the same in terms of physical block accesses. As with insertions, however, both key and associated data in a leaf node are deleted together, so no extra block rewrite is needed for data, whereas in a B-tree it is needed [see Eq. (14-37)].

Example 14-1: Given a database with 10^8 records, each with a unique key value, compare B-tree and B*-tree bounds on performance for random retrieval, sequential processing, insertion, and deletion for order 10 ($k = 10$). Plot random retrieval for $k = 1, 10, 100, 1000$. We can directly apply the equations derived for Table 14-5. The results are summarized and plotted in Table 14-6 and Fig. 14-20.

$$h_1 = \log_{21}(10^8 + 1) = 7, \quad h_2 = \log_{11}\left[\frac{(10^8 + 1)}{2} + 1\right] = 8, \text{ the bounds on B-tree height.}$$

TABLE 14-5 Database Operation Cost (PBA) for B-Trees and B*-Trees of Order k

	B-tree	B*-tree
GET UNIQUE	UB: $\left\lfloor \log_{k+1}\left(\dfrac{NR+1}{2}\right)\right\rfloor + 2$ rba LB: 2 rba	$\left\lfloor \log_{k+1}\left(\dfrac{NR+1}{2}\right)\right\rfloor + 1$ rba
GET UNIQUE'	$\left\lfloor \log_{k+1}\left(\dfrac{NR+1}{2}\right)\right\rfloor + 1$ rba	Same as GET UNIQUE
GET NEXT GET PRIOR	PBA(GET ALL)/NR	1 rba
GET ALL	UB: NR$(1 + 1/k)$ rba LB: NR$(1 + 1/2k)$ rba	UB: NR/k rba LB: NR/$2k$ rba
GET BATCH (RPBR records)	PBA(GET ALL) − (NR − RPBR) rba	Same as linked sequential with blocking

After the search is completed:

	B-tree	B*-tree
CHANGE nonkey	1 sba	Same as B-tree
CHANGE key	UB: DELETE index + GET UNIQUE + INSERT index + rewrite data block LB: 2 sba	UB: Same form as B-tree LB: 1 sba
INSERT	UB: 2 sba + h(1 rba + 1 sba) + 1 rba LB: 2 sba	UB: 1 sba + h(1 rba + 1 sba) LB: 1 sba
DELETE	UB: 1 sba + $(h-1)$(1 rba + 1 sba) LB: 1 sba	UB: $(h-1)$(1 rba + 1 sba) LB: 1 sba
UPDATE BATCH	Sum of individual updates	Same as B-tree

Since $2k$ represents the blocking factor in B-tree nodes, Fig. 14-20 suggests that the optimal k is perhaps as large as NR/2. The search time decreases as k increases. However, as in physical sequential files, the upper limit on blocking factor usually depends on other things such as physical device constraints (e.g., track size), buffer size in the system, or standard convention by the user installation. Buffer size is limited to some extent in a multiuser environment, so that a single application does not dominate the physical resources of the computer system.

TABLE 14-6 Comparative Performance for B-Trees and B*-Trees of Order 10

	B-tree		B*-tree	
	Lower Bound	Upper Bound	Lower Bound	Upper Bound
GET UNIQUE	2 rba	9 rba	8 rba	8 rba
GET ALL	1.05×10^8 rba	1.1×10^8 rba	0.05×10^8 rba	0.1×10^8 rba
INSERT	2 sba	9 rba + 10 sba	1 sba	8 rba + 9 sba
DELETE	1 sba	7 rba + 8 sba	1 sba	7 rba + 7 sba

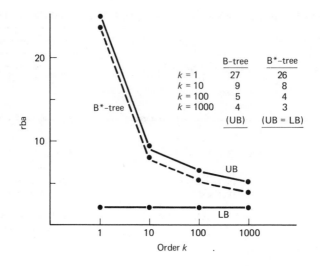

FIGURE 14-20 Comparative random retrieval for B-trees and B*-trees.

14-2-5 Prefix B*-Trees

Bayer and Unterauer [1977] describe two modifications to B-trees, simple prefix B*-trees and prefix B*-trees, which take advantage of the fact that the full-length keys need not be used in the B* index. The *simple prefix B*-tree* extends the concept of B*-tree to use unique prefixes of keys in the index to save storage space and reduce retrieval time. In *prefix B*-trees* the prefixes are not explicitly stored, but dynamically reconstructed as the search mechanism proceeds. We concentrate our discussion on the simple prefix B*-tree, or SPB*-tree for simplicity.

The SPB*-tree has the same basic characteristics as the B*-tree (see Section 14-2-4) except that the index is replaced by a B-tree of variable-length separators. The separators range from a single character to a full-length key value, depending on the values of adjacent (ordered) keys in the data records.

The means of choosing appropriate separators is illustrated in Fig. 14-21, where leaf node keys are alphabetic names from a customer file. If the node is to be split due to, say the insertion of a new name, "Jung," the normal B*-tree redistribution would occur between Johns and Johnson, with Johnson being the key that is duplicated in the

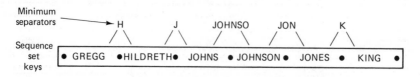

FIGURE 14-21 Potential separators for a leaf node in a SPB*-tree of order 3.

parent node in the index. If the SPB*-tree used the same split point, the shortest prefix between Johns and Johnson is "Johnso." However, moving the split point one in either direction would reduce the prefix, and the move to the left would produce the minimum possible prefix of length 1, "J." The SPB*-tree is defined to have a *split interval* σ_l for the leaf nodes (and σ_b for the branch nodes) that specifies the number of bytes or keys to either side of the middle of the node that might be considered for a split point. The split point is chosen within the split interval such that the length of the separator for the node is minimized. Increasing σ_l and σ_b allows one a greater choice of separators and therefore reduces the size of separators, but it also creates nodes with less than 50% utilization and may result in more storage space. Bayer and Unterauer recognize the conflict and propose future analysis of the effect of σ_l and σ_b on SPB*-tree performance relative to B*-trees. They then derive relationships for the expected length of separators in an SPB*-tree and how the reduced index size decreases the height of a corresponding B*-tree.

Comparing the basic database operations between an SPB*-tree and a B*-tree on an intuitive basis, the random retrieval cost is less with an SPB*-tree because of the potential reduction in height with smaller separators. Sequential processing is the same (as in GET NEXT and GET PRIOR) because the sequence set data are stored in the same way. Insertion is the same procedure in both cases except that the minimum separator is chosen for the parent node in an SPB*-tree; deletion is also the same procedure for both organizations. It is possible that there might be occasions where insertions or deletions may allow a smaller separator to replace a larger one, but Bayer and Unterauer do not recommend making the additional effort to do this because the improvement in performance is probably only marginal. In summary, the biggest advantage to SPB*-trees is the potential reduction in random retrieval cost for very large databases.

Many hybrid tree organizations are proposed in the literature that combine some of the best qualities of hashing, binary trees, B-trees, and the many variants of these. Among them are hash trees [Coffman and Eve, 1970; Severance, 1974], extendible hashing [Fagin et al., 1979], virtual B-trees [Bayer, 1972; Knuth, 1973], binary B-trees [Bayer and McCreight, 1972], and 2-3 trees [Yao, 1978]. The reader is directed to the original papers for details.

14-3 TRIE STRUCTURES

Indexing techniques for large databases or files have been based, for the most part, on full key values stored at different levels of search trees. The variants of the B*-tree represent the most obvious exceptions to this trend. Another class of access methods, called TRIE ("try") access methods, view a primary key as an ordered sequence (or string) of characters from a vocabulary of size V. The TRIE utilizes a multiway tree structure in which each branch node has exactly V exits, one for each possible value of a single character in the key string. If a key has KS characters (bytes) in the string, KS nodes must be traversed in the search for the corresponding data record to determine whether or not the record exists. If it exists, one additional block access is needed to access the record. In effect, the leaves of the TRIE structure correspond to the data records. The TRIE structure has the advantage of fast random retrieval at the expense of potentially large storage space overhead.

The most prominent early TRIE implementations were proposed by Fredkin [1960] and de la Briandais [1959]. Fredkin derived the term TRIE from re*trie*val. His implementation consists of multiple levels of nodes, with each node containing V pointer fields plus a flag, as shown in Fig. 14-22(a). The ith character in the key can have V possible values, and each value represents a position in a node at the ith level of the tree structure. This is a local form of direct addressing in which the character value implicitly determines the position in the node where the branching pointer can be found. The pointer locates the node at the next level that represents the possible values for the $i + 1$st character, and so on. Thus, a KS-character key involves searching KS nodes, one at each of KS levels of the tree. Because key lengths may be variable, the TRIE structure is normally unbalanced; that is, if KS_j is the length of key j, leaf nodes of a TRIE exist at different levels KS_j for different j.

The flag associated with each node in a TRIE indicates when the node is the path end for the key value. In a practical implementation of the flag, it contains the value k that represents the kth position of the character value that completes a full key. Then the kth data pointer is used to locate the data record, and the branch pointer locates the index node at the next level. This effectively ''prunes'' the tree at this level for one combination of character values that represents a complete key, but it allows other key values with the same prefix as the complete key to be accessed below this point in the tree. If more than one key value terminates at this node, the flag can be set to a sum that decodes to the proper (multiple) positions of complete key values. An example of the use of a TRIE index is illustrated in Fig. 14-22.

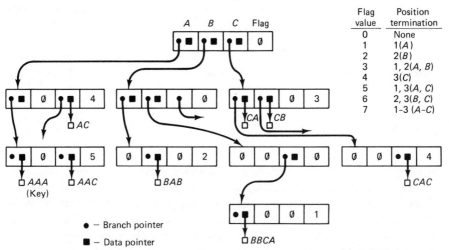

FIGURE 14-22   TRIE index structure for variable length key values (NR = 8).

Although each node allocates space for V possible character values, there are often many combinations of characters that are not used for key identifiers. Consequently, a great deal of unused space is possible. When a particular character value is not used, its pointer space is filled with a null ($\emptyset$) value indicating that the subtree corresponding to this prefix of values is empty. This prunes the tree at the earliest opportunity and eliminates the need to allocate storage space for the empty subtree.

The TRIE configuration where each branch node contains a branch pointer for each single character value represents one end of a spectrum of digital search tree configurations. It is possible for each branch pointer to represent combinations of values for two, three, and up to KS key characters. At KS characters for primary keys, the branch node contains the entire key, and thus we have direct access with the TRIE structure. Remember, however, that direct access incurs an intolerable storage space overhead for most databases, and the sequential search is intolerably long for random retrieval applications. Other combinations of two or more characters also have tradeoffs involving storage space and random retrieval, and they can be investigated similarly to the single-character case. Here it suffices to note that the maximum number of branch nodes at each level quickly increases, but the rate of increase is lowest for the single character configuration. The number of nodes at the various levels is summarized in Table 14-7.

TABLE 14-7   Number of Branch Nodes per Level in TRIE Structures with Different Numbers of Key Characters per Branch Node

Level	1 Char/Node	2 Char/Node	3 Char/Node	KS-Char/Node
1	1	1	1	1
2	V	V^2	V^3	V^{KS}
3	V^2	V^4	V^6	—
4	V^3	V^6	V^9	—
$\vdots$	$\vdots$	$\vdots$	$\vdots$	$\vdots$
i	V^{i-1}	V^{2i-2}	V^{3i-3}	—
Total nodes	$\dfrac{V^{KS} - 1}{V - 1}$	$\dfrac{V^{KS} - 1}{V^2 - 1}$	$\dfrac{V^{KS} - 1}{V^3 - 1}$	$V^{KS} + 1$

The major factors to be addressed in the design of TRIE structures are summarized from the discussion above:

- *Type of work load*. Random retrieval and update are most appropriate.
- *Data volatility*. Affects choice of TRIE implementations.
- *Vocabulary size, V*. Affects the choice of TRIE structures; determines total tree size.
- *Key string length, KS*. Determines path length for retrieval.
- *Pointer size*. Affects node size, blocking factor.

14-3-1 Retrieval Performance

Random retrieval is very fast using TRIE structures. In each case there is a series of random block accesses from the root to the leaf node containing the data record desired. In a TRIE, KS + 1 nodes must always be accessed in a successful search, whereas an unsuccessful search could end at any point a null pointer is encountered or if the search key has been exhausted and the TRIE search does not terminate. We assume that the TRIE nodes are in separate blocks, but typical implementations provide extensive blocking to reduce the number of block accesses required. The grouped allocation feature of binary search trees, where new nodes are clustered near their parent nodes, is commonly implemented for TRIE structures. In the best case all the index nodes are blocked together and the data block is separate. This case is only reasonable for very small indexes, however.

$$\text{PBA(GET UNIQUE, TRIE, unblocked)} = KS + 1 \text{ rba} \qquad (14\text{-}42)$$

$$\text{PBA(GET UNIQUE, TRIE, grouped alloc.)} = \begin{cases} KS + 1 \text{ rba (max.)} \\ 2 \text{ rba (min.)} \end{cases} \qquad (14\text{-}43)$$

$$\text{PBA(GET UNIQUE}', \text{TRIE)} = \begin{cases} KS \text{ rba (max.)} \\ 1 \text{ rba (min.)} \end{cases} \qquad (14\text{-}44)$$

Sequential processing is accomplished the same as in any unordered data area, such as an indexed random file.

$$\text{PBA(GET ALL, TRIE)} = \left\lceil \frac{NR}{EBF_2} \right\rceil \text{ sba} \qquad (14\text{-}45)$$

where EBF_2 is the effective blocking factor for the unordered data area. The operations GET NEXT and GET PRIOR are not directly applicable to TRIE implementations because of the random positions of data records. Also, because of the lack of order in the data file, batch processing is not applicable.

14-3-2 Update Performance

It is now a straightforward task to apply our standard update operations to TRIE structures. The simplest operation, the change of a nonkey value, involves a rewrite of the data block changed, assuming that the search time has already been accounted for.

$$\text{PBA(CHANGE nonkey, TRIE)} = 1 \text{ sba} \qquad (14\text{-}46)$$

The change of a key value is much more complicated. In a TRIE it implies that the entire access path to the data must be reevaluated to see if any part of it must be changed to reflect the new key value. Whether or not any pointers must be reset, the entire path from root to leaf (data record) must be traversed twice, once for deletion of the old key path and once for insertion of the new key path:

$$\text{PBA(CHANGE key, TRIE)} = \text{PBA(DELETE old key)} + \text{PBA(GET UNIQUE)}$$
$$+ \text{PBA(INSERT new key)} \qquad (14\text{-}47)$$

Equation (14-47) is expressed in a general form. Its components are derived below.

The insertion of a new key and data record in a TRIE structure requires an initial access of KS index nodes to either allocate pointer space or use existing pointers. In either case all KS nodes must be accessed; this is already accounted for by the original search to the record position. Once the access path has been established, the new record is either inserted into an existing block (and then rewritten) or a new block is allocated:

$$\text{PBA(INSERT, TRIE)} = \begin{cases} 1 \text{ rba} + 1 \text{ sba (insertion to existing block)} \\ 1 \text{ rba (new block allocated)} \end{cases} \qquad (14\text{-}48)$$

The deletion operations for TRIE structures are also quite similar. If the data records are blocked, a single rewrite is needed for the revised block; if unblocked, no data rewrite is necessary. Additionally, whether or not the data are blocked, the branch pointer must be reset in the KS-level index branch node to effectively finalize the deletion. Assuming that the index nodes are still held in buffers, one rewrite of the branch node block is required. If, in a TRIE, no other data records are pointed to by this branch node, the branch node should be deleted. This operation may possibly be propagated back to the root, thus resetting the TRIE structure to an earlier state. In the worst case, KS branch nodes will be deleted from the structure; each branch node deletion involves a rewrite of the parent node after its child pointer is reset.

$$\text{PBA(DELETE, TRIE)} = \begin{cases} 1 \text{ sba} & \text{if unblocked, no index nodes deleted (min.)} \\ 2 \text{ sba} & \text{if blocked, no index nodes deleted} \\ \text{KS sba} & \text{if unblocked, all index nodes deleted} \\ \text{KS} + 1 \text{ sba} & \text{if blocked, all index nodes deleted (max.)} \end{cases} \qquad (14\text{-}49)$$

Recall that the initial access of all index nodes and the data record has already been accounted for with the original GET UNIQUE operation.

14-3-3   Storage Space

The total number of index branch nodes in a single-character TRIE configuration is given in Table 14-7 as $\text{IBNODES} = (V^{KS} - 1)/(V - 1)$. The number of data records is NR.

$$SRS = V \times PS + 1 \qquad \text{bytes} \tag{14-50}$$

$$EBF_i = \left\lfloor \frac{(BKS_i - BOVHD_i) \times LF_i}{SRS} \right\rfloor \tag{9-36}$$

$$BLKSTOR(TRIE) = \left\lceil \frac{IBNODES}{EBF_1} \right\rceil \times BKS_1 + \left\lceil \frac{NR}{EBF_2} \right\rceil \times BKS_2 \qquad \text{bytes} \tag{14-51}$$

where EBF_1 and EBF_2 are the effective blocking factors of the index branch nodes and the unordered data area, respectively.

14-3-4   TRIE B-Tree Trade-offs

The basic trade-off between the TRIE and other tree structures is fast random retrieval versus storage overhead. Let us look at an example to see what practical considerations should be made.

Example 14-2:   A large database consists of 10^8 records of equal size, 100 bytes, and equal format. Each record has a unique nine-digit key of decimal digits from 0 through 9 that can be used for TRIE index construction. If block size is 1000 bytes, and $BOVHD_i = 0$ and $LF_i = 1$ for all i, compare random retrieval performance with the B-tree configurations in Fig. 14-20 and Table 14-6.

Applying Eqs. (14-50) and (14-51) for storage space, we obtain

$$SRS \text{ (TRIE)} = 10 \times 4 + 1 = 41 \text{ bytes}$$

$$EBF_1(TRIE) = \lfloor 1000 / 41 \rfloor = 24$$

$$IBNODES = \frac{10^9 - 1}{10 - 1} = 11{,}111{,}111$$

$$BLKSTOR(TRIE) = \left\lceil \frac{11{,}111{,}111}{24} \right\rceil \times 1000 + \left\lceil \frac{10^8}{10} \right\rceil \times 10^3 \text{ bytes}$$

$$= 462.9 \times 10^6 \text{ bytes (index)} + 10^{10} \text{ bytes (data)}$$

$$= 10.463 \times 10^9 \text{ bytes}$$

Because of the extremely large number of index nodes, only the first two levels of TRIE nodes can be assumed to be blocked together. Therefore, we estimate the total random accesses to be $KS = 9$ rba. This is approximately the same number of random accesses for an order 10 B-tree. The storage space required for the B-tree index is computed from Eqs. (14-36) to (14-41):

$$BKS_1(BNODES) = 20 \times 9 + 41 \times 4 + 0 = 344 \text{ bytes}$$

$$BKS_2(LNODES) = 20 \times 9 + 20 \times 4 + 0 = 260 \text{ bytes}$$

$$BKS_3(\text{data blocks}) = 100 \text{ bytes (for } BF = 1)$$

Assuming that the best case where leaf nodes are dominant and maximum utilization of space occurs:

$$\text{BLKSTOR(B-tree)} = 260 \text{ bytes} \times 10^8 / 20 \text{ nodes} + 100 \times 10^8 \text{ bytes}$$
$$= 13 \times 10^8 + 100 \times 10^8$$
$$= 11.3 \times 10^9 \text{ bytes}$$

Thus, the TRIE structure has lower cost for this case. Note, however, that a full character set key type would require far more storage space in a TRIE structure (i.e., in SRS) but would require no change in B-tree size. Thus, under this condition the B-tree cost (retrieval plus storage space) would be lower than the TRIE structure.

15 SECONDARY ACCESS METHODS

15-1 INTRODUCTION

A rapidly growing class of database applications involves the *query* (GET SOME) operation, in which records are selected based on the value of one or more attributes of the records. An *ad hoc query* is a query whose exact specifications (format, key values, and target record volume) are not known in advance, and therefore cannot be explicitly used to design the database. However, reasonable estimates as to what types of queries will be used should be obtainable from the requirements analysis. We have already studied how primary access methods efficiently retrieve and possibly update data based on the primary key alone. Now we address *secondary access methods* (SAM), a collection of techniques designed to efficiently access all the target records associated with a set of stated secondary key values defined in a query.

The most generalized form of a query is a set of boolean functions consisting of logical conjunctions (*AND*) and disjunctions (*OR*) operators. The basic terminology associated with queries is useful in the analysis of secondary access methods, and it is illustrated in the example below [Cardenas, 1979]. We shall use the SEQUEL language to demonstrate the query components [Chamberlin and Boyce, 1974].

Example Query 15-1:

```
SELECT EMP_NAME,EMP_ADDR    ⎱ operation part; get attributes
FROM EMPLOYEE                ⎰ EMP_NAME and EMP_ADDR from
                               record type EMPLOYEE
WHERE (AGE=21-59 AND CITY='DETROIT' AND JOBCODE⎱ qualification
      ='PROGRAMMER')                            ⎰ part
    OR (AGE < 65 AND JOBCODE='PROG/ANALYST');
```

1. *Atomic condition, AC*
This is the basic qualification condition in a query. It has the form NAME

$\left\{ \begin{matrix} < \\ = \\ > \end{matrix} \right\} \left\{ \begin{matrix} \text{NAME} \\ \text{VALUE} \end{matrix} \right\}$, where NAME is an item type (or domain in a relational data-base) and VALUE is an item value. Combined relational operators are allowable.

2. *Item condition, IC*

An item condition is a disjunction of atomic conditions, $AC_1 OR AC_2 OR . . . OR$ AC_p, such that each AC_i references the same item type, but with a different item value. Alternatively, an item condition is the collection of item values in a *range specification*. For example, the first item condition in Example Query 15-1, AGE=21-59, has a range of 39 values or 39 atomic conditions, each with a different item value. The item condition AGE<65 represents a single atomic condition, although a range is implied. Only explicit ranges of the form VALUE-VALUE are considered as separate atomic conditions in this text. The process of retrieving the records that have values specified within certain ranges is called *range searching*.

3. *Record condition, RC*

A record condition is a conjunction of item conditions, $IC_1 AND IC_2 AND . . .$ $AND IC_q$, such that each IC_j represents a distinct item type (or domain). In Example Query 15-1 the first set of parentheses enclose a single record condition composed of three item conditions; the second set of parentheses enclose another record condition with only two item conditions.

4. *Query condition, QC*

A query condition is a disjunction of record conditions, $RC_1 OR RC_2 OR . . . OR$ RC_r, such that each record condition may refer to the same of different record type. The qualification part of Query 15-1 is a query condition composed of two record conditions.

We will refer to queries of the boolean form defined here as *conjunctive queries*. The application of standard query terminology to secondary access method analysis will enhance our ability to understand and evaluate the cost necessary to satisfy complex query conditions. In this chapter we investigate the basic access methods for query processing: multilist, inverted file, and doubly chained tree. Hybrid cellular structures are introduced to illustrate basic trade-offs in the storage structures for multilist and inverted files.

It is important to note, however, that inverted files and their variants are among a wider class of tools for secondary key retrieval that include primary access methods, associative search schemes, and special coding schemes.

15-2 MULTILIST FILE

Generalized query operations result in the retrieval of a widely variable number of target records. Because data are not ordinarily sorted on the secondary key, the physical locations of query target records, based on secondary key values, are usually unrelated. Consequently, the search mechanisms and storage structures used for primary access are very inefficient for general queries. If a sequential search of the database is used to satisfy the query, the expected search distance for randomly located target records is the entire database; that is, every record must be accessed and checked for a match with each record condition in the query. Fortunately, a combination of the indexing and linked sequential access methods can be made quite useful for query processing.

A *multilist* structure, or file, is defined as a collection of linked sequential structures (linked lists) threading an extent of stored records, where each linked list connects records containing the same value for a particular data item type; furthermore, the lists are indexed to permit rapid access to records related by secondary key values. The multilist file is the forerunner of the inverted file; both organizations may make use of a multiple-level index to find a list of records containing a particular secondary key value. In general, however, the multilist file is often defined or described without having an index structure.

Figure 15-1 illustrates a two-level index multilist organization for satisfying Example Query 15-1 stated above. The level 1 index lists item types assigned to the single record type specified in the file or subfile. Each item type (name) has an associated pointer which locates a partition in the level 2 index; this index lists active item values corresponding to this particular item type. Other forms of indexes are common at level 1, such as a block index to the level 2 index, or any other form allowable in an indexed sequential file [Cardenas, 1975]. Each entry in the level 2 index, an active item value, also has an associated pointer. This pointer acts as the head of a linked list of records containing the same item value associated in the index with this head pointer. Note that a record in the file may be part of many linked lists, the maximum being the number of item types defined for that record type; thus, we have the term "multilist." The record may actually participate in fewer than the maximum number of linked lists when some items are not specified in the record (i.e., null).

The search mechanism for the multilist structure is system dependent. The indexes could be searched sequentially, or if they are ordered, a binary or tree search could be used. The record level search is always sequential because all records in the list, the target records, are to be accessed. Because records are physically unrelated, they may be unblocked in order to minimize the random access time. However, in another application they may be blocked to minimize sequential access time. Justification of the implementation of a multilist structure for an application requires that the cost in total search time to target records must be lower than the cost of sorting the entire subfile on the secondary keys used in the query and sequentially searching the sorted subfile for the contiguous sets of records that meet each record condition in the query. A few sections of a sorted subfile for Example Query 15-1 are illustrated in Fig. 15-2. Because the query has two record conditions and many atomic conditions, a large number of sets of contiguous data records must be accessed. An example query and the relative costs of sequential, multilist, and inverted file search are presented in Section 15-3-4.

The search strategy in a multilist organization for record conditions with more than one item condition is to first keep a count of the number of records in each list and store that value as part of the second-level index entry. Then the minimum search

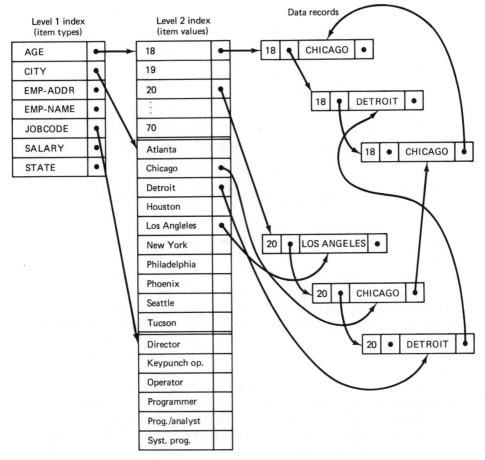

FIGURE 15-1 Multilist structure with a two-level index.

strategy would be to locate each second-level index entry associated with an item condition, determine which list is the shortest from the count value in the index entry, and search that list only. Each record in that list is tested for the correct conjunction of item conditions and is either saved (if it is a target record for the entire record condition) or discarded.

The search strategy for multiple record conditions is to locate the set of target records for each record condition, then merge the lists in the order that best displays the results. Duplicate records, that is, those records satisfying more than one record condition, can be eliminated in the merging process.

Range searching for multiple atomic conditions in an item condition can be handled in several ways. An efficient technique, when the queries are known in advance, would be to make each range of item values a separate entry in the item value (second level) index. This is not practical for ad hoc queries, however, because of the storage space required to account for all possible ranges. A more storage space efficient method, but slower in access time, searches the item value index for each

JOBCODE	CITY	AGE	OTHER
Programmer	Atlanta	20	...
Programmer	Atlanta	21	...
Programmer	Atlanta	23	...
Programmer	Detroit	19	...
Programmer	Detroit	21	...*
Programmer	Detroit	22	...*
Prog./analyst	New York	68	...
Prog./analyst	Philadelphia	22	...*
Prog./analyst	Philadelphia	22	...*
Syst. prog.	Tucson	57	...

*Target record for query

FIGURE 15-2 Sorted subfile based in secondary key values JOBCODE, CITY, AGE for Query 15-1.

value in the range specification. Then the entire set of data record lists for the range values must be accessed. This approach does not increase the I/O significantly if the range is reasonably small and the item value index is ordered; however, more software overhead is needed for the multiple index entry search. Fortunately, more efficient alternative range searching methods, particularly for static files, have recently been developed. The most efficient techniques attempt to reduce the search space through the use of sorted lists of records based on secondary keys, inverted indexes (see Section 15-3), grid or subset searching, and variants of binary tree structures and search mechanisms. Performance is commonly measured in terms of index and data load time, storage space, and query processing time.

To summarize our discussion, the following are the major factors to consider in the design of a multilist organization:

- *Work load.* Generalized queries and updates are most appropriate.
- *Storage space for indexes.*
- *Cost of sorting* (as an alternative for query processing).
- *Query complexity.* Affects access time to target records in a multilist file.
- *Index order.* Affects choice of index search mechanism and the update cost.
- *Record search strategy for multiple item conditions.*
- *Index block size.*

15-2-1 Retrieval Performance for Query Applications

Secondary access methods are specifically designed for secondary key processing (i.e., the GET SOME operation). Other operations could be performed, such as GET UNIQUE or GET ALL, but the storage structure used for them is the primary data area for the multilist. If that area can be regarded as contiguous in extent, it can be organized as either physical sequential or linked sequential, and the analysis of Section 12-2 applies to sequential and random retrieval operations. Our concern in this section is with the generalized query, GET SOME.

Let us assume that indexes are ordered and are searched sequentially. Furthermore, let us assume that the level 1 index is very small and considered to be contained within one physical block. The simplest query consists of a single atomic condition and results in the access of a single record list. Every record in the list is a target record for the query.

$$\text{PBA(GET SOME, 1 AC/IC)} = \text{PBA}_1 \text{ (index}_1 \text{ search)} + \text{PBA}_2 \text{ (index}_2 \text{ search)}$$
$$+ \text{PBA}_3 \text{ (data record search)} \qquad (15\text{-}1)$$

where

$$\text{PBA}_1 = 1 \text{ rba} \qquad (15\text{-}2)$$

$$\text{PBA}_2 = 1 \text{ rba} + \left(\left\lceil \frac{\text{NIV} + 1}{2 \text{ EBF}_2} \right\rceil - 1 \right) \quad \text{sba} \qquad (15\text{-}3)$$

$$\text{PBA}_3 = \text{NRIV rba} \qquad (15\text{-}4)$$

and for a small number of secondary key item types, NIV is the average number of item values per item type, and NRIV the average number of (target) records per item value. If there are multiple (consecutive) atomic conditions or a range specification for a single-item condition, the search is longer in index$_2$ and all potential target record lists must be accessed.

$$\text{PBA(GET SOME, } p \text{ AC/IC)} = \text{PBA}_1 \text{ (index}_1 \text{ search)} + \text{PBA}_{2A} \text{ (index}_2 \text{ search)}$$

$$+ \text{PBA}_{3A} \text{ (data record search)} \qquad (15\text{-}5)$$

where

$$\text{PBA}_1 = 1 \text{ rba}$$

$$\text{PBA}_{2A} = 1 \text{ rba} + \left(\left\lceil \frac{\text{NIV}}{\text{EBF}_2} \right\rceil - 1 \right) \quad \text{sba} \qquad (15\text{-}6)$$

$$\text{PBA}_{3A} = \sum_{i=1}^{p} \text{NRIV}_i \text{ rba}$$

for $p \geq 1$. The first term accounts for the single access to index$_1$. The second term represents the sequential search through index$_2$ for p (possibly nonconsecutive) item values. The third term, a summation, is the total number of accesses for the p target record lists.

Multiple-item conditions add another degree of complexity to the retrieval analysis. If there are q item conditions, each with one atomic condition, one index$_1$ and q index$_2$ searches are required, plus the access of the shortest virtual record list.

$$\text{PBA(GET SOME, } q \text{ IC/RC, 1 AC/IC)} = \text{PBA}_1 + \sum_{j=1}^{q} \text{PBA}_{2j} + \min_{j} (\text{NRIV}_j) \text{ rba}$$

$$(15\text{-}7)$$

for $q \geq 1$, where PBA_{2j} is the number of physical block accesses for the index$_2$ search associated with the jth-item condition. NRIV_j is the number of records associated with the jth-item condition.

Multiple record conditions are separately analyzed and are additive as independent operations. The number of target records for each record condition j is NTR_j, and they are sorted to eliminate duplicate records.

$$\text{PBA(GET SOME, } r \text{ RC/QC)} = \sum_{j=1}^{r} \text{PBA(GET SOME, } q \text{ IC/RC)}_j$$

$$(15\text{-}8)$$

$$+ \text{PBA} \left[\text{SORT} \left(\sum_{j=1}^{r} \text{NTR}_j \right) \right]$$

for $q \geq 1$ and $r \geq 1$.

15-2-2 Generalized Update Performance

Update is performed in multilist organizations after the target records have been accessed. To evaluate update costs properly, we must know the number of target records to be updated, NTR. A change of a primary key value does not affect the secondary indexes, nor does any item value not used as a secondary key affect the secondary indexes. Therefore, once the change is made to the (already accessed) record, only a record rewrite is needed to complete the transaction for the target record.

$$\text{PBA(CHANGE nonkey)} = 1 \text{ sba} \qquad (15\text{-}9)$$

The change of a secondary key value results in a deletion of a record from one access path, with the possible deletion of one index$_2$ entry if the list has no other members, and the insertion of the same record to a new access path and possible insertion of a new index$_2$ entry. Physically, the data record is not moved, but index pointers must be reset. We assume that to maintain a dense, ordered index, any insertion to or deletion from an index requires a read and rewrite of the entire *index fragment,* or index subgroup, associated with the next-higher-level index entry. The multilist $index_1$ fragment is the entire list of NIT entries. The $index_2$ fragments contain NIV entries each.

$$PBA(\text{DELETE data record}) = PBA(\text{rewrite predecessor record's NEXT pointer})$$
$$+ \text{PRDEL} \times PBA(\text{read and rewrite } index_2)$$
$$= 1 \text{ sba} + \text{PRDEL} \times \left\lceil \frac{\text{NIV}}{\text{EBF}_2} \right\rceil \times (2 \text{ sba}) \qquad (15\text{-}10)$$

where PRDEL is the probability that this is the last record in the target list. PRDEL determines the probability that an $index_2$ update is needed.

$$PBA(\text{INSERT data record}) = PBA(\text{write new record and pointer})$$
$$+ PBA(\text{read and rewrite } index_2)$$
$$= 1 \text{ rba} + \text{PRINS} \times \left\lceil \frac{\text{NIV}}{\text{EBF}_2} \right\rceil \times (2 \text{ sba}) \qquad (15\text{-}11)$$

where PRINS is the probability that this is the first record in the target list, and determines whether an $index_2$ update is needed.

$$PBA(\text{reINSERT data record after a change of secondary key})$$
$$= PBA(\text{rewrite record with change and new NEXT pointer})$$
$$+ \text{PRINS} \times PBA(\text{read and rewrite } index_2) \qquad (15\text{-}12)$$
$$= 1 \text{ sba} + \text{PRINS} \times \left\lceil \frac{\text{NIV}}{\text{EBF}_2} \right\rceil \times (2 \text{ sba})$$

$$PBA(\text{CHANGE secondary key, NTR}) = \text{NTR} \times PBA(\text{DELETE data record})$$
$$+ PBA(\text{find new } index_2 \text{ entry})$$
$$+ PBA(\text{reINSERT data record after change}) \qquad (15\text{-}13)$$

A change of a secondary key is illustrated in Fig. 15-3.

15-2-3   Storage Space

Multilist storage space requirements are easily seen as the sum of item type index ($index_1$) blocks, item value index ($index_2$) blocks, and data record blocks. We assumed earlier that $index_1$ consisted of a single block.

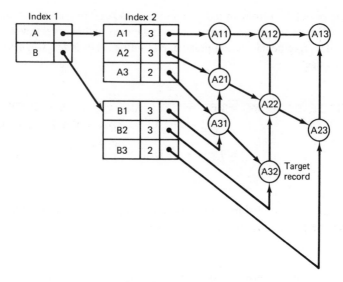

FIGURE 15-3 Record key change in a multilist file.

$$\text{BLKSTOR(multilist file)} = \text{BKS}_1 + \sum_{i=1}^{\text{NIT}} \left\lceil \frac{\text{NIV}_i}{\text{EBF}_{2'}} \right\rceil \times \text{BKS}_2 \tag{15-14}$$

$$+ \left(\sum_{i=1}^{\text{NIT}} \sum_{j=1}^{\text{NIV}} \text{NRIV}_{ij} \right) \times \text{SRS} \qquad \text{bytes}$$

The summations are used instead of expected values because of the potentially extreme variation of record occurrences per item value and item values per item type. If, on the other hand, only the expected values, NIV and NRIV, are known, we have

$$\text{BLKSTOR(multilist file)} = \text{BKS}_1 + \text{NIT} \times \left\lceil \frac{\text{NIV}}{\text{EBF}_2} \right\rceil \times \text{BKS}_2 \tag{15-15}$$

$$+ \text{NIT} \times \text{NIV} \times \text{NRIV} \times \text{SRS} \qquad \text{bytes}$$

where SRS includes NIT pointers in each stored record.

15-2-4 Cellular Multilist

One of the drawbacks of multilist structures is the possibility of long target record lists and therefore a significant number of random accesses to satisfy queries. If there is a strong possibility that some physical clustering exists among records in a target record list, it might be profitable to block data records into so-called "cells," hence the term "cellular." In Fig. 15-4 we see that blocks can be nonhomogeneous in data records; that is, a block may contain records that belong to different record lists.

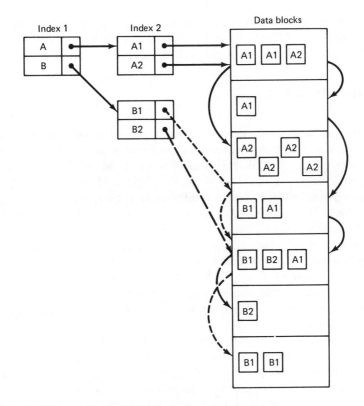

FIGURE 15-4 Cellular multilist organization.

When a block is accessed as part of one record list, the records from other lists, sometimes called false drops, must be identified as such and discarded. This process is done internally and requires CPU overhead. In general, a *false drop* is any record that appears to satisfy a query, based on an index table search, but is not really a target record. This fact is usually discovered upon inspection, using an *inclusion test,* after the record is accessed. False drops often result from secondary access techniques that retrieve more than actual target records in an attempt to increase overall I/O time efficiency.

    Cellular multilist is a multilist organization in which the pointers do not go from record to record, but from physical block to physical block, each of which contains at least one target record. One potential advantage of cellular multilist is that pointer space can be reduced when blocks are allocated with homogeneous or nearly homogeneous records in terms of target record lists; otherwise, the individual pointers must be retained. A more likely advantage is that the number of physical block accesses is reduced when accessing an entire list of records. When blocks are completely homogeneous in target records, the greatest I/O cost reduction will occur. The major disadvantages of cellular multilist are the CPU overhead necessary to maintain the desired degree of block homogeneity and to check each block internally for false drops. The disadvantages can be of major significance; therefore, the implementation of a cellular multilist structure should be preceded by a careful analysis of alternatives and expected performance.

15-3 INVERTED FILE

We have seen how simple queries involving secondary keys can be efficiently satisfied with indexed multilist structures. However, as queries become more complex, involving long boolean functions, Eqs. (15-5) to (15-8) indicate that large multiplication factors are used to specify the physical block accesses required. In particular, as the number of item conditions in a query increases, the multilist structure loses efficiency. For example, in Query 15-1 we may find that the shortest record list is 5000, and only 200, or 4%, of those records are actually target records for the entire query. Thus, a large amount of effort would be spent inspecting nontarget records. A more efficient scheme can be found by maintaining pointer arrays to records instead of record lists. The number of pointers is the same, but their placement is clustered in the pointer arrays, called accession lists. An *accession list* is a physical sequential (linear) list of pointers to records containing identical values for a particular key item.

An *inverted file* is a file organization or structure that permits fast searching for general queries involving secondary key value specifications. It consists of a multiple-level index structure plus a collection of accession lists to data records that meet certain key value criteria. Primary access methods search for a record based on a primary key, and after the record is accessed, the secondary key or nonkey items are investigated. Inverted files (and other secondary access methods) require modification of this process; the secondary key values are now used as a basis to locate a class of data records.

The most common type of inverted file has a two-level index (the same as a multilist file) and associated accession lists, as shown in Fig. 15-5. Data records can be blocked or unblocked (e.g., as determined by the primary access method or for optimizing physical reading of the entire file). Clustering is possible only if the queries are well known in advance; this is not the case in a dynamic database environment.

Some additional terms should be defined to aid in fully describing the inverted file design parameters. The access path model does not explicitly show the difference between partially and fully inverted files. A *fully inverted file* is inverted on every key item type in the record, including primary keys (i.e., NSK = NIT, where NIT is the number of attributes or item types in a record). The primary key index is nothing more than a full index structure (see Section 13-3). Fully inverted files are possible as an option in many DBMSs, including ADABAS and System 2000. They establish fast access to data based on any primary or secondary key values or combinations thereof. The price paid for such complete coverage is a large storage space overhead in the indexes. Hopefully, as storage space becomes less expensive, the effect of this

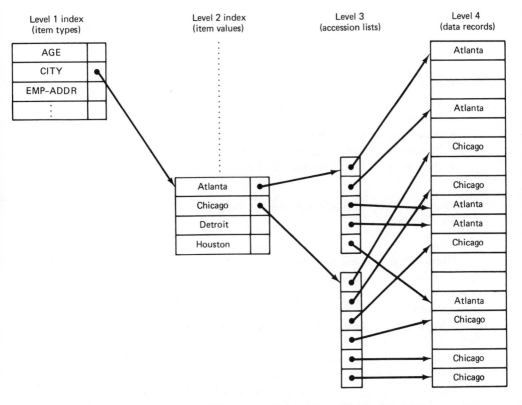

FIGURE 15-5 Inverted file structure with a two-level index for Query 15-1.

overhead will diminish considerably. A *partially inverted file* is inverted on a selected number of key item types (i.e., NSK < NIT). Note that in general,

$$NIT = NSK + NPK + NNK \qquad (15\text{-}16)$$

where NSK is the number of secondary keys, NPK is the number of primary keys, and NNK is the number of nonkeys.

Inverted files have been shown so far to consist of indexes based on single key item types and values. These are referred to as *separate indexes*. (In the literature they are also known as single attribute or single-key indexes.) It is also possible to use *combined indexes* that contain entries with concatenated key item values of different types. (These are also known as multiattribute or multiple-key indexes.) The combined form of indexing is available in IMS, for example, and in other systems. The time/space trade-offs between separate and combined indexes are addressed in Chapter 16.

Let us now summarize the major factors to consider in the design of inverted file organizations:

- Work load (complex conjunctive queries are most appropriate; generalized update of target records)
- Query complexity
- Number of index levels
- Storage space for indexes
- Index order, search mechanism, and blocking factor
- Full or partial inversion
- Secondary index selection
- Separate or combined indexes
- Accession list order, blocking factor

15-3-1 Retrieval Performance for Query Applications

The retrieval analysis for inverted files will concentrate on the GET SOME operation for ad hoc conjunctive queries. Other operations are better serviced with primary access methods. As with multilist files, the inverted file search mechanism is system dependent, particularly in the index levels. If the indexes are sorted, fast index search techniques can be used: binary search, tree search, higher-level indexes, and so on. Accession lists are sequentially processed because all entries (pointers) must be accessed for any atomic condition in the query. Data records are directly accessed on a one-to-one basis from the accession list pointers.

The search strategy for record conditions with more than one item condition is to find, via the indexes, the accession list associated with each item condition. Then the accession lists are merged in a single pass to produce a target accession list which is the conjunction (intersection) of the candidate accession lists. The merge operation can be accomplished only if the accession lists are ordered by physical addresses specified by the pointers. Finally, data records are accessed from the target accession list. This process is much more efficient with an inverted file structure than for a multilist structure (see Example Query 15-2 below).

The search strategy for multiple record conditions is to service each record condition individually, sort the target records, and merge them to eliminate duplicates, if desired. This is basically the same process as for multilist files.

Multiple atomic conditions are treated individually, and the resulting accession lists are merged before considering a new item condition. The hierarchical stepwise merging of accession lists avoids having to resort them and maintains the ordering required for efficient access to target records for multiple item conditions.

The analysis is based on the assumption that all indexes and accession lists are ordered. The simplest query consists of a single atomic condition:

$$
\begin{aligned}
PBA(GET\ SOME,\ 1\ AC/IC) = {}& PBA_1\ (\text{index}_1\ \text{search}) + PBA_2\ (\text{index}_2\ \text{search}) \\
& + PBA_3\ (\text{accession list search}) \qquad (15\text{-}17) \\
& + PBA_4\ (\text{target data record access})
\end{aligned}
$$

where

$$PBA_1 = 1 \text{ rba (single index}_1 \text{ block)} \qquad (15\text{-}18)$$

$$PBA_2 = 1 \text{ rba} + \left(\left\lceil \frac{NIV + 1}{2 \times EBF_2} \right\rceil - 1 \right) \text{ sba} \qquad (15\text{-}19)$$

$$PBA_3 = 1 \text{ rba} + \left(\left\lceil \frac{NRIV}{EBF_3} \right\rceil - 1 \right) \text{ sba} \qquad (15\text{-}20)$$

$$PBA_4 = NRIV \text{ rba} \qquad (15\text{-}21)$$

and where the subscripts denote the search level in the access path representation. For simplicity, let us use the short forms of the search costs, such as PBA_1, PBA_2, and so on.

$$
\begin{aligned}
PBA(\text{GET SOME,} \\
p \text{ AC/IC}) = {} & \left[PBA_1 \right] + \left[1 \text{ rba} + \left(\left\lceil \frac{NRIV}{EBF_2} \right\rceil - 1 \right) \text{ sba} \right. \\
& \left. + \left[p \text{ rba} + \left(\sum_{i=1}^{p} \left\lceil \frac{NRIV_i}{EBF_3} \right\rceil - p \right) \text{ sba} \right] \right. \\
& + \left[\sum_{i=1}^{p} NRIV_i \right] \text{ rba} \qquad (15\text{-}22)
\end{aligned}
$$

The second bracketed term (which we will call PBA_{2A}) shows the access of p nonconsecutive item values across all of index$_2$. The third bracketed term (PBA_{3A}) represents the initial and succeeding accesses to the several (p) accession lists, and the fourth bracketed term is the sum of the data record accesses. Data records are assumed to be unblocked.

Multiple (q) item conditions, each with one atomic condition, require an almost full search of index$_1$, q searches to index$_2$ fragments, q accesses to entire accession lists, the merge of accession lists, and the access to NTR target records that meet all the item conditions in the record condition.

$$
\begin{aligned}
PBA(\text{GET SOME, } q \text{ IC/RC}) = {} & PBA_1 + \sum_{j=1}^{q} PBA_{2j} + \sum_{j=1}^{q} PBA_{3j} \\
& + [NTR \text{ rba}] \qquad (15\text{-}23)
\end{aligned}
$$

where PBA_{2j} is the number of physical block accesses for the index$_2$ search associated with the jth-item condition. PBA_{3j} is similarly defined for the accession list search for the jth-item condition.

If item type A has a given value in a fraction f_A of the records and item type B has a given value in a fraction f_B of the records, then the fraction $f_A \times f_B$ of the records will simultaneously contain these given values for A and B when the item type values are independent. This holds for products of three or more fractions as well. Thus, when the independence assumption holds we can derive NTR for a particular record condition from known parameter values defining each item condition. If the item types are correlated, NTR for the record condition cannot be estimated this way; it must be obtained from empirical data about the known queries.

Multiple-record conditions are additive because the union of target records for individual record conditions is taken. Target records may be sorted to eliminate duplicate records if desired.

$$\text{PBA(GET SOME, } r \text{ RC/QC)} = \sum_{j=1}^{r} \text{PBA(GET SOME, } q \text{ IC/RC, } p \text{ AC/IC})_j$$
$$+ \text{ PBA} \left(\text{SORT} \left(\sum_{j=1}^{r} \text{NTR}_j \right) \right) \tag{15-24}$$

for $r \geq 1$, $q \geq 1$. $\tag{15-25}$

15-3-2   Generalized Update Performance

Inverted files are similar to multilist files in that updates are performed only after the target records have been accessed. Also, the two basic indexes are assumed to function the same way in each case. Let us again define NTR as the number of target records to be updated. If we again assume that primary keys are not represented in secondary indexes, the change of a primary key or any other nonsecondary key is a simple operation, a single data record rewrite:

$$\text{PBA(CHANGE nonkey)} = 1 \text{ sba} \tag{15-26}$$

The change of a secondary key value, represented in index$_2$, results in the rewrite of the target data records, the deletion of the accession list of pointers to those records, and the insertion of the same accession list subordinate to another key value in index$_2$. Each record's physical location remains unchanged. If the old key value is no longer needed (with probability PRDEL), the index$_2$ item value entry is also deleted. Similarly, if the new key item value is not currently in index$_2$ (with probability PRINS), it must be inserted in index$_2$. Any insertion or deletion operation in index$_2$ is assumed to necessitate a read and rewrite of the entire index fragment to maintain density and order. Since the retrieval operation is evaluated separately, the read and rewrite of indexes consists of sequential block accesses only.

$$
\begin{aligned}
\text{PBA(CHANGE secondary key, NTR)} = {}& \text{NTR} \times (\text{PBA(rewrite data record)}) \\
& + \text{PBA(find new accession list position)} \\
& + 2 \times \text{PBA(read and rewrite} \\
& \text{accession list)} + (\text{PRDEL} + \text{PRINS}) \\
& \times \text{PBA(read and rewrite index}_2)
\end{aligned}
$$

$$(15\text{-}27)$$

If NTR includes the entire set of records containing this key value (i.e., NTR = NRIV), Eq. (15-27) is simplified as follows: PRDEL $\dot{=}$ PRINS = 1, and PBA(read and rewrite accession list) = 0. In this case all records are changed, so the accession list is kept intact and only the index$_2$ pointer to it is moved. However, this move is already accounted for in the read and rewrite of the index$_2$ fragments for the old and new key values.

$$
\begin{aligned}
\text{PBA(DELETE data record)} = {}& \text{PBA(read and rewrite accession list)} \\
& + \text{PRDEL} \times \text{PBA(read and rewrite index}_2)
\end{aligned}
$$

$$
= \left\lceil \frac{\text{NRIV}}{\text{EBF}_3} \right\rceil \times (2 \text{ sba}) + \text{PRDEL} \times \left\lceil \frac{\text{NIV}}{\text{EBF}_2} \right\rceil \times (2) \text{ sba})
$$

$$(15\text{-}28)$$

$$
\begin{aligned}
\text{PBA(INSERT data record)} = {}& \text{PBA(write data record)} \\
& + \text{PBA(read and rewrite accession list)} \\
& + \text{PRINS} \times \text{PBA(read and rewrite index}_2)
\end{aligned}
$$

$$
= 1 \text{ rba} + \left\lceil \frac{\text{NRIV}}{\text{EBF}_3} \right\rceil \times (2 \text{ sba}) + \text{PRINS} \times \left\lceil \frac{\text{NIV}}{\text{EBF}_2} \right\rceil \times (2 \text{ sba})
$$

$$(15\text{-}29)$$

15-3-3   Storage Space

Inverted list storage space requirements consist of the item type index block (index$_1$), the item value index blocks (all index$_2$ fragments), accession list blocks, and data blocks:

$$
\text{BLKSTOR(inverted file)} = \text{BKS}_1 + \sum_{i=1}^{\text{NIT}} \left\lceil \frac{\text{NIV}_i}{\text{EBF}_2} \right\rceil \times \text{BKS}_2 + \sum_{i=1}^{\text{NIT}} \sum_{j=1}^{\text{NIV}} \left\lceil \frac{\text{NBIV}_{ij}}{\text{EBF}_3} \right\rceil
$$

$$(15\text{-}30)$$

$$
\times \text{BKS}_3 + \sum_{i=1}^{\text{NIT}} \sum_{j=1}^{\text{NIV}} \text{NRIV}_{ij} \times \text{SRS bytes}
$$

If only the expected values, NIV and NRIV, are known, we have

$$\text{BLKSTOR(inverted file)} = \text{BKS}_1 + \text{NIT} \times \left\lceil \frac{\text{NIV}}{\text{EBF}_2} \right\rceil \times \text{BKS}_2$$

$$+ \text{NIT} \times \text{NIV} \times \left\lceil \frac{\text{NRIV}}{\text{EBF}_3} \right\rceil \times \text{BKS}_3 \qquad (15\text{-}31)$$

$$+ \text{NIT} \times \text{NIV} \times \text{NRIV} \times \text{SRS} \qquad \text{bytes}$$

15-3-4   Trade-offs in Secondary Access Methods

The retrieval analysis for inverted and multilist files can best be illustrated with an example query application. Let us also consider a brute-force sequential processing approach and compare the performance of each access method.

Example Query 15-2: Compare retrieval access cost and storage space requirements for the following query condition and accompanying specifications:

SELECT NAME,ADDRESS,EDUCATION,JOB–HISTORY
FROM EDUCATOR
WHERE CITY = DETROIT *AND* JOB=TEACHER *AND* GRADE=6

NR = 10^6	NIT = 20	NRIV(IC$_1$) = 10,000
SRS = 200 bytes	NIV(CITY) = 100	NRIV(IC$_2$) = 750,000
BKS = 4000 bytes	NIV(JOB) = 5	NRIV(IC$_3$) = 150,000
(indexes and data)	NIV(GRADE) = 13	NTR(RC) = 500 target rec.
BOVHD = 0 for all blocks		
LF = 1 for all blocks		
IS = 6 bytes (average for all item types)		
PS = 4 bytes		

$$\left.\begin{array}{l} \text{TSBA} = 11.7 \text{ ms} \\ \text{TRBA} = 36.7 \text{ ms} \end{array}\right\} \text{ IBM 3350 specifications}$$

Physical sequential file and sequential search:

$$\text{PBA(GET SOME)} = \text{PBA(GET ALL)}$$

$$= \left\lceil \frac{\text{LRA}}{\text{EBF}} \right\rceil = \left\lceil \frac{10^6}{20} \right\rceil = \frac{10^5}{2} \text{ sba}$$

$$\text{TIO} = \frac{10^5}{2} \times \text{TSBA} = \frac{10^5}{2} \times 11.7 \text{ ms} = \underline{585 \text{ seconds}}$$

Multilist file:

PBA(GET SOME, 3 IC/RC)

$$= \text{PBA}_1 + \sum_{j=1}^{3} \text{PBA}_{2j} + \min_j (\text{NRIV}_j) \text{ rba}$$

$$= [1 \text{ rba}] + \left[\left(1 \text{ rba} + \left(\left\lceil \frac{100 + 1}{2 \times 400} \right\rceil - 1 \right) \text{ sba} \right. \right.$$

$$+ \left(1 \text{ rba} + \left(\left\lceil \frac{5 + 1}{2 \times 400} \right\rceil - 1 \right) \text{ sba} \right)$$

$$+ \left(1 \text{ rba} + \left(\left\lceil \frac{13 + 1}{2 \times 400} \right\rceil - 1 \right) \text{ sba} \right)$$

$$+ [10{,}000 \text{ rba}]$$

$$= 10{,}004 \text{ rba} + 1 \text{ sba}$$

TIO $= 10{,}004 \times 36.7 \text{ ms} + 1 \times 11.7 \text{ ms} = \underline{367 \text{ seconds}}$

Inverted file:

$$\text{PBA(GET SOME, 3 IC/RC)} = \text{PBA}_1 + \sum_{j=1}^{3} \text{PBA}_{2j} + \sum_{j=1}^{3} \text{PBA}_{3j}$$
$$+ \text{NTR rba}$$

$$= [1 \text{ rba}] + [3 \text{ rba}] + \left[\left\{ 1 \text{ rba} + \left(\left\lceil \frac{10k}{1k} \right\rceil - 1 \right) \text{ sba} \right\} \right.$$

$$+ \left\{ 1 \text{ rba} + \left(\left\lceil \frac{750k}{1k} \right\rceil - 1 \right) \text{ sba} \right\}$$

$$+ \left. \left\{ 1 \text{ rba} + \left(\left\lceil \frac{150k}{1k} \right\rceil - 1 \right) \text{ sba} \right\} \right] + 500 \text{ rba}$$

$$= 1 \text{ rba} + 3 \text{ rba} + 1 \text{ rba} + 9 \text{ sba} + 1 \text{ rba} + 749 \text{ sba} + 1 \text{ rba}$$
$$+ 149 \text{ sba} + 500 \text{ rba}$$

$$= 507 \text{ rba} + 907 \text{ sba}$$

TIO $= 507 \times 36.7 \text{ ms} + 907 \times 11.7 \text{ ms} = \underline{29 \text{ seconds}}$

The inverted file is a full order of magnitude more efficient than the multilist in terms of query processing time, and both secondary access methods are far superior to sequential processing for this particular query. The storage space breakdown is as follows:

	Index$_1$ (KB)	Index$_2$ (KB)	Accession Lists	Data Records (MB)	Total Storage (MB)
Physical sequential	0	0	0	200.0	200.000
Multilist file	4	4	0	212.0	212.008
Inverted file	4	4	12 MB	200.0	212.008

Although the inverted file requires more storage space, we see that a 6% increase in storage is worth a 12-fold decrease in I/O time relative to the multilist file and an almost 20-fold decrease in I/O time relative to physical sequential processing. The advantage of the inverted file depends on the small set of target records. If there were 30,000 target records, the inverted file I/O time would be approximately 1,112 seconds, which is much larger than the sequential processing time (which is constant regardless of the number of target records). Therefore, for very large sets of target records, the sequential processing approach is more efficient. About 1.5% of the database is the crossover point between the two access methods.

15-3-5   Cellular Inverted File

The *cellular inverted* organization is a variant of the concept of the inverted file in which accession lists consist of pointers to physical blocks that contain at least one data record having the key value represented by the accession list. The justification for this design is that if there is any natural physical clustering of data records that contain the same secondary key values, then many blocks will contain more than one of such records. If this is true, the average accession list length will be greatly reduced and therefore the expected I/O time to service a query will also be reduced. The amount of accession list I/O reduction could be as high as the data blocking factor when the data blocks are completely homogeneous in records containing the same key value (i.e., no false drops). The I/O time for data records is also reduced when they are blocked with some reasonable efficiency. When the accession lists are very long, the cellular inverted organization looks quite promising as a way to increase query processing efficiency. In the worst case, there is only one target record per block, so the accession list is unchanged from the inverted structure and the data block transfer time is conceivably larger if the blocking factor is larger for the cellular inverted case.

Both organizations have an additional overhead in CPU time for the inclusion tests to determine which data records are target records for the entire query; however, the cellular inverted organization tends to have more CPU overhead because of the larger percentage of false drops. The analysis of cellular inverted files should take into account the probable degree of clustering of data records and the extra CPU overhead cost. This is highly system dependent, particularly when the software efficiency must be evaluated.

An example of a cellular inverted structure is shown in Fig. 15-6. It appears to be much simpler to implement than the cellular multilist (see Fig. 15-4) because the data blocks contain no pointers, whereas in cellular multilist structures the data blocks contain a variable number of pointers, depending on the block contents. Thus, more CPU overhead is required to process blocks and maintain those pointers. Cellular inverted structures also have a variable number of pointers, but they are confined to the accession lists.

The retrieval performance is evaluated as follows:

$$\text{PBA(GET SOME, 1 AC/IC)} = \text{PBA}_1 + \text{PBA}_2 + \text{PBA}_{3C} + \text{PBA}_{4C} \qquad (15\text{-}32)$$

where PBA_1 and PBA_2 are the index search costs defined for inverted files in Eqs. (15-18) and (15-19). PBA_{3C} is the accession list search cost for the cellular organization, and PBA_{4C} is the data record search cost:

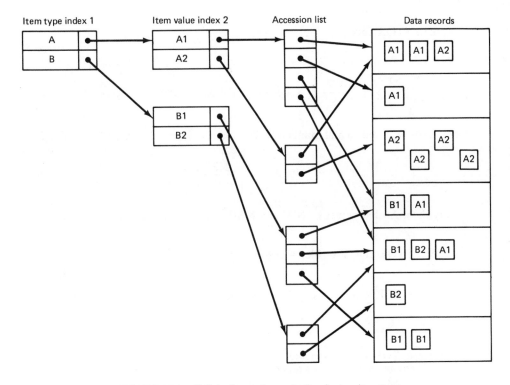

FIGURE 15-6 Cellular inverted organization for two item types.

$$PBA_{3C} = 1 \text{ rba} + \left(\left\lceil \frac{NBIV}{EBF_3} \right\rceil - 1 \right) \text{sba} \tag{15-33}$$

where NBIV is the expected number of blocks containing data records with a particular key item value. In general, NBIV is variable, and if we take individual components for different item types, we can use $NBIV_i$. In Fig. 15-6 $NBIV_i$ has the values 4, 2, 3, and 2 for the four item values listed.

$$PBA_{4C} = NBIV \text{ rba} \tag{15-34}$$

Note that when NBIV = NRIV, the cellular inverted performance is the same as inverted except that data block size is larger (usually) for the cellular inverted structure. Block size, we recall, is accounted for when transforming physical block accesses to I/O service time. Similarly, substitution of NBIV for NRIV in Eq. (15-22) results in an expression for multiple atomic conditions for cellular inverted structures. Equations (15-23) and (15-24) remain unchanged for cellular inverted. Update costs for the cellular inverted organization are evaluated by substituting NBIV for NRIV in Eqs. (15-26) to (15-29). Storage space is given by

$$\text{BLKSTOR(cell. inv. file)} = BKS_1 + \sum_{i=1}^{NIT} \left\lceil \frac{NIV_i}{EBF_2} \right\rceil \times BKS_2$$

(15-35)

$$+ \sum_{i=1}^{NIT} \sum_{j=1}^{NIV} \left\lceil \frac{NBIV_{ij}}{EBF_3} \right\rceil \times BKS_3 + NBLK_4 \times BKS_4 \qquad \text{bytes}$$

where $NBLK_4$ is the actual number of data blocks allocated to the file or subfile.

$$NBLK_4 = \left\lceil \frac{NR}{EBF_4} \right\rceil$$

(15-36)

If only the expected values of NIV and NBIV are known, we have

$$\text{BLKSTOR(cell. inv. file)} = BKS_1 + NIT \times \left\lceil \frac{NIV}{EBF_2} \right\rceil \times BKS_2$$

(15-37)

$$+ NIT \times NIV \times \left\lceil \frac{NBIV}{EBF_3} \right\rceil \times BKS_3 + NBLK_4 \times BKS_4 \qquad \text{bytes}$$

Example Query 15-2 (continued):   Continue the analysis of query retrieval I/O time for Example Query 15-2 using cellular inverted files.

$$NBLK_4 = \left\lceil \frac{10^6}{20} \right\rceil = 50,000$$

Let us assume that each data block of 20 records contains 95% false drops and 5% target records. Then there is one target record per block and NBIV = 500 blocks of target data records.

PBA(GET SOME, 3 IC/RC)

$$= PBA_1 + \sum_{j=1}^{3} PBA_{2j} + \sum_{j=1}^{3} PBA_{3Cj} + NTR \text{ rba}$$

$$= [1 \text{ rba}] + [3 \text{ rba}] + \left\lceil \left\{ 1 \text{ rba} + \left(\left\lceil \frac{10k/20}{1k} \right\rceil - 1 \right) \text{ sba} \right\} \right.$$

$$+ \left\{ 1 \text{ rba} + \left(\left\lceil \frac{750k/20}{1k} \right\rceil - 1 \right) \text{ sba} \right\}$$

$$+ \left\{ 1 \text{ rba} + \left(\left\lceil \frac{150k/20}{1k} \right\rceil - 1 \right) \text{ sba} \right\} \quad + 500 \text{ rba}$$

$$= 1 \text{ rba} + 3 \text{ rba} + 1 \text{ rba} + 0 \text{ sba} + 1 \text{ rba} + 37 \text{ sba} + 1 \text{ rba} + 7 \text{ sba}$$
$$+ 500 \text{ rba}$$

$$= 507 \text{ rba} + 44 \text{ sba}$$

TIO = 507 × 36.7 ms + 44 × 11.7 ms = <u>19 seconds</u>

The cellular inverted file performs 50% better on Example Query 15-2 than the previous best performer, the inverted file. CPU overhead is probably a little higher for cellular inverted, however, and should be investigated.

$$\text{BLKSTOR} = 4\text{ KB}(index_1) + 4\text{ KB}(index_2) + (1 + 75 + 15) \times 4\text{ KB (acc. lists)}$$
$$+ 200\text{ MB(for blocked data records)} \qquad \text{bytes}$$

$$= 4\text{ KB} + 4\text{ KB} + 91 \times 4\text{ KB} + 200\text{ MB}$$

$$= \underline{200.372\text{ MB}}$$

The cellular inverted structure has shorter accession lists, which saves 11.632 MB in storage space.

15-4   DOUBLY CHAINED TREE

The last general secondary access method we will investigate is the doubly chained tree. Its structure differs from inverted and multilist structures in a way analogous to the way a TRIE will differ from a multilevel indexed organization. The *doubly chained tree* is a form of inverted file organization in which the index hierarchy consists of one level for each key item type, the index entries at all levels consist of key item values, and the blocked data records do not contain any of the key items used to index them. The last characteristic reduces storage space in the data blocks considerably relative to inverted and multilist files.

Figure 15-7 illustrates the basic structure of a doubly chained tree by showing a possible implementation for Query 15-1. The three index levels represent the three item types used for storage and retrieval: JOBCODE, CITY, and AGE. The lowest level index entries point to data blocks, or heads of data block lists, containing only those records (i.e., target records) that meet the criteria of all key item values in the index tree path to the data blocks. Using our previous terminology, these blocks are considered to be homogeneous in the records they contain. Maintaining consistency with our previous analysis, we allow only index entries that lead to nonempty target data blocks. If a data block becomes empty through a deletion operation, index entries that do not eventually lead to nonempty blocks are also deleted immediately. We assume that indexes are dynamically reorganized.

Target records for a generalized query in a doubly chained tree may be zero for an unanswerable query, within a single block or block list for one atomic condition, or contained in several blocks for multiple atomic, item, and/or record conditions. In Fig. 15-7 we see that at least eight target records in four target record blocks are found as a result of the query. Data records in doubly chained trees are not duplicated in the access path representation; that is, there are no virtual records. However, sorting of target records may still be necessary for multiple-record conditions when there is overlap among target records for some record conditions. For example, the query condition (JOB=PROGRAMMER $\wedge$ CITY=ATLANTA) $\vee$ (AGE=20) will produce duplicate target records by accessing the leftmost data block in Fig. 15-7 twice.

At level 1 in Fig. 15-7 the number of item values for item type 1, NIV_1, is a

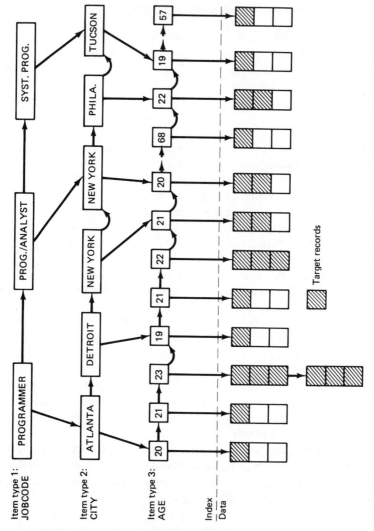

FIGURE 15-7 Doubly chained tree structure for Query 15-1.

Item type 1: JOBCODE

Item type 2: CITY

Item type 3: AGE

Index / Data

PROGRAMMER — PROG./ANALYST — SYST. PROG.

ATLANTA — DETROIT — NEW YORK — NEW YORK — PHILA. — TUCSON

20 — 21 — 23 — 19 — 21 — 22 — 21 — 20 — 68 — 22 — 19 — 57

Target records

constant. However, at level $i \geq 2$, NIV_i is a variable function of the parent item value at level $i - 1$. The value of NIV_i for any index fragment is precisely the number of different item values of type i, associated with all unique ancestor item values at that point in the tree, that have occurred in loaded records thus far. For example, in Fig. 15-7, the first (leftmost) index fragment at level 2 has three nodes to represent the fact that three item values have occurred in records having also the leftmost item value of item type 1 (at level 1). The search length at the data level, NR_{NIL+1}, is equal to the number of target records associated with the precise sequence of item values in the hierarchy from the root to that data block or block list. Target records associated with an actual query would consist of a collection of one or more groups of target records for each sequence of item values.

Strategies for constructing optimal index structures, in terms of storage space efficiency and access-time efficiency, have been analyzed by Cardenas and others [Cardenas, 1973, 1979; Cardenas and Sagamang, 1977; Rotwitt and deMaine, 1971]. The basic rule for minimizing storage space in the index is to order the key items by number of values, NIV_i. Then implement them for level 1 to NIL by increasing value of NIV_i. Because item values become more and more redundant at the lower portion of the tree, this strategy minimizes the size of the upper portion of the tree, and that controls the size of the lower portion. An example is illustrated in Fig. 15-8. It shows a file or subfile with three active item types such that $NIV_1 = 1$, $NIV_2 = 3$, and $NIV_3 = 7$, with eight unique key combinations. The minimum storage configuration is shown in Fig. 15-8(b) when the level assignments are in increasing value of NIV_i. The maximum storage configuration occurs in Fig. 15-8(d) when the level assignments are in decreasing value of NIV_i. Theoretical bounds on the number of nodes in an NIL-level doubly chained tree index can be deduced from Fig. 15-8:

$$\sum_{i=1}^{NIL} NIV_i \leq INODES \leq (NIL - 1) \times UKV + NIV_{max} \qquad (15\text{-}38)$$

where INODES is the number of index nodes, UKV is the number of unique key value combinations in data records, and NIV_{max} is the maximum over NIV_i, for all item types i.

The basic strategy for a doubly chained tree structure to minimize I/O service time to implement item types from level 1 to NIL in order of decreasing frequency of use in known query applications and order of increasing frequency of use in updates. Level 1 then has the most frequently retrieved item type. This tends to minimize the total number of index nodes traversed in many, but not all cases. Additionally, a practical strategy is to design several alternative structures and evaluate each with known retrieval and update operations.

The doubly chained tree has been claimed to have several distinct advantages over inverted files. First, storage space is claimed to be less because secondary keys used in the index are excluded from the data records. Second, because secondary key updates are confined to the index, less I/O processing time is needed to manage the update operations. Inverted file updates of this kind require update to both the index

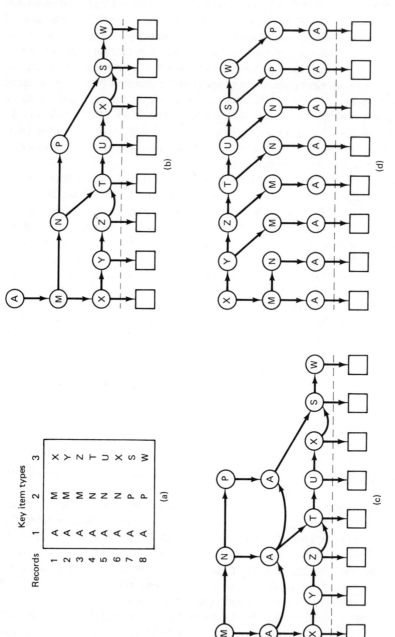

FIGURE 15-8 Doubly chained tree index storage space options: (*a*) sample key item values; (*b*) order of item types: 1, 2, 3 (12 nodes); (*c*) order of item types: 2, 1, 3 (14 nodes); (*d*) order of item types: 3, 2, 1 (23 Nodes).

and the data records. Third, faster query processing can be done when queries are known in advance and a tree can be constructed to minimize index node accesses to a block of target records. Unfortunately, it can be shown that there are configurations and processing requirements in which some of these advantages may not be true. Ad hoc queries may be particularly inefficient with fixed tree index structures. The next sections investigate retrieval and update costs in doubly chained trees, consistent with the previous analysis of multilist and inverted files, so that meaningful comparisons of performance can be made.

The major factors in the design of a doubly chained tree, analyzed further below, are:

- *Work load.* Generalized queries and updates are most appropriate; ad hoc vs. known queries; query complexity.
- *Assignment of key item types to index levels.* Affects storage space and access time efficiency.
- *Frequency of use of specific key items in queries.* Affects the assignment of key item types to index levels.
- *Index ordering*
- *Block size for index and data entries*
- *Storage space restrictions*

15-4-1   Retrieval Performance for Query Applications

Performance relationships for doubly chained tree structures and search mechanisms are derived from the tree representation (Fig. 15-7) and the generalized query definitions of Section 15-1. The basic form of query condition that we start with is the multiple-item condition, single-atomic condition case: $IC_1 \wedge IC_2 \wedge \ldots \wedge IC_3$, where IC_i = item type $\left\{ {\leq \atop >} \right\}$ item value for all i. The search mechanism for this case starts at level 1 and works downward, one level at a time, to level NIL. At each level there are two possible paths. First, if the key item type at level i is included in the query as an item condition, the search proceeds at level i until the specific item value is found. Assuming that a successful search occurs, the expected search length is the midpoint of the index list at level i. Unsuccessful searches are considered later in this section. Second, if the key item type at level i is not included in the query, all key item values are possible and the entire list must be accessed at this level.

As the search mechanism proceeds from level to level, the number of filial sets to be accessed (index fragments) increases sharply. Relative to the previous level, the parent node, there are again two possible situations. First, if the key item type is in the query, there is exactly one node in an index fragment that matches the item condition at level $i - 1$, and it has a filial set fragment at level i. Alternatively, if the key item type is not in the query, all nodes in the index fragment at level $i - 1$ and their filial

sets at level i must be examined. Thus, we can now keep count of the potential search
path length at each level in the index. For $1 \leq q \leq$ NIL,

$$\text{PBA(GET SOME, } q \text{ IC/RC, 1 AC/IC)} = \text{index search} + \text{data block search}$$

$$= \sum_{i=1}^{\text{NIL}} \text{LEN}_i \text{ rba} + \text{NTB rba} \qquad (15\text{-}39)$$

where $\text{LEN}_i = (\prod_{j=1}^{i-1} \text{CARD}_j) \times \text{WID}_i$ is the number of nodes to be accessed at level i.
Also,

$$\text{WID}_i = \begin{cases} \left\lceil \dfrac{1 + \text{NIV}_i}{2} \right\rceil & \text{when item type } i \text{ is in the query} \\[2ex] \text{NIV}_i & \text{otherwise} \end{cases}$$

and

$$\text{CARD}_j = \begin{cases} 1 & \text{when item type } j \text{ is in the query} \\[1ex] \text{NIV}_j & \text{otherwise} \end{cases}$$

The variable NTB represents the number of "target" blocks containing the NTR
records for the query. Note that NTB is at least as large as either $\text{LEN}_{\text{NIL}+1}$ or
$\left\lceil \dfrac{\text{NTR}}{\text{EBF}_{\text{NIL}+1}} \right\rceil$.

Equation (15-39) is greatly simplified when $q = $ NIL, the case when each item
type represented in the index is also specified by an item condition in the query. For
this case we have

$$\text{PBA(GET SOME, } q = \text{NIL IC/RC, 1 AC/IC)} = \sum_{i=1}^{\text{NIL}} \frac{1 + \text{NIV}_i}{2} \text{ rba} + \text{NTB rba}$$
$$(15\text{-}40)$$

Equations (15-39) and (15-40) hold true regardless of how the index level lists are
ordered, assuming that secondary key values and stored key values are independently
selected.

If the search is unsuccessful, it is difficult to find an expected search length. The
lower bound is NR_i, the maximum width of the first level of index. If no match is
found at the end of level 1, the search terminates immediately. The upper bound is
given by Eq. (15-39), except that $\text{WID}_i = \text{NIV}_i$ whether or not the item type i is in the
query.

When there are multiple atomic conditions in addition to multiple-item conditions, there are two possible cases. First, filial index fragments at all levels below the

root (of the access path) must be entirely accessed to check for the atomic conditions. If the index lists are unordered, this is always true. For this case, we apply Eq. (15-39) with restrictions that $WID_i = NIV_i$ and $CARD_j = NIV_j$. Second, when the lists are ordered, it may be possible to reduce the search length to $p_i/(p_i + 1)$ of the maximum, using Theorem 12-1, where p_i is the expected number of atomic conditions per item condition for item type i. However, this marginal reduction in search length is probably not worth the additional overhead to order the query item conditions the same way the index list is ordered. Consequently, the limits on WID_i and $CARD_j$ for the unordered list case are adequate for the ordered case.

Multiple record conditions are considered independently and the I/O access costs for each record condition are simply added. The sort operation can be applied to eliminate redundant target records. For $1 \leq q \leq NIL$ and $p \geq 1$, we have

$$PBA(GET\ SOME,\ r\ RC/QC) = \sum_{j=1}^{r} PBA(GET\ SOME,\ q\ IC/RC,\ p\ AC/IC)_j$$
$$+ SORT\left(\sum_{j=1}^{r} NTR_j\right) \quad (15\text{-}41)$$

15-4-2   Generalized Update Performance

Update operations for doubly chained trees are analyzed in the same manner as multilist and inverted files. We again refer to Fig. 15-7 as our general model, and we assume that the search for a record to be changed or deleted has been successful. Because data records are blocked, the update cost for target records for a query is no longer a linear function of NTR. Blocks may be only partially filled at any given time; consequently, it is difficult to predict how many data blocks are active without having substantial statistical data on past block usage. Such statistics are vital to the expected value analysis; otherwise, we can only compute bounds on performance.

First, we see that a change of a data record for nonkey values involves only a rewrite of the data block where the change occurs.

$$PBA(CHANGE\ nonkey) = \begin{cases} 1\ sba & \text{for 1 record changed} \\ NTB\ sba & \text{for NTR blocked records changed} \end{cases} \quad (15\text{-}42)$$

The deletion of a data record is accomplished by physical deletion within the data block and a rewrite of the updated block. Also, if this was the last record in the block list, occurring with probability $PRDEL_{NIL}$, the index level NIL entry pointing to this block must also be deleted. Index deletions may be propagated up to level 1, but the probability of deletion tends to decrease as one traverses toward level 1, where there are fewer duplicate key values. To delete an index node, which is implemented as a linked sequential structure, the predecessor node's NEXT pointer must be reset. If we assume that the predecessor node (or entry) has been saved in a buffer because it was recently accessed to find the target record to be deleted, only a physical rewrite of that entry need be accomplished.

PBA(DELETE) = PBA(rewrite data block)

$$
\begin{aligned}
&+ \sum_{i=1}^{\text{NIL}} \text{PRDEL}_i \times \text{PBA(rewrite predecessor index entry)} \\
&\qquad\qquad\qquad\qquad\qquad\qquad\qquad\qquad\qquad\qquad (15\text{-}43) \\
&= \begin{cases}
1\ \text{sba} + \sum_{i=1}^{\text{NIL}} \text{PRDEL}_i \times (1\ \text{sba}) & \text{for 1 record deletion} \\[2ex]
0\ \text{sba} + \sum_{i=1}^{\text{NIL}} \text{PRDEL}_i \times (1\ \text{sba}) & \text{for all NTR record} \\
& \qquad\qquad\text{deletions}
\end{cases}
\end{aligned}
$$

The simplest form of insertion of a data record is accomplished by locating the appropriate data block, making the physical insertion into the block, and rewriting the block. There is a certain probability, $\text{PRINS}_{\text{NIL}}$, that no data block yet exists for records meeting the given item conditions. In this case, index entries must be made as well as the allocation and writing of a single data block containing the record to be inserted. The insertion of a new index entry requires a reset of the predecessor's NEXT pointer, a rewrite of the predecessor record, and a write of the new index entry after setting its NEXT pointer.

PBA(INSERT) = PBA(write or rewrite data block)

$$
\begin{aligned}
&+ \sum_{i=1}^{\text{NIL}} \text{PRINS}_i \times \text{PBA(write new index entry + rewrite} \\
&\qquad\qquad\qquad\qquad\qquad\qquad\text{the predecessor record entry)} \\
&\qquad\qquad\qquad\qquad\qquad\qquad\qquad\qquad\qquad\qquad (15\text{-}44) \\
&= [\text{PRINS}_{\text{NIL}} \times (1\ \text{rba}) + (1 - \text{PRINS}_{\text{NIL}}) \times (1\ \text{sba})] \\
&+ \sum_{i=1}^{\text{NIL}} \text{PRINS}_i \times (1\ \text{rba} + 1\ \text{sba})
\end{aligned}
$$

PRINS, like PRDEL, decreases as the propagation proceeds toward level 1.

The change of a secondary key value for a group of records does not affect the physical (stored) records, but only changes the index. After the initial search to the data records, some index pointers to the data are reset:

PBA(CHANGE secondary key) = PBA(DELETE NTR records) + PBA(find new
                              secondary key path for reinsertion)   (15-45)
                              + PBA(INSERT − data block rewrite)

15-4-3   Storage Space

Storage requirements in a doubly chained tree consist of index records and data records. For unblocked index records:

BLKSTOR(doubly chained tree) = index storage space + data storage space

$$= \sum_{i=1}^{NIL} \left(\prod_{j=1}^{i} NIV_j \text{ (active)} \right) \times SRS$$

$$+ \left\lceil \frac{NR}{EBF_2} \right\rceil \times BKS_2 \quad \text{bytes}$$

(15-46)

where the subscript 1 denotes index area and the subscript 2 denotes data area. For blocked index records:

$$\text{BLKSTOR(doubly chained tree)} = \left\lceil \sum_{i=1}^{NIL} \left(\frac{\prod_{j=1}^{i} NIV_j}{EBF_1} \right) \right\rceil \times BKS_1$$

$$+ \left\lceil \frac{NR}{EBF_2} \right\rceil \times BKS_2$$

(15-47)

15-4-4 Comparison with Inverted and Multilist Files

It would be useful to be able to identify conditions under which the doubly chained tree performs better than an inverted or multilist file. Retrieval performance can be compared by continuing Example Query 15-2 (see Sections 15-3-4 and 15-3-5), and update cost comparison will be done with Example Query 15-3 later in this section.

Example Query 15-2 (continued):

NTR = 500 target records

Assume that data blocks are half filled on the average, and completely filled in the minimum (best) case. Let us look at this case in more detail.

$$EBF_2 = \left\lfloor \frac{4000}{200 - 3 \times 6} \right\rfloor = 21 \quad NBLK = \left\lceil \frac{NR}{EBF_2} \right\rceil \times 2 = \left\lceil \frac{10^6}{21} \right\rceil \times 2 = 95,240$$

There is only one query application in this example; therefore, the arrangement of index levels is not critical to retrieval efficiency. However, it will make a difference in storage space. Consequently, let us order the levels by increasing NIV_j.

$$\begin{array}{ll} \text{Level 1} = \text{JOB} & NIV_1 = 5 \\ \text{Level 2} = \text{GRADE} & NIV_2 = 13 \\ \text{Level 3} = \text{CITY} & NIV_3 = 100 \end{array}$$

The average index node size is 6 bytes for the item value and $2 \times (4 \text{ bytes})$ for the two pointers in the minimum configuration.

$$EBF_1 = \left\lfloor \frac{4000}{14} \right\rfloor = 285$$

$$\text{BLKSTOR}_{avg} = \left\lceil \frac{5 + 5 \times 13 + 5 \times 13 \times 100}{285} \right\rceil \times 4000 + 95,240 \times 4000$$

$$= 24 \times 4000 + 95,240 \times 4000 = 381.056 \text{ MB}$$

$$\text{BLKSTOR}_{min} = 24 \times 4000 + \frac{95,240}{2} \times 4000 = 190.076 \text{ MB}$$

The minimum storage requirement is lower by at least 5% than the inverted, cellular inverted, or multilist structures; but the average storage requirement is higher than all the others, and by as much as 90%.

Unblocked index case:

$$\text{PBA(GET SOME, 3 IC/RC)} = \left(\left\lceil \frac{1 + 5}{2} \right\rceil + \left\lceil \frac{1 + 13}{2} \right\rceil + \left\lceil \frac{1 + 100}{2} \right\rceil \right) \text{rba}_1$$
$$+ \text{ NTB rba}_2$$

$$= (3 + 7 + 51) \text{ rba}_1 + 48 \text{ rba}_2$$

$$= 61 \text{ rba}_1 + 48 \text{ rba}_2$$

$$\text{NTB}_{avg} = \left\lceil \frac{\text{NTR}}{\text{EBF}_2} \right\rceil \times 2 = \left\lceil \frac{500}{21} \right\rceil \times 2 = 48$$

$$\text{TIO} = 61 \times 33.4 \text{ ms} + 48 \times 36.7 \text{ ms} = \underline{3.8 \text{ seconds}}$$

Blocked index case:

$$\text{PBA(GET SOME, 3 IC/RC)} = 3 \text{ rba}_2 + 48 \text{ rba}_2 = 51 \text{ rba}_2$$

$$\text{TIO} = 51 \times 36.7 \text{ ms} = \underline{1.9 \text{ seconds}}$$

We now summarize the retrieval performance of the five candidate access methods for Example Query 15-2:

TABLE 15-1   Retrieval I/O cost and storage for Example Query 15-2

	Query I/O time (sec)	Storage space (MB)
Sequential (physical)	585	200.0
Multilist	367	212.0
Inverted	29	212.0
Cellular inverted	19	200.4
Doubly chained tree		
Minimum	1.9–3.8*	190.6
Average	3.6–5.6*	381.1

*Index blocked case to index unblocked case.

Observing Table 15-1, the doubly chained tree becomes significantly lower in I/O time when there is blocking of data records. If, in the worst case, only one target record existed in each data block, there would be NTR = NTB = 500 data blocks and the I/O time range would be considerably higher. The blocking of indexes is significant, but not the order-of-magnitude difference blocked data records makes. The trade-off appears to be in the possibility of a large storage space overhead with the doubly chained tree unless the data blocks can be kept highly loaded.

We have not yet compared the secondary access methods in terms of update cost. Let us look at an update example and use our analytical model to evaluate performance of our candidate secondary access methods.

Example Query 15-3:   Using the configuration in Example Query 15-2, compute the I/O time required to accomplish the following update operations: CHANGE nonkey, DELETE, INSERT, and CHANGE secondary key CITY. Assume that PRDEL = PRINS = 0.1 at all levels, and let NTR = 1 and 100 for the two cases.
   Basic parameters given:

$PRDEL = PRINS = 0.1$ $EBF_1 = EBF_2 = 400$ for $index_1$ and $index_2$
$NTR = 1,100$ $EBF_3 = 1000$ for accession lists
$NIV_{CITY} = 100$ $EBF_4 = 20$ for data blocks (inverted, multilist),
$NRIV_{CITY} = 10,000$ 21 (doubly chained tree)
                $NTB_{avg} = 48$ for doubly chained tree
$NBIV_{CITY} = \dfrac{10,000}{EBF_3} \times 2 = 20$ (half-filled blocks)

The CHANGE secondary key physical block accesses are derived below:
   Multilist:

PBA(CHANGE sec. key) = PBA(DELETE) + PBA(find new $index_2$ entry)
               + PBA(reINSERT)

            = 1.2 sba + 2 rba + 1.2 sba

            = 2.4 sba + 2 rba

   Inverted:

PBA(CHANGE sec. key) = PBA(rewrite data rec.) + PBA(find new acc. list)
               + PBA(read and rewrite acc. list)
               + PBA(read and rewrite $index_2$)
               × (PRDEL + PRINS)

            = 1 sba + 2 rba + 2 × (1 rba + 1 sba)
               + (1 rba + 1 sba) × 0.2

            = 3.2 sba + 4.2 rba

   Cellular inverted:

PBA(CHANGE sec. key) = 1 sba + 2 rba + 2 × (1 rba + 1 sba)
               + (1 rba + 1 sba) × 0.2

            = 3.2 sba + 4.2 rba

   Doubly chained tree:

PBA(CHANGE sec. key) = PBA(DELETE) + PBA(find point for reinsertion)
               + PBA(INSERT–rewrite data block)

            = 1.3 sba + 4 rba + (1.2 sba + 0.4 rba − 1 sba)

            = 1.5 sba + 4.4 rba

Tables 15-2 and 15-3 indicate that no single access method is superior in update performance for all types of update operations. However, if certain types of updates

TABLE 15-2   Update I/O Costs (PBA) for Example Query 15-3 with NTR = 1

	Multilist	Inverted	Cellular Inverted	Doubly Chained Tree
CHANGE nonkey	1 sba	1 sba	1 sba	1 sba
DELETE data record	1.2 sba	2.2 sba	2.2 sba	1.3 sba
INSERT data record	0.2 sba + 1 rba	2.2 sba + 1 rba	2.2 sba + 1 rba	1.2 sba + 0.4 rba
CHANGE secondary key	2.4 sba + 2 rba	3.2 sba + 4.2 rba	3.2 sba + 4.2 rba	1.5 sba + 4.4 rba

TABLE 15-3   Update I/O Cost (PBA) for Example Query 15-3 with NTR = 100

	Multilist	Inverted	Cellular Inverted	Doubly Chained Tree
CHANGE nonkey	100 sba	100 sba	100 sba	10 sba
DELETE data record	1.2 sba	20.2 sba	2.2 sba	0.3 sba
INSERT data record	0.2 sba + 100 rba	20.2 sba + 100 rba	2.2 sba + 20 rba	90.3 sba + 10.3 rba
CHANGE secondary key	101.4 sba + 2 rba	138.2 sba + 4.2 rba	102.2 sba + 2.2 rba	85.6 sba + 61.3 rba

predominate, there could be an obvious choice of access method to implement. For example, when there is an extremely large number of record insertions, the cellular inverted structure and search mechanism is significantly more efficient than all the other methods. Note that the differences in performance become more dramatic for NTR = 100 records than for 1 record. This is due to index and data blocking, which is inefficient for small sets of target records.

15-5   INVERTED INDEX MAINTENANCE ALTERNATIVES

Each secondary access method discussed in this chapter has a unique storage structure. However, the multilist and inverted files use the same basic indexing structure. For future discussion we refer to the inverted file indexing structure as the protoype for comparing various inverted index configurations. Up to this point we have assumed that the item value index fragment (index$_2$) is dense and ordered to facilitate fast retrieval. We have also assumed that the accession list associated with each entry in index$_2$ is also dense and ordered to efficiently find intersections of target records for conjunctive queries. We refer to variations in these assumptions and the update activities associated with them as *index maintenance alternatives*. An extensive list of index maintenance alternatives has been described and analyzed in connection with index selection [Anderson and Berra, 1977], and we extend the concepts here to conform to our model of access methods.

We assume throughout the discussion that index updates are accomplished immediately so that the database is correct for any query. We also assume that database lockout need not be considered for a single-user environment, but it should be analyzed to estimate response time in multiuser configurations [see the QDELAY parameter defined in Chapter 9. This requires a queuing model of database dynamics [Kleinrock, 1975; Kobayashi, 1978].

Let us identify each index maintenance alternative and derive its performance characteristics. Alternatives 1 through 9 specify variations in $index_2$, while accession lists are always dense and ordered.

1. *SORTED/SEQUENTIAL (SSEQ)*

This index structure is the standard prototype for inverted files. Both the item value index ($index_2$) fragments and all accession lists are dense and ordered physical sequential files and allow fast retrieval. A new index entry is inserted at its proper position in the sorted list, after a sequential search, and the remainder of the list is shifted to maintain density and order. Deletion of an index entry also requires a sequential search and reshifting. Retrieval of a specific item from the index may be enhanced by a binary search or multilevel index search mechanism. The important update performance relationships for this alternative are

$$PBA(\text{INSERT data record}) = PBA_1 + PBA_2 + PRINS \times PBA_3 \qquad (15\text{-}48)$$

where $PBA_1 = PBA(\text{write data block})$, $PBA_2 = PBA(\text{read and rewrite an accession list})$, and $PBA_3 = PBA(\text{read and rewrite } index_2)$.

$$PBA(\text{DELETE data record}) = PBA_2 + PRDEL \times PBA_3 \qquad (15\text{-}49)$$

$$
\begin{aligned}
PBA(\text{CHANGE key}) = \; & PBA(\text{DELETE data record}) \\
& + PBA(\text{find new acc. list}) \\
& + PBA(\text{INSERT data record, with rewrite} \\
& \quad \text{instead of write data record})
\end{aligned}
\qquad (15\text{-}50)
$$

We assume that each random (or linked) block read or write is 1 rba, each block rewrite is 1 sba, and that the physical sequential block reads and writes are 1 sba per block.

. 2. *SORTED/FREE SPACE (SFREE)*

The SFREE structure modifies SSEQ to allow index blocks to become nondense. This is accomplished by setting $LF < 1$, so that blocks have some free space to allow for some expansion without having to shift the rest of the index. Deletions are also easier to make because a record can be merely flagged or blanked out to denote deletion. All retrieval can be done using fast primary access methods on index blocks, and update operations can be accomplished more efficiently. Performance differences are shown below:

INSERT data record: Use Eq. (15-48) except that

$$PBA_3 = P_1 \times PBA(\text{rewrite one index}_2 \text{ block})$$
$$+ (1 - P_1) \times PBA(\text{shift index}_2 \text{ entries until} \quad (15\text{-}51)$$
$$\text{available space is found for the new entry})$$

where P_1 = probability that the index block has space available for a new entry. This is a recursive relationship and in the worst case could result in an incremental shifting of the entire index$_2$ fragment, as in Eq. (15-48).

DELETE data record: Use Eq. (15-49) except that

$$PBA_3 = PBA(\text{rewrite one index}_2 \text{ block}) \qquad (15\text{-}52)$$

The CHANGE key expression is constant for all the index maintenance alternatives because it is written at a higher level of abstraction; that is, it is expressed in terms of INSERT and DELETE operations. Therefore, we refer only to Eq. (15-50).

3. *SORTED/SPLIT BLOCK (SSPLIT)*

This alternative modifies SFREE such that if no space is available in an index block for a new entry, either a new block is allocated (as in ISAM) or block splitting is accomplished (as in VSAM). No shifting of index entries across block splitting is necessary. Similarly, deletion is done in place with a flag or blank out and no shifting of data is necessary. If block splitting is done, it may be necessary to delete a block if it is emptied by a DELETE data record operation.

INSERT data record: Use Eq. (15-48) except that

$$PBA_3 = P_1 \times PBA(\text{rewrite one index}_2 \text{ block})$$
$$+ (1 - P_1) \times PBA \text{ split block} \qquad (15\text{-}53)$$

where

$$PBA_4(\text{split block}) = PBA(\text{rewrite old block} + \text{write new block}) \quad (15\text{-}54)$$

DELETE data record: Use Eq. (11-49) except that

$$PBA_3 = P_2 \times PBA(\text{rewrite one index}_2 \text{ block})$$
$$+ (1 - P_2)$$
$$\times PBA(\text{rewrite one index}_2 \text{ block} \qquad (15\text{-}55)$$
$$+ \text{rewrite prior index}_2 \text{ block after its pointer is changed})$$

where P_2 = probability that an index block becomes empty after a DELETE operation.

4. *SORTED/LINKED (SLINK)*

If the index is organized as a sorted linked sequential file, an index update is accomplished by a sequential search to the proper position and a modification of NEXT (and possibly PRIOR) pointers. All retrieval is done via a sequential search. For a one-way linked sequential organization, we have the following:

INSERT data record: Use Eq. (15-48) except that

$$PBA_3 = PBA(\text{modify NEXT pointer of new entry and its}$$
$$\text{predecessor entry and rewrite each entry}) \qquad (15\text{-}56)$$

DELETE data record: Use Eq. (15-49) except that

$$PBA_3 = PBA(\text{modify NEXT pointer of predecessor entry} \atop \text{and rewrite predecessor block}) \tag{15-57}$$

5. *UNSORTED/SEQUENTIAL (UNSEQ)*

If the index is unsorted, but density is to be maintained, new entries are inserted at the end of the last index block. Overflow is handled by allocating a new end block. Deletion of an entry requires a shift of the remaining entries to maintain density. Retrieval is always sequential.

INSERT data record: Use Eq. (15-48) except that

$$PBA_3 = P_1 \times PBA(\text{rewrite last index}_2 \text{ block}) + (1 - P_1) \atop \times PBA(\text{write new index}_2 \text{ block}) \tag{15-58}$$

DELETE data record: Use Eq. (15-49) except that

$$PBA_3 = PBA(\text{read and rewrite index}_2) \tag{15-59}$$

6. *UNSORTED/FREE SPACE (UNFREE)*

UNFREE is the same as SFREE except that retrieval prior to insertion is only to the first block with available free space, and all other retrieval is always sequential.

7. *UNSORTED/SPLIT BLOCK (UNSPLIT)*

UNSPLIT is the same as SSPLIT except that retrieval prior to insertion is only to the first block, and all other retrieval is always sequential.

8. *UNSORTED/LINKED (UNLINK)*

UNLINK is the same as SLINK except that retrieval prior to insertion is only to the head pointer of the index.

9. *UNSORTED/DIRECT (UNDIR)*

UNDIR is the same as UNSEQ except that retrieval prior to insertion is one physical block access to the end block of the $index_2$ fragment. A special pointer is maintained for this purpose.

The accession list alternatives are the same as $index_2$ alternatives 1 through 9, except that with accession lists we need to derive the same set of new expressions for PBA_2 instead of PBA_3.

16 SECONDARY INDEX SELECTION

The traditional secondary access methods that are commonly implemented in DBMS and other software systems were considered in Chapter 15. The multilist and inverted files are examples of single-key (separate) indexing, that is, for index fragments based on values for a single key item type. The doubly chained tree is a hybrid indexing scheme, with each level specified by a single-key item type, but traversal across levels can be considered a multiple-key (combined) index search. All index accesses, both within and across levels, are conceptually seen as linked sequential in a doubly chained tree, although in the actual implementation many of those accesses occur within the same physical block.

Our investigation now turns to some alternative methods of multiple-key indexing and the problem of selecting keys for indexes that will produce the best system performance. Index selection is an important part of the database design process; and it applies to primary keys, secondary keys in separate indexes, and to secondary keys in combined indexes. It is an inexact process which requires a good deal of intuitive thought and enumerative evaluation. Some automatic design tools have been proposed, but they are still in the experimental stage and in practice defer to computer-aided analysis with human intervention or completely manual analysis. In this chapter we continue to use our analytical model of databases to investigate trade-offs among the variety of secondary access methods and selection of keys.

16-1 MULTIPLE-KEY (COMBINED) INDEXING

The inverted file, as an example of single-key indexing, provides excellent retrieval performance for simple queries based on a single key, and reasonable performance for conjunctive queries with multiple-item conditions. In the latter case, extra processing is required to merge accession lists and obtain target records for the complete record condition, but this has been shown in Example Query 15-2 to be much faster still than data record searches for a sequential file or a multilist file. On the other hand, the hybrid combined index technique (doubly chained tree) was even faster than the inverted file for this example. For short accession lists the inverted file would have better retrieval performance relative to the doubly chained tree, and in general is more flexible for ad hoc queries of any complexity. Still, for many query applications it is significantly better to use some form of combined indexes.

An extension of Example Query 15-1 shows the advantage of combined indexes more clearly. Suppose that the query is representative of a class of queries of the same format, although having different values of key items in the item conditions, that were known to occur with reasonably high frequency. Then, because of the static nature of the processing we could improve our retrieval efficiency by setting up a special index that is ordered on the three known item types (CITY, JOB, GRADE), treating the combined keys as a composite single key, and using an appropriate primary access method to find the desired index entry. This would reduce the index search for the entire query to possibly one or just a few block accesses at most. Multiple-record-condition queries would require one index entry retrieval per record condition, but this is still a large improvement over inverted file retrieval.

The total retrieval time could be further reduced if the record condition accession list were eliminated in favor of a bucket of records satisfying the record condition, as is done with the doubly chained tree and partial-match hashing algorithms. An example of a combined index file is shown in Fig. 16-1.

In Example Query 15-1 it is possible that the query could be serviced in three accesses (3 rba) with an indexed sequential search of the combined index, plus $500/20 = 25$ block accesses for the 500 target data records (1 rba + 24 sba at best). The total retrieval time would be (4 rba) $\times$ 36.7 + (24 sba) $\times$ 11.7 = 427.6 milliseconds. This represents a 44:1 improvement over the cellular inverted file and is comparable to performance of a doubly chained tree with blocking of the index.

The dramatic improvement in retrieval performance has its price, as we learned

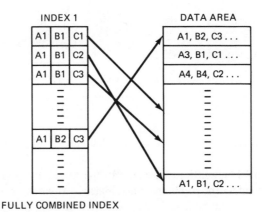

FULLY COMBINED INDEX

FIGURE 16-1   Combined index file.

with the doubly chained tree. The price is twofold: a great deal of redundancy is built into a combined index, and the structure is inflexible for any change in the database contents or type of query applied to it; such changes require the index to be reorganized. The redundancy is analogous to the redundancy in a relational database in first normal form, a flat file for the combined index, compared to second or third normal forms, which are expressed similarly to a collection of single-key indexes. The combined index for Example Query 15-2 has storage of $\prod\limits_{i=1}^{3} NIV_i = 100 \times 5 \times 13 = 6500$ entries. At 6 bytes per value and 4 bytes per pointer (10 bytes per entry), the total becomes 65 kB. Individual single-key indexes have storage of $\sum\limits_{i=1}^{3} NIV_i = 100 + 5 + 13 = 118$ entries, or 1.18 KB. (Note that the analogy with the relational normal forms is not exact. The second and third normal forms also have some redundancy in them.) Although for this example a 65-KB index is acceptable in medium-to-large scale computer systems, the size difference is quite large and for some query classes the combined index could be impractical to implement.

The flexibility issue is illustrated by the added requirement to process queries based on the third key component, GRADE. The inverted file software simply accesses the GRADE value index (index$_2$) and finds the appropriate accession list. The combined index file, because it is not ordered by GRADE, must be scanned sequentially because the data records have been randomly stored. For example, if the item condition GRADE = 10 had 10^5 target records distributed randomly over 50,000 blocks, the number of block accesses for a single-key access method (cellular inverted) and a combined index access method are:

Cellular inverted file:

PBA(GET index$_1$) = 1 rba

PBA(GET index$_2$) = 1 rba

PBA(GET accession list) = 1 rba + $\left(\dfrac{5000}{10^3} - 1 \right)$ sba = 1 rba + 4 sba

PBA(GET data records) = 5000 rba

PBA(GET SOME, total) = 5003 rba + 4 sba   (TIO = 184 seconds)

Combined index file:

PBA(GET ALL, sequential scan) = 50,000 sba   (TIO = 585 seconds)

Inverted files would be inefficient because of the extremely large target record list (TIO = 3670 seconds). The combined index is also inefficient, but it is due to the need to scan the entire file with randomness of the target records. The cellular inverted file is better for large target record lists because it takes advantage of blocking at the data record level. Clearly, the benefit of a combined index is most realized when queries are predetermined, very frequent, and static. Otherwise, there is a dramatic degradation in retrieval performance in addition to the everpresent storage space overhead.

In general, we can classify record conditions into three categories based on how well the query complexity and available indexing match [Anderson and Berra, 1977]. A *serial conjunct* is a record condition that contains only items that are not indexed (i.e., nonkey items). When this occurs, the data records must be sequentially scanned and an inclusion test performed for each record. A *pure conjunct* is a record condition that contains only indexed items, so that the index search (and the accession list merge, if necessary) will be enough to determine the location of target records for the query. A *mixed conjunct* is a record condition that contains both indexed and nonindexed items. When this occurs, the normal strategy is to obtain a list of target records that satisfies the indexed item conditions and then conduct inclusion tests on those items for the nonindexed item conditions. Obviously, the pure conjunct is the most efficient to service, so we make extensive use of known query applications to design indexing schemes.

16-2   CATEGORIZATION OF SECONDARY ACCESS METHODS

The previous discussion has identified clear differences among secondary access methods (SAMs). These differences can be categorized into four groups as follows:

GROUP 1. Index structure. The basic parameters are:
- NIF, the number of index fragments for key values (in index$_2$)
- NKEY, the number of keys per entry in each (key value) index fragment in index$_2$

GROUP 2. Index search techniques

GROUP 3. Index maintenance alternatives

GROUP 4. Data record access methods:
- Accession list for individual target data records
- Accession list for target data blocks only
- Clustered (and blocked) data records with no accession lists
- Unclustered data records, linked sequential

Each group of parameters is considered to be independent; that is, parameters from any group can be added to any combination of parameters from the other groups for a total *SAM configuration*. Groups 1 to 3 are referred to as the *index configuration*.

Let us observe the index structure (Group 1) parameters first. Figure 16-2 shows the potential SAM categories in two-dimensional space defined by NIF and NKEY. Each category is described below in more detail.

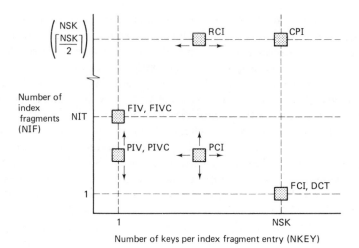

FIGURE 16-2 Categorization of secondary access methods by index structure.

Group 1. Index structure

FIV (fully inverted file): NKEY = 1, NIF = NIT. Full inversion is possible with many current DBMSs, and was a mandatory component of TDMS [Blier and Vorkaus, 1968]. The most common implementation is for the accession list to point to individual target records; the cellular inverted option (FIVC) provides for accession list entries to point to target data blocks. Index search is often done via a higher-level block or track index similar to the indexed sequential access method. Index maintenance rules are system dependent.

PIV (partially inverted file): NKEY = 1, NIF < NIT. Partial inversion is very common in commercial DBMSs [Cardenas, 1979; Sprowls, 1976]; it differs from full inversion only in that not every item type need be inverted (indexed). The cellular inverted option (PIVC) provides an accession list for target data blocks. The multilist structure differs only in the record access method.

FCI (fully combined index) and DCT (doubly chained tree): NKEY = NSK, NIF = 1. Conceptually, the FCI and DCT structures are the same; both encompass a large single index. However, the implementations differ considerably. The FCI index is stored as a physical sequential file and the DCT multiple-level index is stored and searched as a linked sequential file. In each case the best performance is attained when the key item types represented in the index are equivalent to the search keys in the queries. Less storage overhead occurs in the DCT, however, because of the hierarchical nature of the index levels. One type of experimental FCI scheme, called the balanced filing scheme [Ghosh and Abraham, 1968], specified buckets to contain the accession lists; accession list entries were pointers to individual noncontiguous data records.

PCI (partially combined index): 1 ≤ NKEY ≤ NSK, 1 ≤ NIF ≤ NIT. The PCI index structure is the general case from which the fully and partially inverted files and fully combined index structures are defined [Lum et al., 1970]. A SAM with several multiple-key indexes strikes a compromise between the fast retrieval, but high storage and low flexibility FCI and the slower retrieval, but low storage and high flexibility FIV or PIV. Secondary indexing in IMS is an implementation example of a PCI scheme.

CPI (compound indexing): NKEY = NSK, NIF = $\left(\begin{matrix} NSK \\ \lceil NSK/2 \rceil \end{matrix} \right)$. The compound indexing scheme, proposed by Lum [1970], extends the concept of the fully combined index scheme to even greater redundancy to guarantee faster retrieval. Each of several indexes is equivalent to a fully combined index, but differs from other indexes in key order. Although NSK! orderings are possible, Lum shows that only

$$NIF = \left(\begin{matrix} NSK \\ \lceil NSK/2 \rceil \end{matrix} \right) \tag{16-1}$$

orderings are required to guarantee that all possible conjunctive queries on NSK or fewer keys could be answered without resorting to finding the intersection of target record accession lists. For example, if we relabel Example Query 15-2 with item types A, B, and C, and all possible conjunctive queries with 1, 2, or 3, item conditions could be represented by the following 15 cases [Lum, 1970; Shneiderman, 1977 A, B, C, $A \wedge B$, $B \wedge A$, $A \wedge C$, $C \wedge A$, $B \wedge C$, $C \wedge B$, $A \wedge B \wedge C$, $A \wedge C \wedge B$, $B \wedge A \wedge C$, $B \wedge C \wedge A$, $C \wedge A \wedge B$, $C \wedge B \wedge A$.

However, Lum proposed a three-index fragment structure

Index keys	*Queries applicable*
1. *ABC*	A, $A \wedge B$, $B \wedge A$, $A \wedge B \wedge C$, $A \wedge C \wedge B$
2. *BCA*	B, $B \wedge C$, $C \wedge B$, $B \wedge C \wedge A$, $B \wedge A \wedge C$
3. *CAB*	C, $C \wedge A$, $A \wedge C$, $C \wedge A \wedge B$, $C \wedge B \wedge A$

that would answer any of the 15 types of queries without taking intersections of accession lists or scanning the entire index.

Applying Eq. (16-1), we obtain the following values for the number of index fragments as a function of the number of secondary keys:

NSK	2	3	4	5	10
NSK!	2	6	24	120	3,628,800
NIF	2	3	6	10	252

RCI (reduced combined indexes): NKEY ≤ NSK, NIF $= \left(\dfrac{NSK}{\lceil NSK/2 \rceil} \right)$. The reduced combined indexes scheme is a variation of the CPI scheme that reduces the amount of redundancy within the individual indexes [Shneiderman, 1977], although the number of indexes is the same as the CPI scheme. As an example, in the NSK = 3 index in Example Query 15-2 the three indexes proposed by Lum can be reduced in size as shown in Table 16-1, where the RCI indexes are *ABC, BC,* and *CA.*

TABLE 16-1   Number of Entries in Indexes for the CPI and RCI Index Structures for Example Query 15-2 with NSK = 3

Index	CPI	RCI
1. *A B C*	100 × 5 × 13 = 6500	100 × 5 × 13 = 6500
2. *B C A*	6500	5 × 13 = 65
3. *C A B*	6500	13 × 100 = 1300
Total number of entries	19,500	7,865

The indexes necessary for the CPI and RCI schemes are shown in Fig. 16-3. The full indexes represent the CPI scheme, and the partial indexes, which exclude items to the right of the vertical lines, represent the RCI scheme. Shortened indexes mean that the RCI scheme can reduce not only storage space, but also the index search time for target records. Both Lum et al. [1970] and Shneiderman [1977] also discuss variations to their schemes to reduce retrieval time further under special conditions.

Partial match hash algorithms are not really indexing schemes, but conceptually they are similar to a form of the partial combined index (PCI) approach, in which a compound key value is transformed into a physical address of a bucket of data records, each of which contain that whole key value [Aho and Ullman, 1979; Burkhard, 1979]. More research needs to be done comparing indexing and hashing methods of combined indexing.

```
NSK = 2   A   B |              NSK = 5   A   B   C   D   E |
          B | A                          E   A   B   C | D
                                         B   C   D   E | A
NSK = 3   A   B   C |                     B   E   C | A   D
          B   C | A                       B   D   E | A   C
          C | A   B                       C   A   D | E   B
                                          C   E   A | B   D
NSK = 4   A   B   C   D |                 C   D   E | A   B
          B   C   D | A                   D   A   B | E   C
          B   D   A | C                   D   E   A | B   C
          C   A   D | B
          C   D | A   B
          D   A | B   C
```

FIGURE 16-3 Compound and reduced combined indexes for index keys A, B, C, D [Shneiderman, 1977].

Group 2. Index Search Techniques

Candidates for index searching can be drawn from the entire pool of primary access methods discussed in Chapters 12 to 14; sequential search, binary search, block indexing (multilevel), hashing, and tree searching. Analysis is conducted for indexes in their representation as physical sequential or linked sequential files.

Group 3. Index Maintenance Alternatives

The index maintenance alternatives are discussed in Section 15-5. The maintenance options apply to indexes in their representation as physical or linked sequential files.

Group 4. Data Record Access Methods

The data record access methods represent options that could conceivably be attached to any of the indexing configurations described in groups 1 to 3. The accession list with data record pointers is the basic inverted file structure analyzed in Chapter 15. The accession list with data block pointers is the basic cellular inverted file structure. The cluster of data records, related by multiple key values, is the basic form associated with the doubly chained tree organization. It is most efficient for static files and static queries, but loses its efficiency when data and/or queries change over time. The unclustered data records represent the multilist approach. In each of these methods the search mechanism is simply sequential.

These groups and alternatives of SAM configurations are important for proper index selection. We now turn to the index selection problem in more detail.

16-3   THE INDEX SELECTION PROBLEM

Index selection is one of the most complex problems in the entire database design process. We define the *index selection problem* as the problem of choosing primary keys, secondary keys, and index configurations in order to produce reasonably "good" database system performance for all types of applications designated in the requirements statement. *Secondary index selection* is more restrictive; it is the choice of a set of secondary keys and index configurations that support "good" database system performance. We distinguish both of these terms from *optimal secondary index selection* in which one chooses a configuration of secondary keys and index configurations that optimizes database system performance. Index configurations are defined by groups 1 to 3 SAM characteristics in Section 16-2. Performance is measured in terms of the various costs we have described already: retrieval and update I/O time, CPU overhead, storage space, or some subset of these costs.

The difference between index selection and optimal index selection, in practice, is that although some heuristics exist for index selection, there are no design tools to compute the optimal solution to the entire problem. There are several enumerative approaches to optimal solutions for the separate problems of single-key (separate) indexes and multikey (combined) indexes, but not for both types of indexes simultaneously. The enumerative approach is discussed in Section 16-4. One automatic optimum-finding technique has been developed, but it is restricted to the single-key index configuration [Schkolnick, 1975]. Comer has shown that for single-key index selection alone, no algorithm has better than 2^{NIT} steps in the worst case, a potentially difficult problem (i.e., NP-complete) [Comer, 1978]. Although many such problems can be solved in far fewer steps on the average, it may not be worthwhile to use such algorithms in a dynamic environment where index components are to be changed frequently. Comer advocates the study of approximation algorithms for optimal index selection as a means to obtain suboptimal solutions without undue computational costs.

Whether we wish to develop an optimal or "good" solution to the index selection problem, there are a few basic steps in the index selection process:

1. Recognize the types of keys required and generate the candidate keys that satisfy feasibility.
2. Eliminate bad choices of keys (reduce the solution space).
3. Select a subset of the candidate keys that gives a solution of the quality desired.

Let us look into each of these steps in more detail.

STEP 1: GENERATION OF CANDIDATE KEYS

The source of information on potential keys is the logical database structure that satisfies user information and processing requirements. It illustrates data relationships that affect the choice of keys. Data dictionaries or directories that support the logical database structure are also very useful for defining item types precisely.

Primary keys are chosen where the data are to be specifically ordered for efficient handling of sequential (GET ALL) or random (GET UNIQUE) applications. Ordering by primary key also facilitates batch processing of queries or updates. The simplest primary key is the single-attribute (item type) key, which has a unique value for each data record. Customer account number, social security number (SSN), or invoice number are examples of single attribute identifiers. Often the majority of primary keys are identified during the selection of entities and attributes in the conceptual phase of database design, and are verified only at this point.

Sometimes attributes are too long for convenient processing, so only partial attribute keys are used. Unfortunately, there are often duplicate partial keys, and the designer then needs to create a suffix to the keys that provides uniqueness. Thus, we now have concatenation as an option for primary keys. As an example, suppose that the first five characters of last names were used to create partial key values. Duplicate last names or similar last names (e.g., JOHNS, JOHNSON) would result in duplicate partial keys. Some useful suffixes include other keys or partial keys from the rest of the record, sequence numbers, or relative address values. An interesting concatenation suggested by Hoffer [1979] is to add one or more bits to a key to designate whether records have been changed, how often, or what type of change has been made.

Concatenated keys, as implemented in IMS, are useful to keep track of hierarchical data relationships as well as to provide uniqueness. Sometimes hierarchically defined concatenated keys can be quite lengthy and are variable in size. Both of these traits tend to demand extra CPU overhead.

Other suggestions for primary keys involve creating special keys to enhance the sorting of data for a particular report generation requirement, creating indexes to point to data records with null values for certain keys, and moving intersection data (in m:n relationships) to keys instead of residing in separately defined records. The latter possibility requires additional storage space because the intersection data are often duplicated in the keys.

STEP 2: ELIMINATION OF OBVIOUS BAD SOLUTIONS

The examination of candidate keys should first designate the necessary primary keys so that they can be put aside from further consideration. In the selection of secondary keys, we normally want to avoid primary keys or keys with almost all unique values because of the extremely long item value lists and short accession lists. A primary key has an item value list of NR and an accession list of length 1. Primary access methods are recommended for these keys instead. Another class of keys to avoid contains keys with only a few values and has a large number of duplications, such as the item type GENDER. Queries that specify key values of this type are often more efficiently serviced with sequential processing. What candidate keys that remain for index selection are investigated for current as well as potential usage in the dominant query applications.

STEP 3: SELECTION OF THE FINAL SET OF KEYS AND INDEX STRUCTURES

Secondary keys are chosen to facilitate queries that are known or anticipated to occur with reasonable frequency. At one extreme, indexing on every candidate key would ensure that all simple (i.e., one item condition) queries, both now and in the future, could be answered without scanning the entire database. The trade-off with guaranteed fast retrieval is the amount of extra storage overhead and index maintenance required. If the trade-off analysis reveals that inversion of all keys is not reasonable, a more thoughtful approach is needed. Certainly, the list of candidate keys can be reduced to service the dominant known or anticipated queries. While partial secondary keys may cause undue CPU overhead, concatenation of keys to produce combined multikey indexes is certainly feasible, particularly for known queries of greater complexity than one item condition. The choice of candidate secondary keys is based mainly on analysis of processing requirements and feasibility of meeting those requirements in terms of data content. The choice of the final set of secondary keys and how they are to be combined in index configurations is based on performance requirements established by the users.

16-4 OPTIMAL SECONDARY INDEX SELECTION

We have already noted that the problem of selecting an optimal set of secondary keys is computationally difficult. However, we note that for small problems an optimal solution may be computationally feasible, and for many moderate to large problems a nearly optimal solution may also be feasible. Most of the research done in the 1970s concentrated on approximation solutions to single-key (separate) and multiple-key (combined) index selection [Anderson and Berra, 1977; Cardenas, 1975; Hammer and Chan, 1976a, b; Hoffer, 1978; Lum, 1970; Lum et al., 1970, 1971; Schkolnick, 1975; Stonebraker, 1974].

We shall now specify a general secondary index selection method whose foundation is the sequential and random access model and its associated analytical formulation of secondary access method performance. We build on this foundation with the index selection criteria consistent with the theoretical models and algorithms described in the literature. Using the access model we can define any separate or combined index structure specified in Fig. 16-2, including index search and maintenance techniques; the most complex query conditions defined in Section 15-1; and a cost function that includes retrieval, update, and storage. Optimization is done by manual enumeration of candidate solutions. The optimization procedure can be improved by writing a computer algorithm for cost evaluation (using the relationships described here) and superimposing a decision algorithm that eliminates classes of poor solutions. Global optimality of *indexing choice,* the selection of secondary keys and index configuration that minimizes total cost, will remain a research topic for the immediate future.

We shall take a top-down stepwise refinement approach to defining the components of total cost over a standard unit time period:

$$\text{TCOST(index. choice } x) = \sum_{\substack{\text{all} \\ \text{DML} \\ \text{opns.} i}} (CR_i + CU_i) + CS \qquad (16\text{-}2)$$

where CR_i is the retrieval cost, CU_i the update cost for DML operation $i,$ and CS the storage cost. Another objective function that might be used is the cost savings for an indexing choice $x,$ which is the difference in TCOST(no indexes) and TCOST(index, choice x); this function is to be maximized [Anderson and Berra, 1977]. We will use Eq. (16-2) and evaluate the no index (physical sequential) access method as a standard for comparison.

$$CR_i = CR_i(IO) + CR_i(CPU) \qquad (16\text{-}3)$$

$$CR_i(IO) = TIO_i(GET\ SOME) \times C_{IO} \times FGS_i \tag{16-4}$$

$$CR_i(CPU) = TCPU_i(GET\ SOME) \times C_{CPU} \times FGS_i \tag{16-5}$$

where TIO_i(GET SOME), the I/O time associated with servicing query i, is a linear function of PBA_i(GET SOME) as given by Eqs. (9-5) to (9-7), C_{IO} is the unit cost of an I/O second, C_{CPU} is the unit cost of a CPU second, and FGS_i is the frequency of GET SOME (query) operation i. $TCPU_i$(GET SOME) is the total CPU time associated with query i and is defined in more detail below:

$$TCPU_i(GET\ SOME) = CPU.MERGE(c,\ a) + CPU.TEST(q,\ a) \\ + CPU.EXCH \times PBA_i(GET\ SOME) \tag{16-6}$$

$$CPU.MERGE(c,\ a) = CPU\ \text{time to merge } c \text{ ordered lists of } a \text{ elements each} \\ = (c \times a) \times CPU.1 \tag{16-7}$$

where CPU.1 is the average time to make one comparison between two data items.

$$CPU.TEST(q,\ a) = \text{the CPU time to make an inclusion test for} \\ q \text{ item conditions for each of } a \text{ elements} \\ \text{(records) in a list} \tag{16-8}$$

$$= a \times CPU.q$$

where

$$CPU.q = q \times CPU.1 \tag{16-9}$$

CPU.EXCH is the CPU time to execute a channel program for a physical block I/O operation, and PBA_i(GET SOME) is the count of physical block accesses required to service the GET SOME operation i. PBA_i(GET SOME) is the same parameter used in the computation of TIO_i(GET SOME).

    Update costs per unit time period are computed in a similar way, except that there are four types of updates: INSERT (I), DELETE (D), CHANGE key (CK), and CHANGE nonkey (CNK).

$$CU_i = CU_i(IO) + CU_i(CPU) \tag{16-10}$$

$$CU_i(IO) = CI_i(IO) + CD_i(IO) + CCK_i(IO) + CCNK_i(IO) \tag{16-11}$$

$$CU_i(CPU) = CI_i(CPU) + CD_i(CPU) + CCK_i(CPU) + CCNK_i(CPU) \tag{16-12}$$

The individual I/O costs are:

$$CI_i(IO) = TIO_i(INSERT, NTR.\ I) \times C_{IO} \times FI_i \qquad (16\text{-}13)$$

$$CD_i(IO) = TIO_i(DELETE, NTR.D) \times C_{IO} \times FD_i \qquad (16\text{-}14)$$

$$CCK_i(IO) = TIO_i(CHANGE\ key, NTR.CK) \times C_{IO} \times FCK_i \qquad (16\text{-}15)$$

$$CCNK_i(IO) = TIO_i(CHANGE\ nonkey, NTR.CNK) \times C_{IO} \times FCNK_i \qquad (16\text{-}16)$$

The CPU costs are very similar:

$$CI_i(CPU) = TCPU_i(INSERT, NTR.I) \times C_{CPU} \times FI_i \qquad (16\text{-}17)$$

$$CD_i(CPU) = TCPU_i(DELETE, NTR.D) \times C_{CPU} \times FD_i \qquad (16\text{-}18)$$

$$CCK_i(CPU) = TCPU_i(CHANGE\ key, NTR.CK) \times C_{CPU} \times FCK_i \qquad (16\text{-}19)$$

$$CCNK_i(CPU) = TCPU_i(CHANGE\ nonkey, NTR.CNK) \times C_{CPU} \times FCNK_i$$
$$(16\text{-}20)$$

In Eqs. (16-13) to (16-20) the frequency of each type of update operation is specified by "F" followed by the abbreviation for the type of update used. $TCPU_i$ (type of update) represents the total CPU time associated with an update, over and above the CPU time used in the retrieval access of the record to be updated. The NTR prefix specifies the expected number of target records associated with that operation. Rewriting the variables in a simpler form to denote constants, we obtain

$$TCPU_i(INSERT, NTR.I) = CPU.I \times NTR.I_i + CPU.EXCH \\ \times PBA(REWRITE)_i \qquad (16\text{-}21)$$

$$TCPU_i(DELETE, NTR.D) = CPU.D \times NTR.D_i + CPU.EXCH \\ \times PBA(REWRITE)_i \qquad (16\text{-}22)$$

$$TCPU_i(CHANGE\ key, NTR.CK) = CPU.CK \times NTR.CK_i + CPU.EXCH \\ \times PBA(REWRITE)_i \qquad (16\text{-}23)$$

$$TCPU_i(CHANGE\ nonkey, NTR.CNK) = CPU.CNK \times NTR.CNK_i \\ + CPU.EXCH \\ \times PBA(REWRITE)_i \qquad (16\text{-}24)$$

The CPU.-terms are system-dependent times that are functions of CPU speed and software efficiency. Occasionally, opportunities arise to use additional CPU times:

$$CPU.SORT(a) = \text{the CPU time to sort a list of } a \text{ elements} \qquad (16\text{-}25)$$
$$= a \log_2 a \times CPU.1 \text{ (for the } \log_2 a \text{ class} \\ \text{of sort techniques)}$$

CPU.BSEARCH(b, a) = the CPU time to do a binary search of a list
of a elements, once for each of b data
elements to match another list   (16-26)

$$= b \log_2 a \times \text{CPU.1}$$

The combination of sorting and matching for an unordered list (e.g., an accession list) is evaluated by adding Eqs. (16-25) and (16-26). If the sort is not performed, the total matching time is longer:

$$\text{CPU.USEARCH}(b, a) = b \times a \times \text{CPU.1} \qquad (16\text{-}27)$$

The storage cost per unit time period is a very straightforward extension of the BLKSTOR computations in Chapters 12 to 15. Note that the storage cost is not dependent on DML operations.

$$\text{CS} = (\text{BLKSTOR(index)} + \text{BLKSTOR(data)}) \times C_{ST} \qquad (16\text{-}28)$$

where C_{ST} is the unit cost of a byte of storage. This completes the computation of total cost.

Example 16-1:   A database consists of a single record type with 10^5 occurrences. Query and update applications are summarized in Table 16-2. For the given processing volume and database parameter values, find the indexing choice that minimizes total cost as given in Eq. (16-2). The candidate indexing choices are:

1. No index
2. *A* index only
3. *B* index only
4. *A, B* separate indexes ($A - B$)
5. *A, B* combined index (AB)

Database parameters:

NR = 10^5 record occurrences
SRS = 50 bytes
KS = 6 bytes (average)
PS = 4 bytes
BKS = 1000 bytes
LF = 1
BOVHD = 0
PRDEL = PRINS = 0
  (no index$_2$ rewrite)
Fixed index maintenance: sorted,
  dense, sequential (SSEQ)
Fixed accession list ordering
  choice: always ordered
Report generation cost is not
  included (assumed constant)

CPU.EXCH = 10^{-3} second
CPU.1 = 10^{-5} second
CPU.n = $n \times 10^{-5}$ second
$C_{IO} = 1$ ⎫
$C_{CPU} = 10$ ⎬ *
$C_{ST} = 10^{-4}$ ⎭
sba = 10 milliseconds
rba = 40 milliseconds
CPU.I = 10×10^{-5} second
CPU.D = 5×10^{-5} second
CPU.CK = 2×10^{-5} second
CPU.CNK = 2×10^{-5} second

*Michigan Terminal System charge rate.

TABLE 16-2   Processing Volume for Example 16-1 (frequency per unit time)

Keys used in query item condition	GET SOME	I	D	CHK	CHNK	NRIV (NTR)	NIV	NR
A	10	—	—	—	—	10^4	10	10^5
B	10	—	—	—	—	10^2	10^3	10^5
AB	80	10	10	10	10	10	10^4	10^5
Totals	100	10	10	10	10			

The optimal indexing choice for the given set of applications is a combined index on key items A and B (see Table 16-3). Another good indexing choice, one that produces nearly optimal performance, is the single index on B. The dominant costs are for retrieval, and the CPU and I/O retrieval costs are quite close in magnitude. Although storage cost is large, the increase in cost for indexes is not significant for this database. Update costs are quite low when indexing is used; this is due to the fact that update operations are executed on only 10 target records (0.01% of the database), whereas retrieval operations can result in as many as 10^4 records (10% of the database). Creating an index on A is not reasonable because the indexed retrieval of 10^4 records for applications involving item conditions based on A is much more costly in I/O time than a sequential search of the database. However, the two leading indexing choices are far better in performance than the no-index configuration.

TABLE 16-3   Indexing Choice Costs (seconds)

	Indexing Choice				
	1 (no index)	2 (A only)	3 (B only)	4 (A − B)	5 (AB)
CR(IO)	5000	36.5k	870	4370	551
CI(IO)	500	84	6	6	6
CD(IO)	500	80	2	2	2
CCK(IO)	500	165	9	9	9
CCNK(IO)	500	1	1	1	1
CR(CPU)	6800	2616	622	1022	670
CI(CPU)	500	1	1	1	9
CD(CPU)	500	1	1	1	9
CCK(CPU)	500	3	3	3	7
CCNK(CPU)	500	1	1	1	9
CS	500	540	541	581	550
TCOST	16.300k	39.992k	2.057k	5.997k	1.823k

V SPECIAL DESIGN ISSUES

17 REORGANIZATION

17-1 INTRODUCTION

Reorganization is the process of changing either the conceptual, implementation, or physical structure of a database. The change of a conceptual or implementation structure is called *restructuring,* and the change of a physical structure is called *reformatting.* Some examples of reorganization are the adding of an item type to a record, the change in a relationship between two or more record types, switching of data representation from ASCII to EBCDIC, indexing to hashing, or moving overflow records to the primary data area.

Reorganization may be performed for a variety of reasons. It may be useful to reorganize to enhance storage utilization, to reduce retrieval and update time, or to increase database user productivity. Reorganization may also be logically necessary, as shown in the first example below. The following are some examples of circumstances in which reorganization may be appropriate [Sockut and Goldberg, 1979]:

- The definition of information changes. For example, if a company initially requires each of its employees to work on only one project at any time, but later the company's policy is changed to allow an employee to work on several projects simultaneously, then the one : many relationship between projects and employees must be changed to a many : many relationship.
- New types of information are added to the database. This may require increasing the logical (and stored) record size to accommodate a new item types.
- New legislation requires a change. For example, restricting disclosure of information among government agencies may require splitting records into disclosable and nondisclosable segments.
- A new database is created from old databases or files. For example, a company that acquires another company may decide to merge the two customer

databases, which may be associated with different DBMS and which may be in different formats, thus requiring conversion.

- Characteristics of usage change, on either a short-term or long-term basis. For example, if new sociological research using a population database requires access via a particular key, a new secondary index might be added.

- As the amount of data grows, a database may be moved to larger or faster storage devices. This may require modifying the mapping of records to physical locations.

- Observation of database performance may lead to tuning or redesigning physical parameters, such as index maintenance techniques or block size.

Some storage structures may be selected and maintained automatically by a DBMS. Even for such a system, those storage structures, as well as implementation structures, may require manual or automatic reorganization at times.

There are many types of reorganization in the spectrum from physical formatting to conceptual restructuring. In order to categorize them in some meaningful way, let us apply the three major levels of abstraction in database design: conceptual, implementation, and physical.

Conceptual-Level Reorganization

Conceptual-level reorganization may be necessary when information requirements change or the organizational environment evolves significantly. The resulting information structure may show a modification of entities, attributes, and/or relationships. Entities and attributes can be added, deleted, consolidated, split, or renamed. Relationships can be created, deleted, or renamed. Relationship type can also be changed: one : one, one : many, or many : many. Also, in a one : many relationship, certain attributes may be moved between the one side and the many side.

Implementation-Level Reorganization

Every change associated with entities, attributes, and relationships at the conceptual level can also be applied to records, item types, and interrecord relationships at the implementation level. Such changes may be done in response to conceptual-level changes that must be propagated to an implementation schema or they may originate at the implementation level due to changes in processing requirements, integrity constraints, security constraints, and so on. Some examples of item-level changes include changes in scale, level of aggregation (daily hours vs. monthly hours worked), and range of values that can be associated with an item type. Changes in the DBMS schema and subschema also have a direct effect on application program design.

Physical-Level Reorganization

Any change in the format or content of stored records, access method for stored records, blocking, or stored record clustering falls into the category of physical record reorganization, or reformatting. Some specific examples of these and other changes are:

- Pointer options (e.g., hierarchical sequential vs. hierarchical direct in IMS, or adding owner pointers in CODASYL)
- Indexing configuration
- Balancing an index hierarchy
- Security controls added (e.g., CODASYL privacy lock)
- Storing data explicitly vs. deriving the values dynamically (e.g., CODASYL ACTUAL RESULT vs. VIRTUAL RESULT)
- Basic data representation or encoding changes, encryption, and compression
- Item size
- Fixed-length vs. variable-length records
- Access method changes
- Stored record partitioning or clustering
- Maintenance to check for broken chains (missing or incorrect pointers)
- Maintenance to move overflow data to the primary area; compacting the primary area
- Adjust to changing secondary storage devices

17-2 REORGANIZATION STRATEGIES

We now describe four strategies that can be used to reorganize a database [Sockut and Goldberg, 1979]. The first three are commonly used in current DBMS, and the fourth appears to be used only for database unloading in some DBMS. For the first two strategies, the database, or at least the portion to be reorganized, is usually taken off-line (i.e., made unavailable for normal usage) for a few hours.

1. *Reorganization in place.* This is illustrated in Fig. 17-1. In step 1 normal user access is allowed. Then, in step 2, all user access is blocked while reorganization is performed in place. When reorganization is complete, normal access is allowed again. A variation on this strategy which can sometimes be used is merely to change the database definition without performing physical reorganization.

2. *Reorganization by unloading and reloading.* Normal user access is allowed initially, in step 1 (see Fig. 17-2). All user access is then blocked during step 2, unloading onto an unload area, and during step 3, reloading in a reorganized format. When reorganization is complete, normal access is allowed again. A variation on this strategy is to reorganize by copying from one area to another without using an intermediate unload area.

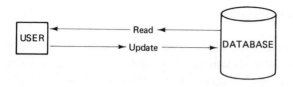

Step 1 Normal access

Step 2 Reorganize in place

FIGURE 17-1 Reorganization in place [Sockut and Goldberg, 1979].

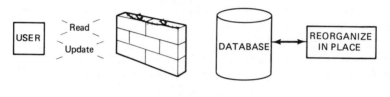

Step 1 Normal access

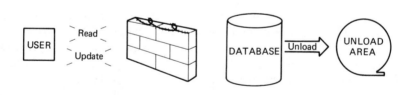

Step 2 Unload

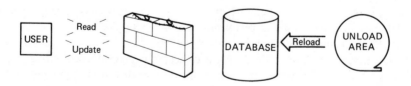

Step 3 Reload and reorganize

FIGURE 17-2 Reorganization by unloading and reloading [Sockut and Goldberg, 1979].

3. *Incremental reorganization.* A strategy that does not involve bringing the database off-line is incremental reorganization performed as data elements are referenced. In this strategy, any needed reorganization occurs incrementally when a user references some unit of data in the database (e.g., moving a hashing synonym to its home bucket when the record that was in its home bucket is deleted).

4. *Concurrent reorganization and usage.* Another strategy that does not involve bringing the database off-line is reorganizing concurrently with usage of the database. Under this strategy, users have access to the reorganized portion of the database while one or more reorganization processes are modifying it, either in place or by unloading and reloading. This strategy is illustrated in Fig. 17-3. An example is the dynamic block splitting technique used in B-tree implementation, including VSAM.

Many of the current commercial DBMS packages include extensive reorganization programs using various combinations of the strategies listed above. An excellent survey is given in [Sockut and Goldberg, 1979].

17-3 THE DATABASE ADMINISTRATOR'S ROLE

Reorganization of a database is usually managed by the database administrator (DBA) [Canning, 1972; DeBlasis and Johnson, 1977, 1978; Lyon, 1976a; Winkler et al., 1976]. The DBA determines that reorganization should be performed, when it is best done, and carries out the implementation with DBMS or in-house software. The following issues are considered by the DBA in carrying out these functions [Sockut and Goldberg, 1979]:

1. Recognize the *need* to reorganize.
2. Decide *what* new structures are to be the final result of reorganization.
3. Decide *when* to perform reorganization. For maintenance, there may be an optimal period between reorganizations. This is discussed further in Section 17-4.
4. Know *how* to execute the reorganization.
   a. Strategies may involve unloading and reloading, reorganizing in place but off-line, reorganizing incrementally as data elements are referenced, or reorganizing concurrently with usage.
   b. The DBA must select the appropriate reorganization facilities.
5. Determine how much the reorganization will *benefit* the whole organization.

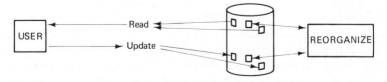

FIGURE 17-3 Concurrent reorganization and usage [Sockut and Goldberg, 1979].

This may include improved performance, increased functional capabilities, or better storage utilization.

6. Assess how much reorganization will *cost*. This includes
   a. Human and computation resources consumed during planning, actual reorganization, any software changes, and any personnel training.
   b. Either the denial of resources to users during off-line reorganization or degraded user performance during concurrent reorganization.

7. Be aware of *who* and *what* will be *affected* by reorganization. A tool that often can determine effects of reorganization is a data dictionary/directory, which maintains information on data elements, their interrelationships, and which applications use them. Some applications may benefit from the reorganization, whereas others may suffer if the database is no longer optimized toward them. The DBA must act as arbitrator in this situation, see that affected software is revised, and ensure that personnel training is provided for any users who are affected.

8. *Document* any changes that result from reorganization. Some of this documentation may be provided by the data dictionary/directory.

9. *Certify* that reorganization yielded the desired result. For example, this can involve checking that new pointers correctly implement a new relationship.

17-4   WHEN TO REORGANIZE: A HEURISTIC RULE

In this section we study the effect of various system and user parameters on the choice of optimal reorganization points. A heuristic rule is introduced that determines a set of nearly optimal reorganization points, based on total cost, where cost is defined in this context as some function of database retrieval, update, and possibly storage costs for a given set of user activities over a time period t. This analysis is a major concern of reorganization for maintenance, such as overflow removal, but not necessarily for one-shot reformatting or restructuring based on a specific new requirement.

An early study on the optimum reorganization points by Shneiderman [1973] assumed a linear cost function, linear database growth rate, and known database lifetime T. A closed-form solution for the optimal fixed length reorganization interval t_s was determined. For a linear growth rate and linearly increasing reorganization cost, t_s was found to be approximately proportional to $T^{1/2}$. As $T \rightarrow \infty$, t_s becomes undefined. The solution of optimal variable-length reorganization intervals for linearly growing databases was later obtained by Tuel [1977].

A definition of database growth in terms of item value occurrences and record occurrences often results in a nonlinear cost function that grows faster than linearly. It can be shown that with nonlinear cost, an unknown database lifetime, and a fixed work-load level, the time between reorganization points increases as the database grows [Yao et al., 1976]. On the other hand, a work-load level proportional to database size (as it increases) results in a series of rapidly decreasing reorganization points. The near-optimality of the heuristic algorithm is demonstrated by comparing total cost with the exact solutions obtained with linear cost models for various values of the database lifetime T.

Assume that a database has an initial search cost of C_0. After the data are accessed, the search time may deteriorate because of insertion and other update operations. Reorganization of the database could be performed periodically to reduce the search cost. For the case of linear deterioration, let Θ_1 be the rate of deterioration of the search cost without reorganization, and Θ_2 be the rate of deterioration of the search cost if the database were constantly being reorganized. Assume further that the reorganization is considered at discrete time periods. Figure 17-4 illustrates the search cost of the database with time. Where C_n is the search cost after the nth time period if no reorganization is performed, C'_n is the search cost after the nth time period when the latest reorganization occurred at the end of the nth time period. R_n is the reorganization cost at the end of the nth time period; R_0 is the initial reorganization cost, and μ is the rate of increase of reorganization cost. In other words, we have

$$C_n = C_0 + \Theta_1 n \qquad (17\text{-}1)$$

$$C'_n = C_0 + \Theta_2 n \qquad (17\text{-}2)$$

$$R_n = R_0 + \mu n \qquad (17\text{-}3)$$

If we assume a linear rate of deterioration, both C_n and C'_n increase as n increases because the search time for a record increases as the database grows over time. R_n also grows because reorganization time is normally an increasing function of the number

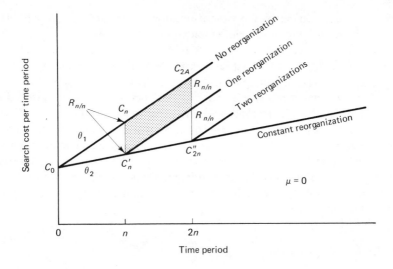

FIGURE 17-4   Search cost per time period as a function of time and reorganization.

of record occurrences in the database. As an example, suppose that the reason for reorganization is to move overflow records back into the primary data area and physically delete those records that have been flagged for deletion. In this case, R_n is the cost of processing all the records of a particular type or types for unloading, including those flagged for deletion, plus the cost to reload the nondeleted records, assuming that the unload and reload strategy is used. If NR is the total number of records in a subfile at the beginning of the first time period and x records are inserted while y records are deleted, then the number of records required to be accessed for reorganization is $NR + x$ and the number of records rewritten is $NR + x - y$. The number of records in overflow just before reorganization is between 0 and x, depending upon the loading factor of the primary area.

The criterion for determining reorganization points that accounts for database growth rate, user activity level, and database lifetime should satisfy optimality and computational efficiency. The optimality criterion requires that total cost be minimized, but if the lifetime of a database is unknown, the total cost is also unknown. Consequently, for a time horizon that is known only at the time of occurrence (or shortly before), the optimal solution can only be approximated. The efficiency in computing the reorganization points should also be considered. The following is an efficient heuristic rule which considers at most the previous and future n time periods.

Dynamic reorganization criterion. The database should be reorganized at the end of the nth time period after the most recent reorganization, where n is defined as the smallest integer for which

$$C_n \geqslant C'_n + R_n / n \tag{17-4}$$

where C_n is the search cost without reorganization, C'_n the search cost with reorganization, and R_n the current reorganization cost.

Let us look at the continuous linear cost problem (linear growth and constant user activity) first. In Fig. 17-4 the first reorganization point occurs at the end of the nth time period. Total search cost up to time t is $\int_o^t C_x dx$, which corresponds to the area under the curve. Between the nth and $2n$th time periods, the cost saving due to reorganization is shown by the shaded area between the parallel lines. When $C_n = C'_n + R_n$ the area is seen to be R_n, the precise cost of the reorganization at the end of period n. Therefore, a reorganization after n time periods results in an overall decrease in total cost only after an additional n time periods. In the limiting case as $\mu = 0$ (i.e., constant reorganization cost), the second reorganization occurs at $2n$.

The total processing cost of the database is the sum of the total search cost and reorganization cost:

$$TC_t = \int_o^t C_x dx + \sum_m R_m \tag{17-5}$$

where the m's are the time periods where reorganization occurred. Figure 17-5 shows the total cost over time for the case $\mu = 0$. The curve for one reorganization crosses

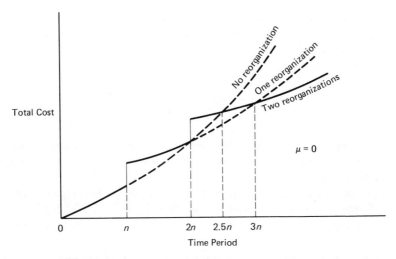

FIGURE 17-5 Total cost with and without reorganization.

over the curve for no reorganization at time $2n$. The second reorganization at $2n$ lowers the search cost to $C'_{2n} = C_{2n} - 2 \times R_n/n$ and doubles the saving in search cost (see Figure 17-4). Therefore, it takes only $n/2$ additional time periods to again decrease total cost below no reorganization and n periods to cross over with one reorganization. Eventually, a steady state is reached where no reorganization always requires higher total cost. For $\mu > 0$ (i.e., linear reorganization cost increases), R_n is increasing over time but the difference between C'_n and C_n does not change; the second reorganization point will occur at some point greater than or equal to $2n$ (see Fig. 17-6). The reorganization requires longer and longer time periods. The cost saving will always result in higher cost beyond a certain point.

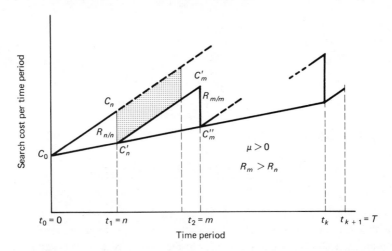

FIGURE 17-6 Search cost per time period with increasing reorganization cost.

For a given database lifetime T and linear database growth rate, it is possible to find an optimal fixed reorganization interval (i.e., fixed-length intervals between reorganization points). The optimal reorganization interval, t_s, was computed in Shneiderman [1973] as

$$t_s = \left(\frac{2 \times R_0 + \mu \times T}{\Theta_1 - \Theta_2} \right)^{\frac{1}{2}} \qquad (17\text{-}6)$$

where R_0 is the original reorganization cost, Θ_1 the growth rate without reorganization, Θ_2 the growth rate with continuous reorganization, and μ the growth rate of R_n in cost per time period.

When the database lifetime T is unknown, the optimal reorganization interval is not obtainable. The dynamic reorganization criterion can be applied for unknown T. The following theorem gives the dynamic reorganization point since the most recent reorganization.

THEOREM 17-1   The reorganization point for the dynamic reorganization criterion is

$$t_n = \frac{\mu + [\mu^2 + 4 \times R_0(\Theta_1 - \Theta_2)]^{\frac{1}{2}}}{2(\Theta_1 - \Theta_2)} \qquad (17\text{-}7)$$

PROOF. From the reorganization criterion

$$C_n \geq C_n' + R_n/n \qquad \text{or} \qquad C_0 + \Theta_1 t_n \geq C_0 + \Theta_2 t_n + (R_0 + \mu t_n)/t_n$$

Multiplying through by t_n and simplifying, we have

$$C_0 t_n + \Theta_1 t_n^2 \geq C_0 t_n + \Theta_2 t_n^2 + R_0 + \mu t_n$$

or

$$\Theta_1 t_n^2 \geq \Theta_2 t_n^2 + R_0 + \mu t$$

At the point of equality, $t_n^2(\Theta_1 - \Theta_2) - t_n(\mu) - R_0 = 0$.

Solving the quadratic, we obtain

$$t_n = \frac{\mu + [\mu^2 + 4 \times R_0(\Theta_1 - \Theta_2)]^{\frac{1}{2}}}{2(\Theta_1 - \Theta_2)}$$

Note that Eq. (17-7) is applied after each reorganization to determine the next reorganization point and that R_0 is reset to the current R_n after reorganization. The reorganization point exists for any given values of $\Theta_1 - \Theta_2$, R_o, and μ. Reorganization is unnecessary only if $t_n \geq T$.

It is shown in Yao et al. [1976] that the total cost for the dynamic reorganization criterion for the case of constant reorganization cost ($\mu = 0$) is at most 6% higher than the optimal total cost of fixed reorganization points [Shneiderman, 1973]. When $\mu > 0$, the dynamic reorganization criterion performs better than the method of fixed reorganization points, although neither approaches are optimal. An optimal policy and a nearly optimal approximation were derived by Tuel [1978], in which reorganization points were no longer constrained to be fixed length. He also showed that the dynamic reorganization criterion was reasonably near optimal, although not as close as his approximate solution. The usefulness of the heuristic approach is for nonideal situations such as unknown database lifetime T, nonlinear database growth rate, or nonlinear growth of database work load.

Experiments with the heuristic approach show that the time between consecutive reorganizations is highly sensitive to the way in which a file is organized. As search (access) cost increases, reorganization intervals tend to decrease unless the cost of reorganization increases at a higher rate. An increase in user database activity (work load) will increase the cost of servicing a user application without increasing the reorganization cost. If the database is not growing, the resulting effect is to rapidly decrease the time between reorganizations. If it is growing, both the application cost and reorganization cost are increasing. Consequently, the time between reorganizations may increase or decrease depending upon the relative values of these growth rates.

In practice, we note that cost functions are not always so easy to define. Reorganization often occurs when either the cost of reorganization is extremely low (possibly during weekend or holiday hours) or just prior to a time when database usage costs are expected to be very high (e.g., just before registration week in a university course registration system). The heuristic rule is still applicable for these situations because it is consistent with the intuitive nature of deciding when to reorganize.

17-5 RESTRUCTURING

The purpose of restructuring is to transform the logical structure of a database to meet new information or processing requirements. Navathe and Fry [1976] developed a category of restructuring operations for the hierarchical class of logical structures. Three fundamental logical structure modifications were defined: naming, relation, and combining; these were refined into several lower-level restructuring operations.

Figure 17-7 illustrates a few hierarchical restructuring operations [Fry, 1978; Fry, 1974]. The first part, section A, depicts a hierarchical relationship among PRESIDENTS, SPOUSES, and CHILDREN. The uppermost box or record type, PRESIDENTS, contains the names of the presidents of the United States. The

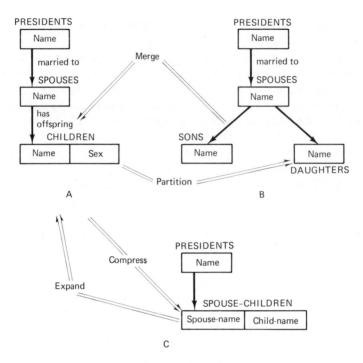

FIGURE 17-7 Restructuring operations.

second-level record type, SPOUSES, is related to PRESIDENTS through the set type "Married to"; this contains the names of all spouses for each president. Thus, the set is a one-to-many mapping over two record types. In a similar fashion, the third-level record type, CHILDREN, is related to SPOUSES and contains the names of the children born to each SPOUSES.

In section B of Fig. 17-7, the source record type CHILDREN has been partitioned into two record types, SONS and DAUGHTERS, based on the data item "sex" (partitioning is a restructuring operation in which the occurrences of a record type are divided into two or more distinct record types based on the value of one or more data items). Notice that "sex" has been eliminated in the logical structure of section A because this information is now represented by the target logical structure (section B).

The dual restructuring operation of partitioning is merging. The merging operation consolidates occurrences from two or more record types into a single record type. Often, a data item is added to the record type to preserve information previously represented by the logical structure. In Fig. 17-7, the occurrences of the two record types, SONS and DAUGHTERS, have been merged into a single record type, CHILDREN. The terms "source" and "target" are relative and depend on the direction of the restructuring transformation. Section A represents the source logical structure for the partitioning example and the target database for the merging example. The item type "sex" has been added to contain the information previously represented semantically by the source logical structure of section B.

Another form of restructuring involves the compression of two or more hierarchical levels into one. In Fig. 17-7, the two source records, SPOUSES and CHILDREN, have been compressed into a single record type, SPOUSE–CHILDREN. On the record occurrence level, this operation would be accomplished by replicating the associated SPOUSE record occurrence for every CHILD record occurrence. The dual operation, expansion, expands one level of hierarchy into two or more by factoring out selected data items. This procedure is illustrated in section C, where the SPOUSE–CHILDREN record type has been factored into two levels.

17-5-1   Network Restructuring

Restructuring operations are more difficult to categorize in the network class of logical structures. This is due primarily to the variety and complexity of the structures involved. For example, an important network restructuring operation, changing the implementation of many-to-many relationships, is illustrated by the restructuring transform of Fig. 17-8. The source logical structure represents information on students, their class standing, all courses taken by each student, and the final grade received in each course. The target logical structure represents the same information except the association between students, course, and grades is achieved using a LINK record type. This example is typical of the restructuring operations that may be posed in a network environment—those that involve several record and set types.

Another operation that might enhance processing is the addition of indexing sets or record types. This could be achieved by migrating the data item "class" to the record type CLASS-STANDING. This migration would serve to segment the students into graduate, undergraduate, special, foreign exchange, and so on (Fig. 17-9). Note that this operation is actually an expansion performed on a hierarchical substructure of the target structure.

Yet another important network restructuring operation is the ability to extract not only the actual data in the source database, but also the implicit data (implicit data is information that may be inferred from actual source data). An example of the

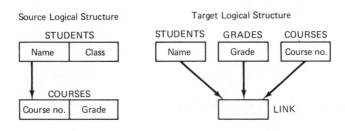

FIGURE 17-8   Network restructuring example.

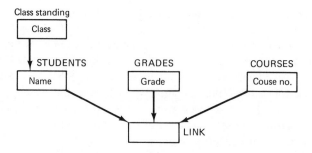

FIGURE 17-9 Addition of indexing sets.

difference between implicit and explicit information is described in the hypothetical restructuring transform of Fig. 17-10.

The example describes a source database containing two record types, PERSONS and LINK. The PERSONS record type contains name and sex item types; the LINK record type contains no data but provides relationship information in conjunction with sets, PARENTS and CHILDREN. The target structure also contains the PERSONS record type; construction of target PERSONS records involves the extraction of data explicitly resident in the source file, PERSONS record type. In contrast, target record types, PARENTS and GRANDFATHERS, do not correspond directly to any source file record type; they contain information that is represented implicitly in the source file. Needless to say, this transformation cannot be described by operations on hierarchical substructures.

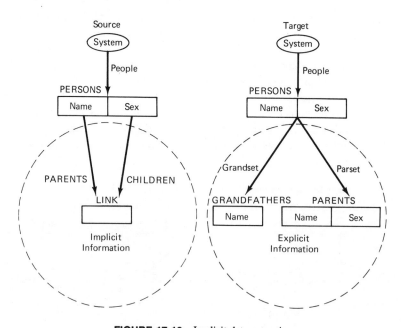

FIGURE 17-10 Implicit data extraction.

17-5-2 Technical Approaches to Restructuring

The Elementary Operations Approach

An interesting analogy exists between restructuring systems and high-level query systems. In fact, we can consider a query as a restricted restructuring transformation in which the target is not a database but some other form of information representation. Efficient, easy-to-use query languages for the hierarchical class of logical structures have been built through the use of elementary operations [Shoshani, 1975; Shoshani and Brandon, 1975; Shu et al., 1975]. These systems allow a user to specify a sequence of elementary operations on hierarchical structures that will answer a query. Such languages are easy to learn and use because they employ a few rather simple operations to perform most queries.

Several research efforts have addressed the problems of restructuring and restructuring language specification through the elementary operations approach. CONVERT, a high-level translation language, provides a generalized restructuring capability for hierarchical structures [Shu et al., 1975]. This approach is based on the concept of a "data form" in conjunction with a set of restructuring functions called "form operations." Shoshani [1975; Shoshani and Brandon, 1975] takes a similar approach to restructuring using a set of "conversion functions" to specify restructuring operations.

In the elementary operations approach, the source database is viewed as a collection of data in a specific logical structure and format. The target database is viewed as essentially the same data in a different logical structure and format. Restructuring, therefore, is the process of manipulating the source data to conform to the target logical structure and format.

Researchers investigating the elementary operations approach to restructuring have developed low-level (primitive) operations that transform occurrences from one logical structure to another. One advantage of such an approach is that the architecture of the restructuring software system is greatly simplified; it defaults to a set of low-level subroutines that correspond directly to the elementary operations. Thus, a restructuring specification consists of a sequence of primitives that may be directly converted to a sequence of subroutine calls; the subroutine calls perform the actual restructuring. Unfortunately, users are not shielded from any aspects of the restructuring. They must thoroughly understand the function of each operation in order to use it. Consequently, the language, although high level, still requires the user to treat restructuring as a sequence of low-level steps.

Several other problems arise when the elementary operations approach is applied to restructuring network databases. In general, elementary operations are designed to operate on small, logical substructures (consisting of one or two record types and a set) to produce a new, logical substructure. Because only a limited number of operations may be defined, only a finite number of source substructures can be valid candidates for restructuring. The more complex the structure, the greater the probability it will contain substructures that are not valid candidates for the set of available operations. For this reason, elementary operations are not particularly well suited to describing restructuring transformations on complex network logical structures. In addition, a complex restructuring transformation (assuming that it can be performed by elementary operations) requires the specification of a complex sequence of elementary operations that is difficult to analyze.

Another class of restructuring transformations that is difficult to accomplish with elementary operations is the extraction of implicit information. We have indicated that such transformations (as in the example of Fig. 17-10) cannot usually be described by a sequence of operations on hierarchical substructures. Even if such transformations can be described by sequences of elementary operations on network substructures, such descriptions are generally long and complicated. There is also reason to believe that, in time, designers of network databases will produce enough intricate methods of storing information implicitly to exhaust any set of elementary operations.

Following our analogy, it is very difficult to apply the elementary operations of high-level query systems to network databases. The elementary operations approach to developing a query system for network databases tends to be less powerful and more cumbersome than its hierarchical counterparts. In general, they suffer from the problems cited above—limited allowable input structures, overly complex specifications, and difficulties with link records and other implicit information storage techniques. The high-level access path approach to restructuring grew from attempts to develop a restructuring strategy better suited to network databases.

The Access Path Approach

Following a current trend in host language database systems that process the network structure databases, we chose the high-level "access path" approach to restructuring. The source database is viewed as a body of information, some of which is represented explicitly by data and some of which is represented implicitly. Similarly, it is assumed that the target database contains a subset of information represented by the source; these data are created from information provided by the source data. Executing a restructuring transformation, then, is simply the process of traversing the source database to obtain the information needed to create the target database and storing it according to the target logical structure.

There are numerous consequences of this approach. For one, researchers in restructuring specification are attempting to develop restructuring specification languages based on the concepts of access strategies and selection criteria. Because this area is closely related to query-language development, certain concepts from previous research in this area may be utilized. The access path approach has also affected the development of the actual restructuring algorithm. Algorithms are being developed that access the source database efficiently and exhaustively; they also perform tests on the data following externally specified access strategies and test criteria. This is a radical change from the elementary operations approach that tends to develop low-level subroutines.

The most important consequence of this approach is that it produces powerful, generalized network restructuring capabilities. Since restructuring is viewed as an operation that accesses information (rather than manipulates data), the approach is unaffected by the logical structure of the database. This independence ensures that any database is a valid candidate for restructuring, regardless of the complexity of the logical structure (hierarchical, network, and so on). Furthermore, source and target logical structures need not resemble each other because the target is derived from information provided by the source rather than from the source structure itself. Also (unlike the elementary operations approach), implicit information may be extracted and restructured as easily as explicit information (as in Fig. 17-10). Thus, explicit information may become implicit, and vice versa.

Finally, the system is inherently simple. Users familiar with databases and applications should easily comprehend a restructuring specification language based on such application-oriented concepts as access strategies and selection criteria. Even more complex restructuring transformations should not cause confusion because all restructuring operations are expressed as information-accessing problems. An algorithm designed to carry out this process is also simple, straightforward, and dependable.

All restructuring is performed in the same sequence of steps, regardless of the particular transformation:

- Thoroughly access the source data according to access specifications
- Test data on the basis of selection criteria
- Create target record occurrences containing the relevant data

For a more complete discussion of the theoretical foundations of this approach, see [Deppe, 1976].

Access Path Specification Language
Architecture

The architecture of the Access Path Specification Language (APSL) is based on the high-level specification of access paths. The major components of the language describe access strategies and selection criteria. Access strategies are described in an access path statement. This statement specifies the traversal scheme required to obtain data for each target record type. The selection criteria establish the source (and, indirectly, the target) data requirements. A detailed description of APSL is beyond the scope of this text (see [Swartwout et al., 1977b]); however, the major points of the language will be illustrated here.

The APSL is essentially a block-structured language in which each "block" contains a single target record statement. There is one target record statement for each record type in the target database. This structure reflects the access path approach because each target record type represents a certain quantity of information that may be obtained from the source database. Consequently, each target record description contains the specifications for the source database assessing scheme as well as for the selection criteria.

The second level of structure in the APSL is the target set statement (see Fig. 17-11 for the APSL structure). Each target record statement includes one or more target set statements that identify the sets of which the target record type is a member.

The third level of APSL structure is the access path statement. This specifies exactly how the source logical structure is to be traversed in order to obtain the information necessary to create an occurrence of the target record type. There may be individual access path statements—one or more for each target set statement. This is because the information contributing to the target record type may come from several different source record types.

There are two types of APSL statements at the fourth level of structure, the new target item statement and the source record statement. There may be zero or more new target item statements for each access path statement. Such a statement indicates a target item that receives a constant value each time a target record occurrence is constructed using the specified access path. Because access paths indicate structure in the source database, the new item statement is useful when information represented semantically in the source structure is converted to actual data values in the target structure.

The second APSL statement at the fourth level of structure is the source record statement. This identifies the source record(s) on the access path that will be used in the creation of a target record occurrence to obtain item values and/or to test the source data. There may be one or more source record statements for each access path statement because data may be obtained or examined from several different source record types. Furthermore, each source record type may be assigned an optional index number. The index number uniquely identifies a source record within an access path

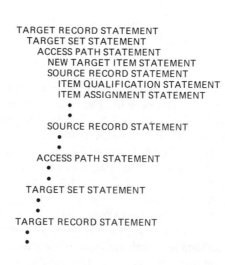

FIGURE 17-11   Structure of APSL Specification.

that "cycles" or "loops" back on itself, thus causing the same source record type to appear more than once.

At the fifth and final level of the APSL structure are two statement types, the item qualification statement and the item assignment statement. Item qualification statements are used to establish the selection criteria used in testing the source data. Thus, one may specify a constant value to be compared against a source item value that will determine whether a target record occurrence is to be created using the current set of source data. The item assignment statement is used to obtain source item values and then assign them to the proper target items.

It should be noted that the APSL does not explicitly describe the logical structure of either the source or target database. The Michigan Data Translator obtains appropriate descriptions of the source and target databases without referring to the restructuring specifications. The APSL, therefore, describes only information relevant to the actual transformation from source to target. It is assumed that the logical structures of the databases have been previously defined and are available to the restructurer.

An APSL Restructuring Example

An APSL example has been chosen to illustrate the capability of the language to specify restructuring capabilities that cannot be classified in terms of hierarchical structures or elementary operations. The example involves the extraction of implicit information from a network structure and is taken from Fig. 17-10. This example is reproduced in Fig. 17-12 for convenience. The APSL required to accomplish the necessary transformation is documented in Fig. 17-13. The form of the APSL has

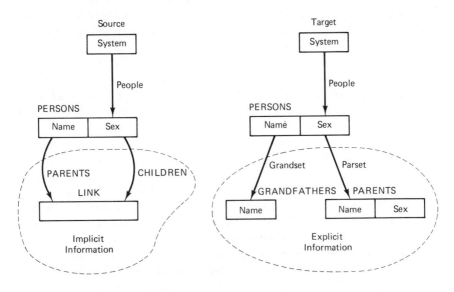

FIGURE 17-12   APSL restructuring example.

```
1.   TARGET RECORD PERSONS
2.      TDLAP PERSONS
3.        SOURCE RECORD PERSONS ACCESS VIA PEOPLE
4.          ACTUAL DATA IN ORDER
5.   TARGET RECORD PARENTS
6.      TDLAP PARENTS
7.        SOURCE RECORD PERSONS ID=KID ACCESS VIA PEOPLE
8.          NAME ASSIGN TO NAME <PARSET>
9.        SOURCE RECORD LINK ACCESS VIA PARENTS FROM ID=KID
10.       SOURCE RECORD PERSONS ID = PARENT ACCESS VIA CHILDREN
11.         ACTUAL DATA IN ORDER
12.  TARGET RECORD GRANDFATHERS
13.     TDLAP GRNDAD
14.       SOURCE RECORD PERSONS ID=GRNDAD ACCESS VIA PEOPLE
15.         SEX SELECT IF EQ 'MALE'
16.         NAME ASSIGN TO NAME
17.       SOURCE RECORD LINK ID=STEP 1 ACCESS VIA CHILDREN FROM ID=GRNDAD
18.       SOURCE RECORD PERSONS ID=PARENT ACCESS VIA PARENTS FROM ID=STEP 1
19.       SOURCE RECORD LINK ID=STEP 2 ACCESS VIA CHILDREN FROM ID=PARENT
20.         NAME <PARENTS> ASSIGN TO NAME <GRANDSET>
```

FIGURE 17-13   APSL required for transformation.

been simplified slightly for clarity. The block structure of the language may be easily observed.

Because there are three target record types, there are three target record statements. Statement 1 begins the APSL description for the target record type PERSONS. PERSONS is a member of only one set (from the system access level); as a consequence, there is only one access path statement (2). Statement 3 specifies the source access path to be used in locating the data necessary to create the target record type. ACCESS VIA PEOPLE describes an access path from the source SYSTEM node along the set PEOPLE to record type PERSONS. Statement 4 assigns the data from the source record to the target record. ACTUAL DATA IN ORDER indicates the values in source record item types "name" and "sex" are to be assigned to the target item types "name" and "sex."

The APSL description for the record type GRANDFATHERS begins with statement 12. As before, there is only one access path statement (13) because the record type is a member of only one set (GRAND-SET). Statements 14, 17, 18, and 19 specify the source access path strategy to be used to obtain the desired information. (Note that this is one of three possible alternatives.)

This access strategy may be summarized as follows. The LINK record type in the source models the relationship between parents and children. Given a particular PERSONS record occurrence, parents can be accessed by using the set types PARENTS and CHILDREN in conjunction with the LINK record type. Similarly, all grandparents of a person are obtained by accessing all parents of parents. The access path statements on lines 14, 17, 18, and 19 describe the essence of this strategy. Use PEOPLE set to reach the PERSONS record type (identifier is GRNDAD). Follow CHILDREN set to the LINK record type (identifier is Step 1), then follow the parents set back to the PERSONS record type (identifier is PARENT). Next, follow children set back to the LINK record type (identifier is Step 2) and finally, follow PARENTS back to the PERSONS record type (identifier is KID).

Note that the source record type PERSONS is used twice in the access path specification. Consequently, each time it is used, the source record statement must indicate which source group PERSONS or LINK is to be used. The PERSONS record is assigned the identifier GRNDAD the first time it is used and the identifier PARENT the second time. In the same manner, LINK is also distinguished. Statement 15 is an item qualification statement used to select only male grandparents to yield grandfathers, the desired target record information. Statement 16 assigns the value in the source item type "name" to the target item type "name."

It should be clear that the target record type PARENTS is created in a manner similar to that of GRANDFATHERS, except that the accessing strategy is simpler and no selection criterion is required.

In summary, significant results have been achieved in the implementation of a generalized restructurer. Although a generalized restructurer is technically feasible, it is too early to predict the overall savings in human and machine resources. There is some concern in the case of large databases because restructurer performance is proportional to size. However, optimization efforts have been initiated that should greatly improve the efficiency of this process. Complete generality in the physical transformation process has yet to be achieved as well. It appears much more difficult because the deeper one goes into the actual representation, the more complex the description process and the implementation of the physical transformation modules become.

18 DISTRIBUTED DATABASE DESIGN: AN OVERVIEW

18-1 INTRODUCTION

Beginning with intercomputer communications technology and continuing through the recent minicomputer explosion, a trend has developed in information systems: a migration from the highly centralized systems of the early 1970s to distributed information systems for the 1980s.

To discuss distributed systems in general, we must distinguish between distributed database systems and distributed systems. A *distributed database system* subsets the database over several computer sites and provides sufficient accessing power to manipulate these subsets. In contrast is the *distributed processing system,* which typically has a centralized database but has software and processing power distributed throughout the interconnected computer sites.

In this chapter we focus exclusively on distributed database systems. Our purpose is to identify the trade-offs implicit in the design and implementation of distributed database systems, and to define a framework for distributed database design.

The overall goal of a distributed database system is the controlled access to and the sharability of the data distributed across a computer network. Controlled access refers to the degree of security necessary to protect the data from unauthorized user access. Sharability implies users accessing data from different, perhaps remote, computing facilities. A computer network is a collection of heterogeneous computing facilities connected by high-speed communication lines.

To provide sharability of data, the various accessing mechanisms and database management systems must cooperate with one another to share the data under their control. The technology for distributed databases is progressing rapidly.

The technological issues in distributed database systems can be divided into two major categories according to when they arise. Those issues that take place during the design phase, be it the design of the network, database management system or the database, are identified as *design issues*. In a similar manner those issues that affect the operation of a distributed system are labeled *implementation issues*. Although these issues can be categorized for descriptive purposes, it should be noted that they do bear a direct causal relationship. Since design is performed prior to implementation, decisions made at this stage directly affect the implementation decisions and subsequent operation of the system. The decisions made concerning the design issues—system architecture, data allocation, network directory distribution, and the environment's homogeneity—directly affect the implementation issues of control, synchronization, locking, and translation. Although state-of-the-art technical solutions have been proposed and some even implemented, their impact on system performance is not widely understood. Finally, the emergence of new technology will have a major effect on today's technical solutions and system performance.

18-2   DISTRIBUTED DBMS ARCHITECTURE

A general multilevel architecture is frequently chosen for distributed database management system (D-DBMS) software [Astrahan et al., 1976; Rothnie et al., 1980; Stonebraker and Neuhold, 1977]. As depicted in Fig. 18-1, there are five levels to this architecture, which can be divided into two major parts. The top four levels—the user view processor, the global logical view processor, the fragmented view processor, and the distributed view processor—can be grouped together and called the network DBMS. The lowest level, the nodal view processor, can be called the local DBMS. Internode communication is from the network DBMS at one node to the local DBMS of another node, and vice versa.

Each of these levels supports a different "view" or perspective of the database. Each level interacts only with other levels that are its immediate neighbors. On top of the entire structure is either an application program interface or a query processor interface.

Each view of the database exists in order to make explicit another aspect of the database's logical or physical structure. An extended example is given in Figs. 18-2 to 18-6 to help describe these various aspects of the database. For this example the database can be thought of as several tables that support several "views." The first view, called the global logical view, is the logical database structure of the total network database as seen from the perspective of the database administrator. The global logical view is similar to the conceptual view [ANSI, 1978]. In Fig. 18-2 the global logical view of the database is given. This consists of three tables (relations) which are used to model the organization's three plants. Each table contains data related to each of the three plants. The next view is called the user view because it describes the portion of the database that a particular user is permitted to process. It is a subset of the global logical view and is similar to the external view [ANSI, 1978]. Each user may have a different user view based on need-to-know and security requirements. Figure 18-3 gives one example of a user view that provides several

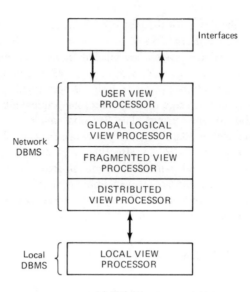

FIGURE 18-1   D-DBMS architecture.

points. The first point is that not all of the tables in the global logical view may be available to a particular user. In the example, the table RAW-MATERIALS is not contained in the sample user view, meaning that a user view need not contain all of the tables from the global logical view. The second point is that a user view may be further refined by allowing only a subset of the tables' columns. The RATE column of the EMPLOYEE table is not included in the given user view. The last point is that a user view may include only a subset of the rows of a table. In the example the user view's EMPLOYEE table only contains rows where PLANT-NO is 3.

The third and fourth views exist because of the distributed nature of the database and the decision to use controlled redundancy. The third view is the fragmented view. Through the use of this view the DBA defines disjoint subsets of the database, called *logical fragments,* each of which is a subset of the rows of a table. Figure 18-4 shows the logical fragments of the example database. In the example the PLANT table is divided into three logical fragments, one for each value of PLANT-NO. The geographic location of each physical occurrence of each fragment is defined in the fourth view, the distributed view. This view allows multiple physical copies of one fragment. Figure 18-5 shows one alternative for the distribution and duplication of stored fragments on the three node system. *Stored fragments* are the physical implementation of logical fragments. The example assumes that plant 1 also is the headquarters for the organization, so it is desirable for plant 1 to have efficient access to portions of the database that describe the other plants. Plants 2 and 3 are mainly concerned with themselves. For this reason all three fragments of the EMPLOYEE table have a copy at plant 1, whereas plants 2 and 3 only have a copy of the respective fragment that concerns them. It should be noted that the choice of controlled redundancy allows great flexibility. The PLANT table is totally duplicated, the RAW-MATERIALS

EMPLOYEE

E-NO	NAME	PLANT-NO	RATE
100	BILL	1	6.00
101	JIM	1	6.00
102	MIKE	2	10.00
103	HOUTAN	2	12.00
104	DON	3	2.90
105	STEVE	3	3.00

PLANT

P-NO	P-NAME
1	ANN ARBOR
2	DETROIT
3	NEW YORK

RAW-MATERIALS

P-NO	ITEM	QUANTITY
1	CLAY	500
1	GYPSUM	100
2	COAL	940
3	CLAY	75

FIGURE 18-2 Global logical view.

EMPLOYEE

E-NO	NAME	PLANT-NO
104	DON	3
105	STEVE	3

PLANT

P-NO	P-NAME
1	ANN ARBOR
2	DETROIT
3	NEW YORK

FIGURE 18-3 User view.

EMPLOYEE

	E–NO	NAME	PLANT–NO	RATE
FRAGMENT 1	100	BILL	1	6.00
	101	JIM	1	6.00
FRAGMENT 2	102	MIKE	2	10.00
	103	HOUTAN	2	12.00
FRAGMENT 3	104	DON	3	2.90
	105	STEVE	3	3.00

PLANT

	P–NO	P–NAME
FRAGMENT a	1	ANN ARBOR
	2	DETROIT
	3	NEW YORK

RAW–MATERIALS

	P–NO	ITEM	QUANTITY
FRAGMENT A	1	CLAY	500
	1	GYPSUM	100
FRAGMENT B	2	COAL	940
FRAGMENT C	3	CLAY	75

FIGURE 18-4 Fragmented view.

table is partitioned but not duplicated, and the EMPLOYEE table is distributed using a combination of partitioning and duplication.

The final view, the local view, is the view of the portion of a database existing at a particular node (hence "local"). In other words, it describes the database available to the local DBMS. Figure 18-6 shows the local view of the database from node 3 of Fig. 18-5. Of course, the database at a node can be viewed either from a logical or physical structure perspective. The local view, as defined, is the logical structure, but the physical structure is hidden underneath. The local DBMS could alternatively be divided into several levels, but this detail is not needed at this stage.

Logical Database Structure

The data model supporting the logical database structure, a variant of the relational model, is powerful enough to support relational structures but also the logical structure of other data models. In the extended relational model, EMOD, the

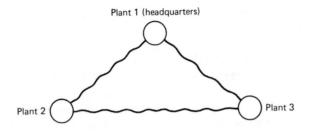

Plant 1 (headquarters)

Plant 2   Plant 3

TABLE	FRAGMENT	LOCATION
EMPLOYEE	1 2 3	1 1, 2 1, 3
PLANT	a	1, 2, 3
RAW–MATERIALS	A B C	1 2 3

FIGURE 18-5 Distributed view.

EMPLOYEE

	E-NO	NAME	PLANT-NO	RATE
FRAGMENT 3	104	DON	3	2.90
	105	STEVE	3	3.00

PLANT

	P-NO	P-NAME
FRAGMENT a	1	ANN ARBOR
	2	DETROIT
	3	NEW YORK

RAW-MATERIALS

	P-NO	ITEM	QUANTITY
FRAGMENT C	3	CLAY	75

FIGURE 18-6 Local view at plant 3.

database consists of several tables. Given sets of values $D_1, D_2, \ldots, D_n$, a table is defined as a set of rows, each of which has its first element from D_1, its second from $D_2, \ldots$, and its nth element from D_n. The sets D_i are called domains of the columns of the table. Valid data types for these domains are character strings, integers, real numbers, and logical variables. Each table must have a primary key, one or more columns whose values uniquely identify a row. All rows of the tables are distinct (no duplicate primary keys) and may have one or more ordering sequences specified.

Tree-structured databases are explicitly defined at data definition time by an intermediate table called an association. Associations are explicit relationships between two tables and are used to represent the one-to-many $(1 : M)$ relationship in tree-structured databases. In this relationship, one table may be called the ''owner'' and the other the ''member.'' One or more ordering criteria may be specified for the rows of a member table that are associated with the rows of the owner table.

As described in the example there are two types of perspectives of the logical database structure: the global logical view and the user view. The global logical view contains the logical database structure of the entire distributed database. The user view is the subset of the global logical view that is permitted to an individual user by the database administrator. This simplified view includes only those tables, columns, and rows that are needed for specific user. Several user views may be associated with the same global logical view. To the database administrator, a user view is a means of control and also security. To the user it provides a means of simplifying the database structure.

Physical Database Structure

The unit of database distribution to a node is called a stored fragment. A stored fragment, as an implementation of a logical fragment, contains a subset of the rows of a table. The collection of fragments for a table must be disjoint and collectively exhaust the table. The smallest fragment of a table is a single row. Each row of a fragment is complete in that it contains all the columns defined for the table. A fragment can be replicated to improve reliability and performance. There can be any number of copies of a single fragment, each located at a different node. When a table is requested it is first necessary to determine which fragments of the table may contain requested rows. Then it is necessary to locate the ''best'' copy(s) of the fragments(s).

Design flexibility is therefore provided by allowing a combination of database replication and database partitioning. Defining logical fragments and the location of stored fragment copies allows the designer to meet response time and reliability needs while controlling database duplication.

18-3 DESIGN ISSUES IN A DISTRIBUTED DATABASE ENVIRONMENT

The multiplicity of the design options of distributed database systems indicates a diversity in system goals and a pervasiveness of the design issues. Although there is a large volume of technical literature, the majority of the research is directed to the modeling of data distribution strategies under stringent assumptions, with very little being reported on the solutions to existing implementation problems.

18-3-1 Data Distribution Strategies

Strategies for the distribution of data to the nodes of a computer network can be classified as to whether one or more than one node contains data and by the existence or nonexistence of data duplication. The allowable strategies are defined by the system architecture and the network database management system software. A particular implementation of the data distribution strategy is usually determined during database design. Let us consider the following four alternative data distribution strategies:

1. Centralized (single copy of the database, located at one node)
2. Partitioned (single copy of the database, disjoint subsets located at various nodes)
3. Replicated (multiple copies of the database, a complete copy per data node)
4. Hybrid (multiple copies of subsets of the database, each node may have an arbitrary fraction of the database)

A distributed database management system that allows only a centralized database is the simplest, and one that allows hybrid data distribution is the most complex. The partitioned strategy and the replicated strategy are each more complex than the centralized strategy, but in different ways. In the partitioned strategy there is only one copy of the database, but it is necessary to know what part of the database is located at each node. In the replicated strategy every data node has a complete copy of the database and all copies must be synchronized to guarantee consistency and integrity. The hybrid strategy combines the complexities of the other two distributed strategies to gain flexibility and the advantages of both. The network database management system (network or distributed DBMS) may need to keep track of the number of copies of each subset of the database as well as the location of each copy.

A distinction can be made between the data distribution strategy allowed by the network DBMS and the strategy employed in a particular database implementation. A particular database implementation may not exploit the full capabilities of the network DBMS. For example, a centralized database may be implemented even though the network DBMS allows one of the three distributed data strategies. Another, more interesting, example is the case where the network DBMS supports the hybrid strategy but the database implementation uses only one of the degenerate cases: partitioned or replicated data distribution. If the database implemented is a degenerate case of that allowed by the network DBMS, the result will generally be wasted resources both in terms of unnecessary software complexity and run-time efficiency. The amount of wasted resources will vary greatly from one implementation to another. Having a more flexible network DBMS does have advantages in terms of future modifications, however, even if its full capabilities are not used immediately.

The rest of this section assumes that the four data distribution strategies describe the capabilities of classes of network DBMSs and not a particular database implementation. The reader can easily extrapolate to the situations involving degenerate cases.

There are advantages and disadvantages to each of the four data distribution strategies. Considerations include reliability, data storage, response time for both retrievals and updates, and the various control mechanisms required with their concomitant costs in software and communication. We now focus on the advantages and disadvantages of each strategy together with typical situations where each would be appropriate.

Centralized

The main advantage of a centralized database is, of course, simplicity. All activity is under the control of a single node and the problems and operation are well understood, at least relative to distributed databases. The distributed strategies must prove themselves in overcoming some of the disadvantages of the centralized approach in order to be viable alternatives. Since, in the centralized database approach, all the data are located at a single node, the availability of secondary storage at that node limits the size of possible databases. All retrievals and updates must be directed to the central node with the accompanying communication costs and time delay. If a node consisting of a single computer is assumed, there is limited opportunity for parallel processing; thus, the rate of activity is limited by the processor speed. The central node is also susceptible to communication bottlenecks even though the rest of the network is operating normally. One of the major problems of this strategy is limited availability and reliability. The database may become unavailable from any of the remote nodes when communication failures occur, and the database system fails totally when the central node fails. Each of the other three data distribution strategies overcomes some of these disadvantages, but at a price.

Partitioned

The partitioned data distribution strategy allocates the database over a number of nodes of the network but does not allow multiple copies. As described earlier, the database is partitioned into disjoint subsets called logical fragments, and each logical fragment is assigned to a particular node. This approach has several advantages over the centralized strategy. The size of the database is now limited only by the secondary storage available on the network as a whole, not by the storage available at a particular node. Since retrievals and updates are directed to the node on which the needed data are located, communication costs may be lowered due to a greater percentage of database accesses being local. On the other hand, a request may require access to all the nodes of the network with even greater communication costs and delay than with the centralized database. Response time may be less than for a centralized database even when communication is needed, if the network DBMS exploits the possible parallelism. The system should also be less susceptible to communication bottlenecks at any one node since the communication load should be more evenly distributed across the entire network.

Database reliability and availability may be enhanced compared to the centralized approach. Even if part or all of the communication facility fails or if one or more nodes fail, the system may be at least partially functional. The part of the database that is local or located on nodes still on the network may still be available. A key factor influencing database reliability and availability is what is termed locality of reference (i.e., the location of data required to satisfy user requests). If the database is partitioned across the network such that the data located on a node are used almost exclusively by users at that node, there is said to be a high degree of locality of reference. If such a partitioning of the database is not possible, there is said to be little locality of reference. A higher degree of locality of reference generally implies greater database availability. For example, if a user request can be satisfied with data stored locally, the failures of other nodes or failure in communication do not affect that request. If there is little locality of reference or if a user request is complex, data stored on many nodes may be required. If one node is unavailable, it may be impossible to satisfy the request. In this case database availability may be worse than in the centralized strategy. The probability of at least one node of the network being unavailable is clearly greater than the probability of a single node failing. Hence, the database can be available a lower percentage of the time than when using the centralized strategy.

In summary, the partitioned strategy is particularly appropriate where either local secondary storage is limited compared to the database size (such as in a minicomputer environment), where the reliability of a centralized database is not sufficient, or where operating efficiencies can be gained. Operating efficiencies can generally be gained when database access patterns are such that there is a high degree of locality of reference. If there is no locality of reference, efficiency can degenerate quite rapidly, owing to the high volume of communication.

Replicated

The replicated data distribution strategy allocates a complete copy of the database to each data node of the network (i.e., each node that has data has the entire database). The network database management system must coordinate multiple copies of data, but there is not the problem of figuring out which node contains a particular part of the database, as there is in the partitioned strategy. These two strategies have different problems to be dealt with and therefore cannot be compared directly to determine which is more complex. The major advantages of the replicated strategy lie in the areas of reliability, availability, and retrieval efficiency. The degree of reliability is the highest available but with the obvious cost of secondary storage usage. The database size is again limited by the secondary storage available at each node. A large part of the processing may be done locally, but synchronization of the multiple copies must occur in some fashion. How this syncrhonization is accomplished will vary widely from system to system, and the amount of overhead incurred (communication and processor) will depend on the level of data consistency provided. This strategy, in general, is not as amenable to the parallel processing of a single request as is the partitioned strategy, because of the synchronization and control complexities, but each node may asynchronously process different requests. Faster responses to user requests are possible, especially in situations where internode communication for synchronization is not needed, such as in a retrieval-only database. Communication should again be fairly well distributed over the network in many cases. Reliability is not only high in terms of data availability when a node or part of the network has failed, but it is also easy to replace a copy of the database that has been destroyed or to continue despite a destroyed node. Another advantage of the replicated strategy is the simplicity of backup and recovery operations. A consistent copy of the database can be obtained from any other operational node. When part of the network is unavailable for some reason, it may be necessary to restrict the operations (i.e., updates) that can be performed in order to maintain database consistency. That is, if two updates are allowed to take place on two different nodes when no synchronization is being performed, inconsistency may result when the network resumes normal operation. In summary, the totally redundant distributed data strategy is particularly appropriate where reliability is critical, the database is small, and update inefficiency can be tolerated (e.g., a retrieval-intensive database). This is a clear example of where an implementation issue, such as choice of synchronization technique, has a significant effect on database distribution efficiency. The quantification of this interdependence is an important research topic today.

Hybrid

The hybrid data distribution strategy combines the partitioned and replicated approaches in order to gain some of the advantages of each but, unfortunately, also requires some of the complexity of each. This strategy divides the database into logical fragments (disjoint subsets) as is done in the partitioned strategy, but additionally allows an arbitrary number of physical copies of each logical fragment, called the stored fragments. This strategy is totally general in that each part of the database can be duplicated any number of times and each node can have exactly the part of the database desired. Unfortunately, the network DBMS must both keep track of where data exist on the network and synchronize the arbitrary number of stored fragments associated with each logical fragment. Query processing and query optimization are nontrivial tasks when using the hybrid strategy.

Flexibility is the key advantage of this strategy. For example, trade-offs can be made between the amount of storage used in total and at each node, the reliability provided, and various efficiency measures. For example, data that are archival and hence noncritical need be stored only once, whereas data that are more critical can be duplicated as desired to meet the required level of reliability. When a logical fragment is duplicated (more than one stored fragment), synchronization costs, including communication costs, are increased; however, more data are available locally, which has the result of lowering the amount of communication needed for retrievals. This is due to the fact that the degree of locality of reference can be increased via duplication. Again we have a system where parallel processing can be exploited relatively easily, making lower response times possible. Communication bottlenecks can also be avoided in many instances. Since each node of the network can have an arbitrary subset of the database there can be any amount of reliability in the event of communication or node failures. Operation can continue although only a reduced functionality may be available. As may be the case in the replicated strategy, operations involving updates may be restricted so that database consistency can be brought about automatically when the network resumes full operation.

Although a distributed DBMS that allows the hybrid strategy is extremely flexible, the problem is the interdependence of the various factors that affect system performance, reliability, and storage requirements. It is difficult to isolate one factor from the others. The mechanisms used by the distributed DBMS have a large effect on performance and other system metrics. Assumptions concerning database usage also have a large impact on the value of the trade-offs and the resulting data distribution. One way to describe the situations where the hybrid strategy is appropriate is when none of the simpler strategies work well. This may occur quite often. One example would be where there was a large database with only certain designated portions of it requiring high reliability. Each node may access some fraction of the database frequently but other fractions infrequently (i.e., variability in locality of reference). In this case the partitioned strategy may not provide sufficient reliability and the replicated strategy may be impractical or impossible because of the secondary storage needed.

18-3-2   Network Data Directory Distribution

The network data directory can be distributed among the nodes of a network via any of the four strategies used for the database itself: centralized, partitioned, replicated, or hybrid. Which strategy is appropriate is usually dictated by a combination of the data distribution strategy used by the network DBMS and assumptions concerning the requirements of the database systems (by users and applications). This means that the basic strategy will usually be predefined by the network DBMS, and hence its effects must be evaluated prior to network DBMS selection. Much of the discussion concerning data distribution can be extended to directory distribution. Multiple copies of the directory, for example, imply the need for synchronization if the directory is to be modified.

Although in theory any directory distribution strategy can be used with any data distribution strategy, in practice several of the combinations are of limited value. The use of a centralized network data directory with a hybrid database would result in the loss of many of the advantages of data distribution. It should be noted that the pattern of accesses to the network directory, the ratio of updates to retrievals (volatility), and other factors important in choosing a distribution strategy may be quite different for the network directory than they are for the database controlled by that directory.

Retrievals from the directory occur during the processing of every user request, thus encouraging the distribution and duplication of the directory. If the hybrid data distribution strategy is supported, a ''directory'' to the directory is required to allow the network DBMS to locate the needed portion of the directory. In SDD-1 [Rothnie et al., 1980] this directory is called the directory locator and is replicated at every node. In summary, the network data directory must be viewed as a part of the network DBMS and not as an independent entity. The directory distribution strategy employed must be seen in light of the data distribution strategy and the purpose of the database system.

Network directory design during database implementation may still be required, although there may be more restrictions on what is allowed in comparison to database design. Some network DBMSs may allow network directory allocation to be defined similar to the way in which distributed data are defined. In other words, the network directory may be divided into logical fragments, or disjoint subsets, and then the logical fragments can be allocated to nodes of the network, possibly with redundancy. If the directory is treated the same as the database, all of the mechanisms used to support the database, such as concurrency control and security, also support the directory. Factors such as storage costs, reliability, and performance measures need to be evaluated once again.

The location of the data directories in a distributed data system was researched by Wesley Chu [1976] at the University of California at Los Angeles. This research is directed toward the analysis of directory location schemes under various situations.

At Bolt, Beranek and Newman, Sutherland [1974] envisioned the data directory function as a binding between names of ''entities'' and their location within the distributed data system. Two approaches to this issue are the ''full access name'' and the cataloging function. The full access name accomplishes the binding simply by providing a distributed data system location field within every file name, thereby explicitly specifying the location. The cataloging function provides for a distributed data sharing system to maintain internally the name-to-location bindings such that a user need not know the location of the file.

18-3-3   Homogeneous versus Heterogeneous Environment

Distributed systems are often used as means of ''integrating'' dissimilar hardware and software systems. Consequently, decisions have to be made as to whether to allow homogeneous or heterogeneous hardware systems.

First it is necessary to define the relationship of the network DBMS to a local DBMS. In the homogeneous DMBS case there is little question as to the data model, query language, and so on, that should be presented to the users: it is the same as that supported by the local DBMS. There may be some question, however, as to whether all users should interact with the network DBMS software or whether users who need purely local data should interact directly with the local DBMS. Since the facilities available to a user of the network DBMS would be equivalent, or at least very similar, the question is one mainly of software architecture and the advantages of a common software interface versus the overhead involved in the network DBMS. When the distributed database system supports heterogeneous DBMSs, the questions become more complex. The use of heterogeneous DBMSs would generally be the result of forming a distributed database system from several previously existing autonomous database systems. The stated goal is to do more than just provide access to remote DBMSs and the databases under their control; the goal is to provide transparency. Transparency means that the location of data is not known by users, or at least that such knowledge is not required. In a heterogeneous DBMS environment this is possible only if the local DMBS controlling that data is also "transparent"; that is, users do not know which local DBMS is being used to satisfy their requests. This can be accomplished in two fundamentally different ways. One way is to have the users at each node continue with the user interface provided by the local DBMS. The schema available would be extended to include the data available at other nodes, but users would continue as if the remote data had been added to the local database. The problem is that the network DBMS software at each node needs to be able to access data at every other node no matter what the data model and other factors. As the number of dissimilar local DBMSs increases, the number of translation schemes required grows rapidly. If there are n local DBMSs there are $n(n - 1)$ translation schemes needed—not a very efficient approach.

The use of a standard, network-wide user interface and a standard internal form reduces the data translation problem. In this approach all users, or at least those who need remote data, use a common interface which may be different from that provided by any of the local DBMSs. There is one schema of the network database, not a different schema at each node that depends on the local DBMS. There must be a translation scheme from each local DBMS type to the common form, but this involves only n translation schemes for n dissimilar DBMSs versus the $n(n - 1)$ translation schemes required for the previous approach. The disadvantage is that users must learn a new system, the network DBMS. Also, there is still the question of whether to allow users who need only local data to use the local DBMS directly or to force everyone to use the network standard. The latter alternative is probably not managerially possible or effective but may have technological advantages in areas such as concurrency control.

Another problem is that the present state of the art deals with only half the problem, the retrieval aspect. The mapping of updates across heterogeneous DBMSs is an unsolved research problem, at least in its general form.

Most of the research in this area has assumed that data translation would be performed in a static environment, that is, the database being unavailable to users while a database in one form is translated into a database of another form. The performance requirements involved in dynamic data translation make it difficult to apply the schemes that work well in the static case. In summary, it can be said that the technical issues involved in data translation become increasingly more difficult as the database system becomes more heterogeneous.

18-4 A FRAMEWORK FOR DISTRIBUTED
DATABASE DESIGN

A stepwise methodology for centralized database design has been proposed in Chapter 1 and elaborated upon throughout this text. This section discusses a potential extension of this methodology to accommodate distributed database design as well [Chang, 1980; Mohan and Yeh, 1979]. In a distributed database system, a logically integrated database may be fragmented and widely dispersed in order to improve system performance. Fragmentation and dispersion of a database without careful central planning often creates confusion and inconsistency in database applications. The following proposed stepwise distributed database design procedure realizes this important fact and the sequence of steps include those that require a central monitor.

The basic steps in the stepwise distributed database sequence are illustrated in Fig. 18-7. We assume that the distributed DBMS (D-DBMS) under consideration is capable of defining the whole database structure as well as database partition and allocation, and is capable of automatically processing database applications no matter how the stored fragments are distributed. An example of this kind of D-DBMS has been proposed in DeSmith et al. [1979]. A D-DBMS with this capability usually uses the same data model describing every global database entering the system and in some way maintains a directory for database partition and allocation. Noting this fact, and letting a system designer perform Step 1 to Step 5, applications can take advantage of the homogeneity in every database structure and can enforce consistency of databases as well as impose system-wide standards on databases preferred by the particular organization that owns the system. Step 6 (physical design), on the other hand, may be carried out locally so that features peculiar to local computers would be accounted for, and consequently a better design could be resulted.

Observing that Steps 1, 2, 3, and 6 are similar to the centralized database design Steps 1 to 4 in Chapter 2, in the following sections we explore further only Steps 4 and 5.

18-4-1 Database Partitioning

The database partition step is concerned with the partitioning of the global database and synthesis of diverse database applications into usage patterns using the partitions. As shown in Fig. 18-8, there are three classes of outputs: (1) a partition, (2) size of each member of the partition, and (3) usage patterns and frequencies. In the following paragraphs we describe these output classes and briefly discuss some aspects relevant to them.

A partition $\{F_1, \ldots, F_n\}$. The input global database to this design step is partitioned into a set of subfiles $\{F_1, \ldots, F_n\}$. The partition is required to contain the exact information present in the global database. Beside this information-preserving requirement, a database structure compatability constraint for database partition is often desired. Generally speaking, database structure compatibility supplies the

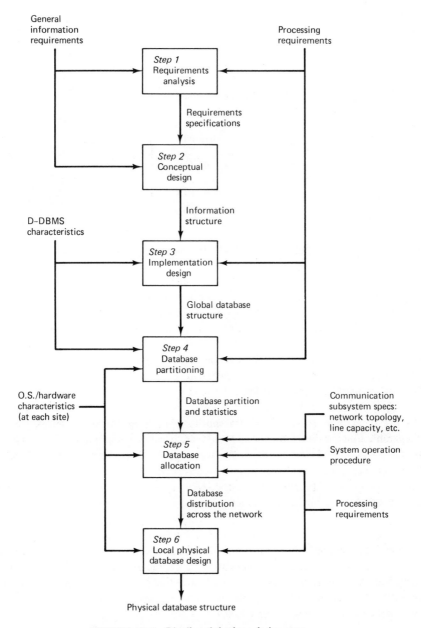

FIGURE 18-7 Distributed database design steps.

building blocks (or units) for all structurally feasible partitions. The building blocks could be as small as tuples (record occurrences) in the relational data model, or as large as connected components (via owner–member relationship) in the network data model. To form database partitions from the building blocks, there are two more considerations that further restrict possible database partition output. One is size

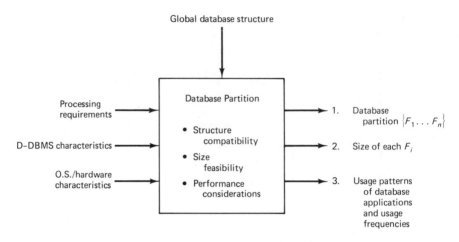

FIGURE 18-8   Distributed database partition step (Step 4).

feasibility and the other is performance considerations. For the performance considerations, roughly speaking, there are two major factors that should be dealt with: responsiveness and reliability of the system. One likes to cluster in a subfile those records used together so that the subfile can be distributed to the place where it is referenced most often, to improve system responsiveness. When using redundancy for reliability, we would like to achieve the desired degree of reliability with as small an amount of data duplication as possible. This goal can be reached reasonably only for some properly chosen partitions.

Size of each member, F_i. Every subfile in the partition is to be taken as an inseparable unit for data allocation. Moreover, if every computer site in the system has fixed and limited storage space, this would place certain restrictions on the class of feasible partitions (i.e., size feasibility constraints on partitions). A simple example of such constraints is that no subfile sizes are allowed to exceed the maximum storage space available at various sites.

Usage patterns and usage frequencies. How database applications utilize the feasible database partitions is also analyzed in this step. The relationship between database partition and database applications is characterized by an application-type identification, identification of the network node that originates the application (i.e., transaction), frequency of the application, and application pattern.

Application patterns can be classified as follows:

1. Single-subfile applications
2. Multiple-subfile applications:
   a. Pure parallel processing applications.
   b. Synchronizing processing applications. The processing cost and side effects of synchronization have an important bearing on the performance of

424

the database, together with the database partitioning and allocation. An understanding of these interrelationships is critical to the distributed database design process.

18-4-2   Database Allocation

The stepwise methodology differs from the classical approaches at least in the following two aspects:

1. The database partition is considered to be an integral part of the problem. The classical database allocation problem assumes that database partition is given. In the database partition step we use as many constraints as reasonable to narrow the class of feasible partitions. Nevertheless, we cannot in general single out a unique partitioning in Step 4. To obtain a better structure, one can repeat Step 5 for every feasible partition output from Step 4 until a satisfactory result is reached or all the feasible partitions are exhausted.

2. Instead of assuming only single-file applications as stated in the classical approaches (i.e., programs use at most one data file), the assumption on transactions resulting from Step 4 should account for multiple-file applications. A new model is needed to deal with this generalization.

Distributed database allocation is a challenging task. If the network database management system supports either the partitioned or hybrid data distribution strategies, the number of implementation options available to a database designer is immense. If possible, a gross evaluation of user and system needs should be performed prior to database management system selection to determine which data distribution strategy is most appropriate. Assumptions that simplify the network database management system may also be discovered, such as updates originating from only one node or the fact that temporary database inconsistency is acceptable. Within any of the four data distribution strategies, assumptions of this type will have a large impact on the particular network database management system chosen, which in turn affects the distributed database design phase. What is needed is information concerning the data, the nodes, the applications, and their relationships as well as requirements for response time and reliability and the constraints imposed by the network hardware and software. It may be necessary to perform iterations in the design even at this high level of detail until an acceptable compromise is achieved.

Once a data distribution strategy is selected and a particular network database management system is chosen, the task is to allocate the data to nodes in a nearly optimal or at least "reasonable" manner. At this point it is assumed that the logical database structure, or schema, is fixed.

The allocation of data to the nodes of the network is relatively simple for two of the four data distribution strategies. If the centralized strategy is being employed, the only possible question is which node should be the central database node. In most cases even this will be obvious due to the network architecture or secondary storage availability. For the replicated strategy the option at each node is either to have a copy of the entire database or to have none of it. Some combination of user requirements, enumeration of alternatives, and common sense will solve many problems or at least reduce the number of alternatives so that each can be investigated further.

The allocation of data to the nodes of the network is more difficult for the partition strategy and much more difficult for the hybrid strategy. In the partitioned case the decisions are (1) how to divide the database into logical fragments or disjoint subsets (Step 4 in Fig. 18-7) and (2) how to assign each logical fragment to a specific node [i.e., one stored fragment (Step 5 in Fig. 18-7)]. When the hybrid strategy is allowed, the decision is even more complex because each logical fragment can be assigned to any number of nodes (multiple stored fragments). An equivalent way of viewing the decisions is deciding what part of the database should be at each node. The number of permutations of logical fragment definitions and stored fragment allocations grow quite rapidly. This is one reason why a "reasonable" data allocation scheme and not an optimal one is often the goal. Evaluation of a manually generated distributed database structure is difficult enough, much less the automatic design of a distributed database. Additional complexities, such as the design of a network data directory and its effects on performance, have been completely overlooked in this section in order to focus on the database itself, but must be considered in the database implementation process.

The question of how to allocate the database has been addressed by several researchers. Most of the work done applies simply to a collection of data files which are not necessarily structured into a logical schema. The term "file" which is used in the literature may also be correctly referred to as a logical fragment. The term "copy" is equivalent to a stored fragment.

Early significant work in the area of physical data distribution was provided by Chu's [1973] investigation of a linear programming solution to optimize the allocation of files in a network. Under the assumptions that (1) the number of file copies is known, (2) queries are routed to all files, (3) query patterns are known, and (4) a Poisson queuing discipline is used, he formulated a zero–one linear programming solution. It is well known that such a solution approach is feasible only for small problems since the number of variables and constraints increases rapidly as the number of nodes in the problem increases. Whitney's [1970] Ph.D. dissertation addressed the broader problem of computer communication system design but applied Chu's approach to the optimal allocation of files. Casey [1972, 1973a,b] relaxed limitations set by Chu's model and showed that the proportions of update traffic to query traffic determine an upper bound for the number of file copies that are maintained in the network. Mahmoud et al. [1979] developed a heuristic algorithm to solve the combined problem of network file allocation and channel capacity allocation in a fixed topology network. Both Whitney and Casey combined file allocation and communication network design but restricted themselves to tree and network topologies. Khabbaz [1979] investigated other network topologies which may provide higher reliability at lower cost. A heuristic procedure is used to minimize the total cost of database storage and communication channels, subject to given constraints of network reliability, file availability, and communication delay.

The distribution of data in a network is not independent of the programs that use the data. Morgan and Levin [1977] extended the data distribution strategies by considering the effect of programs. A model that considered the effect of the dependencies between programs and data and their optimal allocation in a network was formulated. The allocation problem was partitioned into three levels. The first level assumed that the access patterns were static and known over time. A zero–one linear programming solution was developed for the optimal allocation of files. In the second level, the assumption that the access request patterns were known was relaxed and a dynamic programming solution approach was formulated. The third and final level addressed the situations where the access request patterns are initially unknown. A statistical procedure for the estimation of these patterns was developed and incorporated into the file allocation model. This would be useful in the adaptive reassignment of files in the network.

18-5   DIFFERENTIAL FILES

A differential file for a database is analogous to an errata list for a book. Rather than print a new edition of a book each time a change in text is desired, a publisher identifies corrections by page and line number, collecting them into an errata list which is distributed with each book. This procedure significantly reduces publication costs. To reference the corrected version of the book, however, readers must consult the errata list before any reading of the main text. An increase in access time is thus traded for a decrease in maintenance cost. If text changes are continued, the errata list grows to sufficient length that reorganization costs are justified. All changes would then be incorporated into the book, forming a new physical edition.

Updating a large database poses a similar problem. As with a book, it is generally simplest and least expensive to accumulate changes over a period of time and to post them en masse when creating a new database edition (generation). It is more expensive, as measured in terms of storage costs, maintenance time, and overall system complexity, to modify the database directly with each update transaction. As a compromise, a differential file can be used like an errata list to identify and collect pending record changes. Consulting the differential file as a first step in data retrieval effectively yields an up-to-date database. At a cost of increased access time, database update costs may be reduced. When the differential file grows sufficiently large, a reorganization incorporates all changes into a new generation of the database, and the now empty differential file can begin accumulating changes anew.

The concept of a differential file has been rediscovered many times, and is applicable to distributed database systems [Severance and Duhne, 1976]. Three documented systems will be described. First, Turnburke [1963] outlines a differential structure for tape systems which is designed to avoid the writing of unchanged data records while sequentially processing batched updates. A data file is decomposed into similarly ordered subfiles: a large collection of read-only records is stored on one tape, while a smaller collection of modified records is maintained on a separate "change tape." To update the data file, both tapes are merged with a transaction file and a new change tape is output. Unchanged records from the read-only tape are never written. First, Turnburke recommends data file reorganization when one-half of all records have been modified.

Roycroft [1968] suggests a direct access file organization which also makes use of a differential file concept to process file changes. The system addresses records via unique identifiers, and every data reference passes through a database index which points to all records. Once created, the main data file is never modified. New database records are accessed through the index, but are stored in a separate overflow area. All record modifications are treated as record additions. A new copy of the record is created and the index is updated to point into the overflow area. The old record is not destroyed, but rather maintained as a before-image and pointed to by the new record to grow in size as a result of an update without disturbing the positioning of neighboring records.

A system with a similar structure is described by Rappaport [1975]. It was developed to facilitate database recovery after an electrical power failure. Again all database records are accessed through a system index, and all modifications are physically separated into a file of changes called a MODFILE. Each changed record points back to its before-image. In the event of a power loss, information in a transaction log is used in conjunction with the MODFILE to undo partially completed update transactions.

Whenever a record is updated in either the Roycroft or Rappaport system, a record search mechanism (initially associated with only the main data file) is modified to address a new record copy, which is stored in what is essentially a differential file. As depicted by Fig. 18-9(a), the current version of any identified record, whether in the main file or the differential file, is accessed via a common search mechanism—the system index.

A generalization of this record accessing strategy is shown in Fig. 18-9(b). Here, given the identifier for any database record, the differential file is always searched first for that record; in the event that the record is not found, it is then retrieved from the main data file. Implicit in this diagram is the fact that each file may utilize a separate search mechanism. The main file index is then static and can be quickly recovered from a backup copy in the event of a loss. Index volatility is shifted to a smaller, and therefore more quickly recoverable differential file index.

To isolate the main file and its search mechanism from change, an overhead in the form of a differential file search is paid for every record retrieval. If the two data files and their search mechanisms can be assigned to different devices and accessed via separate channels, both file searches may proceed in parallel, and system users will not perceive an additional delay. When such overlap is impossible, one can expect the average time of data record retrieval (assuming a judicious selection of the differential file search strategy [Severance and Duhne, 1976; Severance and Lohman, 1976]) to increase by the amount of time required for a random access to secondary memory.

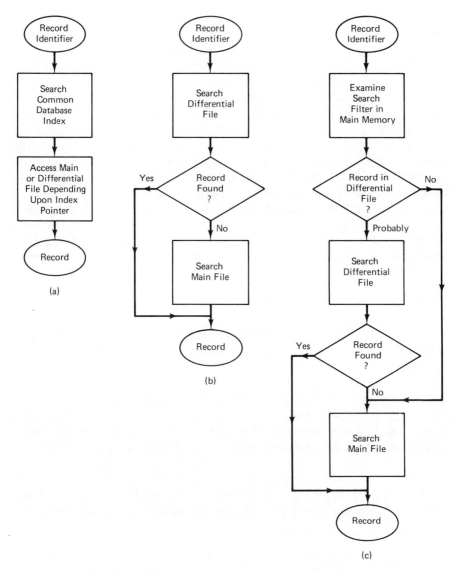

FIGURE 18-9 Alternative access strategies: (*a*) common index; (*b*) separate indexes; (*c*) separate indexes and search filter.

This additional access time may be comparatively large and can seriously degrade system performance.

For an operating environment in which a significant increase in retrieval time is intolerable, Fig. 18-9(c) suggests modified search strategy which uses a presearch filtering algorithm to reduce the number of unnecessary searches of the differential file. A *filtering scheme*, devised by Bloom [1970] to detect the occurrence of rare events, can be used to nearly eliminate unsuccessful searches. The Bloom technique associates the differential file with a main memory bit vector B of length M, and some number X of hashing functions which map record identifiers into bit addresses. When the differential file is initially empty, all bits in B are set to zero. Whenever a record is stored in the differential file, each transformation is applied to the record identifier and each of the X bits addressed is set to 1.

Retrieval of a database record now proceeds as follows. The identifier of a record to be retrieved is mapped through each transformation and the logical AND operator is applied to the X bits that are addressed. The resulting bit value is either 0 or 1. The value 0 is a certain indication that the most recent version of the record still resides in the main data file; the differential file search is skipped and the main file is immediately accessed. A resulting value of 1 is an indication that an updated copy of the record will probably be found in the differential file, which is therefore searched. There is a possibility that this search will prove fruitless, since the bits associated with a given identifier might be set to 1 coincidentally by mappings from other updated records. Only in the event of such a filtering error are both files searched during a record retrieval.

Advantages of a Differential File

The history of database development efforts shows design simplicity to be a dominant characteristic of successful implementations. And although the notion of a differential file is conceptually rather simple, in practice any additional system complexity must be justified by tangible benefits. The potential advantages of a differentially organized database are not widely appreciated; even existing systems are rather narrowly motivated. This section therefore collects and discusses eight general benefits that can be realized. Five relate to database integrity and show that a differential file can reduce backup costs, speed recovery, and even minimize the chances of a serious data loss. The final three advantages are operational; a differential file can produce increased data availability and simultaneously reduce storage and retrieval costs. In total these benefits constitute a strong argument for a much wider use of differential files, especially for the maintenance of very large databases.

1. *Reduces database dumping costs*

In general, to recover a database that has been physically damaged, some form of roll-forward procedure [Yourdon, 1972] is employed: The status of the database, saved at a previous point in time, is first reloaded; the cumulative effect of all update transactions processed since that time is then reestablished via some abbreviated form of reprocessing. The frequency with which the database is copied to its backup file is a critical parameter in designing such a procedure [Chandy et al., 1975; Drake and Smith, 1971]. Frequent dumping permits fast recovery but is associated with high system overhead.

Since the time required for a dump is proportional to the volume of data copied [Innovation Data Processing, 1973], a differential file can drastically reduce the cost to back up a large database, particularly when the proportion of records changed during a backup period is small. Consider, for example, a database with 10^7 500-character records stored in track-size blocks on an IBM 3330 disk facility. Suppose that updates are applied 5 days per week, 10 hours per day, at a rate of 100 changes per hour. Using a fast dump/restore utility [Innovation Data Processing, 1973], a full database dump would require over 6 hours to accomplish. On the other hand, even after a full week of processing, a differential file, its bit vector, and the data required by a reasonable search mechanism could be dumped in less than 2 minutes. In total, they would occupy less than 300 tracks of storage, as compared to 51 disk packs.

2. Facilitates incremental dumping

It is sometimes impractical to dump an entire database at one time. An incremental dumping strategy [Sayani, 1974], also called "differential disk dumping" by Yourdon [1972], will sequence through physical sections of a database, periodically dumping each section that has changed. A differential file implementation in which new records are sequentially allocated in secondary storage (for example, Rappaport's system [1975]) lends itself naturally to such a strategy. To provide a complete database backup at any time, one need only append to the current backup file those differential file records created since the last dump. With each incremental dump, one might also choose to save the current status of the differential file bit vector and search index. Alternatively, both could be recovered with a single scan of the restored differential file.

3. Permits both real-time dumping and reorganization with concurrent updates

Since a dump represents the instantaneous status of a database at a fixed point in time, conventional backup procedures will prohibit all changes while this snapshot is developed. By dumping only a small differential file, the time during which update transactions are prohibited can be substantially reduced. More important, one can avoid completely the need to inhibit change by building a "differential-differential" file to store record updates which are generated during the differential file dumping process. For most applications, this file will be quite small and can be reasonably held in main memory. Acting as a "cache" store during the dump, it would be scanned before every retrieval. When the dump has been completed, its records would be incorporated into the main differential file. Clearly, the same basic idea permits on-line reorganization. Since the generation of a new main file might require a significant amount of time, the differential-differential file would be maintained in secondary memory. It replaces the old differential file when reorganization is complete.

These procedures for dumping and reorganizing a database are particularly appropriate for applications such as airline reservation systems, which require 24-hour on-line availability, but which experience periods of reduced traffic intensity. Without locking out updates, either procedure could be activated during a slack period and would act to level the system load.

4. *Speeds recovery from data loss*

Damage to storage hardware is not the only cause of data loss. A user program may incorrectly modify a database; or a program error, a system deadlock, or a machine failure may abort the processing of an update transaction in the midst of a multistep procedure (such as a transfer of funds between bank accounts). The content and/or structural integrity of the database may be damaged by either type of error. Rappaport's Vehicle and Drive Information System [1975] provides a working example of a differential file (used in the maintenance of an on-line before-image log) which permits rapid system recovery through the rollback of incorrectly processed or partially completed transactions.

5. *Reduces the risk of a serious data loss*

When recovering a database, a properly tuned dump-restore utility can reload a physical dump at nearly the maximum transfer rate of available hardware (on the order of 10^5 characters/second). The major portion of recovery time is then spent individually reapplying updates to a small fraction of the records restored. This small subset of changed records constitutes an "Achilles' heel." Traditional update-in-place file organizations distributed changed records widely over secondary storage; this practice guarantees that even localized physical damage (e.g., a track loss or head crash on a single device of a very large database) will require a lengthy recovery procedure. By concentrating updates in a small physical area, a differential file offers three potential advantages:

a. The critical exposure area of a database is minimized. Most physical damage can be quickly repaired with a localized backup copy procedure.
b. The critical area may be allocated to a more reliable device type than is practical for the larger main file.
c. The small critical area may be duplexed to provide the most valuable redundancy for a marginal increase in operating costs.

6. *Supports "memo files" efficiently*

Accurate on-line updating of a database requires complex software to provide multiuser access control and to assure data recoverability [King and Collmeyer, 1973]. To avoid the substantial overhead associated with such software, many "on-line" systems will actually batch updates for end-of-day processing. Inventory control systems, for example, can generally tolerate some loss of accuracy during the batching cycle provided that database integrity is reestablished with each batch run. In systems where a predictible information lag might be exploited (in a banking system, for example), the memo file concept of Davis [1974] can be used to maintain "probably accurate" data without the need for complex software. The idea is to permit software that does not defend against improbable events (such as concurrent update, system failure, head crash) to update a "scratch pad" copy of the database. At end-of-day the copy is discarded and the updates are reapplied to the "real" database. The use for a differential file here is obvious.

7. Simplifies software development

Since the main data file and its associated index are unaffected by updates in a differential file system, this affords a natural environment for the development and testing of new data processing software. Using two differential files, one can imagine a developmental system and a production system running in parallel, with both accessing the same main file but modifying their own differential files. To debug new software, on-line comparisons could be made between the data values maintained by both systems. For very large databases, where it is either infeasible to create a duplicate copy of the database for experimentation or at least impossible for both copies to be on-line simultaneously, this use of differential files is particularly important.

Because the main file is static between reorganizations, the structures required for its storage are inherently simple and efficient. Neither free space nor record linkages are allocated to accommodate record growth, and a greater density of data storage can be achieved when the database is initially loaded [Roycroft, 1968]. Since the main file is read-only, multiple access requests may be handled concurrently without requiring the use of a complex protocol to avoid deadlock or errors due to simultaneous write access [Brinch Hansen, 1973]. Thus, if a user program requires access to data that are either known to be constant or are relatively stable, so that absolute currency is noncritical, such requests may bypass the differential file and safely access only the main file without queuing for private access.

8. Reduces future database storage costs

In the foreseeable future, trillion-bit random access mass storage devices will be provided by at least one of several competing technologies. The cost for a dynamic read–write capability is expected to be an order of magnitude greater than the cost of a read-only memory. The application of the differential file concept in such an operating environment is obvious: The large main data file is read-only. The cost reduction that differential files provide will greatly enlarge the realm of feasible computer-based information systems.

APPENDICES

A EXERCISES IN CONCEPTUAL AND IMPLEMENTATION SCHEMA DESIGN

Eight fundamental activities in the development of conceptual and implementation schemas from information requirements specifications are given below in the form of exercises. Each of these exercises (or any subset of them) can be applied to the design problems defined subsequently.

The objective of these exercises is to gain experience in designing databases and application programs to support sets of data and processing requirements. Various technical and management constraints and considerations will influence the available design alternatives, decision criteria, and decisions.

Exercise A1. Conceptual Design

Design a DBMS-independent structure that designates the information content of the database. The information structure may be specified in terms of an entity–attribute–relationship diagram, normalized relations, or some comparable conceptual data model.

If entity–attribute–relationship diagrams are used, sketch out a rough diagram of entities and relationships based on the information requirements alone. If the entities are not easily definable, develop a diagram of all data elements and their inter-relationships.

Exercise A2. Local Information Structures

Using your initial diagram for perspective, develop a set of local information structures (entity diagrams), one for each of the major processing applications. Each local structure should consist of entities (in boxes), attributes (listed outside the entity boxes), and relationships (with arcs and arrows) such that the application can be satisfied by traversing some access path shown in the diagram. Alternatively, if the relational model is favored, develop the appropriate functional dependency relation-ships.

Exercise A3. Consolidated Structures

Consolidate all the local information structures into a single global structure that eliminates redundant entities and attributes and still satisfies the accessing needed for the processing applications.

Note that we are not concerned with accessing efficiency at this point, but only the feasibility of satisfying the information content of the processing requirements.

Exercise A4. Processing Activity

Using two or three of the reports and two or three of the transaction types as examples, indicate how the processing requirements would be satisfied with the specific information structure.

Exercise A5. Logical Database Structure

Your objective is to design a DBMS-dependent logical database structure that is efficient. Use your newly formed global information structure as a starting point; incorporate data volume, processing frequencies, and DBMS constraints in whatever order you feel most comfortable with, continually refining the structure to a final state. Design decisions are to be based on minimization of (some combination of) logical record accesses, transport volume (i.e., total bytes accessed), and storage space.

In your final diagram, show your database entry points and specify record ordering. Produce a table of processing applications and record types that shows how you computed logical record accesses, designating the number of accesses of each record type.

Exercise A6. Alternative Data Models

Derive DBMS-dependent logical database structures for alternative data models among the classes of hierarchical, network, and relational systems; that is, transform the structure developed above into one compatible with specific systems representing the other major data models.

Exercise A7. Application Program Design

Sketch high-level flowcharts or Warnier–Orr diagrams of the application programs designated or implied in the stated processing requirements.

Exercise A8. Additional Design Issues

Discuss alternative solutions for the following problems and/or situations.

1. If retrieval transactions could be held until specific times in the day, what effect would this have on the database and application programs?
2. If update transactions could be held until specific times in the day, what effect would this have on the database and application programs?
3. What effect would specifying security or integrity requirements on the system have on the application programs and databases?

4. What types of additional report or transaction requests would have a significant effect on the database and application program specifications?

DESIGN PROBLEMS

Design Problem 1. Student Registration System

A computer-based student registration system is desired for a large university. The university has a stable population of 35,000 students, 3000 faculty, 100 departments, and 4000 courses. Assume that they are all evenly distributed throughout the university. Each student averages four courses per semester. The system to generate the following reports and query, replies in an efficient manner. Frequency of each application is in parentheses.

  a. List all students in a given section of a particular course (1000 per day).
  b. List all instructors, office numbers, and courses they are currently teaching for a given department (20 per day).
  c. List all the course offerings for a given department (100 per day).
  d. Determine if a student has the proper prerequisites for a course (5000 per day).
  e. Add/drop a student to/from a section of a course (20,000 per day).
  f. List a student's final schedule for the term (5000 per day).

Design Problem 2. Order entry system

Company D is a distributor that purchases products from vendors, puts them in storage, and resells them to customers. Each product may have several models. A particular product model may be offered by several vendors with different prices. The order entry system must keep track of information related to vendors, products, customers, orders, and so on.

Specific Processing Activity

The order entry system is required to support several types of applications, each of which produces a report. Sample reports/queries include the following:

  R1. *Customer Report.* For each customer, list all order numbers and product models ordered.
  R2. *Vendor Report.* For each vendor, list all the catalog names, product model names, product model numbers, and prices.
  R3. *Customer Order Inquiry.* Given a product model number, list all customers that have an open order for that product model.
  R4. *Stock Status.* For each product model for which the quantity on hand is less than or equal to the reorder quantity, print product model name, number, suppliers, quantity on hand, and reorder quantity. (Occurs 10% of the time.)
  R5. *Vendor Inquiry.* Given a product model number, list the following information on each vendor that can supply the product model: name, number, address, prices, and expected lead time for delivery.
  R6. *Customer Inquiry.* Given a customer name or number, retrieve the descriptive information on customer.

The system is also expected to process a number of transaction types, including the following:

T1. *Order Entry.* Customer orders are most often phoned in by a customer or a salesperson. The order should be entered into the system. Following the entry of the order, stock availability should be determined for each line item. Back orders should be filled. After a credit check is performed, an invoice should be produced and a picking list generated. The line items on the invoice should be ordered as they were on the original order, while the picking list should be ordered to facilitate order filling.

T2. *New Customer.* For each new customer enter number, name, credit limit, address, and so on.

T3. *New Products.* For each new product model, enter information which describes the product model, identifies its suppliers, and identifies its bin location(s). Product may be added or deleted.

T4. *New Vendor.* For each new vendor, enter general descriptive information and update the database. Vendors may be added or deleted.

T5. *Receipt of Goods.* For each item received, identify bin location of storage and update the database.

Data and Processing Volume

APPLICATIONS		FREQUENCY OF USE	
T1	Order Entry	1000	new customer orders per day
T2	New Customer	50	per day
T3	Product Models		{ Add one per day
			{ Delete one per day
T4	Vendors		{ Add one per day
			{ Delete one per 10 days
T5	Receipt of Goods	100	items per day
R1	Customer Report		Once per 100 days
R2	Vendor Report		Once per 10 days
R3	Customer Order Inquiry	100	per day
R4	Stock Status	1	per day
R5	Vendor Inquiry	100	per day
R6	Customer Inquiry	1200	per day

DATA VOLUME INFORMATION (CURRENT STATUS)

40	Vendors
50,000	Customers
1,000	Product models
5,000	Average quantity-on-hand-per model
80	Catalogs
200	Average entries per catalog (no duplication of entries across catalogs for a given vendor)
10	Storage bins per product model (average)
2,000	Storage bins (total)
150,000	Orders
4	Lines per order (average)
2	Customer locations per customer (average)
16	Vendors per product model (average)
400	Product models per vendor (average)

Design Problem 3. Space Federation Database

The following tasks represent increasingly difficult conceptual and implementation database design problems for a fictitious environment based roughly on the *Star Trek* concept.

Task 3A

Data environment. The Space Federation governs 100 galactic sectors which it patrols with 25 starships assigned to approximately four sectors apiece.

Usage patterns

1. Whenever a galactic sector appears to be having some difficulty such as an interplanetary war, the starship associated with that sector is found and called in to resolve the problem (frequency, 20%)
2. The governing counsel often wants to know what galactic sectors are governed by a given starship, in particular, the starship *Enterprise* (frequency, 80%).

Task 3B

Data environment. The Space Federation has 25 starships stationed throughout known space. One hundred cargo ships are assigned the task of bringing fuel, equipment, and supplies to these starships. Because each starship is unique, cargo ships must be specially built to service each one and cannot service any other starship. More than one cargo ship is assigned to a starship to assure continued maintenance.

To aid in dispatching cargo ships and assigning crewmembers for relief, the Federation keeps a record of all coordinates and crew rosters for each ship.

Usage patterns

1. When a starship needs servicing it is necessary to find the closest cargo ship capable of performing the service (frequency, 90%).
2. Whenever a cargo ship is assigned a service operation, the Federation distributes notices to those crew members on both ships who will find relatives on the other ship. This is done by obtaining a report of all crew members with the same last names on both ships (frequency, 10%).

Task 3C

Data environment. Each cargo ship belonging to the Space Federation is divided into five sections. These sections are assigned specific maintenance, navigation, and cargo manipulation duties. Each section performs an average of three different duties.

Fifty crew members are assigned to a ship and each crew member works in two sections, on the average. The Federation maintains a set of personal information for each crew member.

1. The commander of the ship often wants to know the personal data about the individual assigned to a given section (frequency, 90%).
2. Every now and then, the ship is short a crew member. Other crew members are examined for replacement possibilities. What is typically looked at is the set of duties the crew member already performs (frequency, 10%).

Task 3D

Data environment. The organization of the starship *Enterprise* is fairly simple. The starship is divided into several divisions, each of which has a division leader. Associated with each division are a number of tasks; these tasks are performed by crew members. Although a crew member will, in general, perform more than one task, no crew member performs tasks from more than one division.

Some tasks require several crew members. Associated with each person on the ship (division leader and crew member) is a set of personal information. A rating of how well a task is performed is associated with the crew member and the tasks.

Usage patterns

1. Find the personal information and names of all crewmembers capable of doing task T in division D, with a rating of R or better (frequency, 50%).
2. Find the names of those crew members who are capable of doing all the tasks in a subset of division D's tasks (frequency, 10%).
3. Find the names of all the crew members commanded by a specific leader (frequency, 40%).

Task 3E

Data environment. The sick bay of the starship *Enterprise* keeps the following information about its 10 physicians and the 100 crew members they treat: Each physician treats an average of 400 crew members. For each crew member, the physician maintains a history of the diseases contracted and a record of drug allergies. A crew member averages five of each of these sick log entries. The physician also notes the planets the crew member has visited (an average of 10). Associated with each planet is a list of known diseases indigenous to the planet and a description of their symptoms and treatment.

Usage patterns

1. Find the names of all the crew members that a given physician has treated (frequency, 20%).
2. Find the names of all the planets a given crew member has visited and list out their diseases, symptoms, and treatments (frequency, 50%).

3. Find the specified treatment for a given disease and list all crew members who are known to be allergic to this treatment (frequency, 30%).

Task 3F

Data environment. The Klingons are colonizing the universe! They have already captured 500 solar systems. Each of these has an average of three inhabitable planets. For each planet captured, the Klingons assign a governor and a puppet ruler. A record of service and commendations is kept on each governor for promotion purposes. In contrast, a record of loyalty information is kept on the puppet ruler.

The governor is assigned to record data on the planet's exploitable resources and the population's usable skills. Each planet has an average population of 1 million people. Because of underpopulation, every individual on the planet has, on the average, three skills that interest the Klingons. Ratings are taken on these skills.

Usage patterns

1. Find the inhabited planets of a specified solar system and retrieve a list of its resources and the names of the local governors and puppet rulers (frequency, 30%).
2. Given a solar system and a specific planet, list all the information associated with its governor and its puppet ruler (frequency, 10%).
3. The Klingons badly need a specific skill. Therefore, they want the names and ratings of every individual in the Klingon Empire who can perform this skill (frequency, 60%).

Task 3G

Data environment. Space is not easy on starships. To keep them in top shape, the Federation maintains 10,000 space stations. Each is located at what has been determined to be an optimal set of coordinates for servicing the fleet, and each has been given the name of a famous captain or courageous cadet who died in battle.

The starship manuals define 1000 standard starship repairs. Because of their complexity and special equipment requirements, each space station is only constructed to handle 50 of these repairs. Thus, any given repair can only take place at 500 of the stations.

Approximately 100 mechanics work at each station. They are trained on 10 different repairs and are given a rating level associated with each specialty.

The 25 Federation starships show up at these various stations for routine maintenance and whenever major difficulties that cannot be fixed by the starship engineering staff occur. The Federation keeps records of these repairs. About 1000 such repair stops have been made at each station.

Usage patterns

1. A starship is due for maintenance on a specific control system. The captain wants to find the repair station closest to its coordinates that is capable of performing the repair (frequency, 30%).
2. The Federation periodically checks usage patterns to see if its repair stations are appropriately distributed. It does this by listing all the starships that have had a given repair at a given station (frequency, 40%).
3. The *Enterprise* needs a very tricky repair. The Federation office wants to find the best mechanic for this job and the station where the mechanic works (frequency, 30%).

B   EXERCISES IN PHYSICAL DATABASE DESIGN

Exercise B1

For the conceptual and implementation design problems specified in Appendix A, specify appropriate physical parameter values to implement your DBMS-dependent logical database structure efficiently, assuming that the logical structure is fixed at this point. Consider performance criteria such as I/O time and storage space in your design. Consider CPU time if it can be reasonably estimated by your DBMS and O.S.

Design for the following parameter classes:

a. Pointer options
b. Access methods (indexed, random, etc.)
c. Secondary indexes
d. Clustering (areas, subfiles, secondary data set groups)
e. Block size
f. Any others specific to your DBMS (e.g., buffer allocation, secondary storage allocation, archival vs. on-line storage, compression, etc.)

Exercise B2

The following instructor/course/student database structure is represented by a "simple" network schema. Extend the attached schema to implement each of the following access methods. Assume that the DBMS has no indexes and it is up to the user to create special record types to do the indexing.

a. Indexed sequential access to instructor records.
b. Indexed random access to course records based on course number.
c. Inverted access to students based on the department they are in.
d. B-tree index to instructor records.
e. TRIE index to course records.

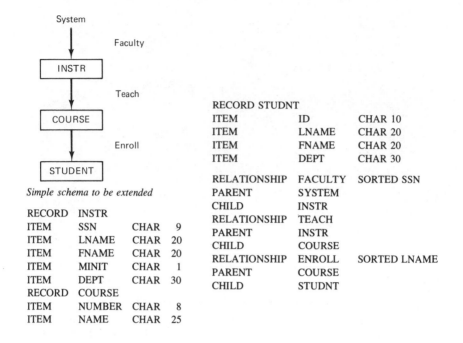

System

Faculty

INSTR

Teach

COURSE

Enroll

STUDENT

Simple schema to be extended

RECORD INSTR
ITEM   SSN   CHAR 9
ITEM   LNAME   CHAR 20
ITEM   FNAME   CHAR 20
ITEM   MINIT   CHAR 1
ITEM   DEPT   CHAR 30
RECORD COURSE
ITEM   NUMBER CHAR 8
ITEM   NAME   CHAR 25

RECORD STUDNT
ITEM   ID   CHAR 10
ITEM   LNAME   CHAR 20
ITEM   FNAME   CHAR 20
ITEM   DEPT   CHAR 30
RELATIONSHIP   FACULTY   SORTED SSN
PARENT   SYSTEM
CHILD   INSTR
RELATIONSHIP   TEACH
PARENT   INSTR
CHILD   COURSE
RELATIONSHIP   ENROLL   SORTED LNAME
PARENT   COURSE
CHILD   STUDNT

Exercise B3

a. Given that a single-file-type organization is desired for the university employee example given below, design an organization for each of the six access methods listed. Define each organization in diagram form. Each of the six organizations should be able to at least satisfy the following three retrieval/query transactions, regardless of efficiency. Try to be efficient if you can, however.

Access methods: 1. Sequential   4. Indexed sequential
                  2. Random (hashing)   5. Inverted
                  3. Indexed random   6. Doubly chained tree
                                           7. B-tree

Application A: List all employees by name in alphabetical order. (10%)
Application B: Print all employee data for ID-NUMBER = XXX. (50%)
Application C: Print the name and department of employees in age group XXX and holding degree YYY. (40%)

b. Compare your access methods in terms of total storage space required and total access time to satisfy each application. Derive total access time in terms of random block access time (TRBA) and sequential block access time (TSBA). Disk storage is assumed, but there is no need to go into any detail beyond the variables specified here. Put your results in a table:

	Applic. A	Applic. B	Applic. C	Storage Space
Sequential				
Random				
etc.				

c. Which access method minimizes total access time for all three types of applications? If all record accesses for Application B also involved changing the value of age, department, or degree, would this method still be the most efficient? Justify your answer.

Supporting data:

Number of employees = 5000
Number of departments = 100
Number of degree types = 3
Number of age groups = 10 (up through 70)

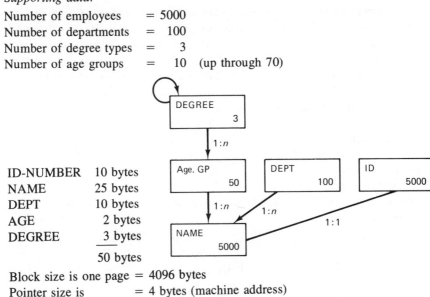

ID-NUMBER 10 bytes
NAME 25 bytes
DEPT 10 bytes
AGE 2 bytes
DEGREE 3 bytes
50 bytes

Block size is one page = 4096 bytes
Pointer size is = 4 bytes (machine address)

Exercise B4

A simple sequential file has been established for a governmental research group to keep track of the current location of maritime vessels associated with various research projects. The file contains 25,000 records of 80 bytes each, and is stored contiguously on a movable-head disk. The timing characteristics of the disk will be supplied. The user activity on the file consists of batch update operations for 20% of the runs and individual queries for 80% of the runs. Batch update runs average 600 transactions per batch. The average query results in 2000 "hits" or logical records actually meeting all the conditions specified in the query.

1. If the user activity were only queries, which access method and structure would minimize elapsed I/O time: sequential, indexed sequential, or in-

verted? The inverted file specifications are 8 item types, each of which has an average of 25 possible values. Plot elapsed I/O time vs. number of ''hits'' per query before answering the question.

2. When batch updates *and* queries are accounted for, which access method and structure would minimize elapsed I/O time? Plot elapsed I/O time vs. % batch update for 0 to 100%.

3. How are the results in 1 and 2 above sensitive to data block size? to index block size? to the number of ''hits'' in a query? to the type of interference for a shared disk vs. a dedicated disk?

Exercise B5. Response-time Reduction

A computer service division is currently in the process of acquiring on-line terminals, doubling the size of main memory to 1 megabyte, and upgrading the speed and capacity of its disk storage devices. One justification for the new hardware was the need for a 1-minute response for a specific set of file retrieval applications. Currently, the turnaround time in batch for the application is from 1 to 4 hours. The run time for the job, which is conjectured to be totally I/O bound, is approximately 4 minutes. Your task is to suggest alternative methods for reformatting the database to provide the promised support, outlining relative advantages and disadvantages of these alternatives.

The current application is depicted in Fig. B-1. It is designed to first parse an arbitrary record selection criteria, and then to read a sequential file of fixed length, formatted records, gathering desired statistics from qualified records. Because of stringent core limitations, the application was designed with a blocking factor of 5 and a single buffer region.

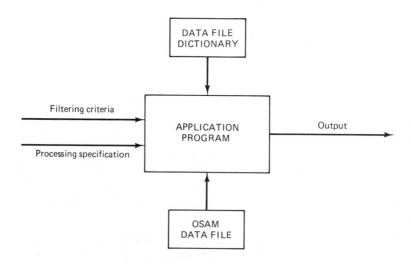

FIGURE B-1 Current application input.

Data Set Specification	
Logical records	30,000
Number of data items	200
Average value length	3
Logical record length	690
Identifier length (numeric)	6

Data Set Volatility	
Deletions	2,500/month
Modifications	none
Additions	2,500/month
(Currency of database is not critical, additions are inserted in batch once a month, and the oldest transactions are retired in a history tape.)	

Data set usage

Between 5 and 50 users per day gather summary statistics (such as counts or totals) from a specified subset of records (typically 0.1% to 10% of the total set). While arbitrary record selection criteria must be supported, in any given month 80% of record selection tends to concentrate on 5 to 10 specific attributes. Typically, 10 to 100 keys (i.e., boolean combinations of attribute–value range pairs) are actively used. The attributes of interest tend to change over the period of a year.

Hardware	Current Disk	New Disk	Current Tape
Rotation time	25 ms	17 ms	
Access			
Min.	25 ms	10 ms	start/stop 4 ms
Avg.	75 ms	16.7 ms	nonstop 3 ms
Char/track	7294	13,030	1600 bits/inch
Tracks/cyl	20	19	
Data transfer rate	312 kB/sec	806 kB/sec	320 kB/sec

	Maximum Bytes per Physical Block Keys	
Physical Blocks per Track	Current Disk	New Disk
1	7,294	13,030
2	3,521	6,447
3	2,298	4,253
4	1,693	3,156
5	1,332	2,498
6	1,092	2,059
7	921	1,745
8	793	1,510
9	694	1,327
10	615	1,181
11	550	1,061
12	496	962
13	450	877
14	411	805
15	377	742
16	347	687

With the new hardware assume enough channels, control units, and devices to make contention negligible. In addition, it will be possible to expand the application program core size by as much as 50K.

Areas for analysis

1. How long does it currently take to analyze the file?
2. How will the increased speed of the new device affect this time?
3. Compare this time with that required to analyze a history tape with 30,000 records.
4. How will an increase in either blocking factor or number of buffers affect these timings?
5. How can a multilist or inverted list organization be used to reduce response time? Which lists should be maintained, how will they be constructed, what should be used to "point to" a data record, and how will these pointers be translated? Discuss some options.

Exercise B6. Design of a record retrieval algorithm

Consider an on-line database of 100,000 150-character records which are to be stored on a 3330 disk facility at a cost of $0.50/track/month. Characteristics are given below. Individual data records will be retrieved from 600 on-line terminals using a six-digit record identifier. The retrieval rate will be 1 retrieval/terminal/minute, which is 10 retrievals/second, or 100 retrievals/record/month. All input/output time is charged at the rate of $0.02/second and delay in terminal response time is valued at $0.03/second.

Design an efficient record retrieval algorithm for this problem. Consider the use of an ISAM-type search as well as a hashing transformation. How would you do hashing if the identifiers were six-character alphabetic strings?

Hardware			Maximum Bytes per Physical Block	
Rotation time	16.7 ms	*Physical Blocks*		
Access		*per Track*	*3330*	
Min.	10 ms			
Avg.	30 ms	1	13,030	
Char/track	13,030	2	6,447	
Tracks/cyl	19	3	4,253	
Data transfer rate	806 kB/sec	4	3,156	
Hardware rec. addrs.	4 bytes	5	2,498	
		6	2,059	
		7	1,745	
		8	1,510	
		9	1,327	
		10	1,181	
		11	1,061	
		12	962	
		13	877	
		14	805	
		15	742	
		16	687	

Exercise B7

This design problem provides an opportunity to utilize the prescriptive taxonomy for file design suggested by Severance and Carlis (1977). Devise a database structure for the problem given below. Sections of the problem description cover: the file and record content, record updates, database retrievals, and storage hardware.

a. *File and record content*

An insurance company maintains an auto policy file which contains about 200,000 records, one for each auto policy issued. The file is stored on disk to permit on-line processing.

Policy record attributes can be classed into seven groups: policy, premium data, policyholder, automobile description, agent, claims, related company policies. The value of the policy number attribute is used as the record identifier. The claims segment of the policy is a repeating group of length 150 bytes. There is an average of two claims per policy. The average total record length is 468 bytes.

b. *Updates*

The growth of 6,000 policies per year is the net result of adding 1,000 new policies each month while retiring 500 existing policies. Each day 300 claims are processed; each requires a record update. An average of 80 record changes per day are initiated by customers (changing address, coverage, auto, etc.). Customer payments of quarterly billings arrive at a fairly constant rate of 16,000 per week.

c. *Retrievals*

Calls from agents and customers account for about 600 record retrievals per day. The 15-digit policy number is unknown in approximately one-third of the inquiries and the policyholder's phonetic name is used for retrieval. (The generation of a soundex code, a form of hashing, is explained below.) Management demands a daily sale and claims activity report and a weekly report for premium payments. Other reports are required infrequently and may be ignored here.

d. *Hardware (IBM 3330 Disk)*

Rotation time	16.7 ms
Access	
Min.	10 ms
Avg.	30 ms
Tracks/cyl	19
Data transfer rate	806 kB/sec
Hardware rec. addrs.	4 bytes
Track capacity	(See table for Exercise B6)

Soundex coding algorithm (Remington Rand)

1. Given any name, retain the first letter
2. Delete the following: A E I O U Y W H
3. Assign code numbers to the remaining letters

Code	Letters
1	B F P V
2	C G J K Q S X Z
3	D T
4	L
5	M N
6	R

4. Truncate or pad with "0" to bring to length of 4

Examples

Suggested steps in selecting a database design:

a. Determine the dominant retrieval activity and select an appropriate access path.
b. Select a strategy for maintenance.
c. If necessary, select secondary structures for other retrievals.
d. Select pointer types for supported structures.
e. Calculate total system space requirements.

Exercise B8

Frequently, Blue Cross subscribers make inquiries regarding their claims and membership without their Blue Cross Identification number. When this occurs, the clerk handling the inquiry must be able to obtain the subscriber's ID number. This is done by an inquiry transaction against an ALPHA database where the primary key is the subscriber's last name.

The current database implementation is acceptable with regard to inquiry response time but does not provide for daily updating. The database is reloaded on a monthly basis. Design a file access method (i.e., storage structure and search mechanism) that would not degrade inquiry response time but would allow for daily batch updating.

Processing Specifications

1. Inquiry only (4200/day)
   Be able to retrieve on
   a. Last name only (10%)
   b. Last name, first name (59%)
   c. Last name, street address (30%)
   d. Last name, first name, street address (1%)
2. Batch Update
   a. Updating will occur daily
      (1) 26 K adds/month

(2) 3,700 last name changes/month
(3) 19K address changes/month
(4) 2,300 first name changes/month
(5) 20K deletes/month

b. Reorganization can occur as needed
c. Deletes monthly

Data Items

Title	Length (chars)
Last name	15
First name	8
Middle initial	1
Address line 1	16
Address line 2	16
ID number	9
Last name suffix	3
	68

Distribution of Data Occurrences

Number of names	With this range of occurrences		Total occurrences in this range
85,420	1–	1	85,420
112,402	2–	100	1,011,839
1,711	100–	200	236,271
633	200–	300	154,435
320	300–	400	109,690
214	400–	500	95,960
146	500–	600	79,629
101	600–	700	64,894
63	700–	800	46,313
61	800–	900	51,789
47	900–	1,000	44,949
292	1,001–16,410		619,105
			2,600,294

Some Specific Extremes of the Distribution

Number of occurrences	First initial and last name	Surname totals
1,725	R. Smith	16,410 total Smiths
1,565	M. Smith	
1,482	J. Smith	
1,333	D. Smith	
1,217	E. Smith	
1,300	R. Johnson	11,350 total Johnsons
1,773	J. Sullivan	10,341 total Sullivans
1,660	M. Sullivan	
739	E. Sullivan	

Exercise B9

Apply the overflow models for hashing and indexed sequential and plot the degradation of retrieval time as a function of database growth due to insertions.

Exercise B10

Compare SPB*-tree and B*-tree performance in retrieval and update for separator length $= \frac{1}{2}$ key length (see Chapter 14).

Exercise B11

Derive an expression for (physical block) storage space for B*-tree and compare it with B-tree storage space.

Exercise B12

Determine the relationship between block size and the optimal clustering using Schkolnick's clustering method (see Chapter 11).

C   LIST OF VARIABLES

ANC	Average number of child record occurrences per parent
BA	Number of bucket accesses
BF	Blocking factor
BKS	Block size (bytes)
BLKPC	Number of physical blocks per cylinder
BLKPT	Number of physical blocks per track
BLKSTOR	Total block storage in a database (bytes)
BNODES	Number of branch nodes in a B-tree
BOND	Nearest-neighbor bond strength
BOVHD	Block overhead (bytes)
BPT	Number of bytes per track (maximum track size)
C	Search cost
CA	Cost of a single block access
CCK	Cost of a CHANGE key operation
CCNK	Cost of a CHANGE nonkey operation
CD	Cost of a DELETE operation
CI	Cost of an INSERT operation
CIO	I/O processing cost
COMMDELAY	Expected total communication delay
COMPR	Compression ratio
CPD	Number of usable cylinders per disk

CPU. BSEARCH	CPU time for binary search
CPU. EXCH	CPU time to execute a channel program for a read or write I/O operation
CPU. MERGE (c,a)	CPU time to merge c ordered lists with a elements in each
CPU.1	CPU time to make one comparison between two data item values
CPU. SORT(a)	CPU time to sort a list of a elements
CPU. TEST	CPU time for an inclusion test in a query
CPU. USEARCH	CPU time for a sequential search of an unordered list
CR	Cost of all retrieval operations
CS	Cost of storage space (per byte)
CSORT	Cost of a sort procedure
CT	Cost of data transfer (per byte)
CU	Cost of all update operations
D	Expected distance between record occurrences (in clustering algorithms)
DSTOR	Data storage space (bytes)
EBF	Effective blocking factor
EBKS	Effective block size
ESRS	Expected stored record size over all record types in a database
F	Frequency of execution of a database application
FCK	Frequency of CHANGE key operations
FCNK	Frequency of CHANGE nonkey operations
FD	Frequency of DELETE operations
FGS	Frequency of GET SOME operation
FI	Frequency of DELETE operations
IBNODES	Number of index branch nodes in a TRIE index
INODES	Number of index nodes in a doubly chained tree
IS	Item size (bytes)
KS	Key (item) size (bytes)
LEN	Number of nodes to be accessed at a particular index level (doubly chained tree)
LF	Loading factor
LNODES	Number of leaf nodes in a B-tree
LRA	Logical record accesses

LRAB	Logical record accesses in a bucket search
MAXSK	Maximum seek distance over CPD-1 cylinders
MINSK	Minimum seek time to traverse one cylinder
NB	Number of buckets in a random access file
NBIV	Expected number of blocks containing data records with a particular item value
NBLK	Number of blocks necessary to contain a database; number of blocks of a given size in the database
NBLKC	Number of blocks in the cylinder index
NBLKOV	Number of physical blocks allocated to the overflow area
NBLKT	Number of blocks in the track indexes
NBUF	Number of buffers allocated to an application
NCYL	Number of contiguous disk cylinders needed to store a database
NIL	Number of index levels in an access method
NIT	Number of item types in the database
NIV	Number of occurrences of particular item type in the database; average number of item values per item type
NPTR	Average number of pointers stored in a record
NR	Number of records in a file or database
NREC	Number of occurrences of a record
NRIV	Expected number of records containing a particular item value
NTB	Number of target blocks containing the NTR target records in a query
NTR	Number of target records in a query
NTRK	Number of tracks needed to contain a database
NVAL	Number of values of an item type required by an application
OVFLCH	Expected overflow chain length
OVFLPR	Probability of bucket overflow
OVPBA	Overflow physical block accesses
P	Probability of occurrence of an event
PBA	Physical block access
PMS	Probability that the next random block requested is already in a buffer in main storage
PRDEL	Probability that an old key value must be deleted from the index

PRI	Probability that a bucket will contain at least i records
PRINS	Probability that a new key value must be added to the index
PRMV	Probability that a data record must be moved to a new block
PS	Pointer size (bytes)
PTRSTOR	Pointer storage space (bytes)
R	Cost of reorganization
RECSIZE	Average size of a logical record (bytes)
REDUC	Expected data size reduction due to compression
ROT	Full rotation time for disk
ROVHD	Record overhead (bytes)
RPB	Average number of stored records per bucket
RPBD	Number of records per batch delete
RPBI	Number of records per batch insertion
RPBR	Number of records per batch retrieval
RSPB	Record slots per bucket
S	Similarity measure
SDIST	Seek distance (on disk)
SEEK(CPD)	Expected seek time over the entire disk of CPD cylinders
SEEK(NCYL)	Expected seek time over a database of NCYL contiguous cylinders
SRS	Stored record size
SRSTOR	Total storage due to stored records
TC	Total processing cost of a database (search cost plus re-organization cost)
TCOST	Total cost to execute a sequence of applications on a database
TCPU	Total CPU time
TCPUB	Expected CPU time to process data in a physical block
TFBA	Expected time to transfer a sequentially accessed physical block from disk to main storage
TIO	I/O service time, in seconds
TPC	Number of usable tracks per cylinder
TR	Data transfer rate to/from disk (bytes per second)
TRBA	Expected time to access and transfer a randomly accessed physical block from disk to main storage
TRESP	Response time

TRKSTOR	Track storage space needed to contain a database (bytes)
TRVOL	Transport volume (bytes)
TSBA	Expected time to access and transfer a sequentially accessed physical block from disk to main storage
UKV	Number of unique key value combinations in records in a doubly chained tree
USED	Actual used space in a block
V	Number of possible character values in an alphabet
WAIT	Expected total wait time in resource queues, including lockout delays

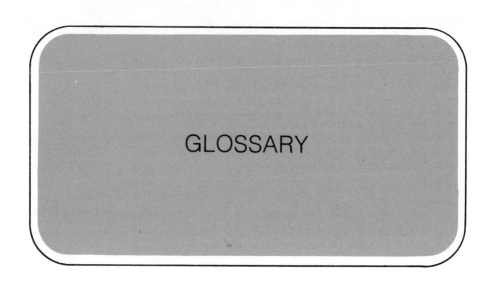

GLOSSARY

Accession list. A physical sequential list of pointers to records containing identical values for a particular key item.

Access method. A technique that provides storage and retrieval capabilities for data stored on physical devices, normally secondary storage.

Access path length. The number of entity occurrences or logical records accessed to execute a given database application.

Access time. The elapsed time between invoking a command to access some data and the actual availability of the data for processing.

Ad hoc query. A query whose exact specifications (format, key values, and target record volume) are not known in advance.

Aggregation. An abstraction in which a relationship between objects is regarded as a higher-level object.

Analysis and/or design tool (ADT). Manual or automatic database design tool.

Anomalies (add, delete, update). Three kinds of irregularities due to a relation not being in normal form. It could involve loss of information about a relationship between data items if the last occurrence of that relationship is deleted.

ANSI/SPARC model. Architecture for a database system represented by three levels of schemas (external, conceptual, internal), based on the ANSI/X3/SPARC study group on DBMSs 1975 report, attempting to define standards for database systems. The external schema is based on the application programmer's view, the conceptual schema is a higher-level view of all records in the database, and the internal schema is the stored data view [Date, 1975].

Area. A database subdivision; a named portion of the total addressable physical space in which the database is stored; the area (CODASYL) may contain occurrences of different records, sets, or parts of sets, as defined by the database administrator.

Atomic condition. The basic qualification condition in a query. It has the form name $\{ < = > \}$ value, where name is an item type and value is an item value.

Attribute. Descriptive information about an entity that might serve as an identifier for an entity. In a stored record an attribute is an item type, which can be used as a primary key, secondary key, or a nonkey.

Attribute relationship. An unqualified ownership between attributes which belong to the same entity or entity relationship.

Audit trail. A log in some journal of all changes made to the database.

AVL tree. A height-balanced tree in which the height of its left and right subtrees differ by at most 1.

Balanced tree. A tree is considered balanced when the difference in height between the root and any two leaves (terminal nodes) is at most 1.

Binary search. A method of searching a physical sequential file. The procedure involves selecting the upper or lower half based upon an examination of its midpoint value. The portion selected is then similarly halved, and so on until the required item is found.

Binary search tree. A binary tree in which each node is labeled with a distinct name and is in lexicographic order, that is, for any node i, the names of nodes in its left subtree lexicographically precede node i and the names of nodes in its right subtree.

Blocking factor. The number of logical records per physical block.

Block index. An ordered index of primary key values, where each value represents the highest key value of all records in a given block. Associated with each key value in the index is a pointer to that block. This forms the basis for the indexed sequential access method.

Block size. The number of bytes per block.

B-tree. A generalization of a binary tree in which two or more branches may be taken from each node.

B*-tree. A variant of the B-tree in which all the keys and associated data reside in the leaf nodes and are accessed via a B-tree index.

Bucket. An area of storage that may contain more than one record and which is referred to as a whole by some addressing technique. The basic unit of storage addressing used by hashing (random or calc) functions.

Calc chain (CODASYL). A linked list of logical records that hash (calc) to the same physical block. This allows for keeping track of overflow records.

Candidate key. Items such that the instances of those items in a group are in one-to-one correspondence to an instance of the entity; an identifier.

Cardinality (of a relation). The number of tuples in a relation.

Cellular inverted. An inverted organization in which accession list entries point to physical blocks that contain at least one record that meets the key value criterion.

Cellular multilist. A multilist organization in which the pointers do not go from record to record, but only between physical blocks that contain at least one record that meets the key value criterion.

Certification (validation). Error checking of database creation data, before and after database creation. Tests for proper format, value range, uniqueness of key field, and number of occurrences are included.

Chain. A linked list in which the last node has a null link field, or pointer; it may be singly or doubly linked.

Clustering. The placement of data near related data to improve efficiency of access. Logical clustering places certain items together in records; physical clustering places the same or different record types together in blocks, areas, or storage devices.

Coalesced chaining. A method of chaining for hashing that maintains a global free space list for all the addressable buckets. Each bucket has its own chain, but the next chain entry may reside in any available bucket designated by the free space list head pointer.

CODASYL DBTG. Data Base Task Group, a special committee of CODASYL formed in the late 1960s to propose a standard for modern database management systems.

Collision. The transformation of a key value to a physical address that is already occupied.

Combined index. An index in which each entry consists of a concatenation of key item values of different item types. A fully combined index contains positions (and values) for all item types in the records, and a partially combined index only contains positions for a subset of the item types in the records.

Compound indexing. Multiple fully combined indexes, each based on a different order of item types so that each possible order is represented.

Compression. Data item encoding in which the size of the data is reduced from the normal representation method without destroying any information content.

Concatenation. The consolidation of two less-than-half-filled nodes in a B-tree to a single node, particularly upon deletion of a key.

Conceptual design. Analysis of formally specified processing-independent information requirements and the formulation of a DBMS-independent information structure, or conceptual schema, that accurately models the real-world organization and its important data elements and relationships.

Conceptual schema (ANSI/SPARC). The highest-level user view of data, usually represented by entities and relationships (i.e., an information structure).

Concurrent reorganization. A reorganization strategy in which users have access to the reorganized portion of the database while one or more reorganization processes are modifying it.

Conjunct. A record condition, a conjunction (AND function) of item conditions in a query. A conjunctive query is any query of Boolean form of conjunctions and disjunctions of data elements.

Consistency. A property of databases, particularly those with duplicate data and multiple users, such that at any instant in time the database will respond with the same result to a query for all users. To maintain consistency when updating occurs, read operations are restricted from the changing data until all copies are updated properly.

Containment. The placement of repeating groups within logical records, the only recourse available with flat file organizations.

Currency. Method of saving the addresses of the most recently accessed record occurrences of each type or set occurrences (in CODASYL) of each type (i.e., owner record, etc.) so that they can be quickly retrieved if database navigation is to be continued from one or more of those points at a later time.

Data. Something that is either known from being experientially encountered or from being admitted or assumed for specific purposes; a fact or principle granted; something upon which an inference or an argument is based or from which an intellectual system of any sort is constructed.

Database. A computerized collection of stored operational data that serves the needs of multiple users within an organization or some defined subset of the organization.

Database administrator (DBA). An individual, possibly aided by a staff, who manages the organization's database resource over the life cycle of database applications.

Database design. The process of developing an implementable database structure from user requirements.

Database design methodology. A collection of tools and techniques employed within an organizational framework that can be consistently applied to successive database structure development projects.

Database key. A unique identifier which is associated with every record occurrence in the database.

Database management system (DBMS). A generalized tool for manipulating large databases; it is made available through special software for the interrogation, maintenance, and analysis of data. Its interfaces generally provide a broad range of language to aid all users—from clerk to data administrator.

Database system. The combination of DBMS software, applications software, database, and operating system–hardware environment brought together to provide information services for users.

Database system life cycle. The major steps in the process of designing, implementing, and reorganizing a database and its application software.

Data definition. Generally consists of a statement of the names of elements, their properties (such as character or numerical type), and their relationship to other elements (including complex grouping) that make up the database.

Data definition language (DDL). A language for defining a data model together with (part of) its mapping to storage; a subschema DDL is a language for defining a data submodel.

Data dictionary. A catalog of all data elements in a database, giving their definition, format, source, and usage; frequently computer-based.

Data element. A primitive data object in the real world; an entity.

Data independence. The ability to modify the database structure without having to revise application programs that access that database. Logical data independence implies the ability to change the logical database structure (implementation schema) without affecting application programs, and physical data independence implies the ability to change physical structure without affecting application programs.

Data item. The smallest unit of data that has meaning in describing information; the smallest unit of named data.

Data manipulation language (DML). The language that the programmer uses to load, access, and update a database.

Data model. A representation of data and its interrelationships which describes ideas about the real world. A data model may present either a conceptual view or an implementation view of data.

Data translation. The modification of the physical (and sometimes logical) representation of data used in one hardware/software environment so that it is compatible with a different hardware/software environment.

Data volume. The number of occurrences of each record type currently stored in the database.

Dedicated device. A secondary storage device (disk) dedicated to a single-user application, thus allowing the application to be designed to run efficiently, taking advantage of the physical characteristics of the device.

Designer. A software package that produces either a feasible database structure (logical or physical), given some requirements, or produces a database structure that optimizes on some clearly defined measure or measures.

Design review. A walkthrough of the current design specifications for a database structure. It is often conducted in conjunction with a review of the applications software for a database system.

Design tool. Any analytical, heuristic, or procedural technique relevant to database design that is implementable in software.

DIAM model. The data-independent accessing model is a formal conception of data in a DBMS based on a four-level architecture from a logical (entity) model to a physical device model.

Direct access method. A method for mapping every possible value of a primary key identifier to a unique position in storage. Tends to be high on storage overhead, but quite useful for entry-point access when there are very few primary key values.

Displacement. The number of buckets accessed in a linear probe before a new record can be stored.

Distributed database. A single database partitioned into disjoint (or redundant and overlapping) subunits at separate locations.

Domain. The collection of data items (fields) of the same type in a relation.

Doubly chained tree. An inverted file organization in which the index hierarchy consists of one level for each key item type, the index entries consist of key item values, and the data records do not contain the key item values used to index them.

Entity. A primitive data object that represents elements of the real world (persons, places, things).

Entity–attribute relationship. A functional dependency between an entity and one of its attributes.

Entity relationship. The property of qualified or unqualified ownership between entities of different type.

Evaluator. A software package that evaluates a given database structure (logical or physical) in terms of one or more clearly defined performance measures.

Extent. A contiguous area of data storage.

External schema (ANSI-SPARC). The application programmer view of data, usually represented in an implementation schema, a logical database structure.

False drop. A record that appears to satisfy a query, based on index pointers to a block, but is not a target record of that query.

Field. An item type (IMS).

Filial set. The set of all existing child nodes for a parent node.

File. A set of similarly constructed stored records of a single type and either fixed or variable size.

File organization. A representation of data records that make up a file that shows the interrecord relationships and accounts for physical parameters such as pointers and indices.

Flat file. A physical sequential structure, a file.

Full functional dependence. Attribute Y is fully functionally dependent on attribute X if it is functionally dependent on X and not functionally dependent on any subset of X (X must be composite).

Full index. A file organization in which an index entry is necessary for each individual record occurrence in the file. An index entry consists of a primary key value and a pointer to the record containing that value. Normally, this method is too high on storage overhead to be practical, except for small files. It is also known as the indexed random organization.

Fully concatenated key (IMS). The concatenation of the sequence field values of all segments in the hierarchical path from the root down to the retrieved segment.

Functional dependency (FD). Given a relation R, a set of attributes B of relation R is functionally dependent on a set of attributes A if, at every instant of time, each A value in R is associated with only one B value.

Generalization. An abstraction in which a set of similar objects is regarded as a generic object.

Global information structure. An efficient consolidation of two or more local information structures that minimizes redundancy and record access path length.

Hashing. An access method that directly addresses data by transforming, through a randomization function, a key value into a relative or absolute physical address.

Hierarchical order (or sequence). For an IMS database, it is the sequence of segment occurrences defined by ascending values of the hierarchical sequence key, which consists of the sequence field value for that segment, prefixed with the type code for that segment, prefixed with hierarchical sequence key value of its parent, if any.

Hit ratio. The ratio of the number of records in the file or database that satisfy a query to the total number of records in the file or database.

Identifier. An attribute that uniquely defines each occurrence of some real-world entity; an item type that uniquely identifies occurrences of a particular record type (i.e., a primary key).

Implementation design. The phase of database design that transforms and refines a conceptual schema into a DBMS-processible schema.

Index. A table containing information on records or data items and their location.

Indexed random. Full index.

Indexed sequential access method. An access method associated with an ordered sequential file that uses a hierarchy of block indexes, each ordered by primary key values (same way the data are ordered), to reduce the access time for randomly requested records while maintaining efficiency for sequential processing. When overflow occurs due to database additions, the efficiency goes down quickly.

Information. Knowledge communicated by others or obtained from investigation, study, or instruction; knowledge gained from data [Webster's, 1974].

Information processing system. A computer system and its collection of user programs and data.

Information requirements. Process-independent information requirements are requirements that certain types of data be represented in the database to represent the organization accurately, not necessarily to satisfy the current applications, integrity, and security constraints. Process-dependent requirements include the efficient and correct execution of application programs using the final database structure.

Information structure. Diagram of primitive data objects or entities and their relationships that is totally independent of DBMS characteristics. Entities are normally represented by boxes and relationships by arcs or arrows.

Information structure perspective (ISP). Information describing the natural and conceptual relationships of all data in the database and not bound to any applications; process-independent information.

Integrity. A database is defined to have the integrity property when it satisfies data value (range) constraints and preserves this property under all modifications of the database.

Internal schema (ANSI-SPARC). The physical structure of data; the system view of data as they actually appear in the storage media, usually represented in a storage structure.

Inverted file. A file organization that permits fast searching for general queries based on secondary key item values. It consists of a multiple-level index structure plus a collection of accession lists pointing to data that meet specific key item value criteria. A partially inverted file is inverted on (has index entries for) some item types, and a fully inverted file is inverted on all item types.

I/O time. The access time to retrieve data from secondary storage to main storage; includes the data transfer time.

Item type. A data item type or field. The basic unit of data that describes an entity; the basic component of a record.

Item value. A value of an item in a record occurrence.

Key. A data item used to identify or locate a record. Organization in which stored record occurrences are accessed via a chain (linked list). Logical ordering may or may not be maintained in the chain.

Loading factor. A fraction specifying the maximum proportion of usable space in a physical block after block overhead is accounted for.

Local information structure. An information structure that satisfies the basic processing requirement for individual application.

Logical database structure. A DBMS-processable schema or data definition which results from implementation design.

M : N relationship. Two entities *A* and *B* are *M : N* related if elements of *A* are associated with several elements of *B* and also elements of *B* are associated with several elements of *A*.

Multilist file. A collection of linked sequential structures (linked lists), each consisting of stored records containing the same value for a particular item type. Typically, the lists are indexed to permit rapid access to records related by secondary key values.

Network structure. A relationship between records (or other groupings) in which a child record can have more than one parent record.

Normalization. The decomposition of complex data structures into a set of one or more flat files (relations); analysis of functional dependencies is necessary to formulate the different levels of normalization (i.e., normal forms).

Occurrence. An individual instance of an entity, record, item, CODASYL set, and so on, containing a set of values for its constituent parts.

Overflow area. A physical extent in which data are placed when there is no available space in the primary data area. Overflow areas may be allocated within stored records, physical blocks, disk tracks, or disk cylinders.

Percent fill. A parameter (0 to 100%) that specifies how much each physical block is to be allocated for data at the initial load of the file or database. It allows for subsequent database growth such that new records that are to be inserted in a particular order or clustered near each other reside in their proper block without having to resort to overflow.

Physical block accesses (PBAs). The total number of physical blocks accessed to execute a database application. Sequential block accesses (sba) on disk incur a rotational delay plus transfer time (I/O time); random or pointer block accesses (rba) incur an additional average seek delay.

Physical database. A collection of interrelated data stored as one or more types of stored record.

Physical database structure. Stored record format, logical and physical ordering of stored records, access paths, and device allocation for a multiple-record-type database.

Physical sequential organization. A file or physical database organization in which records are stored in contiguous locations so that logical and physical ordering coincide.

Pointer. An indicator that leads to a given record from another location in the database; a pointer may be a machine address, a relative record address, or a symbolic identifier of a record.

Pointer array. A list of pointers to records meeting a specific criterion; an accession list.

Populating (a database). Initial loading of data into the database.

Primary key. A key that uniquely identifies a record.

Processing frequency. The frequency at which an individual query or update transaction (database application) is estimated to be executed.

Processing volume. The combination of processing frequency and data volume.

Program translation. Modification of source program code written originally to manipulate data in one hardware/software environment, so that it can do the equivalent functions on the translated data when running in a new hardware/software environment.

Protocol. Rules for software communication among nodes in a computer network.

Query. A retrieval request for specific data from a database, often generalized in terms of Boolean functions consisting of logical conjunctions (AND) and disjunctions (OR).

Query language. A high-level data manipulation language for interacting with the file or database.

Random access method. Access method utilizing a hashing function to derive record addresses from key item values.

Random processing. The combination of database organization and target record selection by user applications that result in a random target record physical location with respect to the previous record accessed.

Record. A named collection of related data items treated as a unit by an application program.

Record clustering. The clustering of stored records in a collection of contiguous extents.

Record segmentation. Record partitioning; the allocation of individual data items in a stored record to separate physical extents, possibly on different physical devices.

Recovery. The designed capability of a DBMS to restore the integrity (correct state) of a database following any type of system failure.

Redundancy. Duplication of data items and/or records.

Reformatting. Physical reorganization of data (e.g., changing character representation, word length, or purging overflow records back into the primary data area).

Relation. A flat file or table; a file whose records (called tuples) cannot have repeating groups.

Relational algebra. A collection of data manipulation operations that operate on one or more relations as its operands and produces a relation as its result.

Relationship. An association between occurrences of primitive or aggregated data objects (entities or records) (e.g., $1 : 1$, $1 : m$, $m : n$).

Reorganization. The process of changing the conceptual, implementation (logical), or physical structure of a database. The change of a logical structure is called restructuring, and the change of a physical structure is called reformatting.

Repeating group. A named collection of data items that has a variable number of occurrences.

Response time. The total time elapsed between the statement of a database query on the computer until the query is completed and the results displayed.

Restructuring. Logical reorganization of data (e.g., schema redesign). A restructurer is a software package that reorganizes record occurrences to be compatible with a modified schema.

Scatter table. A pointer array associated with a hashing function that allows one level of indirection to data to be randomly accessed, and thus facilitates flexibility in the physical ordering of the data areas.

Schema. A diagram or formal definition of logical database structure. In CODASYL systems a schema consists of data definition language entries.

Search key. The key or identifier used in a query upon which data are searched. A complete description of all record types, set types, data item types as they exist in the database. Many DBMS implementations include physical structure in their schemas; however, we refer to (logical or implementation) schema as separate from the physical schema in the analysis.

Search mechanism. An algorithm that defines a specific access path to be taken in a database structure and traverses that access path for transactions that invoke it.

Secondary access method. A collection of techniques designed to access efficiently all the target records associated with a set of stated secondary key values in a query.

Secondary data set group (IMS). A physical clustering of segments that does not contain the root segment (IMS).

Secondary key. An attribute or item type that is used to index records but does not necessarily uniquely identify those records (i.e., the same key value can appear in more than one record occurrence).

Security. The protection of data against intentional or unintentional disclosure, modification, or loss.

Segment (IMS). A named collection of data containing one or more fields; a record.

Sequential access method. The sequential processing of a sequential file.

Sequential file. A file stored in contiguous physical addresses.

Set (CODASYL). A relationship; a named collection of parent and child record types.

Shared device. Secondary storage device used in a multiuser environment; thus experiences possible randomization of addresses for retrieval due to interference. For example, processing a sequential application on a shared disk could result in a random seek of the disk arm for every physical block accessed.

Storage structure. Describes the way data are physically stored in the system: pointers, character representations, floating point, blocking, access method, and so on.

Stored record. A collection of related data items that correspond to one or more logical records and includes all necessary pointers, record length and other overhead data, and coding schemes for character representation.

Subschema. Definition of an individual user (programmer) view of data; possibly a subset of the schema.

Target record. A record that satisfies the qualification conditions of a query.

Transaction. A database application program; typically an update program.

Transport volume. The total number of bytes transferred to satisfy (execute) a database application.

Trie structure. A random access method based on individual character values in the primary key; it utilizes a multiway tree structure at each level, corresponding to the many possible values of character $i + 1$, given a particular value of character i.

Unnormalized relation. A relation that is not in first normal form.

Update. Any modification of a database, whether via additions, deletions, or changes to data.

Usage perspective (UP). Information describing the processing requirements; process-dependent information.

View integration. Consolidation of individual users' requirements and representation of those requirements in a common form. It may or may not be done separately for process-independent and process-dependent requirements.

Virtual field (or record). A field or record that appears to be but is not physically stored; rather, it is formulated physically when its value is requested by an application program. It is constructed or derived from existing physical data.

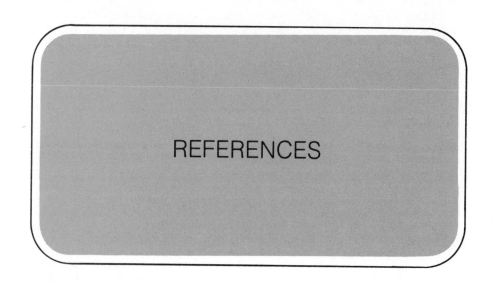

REFERENCES

AANSTAD, P. S., SKYLSTAD, G., AND SOLVBERG, A., "CASCADE—A Computer-Based Documentation System," *Computer-Aided Information Systems, Analysis and Design*, J. A. Bubenko, B. Langefors, and A. Solvberg, eds., Lund, Sweden, 1972, pp. 93–112.

ACM/NBS, "Data Base Directions: The Next Steps," NBS/ACM Workshop, J. Berg, ed., NBS Spec. Pub 451, U.S. Dept. of Commerce, Washington, DC, 1976.

ADELSON-VELSKII, G. M., AND LANDIS, Y. M., "An Algorithm for the Organization of Information," *Dokl. Akad, Nauk SSSR* 146 (1962), pp. 263–66 (in Russian). English translation: *Sov. Math. Dokl.* 3(1962), pp. 1259–62.

AHO, A. V., AND ULLMAN, J. D., "Optimal Partial-Match Retrieval When Fields Are Independently Specified," *ACM TODS* 4,2(June 1979), pp. 168–79.

AIGNER, M., *Combinatorial Theory*, Springer-Verlag, New York, 1979, p. 92.

ALFORD, M. W., "A Requirements Engineering Methodology for Real-Time Processing Requirements," *IEEE Trans. Softw. Eng.* SE-3, 1(1977), pp. 60–69.

ANDERSON, H. D., AND BERRA, P. B., "Minimum Cost Selection of Secondary Indexes for Formatted Files," *ACM Trans. Database Syst.* 2,1(1977), pp. 68–90.

ANSI/X3/SPARC/STUDY GROUP-DATABASE MANAGEMENT SYSTEMS, "The ANSI/X3/SPARC DBMS Framework," *Inf. Syst.* 3,3(1978), pp. 173–91.

ARONSON, J., "Data Compression: A Comparison of Methods," in U.S. Dept. of Commerce, Washington, DC, *Computer Science and Technology*, NBS Spec. Publ. 500–12, June 1977, 31 pp.

ASCHIM, F., "Some Design and Analysis Tools for Design of Databases for Database Oriented Information Systems," Central Institute for Industrial Research, Oslo, Norway, Feb. 1975.

ASHANY, R., "Application of Sparse Matrix Techniques to Search, Retrieval, Classification and Relationship Analysis in Large Database Systems," *Proc. 4th Int. Conf. Very Large Data Bases* (ACM), 1978, pp. 499–516.

ASTRAHAN, M. M., AND CHAMBERLIN, D. D., "Implementation of a Structured English Query Language," *Commun. ACM* 18,10(Oct. 1975), pp. 580–88.

ASTRAHAN, M. M., et al., "System R: Relational Approach to Database Management," *ACM TODS*, 1,2(1976), pp. 97–137.

BABAD, J. M., "A Record and File Partitioning Model," *Commun. ACM* 20,1(Jan. 1977), pp. 22–31.

BACH, T. J., COGUEN, N. H., AND KAPLAN, M. M., "The ADAPT System: A

Generalized Approach towards Data Conversion," *Proc. 5th Int. Conf. Very Large Data Bases* (ACM), 1979, pp. 183–93.

BACHMAN, C. W., "Data Structure Diagrams," *Database* 1,2(1969), pp. 4–10.

BACHMAN, C. W., "The Evolution of Storage Structures," *Commun. ACM* 15,7(1972), pp. 628–34.

BACHMAN, C. W., "Implementation Techniques for Data Structure Sets," in *Data Base Management Systems,* D. A. Jardine, ed., North-Holland, Amsterdam, 1974.

BACHMAN, C. W., AND DAYA, M., "The Role Concept in Data Models," *Proc. 3rd Int. Conf. Very Large Data Bases* (ACM), 1977, pp. 464–76.

BAYER, R., "Symmetric Binary B-trees: Data Structure and Maintenance Algorithms," *Acta Inf.* 1,4(1972), pp. 290–306.

BAYER, R., AND MCCREIGHT, E., "Organization and Maintenance of Large Ordered Indexes," *Acta Inf.* 1,3(1972), pp. 173–89.

BAYER, R., AND SCHKOLNICK, M., "Concurrency of Operations on B-Trees," *Acta Inf.* 9,1(1977), pp. 1–21.

BAYER, R., AND UNTERAUER, K., "Prefix B-trees," *ACM TODS* 2,1(Mar. 1977), pp. 11–26.

BELFORD, G., "Dynamic Data Clustering," Research in Data Management and Resource Sharing, University of Illinois at Urbana-Champaign, May 1975.

BELL, T. E., BIXLER, D. C., AND DYER, M. E., "An Extendable Approach to Computer-Aided Software Requirements Engineering." *IEEE Trans. Softw. Eng.* SE-3,1(1977), pp. 49–60.

BENTLEY, J. L., AND FRIEDMAN, J. H., "Data Structures for Range Searching," *ACM Comp. Surv.* 11,4(Dec. 1979), pp. 397–409.

BERELIAN, E., AND IRANI, K. B., "Evaluation and Optimization," *Proc. 3rd Int. Conf. Very Large Data Bases* (ACM), 1977, pp. 545–55.

BERNSTEIN, P. A., "Synthesizing Third Normal Form Relations from Functional Dependencies," *ACM Trans. Database Syst.* 1,4(1976), pp. 277–98.

BERNSTEIN, P. A., AND GOODMAN, N., "Concurrency Control in Distributed Database Systems," ACM *Comput. Surv.* 13,2(1981), pp. 185–221.

BERNSTEIN, P. A., SWENSON, J. R., AND TSICHRITZIS, D. C., "A Unified Approach to Functional Dependencies and Relations," *Proc. ACM-SIGMOD Int. Conf. Manage. Data* (ACM), 1975, pp. 237–45.

BERNSTEIN, P. A., SHIPMAN, D. W., AND WONG, W. S., "Formal Aspects of Serializability in Database Concurrency Control," *IEEE Trans. Softw. Eng.* SE-5,3(1979), pp. 203–16.

BERNSTEIN, P. A., SHIPMAN, D. W., AND ROTHNIE, J. B., "Concurrency Control in a System for Distributed Databases, (SDD-1)," *ACM TODS* 5,1(1980), pp. 18–51.

BIRSS, E. W., AND FRY, J. P., "Generalized Software for Translating Data," *Proc. 1976 Nat. Comput. Conf.* AFIPS Press, Arlington, VA, 1976, pp. 889–99.

BLASGEN, M. W., AND ESWARAN, K. P., "Storage Access in Relational Data Bases," *IBM Syst. J.* 4(1977), pp. 363–77.

BLIER, R., AND VORKAUS, A., "File Organization in the SDC Time Shared Data Management (TDMS) System," *Proc. IFIP Congr.,* 1968, pp. F92–F97.

BLOOM, B. H., "Space/Time Trade-offs in Hash Coding with Allowable Errors," *Commun. ACM* 13,7(July 1970), pp. 422–26.

BOEHM, B. W., "Software and Its Impact: A Quantitative Assessment," *Datamation,* May 1973, pp. 48–59.

BOEHM, B. W., "Software Engineering," TRW Tech. Rep. TRW-SS-76-98, Oct. 1976, 40 pp.

BOLOUR, A., "Optimality Properties of Multiple Key Hashing Functions," *J. ACM* 26,2(Apr. 1979), pp. 196–210.

BRINCH HANSEN, P., *Operating System Principles,* Prentice-Hall, Englewood Cliffs, NJ, 1973, pp. 55–131.

BRITISH COMPUTER SOCIETY, "Data Dictionary Systems Working Party," *Data Base* 9,2(1977) and *SIGMOD Record* 9,4(1977), p. 24.

BROWN, L., "Data Base Review Methodology and IMS On-Line Performance Guidelines," Data Systems Center, University of Michigan, Ann Arbor, MI, Mar. 1977.

BUBENKO, J. A., "IAM: An Inferential Abstract Modeling Approach to Design of Conceptual Schema," *Proc. ACM/SIGMOD Int. Conf. Manage. Data* (ACM), 1977a, pp. 62–74.

BUBENKO, J. A., "IAM: Inferential Abstract Modeling—An Approach to Design of Information Models for Large Shared Data Bases," IBM Res. Rep. No. RC6343 (27297), Jan. 4, 1977b, 79 pp.

BUBENKO, J. A., "Validity and Verification Aspects of Information Modeling," *Proc. 3rd Int. Conf. Very Large Data Bases,* Tokyo, (ACM), 1977c, pp. 556–65.

BUBENKO, J., BERILD, S., LINDENCRONA-OHLIN, E. AND NACHMENS, S. A., "From Information Requirements to DBTG Data Structures," *Proc. ACM/SIGMOD/SIGPLAN Conf. Data: Abstraction, Definition and Structure* (ACM), 1976, pp. 73–85.

BUCHHOLZ, W., "File Organization and Addressing," *IBM Syst. J.* 2(June 1963), pp. 86–111.

BURKHARD, W. A., "Hashing and Trie Algorithms for Partial-Match Retrieval," *ACM TODS* 1,2(June 1976), pp. 175–87.

BURKHARD, W. A., "Partial-Match Hash Coding: Benefits of Redundancy," *ACM TODS* 4,2(June 1979), pp. 228–39.

BURROUGHS CORPORATION, "B6700/B7700 DMS II Data and Structure Definition Language (DASDL) Reference Manual," Burroughs, Corp., Detroit, MI, 1974.

CAINE, S. H., AND GORDON, E. K., "PDL: A Tool for Software Design," *Proc. 1975 Natl. Comput. Conf.* (AFIPS), Vol. 44, AFIPS Press, Montvale, NJ, 1975, pp. 271–276.

CANNING, R. G., "The Data Administrator Function," *EDP Anal.* 10,11(Nov. 1972).

CANNING, R. G., "The Data Dictionary/Directory Function," *EDP Anal.* 12,10(1974).

CANNING, R. G., "Getting the Requirements Right," *EDP Anal.* 15,7(1977).

CANNING, R. G., "Installing a Data Dictionary," *EDP Anal.* 16,1(1978).

CARDENAS, A. F., "Evaluation and Selection of File Organization—A Model and System," *Commun. ACM* 16,9(1973), pp. 540–48.

CARDENAS, A. F., "Analysis and Performance of Inverted Data Base Structures," *Commun. ACM* 13,5(1975), pp. 253–64.

CARDENAS, A. F., *Data Base Management Systems,* Allyn and Bacon, Boston, 1979.

CARDENAS, A. F., AND SAGAMANG, J. P., "Doubly-Chained Tree Data Base Organization—Analysis and Design Strategies," *Comput. J.* 20,1(1977), pp. 15–26.

CASEY, R. B., "Allocation of Copies of a File in an Information Network," *Proc. AFIPS Spring Joint Comput. Conf.,* Vol. 40, AFIPS Press, Arlington, VA, 1972, pp. 617–25.

CASEY, R. G., "Design of Tree Networks for Distributed Data," *AFIPS NCC Proc.* 42(1973a), pp. 251–57.

CASEY, R. G., "Design of Tree Structures for Efficient Querying," *Commun. ACM* 16(1973b), pp. 549–56.

CHAMBERLIN, D., "Relational Data-Base Management Systems," *Comput. Surv.* 8,1(1976), pp. 43–66.

CHAMBERLIN, D. D., AND BOYCE, R. F., "Sequel: A Structured English Query Language," *Proc. 1974 ACM SIGFIDET Workshop,* Apr. 1974, pp. 249–64.

CHANDY, K. M., BROWN, J. C., DISSLY, C. W., AND UHRIG, M. R., "Analytic Models for Rollback and Recovery Strategies in Database Systems," *IEEE Trans. Softw. Eng. SE-1,* 1(Mar. 1975), pp. 100–10.

CHANG, D., "A Stepwise Distributed Database Design," Database Systems Research Group Tech. Memo 79DS 1.1(R), University of Michigan, Ann Arbor, MI, May 6, 1980.

CHANG, S.-K., AND CHENG, W.-H., "Database Skeleton and Its Application to Logical Database Synthesis," *IEEE Trans. Softw. Eng.* SE-4, 1(1978), pp. 18–30.

CHEN, P., "The Entity-Relationship Model—Towards a Unified View of Data" *ACM TODS* 1,1(Mar. 1976), pp. 9–36.

CHEN, P., "The Entity-Relationship Model—A Basis for the Enterprise View of Data," *Proc. AFIPS Conf.,* Vol. 46, AFIPS Press, Arlington, VA, 1977a, pp. 77–84.

CHEN, P., "The Entity-Relationship Approach to Logical Data Base Design," Q.E.D. Monograph Series, Wellesley, MA, 1977b.

CHEN, P., "Applications of the Entity-Relationship Model," *NYU Symp. Database Design,* May 1978, pp. 25–33.

CHEN, P., AND YAO, S. B., "Design and Performance Tools for Database Systems," *Proc. 3rd Int. Conf. Very Large Data Bases* (ACM), 1977, pp. 3–15.

CHEN, D. D., FRY, J. P., AND TEOREY, T. J., "The Hierarchical Evaluator," Rep. No. DSRG 79DE6.2, Database Syst. Res. Group, University of Michigan, Ann Arbor, MI, Aug. 1979.

CHU, W. H. W., "Optimal File Placement in a Computer Network," *Computer Communication Networks,* N. Abramson and F. Kuo, eds., Prentice-Hall, Englewood Cliffs, NJ, 1973, pp. 82–94.

CHU, W. H. W., "Performance of File Directory Systems for Databases in Distributed Networks," *Proc. 1976 Natl. Comput. Conf.* (ACM), Vol. 45(1976), pp. 577–87.

CLARK, J. D., "An Attribute Access Probability Determination Procedure," Ph.D. thesis, Case Western Reserve University, School of Management, June 1977.

CLARK, J. D., AND HOFFER, J. A., "A Procedure for the Determination of Attribute Access Probabilities," *Proc. ACM/SIGMOD Int. Conf. Manage. Data* (ACM), 1978, pp. 110–17.

CLARK, J. D., AND HOFFER, J. A., *Physical Database Record Design,* Q.E.D. Monograph Series, Q.E.D. Information Systems, Inc., Wellesley, MA, 1979, 110 pp.

CODASYL—STORAGE STRUCTURE DEFINITION LANGUAGE TASK GROUP (SSDLTG) OF CODASYL SYSTEMS COMMITTEE, "Introduction to Storage Structure Definition," (by J. P. Fry); "Informal Definitions for the Development of a Storage Structure Definition Language," (by W. C. McGee); "A Procedural Approach to File Translation" (by J. W. Young, Jr.); "Preliminary Discussion of a General Data to Storage Structure Mapping Language" (by E. H. Sibley and R. W. Taylor), *Proc. ACM-SIGFIDET Workshop Data Description, Access, Control,* E. F. Codd, ed., ACM, New York, Nov. 1970, pp. 368–80.

CODASYL DATA BASE TASK GROUP, *April 1971 Report,* ACM, New York, 1971a.

CODASYL SYSTEMS COMMITTEE, *Feature Analysis of Generalized Data Base Management Systems,* ACM, New York, 1971b.

CODASYL Systems Committee, *Selection and Acquisition of Data Base Management Systems,* ACM, New York, Mar. 1976.

CODASYL—The Stored-Data Definition and Translation Task Group, "Stored-Data Description and Data Translation: A Model and Language," *Inf. Syst.* 2,3(1977), pp. 95–148.

CODASYL DATA DESCRIPTION LANGUAGE COMMITTEE, *J. Dev.,* 1978.

CODD, E. F., "A Relational Model of Data for Large Shared Data Banks," *Commun. ACM* 13,6(1970), pp. 377–87.

COFFMAN, E. G., AND EVE, J., "File Structures Using Hashing Functions," *Commun. ACM* 13,7(July 1970), pp. 427–32.

COMER, D., "The Difficulty of Optimum Index Selection," *ACM TODS* 3,4(Dec. 1978), pp. 440–45.

COMER, D., "Heuristics for Trie Index Minimization," *ACM TODS* 4,3(Sept. 1979a), pp. 383–95.

COMER, D., "The Ubiquitous B-Tree," *ACM Comput. Surv.* 11,2(June 1979b), pp. 121–37.

CURTICE, R. M., "Data Base Design Using IMS/360," *Proc. AFIPS 1972 Fall Joint*

Comput. Conf., Vol. 41, Thompson Book Co., Washington, DC, pp. 1105–10.

CURTICE, R. M., "Data Base Design Using a CODASYL System," *Proc. 1974 Natl. Comput. Conf.* (ACM), Vol. 43, AFIPS Press, Arlington, VA, pp. 473–80.

CURTICE, R. M., *Access Mechanisms and Data Structure Support in Data Base Management Systems,* Q.E.D. Monograph Series No. 1, Q.E.D. Information Systems, Inc., Wellesley, MA, 1975.

CURTICE, R. M., AND JONES, P. E., "Key Steps in the Logical Design of Data Bases," *NYU Symp. Database Design,* May 1978, pp. 51–66.

DAS, K. SUNDAR, "A Scheduling Methodology for Computer Operations," Ph.D. thesis, Dept. of Industrial and Operations Engineering, University of Michigan, Ann Arbor, 1977.

DATABASE ADMINISTRATION WORKING GROUP, "B.C.S./CODASYL DDIC," Rep. British Computer Society, London, June 1975.

"Data Dictionary System, Technical Overview," International Computers Ltd., London, 1977.

DATE, C. J., *An Introduction to Database Systems,* Addison-Wesley, Reading, MA, 1975.

DAVENPORT, R.A., "Data Analysis for Database Design," *Aust. Comput. J.,* 10,4(Nov. 1978), pp. 122–37.

DAVENPORT, R. A., "Design of Distributed Database Systems," *Infotech State of the Art Report: Distributed Databases,* Vol. 2, Infotech International, Maidenhead, Berkshire, England, 1979, pp. 87–114.

DAVIS, G. B., *Management Information Systems: Conceptual Foundations, Structure and Development,* McGraw-Hill, New York, 1974, p. 278.

DAVIS, C. G., AND VICK, C. R., "The Software Development System," *IEEE Trans. Softw. Eng. SE-3,* 1(1977), pp. 70–84.

DEBLASIS, J. P., AND JOHNSON, T. H., "Database Administration—Classical Pattern, Some Experiences and Trends," *Proc. AFIPS NCC,* Vol. 46, AFIPS Press, Arlington, VA, 1977, pp. 1–7.

DEBLASIS, J. P., AND JOHNSON, T. H., "Review of Database Administrators Functions from a Survey," *Proc. ACM/SIGMOD Int. Conf. Manage. Data* (ACM), 1978, pp. 101–09.

DE LA BRIANDAIS, R., "File Searching Using Variable Length Keys," *Proc. 1959 West. Joint Comput. Conf.,* pp. 295–98.

DENNING, D. E., AND DENNING, P. J., "Data Security," *ACM Comput. Surv.* 11,3(Sept. 1978), pp. 227–49.

DEPPE, M. E., "A Relational Interface Model for Database Restructuring," Tech. Rep. 76 DT 3, Data Translation Project, Graduate School of Business Administration, University of Michigan, Ann Arbor, MI 1976.

DESMITH, D., AND FRY, J. P., "CODASYL Report on Distributed Database Systems," 1980.

DESMITH, D. A., AGHILI, H., GROCOCK, M., AND MATTHEWS, W., "A Distributed Database Management System for the IBM Series/1: Functional Capabilities," 79DS8.1(R), Database Systems Research Group, University of Michigan, Ann Arbor, MI, 1979.

DIJKSTRA, E. W. *A Discipline of Programming,* Prentice-Hall, Englewood Cliffs, NJ, 1976.

DRAKE, R. W., AND SMITH, J. L., "Some Techniques for File Recovery," *Aust. Comput. J.* 3,4(Nov. 1971), pp. 162–70.

EISNER, M. J., AND SEVERANCE, D. G., "Mathematical Techniques for Efficient Record Segmentation in Large Shared Databases," *J. ACM* 23,4(1976), pp. 619–35.

EVEREST, G. C., "Characteristics of Inter-entity Relationships and a Graphical Notation," MISRC-WP-77-04, Graduate School of Business Administration, University of Minnesota, Minneapolis, MN, June 1977.

FAGIN, R., "Multi-valued Dependencies and a New Normal Form for Relational Databases," *ACM Trans. Database Syst.* 2,3(1977), pp. 262–78.

FAGIN, R., "Normal Forms and Relational Database Operations," *Proc. ACM/SIGMOD Int. Conf. Manage. Data* (ACM), 1979, pp. 153–60.

FAGIN, R., NIEVERGELT, J., PIPPENGER, N., AND STRONG, H. R., "Extendible Hashing—A Fast Access Method for Dynamic Files," *ACM TODS* 4,3(Sept. 1979), pp. 315–44.

FALKENBERG, E., "Concepts for Modelling Information," in *Modelling in Data Base Management Systems*, G. M. Nijssen, ed., IFIP '76, North-Holland, Amsterdam, 1976, pp. 95–110.

FOSTER, C. C., "Information Storage and Retrieval Using AVL Trees", *Proc. ACM 20th Natl. Conf.*, 1965, pp. 192–205.

FOSTER, C. C., "A Generalization of AVL Trees," *Commun. ACM* 16,8(Aug. 1973), pp. 513–17.

FREDKIN, E., "Trie Memory," *Commun. ACM* 3,9(Sept. 1960), pp. 490–500.

FRY, J. P., PREP., The Technology of Data Base Translation—Data Base Restructuring," *Auerbach Information Management Series: Current Directions in DBM Development (24-01-11)*, Auerbach Publishers, Pennsauken, NJ, 1978.

FRY, J. P., AND DEPPE, M. E., "Distributed Data Bases: A Summary of Research," *Comput. Networks* 1,2(1976), pp. 1–13.

FRY, J. P., AND JERIS, D., "Towards a Formulation of Data Reorganization," *Proc. 1974 ACM/SIGMOD Workshop Data Description, Access, Control*, R. Rustin, ed., ACM, New York, pp. 83–100.

FRY, J. P., AND KAHN, B. K., "A Stepwise Approach to Database Design," *Proc. ACM Southeast Reg. Conf.*, 1976, pp. 34–43.

FRY, J. P., AND MAURER, J., "Operational and Technological Issues in Distributed Databases," Auerbach Database Management Series, Portfolio No. 24-01-02, 1977.

FRY, J. P., AND SIBLEY, E. A., "Evolution of Database Management Systems," *Comput. Surv.* 8,1(Mar. 1976), pp. 7–42.

FRY, J. P., TEOREY, T. J., DeSMITH, D. A., AND OBERLANDER, L. B., "Survey of State-of-the-Art Database Administration Tools: Survey Results and Evaluation," with Appendixes A, B, and C, DSRG Tech. Rep. 78DE14.2, Database Systems Research Group, Graduate School of Business Administration, University of Michigan, Ann Arbor, MI, 1978a.

FRY, J. P., DeSMITH, D. A., AND OBERLANDER, L. B., "Database Research and Systems Bibliography," attachment to DSRG Tech. Rep. 78DE14.2, Database Systems Research Group, Graduate School of Business Administration, University of Michigan, Ann Arbor, MI, 1978b.

GAMBINO, T.J., AND GERRITSEN, R., "A Data Base Design Decision Support System," *Proc. 3rd Int. Conf. Very Large Data Bases* (ACM), 1977, pp. 534–44.

GANE, C., AND SARSON, T. *Structured System Analysis*, Prentice-Hall, Englewood Cliffs, NJ, 1979.

GERRITSEN, R., *Understanding Data Structures*, NTIS AD-A008-937, Springfield, VA, 1975a.

GERRITSEN, R., "A Preliminary System for the Design of DBTG Data Structures," *Commun. ACM* 18,10(Oct. 1975b), pp. 557–67.

GERRITSEN, R., "Steps toward the Automation of Database Design," *NYU Symp. Database Design*, May 1978, pp. 91–99.

GHOSH, S., *Data Base Organization for Data Management*, Academic Press, New York, 1976.

GHOSH, S. P., AND ABRAHAM, C. T., "Application of Finite Geometry in File Organization for Records with Multiple-Valued Attributes," *IBM. J. Res. Dev.* 12,2(1968), pp. 180–87.

GRAY, J. N., "Notes on Database Operating Systems," *Operating Systems—An Advanced Course*, Vol. 60, *Lecture Notes in Computer Science*, Springer-Verlag, New York, 1978, pp. 393–481.

GRAY, J. N., LORIE, R. A., AND PUTZOLU, G. R., "Granularity of Locks and Degrees of Consistency in a Shared Database," *Proc. 1st Int. Conf. Very Large Data Bases* (ACM), Sept. 1975, pp. 428–451.

GUIDE INTERNATIONAL, "Comparison of Data Base Management Systems," Oct. 1971.

GUIDE INTERNATIONAL, "The Data Base Administrator," Nov. 1972.

GUIDE INTERNATIONAL, "The Data Base Design Guide," Aug. 1974.

HAERDER, T., "Implementing a Generalized Access Path Structure for a Relational Database System," *ACM Trans. Database Syst.* 3,3(1978), pp. 285–98.

HALL, P., OWLETT, J., AND TODD, S. "Relations and Entities," in *Modelling in Data Base Management Systems*, G. M. Nijssen, ed., North-Holland, New York, 1976.

HAMMAD, P., AND RAVIART, T., "Formulation of Choice Criterions for File Organizations," *Inf. Syst.* 3,2(1978), 123–30.

HAMMER, M., AND CHAN, A., "Index Selection in a Self-Adaptive Data Base Management System," *Proc. ACM/SIGMOD Int. Conf. Manage. Data* (ACM), 1976a, pp. 1–8.

HAMMER, M., AND CHAN, A., "Acquisition and Utilization of Access Patterns in a Relational Data Base Implementation," in *Pattern Recognition and Artificial Intelligence*. Academic Press, New York, 1976b, pp. 292–313.

HAMMER, M., AND NIAMIR, B., "A Heuristic Approach to Attribute Partitioning," *Proc. ACM/SIGMOD Int. Conf. Manage. Data* (ACM), 1979, pp. 93–100.

HARDGRAVE, W. T., "A Technique for Implementing a Set Processor," *Proc. ACM/ SIGMOD/SIGPLAN Conf. Data: Abstraction, Definition and Structure,* Mar. 1976, pp. 86–94.

HEBALKAR, P. G., AND ZILLES, S. M., "Graphical Representation and Analysis Information Systems Design," IBM Res. Rep. RJ2465, Jan. 1979.

HELD, G., AND STONEBRAKER, M., "B-trees Reexamined," *Commun. ACM* 12,2(Feb. 1978), pp. 139–43.

HELLERMAN, H., AND SMITH, JR., H. J., "Throughput Analysis of Some Idealized Input, Output, and Compute Overlap Configurations," *ACM Comput. Surv.* 2,2(June 1970), pp. 111–18.

HERSHEY, E. A. ET AL., "Problem Statement Language Version 3.0 Language Reference Manual," Working Paper 68, ISDOS Research Project, University of Michigan, Ann Arbor, MI, May 1975.

HIBBARD, T., "Some Combinatorial Properties of Certain Trees with Applications to Searching and Sorting," *J. ACM* 9,1(Jan. 1962), pp. 13–28.

HOFFER, J. A., "A Clustering Approach to the Generation of Subfiles for the Design of a Computer Database," Ph.D. thesis, Dept. of Operations Research, Cornell University, Jan. 1975.

HOFFER, J. A., "Selection of Secondary Indexes in a Minicomputer Environment," Tech. Rep., Case Western Reserve University, 1978.

HOFFER, J. A., "A Survey of Primary and Secondary Keys through a Case Study," *Inf. Manage.* 2(1979), pp. 99–106.

HOFFER, J. A., AND SEVERANCE, D. G., "The Use of Cluster Analysis in Physical Data Base Design," *Proc. First Intl. Conf. VLDB,* Framingham, MA, Sept. 1975, ACM, New York, pp. 69–86.

HOUSEL, B. C., WADDLE, V., AND YAO, S. B. "The Functional Dependency Model for Logical Database Design" *Proc. 5th Int. Conf. Very Large Data Bases* (ACM), Oct. 3–5, 1979, pp. 194–203.

HSIAO, D., AND HARARY, F., "A Formal System for Information Retrieval from Files," *Commun. ACM* 14,2(1970), pp. 67–73.

HUBBARD, G. U., "Technique for Automated Logical Database Design," *NYU Symp. Database Design,* May 1978, pp. 85–90.

HUBBARD, G., AND RAVER, N., "Automating Logical File Design," in *Proc. 1st Int. Conf. Very Large Data Bases* (ACM), 1975, pp. 227–53.

HUFFMAN, D. A., "A Method for the Construction of Minimum Redundancy Codes," *Proc. IRE 40*(Sept. 1952), pp. 1098–1104.

HULTEN, C., AND SODERLUND, L., "A Simulation Model for Performance Analysis of Large Shared Data Bases," *Proc. 3rd Int. Conf. Very Large Data Bases* (ACM), 1977, pp. 524–32.

IBM. DBPROTOTYPE General Information Manual GH20-1272-0, IBM Mechanicsburg, PA, 1973.

IBM, *IBM Data Base Design Aid-A Designer's Guide,* Program No. 5748-XX4, GH20-1627-0, 1975.

IBM, "Structured Walk-Throughs: A Project Management Tool," IBM, Aug. 1973.

IBM, "IMS/VS System/Application Design Guide," SH20-0910, IBM, 1974.

IBM, "OS/VS Virtual Storage Access Method (VSAM) Programmer's Guide," IBM GC26-3838-2, 1976.

IBM, "Planning for Enhanced VSAM under OS/VS," IBM GC26-3842-2, 1977.

IBM, "IBM 3350 Direct Access Storage," GA26-1638, rev. 1979.

IBM, "Introduction to IBM System/360 Direct Access Storage Devices and Organization Methods," IBM C20-1649-4, 1966.

INFOTECH, "Database Technology," *INFOTECH State of the Art Report,* INFOTECH International, Maidenhead, Berkshire, England, 1978.

INNOVATION DATA PROCESSING, INC. "Fast Dump Restore and Data Set Functions, User Documentation," Innovation Data Processing, Inc., Clifton, NJ, July 1973.

IRANI, K., PURKAYASTHA, S., AND TEOREY, T. J., "A Designer for DBMS-Processable Logical Database Structures," *Proc. 5th Int. Conf. Very Large Data Bases* (ACM), Oct. 3–5, 1979, pp. 219–31.

JACKSON, M. A., *Principles of Program Design,* Academic Press, New York, 1975.

JANNING, M., NACHMENS, S., AND BERILD, S., *CS4: An Introduction to Associative Data Bases and the CS4-System,* Studentlitteratur, Lund, Sweden, ISBN 91-44-17111-0, 1981, 251 pp.

JONES, P. E., "Data Base Design Methodology—Logical Framework," Q.E.D. Monograph Series, Q.E.D. Information Systems, Inc., Wellesley, MA, 1976.

KAHN, B. K., "A Method for Describing the Information Required by the Data Base Design Process," *Proc. Int. ACM/SIGMOD Conf. Manage. Data,* 1976, pp. 53–64.

KAHN, B., "A Structured Logical Data-Base Design Methodology," in *NYU Symp. Database Design,* May 1978, pp. 15–24.

KARLTON, P., FULLER, S., SCROGGS, R., AND KACHLER, E., "Performance of Height Balanced Trees," *Commun. ACM* 19,1(Jan. 1976), pp. 23–28.

KEEHN, D., AND LACY, J., "VSAM Data Set Design Parameters," *IBM Syst. J.* 13,3(1974), pp. 186–212.

KENT, W., "Entities and Relationships in Information," in *Architecture and Models in Data Base Management Systems,* G. Nijssen, ed. North-Holland, Amsterdam, 1977.

KENT, W., *Data and Reality: Basic Assumptions in Data Processing Reconsidered,* North-Holland, Amsterdam, 1978, p. 211.

KERSCHBERG, L., ET AL., "A Taxonomy of Data Models," Tr. Csrb-70, Computer System Research Group, University of Toronto, Toronto, May 1976.

KHABBAZ, N. G., "A Combined Communication Network Design and File Allocation for Distributed Databases," Ph.D. dissertation, University of Michigan, Ann Arbor, 1979.

KING, P. F., AND COLLMEYER, A. J., "Database Sharing—An Efficient Mechanism for Supporting Concurrent Processes," *Proc. AFIPS 1973 NCC,* Vol. 42, AFIPS Press, Montvale NJ, 1973, pp. 271–75.

KING, W. F., "On the Selection of Indices for a File," *IBM Tech. Rep. RJ 1341,* San Jose, CA, 1974.

KLEINROCK, L., *Queuing Systems,* Wiley, New York, 1975.

KNUTH, D. E., *The Art of Computer Programming*, Vol. 1: *Fundamental Algorithms*, Addison-Wesley, Reading, MA, 1968.

KNUTH, D. E., *The Art of Computer Programming*, Vol. 3: *Sorting and Searching*, Addison-Wesley, Reading, MA, 1973.

KOBAYASHI, H., *Modeling and Analysis: An Introduction to System Performance Evaluation Methodology*, Addison-Wesley, Reading, MA, 1978, 446 pp.

LAMPSON, B., AND STURGIS, H., "Crash Recovery in a Distributed Data Storage System," Tech. Rep., Comp. Sci. Lab., Xerox Palo Alto Research Center, Palo Alto, CA., 1976.

LANDAUER, W. I., "The Balanced Tree and Its Utilization in Information Retrieval," *IEEE Trans. Electron. Comput.* EC-12,5(Dec. 1963), pp. 863–71.

LANGEFORS, B., "Information Systems," *Proc. IFIP Congr.*, North-Holland, Amsterdam, 1974, pp. 937–45.

LEFKOVITZ, D., *File Structures for Online Systems*, Spartan Books, Rochelle Park, NJ, 1969.

LEFKOVITZ, D., *Data Management for Online System*, Hayden, Rochelle Park, NJ, 1974.

LEONG-HONG, B., AND MARRON, B., "Technical Profile of Seven Data Element Dictionary Directory Systems," NBS Spec. Publ. 500–3, U.S. Dept. of Commerce, Washington, DC, Feb. 1977.

LEONG-HONG, B., AND MARRON, B., "Database Administration: Concepts, Tools, Experiences, and Problems," NBS Spec. Publ. 500–28, U.S. Dept. of Commerce, Washington, DC, Mar. 1978.

LIOU, J. H., AND YAO, S. B., "Multidimensional Clustering for Data Base Organizations," *Inf. Syst.* 2,4(1977), pp. 187–98.

LIU, J. W. S., "Algorithms for Parsing Search Queries in Systems with Inverted File Organizations," *ACM TODS* 1,4(Dec. 1976), pp. 299–316.

LOHMAN, G. M., AND MUCKSTADT, J. A., "Optimal Policy for Batch Operations: Backup, Checkpointing, Reorganization, and Updating," *ACM Trans. Database Syst.* 2,3(1977), pp. 209–22.

LOWE, T. C., "The Influence of Data Base Characteristics and Usage on Direct Access File Organization," *J. ACM* 15,4(1968), pp. 535–48.

LUM, V. Y., "Multi-attribute Retrieval with Combined Indexes," *Commun. ACM* 13,11(Nov. 1970), pp. 660–65.

LUM, V. Y., AND YUEN, P.S.T., "Additional Results on Key-To-Address Transform Techniques," *Commun. ACM* 15,11(1972), pp. 996–7.

LUM, V. Y., LING, H., AND SENKO, M. E., "Analysis of a Complex Data Management Access Method by Simulation Modeling," *Proc. AFIPS 1970 Fall Joint Comput. Conf.* AFIPS Press, Arlington, VA, 1970, pp. 211–22.

LUM, V. Y., YUEN, P. S. T., AND DODD, M., "Key-To-Address Transformation Techniques: A Fundamental Performance Study on Large Existing Formatted Files," *Commun. ACM* 14,4(1971), pp. 228–39.

LUM, V. Y., SENKO, M. E., WANG, C. P., AND LING, H., "A Cost Oriented Algorithm for Data Set Allocation in Storage Hierarchies," *Commun. ACM*, 18,6(June 1975), pp. 318–32.

LUM, V., ET AL., "1978 New Orleans Data Base Design Workshop Report," IBM Tech. Rep. No. RJ2554(33154), July 1979a.

LUM, V. Y., ET AL., "1978 New Orleans Data Base Design Workshop Report," *Proc. 5th Int. Conf. Very Large Data Bases* (ACM), Oct. 3–5, 1979b, pp. 328–39.

LYON, J. K., *Data Base Administrator*, Wiley-Interscience, New York, 1976a.

LYON, J. K., *Introduction to Data Base Design*, Wiley Interscience Communigraph Series on Business Data Processing, Wiley-Interscience, New York, 1976b.

MAHMOUD, S. A., RIORDON, J. S., AND TOTH, K. C., "Distributed Database Partitioning and Query Processing," *Proc. IFIP TC-2 Working Conf. Database Architecture*, Venice, Italy, June 1979.

MANOLA, F., "An Evaluation of the New CODASYL and ANSI/SPARC Database Proposals," *Infotech State of the Art Report: Data Base Technology,* Vol. 2, Infotech International, Maidenhead, Berkshire, England, 1978, pp. 131–50.

MARCH, S. T., "Models of Storage Structures and the Design of Database Records Based upon a User Characterization," Ph.D. dissertation, Cornell University, 1978.

MARCH, S. T., AND SEVERANCE, D. G., "The Determination of Efficient Record Segmentations and Blocking Factors for Shared Files," *ACM Trans. Database Syst.* 2,3(1977), pp. 279–96.

MARCH, S. T., AND SEVERANCE, D. G., "A Mathematical Modeling Approach to the Automatic Selection of Database Designs," *Proc. ACM/SIGMOD Int. Conf. Manage. Data,* 1978, pp. 52–65.

MARCH, S. T., SEVERANCE, D. G., AND WILENS, M. E., "Frame-Memory: A Storage Architecture to Support Rapid Design and Implementation of Efficient Databases," ACM TODS 6,3(1981), pp. 441–63.

MARTIN, J., *Design of Real-Time Computer Systems,* Prentice-Hall, Englewood Cliffs, NJ, 1967.

MARTIN, J., *Teleprocessing Network Organization,* Prentice-Hall, Englewood Cliffs, NJ, 1970.

MARTIN, J., *Computer Data-Base Organization,* 2nd ed., Prentice-Hall, Englewood Cliffs, NJ, 1977.

MARYANSKI, F. J., AND FISHER, P. S., "Rollback and Recovery in Distributed Database Management Systems," *Proc. 1977 ACM Annu. Conf.,* 1977, pp. 33–38.

MAURER, W. D., "An Improved Hash Code for Scatter Storage," *Commun. ACM* 11,1(Jan. 1968), pp. 35–38.

MAXWELL, W. L., AND SEVERANCE, D. G., "Comparison of Alternatives for the Representation of Data Items Values in an Information System," *Proc. Wharton Conf. Res. Comput. Organ. Oper. Res.* 20-5 (1973), 16 pp.

MCCORMICK, W. T., JR., SWEITZER, P. J., AND WHITE, T. W., "Problem Decomposition and Data Reorganization by a Clustering Technique," *Oper. Res.* 20,5(Sept.–Oct. 1972), pp. 993–1009.

MCILROY, M. D., "A Variant Method of File Searching," *Commun. ACM* 6,1(Jan. 1963), p. 101.

MENASCE, D. A., POPEK, G. J., AND MUNTZ, R., "A Locking Protocol for Resource Coordination in Distributed Database Systems," Supplement to *ACM SIGMOD 1978,* pp. 1–4.

METHLIE, L. B., "Schema Design Using a Data Structure Matrix," *Inf. Syst.* 3,2(1978), pp. 81–91.

MILLER, G. A., "The Magical Number Seven, Plus-or-minus Two: Some Limits on Our Capacity for Processing Information," *Psychol. Rev.* 63,2(Mar. 1956), pp. 81–97.

MILLS, H. D., "Mathematical Foundations for Structured Programming," IBM Tech. Rep. FSC72-6012, Feb. 1972.

MITOMA, M. F., "Optimal Data Base Schema Design," Ph.D. dissertation, University of Michigan, Ann Arbor, 1975.

MITOMA, M. F., AND IRANI, K. B., "Automatic Data Base Schema Design," *Proc. 1st Int. Conf. Very Large Data Bases* (ACM), 1975, pp. 286–321.

MOHAN, C., AND YEH, R. T., "Distributed Database Systems—A Framework for Database Design," *INFOTECH State of the Art Report: Distributed Database,* Vol. 2, INFOTECH International, Maidenhead, Berkshire, England, 1979, pp. 237–56.

MOMMENS, J., AND SMITH, S., "Automatic Generation of Physical Data Base Structures," *Proc. Int. ACM/SIGMOD Conf. on Manage. Data,* 1975, pp. 157–65.

MORGAN, H. L., AND LEVIN, H. D., "Optimal Program and Data Locations in Computer Networks," *Commun. ACM* 20,5(1977), pp. 315–22.

MORRIS, R., "Scatter Storage Techniques," *Commun. ACM* 11,1(1968), pp. 38–43.

MUNTZ, R., AND UZGALIS, R., "Dynamic Storage Allocation for Binary Search Trees in a Two-Level Memory," *Proc. 4th Annu. Princeton Conf.,* Princeton, NJ, 1970, pp. 539–49.

NAKAMURA, F., YOSHIDA, I., AND KANDO, H., "A Simulation Model for Data Base System Performance Evaluation," *Proc. 1975 Natl. Comput. Conf.*, Vol. 44, AFIPS Press, Montvale, NJ, pp. 459–65.

NAVATHE, S. B., AND FRY, J. P., "Restructuring for Large Data Bases: Three Levels of Abstraction," *ACM Trans. Database Syst.* 1,2(1976), pp. 138–58.

NAVATHE, S. B., AND GADGIL, S. G., "A Methodology for View Integration in Logical Database Design," Database Systems Research and Development Center Tech. Rep. University of Florida, 1980.

NAVATHE, S. B., AND SCHKOLNICK, M., "View Representation in Logical Database Design," *Proc. ACM/SIGMOD Int. Conf. Manage. Data,* 1978, pp. 144–56.

NIAMIR, B., "Attribute Partitioning in a Self-Adaptive Relational Database System," MIT Lab. Comput. Sci. Tech. Rep. 192, Cambridge, MA, Jan. 1978.

NIEVERGELT, J., "Binary Search Trees and File Organization," *ACM Comput. Surv.* 6,3(Sept. 1974), pp. 195–207.

NIEVERGELT, J., AND REINGOLD, E. M., "Binary Search Trees of Bounded Balance," *SIAM J. Comput.* 2,1(Mar. 1973), pp. 33–43.

NIJSSEN, G. M., "Current Issues in Conceptual Schema Concepts," *Proc. IFIP TC2 Conf.*, Nice, France, North-Holland, Amsterdam, Jan. 1977.

NOVAK, D., AND FRY, J., "The State of the Art of Logical Database Design," *Proc. 5th Texas Conf. Comput. Syst.* (IEEE), Long Beach CA, 1976, pp. 30–39.

OBERLANDER, L. B., "Physical Design of Database Structures," Ph.D. thesis, Dept. of Computer and Communications Science, University of Michigan, Ann Arbor, 1979.

OLLE, W. T., "UL-1—A Non-procedural Language for Retrieving Information from Data Bases," *Information Processing—68,* North-Holland, Amsterdam, (1968), pp. 572–78.

OLSON, C. A., "Random Access File Organization for Indirectly Addressed Records," *Proc. 1969 ACM Natl. Conf.*, pp. 539–49.

OREN, O. A., AND ASCHIM, F., "Statistics for the Usage of a Conceptual Data Model as a Basis for Logical Data Base Design," *Proc. 5th Int. Conf. Very Large Data Bases* (ACM), Oct. 3–5, 1979, pp. 140–45.

ORR, K. T., *Structured Systems Design,* Langston Kitch and Associates, Topeka, Kans., 1976.

PALMER, I., "Practicalities in Applying a Formal Methodology to Data Analysis," *NYU Symp. Database Design,* May 1978, pp. 67–84.

PARNAS, D. L., "On the Criteria to be Used in Decomposing Systems into Models" *Commun. ACM* 15,12(Dec. 1972), pp. 1053–58.

PETERSON, W. W., "Addressing for Random Access Storage," *IBM J. Res. Dev.* 1(Apr. 1957), pp. 130–46.

Proceedings of Wharton Seminar on Database Administration, University of Pennsylvania Press, Philadelphia, 1977.

RAMERIZ, J. A., RIN, N. A., AND PRYWES, N. S., "Automatic Conversion of Data Conversion Programs Using a Data Description Language, Access and Control," *Proc. ACM/SIGFIDET Workshop Data Description* (ACM), 1974, pp. 207–25.

RAPPAPORT, R. L., "File Structure Design to Facilitate On-Line Instantaneous Updating," *Proc. 1975 ACM/SIGMOD Conf.*, pp. 1–14.

RIES, D. R., AND STONEBRAKER, M. R., "Locking Granularity Revisited," *ACM Trans. Database Syst.* 4,2(June 1979), pp. 210–27.

RIVEST, R. L., "Partial Match Retrieval Algorithms," *SIAM J. Comput.*, 5,1(Mar. 1976), pp. 19–50.

ROCHE, D. J. M., "Practical Aspects of Randomizing," *IFIP, ADP Group, IAG, File Organization and Search Techniques Seminar Notes,* Nov. 1969, pp. C-1–C-24.

ROSENKRANTZ, D., STERNS, R., AND LEWIS, R., "A System Level Concurrency Control for Distributed Database Systems," *Proc. 2nd Berkeley Workshop,* May 22–27, 1977.

ROSS, D. T., "Structured Analysis (SA): A Language for Communicating Ideas," *IEEE Trans. Softw. Eng.* SE-3,1(1977), pp. 16–34.

Ross, D. T., AND SCHOMAN, K. B., JR., "Structured Analysis for Requirements Definition," *IEEE Trans. Softw. Eng.* SE-3, 1 (Jan. 1977), pp. 6–15.

ROTHNIE, J. B., AND GOODMAN, N., "An Overview of the Preliminary Design of SDD-1: A System for Distributed Database," *Proc. 1977 Berkeley Workshop Data Manage. Comput. Networks,* Lawrence Berkeley Lab., University of California, Berkeley, CA, May 1977, pp. 39–57.

ROTHNIE, J. B., ET AL., "Introduction to a System for Distributed Databases (SDD-1)," *ACM Trans. Database Syst.* 5,1(1980), pp. 1–17.

ROTWITT, T., AND DeMAINE, P. A. D., "Storage Optimization of Tree Structured Files Representing Descriptor Sets," *Proc. 1971 SIGFIDET (SIGMOD) Workshop,* San Diego, CA.

ROYCROFT, A. J., "Techniques for Handling Variable Length Logical Records on IBM Direct Access Storage Devices," *Proc. FILE68 Int. Seminar File Org.,* Copenhagen, 1968, pp. 701–20.

RUBIN, F., "Experiments in Text File Compression," *Commun. ACM* 19,11(Nov. 1976), pp. 617–23.

RUND, D. S., "Data Base Design Methodology—Parts I & II," Auerbach Data Base Management Series, Portfolios Nos. 23-01-01 and -02, 1977.

SALTON, G., AND WANG, A., "Generation and Search of Clustered Files," *ACM Trans. Database Syst.* 3,4(1978), pp. 321–46.

SAYANI, H. H., "Restart and Recovery in Transaction-Oriented Information Processing System," *Proc. 1974 ACM/SIGMOD Workshop Data Description, Access, Control,* May 1974, pp. 351–66.

SCHKOLNICK, M., "The Optimal Selection of Secondary Indices for Files," *Inf. Syst.* 1(1975), pp. 141–46.

SCHKOLNICK, M., "A Clustering Algorithm for Hierarchical Structures," *ACM Trans. Database Syst.* 2,1(1977), pp. 27–44.

SCHKOLNICK, M., "Physical Database Design Techniques," *NYU Symp. Database Design,* May 1978, pp. 99–110.

SCIDMORE, A. K., AND WEINBERG, B. L., "Storage and Search Properties of a Tree-organized Memory System," *Commun. ACM* 6,1(Jan. 1963), pp. 28–31.

SELINGER, M. M., ASTRAHAN, M. M., CHAMBERLIN, D. D., LORIE, R. A., AND PRICE, T. G., "Access Path Selection in a Relational Database Management System," *Proc. ACM/SIGMOD Int. Conf. Manage. Data,* 1979, pp. 23–34.

SENKO, M. E., LUM, V. Y., AND OWENS, P. J., "A File Organization Evaluation Model (FOREM)," *Proc. 1968 IFIP Cong.,* Spartan Books, Washington, DC, pp. C19–C23.

SENKO, M., ET AL., "Data Structures and Accessing in Data-base Systems," *IBM Syst. J.* 12,1(1973), pp. 30–93.

SEVERANCE, D. G., "Some Generalized Modeling Structures for Use in Design of File Organization," Ph.D. dissertation, University of Michigan, Ann Arbor, 1972.

SEVERANCE, D. G., "Identifier Search Mechanisms: A Survey and Generalized Model," *Comput. Surv.* 6,3(1974), pp. 175–94.

SEVERANCE, D. G., AND CARLIS, J. V., "A Practical Approach to Selecting Record Access Paths," *ACM Comput. Surv.* 9,4(1977), pp. 259–72.

SEVERANCE, D. G., AND DUHNE, R. A., "A Practitioner's Guide to Addressing Algorithms," *Commun. ACM* 19,6(1976), pp. 314–26.

SEVERANCE, D. G., AND LOHMAN, G. M., "Differential Files: Their Application to the Maintenance of Large Databases," *ACM TODS,* 1,3(Sept. 1976), pp. 256–67.

SHARMEN, G., AND WINTERBOTTOM, N., "The Data Dictionary Facilities of NDB," in *Proc. 4th Int. Conf. Very Large Data Bases* (ACM), 1978, pp. 186–97.

SHEPPARD, D. L., "Data Base: A Business Approach to System Design," CONCOM Systems, Inc., Cincinnati, OH, Aug. 1974.

SHERMAN, S. W., AND BRICE, R. S., "Performance of a Database Manager in a Virtual Memory System" *ACM Trans. Database Syst.* 1,4(1976a), pp. 317–43.

SHERMAN, S. W., AND BRICE, R. S., "An Extension of the Performance of a Database

Manager in a Virtual Memory System Using Partially Locked Virtual Buffers," *ACM Trans. Database Syst.* 2,2(1977b), pp. 196–207.

SHNEIDERMAN, B., "Optimum Data Base Reorganization Points," *Commun. ACM* 16,6(1973), pp. 363–65.

SHNEIDERMAN, B., "Reduced Combined Indexes for Efficient Multiple Attribute Retrieval," *Inf. Syst.* 2,4(1977), Pergamon Press, Oxford, pp. 149–54.

SHOSHANI, A., "A Logical-Level Approach to Data Base Conversion," *Proc. 1975 ACM/SIGMOD Int. Conf. Manage. Data* (ACM), pp. 112–22.

SHOSHANI, A., AND BRANDON, K., "On the Implementation of a Logical Data Base Converter," *Proc. First Int. Conf. Very Large Data Bases* (ACM), 1975, pp. 529–31.

SHU, N. C., HOUSEL, B. C., AND LUM, V. Y., "CONVERT: A High-Level Translation Language for Data Conversion," *Commun. ACM* 18,10(1975), pp. 557–67.

SHU, N. C., ET AL., "EXPRESS: A Data Extraction, Processing, and Restructuring System," *ACM TODS*, June 1977, pp. 134–74.

SILER, K. F., "A Stochastic Evaluation Model for Database Organizations in Data Retrieval Systems," *Commun. ACM* 19,2(Feb. 1976), pp. 84–95.

SMITH, J. M., AND SMITH, D. C. P., "Database Abstractions: Aggregation and Generalization," *ACM Trans. Database Syst.* 2,2(1977a), pp. 105–33.

SMITH, J. M., AND SMITH, D. C. P., "Database Abstractions: Aggregation," *Commun. ACM* 20,6(June 1977b), pp. 405–13.

SMITH, J. M., AND SMITH, D. C. P., "Principles of Database Design," *NYU Symp. Database Design*, May 1978, pp. 35–50.

SOCKUT, G. H., AND GOLDBERG R. P., "Database Reorganization—Principles and Practice," *ACM Comput. Surv.* 11,4(Dec. 1979), pp. 371–95.

SODERLUND, LARS, "A Study on Concurrent Database Reorganization," Ph.D. thesis, of Information Processing and Computer Science, The Royal Institute of Technology and The University of Stockholm, Sweden, ISBN 91-85212-57-1, 1980.

SOWA, J., "Conceptual Graphs for a Data Base Interface," *IBM J. Res. Dev.* 20,4(1976), pp. 336–357.

SPERRY UNIVAC, "Data Management System (DMS1100) Level 8R1 System Support Functions Data Administrator Reference," Univac Publ. UP 7909.1, 1978.

SPROWLS, R. C., *Management Data Bases,* Wiley/Hamilton, Santa Barbara, CA 1976.

STONE, H. S., "Multiprocessor Scheduling with the Aid of Network Flow Algorithms," *IEEE Trans. Softw. Eng.,* SE-3,1(Jan. 1977), pp. 85–93.

STONEBRAKER, M., "The Choice of Partial Inversions and Combined Indices," *J. Comput. Inf. Sci.* 3,2(1974), pp. 167–88.

STONEBRAKER, M., "Concurrency Control and Consistency of Multiple Copies of Data in Distributed INGRES," *IEEE Trans. Softw. Eng.,* SE-5,3, 1979, pp. 188–94.

STONEBRAKER, M., AND NEUHOLD, E., "A Distributed Data Base Version of IN-GRES," *Proc. Berkeley Workshop Distributed Data Manage. Comput. Networks,* 1977, pp. 19–36.

STONEBRAKER, M., ET AL., "The Design and Implementation of INGRES," *ACM TODS*, Sept. 1976, pp. 189–222.

STRONG, H. R., MARKOWSKY, G., AND CHANDRA, A. K., "Search within a Page," *J. ACM* 26,2(July 1979), pp. 457–82.

SUNDGREN, B., "An Infological Approach to Databases," Ph.D. dissertation, University of Stockholm, Sweden, 1973.

SUNDGREN, B., "Data Base Design in Theory and Practice—Towards an Integrated Methodology," *Proc. 4th Conf. Very Large Data Bases* (ACM), 1978, pp. 3–26 (with comments pp. 17–30).

SUSSENGUTH, E. H., JR., "Use of Tree Structures for Processing Files," *Commun. ACM* 6,5(May 1963), pp. 272–79.

SUTHERLAND, W. R., "Distributed Computation Research at BBN," III BBN Tech. Rep. 2976, Bolt, Beranek and Newman, Dec. 1974.

SWARTWOUT, D., "An Access Path Specification Language for Restructuring Network Databases,"*Proc. 1977 ACM/SIGMOD Int. Conf. Manage. Data* (ACM), 1977, pp. 88–101.

SWARTWOUT, D. E., DEPPE, M. E., AND FRY, J. P., "Operational Software for Restructuring Network Databases," *Proc. 1977 Natl. Comput. Conf.*, Vol. 46, AFIPS Press, Arlington, VA, 1977a, pp. 499–508.

SWARTWOUT, D. E., WOLFE, G. J., AND BURPEE, C. E., "Translation Definition Language Reference Manual for Version IIa Translator, Release 3," Working Paper 77 DT 5.3, Data Translation Project, University of Michigan, Ann Arbor, MI, 1977b.

TAGGART, W. M., JR., AND THARP, M. O., "A survey of Information Requirements Analysis Techniques," *ACM Comput. Surv.* 9,4(Dec. 1977), pp. 273–90.

TAYLOR, R., ET AL., "Database Program Conversion: A Framework for Research," *Proc. 5th Int. Conf. Very Large Data Bases* (ACM), 1979, pp. 299–312.

TEICHROEW, D., AND HERSHEY, E. A., "PSL/PSA: A Computer Aided Technique for Structured Documentation and Analysis of Information Processing Systems," *IEEE Trans. Softw. Eng.* SE-3,1(1977), pp. 41–48.

TEICHROEW, D., AND SAYANI, H., "Automation of System Building," *Datamation,* Aug. 1971, pp. 25–30.

TEICHROEW, D., HERSHEY, E. A., III, AND BASTARCHE, M. J., "An Introduction to PSL/PSA," ISDOS Workshop Paper 86, University of Michigan, Ann Arbor, MI, 1974.

TEOREY, T. J., "General Equations for Idealized CPU-I/O Overlap Configurations," *Commun. ACM* 21,6(June 1978), pp. 500–507.

TEOREY, T. J., AND DAS, K. S., "Application of an Analytical Model to Evaluate Storage Structures," *Proc. Int. ACM/SIGMOD Conf. Manage. Data,* 1976, pp. 9–20.

TEOREY, T. J., AND FRY, J. P., "Logical Database Design: A Pragmatic Approach," *INFOTECH State of the Art Report,* INFOTECH International, Maidenhead, Berkshire, England, 1978, pp. 357–83.

TEOREY, T. J., AND FRY, J. P. "The Logical Record Access Approach to Database Design,"*ACM Comput. Surv.* 12,2(1980), pp. 179–211. Corrigendum 12,4(1980), p. 465.

TEOREY, T. J., AND OBERLANDER, L. B., "Network Database Evaluation Using Analytical Modeling,"*Proc. 1978 Natl. Comput. Conf.*, Vol. 47, AFIPS Press, Arlington, VA, 1978, pp. 833–42.

TOTH, K. C., MAHMOUD, S. A., RIORDON, J. S., AND SHERIF, O., "The ADD System: An Architecture for Distributed Databases," *Proc. 4th Int. Conf. Very Large Data Bases* (ACM), 1978, pp. 462–71.

TOWSLEY, D., CHANDY, K. M., AND BROWNE, J. C., "Models for Parallel Processing within Programs: Application to CPU:I/O and I/O:I/O Overlap," *Commun. ACM* 21,10(Oct. 1978), pp. 821–31.

TOZER, E. F., "Data Systems Analysis and Design," *Proc. I Conf. European Coop. Informatics,* K. Samelson, ed., *Lecture Notes in Computer Science,* Springer-Verlag, New York, 1976, pp. 193–224.

TREMBLAY, J., AND SORENSON, P. G., *An Introduction to Data Structures with Applications,* McGraw-Hill, New York, 1976.

TUEL, W. G., JR., "Optimum Reorganization Points for Linearly Growing Files,"*ACM Trans. Database Syst.* 2,3(1977), pp. 32–40.

TURNBURKE, V. P., JR., "Sequential Data Processing Design," *IBM Syst. J.* 2(Mar. 1963), pp. 37–48.

UHROWCZIK, P. P., "Data Dictionary/Directories,"*IBM Syst. J.* 12,4(1973), pp. 332–50.

VERHOFSTAD, J. J. M., "Recovery Techniques for Database Systems," *ACM Comput. Surv.* 10,2(June 1978), pp. 167–95.

WAGNER, R. E., "Indexing Design Considerations," *IBM Syst. J.,* 12,4(1973), pp. 351–67.

WANG, C. P., AND WEDEKIND, H. H., "Segment Synthesis in Logical Data Base Design," *IBM J. Res. Dev.* 19,1(1975), pp. 71–77.

WASSERMAN, A. I., "Information System Design Methodology," *J. Am. Soc. Inf. Sci.* 31,1(Jan. 1980).

Webster's New World Dictionary of the American Language, D. B. Guralnik, ed., William Collins and World Publishing Co., New York, 1974.

WEDEKIND, H., "On the Selection of Access Paths in a Data Base System," in *Data Base Management,* J. W. Klimbie and K. L. Koffeman, eds., North-Holland, Amsterdam, 1974, pp. 385–97.

WHITNEY, V. K. M., "A Study of Optimal File Assignment and Communication Network Configuration," Ph.D. thesis, University of Michigan, Ann Arbor, 1970.

WIEDERHOLD, G., *Database Design,* McGraw-Hill, New York, 1977.

WILENS, M. E., VOLZ, R. A., AND FRY, J. P., "Interactive Database Design Laboratory," Tech. Rep. 78 DE 13, Database Systems Research Group, Graduate School of Business Administration, University of Michigan, Ann Arbor, MI, Apr. 1978.

WINKLER, A., ET AL., *The Data Administrator's Handbook,* U.S. Air Force Academy Unclassified Rep. USAF-TR-76-1, National Technical Information Service, Springfield, VA, Jan. 1976.

WIRTH, N. "Program Development by Stepwise Refinement," *Commun. ACM* 14,4(Apr. 1971), pp. 221–227.

WIRTH, N., "On the Composition of Well-Structure Programs," *ACM Comput. Surv.* 6,4(Dec. 1974), pp. 247–259.

WONG, E., AND YOUSSEFI, K., "Decomposition—A Strategy for Query Processing," *ACM TODS* 1,3(Sept. 1976), pp. 223–41.

YAMAMOTO, S., TAZAWA, S., USHIO, K., AND IKEDA, H., "Design of a Generalized Balanced Multiple-Valued File Organization Scheme of Order Two," *Proc. ACM/SIGMOD Int. Conf. Manage. Data,* 1978, pp. 47–51.

YANG, C., "A Class of Hybrid List File Organizations," *Inf. Syst.* 3,(1978), pp. 49–58.

YAO, S. B., "Evaluation and Optimization of File Organizations through Analytic Modeling," Ph.D. dissertation, University of Michigan, Ann Arbor, 1974.

YAO, S. B., "An Attribute Based Model for Database Access Cost Analysis," *ACM Trans. Database Systems,* 2,1(1977a), pp. 45–67.

YAO, S. B., "Approximating Block Accesses in Database Organizations, *Commun. ACM* 20,4(1977b), pp. 260–61.

YAO, A., "On Random 2–3 Trees," *Acta. Inf.* 9,2(1978), pp. 159–70.

YAO, S. B., "Optimization of Query Evaluation Algorithms," *ACM TODS* 4,2(June 1979), pp. 133–55.

YAO, S. B., AND DE JONG, D., "Evaluation of Database Access Paths," *Proc. ACM/SIGMOD Int. Conf. Manage. Data,* 1978, pp. 66–77.

YAO, S. B., DAS, K. S., AND TEOREY, T. J., "A Dynamic Data Base Reorganization Algorithm," *ACM Trans. Database Syst.* 1,2(1976), pp. 159–74.

YAO, S. B., NAVATHE, S. B., AND WELDON, J. L., "An Integrated Approach to Logical Database Design," *NYU Symp. Database Design,* May 1978, pp. 1–14.

YEH, R. T., ROUSSOPOULOS, N., AND CHANG, P., "Data Base Design—An Approach to Logical Database Design," *INFOTECH State of the Art Report on Data Base Technology,* INFOTECH International, Maidenhead, Berkshire, England, 1978a, pp. 443–77.

YEH, R. T., CHANG, P., AND MOHAN, C., "A Multi-level Data Base Design Approach," *Proc. COMPSAC 1978,* Chicago, 1978b, pp. 370–75.

YOURDON, E., *Design of On-Line Computer Systems,* Prentice-Hall, Englewood Cliffs, NJ, 1972, pp. 340–53, 515–42.

YOURDON, E., AND CONSTANTINE, L. L., *Structured Design,* Prentice-Hall, Englewood Cliffs, NJ, 1979.

ZLOOF, M. M., "Query by Example," *Proc. NCC,* 1975, AFIPS Press, pp. 431–38.

INDEX